ROYAL HISTORICAL SOCIETY

STUDIES IN HISTORY

New Series

SOLDIER AND PEASANT IN FRENCH POPULAR CULTURE, 1766–1870

PAST & PRESENT
a journal of historical studies

SOLDIER AND PEASANT IN FRENCH POPULAR CULTURE, 1766–1870

David M. Hopkin

THE ROYAL HISTORICAL SOCIETY
THE BOYDELL PRESS

First published 2002
The Royal Historical Society, London
in association with
The Boydell Press, Woodbridge
Paperback edition 2013
The Boydell Press, Woodbridge

ISBN   978 0 86193 258 0 hardback
ISBN   978 1 84383 843 2 paperback

Transferred to digital printing

The Boydell Press is an imprint of Boydell & Brewer Ltd
PO Box 9, Woodbridge, Suffolk IP12 3DF, UK
and of Boydell & Brewer Inc,
668 Mt Hope Avenue, Rochester, NY 14620–2731, USA
website: www.boydellandbrewer.com

A CIP catalogue record for this book is available
from the British Library

Library of Congress Catalog Card Number: 2002008046

This publication is printed on acid-free paper

I FY NHAD

Les Quatre Vérités du siècle (detail): Gangel (Metz), 1854
This block was originally engraved by Charles Boulay
of Epinal for Jean-Pierre Clerc (Belfort), c. 1830.
Reproduced by permission of the Archives départmentales de la Moselle.

Contents

List of Illustrations

Frontispiece/jacket illustration: *Les Quatre Vérités du siècle* (detail): Gangel (Metz), 1854

Photographic Acknowledgements

The frontispiece/jacket illustration and plates 36, 44, 46 and 51 are reproduced by permission of the Archives départementales de la Moselle; plates
1–2, 7–9, 11–14, 16, 19, 21, 23–4, 26–33, 39–43, 45, 47–50, 52 and 54 by
permission of the Musée départemental d'art ancien et contemporain, Epinal;
plates 3, 4, 5 and 53 by permission of the Réunion des musées nationaux;
plates 6, 10, 17, 18, 34 and 35 by permission of the Bibliothèque nationale de
France, Paris; plate 15 by permission of Glasgow University Library (Special
Collections); plate 20 by permission of the Mediathèque du Pontiffroy, Metz;
and plates 22, 25 and 37–8 by permission of the Archives départementales
des Vosges.

Acknowledgements

My interest in European history, and the Franco-German borderlands in particular, was kindled by the friendship of Kathy von Bülow. But the origin of the particular topic for this book lies in a question posed by Peter Burke in his study of European popular culture: 'Does the frequency with which soldiers turn up in eighteenth-century popular art mean that ordinary people approved of wars?' I am very grateful to Professor Burke for supervising my PhD and for all his encouragement.

I have become indebted to many people in many institutions over the last few years, not least the Economic and Social Research Council for giving me the opportunity to spend several months in the archives and museums of Lorraine. Mark Goldie, Vice Master of Churchill College, Cambridge, was unstinting in his support. In France I would have been lost without the expertise of museum curators, librarians and archivists. From Alençon to Metz I found them uniformly considerate and enthusiastic, but I must extend a special thanks to the staff of three institutions without whose assistance I would never have completed my research: the Bibliothèque municipale in Nancy, the Musée national des arts et traditions populaires in Neuilly, and in particular Bernard Huin and his *équipe* at the Musée départemental d'art ancien et contemporain who made my stay in Epinal a real pleasure. In Britain I have benefited enormously from the collective wisdom of the Folklore Society, the fount of which is the society's librarian Caroline Oates. Significant parts of chapter 3 were published in *Modern and Contemporary France* ix (2001), 19–36, of chapter 4 in *War in History* ix (2002), 251–78, and of chapter 5 in *French History* xiv (2000), 115–49. I am grateful to the editors of both journals for permission to use this material here.

Bob Scribner, Martin Daunton, Colin Jones, Alan Forrest, Tim Blanning, Chris Linehan, Roger Magraw, Edward Ryan, Neil and Kate Colyer are just some of the individuals who have helped bring this project to fruition, but above all I must thank my parents for their unflagging support, material and otherwise, and my wife who, during the time it took to write this book, brought two boys into the world, and with less fuss.

merci à tous

David Hopkin

Publication of this volume was aided by a grant from the Scouloudi Foundation, in association with the Institute of Historical Research.

Abbreviations

AT	Aarne-Thompson index of folktale types [Antti Aarne, *The types of the folktale: a classification and bibliography* (Folklore Fellows Communications iii), Helsinki 1910; rev. Stith Thompson (Folklore Fellows Communications clxxxiv), Helsinki 1961]
BN	Bibliothèque nationals, Paris
Nos Traditions	*Nos Traditions: cahiers de la Société du folklore et d'ethnologie de la Moselle*
MDAACE	Musée départemental d'art ancien et contemporain, Epinal
MNATP	Musée national des arts et traditions populaires
Le Vieux Papier	*Bulletin de la Société archéologique, historique et artistique: le vieux papier*

Introduction

The French army is not an understudied institution. In recent decades the Archives de la guerre at Vincennes have been expertly mined by a series of French, British and American scholars. Their writings have contributed both to an understanding of the army as an institution and to much wider questions of French history, for example the public's reaction to the revolution. Historians have considered the impact of conscription on rural communities, they have examined the interaction between soldiers and civilians in garrison towns, they have established the mechanisms by which veterans were reintegrated into society.[1] What, then, can be the justification for another study of the *armée de terre*?

In fact this book is not primarily concerned with the French army. Rather it is a study of popular mentalities through one particular facet, attitudes to the military. I am less concerned with the army's ability to fill its ranks than with what the peasant thought about his son becoming a soldier. Of course the two were likely to be connected, and so I have drawn on the insights and information provided by military and social historians.[2] Without their work I would not have been able to make sense of the image of the soldier presented by my sources. However, because of this different slant, my researches have led me not to the Archives de la guerre but to the cheap prints and folktale collections to be found at the other end of the Parisian métro line 1, in the Musée national des arts et traditions populaires in Neuilly. The choice of source material has produced a rather different picture of the relationship between the civil and military spheres.

The period covered runs from *ancien régime* to the end of the second empire. It thus takes in the years of the revolution which are often credited with creating a new relationship between citizen and soldier. Whether this was the case or not is the subject of this book. I start in 1766, the year which witnessed the 'réunion' of Lorraine with France. Lorraine, together with the contiguous provinces of Alsace, Champagne and Franche-Comté, was the central location for my research. Although I have made use of comparative

---

[1] See the works of Jean-Paul Bertaud, Jean-Pierre Bois, Jean Chagniot, Richard Cobb, André Corvisier, Alan Forrest, Richard Holmes, John A. Lynn, Douglas Porch, Bernard Schnapper, Samuel F. Scott and Isser Woloch listed in the bibliography (to mention just the most obvious examples within the period).
[2] These include a large number of excellent local studies, many unpublished. See, among others, the works of Pierre Boye, Ghislaine Grosdemange, Bernard Kappaun, J.-C. Labate, Camille Maire, Michelle Mignot, Jean-Aimé Morizot, Gabriel Richard, Paul Wiltzer and Gaston Zeller listed in the bibliography.

material from other regions of France and beyond, some readers may feel that this concentration on the eastern borderlands undermines the book's claim to deal with 'French popular culture'. However, there are justifications for this choice: peasant attitudes to the military have been of particular consequence there.

Lorraine: a divided territory

Because Lorraine was for long a disputed region it has been very well mapped. What emerges most clearly from the work of cartographers is the complexity of the *espace lorrain*.[3] In the sixteenth century the largest political unit was the duchy of Lorraine which had the misfortune to straddle the border between two European powers. Most of its inhabitants lived within the borders of the Holy Roman Empire, but in that part known as Bar mouvant the inhabitants owed their ultimate fealty to the king in Paris.[4] The French had toeholds of territory within ducal Lorraine, as did both branches of the Habsburg family. A whole shoal of smaller secular and religious states completed the picture.

The situation was made more complicated when Henry II wrested control of the three imperial bishoprics of Metz, Toul and Verdun in 1552. These city-states became the bulwark of France's eastern defences through the following centuries. The dukes, irritated by the French presence, were driven further into the Habsburg camp. Lorraine became the hub of the network of military corridors collectively known as 'The Spanish Road' that linked the imperial recruiting grounds in Italy and Germany to the battlefields of Flanders.

Lorraine's strategic position determined its fate during the Thirty Years' War. Duke Charles IV was a supporter of the emperor, and was treated accordingly at the hands of France and her allies. No area of Europe suffered more than Lorraine during the war. It has been estimated that more than half the population of the province was lost.[5] It is no coincidence that Jacques Callot, whose print series *Les Misères de la guerre* is often used to illustrate the war's consequences, was a court artist in Nancy, the capital of ducal Lorraine.

Neither the Peace of Westphalia nor the Treaty of the Pyrenees resolved

---

3   Two excellent historical atlases of the region are the Geographical section of Naval Intelligence Division, Naval Staff, Admiralty, *A manual of Alsace-Lorraine atlas*, London 1920, and Georg Wolfram and Werner Gley, *Elsass-lothringischer Atlas: Landeskunde, Geschichte, Kultur und Wirtschaft Elsass-Lothringens*, Frankfurt-am-Main, 1931.

4   Emperor Charles V gave Lorraine its sovereignty in an attempt to create a series of buffer states between France and the empire, but the precise location and nature of the borders of Lorraine were constantly questioned, particularly in the Barrois where minor disputes over jurisdiction could rapidly develop into international incidents.

5   For the scale of the destruction see Stéphane Gaber, *La Lorraine meutrie: les malheurs de la guerre de trente ans*, Nancy 1979.

Lorraine's situation, leaving the French in place as the occupying power for most of the rest of the century.[6] Independence was only regained at the Peace of Ryswick in 1697.[7] However, in 1735, when it appeared likely that Duke François was going to marry the future Empress Maria-Theresa, the French, fearful of renewed Habsburg power on their borders, put pressure on him to relinquish his inheritance. In 1738 he swapped Lorraine for Tuscany. The former passed under the nominal rule of Louis XV's father-in-law, King Stanislas of Poland, but effective power was in the hands of French-appointed intendants. In 1766, on the death of Stanislas, *de facto* control became *de jure* authority, as Lorraine was incorporated into the kingdom of France.

Until the revolution the French merely administered the existing borders: islets of independence, such as the principality of Salm and the county of Saarwerden, still complicated the map. Even after Lorraine, now part of France 'une et indivisible', was reorganised by the revolutionary authorities into the four departments of Meuse, Meurthe, Moselle and the Vosges, its territory was not fixed. Changes were made at both Treaties of Paris, in 1814 and 1815, and minor adjustments took place through territorial exchanges with neighbouring Prussia and Württemberg in 1825, 1830 and 1834. In 1870 north-eastern Lorraine was fought over, conquered and incorporated into the new *Reichsland* of the German empire, only to be won back in 1918, and again in 1945.[8]

While Lorraine's political boundaries have been moveable, the long-term pattern of the success of France over the empire and its successor states is clear. But it is also a region of frontiers that proved more durable than the political ones. The division between germanic and romance language groups, from the ninth to the nineteenth century, ran along the north-east corner of the province, just to the north of Metz but taking in the major towns of Thionville (Diedenhofen) and Saarguemines (Saargemünd). The linguistic (and ethnic) divide was an element in the self-definition of these communities, but certainly not the only factor in their relationship with the states that fought over them.

The border nature of this region accounts for its militarised history. With the exception of the allied invasions of 1792, 1814 and 1815, Lorraine witnessed relatively little actual conflict in the period under examination (compared with what was to come). However, Lorraine was the site of a great deal of military activity, and not only during moments of conflict. As French control extended, Lorraine became an immense garrison and military maga-

---

6 The French withdrew for nine years after 1661, but the army returned in 1670 when Louis XIV was preparing for his war against the Dutch.

7 The French occupied Lorraine for most of the War of Spanish Succession as well.

8 The division of Lorraine in 1871 led to a reorganisation of the departments, which is still in effect. The territory previously occupied by Germany, which included the eastern halves of the old departments of the Meurthe and of the Moselle, is now called Moselle, while the western halves are united in the single department Meurthe-et-Moselle.

zine. The local population was obliged to assist in these defences through taxes in money, goods and labour.

What was the attitude of the civilian inhabitants towards the military, to whose needs their own were so often sacrificed? Did the dominant presence of the French army affect their understanding of their own identity as their territory changed, between 1766 and 1870, from a quasi-independent state into a mere province of their powerful, but politically unstable neighbour? One indication might be the consistently high level of recruitment of Lorrainers into the French army from the early eighteenth century until the Franco-Prussian War. Lorraine was the 'military terrain par excellence of France'.[9] As a proportion of her population more young men of Lorraine volunteered for the army than from almost any other region of France. A number of plausible explanations have been put forward for this over-representation, ranging from relative height to the fact that regiments, responsible for their own recruiting, seldom looked far from their garrisons which were overwhelmingly in the north-eastern corner of the country. However, the military tradition of Lorraine can hardly be reduced to questions of physical aptitude and habit. An alternative proposition is that the tradition of military service was more developed in Lorraine because it enabled the inhabitants to reach a clear definition of themselves, articulated in opposition to 'the other' around them. The army was a fixed point in a changeable environment, and thus it helped Lorrainers to fix their ideas about their own identity.

Such oppositional explanations of the origins of nationalism, in which 'us' can only be defined in relation to 'them', apply particularly well in frontier regions where inhabitants are acutely aware of relatively minor differences. Robert Muchembled, working in the comparably complex border area of Artois, found that people's definitions of themselves as 'Burgundian' or 'French' dwelt less on the shared characteristics of their nation than on shared hatred for the foreigner, who was at the same time their neighbour.[10] Conflict strengthened these identities. It is no coincidence that so many great nationalist leaders have come from regions whose identity was in dispute.[11] It is clear, for example, that the memory of the lost provinces shaped the careers of such Lorrainer politicians and French nationalists in the third republic as Jules Ferry, Maurice Barrès, Raymond Poincaré and Louis Marin.

Consequently 'untypical' frontier regions, which to the detached observer

---

9 Isser Woloch, *The French veteran from the revolution to the restoration*, Chapel Hill, NC 1979, 227. To be pedantic, the term in English for someone from Lorraine is 'Lotharingian', but for the ease of the reader I have adopted the term 'Lorrainer'.

10 Robert Muchembled, *La Violence au village: sociabilité et comportements populaires en Artois du XVe au XVIIe siècle*, Turnhout 1989, 86–95.

11 If historians are right about its location, Joan of Arc lived in the very first house one came to in France after crossing the border from Lorraine.

seem to have more in common with their neighbours over the border, may be more concerned to demonstrate their unity with the larger nation than 'typical' regions of the interior. Local culture may be nationalist long before the existence of a national culture. General Foch made this paradox explicit in his victory address following the recapture of eastern Lorraine in 1918: 'The more you are Lorrainers, the more you will be French.'[12] Peter Sahlins has uncovered an analogous situation in the southern Pyrenees, where the local population was culturally Catalan but divided in their allegiances: 'national identity – as Frenchmen or Spaniards – appeared on the periphery before it was built there by the centre. It appeared less as a result of state intentions than from the local process of adopting and appropriating the nation without abandoning local interests, a local sense of place, or a local identity'. It is true that they often did so in the pursuit of purely local issues, and that they were willing to assert other, sometimes contradictory, identities when these suited their purpose better. However, their initial pragmatic choices were reinforced over time because of the heightened sense of 'us' and 'them' which they created.[13]

The irreducible 'Frenchness' of Lorraine has been a major political issue in the past, particularly in the germanophone north-east of the province. Since 1870 the population of this small corner has changed nationality four times. The competing claims on its allegiance made by France and Germany were made more difficult to resolve (except by armed conflict) because each side was using different concepts of national identity. The inhabitants spoke German, they were largely ethnically German, culturally there was little to distinguish them from their neighbours in the Palatinate. Therefore, according to an 'ethnic' model of nationhood they should be German. However, according to the French 'civic' model such considerations were not important.[14] As one French historian expressed his hopes for the eventual recovery of the lost provinces, 'What distinguishes nations is neither race nor language. Men feel in their hearts that they are one people when they possess a communality of ideas, of interests, of affections, of memories, and of hopes.'[15] Thus Lorrainers were French because they had willingly partici-

---

[12] 'Plus vous serez lorrains, plus vous serez français': Louis Marin, *Les Contes traditionnels en Lorraine*, Paris 1964, 15. The development of this paradoxical situation is explored in Pierre Barral, *L'Esprit lorrain: cet accent singulier du patriotisme français*, Nancy 1989.

[13] Peter Sahlins, *Boundaries: the making of France and Spain in the Pyrenees*, Berkeley–Los Angeles 1989, 9, 267–76.

[14] These definitions – 'civic' and 'ethnic' – of national identity are explained by David Bell, 'Recent works on early modern French national identity', *Journal of Modern History* lxviii (1996), 89.

[15] N. D. Fustel de Coulanges, 'L'Alsace est-elle allemande ou française?', quoted by Daniel Nordman, 'Des Limites d'état aux frontières nationales', in Pierre Nora (ed.), *Les Lieux de memoire*, II: *La nation*, Paris 1986, ii. 56. This is clearly in line with Ernest Renan's answer to *Qu'est-ce-qu'une nation?*: 'To have common glories in the past, a common will in the present; to have accomplished great things together, to wish to do so again, that is the

pated in collective acts of nation-building. By their own choice they were French.

It is open to question to what extent these competing models of national identity were spurs to action, and to what extent they were simply *post-facto* justifications for political acts whose origins lay elsewhere.[16] It is also far from clear whether the differences between the ethnic and civic models of nationality were appreciated at a popular level. The francophone inhabitants of Lorraine used the term 'Allemands' to cover both their fellow Lorrainers who spoke German and the inhabitants of the lands beyond their eastern borders (and held similar prejudices about them).[17] In practice, countries whose concepts of nationality are based on collective will have as much difficulty coping with cultural diversity as those that follow the ethnic model. Nationality may be result of a choice, but minorities can only demonstrate their choice by speaking and behaving more like the ethnic majority. The folklorists of germanophone Lorraine, whose work could hardly fail to highlight ethnic differences, have been criticised in precisely these terms.[18]

The value of the civic model is that it highlights the possible role of the army in nation-building. If French philosophers and historians of nationality usually cite the revolution as the prime example of an act of collective political will which forged the nation, in Lorraine, and especially germanophone Lorraine, the army was the national institution which inspired the greatest loyalty. It was not simply that the army provided the mechanism for learning about, and communicating with, other Frenchmen, although this was true for Lorrainers who had served in the army; their knowledge of France was strengthened through contacts with natives of other regions and tours of duty in different parts of the country. But in Lorraine, where the army was highly visible, its emotive impact was felt throughout society. Lorrainers, above all others, had contributed to the victories of the French army, and suffered for

essential condition for being a nation': John Hutchinson and Anthony D. Smith (eds), *Nationalism*, Oxford 1994, 17.

16 For example, the area of Lorraine seized by the new German empire in 1871 (and again by Hitler in 1940) comprised not only a germanophone population but also a large francophone population, including the important city of Metz. Their incorporation was justified in terms of history (Metz had been an imperial city until 1552) but also by the need to compromise France's defences and the desire to benefit from the area's reserves of coal and iron.

17 For example, the volunteer Joseph-Louis-Gabriel Noël, from Nancy, referred to his German-speaking comrades in the 2nd battalion de la Meurthe as 'têtes d'Allemands' because of their belief in the supernatural: *Au Temps des volontaires: lettres d'un volontaire de 1792*, ed. J. Noël, Paris 1912, 10.

18 François Roth, *La Lorraine annexée: étude sur la presidence de Lorraine dans l'empire allemand (1870–1918)*, Nancy 1976, 258, 493. As Stephen Harp has demonstrated for this very region, administrators of different nationalities, who were also apparently reliant on competing definitions of nationhood, none the less behaved in remarkably similar ways: *Learning to be loyal: primary schooling as nation building in Alsace and Lorraine, 1850–1940*, Dekalb, Ill. 1998, 206.

its defeats. The roll-call of French military heroes was bursting with their compatriots, from Marshal Ney downwards.[19] It was a germanophone Lorrainer who planted the tricolour on the Malakoff Redoubt. Lorrainers remained French, even during half a century of German occupation after 1870, because they were still singing songs about Austerlitz, Algiers and Sebastopol.[20]

If this hypothesis proved correct then it might help explain the relationship between militarism and the dominant ideologies of the late nineteenth century, nationalism and imperialism. Studies in a number of European countries have shown how the image of the soldier in art and literature in the decades before the First World War appealed to the popular imagination and how this success related to the impact of these ideologies.[21] In the run up to the First World War French nationalism became almost indissoluble from 'the cult of the army'; the idea of the nation was bound together with the image of the soldier.[22] My choice of the period before 1870 was made in order to trace the origins of this relationship.

Peasants into Frenchmen?

Is this book, therefore, a further contribution to the 'peasants into Frenchmen' debate initiated a quarter of a century ago by Eugen Weber? Weber himself identified the army as one of the key institutions in the assimilation of the French peasantry into national culture and society in the third republic, alongside schools, roads, railways, the Church, political parties, newspapers, not to mention the changes within agriculture itself as it adapted from a subsistence economy to market needs.[23] The role that most of these factors played in the conversion (or not) of a traditional society into a modern one has been explored in many excellent studies by other historians;

[19] See Paul Despiques, *Soldats de Lorraine*, Nancy–Paris 1899, for many more examples.
[20] This model rather ignores the fact that in 1914 germanophone Lorrainers were also singing victory songs about Leipzig and Sedan.
[21] For example, the Manchester University Press series, *Studies in Imperialism*, edited by John M. Mackenzie, and in particular his *Imperialism and popular culture*, Manchester 1986.
[22] According to the muse of French nationalism, Paul Déroulède, 'L'armée est la grande patronne/Qui nous baptise tous Français': Jean-Jacques Becker and Stéphane Audoin-Rouzeau, *La France, la nation, la guerre: 1850–1920*, Paris 1995, 149.
[23] Eugen Weber, *Peasants into Frenchmen: the modernisation of rural France, 1800–1914*, Stanford, Ca. 1976, ch. xvii. However, one of Weber's main points, that conscription led to migration, has been refuted by Alan Baker: 'Military service and migration in nineteenth-century France: some evidence from Loir-et-Cher', *Transactions of the Institute of British Geographers* n.s. xxiii (1998), 198–206. For the relationship between conscription and mobility in Lorraine see Camille Maire, 'La Mobilité des jeunes lorrains au XIXe siècle: l'exemple des conscrits des cantons d'Albestroff et de Dieuze (1830–70)', *Le Pays lorrain* lxiv (1984), 246–50.

the one obvious exception remains the army.[24] I was, therefore, interested in pursuing Weber's hypothesis (although I felt that, for north- eastern France at least, the chronology needed to be pushed back), and so my attentions focused on the rural population of Lorraine.

The name Lorraine does not conjure rural idylls for contemporary Frenchmen, rather it is usually envisaged as a land marred by heavy industry. Certainly the *haut-pays* around Briey was the heartland of France's iron and steel foundries until the 1980s, powered by the coal from the seams beneath the Sarre. A glance out of the window of the archives high above the city of Metz confirms that industry dominates the entire Moselle valley north towards Thionville. But its development is fairly recent. Although there were mines and ironworks at the time of the Franco-Prussian War these were, with the significant exception of the de Wendel family forges around Hayange, almost artisanal in nature. No one perceived the massive growth that would take place after 1870, certainly not the Germans who undoubtedly would have tried to occupy more of Lorraine had they appreciated its mineral riches. In fact the Franco-Prussian War provided the impetus for industrial development in Lorraine, as it drove many Alsatian entrepreneurs to set up factories in French Lorraine. (This is certainly the case for the textile mills of the valleys of the Vosges, mostly founded by displaced Mulhouse merchants.) The steel mills of the Barrois, which accounted for two-thirds of France's steel production before the First World War, only took off after the discovery of the Thomas Method of iron ore abstraction in 1878. There was, of course, some industry in Lorraine before 1870 – potteries in the west, glass-blowing in the east, salt extraction at Château-Salins, paper mills in the Vosges (whose presence helped prosper the imagery industry, and thus provided a key source for this book) – but nothing on a scale to warrant reclassifying Lorraine as an industrial rather than an agricultural region. Indeed, according to a leading local historian, Lorraine's economy prior to 1850 still belonged in the *ancien régime*.[25] Lorraine was one of the earliest regions in France to experience rural depopulation, but the truly dramatic haemorraghing from villages only became apparent from the 1860s.[26] Up until this time the major centres of population – Nancy, Metz, Verdun, Toul, Thionville, Lunéville, Commercy – were all garrison towns, not industrial centres. In many parts of the Meuse, the Vosgian *plaine*, the Lorraine plateau, the dominance of agriculture was

[24] A bibliography on the tradition versus modernity debate in nineteenth-century rural France would extend over many pages, but key works by historians Maurice Agulhon, Caroline Ford, Peter Jones, Ted Margadant, Peter McPhee, Roger Price and Peter Sahlins, are listed in the bibliography (and one might also usefully consult the works of the ethnologists Claude Karnoouh, Susan Carol Rogers, Yvonne Verdier and Françoise Zonabend). For a helpful attempt to redraw the parameters of this debate see James R. Lehning, *Peasant and French: cultural contact in rural France during the nineteenth century*, Cambridge 1995.

[25] François Baudin, *Histoire économique et sociale de la Lorraine*, i, Nancy 1992, 229.

[26] Xavier de Planhol, *An historical geography of France*, Cambridge 1994, 394–5.

never challenged. Any study of popular mentalities in this period must, therefore, deal primarily with peasants.

Agriculture in Lorraine was a peasant activity. Despite the region being well within reach of grain merchants from the big northern cities, and thus a potential site for the development of capitalist agriculture, nearly 80 per cent of all landholdings were of five hectares or less in 1882, each consisting of dozens of tiny strips as a result of generations of partible inheritance. With the exceptions of the Vosges (where pasture and forestry were very important) and the vineyards which supplied the garrisons with cheap alcohol, agriculture took the form of traditional, subsistence polyculture, practised in open-field triennial (sometimes quadrennial) rotation. Wheat was the dominant crop. The distinctive feature of Lorraine's rural economy was the continued importance of communal land. The woods, which in 1882 accounted for nearly a third of all agricultural land, remain the most highly visible reminder of this. Whether approaching Lorraine from the east through the Vosges or the west through the Argonne, its borders are marked by forest barriers. But the commons included extensive pasturage, for in Lorraine flocks continued to be communal, and subsisted through *vaine pâture*, the right to graze on private land. In 1893, 522 of the 596 communes in the department of Meurthe-et-Moselle still judged this communal right absolutely indispensable, and it continued in many parts until after the Second World War.[27]

The continued vitality of communal rights and practices in Lorraine – in the open fields, pastures and the forests – has been linked to a particular kind of habitation. Most Lorraine peasants (except in the mountains, where the farms were necessarily more dispersed) lived in nucleated villages made up of long, narrow, terraced houses along both sides of a wide road. It is a quite distinctive type of settlement, which with its shallow tiled roofs, looks slightly Mediterranean. It may well be related to Lorraine's militarised past when each village could be turned into a mini-fortress by closing off each end of the street.[28] The village was, in a quite literal sense, inward-looking, and this may also account for the strong sense of communal identity, maintained through collective institutions such as the winter evening wakes (*veillées*). It was at the wakes that the tales and songs, which form some of the sources for this book, were told and sung.

The vitality of communal life should not be mistaken for equality. Everywhere there were social gradations within the village ranging from landless labourers to the large farmers, not to mention the rural artisans who complicated the social picture. However, this social stratification did not easily translate into class divisions because membership of the village community remained the source of group loyalty. There is, on the other hand, some

---

[27] Baudin, *Histoire économique*, i. 23–81.
[28] Xavier de Planhol, 'Aux Origines de l'habitat rural de type lorrain', in Franz Dussart (ed.), *L'Habitat et les paysages ruraux d'Europe*, Liège 1971, 69–92.

evidence to suggest that Lorrainers had what might be termed an 'order consciousness', which united rich and poor peasants in their social identity because they performed one function in society, the provision of food. This had consequences for their relationship to soldiers as we will see.

There were, therefore, some distinctive features to the rural economy of Lorraine prior to 1870, although many aspects were shared with other parts of France. Perhaps as a result Lorraine seems to have been culturally quite homogeneous. Like most of north-eastern France, it was literate and law-abiding, most tellingly in the low levels of resistance to the draft.[29] But other factors separated Lorraine from the Paris basin. For instance, since the revolution most parts of the region had remained relatively pious, which may be reflected in its high fertility rate (although there are other plausible expla-nations).[30] At the same time Lorrainers were committed to a nationalist and authoritarian version of the republic which could readily shade off into Bonapartism. Although there is little evidence of continuing attachment to the Bourbons in Lorraine (whose inhabitants had been subjects of the king of France for less than thirty years at the declaration of the first republic), neither was there any obvious enthusiasm for the more radical alternatives, whether they be Jacobin, demi-soc or socialist.[31] The most obvious cultural division in Lorraine, that of language, only has the effect of emphasising the religious and political trends in Lorraine, the German-speaking population being generally more pious and more right-wing than their francophone neighbours.

This cultural homogeneity is also apparent in Lorrainers' attitudes to the military, although this probably had less to do with the region's social struc-ture or its cultural inheritance than with its militarised history. A dominant influence on peasant cultural attitudes was the presence of the army in their midst, and this affected the Vosgian forester as much as it did the Mosellan vintner. Lorrainer peasants enjoyed, if that is the right word, an enduring relationship with the military. Their production was geared to the needs of soldiers, they were habituated to their comings and goings, they themselves had often served in the ranks and later formed, with other veterans, a social circle within the village. Rural artisans in particular seem to have viewed their time in the army almost as an apprenticeship. They were, therefore, well positioned to form ideas about the soldier's way of life and the army's role in society. But although originally developed in Lorraine, their ideas spread beyond its boundaries and informed the development of the cultural image of the soldier throughout France. In terms of communications networks, Lorraine was pulled into the national orbit long before many areas of the south and west. It was therefore in a position to influence national culture.

---

[29] Robert Tombs, *France, 1814–1914*, London 1996, ch. xvi.

[30] Roger Price, *A social history of nineteenth-century France*, New York 1987, 289; Tombs, *France*, 322–3.

[31] Tombs, *France*, ch. xiv; Planhol, *An historical geography*, 328–37.

The passage of this form of cultural formation in a largely oral society is not easy to trace: one example might be communal behaviour at the time of conscription which seems to have been most fully articulated in eastern France, and subsequently spread to the rest of the country partly through the institution of the army itself (as in contemporary France, many Frenchmen knew Lorraine largely from their garrison days). A more obvious vehicle for cultural diffusion was provided by the cheap print manufactories located in Epinal, Nancy, Metz and other towns of the eastern borderlands, whose coloured woodcuts and lithographs were to be seen on the walls of homes throughout France, and beyond. This is one reason why, although the focus of this study is on Lorraine, its conclusions may have a wider resonance.

Sources for the history of popular culture

To discover whether the peasants of Lorraine, culturally speaking, had become Frenchmen prior to 1870, I planned to examine their attitudes towards soldiers. Evidence of change there, I hypothesised, might be indicative of the development of a clear sense of national identity. The soldier as national symbol was certainly ubiquitous after the Franco-Prussian War, particularly in the graphic arts.[32] In the cheap prints of the third republic the conscript became the idealised representative of the nation. But the soldier's earlier incarnations in popular culture are less well known, although one recent study has made an excellent attempt to rectify this situation.[33] Gérard de Puymège's hunt for the mythical Nicolas Chauvin, Napoleonic veteran and progenitor of the word 'chauvinism', is concerned with representations of the soldier, and the link between them and the origins of militaristic nationalism. However, although his study touches on popular culture, most of his sources are either Parisian in origin or intellectual in content. The history of nationalism tends to focus on the debates of urban intellectuals, such as the authors of the *Encyclopédie*, but national identity, if it is to be meaningful, must be felt by peasants and *philosophes* alike. This thesis may be considered as a provincial counterweight to the domination of the 'Soldat-laboureur' in Parisian discourse.

The study of the relationship between the civilian and military spheres has likewise tended to rely on the evidence of the same select group of elite commentators, but how reflective were their thoughts of the attitudes prevalent at other levels of society? It was on the popular classes that the burden of

---

32 See, for example, Ouriel Reshef, *Guerre, mythes et caricature: au berceau d'une mentalité française*, Paris 1984; Dominique Lerch, 'La Représentation de la guerre par l'imagerie populaire (1854–1945)', *Ethnologie française* xxiv (1994), 263–75; François Roth, 'Nation, armée et politique à travers les images d'Epinal, 1860–1914', *Annales de l'est*, 5th sér. xxxii (1980), 195–213.
33 Gerard de Puymège, *Chauvin, le soldat-laboureur: contribution à l'étude des nationalismes*, Paris 1993.

military service fell most heavily, both in terms of manpower and taxes. When historians have attempted to answer this question they have tended to look at moments of conflict in order to spotlight attitudes to the military, arguing that such crises reveal feelings that in the humdrum history of the everyday would remain unspoken. Local events, such as the billeting of soldiers or the use of troops to quell food riots, produced a spate of actions in the courts and so are left as sources for the historian. But it is equally possible that it is only the crisis itself that engenders the feelings it is supposed to reveal. The immediacy of the issues hide cultural changes which need longer to show themselves.

I have, therefore, chosen those sources that I believe reveal widespread patterns, but which are also indicative of long-term change. In particular I have concentrated on oral literature (folksongs and folktales), the rituals concerning conscription and the cheap woodcut prints for which Lorraine became famous in the nineteenth century. The reasoning behind these choices, their credentials as sources for a history of popular culture, and the methodological problems they pose, are dealt with in chapters 1, 2 and 3 below.

In practice, and somewhat to my surprise, these sources have not proved abundant hunting-grounds for evidence of attitudes about nationality. Folk-lorists, who were players in the creation and assertion of national identities in Lorraine, were disappointed to find little evidence of the symbolic use of the soldier as national figurehead in their material. Théodore de Puymaigre regretted that he had been unable to find any echoes of Béranger's militaristic (and nationalistic) lyrics in the *pays messin*, the area around Metz where he collected folksongs.[34] How can we account for this absence? It may be that, despite the manifold divisions of their territory, Lorrainers were always sure and certain of their own identity and, therefore, never felt the need to say anything about it.[35] Alternatively one might give credence to Eugen Weber's thesis that French national identity was, at least in rural areas, the creation of the third republic. The soldier could not serve as a national symbol before 1870 because there was no nation to symbolise.[36] However, Weber's thesis is at its most convincing when applied to the far south and west of France; in Lorraine literacy, political involvement and nationalist ideas had certainly penetrated the countryside before the Franco-Prussian War. Thirdly, folktales and cheap prints may be the wrong place to look for historical evidence of national identity. Both tend to be conservative genres, self-referential as

---

34 Théodore de Puymaigre, *Folk-lore*, Paris 1885, 144.
35 This is similar to André Corvisier's not altogether convincing explanation for the invisibility of army recruits' patriotism before 1764: 'l'unité spirituelle de la Nation n'est pas en cause, mais il s'agit de sa défense et il se trouve des hommes pour s'enrôler en silence': *L'Armée française de la fin du XVIIe siècle au ministère de Choiseul: le soldat*, Paris 1964, i. 359.

much as reflective on the experience of reality, and with a limited stock of endlessly repeated themes. However, soldiers in other guises than as national heroes are ubiquitous in folklore and imagery, particularly in Lorraine. Peasants had plenty to say about the military, and popular culture had plenty of uses for the soldier.

The character who emerges from the sources is, I believe, more interesting than the two-dimensional heroic representation of the soldier which was so common under the third republic. Soldiers were presented as ambiguous characters, attractive and repulsive by turns. The image of the soldier was at the centre of a whole complex of attitudes about gender, age and sexuality, violence, order and marginality. In as much as these formed an interconnected structure of both conscious and unconscious assumptions, which were widespread and enduring among large groups of the population, one might be entitled to treat them not simply as attitudes but as a mentality.[37] But whatever he was, the soldier was definitely not a peasant. The synthesis of second and third estates proffered by urban intellectuals in the shape of Nicolas Chauvin, the soldier-farmer, found few supporters among the peasantry.

How was it possible for peasants to look on soldiers as so different from themselves, when they supplied the army with its recruits and veterans returned to their home villages and resumed their peacetime occupations at the end of their service? I have arranged my material in chapters 3, 4 and 5 around the life-cycle of the soldier, in order to address this issue. By following the soldier from conscription through to his discharge and beyond we can see how distinctions arose between him and the civilian society from which he was originally drawn.

Having raised questions relating to national identity and popular militarism in this introduction, readers may feel disappointed to find that they are only addressed obliquely in the following chapters. I have posed them here in order to explain the genesis of this book, and my initial choice of period and location. If the sources have led me to give more attention to other issues, I hope readers will find the alternative picture of the soldier sufficient compensation. Yet perhaps the 'peasants into Frenchmen' debate has left its mark on this book, if not quite in the way that Weber and other modernisation theorists originally posited. James Lehning has recently argued that 'peasant' and 'French' represent less the result of material changes in the nineteenth-century countryside than conceptual opposites, mental categories by which contemporaries arranged their experience of transition, and through which they articulated their own sense of identity in a changing society. In urban culture, as represented by writers such as Honoré de Balzac and Emile Zola, the peasant was the archaic, exotic 'other' against which they could articulate their modern, civilised 'Frenchness'. But was the peasants' own exotic other

---

36 Weber, *Peasants into Frenchmen*, 485.
37 This definition of *mentalité* is taken from Peter Burke, 'Strengths and weaknesses of the history of mentalities', *History of European Ideas* vii (1986), 439–52.

the Frenchman? To judge from my sources the answer is no. Instead I suggest that the distinction between 'peasant' and 'French' rests on a more fundamental division whose origins lie much further back in the history of the formation of the nation-state – the division between peasant and soldier.[38]

---

[38] Lehning, *Peasant and French*, 1–34.

1

Images of the Soldier

During the third republic an identity was created in visual terms between the conscript and the nation, expressed most vividly in the cheap prints commonly termed *images d'Epinal* after the most successful brand, but more generally called popular imagery. Pellerin & Cie., the manufacturers of the *images d'Epinal*, produced the tickets for the annual military lottery which, under the third republic, decided which arm of the military the conscript would enter. These showed the conscript beside France's national heroes, from Joan of Arc to General Boulanger.[1] France's national destiny, the tickets implied, lay with the conscript. He was everything that was virtuous in France – brave, loyal, honest, faithful – in opposition to everything rotten in the state – the agitator, the corrupt politician, the priest, the freemason, the Jew (depending on one's point of view).

A particularly powerful and frequently repeated image was the depiction of the conscript as the child of France who, when he grew up, would sacrifice his life in avenging her wounds. At school young boys were given story-sheets such as Pellerin's *L'Histoire d'un paysan* to which the moral read 'Thus, later, when you have become men, if the Fatherland calls her soldiers, you will reply "Present, Mother".'[2] Ouriel Reshef reproduces one such image in his study of modern French mentality: it shows a mother with her infant son pointing to the soldier he will become, while all three are clasped by the Mère-Patrie. Reshef interprets it thus: 'The mother gives birth to her children but it is the Mother-Fatherland which is their real mother. . . . The act of creation does not truly complete itself until the child accomplishes his destiny in sacrificing his life for the Mother-Fatherland.'[3]

If the purpose of this flood of imagery was to inculcate young Frenchmen with the desire to serve the nation, then there are plenty of testimonies to its success.[4] Maurice Barrès, Lorraine's great nationalist writer, recalled how, as a child in the opening months of the Franco-Prussian War, he played with

---

[1] Henri George, 'Conscription, tirage au sort et imagerie populaire', *Le Vieux Papier*, fasc. 279, Paris 1981.

[2] 'Ainsi, plus tard, quand vous serez des hommes, si la Patrie appelle ses soldats, vous répondrez "Présents Mère" ': Roth, 'Nation, armée et politique', 210.

[3] 'La mère donne naissance à ses enfants mais c'est la Mère-Patrie qui est leur véritable mère. . . . L'acte de création ne s'achève vraiment que lorsque l'enfant accomplit son destin en sacrifiant sa vie à la Mère-Patrie': Reshef, *Guerre, mythes et caricature*, 180–1.

[4] According to the military historian Raoul Girardet, who grew up with these images, 'toute cette imagerie pittoresque et sentimentale a marqué pour une génération, la

Plate 1. Military conscription lottery ticket: Pellerin (Epinal), *c.* 1900
At the base two conscripts can be seen cheering on 'the French heroine'.
Reproduced by permission of the Musée départemental d'art
ancien et contemporain, Epinal.

images which predicted victory for us. Our machine-guns and our Turcos were
sweeping away the Prussians. And because it was represented in such vivid
colours, it was already a fact, an insult to them, an immense joy for us. With
what violence and what certitude these powerful and lively images moved me,
affecting my deepest sensibility. They have left their marks there.[5]

sensibilité de notre peuple': *La Société militaire dans la France contemporaine, 1815–1939,*
Paris 1953, 174.
[5] 'images qui nous prédisaient la victoire. Nos mitrailleuses et nos Turcos balayaient les
Prussiens. Et que ce fût représenté avec des couleurs si franches, c'était déjà un fait, un
outrage pour eux, un immense bonheur pour nous. Avec quelle violence et quelle sûreté,
ces puissantes images, vigoureusement coloriées, m'ébranlaient, allaient promouvoir ma
plus profonde sensibilité! Elles y ont laissé leurs traces': Maurice Barrès, preface to René
Perrout, *Les images d'Epinal,* Paris 1912, p. viii. One might detect here, in the contradiction between the vivid images before his eyes and the sad reality on the ground, the origins
of the mentality of the man who dismissed the proof of Dreyfus' innocence on the grounds
that his guilt was necessary in the name of a higher, 'national' truth: Zeev Sternhell,
Maurice Barrès et le nationalisme française, Brussels 1985, 268.

16

For the French-speaking children of eastern Lorraine, annexed by Germany after 1871, sheets of paper French soldiers were an important cultural life-line. Through them they still had access to the incarnation of the French republic, the conscript.[6]

It could be argued that this identification between soldier and nation was not peculiar to France during this period. It was part of a nationalist mind-set that was common to all European nations at the time. Raphael Tuck and Sons of London and J. F. Schreiber of Germany produced militaristic images similar to Pellerin's (though without the emphasis on the conscript). A significant difference between them was, of course, that they were of British or German soldiers, not French. When imagists deigned to print illustrations of soldiers not their own they implied that the foreign soldier, if he was not comical, was the receptacle of everything bestial and vicious, even when, as in Charles Pinot's (Pellerin's competitor) famous lithograph of a Prussian uhlan, all they wanted was a piece of soap.[7] If the domestic soldier represented his own nation we can assume that the foreign soldier did likewise, that is to say the image of the rapacious uhlan was the symbol of the new German empire.

Yet this identity between the soldier and the nation was relatively new; in the graphic arts of previous centuries there was only the vaguest suggestion that the soldier could carry such symbolic importance. The individual foot-soldier had not been considered a fit subject for artists before a flurry of interest among wood engravers in southern Germany and Switzerland at the beginning of the sixteenth century. The woodcut images of the German *Landsknecht*, and of his enemy the Swiss *Reisläufer*, were occasionally used to display support for the imperial cause or cantonal patriotism. However, more common were those images which treated mercenary bands as alternative societies, exciting, threatening and repulsive by turns.[8] The *Landsknecht's* companions were Death and whores, his habits were drinking, gambling and swearing. He was as much a danger to society as to the enemy. No doubt the vicarious excitement the prints offered was part of their attraction.[9]

During the Thirty Years War the soldier appeared, not as the representative of one nation at war with another, but as the representative of a way of life in conflict with the rest of society. In Jacques Callot's series *Les Misères de la guerre*, there are hardly any clues as to whether the marauding troops he

---

6   Jean-Julien Barbé, *L'Imagier de Metz*, Metz 1950, 104.
7   Ouriel Reshef, 'Le Hulan et la paysanne: lectures d'une image éditée chez Pinot et Sagaire', *Gazette des beaux-arts* cix (1987), 76–7. For a typical example of a popular image in which a foreign soldier was presented as laughable see Pellerin's *Histoire du sergent autrichien Fritz Kreutser*.
8   Keith Moxey, *Peasants, warriors and wives: popular imagery in the Reformation*, Chicago 1989, 79–80.
9   See John R. Hale, 'The soldier in Germanic graphic art of the Renaissance', *Journal of Interdisciplinary History* xvii (1986), 85–114, and *Artists and warfare in the Renaissance*, New Haven–London 1990.

depicted were from the French, Swedish or the imperial armies then devastating his native Lorraine. They may have fought for either side (or both). Similarly in Dutch art, as Susannah Fishman discovered in her examination of the theme of *Boerenverdriet* or 'peasant sufferings', the real war was the one between all soldiers and the peasants who, regardless of nationality, they oppressed and destroyed.[10]

The distance between the cosmopolitan marauder of the seventeenth century and the idealised nationalist conscript of the late nineteenth century is considerable. However, it would be wrong to give the impression that the image of the soldier as national standard-bearer was born, like Minerva, ready-armed on the battlefields of 1870–1. Soldiers had been appearing regularly in folk art for at least a hundred years before the Franco-Prussian War. In order to understand what the image of the soldier meant in popular culture before he became so charged with nationalistic feelings we need to trace his development prior to this flowering in the late nineteenth century. One means by which his mutations can be unravelled is through popular imagery. The Pellerin firm was at its most successful under the third republic, but its origins date back to the *ancien régime*. Their production formed part of a tradition of providing cheap prints going back centuries. We can, therefore, hope to find evidence of the development of the image of the soldier over time in the production of Pellerin and other imagists. The transformations undergone by the soldier in their cheap prints could provide a key to understanding the changes undergone by the idea of the soldier in popular culture.

What is popular imagery?

The term popular imagery was coined in the nineteenth century to describe the cheap, coloured, single-sheet prints sold in many European countries from the seventeenth century onwards. In order to reach a complete definition of popular imagery it would be preferable to consider who bought these prints and why, but in practice one is obliged to rely on who produced them and how. For example, the recent catalogue of the collection belonging to the Musée national des arts et traditions populaires limits itself, with a few exceptions, to woodcut prints.[11] In France this technique was originally associated with the engravers of the rue Montorgueil in Paris, whose favourite sources were the paintings of the Fontainebleau school of artists.[12] Around 1600,

---

10 J. Susannah Fishman, *Boerenverdriet: violence between peasants and soldiers in early modern Netherlands art*, Ann Arbor 1982.

11 Nicole Garnier, *L'Imagerie populaire française*, I: *Gravures en taille-douce et en taille-d'épargne: catalogue des fonds du Musée national des arts et traditions populaires*, Paris 1990, 9–11.

12 For the rue Montorgueil wood-engravers see Jean Adhémar, 'La Rue Montorgueil et la formation d'un groupe d'imagiers parisiens au XVIe siècle', *Le Vieux Papier*, fasc. 166, Paris

however, the trade moved to the rue Saint Jacques on the other bank of the Seine, and at the same time dropped the woodcut in favour of copperplate, an engraving technique recently imported from Italy. Though more expensive, copperplate engraving allowed for a more artistic treatment suitable for the kind of works they were reproducing. The woodcut was, with few exceptions, relegated to the provinces where it came to be considered a cheap medium, not fit for real artists.[13] In France, therefore, the identification of the woodcut with popular imagery is, by-and-large, correct.[14]

In the provinces the first people to recognise its potential were the card-makers and the makers of decorative paper (termed *dominotiers*) who used similar techniques in their own work. Pellerin was an example of a card-maker who eventually concentrated on imagery.[15] In the eighteenth century printers and booksellers also became interested in the genre. For many it was only a sideline to their main trade. I have used the term 'imagists' to describe all the editors of popular imagery – that is the persons whose names appear at the foot of the images – even though in some cases they regarded themselves primarily as printers, booksellers or *dominotiers*. Sometimes the person who made the woodcut (technically known as a xylographer, but for ease I prefer the term engraver) also issued it. In other cases the imagists were entrepreneurs who employed engravers, colourists and pedlars as and when they needed their services.

Popular imagery appeared in a number of formats. The first was probably the poster, in which the image occupied the whole sheet with only a line of text engraved on the same block to identify it. Imagists were not allowed by law to use a moveable letterpress (though licensed printers could make imagery), so this was the format of most early images. Later, when the division between printers and imagists became blurred, the 'cantique' form proved popular; the image still dominated, but it was supported at either side

---

1954, 25–34, and Nicole Garnier, 'Aux Origines de l'imagerie populaire: la gravure de la rue Montorgueil à Paris au XVIe siècle', *Revue du Louvre* iv (1989), 225–32.

13 One theory is that the children of the imagists of the rue Montorgueil themselves moved to the provinces, though the evidence is not conclusive: Jean Adhémar, 'Hypothèses sur la formation des imagiers provinciaux français du XVIIe et du XVIIIe siècle', *Arts et traditions populaires* iii (1955), 208–10. The Papillon dynasty of engravers tried to revive the artistic woodcut in eighteenth-century Paris, but without much success.

14 In Italy and Germany copperplate engraving was used for popular imagery: Wolfgang Bruckner, *Imagerie populaire allemande*, Milan 1969; Achille Bertarelli, *L'Imagerie italienne*, Paris 1929. Avignon, because of the richer clerical market, supported a copperplate print market, while the demands of Lille's particular religious and social institutions favoured this more expensive medium: Jean-François Cerquand, 'L'Imagerie populaire à Avignon et dans le Comtat aux XVIIe et XVIIIe siècles', *Mémoires de l'Académie de Vaucluse* i (1882), 45–71; Elise Seguin, 'Images et imagiers à Lille, avant 1800', *Arts et traditions populaires* ix (1961), 27–56, and 'Imagerie et vie sociale à Lille: Louis Melino, 1790–1859', ibid. xvii (1969), 179–232.

15 The firm continued to produce packs of cards alongside images until 1876 when this side of the business was sold to Grimaud of Paris.

by columns of text, usually a song. As imagery moved away from religious to secular subject matter the narrative or 'comic-strip' form became more important. Finally, some sheets were designed for cutting-out. Although different periods had preferences for particular formats, all formats could be found in the imagists' catalogue at any one time.

These formats will be familiar to the student of British broadsides or catch-penny prints, but imagery differs from these in one very important respect, which is why I have not used these terms. Imagery was always coloured: four or five bright hues were added to the black lines of the woodcut using a stencil. Colour was considered by both the retailers and the authorities as the defining element of popular imagery.[16] The cheap coloured woodcut image was, therefore, a recognisable genre. However, if we rely on the means of manufacture as the defining element of imagery, we have to ask to what extent it deserved the adjective popular.

The imagists and their world

According to critic Champfleury, the common folk (at least prior to his own industrialised and degenerate age) were innocent and spiritual, and imagery was their art form. He considered the rough style of the popular woodcut as reflecting the naiveté of the folk-artist, and for him naiveté equalled truth – the proper goal of all art.[17] This characterisation, of the imagist as folk-artist, influenced the first historians of imagery.[18] However, the more detailed work of post-war historians presents a rather different picture. Maurice Jusselin's study of the Chartres imagists and Jean-Marie Dumont's work on the Pellerin firm, both based largely on notarial documents, portray the imagist as a businessman, with a national network of commercial and political contacts. He was less a folk artist, more an entrepreneur. The size of their undertakings belied the folk-artist image. In 1806 Jean-Charles Pellerin boasted that he had 150 employees, and although there is little evidence to support this claim (which he made in the hope of tax relief), his workshop was more like a

---

[16] Because *canards* lack the vital ingredient of colour, and therefore clearly belong to a different genre, I have felt justified in not making them part of the core study. The *canard*, usually reporting some horrible crime or extraordinary event, consisted largely of text, onto which an image was tacked by way of illustration. The format was very different from imagery, in which the text was secondary. On the whole editors seem to have plumped either for imagery or *canards*. Pellerin is known to have accepted commissions from pedlars for a few *canards* around 1820, but usually he left this work to his neighbour Vautrin, or to Mongel in the nearby town of Charmes.

[17] 'Champfleury' [Jules-François-Félix Husson], *Histoire de l'imagerie populaire*, Paris 1869, 286–301.

[18] Imagery, although a mass-produced commercial article, was included alongside Scandinavian peasant murals and Romanian glass-paintings at the Congrès international des arts populaires held at Prague in 1928.

factory than a craftsman's bench.[19] In 1845 his son was employing thirty-eight adults and fifty children, mostly unskilled seasonal workers on piece-rate wages.[20] The Pellerin works at this period were comparable in size with those of their main competitors in Metz and Wissembourg.

This new picture of the imagist upset a lot of dearly held preconceptions about the artisanal nature of imagery. In order to avoid giving them up completely, attention switched away from the imagist to the engraver whom he employed. Adolphe Aynaud was the leading hunter after the elusive engravers, and the leading defender of the notion of imagery as folk-art. He could not bring himself to believe that the bourgeois Jean-Charles Pellerin revealed by Dumont's researches had actually engraved his own images. Could Pellerin, factory-owner with a summer-house in the country, head of the local Masonic lodge, also be the artist (and therefore by Aynaud's definition 'a man of the people') of these naive woodcuts? 'Eh bien non!'[21] While there is no definitive proof that Pellerin was an engraver, one cannot assume that he was not simply because he does not fit our notions of a folk-artist. Imagery may have been art for the people, but it was not necessarily by the people. It was, above all, a commercial undertaking, designed for a market with which the imagists themselves might have little in common. Jean-Charles Pellerin was probably typical of the kind of businessman involved.

The Pellerin family first arrived in Epinal as part of the occupying French army of 1692. It was there that Charles Pellerin, *carabinier*, met Catherine Tisserand. The following year they had their first child, though Pellerin was not given his officer's permission to marry until several months later. The Tisserand family were important citizens in Epinal and the scandal was considerable, which may be why the young couple moved back to Pellerin's home village near Vaucouleurs. However, they must have kept in contact with the family in Epinal because two of their sons made their homes there. Nicolas Pellerin arrived sometime before his marriage to Elizabeth Dondaine in 1735, his brother Gabriel had to wait for his discharge from the Béarn infantry in 1752. Nicolas was a card-maker, as had been his maternal grandfather Charles Tisserand. He was probably trained in the business by his uncle Dominique-Ignace Tisserand. His son Jean-Charles followed in his career as card-maker, combining this trade with groceries and clock-making. Jean-Charles Pellerin went on to found the imagery firm that still bears his

---

19 Jean-Marie Dumont, *La Vie et l'oeuvre de Jean-Charles Pellerin (1756–1836)*, Epinal 1956, 36.

20 Charles Charton and Henri Lepage, *Le Département des Vosges, statistique historique et administrative*, Epinal 1845, i. 1026. The difficult life of the seasonal staff employed by Pellerin is described by François Mathias, *Notice sur l'imagerie d'Epinal*, Epinal 1904, 29.

21 Adolphe Aynaud, 'Notes sur l'imagerie d'Epinal', *Le Vieux Papier*, fasc. 178, Paris 1956, 340. Aynaud's article caused a bitter row with the doyen of imagery historians, Pierre-Louis Duchartre, whose response appeared in his preface to Jean-Marie Dumont's *Les Maîtres graveurs populaires, 1800–1850*, Epinal 1965. Aynaud hit back in 'Notes sur l'imagerie d'Epinal (suite et fin)', extract from *Le Vieux Papier*, Paris 1966.

family's name. The firm remained in the hands of the Pellerins until 1918, and in the hands of Jean-Charles's direct descendants until the 1980s.

Many years before, in the 1660s, Charles Tisserand had lent money to a printer, Claude Cardinet. Cardinet also produced some imagery, but the immediate aftermath of the wars which had devastated Epinal was not a good time to start a business in the town and Cardinet soon went broke. As part of the debt settlement Tisserand received several woodblocks engraved for Cardinet by Mathurin Verneuil. It is not clear whether any member of the Tisserand family (or the Pellerin family before Jean-Charles) ever made use of these blocks, but Verneuil's blocks were part of Jean-Charles Pellerin's catalogue in the first quarter of the nineteenth century. Nor was this the Pellerin's only link with other imagists in the town. His father's first wife, Elizabeth Dondaine, was aunt to the wife of the card-maker and imagist Jean-Charles Didier. The Didiers were the main rivals of the Pellerin clan in the eighteenth century, but the last surviving son, also called Jean-Charles, died in 1786.[22] Later, Jean-Charles's grandson and successor, Charles-Nicolas Pellerin, was to marry the daughter of the local printer Nicolas-Edouard Gley, just one of several connections between these two families.[23]

The Pellerin family's social and commercial connections were, therefore, with other bourgeois families engaged in similar trades. Jusselin's study of the Chartrian imagists found similar networks of relationships in that city. Imagists belonged to the urban commercial and artisanal classes, and their friends and family came from the same backgrounds as themselves. Their skills as wood-engravers were also required in card-making, producing wall-paper and printed cloth (indiennes), and they often had family connections with these trades, or in the print trades. The circle of connections of the Chartres imagists, as indicated through marriage and baptismal records, was among this group of related crafts, and in particular with other imagists. When the engraver Marin Allabre, founder of the town's most successful firms of imagists, married in 1774, his witnesses were Pierre Hoyau and André-Sébastian Barc, both imagists for whom he had worked and with whom he would soon be in competition. When he set up on his own account in 1781 he worked in partnership with his three brothers, and he was succeeded on his death by his son-in-law.[24] Imagery was a family concern.

Although the imagists' social world was quite a small one, limited to other members of the bourgeois commercial classes engaged in the same or similar trades, their knowledge of the world was likely to be considerable. They had

[22] His brother-in-law Marcel Raguin succeeded him. Raguin does not appear to have been an imagist for long, no doubt due to the harsh attitude taken towards the industry by the revolutionary authorities.

[23] The information on the Pellerin family comes primarily from Jean-Marie Dumont's two works, La Vie et l'oeuvre, and Les Maîtres graveurs.

[24] Maurice Jusselin, Imagiers et cartiers à Chartres, Chartres 1957, 84, 119, 148.

travelled, perhaps lived in Paris, they had networks of correspondents in other cities, and they kept abreast of news and fashions emanating from the great metropolitan centres. The same could be said for their skilled staff, the designers and engravers, who resembled the imagists in terms of family and social connections, and who might hope to become imagists in their turn. The apprentice *garçon-dominotier* could aspire to becoming a *maître-imagier*, particularly if he married the boss's daughter. This was Jacques-Pierre Garnier's pathway to success. Employed as a journeyman- engraver by Marin Allabre of Chartres after an apprenticeship with Basset, the Parisian copperplate print-house, he married Allabre's daughter to form the firm Garnier-Allabre.[25]

Wood-engraving was a craft handed down within families. Charles-Nicolas Canivet of Nancy and his son François-Marc both produced woodblocks for Jean-Charles Pellerin. François Georgin, Pellerin's most famous engraver, was unusual in that, before he joined the firm, he had no family connection with the trade. He was also unusual in that he never left Epinal, and that, apart from the last three years of his life, he never worked for any firm other than Pellerin. Charles Boulay, who was apprenticed alongside Georgin, was far more typical. His father was a journeyman card-maker employed by Pellerin; Jean-Charles Pellerin and his wife were witnesses to the birth of his son. In his teens Charles moved from Epinal to Montbéliard where he was employed by the local imagists, the Deckherr brothers. Both Théophile and Rodolphe Deckherr were witnesses to his wedding in the town in 1820. Subsequently he worked for Jean-Pierre Clerc's imagery in neighbouring Belfort, though he continued to reside in Montbéliard until 1836 when the family moved to Paris. There his daughter, Caroline, carried on the family trade as a wood-engraver.[26] The Boulay family's history of travels, of connections with other firms, of sons (and sometimes daughters) following in their father's footsteps, is typical of the small world of imagists and their staff.[27]

Therefore, if one wishes to define imagists as 'of the people', it must first be admitted that the people to whom they belonged were drawn from a fairly

---

25 Jacques-Marin Garnier, *Histoire de l'imagerie populaire et des cartes à jouer à Chartres*, Toulouse 1991, 21.
26 For information on Georgin and Boulay see Dumont, *Les Maîtres graveurs*, 25–44, and Dominique Lerch, *Almanachs, bibliothèque bleue, imagerie: une famille d'éditeurs de la France de l'est, les frères Deckherr de Montbéliard*, Montbéliard 1990, 240–1. Caroline Boulay's engravings are included alongside her father's in BN, département des estampes, SNR Boulay.
27 The Thiébault brothers, the apprentices of François Desfeuilles, provide further examples of the interconnection between training, travel and family, which are documented in a whole series of articles by André Desfeuilles (a distant relative of François) listed in the bibliography. To these should be added two articles by Adolphe Aynaud: 'Les Thiébault, graveurs nancéiens', *Le Vieux Papier*, fasc. 170, Paris 1955, 105–10, and 'Notes sur l'imagerie de Nancy', *Le Vieux Papier*, fasc. 181, Paris 1957, 3–6.

limited group. It is not simply that they were townsfolk and that their market was largely rural, that they were craftsmen and businessmen while their customers were peasants: even within their urban commercial world they were further limited to craft-relationships, in which their titles as apprentice, journeyman and master indicated their level of social success. Because their trade involved them in book-selling and in contacts in Paris and beyond, they were likely to be far more informed about the world than their customers.

Considering what we know about the imagists and engravers, it would be interesting to see if their experiences and attitudes inspired their woodcuts. Many imagists had family or social connections with the army: the Pellerins arrived in Epinal in the military garrison, as did the family of Charles Pinot, their major local rival after 1860. Others had pronounced political views, which often got them into trouble with the authorities. Can traces of these be found in their imagery?

Jean-Charles Pellerin's uncle, grandfather and great-grandfather were all professional soldiers. Jean-Charles shared his home with another soldier, his brother-in-law Philippe Urbain. He was a leading figure in the local Masonic lodge, membership of which was mostly made up of officers from the garrison. His eldest son, Charles, died in the army in 1804. The Pellerin family was, therefore, well acquainted with the military. Jean-Charles's youngest son and successor, Nicholas, managed to avoid the draft but served as a lieutenant in the National Guard during the Hundred Days. However, his brother-in-law and partner in the firm, Pierre-Germain Vadet, was an altogether more dashing character.

The Vadets were, like the Pellerins, a military family from the Meuse. Pierre-Germain's elder brother, Etienne-Augustin Vadet had distinguished himself in the armies of the revolution. By the time of the Battle of Essling in 1809 he was a major in the 16th *chasseurs à cheval*. Serving in his squadron that day was his twenty-two-year-old brother, Pierre-Germain, recently promoted to lieutenant. Both brothers were severely injured during the battle; Pierre-Germain lost his leg. However, their devotion to the emperor did not go unrewarded. Pierre-Germain was made a Chevalier of the *Legion d'honneur* alongside his brother, and the pair were both given jobs as superintendents of the tobacco warehouses at Remiremont and Epinal, typical of the kind of positions given to wounded veterans of the *grande armée*. During the allied invasion of the Vosges in 1814, the brothers led the partisans defending the pass at Remiremont. When Napoleon returned in 1815 they were both, despite their injuries, given commands in local battalions of *franc-tireurs*.

Such die-hard Bonapartists came in for severe scrutiny at the restoration. Both brothers lost their jobs and Pierre-Germain was constantly harassed by the authorities for his political views. Despite his difficulties, he must have been a well-known figure around town, not least because he continued to sport the uniform of an imperial officer. A confidential prefectorial note provides a glamorous description: 'Captain in the partisans. Out-and-out

Bonapartist. . . . He is all the more dangerous in that he has means, spirit and good looks.' He certainly caught the eye of Marie-Marguerite Pellerin, daughter of the imagist and herself a bit 'outré'.[28] She married Vadet in 1818 and, a few years later, he became a partner in the family firm. Vadet apparently never wavered in his loyalty to the emperor. He left a stirring account of his part in the Essling campaign, written with the endearing lack of modesty that characterises officers' memoirs of the period.[29]

Vadet was not the only Napoleonic veteran to whom Pellerin gave shelter. The first full-time engraver known to have been employed in the workshop was Antoine Reveillé. A Spinalian born and bred, he was conscripted in 1807 and only returned to his home town in 1814. Reveillé did not last long as an engraver – he did not have the talent for it –but stayed with the firm as a paint-mixer and typesetter. Fellow employees gave him the character of a typical grognard, always ready to tell stories of his military career and, like Vadet, devoted to the memory of the emperor. He was not himself responsible for engraving Pellerin's famous Napoleonic imagery but he trained the youth who was, François Georgin, the nephew of another Napoleonic veteran living on his pension in the town. According to local legend Reveillé inspired Georgin with his own enthusiasm for the empire. And when Georgin died in 1863, Reveillé threw his grenadier's hackle after the coffin into the grave.[30]

The management and staff of the Pellerin firm had between them, therefore, considerable experience of military matters. Did any of this find its way into their imagery? Certainly Pellerin & Cie had a reputation as a producer of military, and in particular Napoleonic, imagery. The imperial legend accounted for 20 per cent of the firm's new images in 1831, 40 per cent in 1832, 66 per cent in 1833 and 100 per cent in 1834, although thereafter it rapidly declined.[31] It is tempting to see the hand of Vadet, then in charge of the firm's commercial policy, as responsible for this temporary flourishing. It has even been suggested that Pellerin, Vadet and Georgin together helped

---

[28] When the family home was raided by the police in 1816 a portrait of the emperor was found in her bedroom: André Philippe, 'Jean-Charles Pellerin poursuivi pour vente d'images séditieuses (1816)', La Révolution dans les Vosges xv (1926–7), 6.

[29] Details of the Vadet brothers' military careers can be found in M. Muller, La Défense des Vosges en 1814–1815: Wolff, Brice, les frères Vadet, Vatot et Rouyer, Epinal 1911. Vadet's description of the Battle of Essling is reproduced in Perrout, Trésors, 97–9. His part in the running of the Pellerin firm is detailed in Dumont, Les Maîtres graveurs, 3–8.

[30] For the history of the relationship between Reveillé and Georgin see Perrout, Trésors, 40–2. Lucien Descaves, author of a biography of Georgin, wrote that according to factory legend he had been trained by a certain Roy, whose son also worked for the firm, but there is no conclusive evidence that Roy père had been employed by Pellerin.

[31] Edith Mauriange, 'Sources d'inspiration de François Georgin pour quelques estampes de l'épopée napoléonienne', in Adolphe Riff (ed.), Art populaire de la France de l'est, Strasbourg–Paris 1969, 368.

create the right conditions for Napoleon III's *coup d'état*.[32] Napoleon III himself belatedly acknowledged the usefulness of *imagerie d'Epinal*, by making the firm 'by appointment to Her Majesty the Empress' in 1866.[33] On the other hand, there was very little that was personal in the images themselves. Reveillé was a veteran of the Russian campaign, but there is nothing in his image of the *Retraite de Moscow* to suggest that he had been a witness to the events depicted.[34] Similarly Georgin's series of battle scenes were not based on the veterans' stories heard around the factory, but on Parisian copperplate engravings, in particular the illustrations to Tissot's multi-volume *Trophées des armées françaises de 1792 à 1815*.[35] One of the few exceptions was Georgin's 1829 engraving of the Battle of Essling, the first in his series. In the foreground, next to the dying Marshall Lannes, is an officer of the 16th *chasseurs* in the act of falling from his horse. This image was displayed on the wall of the workshop with the legend underneath 'Bataille où M. Vadet a été blessé'.[36]

Such personal touches can seldom be detected. Even the choice of subject matter was less the result of the imagist's tastes than of commercial imperative. In 1828 Nicolas Pellerin was involved in an extended exchange of letters with the Prefecture and the ministry of the interior, over his proposed image of *Napoléon-le-grand*. His justification for the image was neither historical nor political but commercial; a competitor had been allowed to produce such an image, which was eating into his market share.[37] The same logic applies to the outpouring of Napoleonic imagery in the 1830s. Pellerin was not alone in dedicating himself to the imperial legend. Lacour of Nancy showed the same single-mindedness: Napoleonic imagery accounted for a third of his production in 1832, 100 per cent in 1833, 60 per cent in 1834 and 50 per cent in 1835.[38] Pellerin had to match his competitors if he was to survive commercially.

[32] This oft-repeated assertion has been given firmer credentials by Barbara Day-Hickman's study of the Pellerin firm's role in spreading Bonapartist mythology, which unfortunately appeared to late to be fully incorporated into this chapter: *Napoleonic art: nationalism and the spirit of rebellion in France (1815–1848)*, Newark 1999.
[33] The rival firm of Pinot & Sagaire had received the emperor's own patronage the year before, which must have hurt Pellerin & Cie.
[34] Reproduced in Dumont, *Les Maîtres graveurs*, plate vi.
[35] Mauriange, 'Sources d'inspiration', 369–70.
[36] François Blaudez, Jean Mistler and André Jacquemin, *Epinal et l'imagerie populaire*, Paris 1961, 115.
[37] As the prefect explained to the minister on Pellerin's behalf, 'beaucoup de marchands lui en avaient demandé des exemplaires. . . . qu'ils se les sont procurés ailleurs et qu'il en est résulté pour lui un dommage considérable, non seulement en ne plaçant pas cette image, mais en perdant l'occasion d'en vendre un grand nombre d'autres aux mêmes pratiques': Dumont, *Les Maîtres graveurs*, 56–9. The minister was unrelenting: 'C'est précisément parce que cette estampe pouvait être distribuée à un grand nombre d'exemplaires à cause de la modicité de son prix, que je n'ai pas cru devoir l'autoriser.'
[38] Figures taken from the Registre d'inscription des titres de gravures, cartes, plans, 1823–57, Archives départementales de Meurthe-et-Moselle, Nancy, 1/T/1233.

Similarly, it is difficult to find any evidence of the Pellerins' political beliefs in their imagery. The family had been an object of suspicion to the restored royalist authorities well before Marie-Marguerite's marriage to Vadet. On 5 July 1816, acting on information received from one of Pellerin's clients in Châlon-sur-Saône, the prefect of the Vosges ordered a raid on Jean-Charles Pellerin's workshop and home, to search for prints recalling the reign of the 'usurper'. The gendarmes found 600 images of imperial soldiers in the workshop. At the same time Pellerin's list of clients was seized, and they in turn were visited by the police. The result was the discovery of dozens of Napoleonic images. Worse, many had been dispatched from Epinal after February 1816, when the law that banned republican and Bonapartist symbols came into effect. Pellerin probably had no subversive intention in distributing these images. Images were made in long print runs and kept in store for years. The restoration found Pellerin unprepared with large stocks of now unsaleable images, and it appears that he tried to pass on the burden to his regular customers, such as Thierry in Châlon-sur-Saône, who not unnaturally complained. The authorities took a dim view of this kind of behaviour and Pellerin was initially sentenced to four months in prison and a fine of 600 francs. The prison sentence was waived on appeal.[39] But thereafter the ministry of the interior kept a close eye on Pellerin.[40]

Despite the ministry's worries, one searches in vain through Pellerin's imagery for a personal political statement. It is true that he had produced portraits of the imperial family during the empire, but he also produced portraits of the Bourbon family after the restoration. During the 1820s Pellerin's output was almost entirely religious; in the firm's 1842 catalogue the 610 religious images outnumbered all the other genres put together (530 images), but no one has suggested that this was the result of the family's

---

[39] This was not the only occasion on which Pellerin had difficulties with the royalist authorities. In 1821 an anonymous letter denounced him to the minister of the interior for allegedly distributing Reveillé's image of the *Retraite de Moscow* free to peasants in the surrounding villages. Actually the image had been approved by the prefect and was quite legally on sale. A prefectorial enquiry failed to find any proof that Pellerin had been giving it away free. The details of this case can be found in Philippe, 'Jean-Charles Pellerin', 96–107.

[40] Details of this case can be found in Dumont, *La Vie et l'oeuvre*, 60–2. In 1822, when Jean-Charles Pellerin wished to pass on his permits to print and sell books to his son Nicolas, the ministry refused on political grounds, as a note in the margin of the Pellerin file explains: 'Le sieur Pellerin appartient à une famille qui n'a point de principes religieux, et dont la conduite dans la révolution n'a pas été bonne. De plus, on le croit franc-maçon ainsi que son père. En résultat, on ne pense pas que cet homme soit digne de la confiance du gouvernement et tout porte à croire, au contraire, que s'il avait un brevet, il imprimerait volontiers toute espèce d'ouvrages dirigés contre la Religion et le Roi': Jean Adhémar, 'Pellerin était un dangereux franc-maçon', *Le Vieux Papier*, fasc. 167, Paris 1954, 172. It took six years, and the deployment of considerable political influence by the Pellerins, before the government was persuaded to think again.

deeply held religious convictions.[41] Imagists do not seem to have been concerned with the propaganda potential of their work. Nicolas's son, Charles, who ran the firm from 1854 to 1887, was an avowed republican, but this did not stop him from producing, on commission, party political material for Bourbonists, Orléanists and Bonapartists. He was, he explained when challenged by fellow republicans in 1885, a businessman, not a politician.[42] Market pressures decided Pellerin's commercial policy.[43] Imagery was not a vehicle for individual expression, but an object of trade. We must look elsewhere for the imagist's sources.

If personal experience did not give rise to an engraver's images, how about his local environment? The same eastern towns that were home to the main imagists were all garrison towns. Was the highly visible presence of the army reflected in their imagery? The imagist Joseph-Alexandre Martin of Lille, another garrison city, apparently made the sketches for his blocks of soldiers on the city's Champ-de-Mars.[44] How many other imagists were similarly inspired by their locality?

Imagery appears to be a highly localised art form. Images are known by the town that they come from, the address of the imagist appeared at the bottom of the sheet. Yet in terms of iconography it is hard to identify local influences. Georgin provides a couple of exceptions. In 1830 he engraved a *Bataille des Pyramides* and a portrait of *Général Lafayette* leading the newly formed National Guard in the Place de Grêve in Paris. However, as he had never visited either place, he covered his ignorance with local colour. Behind the Mameluke warriors appears a Vosgian village, with a tiny crescent moon of Islam atop the church spire; General Lafayette's horse prances outside, not the *hôtel-de-ville* in Paris, but Epinal town hall.[45]

It is easier to see local influences at work in the choice of themes imagists made. Local saints and pilgrimage cults were among the most popular items in any imagist's catalogue. Between 1825 and 1875 the Pellerin firm issued four versions of *Notre-Dame de Bon Secours*, a popular cult in Lorraine since the miserable years following the Thirty Years War.[46] However, this is more a case

---

[41] Henri George, 'Un catalogue de l'imagerie Pellerin d'Epinal de 1842', *Le Vieux Papier*, fasc. 340, Paris 1996, 260–1.

[42] Roth, 'Nation, armée et politique', 205–7.

[43] The Pellerins were not the only imagists to be troubled by the Restoration government. Jean-Pierre Clerc, described by the deputy-prefect for Belfort as an 'homme faux, connu dans toute la ville pour l'exagération de ses opinions hostiles au gouvernement et pour d'anciennes opinions républicaines', actually went to prison in 1824 for printing an 'apologie indirecte du régicide'. But in his imagery he put his beliefs to one side, even calling his firm 'Imprimerie catholique': Léon Delarbre, 'L'Imagerie populaire belfortaine', in Adolphe Riff (ed.), *Art populaire de France*, Strasbourg 1960, 185.

[44] Pierre-Louis Duchartre and René Saulnier, *L'Imagerie populaire*, Paris 1925, 233.

[45] Nicole Garnier-Pelle, *L'Imagerie populaire française*, II: *Images d'Epinal gravées sur bois*, Paris 1996, 22, and Musée Carnavalet, *Paris raconté par l'image d'Epinal*, Paris 1990 (exhibition catalogue), 41.

[46] Garnier-Pelle, *L'Imagerie populaire française*, ii, nos 76–80.

of local demand and supply, than a source of inspiration. Most of the common themes illustrated by imagists were national, if not international. Imagists, and presumably their clients, seem to have enjoyed exotic items – portraits of the emperors of Turkey and China, views of the cities of Italy, the confessions of Parisian murderers – as much as purely local material.

If imagery was inspired neither by personal experience nor by the local environment, then it must have been copied from someone else's original idea. Imagists were copyists; almost every theme they chose to depict had a history before it became a popular woodcut. Only when they made the switch to lithography did firms like Pellerin's begin to employ staff to come up with original ideas. Pinot, who joined the firm in 1847, was the first of a new breed of professional imagery designers.

The most important sources for imagists were copperplate prints from the better quality end of the print market. François Desfeuilles of Nancy faithfully copied engravings by Barthel of Strasbourg, Engelbrecht of Augsburg, and Campe of Nuremberg. Above all imagists copied the engravers of Paris.[47] Almost every major theme that proved popular in provincial woodcut imagery had previously appeared in the semi-fine copperplates of the rue Saint-Jacques. Provincial imagists had their favourites among the Parisian engravers; Desfeuilles was particularly attached to the work of the Basset print-house; Pellerin seems to have been keener on Basset's near neighbour and rival Jean, though he also copied from other Parisian engravers such Noël and Chereau.[48] The Parisians themselves were seldom original. They copied their images from other metropolitan centres, from the pictures exhibited in the Salon that year, and from better quality Parisian engravings of Italian old masters. The result is that behind many cheap woodcuts of the eighteenth and nineteenth centuries lurks a Raphael Madonna. Pellerin's Le Lion de Florence, for example, was based on a nineteenth-century Parisian copperplate print of Monsiau's seventeenth-century painting.[49]

The imagists did not, however, simply copy the engravings of the rue Saint-Jacques. They altered them to suit their market. Some alterations were necessarily due to the change in medium. A pear-wood block was far harder to manipulate than copperplate, so wood-engravers preferred sharp outlines to chiaroscuro, and avoided any extraneous detail. Another important difference was the use of colour; the Parisian sources were often black-and-white, or used colour in a naturalistic manner. Popular imagists always used colour, but in a manner that to modern eyes recalls Kandinsky – great blocks often

---

[47] For the history of the rue Saint Jacques engravers see Pierre-Louis Duchartre and René Saulnier, L'Imagerie parisienne: l'imagerie de la rue Saint-Jacques, Paris 1944.

[48] Images bought by Pellerin from Noël to serve as models were among the items seized when his workshop was raided in 1816: Philippe, 'Jean-Charles Pellerin', 98.

[49] Musée du Louvre, Nouvelles Acquisitions du département des peintures, 1983–6, Paris 1987, 129.

applied with little regard to the black-line image.[50] Further, the imagist would often add a text, a hymn or a song and a brief explanatory text. Thereafter it might be kept as a song-sheet or a source of information. Popular woodcut imagery was not purely decorative in the way Parisian copperplates could afford to be. In the changes wrought in turning a copperplate print into imagery, in terms of style, message and the use to which the final print was put, we can begin to see why the appellation 'popular' was appropriate.

The next most important source for imagists was each others' work. If an imagist had a success then others would immediately follow; copyright was set at nought. Several of Pellerin's earliest images were copied from Hurez of Cambrai (and at least two of these had been originally copied from Engelbrecht of Augsburg).[51] Later Georgin used several of Desfeuilles's images as his models.[52] Desfeuilles complained to the prefect that 'for a long time I have perceived nothing but the other makers rushing to grab the new subjects which appear in this genre in order to copy them for their profit without any artistic expenses'.[53] However, he was hardly in a position to throw stones as several of his sheets had been copied straight from Pellerin's.[54] Both Pellerin and Desfeuilles were also copying Boulay's engravings for the Deckherr brothers, but simultaneously Boulay was recreating in Montbéliard many of the images he had seen or worked on in Epinal, including *Le Lion de Florence*.[55] This behaviour was commonplace, but it makes it very difficult to be certain who was borrowing from whom. When Desfeuilles of Nancy issued a series of mounted sovereigns of the world which proved popular, both his local competitors, Lacour and Noël, immediately followed suit, and poached his staff in order to replicate them more exactly.[56] Little effort was made to disguise such plagiarism, even though technically once an image had been

---

50 The similarities between modern paintings and popular imagery are not accidental. Modernist painters from Courbet to Warhol have found popular images inspiring.
51 Garnier-Pelle, *L'Imagerie populaire française*, ii, nos 27, 945, 1170, 1838, 1984, among others. No. 1984 (and another image not listed by Garnier-Pelle but in Pellerin's 1814 catalogue, *Mamelucks et Tartares*) were based on Englebrecht copperplate engravings.
52 Ibid. nos 1205, 1709
53 'depuis longtemps aussi je n'apperçois que l'autres fabricants s'empressent de saisir les nouveaux sujets qui paraissent en ce genre pour les calquer à leur profit sans autre frais d'esprit': François Desfeuilles to the prefect of the Meurthe, 25 Jan. 1825, Archives départementales de Meurthe-et-Moselle, 1/T/1207.
54 Desfeuilles's *Musique française no. 1*, *Grenadiers français no. 17*, *Chasseurs français no. 19* and *Lanciers français no. 38*, were copied from Pellerin's images reproduced in Garnier-Pelle, *L'Imagerie populaire française*, ii, nos 1933, 1714, 1660, 1916 respectively. Desfeuilles even faithfully included the botched replacement flag Pellerin had inserted into his Napoleonic block after the original imperial eagle became unfashionable in 1815.
55 An incomplete list of Boulay's images for Deckherr has been compiled by Lerch: *Almanachs, bibliothèque bleue, imagerie*, 290–2.
56 Nicole Garnier, 'Les Bois d'imagerie populaire de François Desfeuilles de Nancy (1800–1837)', *La Revue du Louvre et des musées de France* v–vi (1987), 390–1.

deposited in the *dépôt légal* it was protected by law. Dembour's images carried the bold legend 'Property of the editor (I will pursue the counterfeiter)' but it is not clear if that made any difference.[57]

The third most important source for an imagist was his own stock of woodblocks. Unlike copperplates, which begin to show signs of wear after a few hundred impressions, a woodblock could lead a useful life for a century or more. As we have seen, Pellerin reused during the first empire several seven-teenth-century blocks he had inherited from his great-great-grandfather, and this was not unusual.[58] None the less a time would come when the block would be too worn and a new one had to be made. In 1812 Jacques-Marin Garnier witnessed his great-uncle recutting an image originally engraved by his grandfather in 1772.[59] It is difficult to say, in the absence of the original, how closely his version was modelled on the earlier one, but often they were straight copies. The engraver's unwillingness to deviate from his model is one explanation for the anachronisms that are a feature of popular imagery. Figures in images known to have been engraved in the eighteenth century wear the costumes of the seventeenth.[60]

A woodblock could last a long time, but it also took a long time to engrave. Therefore, it was a valuable asset, not to be thrown away lightly. Imagists were loath to abandon a block if a slight alteration, or even major surgery, could produce a marketable new image. This was particularly true in the changeable political climate of the nineteenth century. Each new regime required its own images, but few imagists could afford a whole new set of blocks. An example of how they got round this problem is the image of *Marlborough* from Picard-Guérin of Caen. Although it purports to be a portrait of the famous British general – the subject of a favourite nursery rhyme – with his baton and cocked hat, he looks more like a Napoleonic marshal. In fact exactly the same figure had been used for a portrait of *Le Général Foy*. Foy had been an unsuccessful general under Napoleon, but a favourite leader of the liberal opposition during the restoration. When Foy disappeared from the public mind the imagist had reused the block for a song-sheet. But Foy had probably not been the first incarnation of the block;

---

[57] Not a single case of one imagist suing another for breach of copyright is known, although Pierret of Rennes did once burn several of his blocks fearing that Pellerin was about to prosecute him: Musée départemental breton à Quimper, *L'Imagerie populaire bretonne*, Quimper 1992 (exhibition catalogue), 62.

[58] Some of the blocks used by the firm Garnier-Allabre were inherited from their prede-cessor Barc, who himself inherited the majority from Hoyau: Jusselin, *Imagiers et cartiers à Chartres*, 68, 94, 134, 151.

[59] Garnier, *Histoire de l'imagerie populaire*, 71.

[60] A Châlonnais image of Saint Alexis, which bears the signature of a printer active in the first quarter of the eighteenth century, is none the less dressed in the costumes of the Fronde period: Louis Ferrand, *Les Bois gravés châlonnais préservé au Musée de Châlon-sur-Saône*, Châlon-sur-Saône 1973, p. xvi.

31

he too was a reissue of an image that had first portrayed Murat or Lasalle.[61] This kind of salvage was common. In 1830 a new face and tricolour plume metamorphosed Pellerin's Charles X into King Louis-Philippe.[62]

Because blocks were valuable assets they could be bought and sold. When Lacour set up in competition to Desfeuilles in Nancy in 1830 he did so with the old stock of Dupont-Diot of Beauvais. He in turn sold his imagery to Dembour of Metz.[63] A few years later Dembour was buying up the stock of Clerc of Belfort.[64] Blocks regularly changed hands, sometimes more than once. The new owner changed its name and business address, and often cut out any identifying marks. This often makes it difficult to be sure whether the similarities between the images were the result of careful copying or trade.

Imagery cannot, therefore, be defined as popular in terms of its sources. The iconography of an image can usually be traced, if indirectly, to a painting or print produced for an elite market, possibly several generations before. The immediate source might be from among the same small group of artisans and merchants who formed the imagists' network of trade and social relations. Imagery should not be treated as folk art, but rather as one of the earliest manifestations of mass culture, both in the sense of quantity of production and the extent of its distribution, and arguably in its effects.[65] This does not necessarily detract from its value as a historical source. Objects of mass culture are very revealing about the mentality of the groups in which they circulate. In order to be successful they must appeal to the widest possible market. We can therefore expect them to be attuned to the public taste. However, it is as well to be aware of the distance between the culture producing imagery and the culture receiving it.

Imagery does display one of the characteristics of folk-art – fidelity to tradition. Many of the most popular themes in the imagists' repertoire in the 1840s had already been there for centuries. This conservatism may have been due to the imagist's own traditionalism, or even the public's nostalgic taste. But we have also seen how if one imagist, more daring than his fellows, discovered a popular new line, he would soon be followed by the rest. Imagists were only slow about new subjects until someone else had tried them; they had no objection to novelty as such. Pellerin's clients were constantly clam-

---

61 Lucien Crick, 'Monsieur de Marlborough', *Bulletin des musées royaux d'art et d'histoire* 3rd ser. iii (1931), 117–22.

62 In many cases all that was required was a new title; one saintly bishop or virgin martyr looked much like another, so by simply renaming them a new image was created. Thus the *Siège de Rome* in 1849 could be reissued as the *Siège de Sebastopol* in 1855. Compare no. 672 with 697, and no. 868 with 883, in Garnier-Pelle, *L'Imagerie populaire française*, ii.

63 Adolphe Aynaud, 'L'Imagerie de Beauvais', *Le Vieux Papier*, fasc. 156, Paris 1951, 148.

64 Delarbre, 'L'Imagerie populaire belfortaine', 185.

65 Robert Muchembled, *Culture populaire et culture des élites dans la France moderne (XVe–XVIIIe siècle)*, Paris 1978, 348–53.

ouring for new, fresh subjects, but he remained cautious.[66] Such a policy seems very wise when we have seen how closely successive governments supervised their production.

The censors

Under the *ancien régime* imagery was relatively free of bureaucratic control. Imagists were not part of a gild, nor, unlike printers and card-makers, were they regulated by any government office. They could not use a moveable letterpress, but many solved this problem by contracting out work to local printers. Certainly they could produce nothing considered to be offensive to either the monarchy or the Church, but otherwise they enjoyed considerable liberty.[67]

The revolution completely changed the situation. The imagists' subjects had largely consisted of saints and kings, which were inimical to the new authorities. In 1792 Marin Allabre of Chartres was ordered to destroy his 'blocks which depict the former slavery, or the face of the tyrants whom we have destroyed [or] the farces of a religion which philosophy and reason have annihilated for ever'.[68] His firm was shut down, his blocks supposedly burnt; he was given the job of gatekeeper in consolation. Very few other imagists were able to adapt to the new conditions; the lonely exception was Letourmy of Orleans, who renounced his holy images and portraits of the royal family in favour of anticlerical squibs and mementoes of the storming of the Bastille. The imagery industry did not take off again until after the First Consul established freedom of religion in 1800.[69] A few pre-revolutionary imageries made it through this difficult period; Allabre dug up his blocks from their hiding place and went back into production. Unfortunately, few were able to follow suit, and the baton passed to a new generation of imagists, including Pellerin.

Napoleon may have granted freedom of religion, but he had no intention

---

66 Some orders from Pellerin's clients are reproduced in Dumont, *La Vie et l'oeuvre*, 52–4.

67 In theory this liberty was enjoyed by post-revolutionary imagists. When Lacour applied to the prefecture of the Meurthe for a licence as an imagist, he received the reply from the ministry of the interior that 'les moyens d'execution qu'emploient les imagers et dominotiers ne sont soumis par la loi à aucune formalité'. In practice, however, a bookseller's and printer's licence were vital: Archives départementales de Meurthe-et-Moselle, 1/T/1210.

68 'les tableaux qui retracent l'ancien esclavage ou la figure des tirans que nous avons detruit sont proscrits et brulés. Bientôt une pareille proscription va tomber sur les images qui représentent les momeries d'une religion que la philosophe et la raison ont anéantie à jamais': procureur de la commune to the conseil général de la commune de Chartres, 24 brumaire Year II, quoted in Garnier, *Histoire de l'imagerie populaire*, 50–1.

69 Not surprisingly, a number of imagists, such as Leloup of le Mans, celebrated Napoleon's reconciliation with Rome in their prints: Garnier, *L'Imagerie populaire française*, i. 151. Pellerin also published, in 1811, an image entitled *Le Christianisme, affermi par Napoléon Ier*.

of restoring liberty of the press: 'The press is a weapon that it is important not to put into the hands of just anybody.'[70] The bureaucratic controls that Napoleon established over printing remained in place for most of the rest of the century. In order to sell images one needed, in practice, a *brevet de libraire*; in order to print the text one needed a *brevet d'imprimeur*.[71] In order to obtain both one needed a certificate of good conduct from one's mayor and a certificate of competence from four men of the same occupation. These were forwarded to the prefecture of the department, whose agreement was necessary before the ministry made the final award. Dominique Lerch has documented Wentzel of Wissembourg's twenty-year struggle, from 1831 to 1851, to obtain these two pieces of paper.[72] In both Pellerin's and Wentzel's cases, the certificates of competence and good conduct mattered little: what the authorities wanted was an assurance of political reliability. When Hinzelin (Desfeuilles's successor) applied for a printer's permit in 1830, the ministry asked for information, not about his ability or character, but about his political opinions.[73]

The authorities exercised strict controls not only over the imagists but also over their production. The main weapon of the censors was the *dépôt légal*. The *dépôt légal* had existed in one form or another since 1537. One of the restored monarchy's first concerns in 1814 was to ensure its good working. It was the means by which the government registered all printed matter. All publishers had to submit copies of their publications, partly to protect their own copyright, partly to enable the government to build up a library, but mainly so that the authorities could check the contents. The prince-president's minister of the interior explained in 1851 that 'The *dépôt légal* has always been, first and foremost, an institution related to public order.'[74] Theoretically engravers and imagists had fallen within its remit since 1762, but in practice they seem to have escaped its operation until the law of 25 March 1822.[75] The restoration government deliberately included popular imagery within the new law's remit because, as the minister of the interior explained to prefects, 'If freedom of the press has always been the support of

---

[70] 'L'imprimerie est un arsenal qu'il importe de ne pas mettre entre les mains de tout le monde': Dominique Lerch, *Imagerie et société: l'imagerie Wentzel de Wissembourg au XIXe siècle*, Strasbourg 1982, 23.

[71] It was these licences that the ministry of the interior refused to grant to Nicolas Pellerin in 1822.

[72] Lerch, *Imagerie et société*, 23–33.

[73] Prefect of the Meurthe to mayor of Nancy, 7 Mar. 1830, Archives départementales de Meurthe-et-Moselle, 1/T/1210.

[74] 'Le dépôt légal a été de tout temps et avant tout une institution qui se rapporte à la sûreté générale': Lerch, *Imagerie et société*, 69–72.

[75] Duchartre and Saulnier, *L'Imagerie parisienne*, 33. However, before 1822 prefects had kept an eye on imagists' production. In a letter of February 1811 the prefect of the Vosges gave his approval to thirteen new Pellerin images, ordered changes to another, and suppressed the last – *Le Conard volontaire* – on grounds of obscenity: Dumont, *La Vie et l'oeuvre*, 46.

troublemakers, freedom of imagery is much more dangerous, because prints work directly on the people, and may lead them to revolt, or at least into contempt for the most respectable things.'[76] Prefects were ordered to censor all images which were

> contrary to decency or religion; those which contain allusions against the king or members of the royal family, or insults against public functionaries or even private persons; [those which contain] emblems and rallying signs banned by law . . . but beyond that everything which seems to you might exercise a unfortunate influence on people's minds and thus threaten the public peace.[77]

Failure to process an image through the *dépôt légal* could result in imprisonment, a fine or forced closure.[78]

The second empire saw the imposition of yet further controls. The turbulent period of French history that immediately preceded Napoleon III's *coup d'état* was ascribed by many politicians to the subversive influence of cheap print. Anxious to avoid further revolutions, the government set up a *Commission du colportage* to oversee all printed matter designed to be carried by pedlars, including imagery. The commission had the right to order changes or ban any item, without explanation or appeal. Their premise was that almost everything then being carried by pedlars was objectionable, if not on political grounds then on moral ones.[79] Many of the most popular and centuries-old items in the imagists' repertoire fell foul of the commission, including such apparently innocuous images as *L'Arbre d'amour*, *Adelaïde et Ferdinand* and *Les Trois Chemins de l'eternité*.[80] The objections of the commission and prefects to individual images are sometimes hard to fathom: they were usually political, but the censors also regarded themselves as the guardians of the morality of the popular classes (who could not be expected to look after themselves).[81]

---

[76] 'si la licence de la presse a toujours été auxiliaire des factieux, la licence des gravures est encore plus dangereuse, parce qu'elle agit directement sur le peuple, et peut l'entraîner à la révolte, ou du moins au mépris des choses les plus respectables': ministerial circular, 20 May 1822, Archives départementales de Meurthe-et-Moselle, 1/T/1207.

[77] 'contraires aux bonnes moeurs et à la morale religieuse; sur celles qui renferment des allusions contre le Roi et les membres de la famille royale, des outrages contre les fonctionnaires publiés où même les simple particuliers; des emblêmes et des signes de railliement proscrits par les lois . . . mais encore tout ce qui vous paraîtra devoir exercer sur les esprits une influence fâcheuse et porter atteinte à tranquilité publique': ministerial circular, 22 Apr. 1822, Archives départementales de Meurthe-et-Moselle, 1/T/1207.

[78] Heitz, a Strasbourg printer, had his workshop sealed for six months for failure to comply with the *dépôt légal*: Lerch, *Imagerie et société*, 71.

[79] The history of the Commission permanente des livres de colportage is given in Jean-Jacques Darmon, *Le Colportage de librarie en France sous le second empire: grand colporteurs et culture populaire*, Paris 1972, 97–136.

[80] Gangel to his clients, 29 Nov. 1853, reproduced in Gérard Bode, *L'Imagerie messine, 1838–1871: exposition d'images conservées aux archives départementales*, Metz 1987, 243. An image of *L'Enfant prodigue* by one of Gangel's competitors, Thomas, was banned in 1860!

[81] Hence, in 1859, the prefect of the Bas-Rhin ordered the destruction of one of Wentzel's

The need to submit all their production to the authorities for approval and stamping infuriated the imagists. Wentzel constantly complained that he lost ten days every month by having to send all his images down to Strasbourg.[82] The absurd level of scrutiny to which they were subjected obliged imagists to take up a combative stance when in reality they were, as commercially minded businessmen, usually friendly to the forces of law and order. The climate engendered had the effect of making imagists into their own censors. Only 2 per cent of Dembour & Gangel's images, and only 0.5 per cent of Wentzel's, were banned.[83] When one considers that the most innocent of images might be refused for the flimsiest of reasons, this success rate can only be explained by the imagists vetting their own production. The conservatism of imagists should not necessarily be condemned as lack of imagination. They preferred copying to originality because it ran fewer risks. But it also means that when we consider imagery as a historical source, we should always be aware that we are looking at the authorised image.

For the historian, the controls on the industry have at least had the advantage of saving many images which would otherwise have been lost. We only know so much about Pellerin's imperial imagery because it was seized as evidence in 1816.[84] The *dépôt légal*, though it is not absolutely reliable as a complete record of production, at least ensured that a large number of images have been preserved in departmental archives and in the Bibliothèque nationale. Without such measures they would mostly have been destroyed, for imagery was, by its nature, ephemeral. When the Epinal imagist Jean-Charles Didier died in 1772 he left a stock of 56,000 images, which represents only a fraction of the Didier family's production over three generations. Today only ten Didier images are known.[85] Therefore those images that have survived are not necessarily representative of the bulk of production at any one time. They have escaped the usual fate of imagery because they were not used for their original purpose. However, their ephemeral nature also suggests that images were more than decorations; they were designed to be consumed, and as Roger Chartier has taught us, consumption is also a means of cultural production.[86]

images, *Les Autrichiens dans le Pô*, which contained a distasteful pun on the Austrians' misfortunes in Italy. According to the prefect 'le peuple français mérite mieux pour ses plaisirs qu'une grossière équivoque': Lerch, *Imagerie et société*, 74.

[82] However, Wentzel got into serious trouble in 1866 when he tried to circumvent the system and have his image of the battle of Lissa stamped before it had been approved by the committee. It was banned because it depicted an Italian defeat: ibid. 74.

[83] Ibid. 73; Bode, *L'Imagerie messine*, 219.

[84] The images seized are reproduced in André Philippe, 'Les Débuts de l'imagerie populaire à Epinal: images napoléoniennes de Jean-Charles Pellerin (1810–1815)', *L'Art populaire en France* i (1929), 161–78.

[85] Garnier-Pelle, *L'Imagerie populaire française*, ii. 35–8.

[86] Roger Chartier, *The cultural uses of print in early modern France*, Princeton, NJ 1987, 11.

The consumers of imagery

Neither the imagists nor the censors had any doubts as to the nature of the market: imagery was for the poor, particularly the rural poor. Nicolas Pellerin wrote that 'these modest images are not destined to decorate the drawing rooms of the rich, but are made for the working class, for that interesting class – the poor inhabitants of the countryside'.[87] The authorities (representatives of a different class) disdained them: the prefect of the Vosges described Pellerin's images in 1820 as 'of the lowest quality, of very little value, and for this reason principally sold in the countryside'.[88] However, from their point of view this was precisely the problem; it was not just the content which worried the authorities, but the person to whom it was addressed. The *directeur de la police (Libraire)* made this very clear in a letter to the prefect of the Meurthe in 1827 after the latter had approved Desfeuilles's image of *Napoléon-le-grand*:

> I very much regret that you did not notice that this crude image, designed to be coloured and spread among the lower orders, cannot be sold without incon-veniences. The government's principle is never to authorise such prints, unless they will be of such a high price that they will obviously be out of the reach of the inferior classes.[89]

Particular types of print were, therefore, associated with particular consumers. The authorities used three criteria to judge the intended audience for a print: style, colour and price. Imagery was cheap: in 1814 Pellerin sold wholesale at fourteen *francs* a ream of 500 or 1,000 images, depending on the size. This was slightly more expensive than his main competitors but still left sufficient margin for profit for the retailer if sold at the traditional price of five *centimes* or one *sou* (so traditional that they were regularly referred to as *images d'un sou*; Verlaine wrote a pamphlet with that title in 1873).[90] At that price they

---

87 Philippe Picoche, *Le Monde des chamagnons et des colporteurs au XIXe siècle dans les Vosges*, Raon-l'Étape 1992, 145.
88 'd'un travail des plus commun, de très mince valeur, et qui par cette raison se débitent principalement dans les campagnes': Dumont, *La Vie et l'oeuvre*, 61. A functionary of the prefecture of the Bas-Rhin described the lithographs of Pellerin's competitor Wentzel as 'grossièrement faites et n'ont aucun caractère artistique: elles ne peuvent dès lors convenir qu'à orner les auberges de campagne et les habitations ouvrières': Lerch, *Imagerie et société*, 12.
89 'Je regrette beaucoup que vous n'avez pas remarqué que cette gravure grossière destinée à être coloriée et à se repandue dans le bas peuple, ne pouvoir circuler sans inconvéniences. L'administration a pour principe de ne point autoriser ces publications, à moins qu'elles ne soient d'un prix élevé et évidemmen [sic] hors de la portée de la classe inférieure': Archives départementales de Meurthe-et-Moselle, 1/T/1207. This was the image that Pellerin presented to the minister in support of his case after his own image of Napoleon had been banned by the prefect.
90 Dumont, *La Vie et l'oeuvre*, 53. In Pellerin's 1842 catalogue the price had gone down to twelve *francs* per ream.

Plate 2. *Napoléon*: Desfeuilles (Nancy), 1827
The writing in the top right-hand corner is the signature of approval granted
by the prefect of the Meurthe, to the fury of the minister of the interior.
Reproduced by permission of the Musée départemental d'art
ancien et contemporain, Epinal.

were within reach of all but the very poorest members of society. It also meant that, unlike copperplate engravings or lithographs, they had no intrinsic value and, therefore, were not framed or protected with glass, but simply nailed to the wall. As the last Chartrian imagist, Jacques-Marin Garnier, explained: 'It was their destiny to be bought by children in whose hands they lasted just as long as any piece of paper, or to plaster the walls of the cottage, the village inn, or the artisan's workshop, where their destruction was the work of time and smoke.'[91]

The price of imagery put it within reach of the poorer elements of society, but to judge it by its style and colour, as the authorities did, suggests the exercise of taste. Was it poverty or preference that led the popular classes to buy particular types of prints? This is a difficult question to resolve, but we do know the importance that producers and retailers attached to the use of colour as a means to attract their chosen market. Pellerin announced in his 1814 catalogue that 'all the images are decorated in very bright colours', and it was this which allowed him to charge more than his competitors for he knew from his agents that his images were sought for the 'liveliness of the colours'.[92] Their vividness was certainly what stuck in the mind of the schoolboy Ponchon when a Lorrainer pedlar set up his stall in front of his school in the 1860s: 'Heavens, what colours! Red, blue, yellow and, oh ecstasy for the eyes, gold which glittered in the sunlight and made one instantly think of handsome lancers.'[93] Colour was a very important element of a print in the judgement of its purchasers, if only for practical considerations. Balzac might abhor an image 'of a colour that would make Delacroix faint', but in a cottage lit only by smoky rush-lights anything less bright would rapidly become invisible. Paintings of peasant homes by nineteenth-century realists, such as Decamps's *The card-players*, clearly illustrate this necessity.[94]

The authorities were also right to associate imagery with a particular style. They called it 'crude', but collectors prefer the term 'gothic', because the thick black outlines and the absence of shading recall the stained glass windows of medieval cathedrals. The immutability of this style in part derives from the materials: a block of pear-wood gouged out with a nail simply does not allow for the delicacy of a boxwood engraving or the half-tones of a litho-

91 'il entrait dans leur destinée d'être achetées par des enfants dans les mains desquels elles duraient de que vit une feuille de papier, ou bien de tapisser les murailles de la chaumière, le cabaret du village et la boutique de l'artisan; leur destruction était alors l'oeuvre du temps et de la fumée': Garnier, *Histoire de l'imagerie populaire*, 45.

92 'toutes les images sont enluminées de couleurs très vives': Dumont, *La Vie et l'oeuvre*, 53.

93 'Ciel! quelles couleurs éclatantes: du rouge, du bleu, du jaune, et, extase des yeux! des ors qui luisent au soleil et font penser subitement aux beaux lanciers': Alexandre Ponchon, ' "A l'Veille!": la veillée vers 1850: contribution à l'étude des traditions populaires de l'Amienois', *Conference des rosatis picards* xli (1909), 11.

94 'd'une couleur à faire évanouir Delacroix': quoted by Meyer Schapiro, 'Courbet and popular imagery', *Journal of the Warburg and Courtauld Institutes* iv (1940), 177.

graph. However, it is also possible that these elements were the deliberate policy of the imagist, conscious of their market's loyalty to older forms. Dembour of Metz, for example, started life as a lithographer but, when he expanded into imagery in 1836, he reverted to the traditional woodcut method and style of production. Similarly, although Pellerin introduced the lithograph in 1854, new woodblocks were being carved well into the third republic; indeed they were the majority of new production in many years.[95] These examples suggest that there was a continuing consumer taste for 'crude images', even when prints in more fashionable Parisian styles were widely available at the same or similar prices.

Given the nature of the market for imagery, we are entitled to call it 'popular' not in terms of who created it but in terms of who bought it. This is not to ignore the fact that some members of all social classes were attracted to imagery. Because of the way imagery was sold, and the ways it was used, its themes were probably familiar to every level of society.[96] However, this does not necessarily detract from its value as a historical source for a particular social group. Imagists lived by their commercial success in making their products appeal to the widest possible market, which in pre-1870 France meant the peasant market. The sources may have belonged to more elite settings, but it was the peasant who chose the themes that made the transfer from the Parisian salons to the *cabaret*. It was the peasant who chose the style, crude but colourful, in which these themes were illustrated. Even if it is true that imagery was not exclusively for rural consumption, it was in the village that it was most visible and where, for want of other stimuli, it had its greatest impact. Popular imagery offers an insight into the mentality of the 'working class' of the countryside through the choices its members exercised as consumers.

We should, however, be cautious of seeing imagery as merely reflective of the preferences of a particular social group. Like all art (and more obviously than most because of the addition of a didactic text) imagery was designed to impart meaning. What ideas did the viewer draw, what lessons did the reader learn from imagery? Imagery cannot be treated just as a measure of cultural change, but as an active participant in that process. The authorities were convinced of its dangers, but others were equally keen on its positive benefits. Michelet, for example, believed that coloured posters were the ideal way to spread republican politics among the lower classes.[97] Imagery was used by

[95] The Pellerin company even used lithographs as models for woodblock engravings, as in the case of song no. 125, *Le Départ du conscrit*, issued in 1875 but faithfully copied from a lithograph published in 1866: Garnier-Pelle, *L'Imagerie populaire française*, ii, no. 1174.

[96] French popular imagery might be considered in the same way as the English cheap print examined by Tessa Watt, as 'an instrument of social cohesion . . . as stories, images and values permeated the multiple tiers of English society': *Cheap print and popular piety, 1550–1640*, Cambridge 1991, 5.

[97] Chantal Georgel, *L'Enfant et l'image au XIXe siècle*, Paris 1988 (Musée d'Orsay exhibition catalogue), 8.

schoolteachers, priests, imperialists and missionaries to inculcate their messages. However, the potential propaganda value of imagery does not mean that it was simply a weapon in a war of acculturation. The peasant purchaser was not a passive recipient of a finished product, imagery was to be used, and it is in the way he used it, the way he 'appropriated' it, that much of its value as a historical source lies.

The uses of imagery

It seems likely that wood-engraving was introduced to France by monks of the Benedictine and Cistercian orders, who distributed their prints during pilgrimages and the sale of indulgences.[98] Its initial purpose was part of the established tradition of using images as an aid to devotion, and they continued in this role long after imagery production had fallen into secular hands. Most religious imagery, in the nineteenth century at least, included prayers and hymns, while others contained direct instructions for use. Desfeuilles's 1824 image entitled *Bénédiction des maisons* (a crucifixion scene), contains the stern injunction 'Prostrate yourself before the image of our saviour Jesus Christ'.[99] The link between imagery and devotion is most clear in the case of pilgrimage images.[100] Pilgrimage imagery remained in the catalogue of all imagists up until the end of the period, just as the pedlar selling imagery remained a feature of pilgrimages themselves. In 1870 Wentzel sent 60,000 images to the pilgrimage centre of Czestochowa in Poland, 8 per cent of his total production in that troubled year.[101] Pellerin's 1814 catalogue contained no less than six images of miracle-working statues of the Virgin, including the *Véritable Portrait de Notre-Dame de Sion*, a popular local pilgrimage, which instructed the viewer to 'plead for the intercession of the holy Virgin before her miraculous image'.[102] Whether the miraculous image referred to is the actual statue at Sion or the paper reproduction is not made

[98]   The oldest surviving woodblock, at least according to some experts, is the 'bois Protat' which originated in the Benedictine abbey at La Ferté-sur-Grosne: Henri Bouchot, *Le Bois Protat, un ancêtre de la gravure sur bois: étude sur un xylographe taillé en Bourgogne vers 1370*, Paris 1902.

[99]   BN (estampes), Li 11 folio, imagerie populaire de Nancy: Desfeuilles; imagerie populaire de Montbéliard (Doubs): Deckherr. Another crucifixion from Pellerin is more of a private religious exercise, inviting the viewer to 'Arretez et considerez s'il y a douleur semblable à la mienne': Garnier-Pelle, *L'Imagerie populaire française*, ii, no. 185. For the history of one ever-popular religious exercise in print form see Anne Sauvy, *Le Miroir du coeur: quatre siècles d'images savantes et populaires*, Paris 1989. For a more general theory of religious imagery, consult David Morgan, *Visual piety: a history and theory of popular religious images*, Berkeley–Los Angeles, 1998.

[100]   In their review of provincial imagery centres Duchartre and Saulnier pointed out that most were on pilgrimage routes (even Epinal drew pilgrims to its relics of Saint Goëry).

[101]   Lerch, *Imagerie et société*, 172.

[102]   Garnier-Pelle, *L'Imagerie populaire française*, ii, no. 137.

clear, nor is the question resolved by the inclusion of kneeling worshippers in the picture itself, a very common detail and one surely designed to inspire imitation. That imagery was treated with this devotion we know from Stendhal, who wrote of 'those coloured prints that one sees modestly displayed at our country fairs, and which the peasant buys in order to kneel before them'.[103] The folklorist Luzel, during his tours of upper Brittany, found that the peasants were very unwilling to part with their images however old and dirty, because of their religious attachment.[104] Many people testified to the importance of imagery in their own religious life; Chateaubriand wrote that his nurse's woodcut print of the Virgin Mary 'inspired in me more devotion than a Raphael Madonna'.[105] The importance that some purchasers attached to them might have worried the Catholic hierarchy for, in some cases, it is clear that the image was no longer considered simply as representative of the person but as imbued with their real presence. A local legend tells of a peasant woman hanging round the imagery stall in Epinal market in order, she told the stall-holder, 'to see saint Peter in order that he might know me when I arrive up above'.[106] The image was truth materialised rather than merely depicted.

Because the holy figure was actually present in the image, it might be obliged to earn the devotion it enjoyed by protecting the house and its members. The oldest dated image is a Madonna and Child from 1418, found on the inside of the lid of a chest at Malines, and many other early images have been found in similar locations. In the first decade of this century Perrout was still finding eighteenth-century images on the inside of Vosgian cottage cupboard doors.[107] The placing of religious imagery inside furniture, and thus usually invisible, underlines the fact that imagery had functions beyond the decorative, presumably in these cases to guard the valuables contained within. A strict demarcation between devotional and protective uses of imagery is impossible to maintain. Desfeuilles's *Bénédiction des maisons* might have demanded that the viewer bow before it, but its title suggests that its main function was to protect the household.[108] Each image had a special position in the house because each had a specific task. In Catholic Alsace, for

103 'ces estampes coloriées que l'on voit modestement étalées à terre, dans nos foires de campagne, et que le paysan achète pour s'agenouiller devant elles': Henri Beyle ['Stendhal'], *Histoire de la peinture en Italie*, Geneva–Paris 1969, 11.
104 Paul Sébillot, 'L'Imagerie populaire: l'imagerie en Basse-Bretagne', *Revue des traditions populaires* iii (1888), 311.
105 Gabriel Magnien, 'Les Ecrivains romantiques et l'imagerie populaire', *Le Vieux Papier*, fasc. 194, Paris 1961, 27. Saint Thérèse de Lisieux was brought to an awareness of her vocation through imagery.
106 Blaudez, *Epinal et l'imagerie populaire*, 73.
107 Perrout, *Trésors*, 15, 28–9.
108 Archives départementales de Meurthe-et-Moselle, 1/T/1233. Deckherr's *Heureuse Bénédiction des familles et des maisons* was headed 'Que Dieu préserve de toute adversité la maison ou sera cette image adorable!': BN (estampes), Li 11 folio, imagerie populaire de Nancy: Desfeuilles; imagerie populaire de Montbéliard (Doubs): Deckherr. Another image

instance, Saint Agatha was placed above the door to protect the house from fire (in Lorraine Saint Donat had this job), Christ watched over the parents' bed but John the Baptist over the children (in Lorraine Saint Nicolas took his place), while Saint Blaise was relegated to the barn because he was responsible for the animals.[109] The texts accompanying the images invoked their special role, Pellerin's numerous images of Saint Blaise and Saint Guérin all contain the request that they should 'Pray to God for the conservation of our cattle'. The supposed protective power of these images, in some cases attested by representatives of the Church, made them immensely popular items in the imagists' catalogues.[110] Deckherr's *Heureuse Bénédiction* was printed six times, and his *Sainte Agathe* five, more than any other image the firm produced.[111] The function of other saints meant that their images were only called upon occasionally. For example, women in childbirth would have Saint Margaret watching over their bed. Garnier recalled hastily running off a Saint Sebastian, a saint with a long history of combating plague, when cholera struck Chartres in 1832. Both Dembour & Gangel and Pellerin issued special protective images against new cholera epidemics in 1849 and 1854.[112]

One begins to see how a cottage, like those Breton interiors depicted by the painters Guérard and Villard, might fill up with images.[113] But we still need room for yet more to include the whole panoply of individual and group patrons whose protection was also invoked. In a Vosgian household the folklorist Richard noted, alongside the *Mariage de la sainte Vierge* and the *Bon Pasteur*, the patron saints of the members of the family.[114] Local or regional patrons might also be honoured; in Franche-Comté conscripts received an image of their village's patron.[115] At the beginning of the nineteenth century the inhabitants of the Comtois town of Gray annually replaced the images of their patron before his feast-day.[116]

Such behaviour is reminiscent of pre-revolutionary gilds and confraterni-

---

issued by the firm in the same year on the same theme was entitled *Dieu benira la maison où l'image de Jesus Christ sera posée*.

[109] Dominique Lerch, 'Du Colportage à l'errance: réflexions sur le colportage en Alsace au XIXe siècle', *Revue d'Alsace* cxiii (1987), 176, and J. Joachim, 'Les Images de Sainte Agathe en Alsace', in Adolphe Riff (ed.), *Art populaire d'Alsace*, Strasbourg–Paris 1963, 133–55.

[110] Pellerin had the approval of Cardinal Fech, bishop of Lyon, for his 1822 *Heureuse Bénédiction des familles et des maisons*: Garnier-Pelle, *L'Imagerie populaire française*, ii, no. 193.

[111] Lerch, *Almanachs, bibliothèque bleue, imagerie*, 51.

[112] Garnier, *Histoire de l'imagerie populaire*, 207.

[113] Musée départemental breton, *L'Imagerie populaire bretonne*, nos 1, 2.

[114] Nicolas-Louis-Antoine Richard, *Traditions populaires, croyances superstitieuses, usages et coutumes de l'ancienne Lorraine*, Remiremont 1848, 149.

[115] This seems to be a fairly recent custom, which only became widespread after the First World War to judge from the orders received by Pellerin (now preserved in the Archives départementales des Vosges).

[116] Duchartre and Saulnier, *L'Imagerie populaire*, 56.

Plate 3. *Les Quatre Saisons: les amusements de l'hiver:* Pellerin (Epinal), 1843
Imagery in a domestic setting – on the back wall of this Vosgian cottage one
can make out an image of a female figure, possibly Saint Geneviève.
Reproduced by permission of the Réunion des musées nationaux.

ties. Each confraternity would commission an image of its patron, to be given
annually to its members on the feast-day and carried in procession to their
chapel. It then replaced last year's image on the wall of their workplace.[117]
Patronal imagery was therefore consumed by use, which accounts for its rarity
today.[118] However, one did not have to be a member of a rich urban confraternity to possess an image of one's patron saint. They made up a significant part
of all imagists catalogues; Pellerin's catalogue of 1814 includes, among others,
Saint Ely for blacksmiths, Saint Vincent for wine-growers, Saint Honoré for
bakers and Saint Crispin and Saint Crispinian for cobblers. As with confraternity imagery they were used to adorn the workshops of artisans and rural
craftsmen, just as we see the image of Saint Honoré nailed to the wall of the
baker's shop in Gangel's image of the song *La Boulangère*.[119] Garnier describes

---

117 Pierre Salies, 'Imagerie populaire et confréries toulousaines', *Gazette des beaux-arts* lix
(1962), 258–76. To a limited extent benefit clubs and friendly societies kept up this
custom after the revolution: Seguin, 'Imagerie et vie sociale', 179–232.
118 J.-M. Papillon calculated that his grandfather's woodblock commissioned for the
Confrérie royale de la charité de Notre-Dame de bonne délivrance was used to print over
half a million images in over a hundred years. Of these only two have survived: Jean
Gaston, *Les Images des confréries parisiennes avant la révolution*, Paris 1909, p. xxiii. Salies
makes the same point about Toulousian imagery.
119 Barbé, *L'Imagier de Metz*, 69.

how the cobbler next door to his father's print shop was 'utterly covered in images', chief among them being his patrons, Saints Crispin and Crispinian, on each side of the most famous cobbler of them all, the Wandering Jew.[120] Were these, like the earlier confraternity images or the patron of Gray, replaced every year? Garnier does not say, but the habit of replacing one's images annually was not limited to confraternities. In Normandy the old and dirty images were thrown out at the end of the year and new ones bought when the pedlar passed through.[121]

The reader may wonder why I have lingered so long over religious imagery, when this study will be concerned almost exclusively with secular themes, but for most of its history imagery was above all religious. In Lorraine images were called 'saints' regardless of their actual subject, and this history has left traces on secular imagery.[122] The comparison frequently made between Napoleonic and religious imagery is fully justified by Pellerin's series of imperial marshals entitled *Gloire nationale*, the form of which is identical to his contemporaneous *Galerie religieuse*.[123] And it is not just in the iconography of military imagery that one can find evidence of the religious origins of the industry, but also in the uses to which it was put. Were the colourful eighteenth-century dragoons and hussars, who can be found adorning chests and cupboards, more than merely decorative? Perhaps they had a protective function similar to that of the saints whom they dislodged.

The continuity of function is clearer in the case of secular patronal imagery. I have described patronal imagery largely in terms of its protective role but it was much more than that. The patron's image recalled some aspect of the individual who possessed it. If we look again at the Vosgian cottage described by Richard we see the father-guardian echoed in the image of *Le Bon Pasteur*, the wife and mother in *Le Mariage de la sainte Vierge*. An image might represent a role for an individual, whether as part of an age group, as in the case of conscripts, or as a member of a profession. It was a badge of belonging and a symbol of pride in one's craft or in one's community, and through it one's allegiances were publicly displayed. Religious imagery could serve as an affirmation of self, and so could military imagery.

The symbolic value of imagery was used by authors such as Balzac and Hugo to reveal the personalities of their characters. When, in *Le Peau de chagrin*, Balzac pictured on the wall of a Auvergnat cottage an image of Gren-

---

120 Garnier, *Histoire de l'imagerie populaire*, 66.
121 René Hélot, *Notes sur l'imagerie populaire en Normandie*, Lille 1908, 5.
122 Perrout, *Trésors*, 18.
123 Jean Bauchez, looking at the Napoleonic images produced by Dembour & Gangel of Metz, wrote, 'Ils ressemblent fort, dans leur conception, aux images religieuses; l'empereur y apparait comme un dieu auquel on dédie parfois un chant ou un poème': 'Légende napoléonienne et propagande bonarpartiste à Metz et en Moselle de 1832 à 1852', unpubl. *mémoire de maîtrise*, Metz 1986, 22.

adiers de la garde impériale, the reader knew at once that the owner had retained his loyalty to the emperor.[124] Hugo similarly decorated a fictional servant-girl's Paris garret with meaningful images, for in a dark corner, 'entre la Sainte Vierge et le gui de l'année, quatre épingles au mur fixaient Napoléon'.[125] In reality, as in fiction, imagery could be used to express private allegiance. This is demonstrated by an image which straddled the divide between religious and secular – *Saint Napoléon, patron des guerriers*. Though it apparently concerned an officer and martyr of the reign of Diocletian (or a knight of Saint Louis, depending on the imagist's imagination), Saint Napoleon had no basis in history or legend. He was an invention of the Concordat, the symbol of the *rapprochement* between the past-revolutionary state and the papacy. As such his image was outlawed on the return of the Bourbons.[126] On the 18 June 1817 a young pedlar was arrested in a poor quarter of Le Mans for selling images of Saint Napoleon. Neither the arresting officer, the boy or his customers seem to have been in any doubt that this was not just another saint, but rather Bonapartist propaganda, reinforced by the inclusion of a little vignette depicting the Roman soldier in prison, just as Napoleon then was on Saint Helena. The police subsequently visited the homes of those persons known to have purchased a copy, including a certain De Fontaine, 'who had stuck it up in his house'. Like many others he refused to give it up.[127]

During the restoration Bonapartist images were usually kept out of the public's gaze, but other expressions of political allegiance were not so secret. 1814 had seen a flood of royalist imagery from almost every print house: the engraver Godard was kept especially busy with commissions for portraits of Louis XVIII.[128] One can readily understand the need to demonstrate one's loyalty to the returning regime which prompted this outpouring. (Of course in time Bourbon images became subversive, and a royalist black- market was created similar to, if smaller than, the Napoleonic one during the restoration.) Imagery affirmed the public self as well as the private self. Indeed, as it was designed to be shown, it was better suited for advertising one's beliefs and opinions – or at least what one wished to be thought of as one's beliefs and opinions. It is, perhaps, inevitable that most descriptions of imagery should be about its public display, but then imagery was a very public form of cultural expression, sold openly on the streets by pedlars, seen on the walls of shops and workrooms, and, above all, decorating the local inn. It was this most

---

124 Honoré de Balzac, *Le Peau de chagrin*, 1st edn, Paris 1831, Paris 1984, 279–80.

125 Victor Hugo, *Les Rayons et les ombres* (1840), no. 4: *Regard jeté dans une mansarde*, in Jean Masson (ed.), *Oeuvres completes: édition chronologique*, vi, Paris 1968, 40.

126 Adolphe Aynaud, 'Le Saint Napoléon', *Le Vieux Papier*, fasc. 209, Paris 1964, 93–7.

127 Paul Cordonnier-Détrie, 'Imagerie et colportage', *Revue historique et archéologique du Maine* 2nd ser. xxxiii (1953), 25–33.

128 Others, for reasons of economy or time, dug out a pre-revolutionary royal portrait and stuck on a new head and title, for example Hurez of Cambrai's *Louis XVIII*: Hayward Gallery, *French popular imagery: five centuries of prints*, London 1974 (exhibition catalogue), 117.

Plate 4. *La Société des amateurs d'eau-de-vie*: Clerc (Belfort), c. 1835–42
Imagery in a public setting – on the wall behind the drinkers is pinned
an encouraging image. Reproduced by permission of the Réunion
des musées nationaux (photo: Danièle Adam).

public of interiors that painters and writers depicted as the home of
imagery.[129]

In a seventeenth-century Parisian copperplate engraving showing the inn
of *Dame Alison et de Lubin, son mary*, two images are depicted on the walls,
one for the confraternity of Saint Nicolas, and one *Crédit est mort*.[130] Three
centuries later, in Pellerin's historiette *Victor le petit berger*, one can spot
Napoleon on the wall of the village cabaret where Victor goes to drink.[131]

---

129 The nineteenth-century painter Meissonier included images in his many representations of inns.
130 René Saulnier and H. Van der Zée, 'La Mort de crédit: image populaire, ses sources
politiques et économiques', *Dawna Sztuka* ii (1939), 12.
131 Garnier-Pelle, *L'Imagerie populaire française*, ii, no. 1430.

Writers concurred about the location of imagery: in 1831 Pellerin-Dobromel, praising the success of his fellow Chartrian Allabre, noted 'you could not enter into a bar or a village inn in the region of Marseilles, Boulogne, Mainz or Strasbourg without finding the productions of our compatriot exposed to the admiration of connaisseurs'.[132] By 1866, when Delvau published his artistic journey *Du Pont des Arts au pont de Kehl*, Allabre's images had been replaced, at least in the case of the inn where he stayed at Plombières, by those of Pellerin.[133] Nineteenth-century writers also concurred about the type of imagery to be seen – humorous, heroic or even holy, they were above all masculine.

Images found in inns might have a number of ostensible purposes, for example *Bonne Bière de mars* advertised the innkeeper's wares. At the same time it reinforced the atmosphere of male drinking camaraderie. A woman might appear in the image as a barmaid, as in the version cited twice by Balzac, but usually only men were shown, and often only soldiers – representatives of an essentially masculine profession.[134] Battle scenes and military imagery from a variety of epochs were also important decorations of the pub. Delvau mentions *La Prise de Constantine* and *Le Passage des portes-de-fer*. In a typical inn of germanophone Lorraine where, according to Angelika Merkelbach-Pinck the 'wall decoration was rich and varied', one would find, among other items, first empire battle scenes, second empire soldiers and images recalling service in the Prussian army since 1870. She also singled out a pair of images which could be found in every local inn and which carried particular messages to their male audience, *Les Dégres des âges* and *Les Quatre Vérités*.[135] The first showed the various life stages of a man (and only a man in the germanophone version) from birth to death; the second would have particularly appealed to the rural clientele for its depiction of the peasant as the 'maintainer of all'. The inn, therefore, was one location where accepted male gender roles, whether as soldier, drinker or farmer, were reinforced.

Did the imagery of the home differ from that of the pub? The relative absence of religious imagery from the bar marked one divide between the domestic and public spheres, but differences were also apparent within secular imagery, both in the choice of themes and the uses to which they were put. Ponchon, describing the room where the *veillées* (wakes) of his youth were held, mentioned 'on the walls, some smoke-blackened images: *The wandering Jew, Henriette et Damon, Marlbrough s'en va-t-en guere, Pirame et*

---

132 'vous ne pouviez entrer dans un cabaret ou une auberge de village aux environs de Marseille, de Boulogne, de Mayence ou de Strasbourg, sans y trouver les productions de notre compatriote exposées à l'admiration des connaisseurs': Garnier, *Histoire de l'imagerie populaire*, 54.
133 Alfred Delvau, *Du Pont des arts au pont de Kehl*, Paris 1866, 208.
134 Jean Adhémar, 'L'Imagerie vue par l'écrivain au siècle dernier', *Le Vieux Papier*, fasc. 270, Paris 1978, 410.
135 Angelika Merkelbach-Pinck, *Brauche und Sitte in Ostlothringen*, Frankfurt-am-Main 1968, 16–17.

Thisbé, Geneviève de Brabant'.[136] These were not just images, they were the titles of songs, and folklorists tell us that they were sung. At the *veillée* in the Meuse 'one sung *Geneviève de Brabant, Pirame et Thisbé, Damon et Henriette*, which an *image d'Epinal*, stuck to the wall, detailed the dramatic and no less veracious history'.[137] The imagist Garnier recalled that these same images were enthusiastically collected by the attendees at the *veillées*; he himself remembered singing them there as a child.[138] The three images mentioned by all these authors, *Geneviève de Brabant, Pirame et Thisbé, Henriette et Damon*, were love stories, perhaps more acceptable to the female audience of the *veillée* than the violent battle scenes in the pub, and were perhaps considered more suitable decorations for the female space of hearth and home. Again, no strict demarcation can be maintained: Richard lists almost exactly the same selection of military (the *Prise de Constantine* and the *Passage des portes de Fer*), bacchic (*Saint Lundi*) and amorous (*Geneviève de Brabant* and *L'Arbre d'amour*) imagery on the walls of the Vosgian cottage as Delvau found in the bar at Plombières. One can only point to a tendency towards differences, linked to gender, rather than a complete separation between the public and private realms. However, the descriptions of imagery in the home show that it was not just the picture that mattered; the text was also important.

Nicolas Pellerin wrote that the purpose of his images was to allow the rural poor 'the pleasure of contemplating the person of their emperor while singing the couplets that are placed under his portrait'.[139] The two elements of an image, picture and text, he believed were equally valuable to his customers. Indeed sometimes it was for the text that an image was kept; Perrout mentions that some owners preserved their images on a cloth roll, so they could refer to them like a song sheet.[140] The prominence of the text has led some commentators to see in the image a major source for folksongs.[141] In germanophone Lorraine there are clear instances of songs that owe their popularity to distribution through imagery.[142] However, if one turns to collec-

---

136 'aux murs, quelques images enfumées: *Le Juif-Errant, Henriette et Damon, Marlbrough s'en va-t-en guerre, Pyrame et Thysbée, Geneviève de Brabant*': Ponchon, ' "A l'Veille" ', 10.
137 'on chantait *Geneviève de Brabant, Pyrame et Thisbé, Damon et Henriette*, dont une image d'Epinal, collée au mur, retraçait la dramatique et non moins véridique histoire': Henri Labourasse, *Anciens Us, coutumes, légendes, superstitions, préjugés, etc. du département de la Meuse*, Bar-le-Duc 1903, 78.
138 Garnier, *Histoire de l'imagerie populaire . . . à Chartres*, 72, 80.
139 'le plaisir de contempler les traits de leur empereur tout en chantant les couplets qui sont en dessous de son portrait': Picoche, *Le Monde des chamagnons*, 145.
140 Perrout, *Trésors*, 15. Although I know of no surviving French examples used in this way, a linen roll (known as the Sykes-Baron roll) covered in broadsides is preserved in the archives of the Centre for English Cultural Tradition and Language at Sheffield.
141 Jacqueline Lesueur, 'La Chanson populaire et les marchands de chansons dans les Vosges au siècle dernier', *Bulletin de la Société philomatique vosgienne* lxxiii (1970), 90.
142 Papa Gerné, a well-known local singer, liked going to Sarreguemines on his father's business, because of the opportunity it gave him to buy a sheet of 'schöne, neue Lieder', and several of his songs were learnt from image pedlars at the fair: Louis Pinck,

tions of folksongs from francophone Lorraine it is much harder to identify the influence of imagery. A popular folksong, such as *Le Petit Mari*, certainly could be found on an *image d'Epinal*, but the song was already old when first recorded in print in the mid-seventeenth century; there is no reason to credit Pellerin with its success.[143]

None the less, the use of images as song sheets does show how the text could be used to impart information. The addition of a text was one of the changes made by imagists when copying a Parisian print. This may seem a little perverse, considering that the imagists' intended audience contained a greater proportion of illiterates than that of their Parisian counterparts; however, the text was important for the pedlars responsible for distributing images, who used it in their sales patter. Images of saints often carried a potted biography of their subject, images of battles related its most salient points.[144]

Dramatic events made good copy for the imagists. Pellerin's 1814 catalogue included images of such (relatively) recent events as the death of Marshal Lannes and the capture of Moscow. The changeable political climate of the nineteenth century gave them plenty of material, from the carbonarist plots of the restoration to the military adventures of Napoleon III. Imagists made great efforts to be first with the news: Dembour & Gangel had their image commemorating the declaration of the republic ready within two days of the news reaching Metz in 1848.[145] But although imagery commemorating events became an increasingly important element in imagists' catalogues during the nineteenth century, genuine news items remained relatively rare. Pellerin's most famous series, the Napoleonic battles engraved by Georgin, was not commenced until 1829.[146] Unlike *canards*, images usually supplied a picture of an event already known from other sources. Their purpose, therefore, was not merely to inform, but like other images to serve as symbols, as affirmations. The veterans at the *veillée* in Sierck pointed to the battle scenes

---

Verklingende Weisen: Lothringer Volkslieder, i, Metz 1926, 276. See also the discussion of the song *ungarischen Braut* at iii. 275.

[143] Garnier-Pelle, *L'Imagerie populaire française*, ii, no. 1067. The song has been studied by the historian of French folksongs, Patrice Coirault, *Formation de nos chansons folkloriques*, Paris 1953–63, iii. 322–7. Coirault traced many folksongs to a print original, but almost always in the small booklets of songs sold by pedlar-singers. To his knowledge only one folksong, *Les Douze Mois de l'année*, which was to be found on a Pellerin image, owed its origin to imagery. He himself remembered learning this song from just such a sheet: *Formation*, iii. 301.

[144] Imagery was not, however, very reliable when it came to history: an image of the Battle of Waterloo by Pellerin gave the victory to the Russians! The error occurs in lithograph no. 2 of a series illustrating the story of *Marie ou le croix d'or* (MDAACE D.37.1393), issued by Pellerin in 1861.

[145] Bode, *L'Imagerie messine*, 35. The declaration of the republic was announced in the Metz *Moniteur* on 27 February, and the image was *déposé* on the 28 February.

[146] The firm's lithographs of the Franco-Prussian War were still in the catalogue in 1914: Lucien Martin, 'Contribution à l'étude des images d'Epinal sous la troisième république, 1870–1914', unpubl. *mémoire de maîtrise*, Tours 1971, 88.

on the walls around them to give credence to their own stories of war, just as the *Bataille d'Essling* hung on the wall of the Pellerin workshop during Vadet's time.[147] Something of the old religious attitude towards images attached even to these secular prints: a representation of a thing made it true and real to the viewer.[148]

The power inherent in imagery becomes clear when one turns to the juvenile market. Because after 1871 imagery became the preserve of children, its historians have taken great pains to demonstrate that they were not its original audience. But it is also true that long before the Parisian imagist Glémarec was reduced to calling himself a 'maker of images for children' some imagery at least was destined for the hands of children.[149] Rag-and-bone men enticed children with images to steal their parents' clothes to swap for images (according to the *procureur du tribunal de Metz* in 1851).[150] The authorities were worried about the dangers posed by imagery, but at the same time those concerned with the education of children tried to take advantage of the attraction. The minister of education was keen to see images in the classroom, and sent a circular of 9 April 1836 to education officers to this effect, which was repeated in 1838, 1855 and 1881.[151] Imagists were already aware of the potential of the market. In 1827 the Lille imagist Blocquel produced a catalogue aimed at 'churchmen charged with teaching the catechism in rural parishes, to the directors of free or charity schools, to teachers and to all charitable persons desirous of inculcating healthy ideas among the people'.[152] Priests and teachers (and folklorists – Elvire de Cerny got the tale of *Fanfan et la Ramée* from a child in return for an image) used images as rewards for children, but at the same time imagery was working for them,

---

147 Angelika Merkelbach-Pinck, *Aus der lothringer Meistube*, Cassel 1943, ii. 441; Blaudez, *Epinal et l'imagerie populaire*, 115.

148 Legends became more 'real' for being available through imagery. For example in the Meuse the legend of the Wandering Jew, subject of many images, 'était toujours accueillie comme article de foi': Labourasse, *Anciens Us*, 78.

149 In parts of Flanders imagery was known as *Stekebeeldeken*, after a children's game in which cut-out images were placed among the leaves of a book, and turns were taken to find them with a pin or knife. The child who won kept the image: Emile M. Van Heurck and Gerrit J. Boekenoogen, *L'Imagerie populaire des Pays-Bas*, Paris 1930, 4–6.

150 Bode, *L'Imagerie messine*, 238.

151 Dominique Lerch, *L'Imagerie populaire en Alsace et dans l'est de la France*, Nancy 1992, 162.

152 'ecclésiastiques chargés de faire le catéchisme dans les paroisses de campagne, aux directeurs des écoles gratuites ou de charité, aux instituteurs et à toutes les personnes charitables qui désirent faire germer les saines doctrines parmi le peuple': Palais des Beaux-Arts, Lille/Musée des arts et traditions populaires, *L'Image de Lille*, Paris 1957 (exhibition catalogue), p. xii. To judge by Blocquel's output the moralising function was certainly more important than the factual content, which was riddled with errors: Roger Collins, 'Simon Blocquel, imagier et éditeur lillois', *Journal de la Société des océanistes* xli (1985), 235–7. Blocquel's cavalier attitude to veracity was matched by other imagists: Gangel's 1853 image of 'Charles 1er, surnommé Charlemagne' records the emperor's conquest of Great Britain! Such errors may not, of course, be mistakes.

imparting 'healthy ideas' and moral messages.[153] We have already noted the stimulus imagery gave to the patriotism of French schoolboys. Other images encouraged hard work, sobriety and respect for order.[154] Readers might recall how Flaubert's satire of bourgeois inanity Pécuchet 'hung on the walls of his room pictures showing the life of the good and bad character, in order to fire [the] imagination' of Victor, his adopted son.[155] Those imagists who assisted the minister of education in this task, such as Wentzel, could expect to be rewarded, just as those whose work was judged morally unsound could expect to be censored.[156]

The influence of imagery

The memoirs of a whole parade of nineteenth-century French writers and artists from Lamartine to Romain Rolland, whose patriotic, religious or aesthetic senses were awakened by images, testify to the power of these cheap prints. But it was not just schoolboys who were learning lessons from imagery. If we take one last look around Richard's Vosgian cottage we find on the walls one of the most familiar of themes, L'Arbre d'amour, 'towards which the curious young village girl frequently throws timid glances'.[157] The image provided a model for the young girl beginning to think of love and marriage; she could imagine herself as one of the coquettes depicted in the print.[158] Earlier we saw how imagery could serve as an expression of the owner's personality, as a sign of membership and a badge of allegiance. Here we see how imagery, by the responses it drew from the viewer, helped create that personality in the first place. Imagery was a kind of magic mirror in which the viewers saw themselves as they might wish to be. Rodolphe Töpffer hinted at this process in his description of the varied crowd before the imagery stall in Geneva market during the 1820s:

> According to age, sex and class, the different subjects of the prints produce different feelings, and reveal in each the characteristics that are proper to him. Thus, while the kid is captivated by the brilliant colour of the uniforms, the young man of twenty-five only sees the deed of honour, and he feels in his heart for the grenadier who gives up his life in defence of the flag or for the

---

153 Elvire de Cerny, Contes et légendes de Bretagne, Paris 1898, 139.
154 See, for example, Karine Chlemaire, 'La Répresentation de la femme dans l'imagerie populaire: exemple de l'imagerie Pellerin', unpubl. mémoire de maîtrise, Paris IV 1993, 86–98.
155 Gustave Flaubert, Bouvard and Pécuchet, 1st edn, Paris 1881; London 1976, 268–9.
156 Garnier, Histoire de l'imagerie populaire, 193.
157 'devant lequel s'arrêtent souvent les regards timides des jeunes villageoises un peu curieuses': Richard, Traditions populaires, 149.
158 This slightly suggestive image was banned from the packs of pedlars in 1853, the authorities being suspicious about its influence on the morals of 'jeunes villageoises': Bode, L'Imagerie messine, 243.

Plate 5. *L'Arbre de l'amour*: Clerc (Belfort), c. 1835–42
This image, which young Vosgian village women found so stimulating
(according to Richard), was banned from being sold by pedlars after 1853.
Reproduced by permission of the Réunion des musées nationaux
(photo: Danièle Adam).

glory of the regiment. Before the Sacred Heart of Our Lady, the poor old woman makes as many signs of the cross as she dares in front of the street-urchins who torment her; the young peasant-girl looks shyly but with a real and sincere interest at the story of *The guilt of Cécile, or the curious maiden* [about a daughter who defied her father and took a lover].[159]

The power of imagery to enthuse young conscripts became a stereotyped scene in images themselves.[160] Like other items of the peddling trade, imagery falls within the category of goods which 'allow the affirmation of self', not only through the outward show of taste and opinions, but because it gave a form to people's ideas about themselves.[161]

As the authorities and commentators recognised at the time, imagery was not just an expression of mentality, it was an influential force in its creation. This was the lesson of the *rapporteur* for the Académie de Metz commenting on Dembour's images: 'The morality which the poor and ignorant man will never search for in a book, can be found in the coloured image with which for the cost of one *sou* he decorates his garret. The eyes are therefore the pathway to the heart.'[162]

Where Blanc talks about morality, the historian might see acculturation. Lerch suggests that Wentzel's commercial territory, which took in much of Catholic Europe from Poland to the Pyrenees, coincided with the creation of a particular mentality characterised by resignation in the face of suffering, to which he has given the name 'Saint-Sulpicien'. Laurence Fontaine took Lerch to task for this assumption:

> the themes of the books and pictures so widely distributed by the Wentzel, Pellerin and Remondini [an Italian competitor] firms contributed to the spread of a common sensibility. However, to go on to say that the consumer of these prints ... recognised himself in the pictures with which he decorated the interior of his house, or in the tasteless and fraudulent images of religious sen-

---

159 'selon l'âge, le sexe, la condition ou les caractères, ces différents sujets produisent des affections différentes, et révèlent chez chacun des traits qui lui sont propres. Là où le gamin est captivé par la brillante enluminure des uniformes, l'homme de vingt-cinq ans ne voit que le trait d'honneur; son coeur se donne au grenadier qui meurt pour la défense du drapeau ou pour la gloire du régiment. Devant le Sacré-Coeur de Marie, une pauvre vieille se signe autant qu'elle l'ose, si près des gamins; et la jeune villageoise regarde timidement, mais avec un intérêt puissant et sincère, *l'histoire de Cécile*': Rodolphe Töppfer, *La Vie et les oeuvres de Töppfer d'après des documents inédits, suivies de fragments de littérature et de critique inédits ou inconnus*, ed. l'abbé Relave, Paris 1886, 344. The article was originally published in 1836.
160 Garnier-Pelle, *L'Imagerie populaire française*, ii, no. 1088: *Les Agréments de la vie militaire* 549.
161 Laurence Fontaine, *History of pedlars in Europe*, Cambridge 1996, 193.
162 'La morale que l'homme ignorant et pauvre n'irait point chercher dans un livre ... il la trouvera à côté de l'image enluminée dont il aura pour un sou décoré son réduit, les yeux seront ici le chemin du coeur': M. Blanc, 'Rapport sur les images de M. Dembour', *Mémoires de l'Académie royale de Metz* xix (1837–8), 361.

sibility which he hung in his home, is a big step to take, for the function of these prints – in their exaltation of the romantic city vision of the countryside, their refusal of industrialisation and their views of foreign cities, in themselves world tours of the imagination – was perhaps more about escapism than identification.[163]

But is this a real distinction? Surely one's hopes and dreams are as much a part of one's personality as any other part of one's mental furniture. In as much as imagery contributed to the furnishing of the mind it both permitted the expression of an individual's sense of self, but at the same time tended towards the standardisation of those expressions. Imagery is a valuable historical source not only as a marker of the tastes and preferences of a particular social group, but as an instrument of cultural formation. As the proud pedlar of *imagerie d'Epinal* explained to T. A. Trollope (father of the novelist), 'les beaux-arts sont les adoucissements les plus nobles de la vie et ceux qui les répandent sont les agents les plus puissants de la civilisation'.[164]

The pedlars of imagery

Like Trollope, most nineteenth-century commentators credited (or blamed) the pedlar for bringing the print to the wall of the cottage. However, the stock carried by an individual pedlar was very small: Lerch's examination of the contents of the packs of Alsatian pedlars in the 1860s showed that they seldom carried more than 100 images at a time, never more than 200.[165] This was at a time when the combined production of the Epinal imagists was more than twelve million images a year.[166] Although the new means of transport available at the end of the second empire partly account for the scale of these enterprises, it would be wrong to think that imagists were limited to small print runs before the coming of the railway. In 1845 Pellerin was already using between 6,000 and 7,000 reams of paper a year, enough for more than three million images.[167] Even in the eighteenth century the scale of production seems more industrial than artisanal. The surviving accounts of the Chartrian imagist Barc between 1777 and 1787 suggest that a single print run could run into thousands, while total production over a ten-year period was more than half a million images.[168]

163 Fontaine, *History of pedlars*, 194.
164 Thomas Adolphus Trollope, *A summer in Brittany*, London 1840, i. 278. As Trollope quoted the pedlar in French so have I.
165 Lerch, *Imagerie et société*, 192.
166 Martin, 'Contribution', 38. This figure was given by the prefect of the Vosges but it is in line with Martin's own estimates for production under the third republic (based on the Pellerin firm's records) of 11.3 million images *per annum*.
167 Charton and Lepage, *Le Département des Vosges*, i. 1026.
168 Duchartre and Saulnier, *L'Imagerie populaire*, 88, and Jusselin, *Imagiers et cartiers à Chartres*, 116.

The area over which this production had to be distributed was equally impressive. We have already heard M. Pellerin-Dobromel's claim for the nationwide popularity of Garnier-Allabre. An article in *Le Temps* from 1866 made even greater claims for Pellerin:

> Imagine the joy and astonishment on entering the log-cabin of the American pioneer, the Negro hut of Madagascar, the Indian wigwam of Nova Scotia, the Eskimos' igloo, to find a red and yellow coloured image representing *Geneviève of Brabant, The Wandering Jew, Tom Thumb, Napoleon I, The holy Virgin, The child Jesus*, all with text in the language of the country, and to read at the bottom of this dirty old paper: *Imagerie d'Epinal (Vosges)*.[169]

Again, although the railway and the steamboat no doubt played their part, such far-flung markets were by no means a novelty of the late nineteenth century: in 1832 the prefect of the Vosges wrote to the minister that Pellerin's images were exported 'in all the countries of Europe'.[170] In the absence of company records for most imagists it is difficult to establish the precise destinations of their products, but the number of languages used in their titles gives some indication. Many of Wentzel's images were produced in multilingual editions, not just in French and German for the local market, but in Italian, English, Spanish, Dutch, Polish, Hungarian and Portuguese, and a mixture of these and other languages also appear on the images of Dembour and Gangel, Pellerin and Pinot.[171] Could the pedlar alone be responsible for shifting such quantities to such widespread markets?

Pedlars certainly were among the imagists' customers. Their presence in the workshop was considered routine and some imagists, such as Wentzel, actually had pedlars on the firm's payroll.[172] However, they were not the only customers. Every imagist had a network of customers to whom he sold wholesale. Pellerin's troubles with the authorities in 1816 revealed the extent of his contacts, from Arras down to Lyon, as the police rifled through his business correspondence. As the firm expanded during the nineteenth century so did its network of contacts, not just within France but beyond.[173] Other imagists

---

[169] 'Jugez de la joie et de l'étonnement qu'on éprouve en entrant dans la maison de bois du pionnier américain, dans la cabane des nègres de Madagascar, dans le wigwam de l'Indien de la Nouvelle-Ecosse, dans la hutte des Esquimaux, de trouver une image enluminée de jaune et de rouge . . . et de lire au bas d'un de ces papiers enfumés: *Imagerie d'Epinal (Vosges)*': Perrout, *Trésors*, 103.
[170] Dumont, *La Vie et l'oeuvre*, 67. In the eighteenth century the head of the Remondini print firm of Bassano in Italy boasted that 'Nos relations s'étendent à toute l'Europe, l'Amérique, la Moscovie d'Europe et d'Asie, ainsi qu'à certaines régions d'Asie et d'Afrique': Paoli Toschi, *L'Imagerie populaire italienne*, Paris 1964, 26.
[171] Lerch, *Imagerie et société*, 148–51. Even Deckherr, whose smaller print runs imply a narrower market, was producing images in Italian during the 1820s: André Philippe, 'Quelques Images des Deckherr de Montbéliard, éditées de 1820 à 1832', *L'Art populaire en France* iv (1932), 111.
[172] Lerch, 'Du Colportage à l'errance', 176.
[173] The Pellerin firm's single most important partnership during the second empire was

such as Gangel and Wentzel set up their own outlets in Paris, and many firms had subsidiaries in other centres. Two of Jean-Charles Pellerin's sons ran an outlet in Metz in the 1820s which competed with Desfeuilles's branch in the city. Although most eighteenth-century imagists could not boast, as Gangel did, that they had an agent in New York, their commercial dealings were also far-flung.[174] Letourmy of Orleans had dealings with more than a hundred retailers in sixty towns and cities, some of whose orders ran into tens of thousands.[175] His brother ran a subsidiary of the firm in Tours.[176] The role played by family members is typical of the way such networks were formed. Imagists dealt with those customers whose reliability (and creditworthiness) was known to them. If they were not relatives they were often former employees or neighbours.[177]

The imagists' largest customers were not, therefore, pedlars but an urban retail network. However, it would be wrong to deduce from the imagists' client-base that imagery was an urban product for an urban market, for the shopkeepers also dealt wholesale. The images in Pellerin's orders seized in 1816 were not primarily for sale in the shop, but, as the widow André of Troyes explained, for 'the large number of pedlars and small merchants' who called on her.[178] Sabourin de Nanton, a visitor to the Pellerin factory in 1857, recorded that the millions of chapbooks and images in circulation in the 1830s and '40s were the achievement of 350 pedlar bosses, each with five or six employees, who 'supplied themselves principally in Epinal, or with the correspondents of the Pellerin firm'.[179] Reconstructing the means by which imagists got their products to the public simply leads us back to the pedlar and his pack.

For contemporaries the pedlar was an obscure, often dubious, figure, but the fears he raised explain why his activities are comparatively well documented. The authorities who kept a close eye on imagists were even more concerned about the distributors of their products. As the minister reminded the prefect of the Vosges in 1816: 'France is covered by pedlars who criss-cross it in every direction, their busy commerce passes through the smallest hamlets and even reaches the most isolated habitations. . . . Among these men those on which you must fix your attention are the merchants of books,

with the Parisian company Le Bailly, itself the second largest French publisher of chapbooks. Pellerin's products made up a third of their business: Darmon, *Le Colportage de libraire*, 72.

174 Barbé, *L'Imagier de Metz*, 20.

175 Auguste Martin, *L'Imagerie orléanaise*, Paris 1928, 13.

176 René Saulnier, *L'Imagerie populaire du Val-de-Loire (Anjou, Maine, Orléanais et Touraine)*, Angers 1945, 90.

177 Charles-Joseph Pierret, for example, a stockist for Pellerin at Rennes, was born in Epinal and probably trained as a card-maker with Pellerin before moving to Brittany: Musée départemental breton, *L'Imagerie populaire bretonne*, 62.

178 Dumont, *La Vie et l'oeuvre*, 53.

179 Sabourin de Nanton, *Epinal et l'imagerie dans les Vosges*, Strasbourg 1868, 15.

almanacs, and songs.'[180] The results of this scrutiny are preserved in the archives, though the picture which emerges from police records is frequently at odds with that put forward by the government to justify their controls.

In 1852, soon after Louis-Napoleon's *coup-d'état*, the minister of police described pedlars of cheap print as an army, which had 'its codes of discipline, is regulations, its words of command, its signs' and whose generals were based in Paris. Its purpose was to attack 'all governments, to seek out and destroy all holy and religious thoughts, to corrupt morals, to sow division and to thus develop the seeds of those guilty passions which profit by disorder'.[181] His words echo those of a royal edict, then already more than 150 years old, which accused pedlars of 'going through the countryside' under the pretext of selling religious texts and little booklets', but really selling 'defamatory libels, pamphlets against the state and religion, illegal and counterfeit books'.[182] The numerous pieces of legislation concerning peddling passed in the intervening period all referred to the same worries, that pedlars traded in articles which undermined religion, morality and, above all, political authority. Even during the early years of the revolution, which supposedly witnessed the liberation of the press, no pedlar could sell his wares without the permission of the local authorities, who had to check his pack to ensure that it contained nothing 'against morality, nor which might awake the spirit of party or deceive the people'.[183]

Political untrustworthiness was not the pedlars' only fault. They were members of criminal networks, the minister's use of the term 'armée' was a standard description since the publication of *La Vie généreuse des mercelots, gueux et bohémiens* in 1596, a frequently reprinted pamphlet which supposedly unmasked the hierarchies of the underworld. Yet despite this level of organisation pedlars were also considered little better than beggars, in whose company they were sure to found and from whom they were largely indistinguishable. Like beggars, wrote the prefect of Bas-Rhin in 1866, pedlars 'live only from theft and lies'.[184] Pedlars were vagabonds who had no stake in the communities through which they passed and in which they allegedly caused so much trouble. And they were untraceable once they had passed on. They were repeatedly referred to as 'men of no known character', and therefore assuredly a bad lot.

---

[180] 'La France est couverte de colporteurs qui la traversent dans tous les sens, leur active industrie parcourt les plus petits hameaux et s'étend même aux habitations les plus isolées. ... Parmi ces hommes, ceux qui doivent le plus fixer votre attention sont les marchands de livres, d'almanachs et de chansons': Lesueur, 'La Chanson populaire', 101.

[181] 'attaquer les gouvernements, en cherchant à déraciner les idées saintes et religieuses, à corrompre les moeurs, à semer la calomnie, et à développer ainsi les germes de ces passions coupables qui ne spéculent que sur les bouleversements': Picoche, *Le Monde des chamagnons*, 146.

[182] Pierre Brochon, *Le Livre de colportage en France depuis le XVIe siècle*, Paris 1954, 12.

[183] Musée départemental breton, *L'Imagerie populaire bretonne*, 17.

[184] 'ne vivent que de maraude et de mendicité': Lerch, 'Du Colportage à l'errance', 168.

The regulatory regime designed to deal with such dangerous characters was at its most onerous during the second empire, but it was only the culmination of a series of attempts at regulation. The preceding political upheavals made the authorities determined to prevent further disturbances, and new laws were introduced in 1849 and 1852 to regulate the supposed fomenters of revolt. Each pedlar was required to have a permit-cum-passport, issued by the prefecture of his home department and presented for approval to the prefecture of each department he passed through. The permit gave a full description of its holder, and listed any apprentices travelling with him. In order to obtain a licence the pedlar had to have four items: his birth certificate; a certificate of 'good behaviour' (meaning, above all, politically) from his mayor; proof of indigence (because peddling was only supposed to be the 'gagnepain' of the destitute); and a complete list of his stock, together with two examples of each item. Another list was carried on him to assist the searches of gendarmes, should he be stopped on the road. Each item would itself have to bear the prefectorial stamp of approval.[185] All agents of authority, from the gendarmerie to the humblest village *garde-champêtre*, could demand to see the pedlar's permit and the contents of his pack. More than 1,000 stop and searches were made in the Vosges between 1863 and 1870, the local *commissaires* competing with each other to attract the approbation of the prefect.[186] Failure to comply could result in losing one's permit, one's stock, fines and even imprisonment.[187] The capriciousness of prefects and the harassment of the gendarmerie were not by-products of badly drafted laws, but fitted exactly the intentions of their framers who made little secret of their wish to regulate pedlars out of business.[188]

The fears that prompted the authorities to take such draconian measures were not entirely without foundation. Pedlars played important roles in the rural criminal gangs operating in eighteenth- and nineteenth-century France, to judge by those whose exploits are related by Richard Cobb.[189] More important, at least as far as the government were concerned, pedlars sometimes were involved in the distribution of seditious material. In the summer months of 1789 the regiments garrisoned in Paris were being politicised by pamphlets sold at the gates of the barracks by pedlars.[190] No sooner had these had their

---

185 Idem, *Imagerie populaire en Alsace*, 187.

186 Picoche, *Le Monde des chamagnons*, 151.

187 Lerch, *Imagerie et société*, 186.

188 Darmon, *Le Colportage de libraire*, 101–5. Whether the authorities' attempt to kill off the peddling trade was effective is not entirely clear; peddling certainly declined in the period but Darmon cites other contributory causes, such as the improved transport system. However, it is hard to imagine that these measures had anything other than a discouraging effect on the trade.

189 Richard Cobb, *Reactions to the French revolution*, London 1972, 181–215, and *Paris and its provinces, 1792–1802*, London 1975, 141–210.

190 Samuel F. Scott, *The response of the royal army to the French revolution: the role and development of the line army, 1787–93*, Oxford 1978, 56.

desired effect, than the new revolutionary authorities were employing the army against the spread of peddled royalist propaganda.[191] Later, under the restored monarchy, pedlars were among those suspected of circulating Bonapartist literature. In November 1829 Pierre Certicat from Haute-Garonne was arrested for selling anonymous images of Napoleon to the garrison at Lunéville.[192] Indeed, much of our knowledge of imagists' production and marketing comes from the interrogation of pedlars and the inventories made of their confiscated packs.[193]

Yet the voluminous records produced by this constant supervision do not really support the image of the pedlar as an *agent provocateur*. Very few of the pedlars stopped and searched in the Vosges ended up in court, and most of those who did were only charged with minor infractions.[194] The Vosgian pedlars, responsible in part for spreading the fame of the house of Pellerin throughout France, were by reputation inveterate criminals, but of the 150 pedlars traced by Jacqueline Lesueur, only two are known to have served prison sentences (and these were not for the kind of political crimes which so worried the government).[195] Those persons who knew them best, the printers and imagists who supplied them, described them as hard-working and sober. Even Charles Nisard, chairman of the *Commission du colportage*, which condemned the vast bulk of pedlar literature as immoral, accepted that the pedlars themselves were not the drunken ne'er-do-wells of repute.[196] As for the material itself, although priests constantly inveighed against its immorality, there is very little evidence that either socialist or pornographic booklets made up any significant part of the pedlar's stock, which was far more likely to contain orthodox religious items.[197] Only eighteen pedlars were convicted of selling 'works contrary to public morality' in the whole period 1850 to 1874.[198]

One of the authorities' most serious misapprehensions with regard to pedlars was to consider them as men without property or status. Peddling was

---

[191] The volunteer Gabriel Noël witnessed the capture of one 'marchand de libelles infâmes contre l'Assemblée nationale' when on guard duty at Sierck in February 1792: *Au Temps des volontaires*, 65.

[192] Barbara A. Day, 'Political dissent and Napoleonic representations during the restoration monarchy', *Historical Reflections – Réflexions historiques* xix (1993), 429.

[193] Cordonnier-Détrie gives details of three such cases: 'Imagerie et colportage', 3–36.

[194] Picoche, *Le Monde des chamagnons*, 19.

[195] Jacqueline Lesueur, 'Une Figure populaire en Lorraine au siècle dernier: le colporteur ou chamagnon', *Bulletin de la Société lorraine des études locales dans l'enseignement public* n.s. xxxvi (1969), 37. Only one Chamagnon appears ever to have been suspected of sedition, Claude Martin, who was supposed to have 'évoqué à haute voix le nom de l'usurpateur' and thus lost his passport in 1817.

[196] Darmon, *Le Colportage de libraire*, 49.

[197] Religion was the dominant genre not only in imagery, as we have seen, but in all areas of the cheap-print trade: Robert Mandrou, *De La Culture populaire aux 17e et 18e siècles: la bibliothèque bleue de Troyes*, Paris 1964, 45.

[198] Darmon, *Le Colportage de libraire*, 95.

seen as an alternative to (or an alternative form of) begging, suitable only for the itinerant poor, even though the government's own records informed them that, on the contrary, most pedlars had permanent homes. Recent research by Laurence Fontaine has revealed how significant the pedlar's position in his original community was to the financing of his business. It was on the basis of his property and reputation that wholesalers advanced him the credit necessary to stock up for his trip. Profits made from peddling were used to purchase property in the village, so that the pedlar improved his credit situation. Although pedlars might appear as men without resources in the communities they visited, at home they were often men of considerable wealth and influence. Pellerin kept himself informed about the reliability of the pedlars who bought from him, and passed this credit information on to his agents.[199] Pedlars were often poor, but they were seldom men 'without character'. They were businessmen, tied by their finances to both their home communities and their commercial suppliers.

In order to make sense of these two different pictures, historians have attempted to classify the variety of pedlars wandering the roads of rural France. Darmon described three types of peddling which he called large, medium and small, according to their itineraries.[200] At the bottom of the heap were the small pedlars who seldom left their home department. They had a very small stock, typically made up of almanacs or a handful of images, but in many cases these were merely a cover for begging. They were not professionals (few reappear in the prefect's records for two consecutive years), they were the destitute scratching a living any way they could.[201] Middle-sized peddling was more of an occupation. Such pedlars bought their stock at the beginning of a tour and carried it over several weeks and months through the neighbouring departments, returning home to restock. Their stock might be larger but the items were similar to those carried by local pedlars; cheap print and religious knick-knacks predominated. At the top end were the long-distance pedlars, who might spend several months, even years, away from home, travelling the entire country and even abroad. The 'great pedlar' was part of a commercial network that supplied his requirements without the need to return home. Their stock included the larger more expensive items, which they might carry by cart or by donkey. They often had a number of apprentice pedlars working for them.

Fontaine's thesis helps explain some of the differences. The 'great pedlar' acquired his stock on credit and his wholesaler would recommend him to other shopkeepers on his route. Because he did not need to pay straightaway for his stock he could afford to offer credit to his customers (hence the more expensive items), and to other pedlars (hence his apprentices). The 'middling pedlar', on the other hand, was under-capitalised. He might have a little

[199] Martin, 'Contribution', 67–74.
[200] Darmon, *Le Colportage de libraire*, 27–9.
[201] Lerch, *Imagerie et société*, 240.

money to invest, or he might acquire enough credit with one or two whole-salers to put together a small stock, but he was tied to these wholesalers and so could not wander too far from his depot. His normal stock-in-trade was cheap items, so there was no point giving credit. The poorest pedlars, whom Darmon terms 'starvation pedlars', had to pay for their stock with ready cash, and so only became pedlars as the chance arose, and quickly rejoined the ranks of the vagabond poor once whatever profits they had made were dissipated.

However, at the time people seldom drew these kind of distinctions, instead labelling pedlars according to their origins. The imagists of eastern France were particularly reliant on the inhabitants of Chamagne for the distribution of their images. Where did the Chamagnons fit into this picture? Chamagne, a village of about 600 souls in the foothills of the Vosges, was proverbially poor. Perrout quotes a couple of local sayings to prove it, like the Chamagnon horse which could only gallop going downhill.[202] Théophile Claudel, the local teacher, wrote more prosaically in 1889 that 'the soil . . . lacked manure and produced little, that's to say not enough to support the population'.[203] Most of the limited arable land was put down to potatoes, the stable diet of Vosgians, but a crop which was periodically subject to blight. The dearths that resulted combined with demographic growth forced the population to consider alternatives to life in the village, in this case peddling. It was a strategy by which the inhabitants could escape absolute poverty while retaining their links with home.

This is the conclusion of Maradan, who has studied the peddling families of Chamagne: 'wandering is nothing but the expression of a desire for rootedness, a battle against definitive migration'. He is not original in claiming that poverty was the spur to peddling, but his statistics give the theory a lot more substance. Although he was wrong to claim that the local tradition owed its origin to the potato famine of 1824 (Chamagnon pedlars had been a familiar sight since at least the beginning of the century), it is none the less noticeable that years of dearth saw a greater proportion of the villagers on the road.[204] Numbers varied, but between 1807 (when the law which required pedlars to hold a passport was introduced) and 1849 (when the new tougher regulations affected the trade), up to a quarter of the popula-tion were regular pedlars. They were from the poorer families in the village, few had any significant landholdings, and unlike pedlars in other centres

---

[202] Perrout, *Trésors*, 256.

[203] 'le sol . . . manquait d'engrais et produisait peu; c'est-à-dire pas assez pour subvenir aux besoins de la population': *mémoire* from Théophile Claudel to the minister of education, 1889, Bibliothèque municipale de Nancy, MS 354 (1662).

[204] 'l'errance n'est que l'expression d'une volonté d'enracinement, d'une lutte contre un exode définitif': B. Maradan, 'Chamagne et les chamagnons: colporteurs en livres', in *Les Intermédiaires culturels: actes du colloque du centre méridional d'histoire sociale, des mentalités et des cultures, 1978*, Aix-en-Provence 1981, 279. Picoche's graphs of the numbers of pass-ports issued in particular years support this theory: *Le Monde des chamagnons*, 33–5.

most remained poor, the profits from their trade seldom enabling them to buy enough land to retire on (as was the case in nearby Bazoilles-sur-Meuse).[205] For Chamagnons peddling was a subsistence measure which they continued until they died, often by the side of the road.[206]

And yet Chamagne was not significantly poorer than its neighbours, so in itself poverty cannot explain the adoption of the pedlar's pack. Other, equally ill-favoured villages seem to have survived without recourse to temporary migration. Nor can the demographic pressures of the early nineteenth century be held responsible: Vosgian pedlars had been well-known figures since the sixteenth century.[207] It was not just a response to poverty but a traditional occupation in which one had to be trained. Young Chamagnons often accompanied their elders on their travels as apprentices. They would be shown the routes, introduced to suppliers, and taught the jargon of their trade and how to deal with harassment from the gendarmerie. The presence of apprentices was not simply for educational purposes but to assist in the sales technique. Typically Chamagnons worked as a pair, one doing the show which drew the crowd, the other handling the sales.[208]

Each tour lasted several months, usually commencing in October or November to coincide with the festive season on which so much of the pedlar's trade depended, though a significant minority waited until after New Year. Those who left in the late autumn could expect to be home by the early summer and thus help in the harvest, and so this departure was favoured by those with their own small plots of land. Those who left in the spring spent the whole of the summer away and only returned to over-winter in Chamagne where, according to teacher Claudel, they rapidly spent the profits of the preceding months in riotous living.[209]

The commercial territory of the Chamagnons extended down the Rhone

[205] Lesueur could find only one 'propriétaire' out of 150 Chamagnons she studied: 'Une Figure populaire', 37.

[206] Picoche, Le Monde des chamagnons, 50; Lesueur, 'Une Figure populaire', 37.

[207] Michel Vernus, 'Colporteurs et marchands merciers dans le Jura au XVIIIe siècle', La Nouvelle Revue franc-comtoise xviii–xix (1980), 210. It has been conjectured that Claude 'Lorrain' Gélée, Chamagne's most famous son, first left his village to train as an engraver in Switzerland while working as a pedlar.

[208] Although I have referred to the pedlar as 'he' throughout, it should be noted that in 13% of cases it was a woman's name on the passport. There is some evidence to suggest that the peddling tradition was handed down in the female line. For example, although Chamagnon pedlars practised a high level of endogamy, when daughters married out of the village their partners frequently took up the family trade: Picoche, Le Monde des chamagnons, 34–6. Peddling meant long absences – even death – for men away from home, so peddling families in many regions practised female inheritance. This is also the case of the street-singers of Germany with whom the Chamagnons had much in common: Tom Cheesman, 'Bänkelsang: seeing, hearing, telling and singing in the German ballad picture show', Lore and Language xii (1994), 42.

[209] Mémoire from Théophile Claudel to the minister of education, 1889, Bibliothèque municipale de Nancy, MS 354 (1662).

valley and across almost the entirety of northern France, but they seldom ventured south of the Loire, into the tip of Brittany or into Alsace.[210] Village tradition credited them with being great wanderers, visiting Belgium, Luxembourg, Bavaria and the Rhineland, but such exotic destinations never turned up on their passports, and these claims were probably just part of the pedlar's self-image.[211] Their market was limited by three factors: language, which excluded them from Alsace, lower Brittany and large areas of the south; religion (their material was only likely to appeal to Catholics); and a certain level of literacy required to appreciate their cheap print items, not then achieved in many areas of the Massif Central and the Pyrenees.[212]

Chamagne was neatly situated in the middle of the map of the main provincial cheap-print houses, allowing them to stock up before the trip began. It was close to Epinal and the Chamagnons were among Pellerin's favoured customers. Moreover they were a vital source of information for Pellerin, keeping him up to date with changing preferences in different regions and the production of his competitors.[213] At least one print firm, Colin & Buffet, established itself next door to Chamagne in Charmes, in order to cater specifically for the Chamagnons' demands for sensationalist literature, the sale of which was one of their specialities.[214] Each trip pivoted on a handful of provincial cities where the Chamagnon was able to restock. Unlike the Gascons who, according to the publisher Noblet, kept to one itinerary over many seasons, the Chamagnons varied theirs, sometimes switching from summer to winter tours.[215] Their stock was sold for cash and not on credit, so there was no need to make return visits to the points-of-sale. Once they had sold out they might change over to a different product altogether.

The Chamagnon should therefore be placed in the middle of Darmon's hierarchy: he was a professional but, without property and the credit it would give him access to, he could not escape the day-to-day struggle for subsistence. The Chamagnon was always in danger of slipping down into the ranks of the destitute. Several Chamagnons were forced to sell what little land they

---

[210] Les Colporteurs de Chamagne: étude d'après leurs passeports, 1824–1861, Chamagne 1990 (exhibition catalogue), 26–31; Picoche, Le Monde des chamagnons, 42. Although both authors were working from the same set of sources their lists of main destinations differ but the general pattern uncovered remains the same.

[211] Perrout, Trésors, 256.

[212] Contrary to frequent statements by historians there was no arrangement, formal or informal, between the Chamagnons and Gascons to carve up their territories. Gascons were to be found in all these areas, even in what the Chamagnons might have felt was their home territory of Lorraine. If the Chamagnons were cautious about venturing into the south and west it was because the market was too small or the competition too fierce to make such trips viable: Picoche, Le Monde des chamagnons, 42.

[213] André Philippe, 'Colportage de fausses nouvelles', La Révolution dans les Vosges xviii (1928–9), 4.

[214] Picoche, Le Monde des chamagnons, 165–8. Some Chamagnons were directly employed as agents by Colin and Buffet.

[215] Darmon, Le Colportage de librairie, 42.

had to fund further trips.[216] Especially towards the end of the period, when new suppliers such as the village grocer were undercutting him, and the enforcement of stricter regulations ate into his limited profits, the Chamagnon appeared a much reduced figure, a mere rag-and-bone man hanging his images on the playground wall to catch the eyes of school-children.

How did the Chamagnon dispose of his stock of images? Garnier gives a graphic description of a Chamagnon couple working the crowd outside the church after mass on Sunday which, like fairs, fêtes and pilgrimages, was one of their favourite spots. On a table stood a cabinet whose doors opened out to form a triptych, revealing inside a wax model of the crucifixion or some other holy scene. In the forefront one might find Saint Hubert on his knees. Behind was unfurled a painted banner depicting Christ's passion. On the table and covering both wings of the triptych was deployed a whole collec-tion of religious knickknacks or 'bigotage': rosary beads, prayer books, holy pendants and rings from the abbey of Saint Hubert. On each side stood the Chamagnon and his wife 'with a pious and contrite air', the man playing a violin, while the woman lugubriously sang a hymn, copies of which she had ready to sell on images or in booklets. At each sale the Chamagnon would take the object and place it briefly in the interior of the box while muttering a blessing and making numerous signs of the cross, before handing it over to the customer.[217]

The box was considered the characteristic prop of the Chamagnon pedlar.[218] Several writers have left descriptions of its use from which we can understand how important the pedlar's apparent religiosity was to his success. Xavier Thiriat recalled one going from door to door in the Vosges with his box before him, pointing out each saint with a stick and extolling their various miracles in a sing-song voice. He ended with Saint Hubert whose medallion he recommended against accidents, lightning, mad dogs and the plague, and as a ticket straight to paradise after death – 'there are no great miracles which the great saint Hubert has not done'.[219] Not surprisingly

---

216 Picoche, Le Monde des chamagnons, 50, 78–9.

217 Garnier, Histoire de l'imagerie populaire, 195–6. A lithograph, which might almost have made to illustrate Garnier's description, was published by the Parisian printer Albert around 1850: Stuttgart Staatsgalerie, Bänkelsang und Moritat, Stuttgart 1975 (exhibition catalogue), 86.

218 Two such boxes have survived: one in the museum at Epinal depicts an Ecce Homo; the other, which found its way into the museum at Champlitte after the death of its Chamagnon owner on the road in Franche-Comté in 1830, depicts Saint Anne.

219 'il n'y a point de si grands miraques [sic] que le grand saint Hubert n'au fait': Xavier Thiriat, La Vallée de Cleurie; statistique, topographie, histoire, moeurs et idiomes des communes du Syndicat de Saint-Ami, de Lalorge, de Cleurie et de quelques localités voisines, canton de Remiremont, Vosges, Mirecourt–Remiremont–Paris 1869, 320–1.

Chamagnons were also known as 'montreurs de saint Hubert', indications of this specialism occasionally appearing on their passports.[220]

Their other prop, the canvas decorated with scenes from a story, would have been familiar to audiences in many parts of Europe for it formed part of the equipment of fair-ground singers and pedlars well beyond the range of the Vosgian pedlar. It might contain pious material but, increasingly, it was also used to tell of a sensational crime from a 'canard'. According to Vital Collet, who witnessed the tail-end of the Chamagnon tradition, each family group had a canvas illustrating some song-sheet they were selling, and while one held the pole to which it was attached, the other pointed out the various stages of the drama with a stick, and sang the relevant verses.[221] Again the Chamagnon's showmanship was evident. He was not relying on his product's ability to sell itself; he created the market by drawing the crowd into the story. Jean Drouillet described how the pedlar caught the crowd's interest on market day in Nevers:

All eyes were fixed on the immense painted canvas fixed on top of a pole, a picture divided into the different scenes of the drama, which the art of the sign-writer had depicted in all the most garish colours. A roll on the drum, a short patter, and then were sung the sinister verses, in the most theatrical of voices, invariably to the tune known as *Fualdés*. . . . Wham! With a thwack of his baton against the canvas which dripped with horror, the showman punctuated the end of each verse which described one episode of the drama illustrated in the picture, as if to affirm the veracity of the story. The song, a long page of emotional outpourings written in the most lachrymose style and illustrated in lively colours, only cost 10 centimes, so customers abounded.[222]

---

220 Picoche, *Le Monde des chamagnons*, 48. However, the illustration which normally accompanies Thiriat's text (which has been reproduced many times), is not of a Chamagnon but of a Tyrolian 'montreur de Saint Hubert', drawn by the local artist Valentin to accompany the article 'L'Hiver dans les Vosges', by 'A. Joanne' [Louis Jouve] in *L'Illustration*, 16 Feb. 1850, 103–7. The association between the Chamagnons and this particular type of pious show was correct, but not every Chamagnon had a box, and not all pedlars who had boxes were Chamagnons. In the eighteenth and early nineteenth centuries Parisian street-singers and 'montreurs de paradis pour un sou' used them. Chateaubriand even found characters from his popular novel *Atala* displayed in this way on the banks of the Seine 'comme on montre des images de la Vierge et des saints à la foire'. And they must have been a common sight in seventeenth-century Italy, to judge by their frequent appearances in the work of the baroque artist Alessandro Magnasco.

221 Vital Collet, *Les Communes du canton de Charmes*, Epinal 1905, 210. In 1842 Pellerin captured this scene of the 'marchand de complaintes' in a sheet of *Scènes de foire* at Nancy: Garnier-Pelle, *L'Imagerie populaire française*, ii, no. 1415.

222 'Tous les yeux étaient fixées sur l'immense toile peinte fixée au haut d'une perche, un tableau compartimenté des différentes scènes du drame, où l'art du peinturlureur s'était dépensé en criantes couleurs. Un roulement de tambour, un court boniment, et sur l'air invariable de Fualdès se déroulaient les sinistres couplets chantés avec force trémolos. . . . V'lan! d'un bref coup de sa longue baguette sur la toile frémissante d'horreur, le forain ponctuait la fin de chaque couplet en décrivant une tranche du drame comme pour en affirmer plus fortement la véracité. . . . La complainte illustrée en couleurs, longue page

Plate 6. *Scènes de foire*: Pellerin (Epinal), 1842
Chamagnon *canardiers* sell their wares outside the church of
Saint Sebastian in Nancy. Reproduced by permission of the
Bibliothèque nationale de France, Paris.

German *Bänkelsänger*, whose tours took in germanophone areas of Lorraine,
worked in very similar ways: mounted on an improvised stage at the fair (the
bench from which they derived their name) with their 'Schild' or storyboard
behind them, the pedlar told and sang his *Moritaten* (moral tales) to the
sound of a barrel-organ.[223]
The Chamagnon, therefore, was typical of a type of pedlar for whom the
act of selling was more important than the product on sale:

d'émotion écrite en un style des plus larmoyants, ne coûtait que deux sous; aussi les clients
abondaient': Jean Drouillet, *Folklore du Nivernais et du Morvan*, La Charité-sur-Loire 1961,
ii. 204.
[223] Pinck, *Verklingende Weisen*, iii. 334. Some pedlars could not afford to invest in a stock
of songs, and relied on the show itself to move the audience to generosity: Raphaël de
Westphalen, *Petit Dictionnaire des traditions populaires messines*, Metz 1934, col. 79.

They put on a show and sold entertainment and dreams. As intermediaries between their public and other worlds, they took their audiences into the realm of the imaginary, into other ways of knowing oneself, to other places, and to new understandings. Ultimately the pedlar was selling himself and all that his words – spoken or sung – could stir in the imagination of his listeners.[224]

What the pedlar had to offer was not his goods, which were usually cheap and tatty, but his knowledge and experience as a well-travelled man. He had, he implied, seen and learnt things beyond the ken of his audience; he was closer to supernatural sources of power. One *Bänkelsanger* emphasised his connection with far-away places by having the magic word 'AMERIKA' painted along the top of his banner.[225] If we consider the pedlar's sales technique as a show, then his character would vary, depending on the occasion and audience. For the stall after mass the pedlar emphasised his piety, displaying the badges of the pilgrimages he had attended, even laying claim to sacramental power. He blessed the objects he sold, he was the intermediary between the customer and the holy figures he displayed.[226] But this show of religiosity was just that, a show; the Chamagnon was no more devout than his customer, probably less so.[227] On other occasions the pedlar's supernatural power had other sources, for in addition to religious items he sold books of spells like *Le petit Albert*. Several Chamagnons gave themselves the title conjurer on their passports, and in some departments the prefects banned them from interpreting dreams, implying that they had held themselves out as fortune-tellers.[228] Chamagnons had a reputation all over northern France for their knowledge of magic. It was a Vosgian pedlar named Lélut who taught the young men of Picardy how to avoid conscription with an incantation: 'his big spectacles and his red wig lent him an air of mystery that made one take him for a sorcerer'.[229]

Because the pedlar traded on his image he must, in part, share the responsibility for his poor reputation. Sometimes he made a show of his poverty (no doubt in many cases genuine) to win the trust of his audience. It was not just

---

[224] Fontaine, *History of pedlars*, 81.

[225] Angelika Merkelbach-Pinck, *Lothringer Volksmärchen*, Cassel 1940, 147.

[226] The curé of Faucogney in Franche-Comté complained to his bishop of this sacrilegious behaviour by a pedlar at the fair of Faucogney in 1837: Jean Christophe Demard, *Tradition et mystères d'un terroir comtois au XIXe siècle: les Vosges méridionales*, Langres 1981, 334.

[227] One priest accused them of passing off straw they picked up off the roadside as the hay in which the infant Jesus was laid in Bethlehem, and other similar impositions on people's piety: Charles Pierfitte, 'Chamagne: les chamagnons', *Bulletin mensuel de la Société d'archéologie lorraine* iii (1903), 282.

[228] Picoche, *Le Monde des chamagnons*, 58–60, and Georges Delarue, 'La Longue Errance d'un chanteur ambulant du XIXe siècle', *Le Monde alpin et rhodanien* x (1982), 359.

[229] 'avec ses grandes lunettes et sa perruque rousse lui donnaient un air mystérieux qui le faisait prendre pour un sorcier': Maurice Crampon, 'Le Culte de l'arbre et de la forêt: essai sur le folklore picard', *Mémoires de la Société des antiquaires de Picardie* xlvi (1936), 282.

that it helped him obtain charity, though it undoubtedly did, but that holy men were expected to be poor.[230] Other pedlars emphasised their strangeness in dress and language, fascinating by their foreignness. A prop by which the Chamagnon in particular enhanced his quality of mysterious stranger was the bushy beard worn by nine out of ten men. The beard was credited as a distinguishing feature not only on the passports but in the memories of those who had seen him passing. Ponchon as a boy remembered the visit of the pedlar 'with the goatee beard' and 'with the airs of Mephisto'. The mystery surrounding this character deepened when he failed to return after the Franco-Prussian War: was he perhaps a Prussian spy?[231]

The audience were ambiguous about the pedlar: they enjoyed the spectacle and the glimpse of new worlds that he offered, but they were dubious about the messenger. For example, pedlars were appreciated as newscasters, yet their news-bearing reputation could get them into trouble: the pedlar Tilliet was arrested in Mirecourt in 1792 for allegedly making alarmist remarks and passing on news concerning baron de Malvoisin, a local émigré. Tilliet argued that, on the contrary, the crowd had accosted him for news.[232] Chamagnons traded on their character as newscasters and tellers of tales, insisting that their *canards* were the very latest stories that they swore were true, even though, as Garnier revealed, they never believed them themselves.[233] This does not mean that the public was always duped. The Vosgian term for cheap-print pedlars was 'menteurs', while Chamagnons went by the title 'marchands de mensonges'.[234] The fears of the *procureur du roi*, who accused Pellerin and his Chamagnon clients in 1822 of playing on 'the blind credulity of the inhabitants of the region' with a patently false report of an earthquake in nearby Baccarat, were probably misplaced.[235] The customers were able to come to their own conclusions about its veracity, but that did not stop them enjoying the story. Pedlars were well known as storytellers; it was part of the showman's talent that they nurtured. The visit of the pedlar 'Père Jean des images' was looked forward to in the southern Vosges for the tales he told at the evening *veillée*.[236] But the stories of pedlars combined both senses of the term 'conte' in French – a narrative but also a lie.

The general public shared the authorities' difficulties in distinguishing between pedlars and beggars, and in reality this was often only a matter of

[230] The Gascon pedlars interviewed by Picoche knew several tricks to earn the sympathy of their potential customers including dropping the handkerchief you were trying to sell in the farmyard mud, then crying that you would be beaten if you took it back to your master in that condition: *Le Monde des chamagnons*, 144.
[231] Ponchon, ' "A l'Veille" ', 11–12.
[232] André Philippe, 'Mésaventures d'un colporteur à Mirecourt (Janvier 1792)', *La Révolution dans les Vosges* xix (1930–1), 34.
[233] Garnier, *Histoire de l'imagerie populaire*, 255–61.
[234] Perrout, *Trésors*, 256; Pierfitte, 'Chamagne', 282.
[235] Philippe, 'Colportages de fausses nouvelles', 7.
[236] Demard, *Tradition et mystères*, 330.

Plate 7. *Almanach du peuple pour l'an 1831*: Dubiez
(Remiremont), 1830
The veteran as cheap-print pedlar. Reproduced by permission of
the Musée départemental d'art ancien et contemporain, Epinal.

degree. In the Vosges the 'montreurs de Saint Hubert' were classed together
with the self-proclaimed wolf-killers and magicians who plagued isolated
farmhouses in winter, hoping for a night's lodging in exchange for a prayer or
to avert a curse.[237] It was not simply that both groups relied on the generosity
of the communities they passed through to survive on the road; they had
other attributes in common. Both traded on their air of mystery, and the
secret knowledge or danger that it implied. Both groups had reputations as
thieves, cheats and lechers, leading a life of pleasure largely at other people's
expense. And because both lived by their wits they were acknowledged trick-

[237] C. Lemasson, 'Anciennes Coutumes de la paroisse de Champ-le-Duc (Vosges)', *Le
Pays lorrain* xxiv (1932), 511–12.

sters. If I have spent too long trying to pin down the pedlar it is because his public reputation had much in common with the character who is the subject of the remainder of this book, the soldier.

Pedlars and soldiers

The connections between the soldier and the pedlar were well established in popular imagery and folklore. The front cover of Pellerin's *Almanach du peuple* showed a one-legged veteran of the revolutionary wars handing a copy to a peasant at his plough. Other local almanacs used variations on the same theme: the *Almanach des campagnes*, started in Rambervilliers in 1833, also featured the veteran-pedlar on the cover. Over the years the pictures were updated, but the pedlar always retained his military aspect.[238] And if the pedlar was expected to have been a soldier, the soldier was also expected to become a pedlar: a folksong about a fed-up soldier ended with his declaration 'I will take a violin,/ Me and my little housekeeper/ Will sell songs'.[239] Soldiers and pedlars in folktales go by the same name, La Ramée, which as we will see in chapter 5, tells us much about both.[240]

Was there, in reality, any connection between the two occupations? The authorities certainly thought so. Discharged soldiers were exactly the right material to form the vagabond class they most feared. Therefore, in 1746, the government forbade 'all soldiers . . . from distributing or peddling any book or printed document'.[241] The end of conflicts produced gluts of veterans, many too disabled to return to their normal peace-time occupation even if they had one, and it is easy to imagine that some became 'starvation pedlars', begging under the guise of peddling their small stock of images, just as they appear on the covers of Vosgian almanacs. Soldiers do turn up throughout the nineteenth century in applications from the destitute for the right to peddle locally. However, even at the lowest end of the peddling hierarchy ex-soldiers were only one element among the general population of the poor.[242] Professional pedlars, such as the Chamagnons, were part of family and regional traditions, trained in youth to follow peddling as a full-time adult occupation.

---

[238] A later addition to Pellerin's stable of almanac titles, the *Almanach lorrain* created in 1864, similarly showed a one-legged veteran selling copies on the banks of the Moselle: Albert Ronsin, 'Almanachs populaires vosgiens au XIXe siècle', in Jacques Choux and Adolphe Riff (eds), *Art populaire de Lorraine*, Strasbourg–Paris 1966, 215–18.

[239] 'prendrai un violòn,/ Moi et ma petite ménagère/ Vendrons des chansons': Théodore de Puymaigre, *Chants populaires recueillis dans le pays messin*, 2nd edn, Paris–Nancy–Metz 1881, ii. 153–4, no. 78: *Le Soldat découragé*.

[240] See, for example, the tale of *Le Sac de la Ramée*, about a Gascon pedlar who conforms very much to stereotype, in Justin-Édouard-Mathieu Cénac-Moncaut, *Littérature populaire de la Gascogne*, Paris 1868, 57.

[241] Brochon, *Le Livre de colportage*, 18.

[242] Lerch, 'Du Colportage à l'errance', 163.

71

Plate 8. *Le Chanteur de cantiques*: Cochin (Paris), *c.* 1770
This eighteenth-century Parisian street-singer uses a box prop
similar to that favoured by Chamagnons. Reproduced by
permission of the Musée départemental d'art ancien
et contemporain, Epinal.

There is no evidence that they were more likely to have been soldiers than those in other occupations.[243]

The connection between soldiers and pedlars was the result, therefore, not so much of a real relationship but rather through perceived, shared character-istics as travellers, adventurers and *rodomontades*. Street-singers adopted the showy dress of the military with plumes and ribbons, they gave themselves soldiers' *noms-de-guerre* like 'Belhumeur', they boasted of their own – some-

[243] In fact it is possible that for some long-distance pedlars, such as those from Gascony and the Massif Central, temporary migrations helped them avoid the draft.

72

times real, sometimes invented – military exploits. They praised the soldier's life as one long round of wine, women and song, very much like the pedlars' own self-portrait. It was no accident that the base of the Parisian street-singers was the quai de la Ferraille, also the home of the freelance recruiters and conscript replacement agencies. Both traded in promises of an alternative, exciting life.[244] By tradition the recruiting party lurked on the fringes of the crowd round the market-place singer. This was one of the well-known dangers of the fair.[245]

As a sign of their status as travellers both soldiers and pedlars carried packs on their backs, which is why in military slang an infantryman was a 'bifin' or rag-collector (who occupied the lowest rank of the imagery pedlars). The pedlar's pack obviously contained his stock, but it was also a prop and proof of his claims to knowledge and experience. In French folklore the soldier's haversack was the place where he stored his own credentials, for it was there that, as we will come to understand, he kept the stories he told.

---

[244] Coirault, *Formation*, i. 77–99. In some cases it is clear that the singers were employed by particular regiments to drum up business and get young men in the right frame of mind for the recruiting sergeant's proposition.

[245] The hero of Erkmann-Chatrian's novel *Histoire d'un paysan* was inveigled into the army after listening to a pedlar-singer at the fair. Cochin's print of the Parisian *chanteur de cantiques* carries the legend 'Chacun y va toujours son train,/ Le Soldat y fait sa recrue,/ Et le filou son coup de main.'

2

The Soldier's Tale

Imagery offers historical insights through its consumption, but the historian will always hope to find more direct evidence of rural culture. A history of popular attitudes must look for a base in the cultural expressions of the peasantry, labourers and artisans who made up the bulk of the population. Yet where can we find such sources considering that it is precisely these groups who have left us so little in the way of a written record? Although literacy was relatively high in Lorraine, the focus of this study, compared with other areas of France, yet most of what was thought and expressed by members of these groups was never written down.[1] We can characterise the culture of the peasants and artisans of Lorraine as predominantly oral in as much as the spoken language was their favoured medium, whatever the literate influences upon it.

Fortunately, the collections of oral literature made by nineteenth-century folklorists present a picture of the concerns and emotions of precisely those sections of the population who left no other record. In theory these texts were taken directly from the mouths of the 'folk', and therefore should be the least mediated source available. According to the notions of their editors, their authorship was communal, and thus relevant to whole sections of the population. In practice neither of these assumptions can be completely upheld, and concerns over hidden biases may be one reason why historians have, with a few notable exceptions, largely neglected folklore. I will return to the issue of the reliability of oral literature as a source, but first let us discover what has been collected of the folklore of Lorraine.

The folklore of Lorraine: sources and problems

It is usual when considering the development of folklore as a discipline to place its origins in the romantic movement. According to this chronology Herder was the first collector of folksongs, and the Grimm brothers the first collectors of folktales.[2] However, songs and stories similar to those found in nineteenth-century oral folklore had been appearing in literature for centu-

---

1 Jean-Paul Aron, Paul Dumont and Emmanuel Le Roy Ladurie, *Anthropologie du conscrit francais*, Paris 1972, maps 53, 54. By 1870 only 10% of the annual military intake in Lorraine was illiterate, less than half of the national percentage: Camille Maire, Le Contingent de 1860 dans le canton de Lorquin', *Les Cahiers lorrains* n.s. xlvi (1984), 35
2 Peter Burke, *Popular culture in early modern Europe*, London 1978, 4.

ries previously. The imperial territories west of the Rhine were particularly rich in these manuscript and print collections of fables, jests and *exempla* from the medieval and Renaissance eras, some of which claimed to be based on the oral tradition of their time, and some of whose contents appear to be related to later oral texts from the same region. Can we rely on these as evidence of the oral tradition before the folklorists got to work in the nineteenth century?

To illustrate the problems of such an approach let us take the example of Jehan de la Haute Selve, a twelfth-century monk in the bishopric of Toul, who wrote down a collection of *exempla* known as *Dolopathos*. It was based on the famous *Historia septem sapientum*, itself a free translation of a collection originally from India, but its adaptation to Lorraine can be found in the story of the seventh sage, who tells of the Knight of the Swan, the supposed ancestor of the local hero, Godefroy de Bouillon.[3] One of the later editors of *Dolopathos*, Gaston Paris, has suggested that the story came from the local oral tradition, which seems plausible, if unverifiable, for it is similar to a well-known fairytale, *The maiden who seeks her brothers* (AT451), a version of which was collected in germanophone Lorraine in 1939.[4] However, because the monk took the material to make an *exemplum*, with the intention of pleasing his patron who was a kinsman of the duke of Lorraine, it is no longer possible to recover the sense of the original oral version. One can, perhaps, rely on *Dolopathos* to show that the theme was familiar in medieval Lorraine, but not to discover by whom it was known, how they treated it or their intention in telling, let alone any genealogical connection between it and the twentieth-century version. Different genres have different methods of production and carry different messages.

Nearer to the period of study it is possible to draw some inferences about the oral tradition of the seventeenth and eighteenth centuries from literary sources such as diaries, chronicles, plays and even legislative texts. Thus the folklore of Elizabethan England has been reconstructed from references in Shakespeare's plays.[5] The literature of Lorraine is less rich in clues but items like the Messin patois classic *Chan Heurlin* do offer some assistance.[6] Local chroniclers' searches for justifications to competing claims to the dukedom offer further pickings. Several manuscript and printed sources from the medieval period to the eighteenth century touch on the legendary history of the

---

3   The Latin text can be found in Johannis de Alta Silva, *Dolopathos sive de rege et septem sapientibus*, ed. Hermann Oesterley, Strasbourg–London 1873. The old French text can be found in Jehan de la Haute Selve, *Li Romans de Dolopathos*, ed. Charles Brunet and Anatole de Montaiglon, Paris 1856.
4   Angelika Merkelbach-Pinck, *Lothringer Volksmärchen*, Dusseldorf–Cologne 1961, no. 27: *Die sieben Schimmelreiter* (AT451).
5   Katherine Briggs, *The anatomy of Puck*, London 1959, and *Pale Hecate's team*, London 1962.
6   Albert Brondex and Didier Mory, *Chan Heurlin ou les fiançailles de Fanchon: poëme patois messin, en sept chants*, ed. Maurice Cressot, Nancy 1948. The first part appeared in 1787.

Church and aristocratic families.[7] Dom Calmet consciously eschewed all such legendary matter in his more famous history of Lorraine, but the same author's investigations into the supernatural – visions, apparitions, ghosts and vampires – do contain references to locally collected stories.[8] However, Calmet, as a theologian, used his material in ways very different from the community in which these legends were narrated, so one is again faced with the problem of deriving the original sense from this new form.

The poem *Chan Heurlin* was just one result of the growing interest in the romance dialects of Lorraine during the eighteenth century; the collections of patois carols which turn up in a number of surviving print and manuscript collections were another. The origins of these carols are difficult to pinpoint but it was almost certainly not among the popular classes, but rather in Franciscan Counter-Reformation activity. Although each edition of *La Grande Bible des noëls* made the same claim to oral authenticity, each can fairly easily be traced to a previous printed version to the extent that even the order of songs remains the same. The original model probably came either from Burgundy or Champagne. These books should perhaps be looked on more as priests' song-sheets than as a record of the existing oral tradition, but they also show the influence literate sources could have on popular culture, for they succeeded in penetrating the countryside. At the end of the nineteenth century folklorists found handwritten copies of the *Grande Bible* kept by peasant families for use during Christmas festivities.[9]

In the nineteenth century Lorrainer amateur philologists, perhaps in reaction to the attempt of their countryman the abbé Grégoire to impose French as the only mother-tongue of the republic (and later to the threat of Germanisation), recorded folklore texts in dialect. Their results include the restoration patois almanacs of Didier Mory followed, around the middle of the century, by those of Jaclot de Saulny and, later still, Frédéric Estre. None had any great success: the normal market for almanacs was closed to them because although peasants spoke patois they could not read it; nor were they welcome among the local intelligentsia. Indeed all three editors ran into difficulties with the censors over the suggestive nature of some of their stories. Although they were genuinely concerned about folklore and solicited their readers for songs and tales, they were also willing, on occasion, to borrow from other sources. Estre, for example, translated one of his own poems from his native Provençal into the Messin dialect.[10] As with the *Grande Bible* it is

---

[7] These chronicles have been helpfully collected by the Société d'archéologie lorraine under the series title *Recueil de documents sur l'histoire de Lorraine*, Nancy 1855–91.

[8] Dom Augustin Calmet, *The phantom world or the philosophy of spirits, apparitions etc*, ed. H. Christmas, London 1850.

[9] A history and bibliography are supplied by Marie Laissy, *Les Noëls populaires lorrains*, Nancy 1977. For the use of carols outside the church see François-Jean-Baptiste Noël, *Mémoires pour servir à l'histoire de Lorraine*, Nancy 1841, ii. 33.

[10] Raphaël de Westphalen, 'Frédéric Estre', *Nos Traditions* i (1938), 20.

possible that the almanacs served more as source books than as a reflection of the indigenous oral tradition.

In 1877, following the partition of the Treaty of Frankfurt, the Académie Stanislas of Nancy organised research into the dialects of the three remaining departments of Lorraine, calling on the services of the schoolteachers of each commune to provide folkloric texts. It is clear that the Académie had in mind orally transmitted material, but this was not how their request was interpreted, for the material they received mostly consisted of printed patois texts such as carols.[11] The quest of the Académie was preceded by that of Louis Jouve, whose three collections of patois songs and carols from the Vosges are an important source. Unlike his predecessors he drew a distinction between those texts he took down himself from oral rendition, and those he took from printed or manuscript sources.[12] Most dialectologists, however, were more interested in grammar and vocabulary than in literature. The major exception was Léon Zéliqzon, whose works on the patois of the Moselle, often prepared in collaboration with the abbé Thiriot, are rich in songs and tales.[13]

The work of philologists continued after the reunification of Lorraine: at the popular level the journal *Nâte tère louran* occasionally printed tales and songs; at the academic level Professor Charles Bruneau co-ordinated research into both ancient texts and modern spoken forms. Bruneau is an example of some of the difficulties posed by philologists for students of oral literature: he was deeply interested in folklore (he reviewed the subject for the *Annales de l'est*), yet he showed little concern for the sources of the material under review. Even if the distinction between the oral and literate traditions was never as clear as the Grimms suggested, the concern for the status of the source which they developed was (and is) absolutely vital as a basis for research into popular culture.

We must, therefore, turn to the work of folklorists following in the tradition of Herder and the Grimms if we are to find a reliable collection of sources. Unfortunately there was no immediate response in either language community to the romantic movement's interest in oral literature. The only Lorrainer folksong collection from before the middle of the nineteenth century owed more to the Versailles-inspired mania for *Marlbrouk s'en va-t'en*

<hr/>

[11] Some of the results were published: Lucien Adam, *Les Patois lorrains*, Nancy–Paris 1881. The majority remain in manuscript: Bibliothèque municipale de Nancy, MSS 341–6 (743).
[12] Louis Jouve, *Noëls patois anciens et nouveaux chantés dans la Meurthe et dans les Vosges*, Paris 1864; *Recueil nouveau de vieux noëls inédites en patois de la Meurthe et des Vosges*, Paris n.d.; *Chansons en patois vosgien, recueillies et annotées avec un glossaire et la musique des aires*, Epinal–Remiremont 1876
[13] A bibliography of the romance dialects of Lorraine (both texts and studies) can be found in Hermann Urtel, 'Lothringen kritischer Uberblick bis 1908', *Revue du dialectologie romane* ii (1910), 131–48, 437–55, and Charles Bruneau, 'Les Parlers lorrains anciens et modernes: bibliographie critique 1908 à 1924', *Revue linguistique romane* i (1925), 348–413.

guerre than to Herder's dictum that folksong reflected the soul of the people –
a local aristocratic family made collecting a hobby, the results of which were
published by a descendant a century later.[14]

In 1852 a ministerial decree ordered the formation of a *Recueil des poésies
populaires de la France*. The Emperor Napoleon III (like his uncle before him)
understood the potential value of folklore to nationalist ideologies. Collection in Lorraine was organised by the Société d'archéologie lorraine, and the
results were poor. The committee, hoping to find some Ossianic remnants of
a distant past, was only interested in historical songs. The small harvest
reflected the distributive power of pedlars rather than any supposed bardic
tradition.[15] It did, however, inspire a more serious folklorist, le comte de
Puymaigre, who in 1865 published his *Chants populaires receuillis dans le pays
messin*. Puymaigre relied on a network of aristocratic contacts throughout
Moselle to supply him with texts. He also noted songs from the
germanophone population, with the intention of publishing a similar collection. However, the immediate aftermath of the Franco-Prussian War was not
an auspicious time and the project was dropped.[16]

The occupation of the Moselle seems to have been an inspiration to many
folklorists determined to preserve the French-speaking population's
'patrimoine'. In 1877 a local writer, René Paquet, visited those communes to
the south of Metz missed by Puymaigre.[17] The abbé Thiriot published a
number of articles on French folksongs in the *Jahrbuch der Gesellschaft für
lothringische Geschichte und Altertumskunde*. An important collection of
French folksongs was made by another member of the society, Raphaël de
Westphalen. As a rural doctor before the First World War he was in an ideal
position to cajole his patients into singing for him.[18] After the war
Westphalen was a founder member of the local folklore group *Nos Traditions*,
set up in response to a similar germanophone organisation in the east of the
department. A fellow member, René Schamber, was responsible for yet
another song collection from the banks of the Moselle.[19] Taken together with
songs from Metz itself, supplied by local historians Charles Abel and
Jean-Julien Barbé, the combined efforts of the collectors of francophone
Moselle must represent the greater part of the song tradition of this region.

Other parts of francophone Lorraine have not been nearly so well covered.

[14] Etienne Fourier de Bacourt, 'Anciens Chants populaires du Barrois', *Bulletin de la
Société d'archéologie lorraine* 3rd ser. xxii–xxvi (1894, 1896, 1898).

[15] L'abbé Laurent Marchal, 'Poésies populaires de la Lorraine', *Bulletins de la Société
d'archéologie lorraine* iv (1853–4), 383–539; 2nd ser. vii (1865), 43–87.

[16] The manuscript German songs are in the Archives départementales de la Moselle,
Metz, fonds Puymaigre, 12/J/102.

[17] 'Nérée Quépat' [René Paquet], *Chants populaires messins, recueillis dans le Val de Metz en
1877*, Paris 1878.

[18] The resulting 390 texts remained unpublished until 1977: Raphaël de Westphalen,
Chansons populaires lorraines, Nancy 1977.

[19] René Schamber, *Chansons du folklore lorrain*, Metz 1953.

Jouve's books are almost the only available collections from the Vosges.[20] Georges Chepfer made a small collection around Chaudeney, and a number of other texts appeared in the pages of *Le Pays lorrain*. The editor of this journal until 1930, Charles Sadoul, was an active collector himself. In a speech in 1910, he claimed to have collected over 400 songs in just six months in the area of Raon-l'Etape.[21] Only a tiny fraction of his total collection, which probably numbered thousands of items, ever appeared in print; his manuscripts were accidentally destroyed by American troops in 1945.

Germanophone Lorraine, after Puymaigre's aborted project, looked as if it would be similarly neglected. The *Gesellschaft für lothringische Geschichte und Altertumskunde* published a couple of articles on German folksongs, but it was not until the *Verband deutscher Vereine für Volkskunde* persuaded the society to contribute to the formation of the *Deutsche Volksliedarchiv* that any serious attempt to record the local tradition was made. A committee was set up in June 1914, and a considerable amount had been achieved before the events of that summer overtook it.[22] One of the members of the committee, the abbé Louis Pinck, continued collecting during and after the war. The four resulting volumes of *Verklingende Weisen*, published between 1926 and 1939, each contain a hundred songs, and the accompanying notes on variants, sources and singers make his achievement not only invaluable to this book but one of the finest folksong collections of any period. Amazingly, they represent only the tip of the iceberg of Pinck's collecting. He also sought out *Liederheften* – the handwritten songbooks of his informants – *fliegende Blätter* or pedlar's song-sheets and popular hymnbooks. Some of this material was destroyed by looting troops in the first months of the Second World War, but much has also been preserved in the *Deutsche Volksliedarchiv* or in the departmental archives in Metz.[23]

If French folklorists were slow on the scene when it came to collecting folksongs, they were even slower than other European countries in developing an interest in folktales. The first real follower of the Grimms in France was Emmanuel Cosquin. Through a servant in his great-uncle's house he was able to make contact with the storytellers of the village of Montiers-sur-Saulx (Meuse). His *Contes populaires de Lorraine*, consisting of eighty-four tales and variants, was only published in its entirety in 1886, but the fieldwork had been done two decades before. Cosquin's work was inspirational to

[20] The exceptions are the very rare J. Minsmer, *Choix de chansons vosgiennes*, Paris 1918, and the Menéstrels de Gérardmer, *Arts et traditions de la vallée des lacs*, Colmar 1978.

[21] Charles Sadoul, 'Les Chansons lorraines', *Le Pays lorrain* xxv (1933), 219.

[22] Archives départementales de la Moselle, 21/J/12, fonds de la Société d'histoire et d'archéologie de la Lorraine.

[23] There is a guide to his collection in the Deutsches Volksliedarchiv in Freiburg: Otto Holzapfel, 'Nachlasse Pinck in Deutschen Volksliedarchiv: Ammerkungen zum deutschen Volkslied in Lothringen', *Jahrbuch für Volksliedforschung* xxii (1977), 119–30. The material in the Archives départementales de la Moselle can be found under codes 42/J/22–5 fonds Pinck.

researchers in other parts of France, where the assumption was that the oral tradition had long since been snuffed out by the Enlightenment and the revolution. In neighbouring regions of Argonne and the Ardennes the abbé Lallement and the newspaper editor Albert Meyrac cited Cosquin's example in their own, more limited collections. In Lorraine, however, he did not have an immediate successor, unless it could have been Charles Sadoul again. Four tales he collected around Raon-l'Etape were published in the *Revue des traditions populaires* in 1904, and it is likely that many others formed part of his lost library. The few other folktale texts from francophone Lorraine are scattered among the dialect texts of Léon Zéliqzon and the abbé Thiriot, and in works of folklorists such as Léopold-François Sauvé who were otherwise more interested in customs and superstitions. Nor did francophone folklorists after Cosquin pay much attention to other prose genres such as legends or religious tales. It could be argued that this dearth suggests that the oral folktale tradition was already dying in Lorraine. One of Sauvé's narrators made exactly this point when he said that he had known more than a hundred tales but had forgotten many because it was twenty years since anyone had asked to hear them: 'The serial-novel has killed the folktale just about everywhere.'[24] However, this was certainly not the case in germanophone Lorraine.

With the exception of Puymaigre, germanophone Lorraine was ignored by both French-speaking and German-speaking folklorists before the Prussian conquest of 1870, and indeed for a considerable time after. It is perhaps surprising that during the occupation, when the authorities were concerned to demonstrate the essential 'Germanness' of the population, so little work was done. The only collection of folktales to appear before the First World War was published in the form of a chapbook.[25] Some legends appeared in Henri Lerond's folklore works concerning castles, monasteries and saints.[26] However, it was not until 1931 when the sister of Louis Pinck, the schoolteacher Angelika Merkelbach-Pinck, started her researches that a serious attempt was made to collect the prose oral literature of the germanophone population. Until the outbreak of the Second World War she dedicated herself to searching out legends and tales from every corner of eastern Moselle, resulting in a collection of three thousand texts. Two hundred of these texts can be described as folktales (almost all of which have now been published). The bulk is made up of local legends and anecdotes, some of which were published during the war.[27]

Looking at this round-up of Lorrainer folklore three issues stand out as

[24] 'Le Roman-feuilleton a tué le conte presque partout': Léopold-François Sauvé, *Le Folklore des Hautes-Vosges: sorcellerie, croyances et coutumes populaires*, Paris 1889, 340.

[25] F. Peters, *Aus Lothringen: Sagen und Märchen*, Leipzig 1887; *Märchen aus Lothringen: dem Volke nächerzählt*, Strasbourg 1888.

[26] Henri Lerond, *Sagenborn lothringischer Burgtrümmer*, Metz 1912–21; *Lothringische Sammelmappe*, Metz 1890–1901.

[27] The remaining unpublished manuscripts are housed in the Zentralarchiv der deutschen Volkserzählung, Marburg.

affecting its usefulness as a source.[28] The first is the leading role played by aristocrats and Catholic priests. Puymaigre was leader of the Bourbonist faction in Moselle, and his contacts were made through monarchist circles.[29] Cosquin, a lawyer and the son of the mayor of Vitry-le-François, was a leading member of a monarchist organisation, the *Cercles catholiques ouvriers*, and a regular contributor to Catholic journals.[30] The interest of these elite groups in folklore might be considered surprising in the light of their historic antagonism to most forms of popular culture, and there are plenty of examples even from the end of the period of priests doing their level best to suppress smutty folksongs and promiscuous dancing. However, during the nineteenth century clerics and aristocrats found themselves lumped together with local traditions as the useless baggage of the past, jettisoned by successive revolutionary governments. The threat of the secularist and centralist policies emanating from Paris forced these social groups to look for new allies and new weapons. Most Lorrainer folklorists were committed to some form of political regionalism, ranging from moderate decentralisation to outright autonomy. The region might possibly have provided traditional elites with a new power-base, but the justification they claimed for it was the need to protect and foster local, traditional cultures. Particularly in Lorraine, with its mosaic of administrative, ethnic and linguistic borders, a shared folklore became the definition of the region. For Puymaigre there was a clear link between his political and folklore activities. He was the author of a pamphlet on *Décentralisation et régime représentif* in which he called for the defence of the local culture for whose individuality he found evidence in folksong. In the aftermath of the Franco-Prussian War his model inspired the Nancy school of regionalists.[31] Their journal, *Le Pays lorrain*, was (under the editorship of Charles Sadoul) an important platform for regionalist ideas before and after the First World War.

It would not do justice to the love of their 'pays' that inspired so many folklorists to suggest that their endeavours were entirely politically motivated. However, when they wrote about regional traditions these were usually linked to a pious, hierarchical society. Both their political and folkloric activities were directed towards its defence. This is implied in the use of the term Lorraine, for the very mention of old provinces either implicitly or explicitly called up the prospect of counter-revolution. The possible slant that this gave to their collecting is something of which historians need to be aware. On the

---

[28] For a more detailed discussion of the political and regionalist motivations of folklorists see David M. Hopkin, 'Identity in a divided province: the folklorists of Lorraine, 1860–1960', *French Historical Studies* xxiii (2000), 639–82.

[29] Jean Eich, 'Un Littérateur et érudit lorrain: Théodore de Puymaigre', *Annuaire de la Société d'histoire et d'archéologie de la Lorraine* liii (1953), 125.

[30] Raymonde Robert, 'Emmanuel Cosquin et les contes lorrains', in Roger Marchal and Bernard Guidot (eds), *Lorraine vivante: hommage à Jean Lanher*, Nancy 1993, 201–7. Hence Cosquin's superb folklore library is now housed in the Institut Catholique in Paris.

[31] Eich, 'Un Littérateur', 117.

other hand the content of their collections cannot easily be described as pious or deferential, and on some occasions is in clear opposition to the political position of the collector (priests and seigneurs may not have appreciated the portraits of themselves in folklore). The collectors' willingness to include material which contradicted their own views makes me more confident about this source.

A second feature is the concentration of folklorists' efforts on just one of the four departments of Lorraine, the one which was incorporated into the German empire in 1871, Moselle. It is clear that the francophone collectors such as Estre, Barbé, Abel, Thiriot and Westphalen were concerned to preserve the romance heritage of their region. Such concern went beyond collecting to irredentist activity. In 1913 the abbé Thiriot published in a collection of folksongs a dialect song composed by Westphalen entitled *Lo Péys messîn*, minus the final verse. In 1920 he included it in another pamphlet accompanying the *Exposition nationale de Metz* with the restored verse, a call for reunification with France. He attached the note that 'one of former masters', the *Kreisdirektor* von Loeper, called it 'a disguised *Marseillaise*. Perhaps he was not altogether mistaken'.[32]

Similar motivations, though from an opposite position, can be ascribed to the Pincks, brother and sister. Abbé Louis Pinck had made himself notorious before the First World War with his outspoken defence of the Catholic culture of eastern Lorraine against the tide of 'Prussianism'. However, after the war, the perceived threat to his 'Heimatland' came from the new French authorities – France was always associated in his mind with free-thinking and secularisation. He was a leading advocate of mother-tongue education and religious schooling. Despite his antagonism towards the Prussian authorities he was convinced that his part of Lorraine belonged to the German cultural sphere, which led to his involvement with nationalist groups. The publication of the later volumes of *Verklingende Weisen* was funded by Nazi sympathisers. When he died soon after the Nazi invasion the occupying forces wanted to give him a state funeral, which only the intervention of his sister and other members of his family prevented.[33] But although Angelika Merkelbach-Pinck could not, as a result of her Catholic convictions, be in complete sympathy with the Nazi regime, she was a willing propagandist for reunion with Germany. Her reputation in Lorraine has suffered in consequence.[34]

Again, it is would be facile to suggest that the Pincks' motivations were entirely religious or political. They wanted to defend the traditions of their

[32] Henri Tribout de Morembert, 'Raphaël de Westphalen (1873–1949)', *Nos Traditions* n.s. ii (1949), 27.

[33] The disputed character of the abbé Pinck has given rise to a number of biographies, the fullest of which is in the introduction to Laurent Mayer, 'La Chanson populaire en Lorraine germanophone d'après le recueil *Verklingende Weisen* de Louis Pinck', unpubl. *thèse doctorale*, Metz 1983.

[34] Henri Hiegel, 'Deux Folkloristes lorrains: Henri Lerond et Angelika Merkelbach', *Les Cahiers lorrains* n.s. xxvii (1975), 111.

homeland, which they considered essentially German and Catholic. They saw no distinction between collecting folklore and agitating for mother-tongue education. However, their political activism has brought their probity as collectors into question. In fact, probably because they were aware of potential hostility from their French counterparts (and the authorities) the Pincks were more meticulous than other local folklorists. Their publications give no text without considerable detail on the person from whom it was collected, sometimes with comparative references to both sides of the linguis-tic divide. None the less, their example demonstrates how important it is to be aware of the folklorist as the mediator; the oral literature as presented on the pages of their collections is only a partial reflection of the oral culture of their time. It is not simply that they may have had a political axe to grind, but as priest or schoolteacher they were representatives of an educated class whose assumptions and prejudices about their sources (many of which they inherited from the scholarly apparatus erected by previous folklorists such as the Grimms) interposed themselves in their selection of texts and the way they presented them. Their informants were sensitive to these social nuances, so that, for instance, knowing the abbé Pinck's authoritarian reputation, many were unwilling to sing anticlerical or erotic songs or to let him have copies of their songbooks which contained them.

The third feature to note is that the majority of texts were only collected at the end of the period under examination, or even a generation or two after-wards. The years after the Franco-Prussian War witnessed the rapid develop-ment of heavy industry in Lorraine on both sides of the new border, accompanied by large-scale migration, from rural Lorraine but also from Italy into Lorraine and from Germany into the Moselle. Folklorists were extremely sensitive to these changes, believing that the culture they recorded was in the process of disappearing. Hence Pinck called his collection 'disappearing melodies'. The folklorists informants were old, and almost entirely drawn from the increasingly depopulated villages of Lorraine rather than its rapidly expanding industrial towns. While it is undoubtedly true that rural society in Lorraine did experience profound shocks in the aftermath of war, yet the folk-lorists' conceptions about what had preceded industrialisation were problem-atic. Rural society was considered as essentially static, its culture unchanging over a very long period (in some cases from pagan times). The texts they wrote down were, therefore, a heritage from some distant past. Modern folk-lorists, however, highlight the relationship of oral narrative to its immediate context and emphasise its adaptability over time. One therefore has to con-sider whether these collections have any relevance to periods other than that in which they were collected. This is a question to which we will return.

One way to redress the biases which affect folklore collections is to avoid reliance on a single text. Any one variant of a folktale may be idiosyncratic. In order to understand its place in the oral tradition, and its relationship to society, one must make comparison between variants. To do so one must first identify the text, for which purpose folklorists have developed some useful tools. Mention has already been made of tale-type AT451: this identification was made with the assistance of the Aarne-Thompson index of folktale types, which categorises each folktale according to its essential motifs.[35] Folktale texts cited in this book will be identified, where possible, by their Aarne-Thompson – or AT – number. We will see shortly that the creation of this index was the result of a particular concept of the folktale that has now been eclipsed, but the continuing value of this tool is undeniable; comparison remains a necessary complement to other approaches to oral literature.

This index is supplemented by national indexes. The most important for this research is the excellent *catalogue raisonné* of all tale-types found within France and the French-speaking New World, started by Paul Delarue in 1957 and continued by Marie-Louise Tenèze ever since.[36] Not only does this give references for all variants of each tale-type, it breaks them down into their principle episodes, for although each type must have some key motifs in order to be classified, yet none are identical.

The indexes are, however, scholarly constructs based on academic notions about oral literature. Would the divisions imposed by Aarne and Thompson be recognised by the original narrators? Does the separate genre of folktales exist outside the boundaries of the index itself? On the occasions when tales were told, such as at the Vosgian *veillée* described by Sauvé, or at the germanophone *Maistube* visited by Merkelbach-Pinck, identifiable tale-types followed from local anecdotes and legends, and in turn gave rise to songs and jokes. It was not simply that folktales had to compete with gossip, games and chapbook readings for the attention of the audience, but that these apparently separate genres interacted with one another to create a continuous experience. What appears to be an identifiable folktale-type can easily slip between genres. A story similar to Cosquin's *Poutin et Poutot* (AT2022 *The death of the little hen*) turns up in the Vosges as a song.[37] As many of the assumptions about the relationship of folktales to their social context are based on the validity of genre systems this fluidity is worrying.

Not only the genre but the individual plot-lines may only exist as scholarly constructs. Tales-types often do not appear in isolation. Cosquin's variant of AT317 develops from AT530 *The princess on the glass mountain*, or rather it combines elements of both tale-types to make a new whole. For Aarne and Thompson such mixing of plots was evidence of a process of decay or 'devolution' during transmission, poor memory and muddle leading to deviations from the true tale-type: 'The tradition is not always coherent and the tellers of the tale apparently do not always understand the significance of what they

35 Antti Aarne, *The types of the folktale: a classification and bibliography* (Folklore Fellows Communications iii), Helsinki 1910; rev. Stith Thompson (Folklore Fellows Communications clxxxiv), Helsinki 1961.
36 Paul Delarue and Marie-Louise Tenèze, *Le Conte populaire français: catalogue raisonné des versions de France et des pays de langue française d'outre-mer*, Paris 1957–2000.
37 Gaston Paris, 'La Chanson du chevreau', *Romania* i (1872), 218–25.

are telling.'[38] Yet it is precisely this ability to combine plots and spin tales out endlessly which narrators boasted was part of their skill. What had appeared to be devolution was in fact part of the variability that was essential to the storytelling tradition. The index puts artificial boundaries on this variety.

And yet the system of genres defined by academics does find some echo among storytelling communities. In Linda Dégh's examination of tale-telling in an Hungarian village she found that while it was permissible for any villager to tell a joke or local legend, only recognised raconteurs were allowed to tell fairytales. These tales demanded narrative skills not given to everyone, and were considered to be the property of their narrator.[39] The situation in Lorraine was similar, individual narrators had preferences for particular kinds of tales, which were known by their audience who recognised their 'authorship'. Nicolas Baro and Viktor Manque, two of Merkelbach-Pinck's best narrators, were close friends and among the audience for each other's tales, but they never poached from the other's repertoire. The terminology used in communities to express these preferences were rather loose; another of Merkelbach-Pinck's narrators, Nicolas Jung, called his tales 'Rätsel' or riddles, but none the less it is clear that this defined for him and his listeners a group of tales roughly corresponding to the sections of the index entitled 'tales of magic' (AT types 300–749) and 'romantic tales' (AT types 850–999).[40]

The indexing of folktales is much more advanced than that for other oral genres. There are various national indexes of folksongs but none with recognised international validity. Le Catalogue de la chanson folklorique française, though useful, is neither as comprehensive nor as detailed as the Delarue-Tenèze catalogue of tale-types.[41] The narrative themes of songs are as widespread as those of tales, but because their form is tied to the language of composition through rhyme and rhythm no easy method of cross-border comparison has been devised.

The concentration of effort on indexing folktales is perhaps the consequence of the high value attached to this prose genre by folklorists. Folktales, and in particular the tales of magic, were (and to a large extent still are) considered the worthiest products of oral creativity, the epitome of the folk's aesthetic achievement. As we have seen with the case of the Merkelbach-Pinck collection, other genres were far more widespread but it was the folktales that got published. This judgement of the relative worth of different

---

38 Stith Thompson, The folktale, New York 1946, 63.

39 Linda Dégh, Folktales and society: story-telling in a Hungarian peasant community, Bloomington, Ind. 1969, 60. An in-depth study of tale-telling in the French community of Newfoundland reached a similar conclusion about the acceptance of genre divisions among narrators: Gerald Thomas, Les Deux Traditions: le conte populaire chez les franco-terreneuviens, Montreal 1983, 60.

40 Angelika Merkelbach-Pinck, 'Wanderungen der Märchen im deutschsprachigen Lothringen', Folk-Liv ii–iii (1939), 227.

41 Conrad Laforte and Edith Champagne, Le Catalogue de la chanson folklorique française, Quebec 1977–84.

genres was, in as much as it can be established, also shared by the people among whom they were collected, but the result has been the relative neglect of other genres by academics. Although in the study itself I will make use of various genres of oral literature, the discussion that follows on its reliability as a source concentrates on the example of fairytales, the interest they have generated making them the most useful entry-point to the subject.

Folktales between fantasy and reality

At the beginning of a Breton tale the narrator warned his audience 'The more I'll tell you/ The more I'll lie to you/ I'm not paid/ To tell you the truth.'[42] Narrators in the Argonne used humorous reworkings of the epistles, 'Lecto libri gando. It was the year that one mowed the vine and picked the meadow' and continued with other images from the world turned upside down. Their audiences knew, therefore, that what followed was not the gospel truth.[43] Tale-telling was lying, this definition was made by the narrators themselves: 'This is a true story, not a fairytale' Merkelbach-Pinck was told, while in francophone Lorraine the very word 'conte' meant a lie.[44]

Storytellers may talk of lies, folklorists prefer the term fantasy. Stith Thompson wrote that 'Contradiction of reality lies at the heart of the folktale' and many folklorists have taken this as the defining element of the genre.[45] Historians who wish to use folktales as a historical source must, therefore, first defend themselves against the charges of folklorists like Alan Dundes: 'Fairy tales, oral and literary, are essentially creatures of fantasy. They do not necessarily represent historical reality. The literal approach in folklore includes mythologists who lead expeditions to Mount Ararat searching for the remains of Noah's ark.'[46] As the folklorist Lutz Röhrich remarked, 'Where

---

42 'Plus je vous en dirai/ Plus je vous mentirai/ Je ne suis pas payé/ Pour vous dire la vérité': Paul Sébillot, Contes populaires de la Haute-Bretagne, iii, Paris 1882, 74. This was a common opening formula in western France: Ariane de Félice, Contes de Haute-Bretagne, Paris 1954, p. vi.

43 'C'ètée l'annéïe qu'on fauchée lè veign' et qu'on vanndagée lè pré': Louis Lallement, Contes rustiques et folklore de l'Argonne, Châlons-sur-Marne 1913, 53.

44 'Dies isch jetzt e wohri G'schicht un kenn Märche': Karl Heinz Langstroff, Lothringer Volksart: Untersuchung zur deutsch-lothringischen Volkserzählung an Hand der Sammlung von Angelika Merkelbach-Pinck, Marburg 1953, 76. See also Léon Zéliqzon, Dictionnaire des patois romans de la Moselle, Strasbourg 1924, 155, and Louis Lavigne, Le Patois de Cumières et du Verdunois, Verdun 1940, 259. Saint Peter, in one Argonne folktale, turns away a supplicant at the gates of heaven with the words: 'That's nothing but a flàve [fable or tale] that you've told us': Lallement, Contes rustiques, 159.

45 Thompson, The folktale, 8. Max Lüthi went even further and called tales 'an antitype of the uncertain, confusing, unclear and irritating world of reality': The European folktale: form and nature, Bloomington, Ind. 1986, 85.

46 Alan Dundes, 'Fairy tales from a folkloristic perspective', in Ruth B. Bottigheimer (ed.), Fairy tales and society: illusion, allusion and paradigm, Philadelphia 1986, 266.

in "reality" do poor woodsmen abandon their children (*Hansel and Gretel*) or do we find a woman so evil that she allows her stepchildren to be killed (*The Juniper Tree* and *Snow White*)?"[47]

As we will see, even such shocking behaviour may not have been very removed from historical reality. What appears to modern readers as fantasy can appear more like the voice of experience when seen through the eyes of a historian. However, it is not my intention to argue that folktales are a simple reflection of reality. Folktales are the works of narrative craftsmen working in a particular form, and should be looked upon as such, but their value as sources is not invalidated even when no claim is made for them as records of fact. Because folktales are generally escapist aesthetic experiences does not mean that no significance can be attached to them. I intend to show that it is possible to recover the social meaning of a tale, and thereby gain access to the mentality of the past.

If we wish to fathom the meaning of folktales then we must first consider the valuable lessons learnt from folklore studies in the last two centuries. Each generation of scholars, starting with the Grimms, has been faced with the same conundrum: tales as a genre, and even individual tale-types, are all but universal. The most famous example of this uniformity also demonstrates the tale's staying power over time: the earliest known variant of *Cinderella* was found in a ninth-century Chinese manuscript.[48] Yet at the same time no two oral variants are the same. The analysis of the elements of the French variants of Cinderella shows boundless variety even within a plot relatively crystal-lised through readily available printed versions. In order to account for this dual facet of folktales – uniformity and variability – scholars have tried to discover the origin of folktales. Their different approaches have given rise to interesting, if sometimes contradictory, conclusions.

The brothers Grimm were nationalists; part of their interest in folktales was to reassert Germany's cultural heritage. From folktales they derived evidence of the religion of their Teutonic forebears. Christianity and the Enlightenment had destroyed this tradition among the elite, but it had been preserved among the German peasants. For example, the smith who traps Death in a tree in *The smith outwits the devil* (AT330, no. 82 of the *Kinder- und Hausmärchen*) is none other than the god Thor.[49] Folktales, it followed, belonged to and were formed by, all the inheritors of the original population;

---

[47] Lutz Röhrich, *Folktales and reality*, Bloomington, Ind. 1991, 3, 93. Röhrich, in fact, argues that historical realities impinge on folkloric texts even if he recoiled from these particular examples.

[48] R. D. Jameson, 'Cinderella in China', in Alan Dundes (ed.), *Cinderella: a casebook*, London 1988, 74–5. Anna B. Rooth, in a consideration of more than 700 variants of this tale-type, found evidence of Cinderella motifs in the Balkans over 2,000 years ago, and there are many other researches which point to the great age of some folktales: *The Cinderella cycle*, Lund 1951, 233.

[49] Richard Dorson, 'Introduction', in Kurt Ranke (ed.), *Folktales of Germany*, Chicago 1966, p. xii.

they were a product of communal creation. The example and encouragement of the Grimms interested other scholars in folktales, and a theory of origins developed – the mythological school – whose leading exponent was the philologist Max Müller. Through etymologies he asserted that folktales were relics of Aryan mythology brought by the Indo-Europeans from their high Asian home: the Gods of the *Vedas* were the same as the characters in European folktales, each of whom could be traced back to 'mythopoeic' man's prayer that the sun would rise again in the morning.[50]

Such a position could only be maintained in the absence of collections from other parts of the world; once the fashion for folklore spread to Europe's imperial possessions the world-wide nature of many motifs and tale-types became clear. This led to the modified position adopted by the English 'anthropological' school. Their argument was that all societies had experienced parallel development from primitive to civilised, if at different time-scales. The culture of any society at a particular stage would be similar, and this accounted for the uniformity of so many customs around the world (folktales being but the record of these customs). Though society evolved, the imprint of its earlier culture was preserved among its most primitive elements, a process Tylor termed 'survivals in culture'. 'In proverbs and riddles, and nursery tales and superstitions, we detect the relics of a stage of thought which is dying out in Europe, but which still exists in many parts of the world', wrote Andrew Lang, the apologist for this school. It followed that everything in folktales, even the most shocking motifs, must at one time have been familiar.[51]

The theories of Tylor and Lang found an echo on the continent where the idea of 'primitive thought' was given its clearest statement by Lévy-Bruhl. Using new information from North America and elsewhere, he maintained that folktales arose from and were intrinsically linked to primitive religious practices. The tales themselves had once been part of the ritual.[52] The premise of parallel development on which such statements were based was equally attractive to Marxist folklorists, such as Vladimir Propp, who came to similar conclusions about the original purpose of folktales: 'The composition of myths and wondertales coincides with the sequence of events during initia-

---

[50] Richard Dorson, *The British folklorists: a history*, Chicago 1968, 160–86.

[51] Andrew Lang, 'The method of folklore', in *Custom and myth*, London 1904, 12–13. One of Lang's followers, Sidney Hartland, took the tale of *The changeling* (migratory legend type 5085) and showed how it related to actual practices among 'primitives' in China and Ireland, as well as to historical incidents in England: *The science of fairy tales*, London 1890, ch. v.

[52] Pierre Saintyves applied this 'théorie liturgique' to the famous *Contes de ma mère l'Oye* of Charles Perrault. He concluded, on the basis of comparing individual motifs with practices in tribal societies, that they were the 'commentaires rituels' that accompanied seasonal and initiation rites: *Les Contes de Perrault et les récits parallèles*, Paris 1923, p. xxi.

tion, which suggests that someone described to the young man the very thing that was happening to him.'[53]

Most contemporary scholars would disavow the whole concept of the unilinear development of societies that underlay this method. Neither would modern anthropologists permit the loose comparison of individual motifs, divorced from their context, which gave rise to many of its conclusions. Yet despite its poor theoretical underpinnings and myriad failures in practice, the concept of 'survivals' remains remarkably attractive, and probably in its more limited applications not altogether wrong. If used over short periods and in related cultures, this method can be revealing, as recently demonstrated by Ronald Hutton.[54] Röhrich points to a number of existing or ancient courting and marriage customs (the bride losing her shoe, identifying the bride by a part of the body, ritual refusals and hiding the 'true bride'), all of which are attested to in Lorraine, and all of which are essential motifs to several tale-types collected there. In order to explain these motifs he turns to the work of anthropologists among non-Europeans who practise similar customs in order to protect the identities of the couple during this liminal period, when they were at most risk from evil spirits.[55]

Examples abound of motifs that have their counterpart in the historical reality of a past era, but accounting for individual elements is a long way from explaining the existence of the whole tale. It is true, for example, that Cosquin's tale *Jean de l'Ours* contains passages very reminiscent of Siberian shamanistic initiation.[56] The temptation exists, particularly in the light of Carlo Ginzburg's 'evidential paradigm', to find a connection between the two, but the problem with this approach is not (or not only) whether any historical link can be made between two widely separated and very different societies, but whether it can be made between two totally different things: an artistic fantasy composed for an audience on the one hand and a personal, secret, effective ceremony on the other.[57] Even if one accepted the hypothesis that tales once were the explanations given to initiates, why were people in societies and ages with no experience of shamanism or tribal initiation still

53 Vladimir Propp, *Theory and history of folklore*, Manchester 1984, 118.
54 Ronald Hutton, 'The English Reformation and the evidence of folklore', *Past and Present* cxlviii (1995), 89–116. Recent applications in oral literature include Francesca Sautman's 'Le Conte 425B: rites de mariage et parcours magique', *Merveilles et contes* iii (1989), 28–44, and Conrad Laforte, 'La Coutume antique et médiévale des couronnes de fleurs retrouvées dans la chanson de tradition orale', *Folklore canadien – Canadian Folklore* xvi (1994), 89–102.
55 Röhrich, *Folktales and reality*, 92–111. For comparative French material see Nicole Belmont, 'The symbolic function of the wedding procession in the popular rituals of marriage', in Robert Forster and Orest Ranum (eds), *Ritual, religion, and the sacred: selections from the Annales: economies, sociétés, civilisations*, Baltimore 1982, 1–7.
56 Mircea Eliade drew attention to these similarities: *Shamanism: archaic techniques of ecstasy*, 2nd edn, London 1989, 180.
57 Carlo Ginzburg, 'Clues: roots of an evidential paradigm', in *Clues, myths and the historical method*, Baltimore 1989, 96–125.

telling the same stories?[58] One cannot totally reject the idea that folklore motifs have their roots in the practices and beliefs of the past, but it does not explain why these motifs were retained in stories long after the institutions in question have disappeared.

A necessary corollary to the theory of 'survivals in culture' is that similar tales arose in many places. Tales were 'polygenetic', their universality the result of each society experiencing identical cultural epochs. An opposing point of view developed at the end of the nineteenth century that saw tales as 'unigenetic', their uniformity a result of diffusion from one source. The exponents of the historical-geographic or 'Finnish' school attempted to piece together the history of each tale-type by assembling as many variants as they could both from oral and literary sources. Then by careful comparison they constructed a genealogy, finally deriving the outline of the ur-form, from which all other variants stemmed. The process of diffusion necessarily gave rise to variants, as each telling altered the original through forgetfulness, emphasis, modernisation and a variety of other processes codified by Kaarle Krohn, the originator of the method.[59] It was his student, Antti Aarne, who established the tale-type index, the essential tool for the historical-geographical method. An example of the application of the method is Reidar Christiansen's study of *The two travellers* (AT613).[60] He posited an Indian origin for this tale. The older, more popular form, AT613A, arrived in Europe from the east; the newer, more moralistic form, AT613B (new being a relative term, for he found the oldest variant of this sub-type in a fifth-century Jewish manuscript), came via Arabia, and finally through Jewish intermediaries into medieval Spain. Doubt has subsequently been cast on the Indian ur-form of the tale with the discovery of close parallels in a third-century Chinese monastery and in thirteenth-century BC Egypt.[61] This illustrates one of the problems of this method: in the absence of historical data huge gaps are filled in with hypotheses about the primariness of particular motifs, about the movements of peoples and about the process of oral transmission itself. Again, the method has more chances of success if its ambitions are limited to charting the history of a tale-type within a limited region in a historical period, as Emmanuel le Roy Ladurie has shown in his recreation of the paths taken by *Godfather Death* (AT332) into southern France.[62]

---

[58] Both Lüthi and Röhrich have suggested that the reason so many clear instances of survivals, such as shamanistic initiation, have survived in the folktale is precisely because its 'status as conscious fiction enables it to maintain and preserve themes, traits and motifs that have ceased to be part of belief': *Folktales and reality*, 73. Legends, which require belief, adapt their material to the practices of the time; tales 'sublimate' their material, turning historical motifs into fantasy, which acts like a kind of bottling alcohol.

[59] Kaarle Krohn, *Folklore methodology*, Austin, Tx 1971.

[60] Reidar T. Christiansen, *The tale of the two travellers or the blinded man: a comparative study* (Folklore Fellows Communications xxiv), Helsinki 1916.

[61] Delarue and Tenèze, *Le Conte populaire français*, ii. 528.

[62] Emmanuel le Roy Ladurie, *Love, death and money in the pays d'oc*, London 1984, 164–8.

If there was an original form for each tale, then there must also have been an author. Implicit in the premise of unigenesis was that the folk were the custodians of folktales, but not their creators. The original source was a poet, and on this basis alone he was often assumed to be from a different social class. However, if the creator was an oral poet, as the Finnish school assumed, there was little chance of discovering his identity. The main attack on this position came from scholars convinced that one could know the original author, because all creation and most diffusion was through written literature. The main proponent of this argument was Albert Wesselski, a medievalist with a thorough knowledge of fables, *exempla* and jest-books. Struck by the similarity of these to stories collected from the oral tradition, he argued that all folktales had their origins in written ones. Studying literary versions was not, as the Finnish school believed, a useful means of tracing the migrations of the oral tradition, it was the only history that the folktale had. He could not believe that oral transmission, consisting of thousands upon thousands of narrations spread over space and time, could preserve a folktale in a recognisable form.[63]

Wesselski received short shrift from the proponents of oral transmission. Nineteenth-century folktale collectors had found their best sources among rural, illiterate populations, far removed from the artistic circles and print-shops of the cities. Indeed their best sources were among those populations that had little or no written literature, such as the Finns and the Bretons. Folklorists who combated Wesselski were able to point to the growing evidence amassed by anthropologists that it was perfectly feasible for a society with no written literature at all to both create and preserve oral literature.

However, the comparison between nineteenth-century Europe and tribal societies is not tenable. When Cosquin was collecting his tales only 10 per cent of young males in the Meuse were illiterate, and for several centuries each village had had at least a handful of inhabitants who could read, and who became sources of information for those who could not. Priests used tales culled from their reading in their sermons; pedlars carried them on images.

If all theories of diffusion offer narrators a limited role in the creation of the stories they tell, the premise that all oral literature was derived from authors of the written word is particularly dismissive and casts doubt on the importance of folktales as sources for social groups who are otherwise voice-

---

63 Albert Wesselski, *Märchen des Mittelalters*, Berlin 1925, 202–9. To demonstrate his argument he got a teacher to tell a story to a class of schoolchildren, and then asked them to repeat it. The garbled responses proved, he believed, that the oral tradition was incapable of transmitting a complete narrative. Walter Anderson, a follower of the Finnish school, responded with his law of self-correction. Each teller, he suggested, had heard the tale from his informant several times, and probably from more than one informant. Given the necessary skill and intelligence he could reconstruct the standard form from these versions: Walter Anderson, *Kaiser und Abt* (Folklore Fellows Communications xlii), Helsinki 1923, 397–403.

less in history. If, as has been asserted, every narrator of *Beauty and the beast* (AT425) learnt the story from a schoolbook version of a Renaissance reworking of Apuleius' *Cupid and Psyche*, then their tales are simply evidence of the hegemonic control of elites.[64] The most doctrinaire position on the primacy of print is hard to maintain considering what we know about the oral tradition from anthropological fieldwork (which does not stop this position being taken by some literary scholars).[65] It is more usual to think in terms of a regular interchange between oral and literary cultures. But even where we can be fairly certain that the written was the original, the form and content in oral versions will be altered to appeal to a different audience and, perhaps, carry a different message.[66]

A few examples here will demonstrate the general pattern. Research on the Grimms' collection has shown how some of their tales, such as *Sleeping Beauty* (AT410), collected from the daughter of a Huguenot immigrant family from Metz, probably derive from Perrault's *Contes de ma mère l'Oye*.[67] Just as some tales in Grimm derive from Perrault, so other collectors frequently found echoes of Grimm in their oral texts.[68] Such examples should hardly surprise us, folktale narrators were interested in their art-form, and sought out material wherever they could.[69] Merkelbach-Pinck mentions a number of other tales which her informants had taken from written versions.[70] Unfortunately few French collectors asked their narrators from

64 Ruth B. Bottigheimer, '*Cupid and Psyche* vs. *Beauty and the beast*: the Milesian and the modern', *Merveilles et contes* iii (1989), 4–44.
65 'The Hellenistic tale of *Cupid and Psyche* provides powerful evidence of the dependency of the genre on texts': Marina Warner, *From the beast to the blonde: on fairytales and their tellers*, London 1994, p. xviii.
66 Ivan N. Rozanov, 'From book to folklore', in Felix Oinas and Stephen Soudakoff (eds), *The study of Russian folklore*, The Hague 1975, 65–75.
67 John M. Ellis, *One fairy story too many: the brothers Grimm and their tales*, Chicago 1983, 32. I have cited Ellis because he made available in English much of the German scholarship on the Grimms, but I do not accept his argument that the Grimms perpetrated a deliberate fraud in claiming the tales came from the simple, native folk of Hesse.
68 Delarue and Tenèze cite several tale-types whose few French variants appear to derive from the Grimms, including AT426, AT431 and AT440: *Le Conte populaire français*, ii. 110–2, 119. Thirteen tales in Merkelbach-Pinck's collection probably derive, indirectly, from the Grimms.
69 There is, for example, the case of the Finnish storyteller Blind Strömberg who got children to borrow books of fairytales from the public library and read them to him. Several items in his repertoire were acquired in this way, but despite his willingness to adopt literary tales, there can be little doubt that he was primarily working in an oral tradition: Gun Herranen, 'A blind storyteller's repertoire', in Reimund Kvideland, Henning Sehmsdorf and Elizabeth Simpson (eds), *Nordic folklore: recent studies*, Bloomington, Ind. 1989, 65.
70 Langstroff estimates that 14% of Merkelbach-Pinck's published folktale collection has traceable written sources. Though in some cases she was unaware of these, Merkelbach-Pinck excluded some tales from publication whose literary origins were obvious. At least one of her informants, Jean Hemmer, seems to have wished to give the impression of oral transmission when in fact most of his tales were derived from published sources: *Lothringer Volksart*, 52–3, 69.

where they had obtained their tales, but the impact of written versions can be detected. To take one example from the Ardennes, *Florine et Truitonne* derives from Mme d'Aulnoy's *L'Oiseau bleu*, first published in 1697 and a popular chapbook tale throughout the eighteenth and nineteenth centuries.[71] However, the oral text has been shortened, the language 'hardened', subplots, characterisations, descriptions of people and places have all been dropped in favour of a straightforward narrative of the actions, as is typical of oral folk-tales. The presence of *L'Oiseau bleu* among the nineteenth-century peasantry is not simply acculturation but appropriation.

There can be no doubt that the literary tradition had introduced new themes and motifs to the oral tradition, but this is a long way from accepting the 'dependency of the genre on texts'. A variant of *The three magic objects and the marvellous fruits* (AT566) from the Argonne is entitled *Tangu*, from which one might guess that it derived from a literary version of the same tale-type by the abbé Bignon, whose hero is also called Tangu. But whereas Bignon's version is about a prince, the Argonne version is about a hermit. This and other adaptations go well beyond the appropriation of the cultural products of one social group for use by another, for, with the exception of the name and some necessary motifs to the tale-type, there is little resemblance between the two. It is not possible, therefore, to insist that the oral derived from the written, but only that a handful of decorative elements were borrowed from the latter.[72] Before Bignon's treatment, this tale-type had been known for centuries in a chapbook, also about a prince, but this time called *Fortunatus*. The *bibliothèque bleue* version was reprinted dozens of times in France (and in other countries), and distributed across the continent. Yet in the oral variants collected in Lorraine, and indeed all over Europe, the heroes (and there are usually three as opposed to the single prince) are typically 'low' types such as soldiers or cobblers. If one were to suggest that the oral versions from Spain to Russia all derived from the written, then each narrator who borrowed the story must have made exactly the same alterations to the tale, changing the hero (and much else besides) to prepare it for oral narration. This idea is only remotely plausible if one first accepted that the oral tradition has laws, such as tripling, to account for these uniform changes, which would mean accepting that the oral tradition was pre-existing.[73] The audience for folk-tales knew the chapbook version because it was read on the same occasions as

---

[71] Albert Meyrac, *Traditions, coutumes, légendes et contes des Ardennes*, Charleville 1890, 478–81 (AT432).

[72] Lallement, *Contes rustiques*, 110–15.

[73] Similar conclusions can be reached by examining many of the other tales popularised by cheap literature: all the oral variants of AT314, *The magic flight, the youth transformed into a horse*, resemble each other more than they do the story of *Robert le diable*, a medieval treatment of the theme that found its way into *bibliothèque bleue*. The same is true of AT706, *The maiden without hands*, when compared to the popular print versions, *La Belle Hélène de Constantinople* or *Geneviève de Brabant*.

fairytale narration.[74] But despite having circulated in the same areas for centuries, the oral and literary versions had by-and-large maintained their distinct identities. Even within nineteenth-century Lorraine the concept of an oral tradition not dependent on written culture was still valid.

While the Finnish school was defending itself against Wesselski they did not even notice an attack from a different direction. Reading through the Afanas'ev's collection of Russian folktales Vladimir Propp discovered that many concerned tests passed by one 'good' daughter and failed by her step-sister: 'But surely it is the same tale! Various characters "test" the step-daughter and reward her each in his own way, but the plot does not change. . . . To Afanas'ev these were different tales because of different characters in them. To me they were identical because the actions of the characters were the same.'[75] Drawing on this inspiration Propp examined the folktale according to the functions of its characters. Functions were not the same as motifs. It did not matter, for example, how the hero acquired the magical agent to perform his tasks, whether by inheritance, theft or as reward, nor whether it was a horse, whistle or tinderbox. It only mattered that he should be in possession of the means to defeat the villain. Propp's discovery was that, though folktales seemed to exist in endless variety, they shared the same functions and in each tale their sequence was identical. All tales were one in regard to their structure.

Claude Lévi-Strauss welcomed Propp's *Morphology* but questioned whether anything could be deduced from it about the purpose of folktales. He characterised Propp's work as 'syntagmatic' or linear structuralism, simply dividing a text into segments, whereas Lévi-Strauss wanted to uncover the paradigms from which the structure was derived and which gave the text its meaning. This could only be done by relating the text to its context.[76] Folklorists have since tried to combine syntagmatic and paradigmatic structural analysis to show how the underlying conflicts, the themes which drive the plot, are resolved in a series of functions. A recent impressive synthesis was provided by Bengt Holbek who argues that all fairytales are basically the story of a misalliance. The themes of the tale are the three paradigmatic oppositions which the hero and heroine must overcome in order to achieve their misalliance: between the generations; between low and high social groups; between the sexes. The pair reach this resolution, their wedding, in five 'syntagmatic' moves in which they interact with six other characters who represent the

---

[74] Perrout, *Trésors*, 246, and J. Lorraine, 'Nos Traditions: décembre et janvier', *L'Austrasie* n.s. xiv (1910), 105. Readers familiar with the literature on chapbooks will be aware of Roger Chartier's insistence that they were not read aloud at the *veillée*. Though this assertion was originally made only about the *ancien régime*, it has taken on the status of a 'received truth' among historians even of nineteenth-century popular culture. However, it is contradicted by almost every folklorist from Lorraine.

[75] Propp, *Theory and history*, 69.

[76] Claude Lévi-Strauss, 'L'Analyse morphologique des contes russes', *International Journal of Slavic Linguistics and Poetics* iii (1960), 137.

oppositional themes – their parents and the false heroes or heroines (additional roles such as donor and villain are created by splitting conflicting aspects of the parental figures).[77]

Another criticism levelled at Propp was that although he had shown the 'constants' underlying the variety, he was unable to show how each variable was generated, for nowhere was the level of functions laid bare, the tale only existed in variants.[78] Alan Dundes gave the name 'motifeme' to the invariable functions and termed the variables that might fill a motifemic slot 'allomotifs'.[79] One allomotif might replace another depending on the audience. Holbek, using Dundes's model, has shown how in *The princess on the glass mountain* (AT530) half the Danish variants have a monster as the guardian of princess and half her father. The monster can be read as the symbolic equivalent of the father, disguised by the well-known folktale technique of splitting the good and bad aspects of a personality.[80]

Holbek's model, of which only a synopsis is presented here, can be used both to explain the symbolic content of the tales themselves, and their value to the tale-telling community. His debt to Propp was, above all, that by revealing the 'syntax' of fairytales, the invariable structure that underlay the variables, he drew an analogy to language. Just as every performance of a speech act is preceded by acquisition of competence in the language, by analogy every folktale narrator had first to acquire a special grammar and vocabulary. Skilled narrators acquired competence in this special poetic language by serving an apprenticeship.

The analogy to language, and the distinction between competence and performance, inspired scholars concerned with other genres of oral literature. Milman Parry and Albert Lord used it to understand the epic tradition of Yugoslavia. The ability of epic singers to recite songs containing thousands of lines of verse did not, they found on examination, rely on strict memorisa-

---

77 Bengt Holbek, 'The language of fairy tales', in Kvideland, Sehmsdorf and Simpson, *Nordic folklore*, 40–62. A much more detailed version (and application) of the model is provided in *Interpretation of fairy tales: Danish folklore in a European perspective* (Folklore Fellows Communications ccxxxix), Helsinki 1987.

78 Propp in fact did outline a theory of 'transformations' whereby the original content, based, he believed, on prehistoric rituals, was altered to fit the expectations of succeeding historical epochs: *Theory and history*, 116–23.

79 Alan Dundes, 'The symbolic equivalence of allomotifs: towards a method of analysing folktales', in Geneviève Calame-Griaule, Veronika Görög-Karady and Michèle Chiche (eds), *Le Conte, pourquoi? Comment? Folktales, why and how? Actes des journées d'études en littérature orale (Paris, 23–26 March, 1982)*, Paris 1984, 187–99.

80 Bengt Holbek, 'Variation and tale type', in Veronika Görög-Karady (ed.), *D'Un Conte . . . à l'autre: la variabilité dans la littérature orale*, Paris 1990, 471–86. A clear example is provided by one of Alessandro Falassi's informants in the shape of an Italian variant of the common folktale test set for young women by giving them animals to look after. In this case the narrator habitually forgot to refer to kittens and instead referred to children, thus making the symbolism abundantly clear: *Folklore by the fireside: text and context of the Tuscan veglia*, Austin, Tx 1980, 47.

tion. An expert singer could take a skeleton of a plot, either heard or read, and turn it into an oral masterpiece. The oral poet could to do this because 'he has learned the phrases and rhythms of a poetic language, the language of tradition, which he can think in almost as easily as we can think in the phrases and rhythms of our prosaic language'.[81] Each performance was therefore different, but each was also part of a tradition which consisted not only of phrases and rhythms ('oral-formulae'), but also what Lord termed a 'tension of essences' – the architectonic patterns which kept each song a recognisable variant of the same plot-type. An apprentice singer acquired knowledge of phrases, motifs and plots, and the skills to manipulate these elements, through observation of other singers, so that creation, transmission and performance were all part of the same action, all occurred at the same time.

If this insight is also valid for folktales, it follows that their troubling variability was an integral element of the oral tradition, it was part of narrators' skill. However, the talent to compose, the competence in the poetic language of oral literature, was not possessed by all. There were a limited number of recognised singers in Yugoslavia, and there were only a limited number of folktale narrators in Lorraine.[82] Their works were only 'folk' literature in the sense of the audience for whom they were performed. This understanding of oral literature turned attention away from the historical origins of tale-types (for if each folklore text exists only in the performance then the quest for the ur-form was doomed) and towards the character of the narrator and his repertoire, and the milieu in which his art took shape.

Tale-telling was the art of the few, which led to an increased interest in the personality and repertoire of individual narrators; their names even began to appear on the title pages alongside those of collectors.[83] Recognition was being given to them as authors similar to that which ethnographers found was accorded to them in their own communities. Expert narrators owned, in some sense, their stories: other people might know them and at a pinch tell them, but they would describe them as 'so-and-so's story'. Repertoires might even be inherited, the narrator passing on the 'rights' to their successor.[84] This did not mean, however, that in passing on the tale it remained unchanged; recognition of the 'authorship' of narrators led to an understanding of how they chose their repertoire and adapted their stories to fit their personality. Holbek has analysed the preferences of a large sample of Danish narrators, looking for examples of gender bias. He found that male narrators, who made up the majority of the sample, mostly told tales about male protagonists: 'The corre-

81 Albert B. Lord, *The singer of tales*, Cambridge, Mass. 1960, 35–6.
82 Holbek, working with a very thorough set of sources for western Jutland, estimated that no more than 0.3% of the population could be classed as folktale narrators: *Interpretation of fairy tales*, 140.
83 See, for example, Gottfried Henssen, *Ueberlieferung und Persönlichkeit: die Erzählungen und Lieder des Egbert Gerrits*, Munster 1951.
84 Dégh, *Folktales and society*, 89.

spondence of the sex of the narrator with the gender of the tale is unmistak-
able.' This conclusion has far-reaching implications: 'It is no longer possible
to neglect the existence of individual preference in oral tradition. And if the
sex of the narrator is important, as we have found, then his or her social status
is hardly less important. We must now also assume that the predilection of
the old rural proletariat for fairy tales is significant.'[85] In other words narrators
told stories which in some way were about themselves. It was no accident that
the best folktale narrators have usually been found among the poorest, least
educated, members of society. The assumption that tales had originally been
aristocratic entertainments which had sunk down to the folk made no sense if
it could be shown that the tales drew their meaning from a particular social
milieu. Storytelling had a function other than the purely aesthetic, it was a
communication which we can only understand by asking, to quote Holbek
again, 'why did *this* man or woman tell *this* story in *this* way?'[86] Only by
looking at the tale in its context can one see that 'what is being recounted in
the stories themselves is precisely a reflection of many of the problems faced
by both performers and listeners'.[87]

By concentrating on the tale as performance we can appreciate its value as
a communication between particular persons. The power of Holbek's model
resides in the fact that the themes which he found underlying fairytales were
precisely the three areas of conflict felt most strongly by members of the rural
proletariat: between the generations, between social groups and between the
sexes. Further, it shows how tales could be manipulated to impart a message to
a particular audience (or a particular person in an audience) on particular
occasions, the primary one being that, by the successful formation of a
love-relationship between two young persons, their other problems could be
overcome.

Holbek also helps us understanding why folktales have their specific form,
in particular the magical and fantastical elements. These, he said, 'convey
emotional impressions of beings, phenomena, and events in the real world,
organised in the form of fictional narratives sequences which allow the
narrator to speak of the problems, hopes and ideas of the community. . . . The
purpose seems to be to permit a vicarious working through of emotional problems that cannot be openly vented'.[88]

If looking at performance emphasises the variable in folk literature, a
totally different line of investigation, the psychoanalytic, emphasises the

---

85 Holbek, *Interpretation of fairy tales*, 169.
86 William Hansen, 'Bengt Holbek: obituary', *Journal of American Folklore* cvi (1993),
185.
87 Falassi, *Folklore by the fireside*, 30.
88 Holbek, 'The language of fairy tales', 56. The same conclusion was reached by James
Taggart working with storytellers in rural Spain: 'Speaking in the metaphorical language of
a story allows them to express deep feelings through the safety of fantasy': *Enchanted
maidens: gender relations in Spanish folktales of courtship and marriage*, Princeton, NJ 1990,
16.

universal. The best-known example is Erich Fromm's reading of *Little Red Riding Hood* in which the hood becomes a symbol of menstruation, and the whole tale can therefore be understood as a young girl's confrontation with adult sexuality in the shape of the wolf.[89] Psychoanalytic interpretations have proved very popular, but have equally often been held up for ridicule. Using atypical variants is a common complaint against psychoanalysts; Fromm's analysis relied on Perrault's version and the elements he attached so much importance to do not regularly occur in the oral tradition.[90] Another is their fundamentally false assumption that folktales in the oral tradition were intended, like contemporary literary collections, for children.[91] The problem is not that the psychoanalysts are necessarily wrong about the usefulness of fairytales in socialisation but that to generalise from this application of tales to an explanation of the whole tale-telling tradition is invalid. Folklorists such as Dundes and Holbek have applied Freudian symbolism to revealing effect, but only to tales within their context. The work of psychoanalysts is of most importance to historians because it rekindled interest in this source within our discipline. Historians sought to prevent psychoanalysts treating tales, in the words of Robert Darnton, 'flattened out, like patients on a couch, in a timeless contemporaneity'.[92] In order to understand their meaning, folktales had to be returned to their historical context.

We can now look again at the question posed by Röhrich above: 'Where in reality do poor woodsmen abandon their children' as happens in *Hansel and Gretel?* It was, by coincidence, the treatment of this tale by the psychoanalyst Bruno Bettelheim which led Eugen Weber to consider the relationship between folktales and historical reality: 'The cunning analyst wants to go beyond the obvious, so one section of Bettelheim's book is called *The Fantasy of the Wicked Stepmother.* But that interpretation simply ignores the grim everyday experience on which the recurrent motif is based.'[93] High mortality among women in childbirth and rapid remarriage of widowers meant that many children before the twentieth century knew what it was like to have a stepmother, and in societies where there was competition for all resources she could prove an enemy to her stepchildren. Weber quotes the example of the Napoleonic veteran Captain Coignet, who in his memoirs told how he had to run away at the age of eight to escape his stepmother's beatings and hired

89 Erich Fromm, *The forgotten language: an introduction to the understanding of dreams, fairy tales and myths*, New York 1951, 235–41.

90 Robert Darnton, *The great cat massacre and other episodes in French cultural history*, London 1984, 18–21.

91 It is true that in the oral tradition some tales, including many of those widely known today such as *Little Red Riding Hood* and *Tom Thumb*, were probably intended for children, but the predominant pattern, at least in northern Europe, was of adults telling for other adults, and in particular men for other men in single-sex work groups.

92 Darnton, *The great cat massacre*, 21.

93 Eugen Weber, 'Fairies and hard facts; the reality of folktales', *Journal of the History of Ideas* xlii (1981), 94.

himself out as a shepherd. His younger siblings were abandoned in a wood, and only survived by being taken in by a miller, another fairytale motif. Whereas Bettelheim describes the fairytale forest as 'the dark, hidden, near-impenetrable world of our unconscious', Weber shows that for peasants before the mid-nineteenth century the forest was indeed a place of danger, from wild animals, from bandits or simply from getting lost and starving to death. The wolves it hid were not necessarily masked male libidos on the prowl, but genuine man-eating monsters like the 'Beast of Gévaudan'.[94]

Analysts, horrified at some of the details in folktales, naturally want them to be symbolic but with greater knowledge of the historical context they can appear as simply the peasant's version of reality, either as he experienced it or as he believed it to be. The metaphors used are drawn from that under-standing of reality. Although Fromm might have been wrong in many of his assumptions about *Little Red Riding Hood*, the metaphor of the wolf for lustful men is one often used in traditional communities themselves, and so the tale certainly can be read as a warning.[95] In a society where sexual experience was prized among unmarried men, but where young women were expected to preserve their virginity, the danger posed by 'wolves' was not only the psychic – or physical – damage of rape, but the social damage. Rather than being directed to the unconscious, the tale's didactic function is all too obvious: wolves were a genuine threat to a girl on her own, so were young men; she would be wise to avoid both. This is not to deny that elements in folktales are open to symbolic interpretation, but that the symbols' power for their original audience was likely to be rooted in experienced reality.

This helps explain why, whatever their later fantastical developments, the initial situation in a folktale was always believable. Holbek found that 'most of the protagonists began their careers in circumstances exactly like those of the storytellers and their audiences'.[96] Falassi, listening to the tale of *Rolando and Brunhilde* in a Tuscan kitchen, was told by a member of the audience that the narrator liked the story 'because she recognizes herself in it. The story seems her own'. Like Brunhilde, she was engaged to be married and an older more powerful man, her employer, had tried to prevent it and even impris-oned her, but she was rescued by her fiancé and they were wed. The only difference was that in the fairystory the couple gain a fortune, while in reality they were both sacked.[97] Folktales remain a fantasy, but one with close links

---

94 There is a modern myth that wolves never posed any danger to man. It is true that, unless driven by extreme hunger (or rabies), wolves would avoid attacking an adult male, but they did not show such regard to undefended children. Case histories abound in Jean-Yves Chauvet, *Les Loups en Lorraine: histoire et témoignages*, Le Coteau 1986.

95 At the same time, in hunters' songs, young men, often using the same analogy with wolves, were being socialised into thinking of young women on their own as fair game: Pinck, *Verklingende Weisen*, ii. 203–4, no. 67: *Spazierende Schäferin*; Westphalen, *Chansons populaires*, i. 198, no. 150: *Il y a bien six mois*.

96 Holbek, 'The language of fairy tales', 42.

97 Falassi, *Folklore by the fireside*, 51–2.

to experienced reality: their value over legends and other genres is precisely that they reveal what people hoped for as well as what they believed to be true.

Fairytales can be seen in terms of real life, but real life could also be interpreted in terms of fairytales. Eugen Weber compared the folktale with the life stories of lower-class autobiographers such as Captain Coignet, but Coignet was also a 'conteur' in the popular definition of the word – a liar. I am not in a position to assert that what he wrote about his family background was untrue, but as a typical soldier-storyteller of the Baron Munchausen type, he undoubtedly chose to emphasise or even invent particular parts of his experiences to fit an imaginative model. The tendency to rewrite one's life history in line with one's own desires (or society's expectations) is well-documented by oral historians; what I want to emphasise here is how folktales could serve as a model. This is particularly noticeable in soldiers' memoirs. Why, for example, should the Lorrainer hussar Georges Bangofsky choose to record, out of more than fifteen years' service in the *grande armée*, the occasions when he saved some 'princesses' from the threats of his comrades (as happens in AT301B), or when he produced from a 'magic' sack food for all a starving family (a motif in a number of tales), or that he paid the debtors of a dead man who had been refused burial (the distinguishing motif of AT506)?[98] Folktales provide the cultural prisms through which people saw their lives, and they cast their own histories in those terms. What would be interesting to know is whether they had in fact lived their lives according to these models; did Bangofsky pay the dead man's debtors because his knowledge of *The rescued princess* (AT506) influenced his actions?

If this proved to be the case, then we would be much nearer to understanding the function of folktales. Historians have not been satisfied to 'show that a substratum of social realism underlay the fantasies and escapist entertainment of folktales'; they also contain strategies for behaviour.[99] This was the discovery of the anthropologist James Taggart among Spanish folktale narrators: 'Men and women tell one another the story of *Blancaflor* which presents a model for how courtship and marriage can work in a culture in which men are different from women.' The tales formed a dialogue in which male and female narrators stated their sometimes conflicting conceptions of love, marriage and family relationships, but also suggested possible resolutions.[100]

One of the very few examples of historians who have looked at tales as strategies is the consideration by Peter Taylor and Hermann Rebel of women's response to the draft in eighteenth-century Hesse. Taylor and Rebel looked at four variants of *Little brother and little sister* (AT450) and *The maiden*

98   Alexandre de Roche du Teilloy, *Les Etapes de Georges Bangofsky, officier lorrain: fragments de son journal de campagnes (1797–1815)*, Paris–Nancy 1905, 51.
99   Darnton, *The great cat massacre*, 45.
100 Taggart, *Enchanted maidens*, 165–99.

who seeks her brother (AT451) in the Grimms' collection, on the assumption that 'fairytales are not entertaining stories about meaningless fantastic events; rather they tie together conceptual events to provide individuals with an intellectual framework by which to interpret the stories they and others about them experienced in their everyday lives'.[101] The basic plot of AT451 is of a father with many sons who wishes for a girl. When a girl is finally born the sons are forced to flee from home and are transformed into birds. When the girl grows up and learns of their fate she sets out to free them. She succeeds at the end of a trial lasting seven years, during which she must not utter a word. During this time she marries a prince and has his children. The spell on her brothers is broken just as she mounts the pyre having been falsely accused by her mother-in-law of murder. These four tales were collected from women living in a German statelet that raised income by hiring its forces to other nations. So lucrative was this business that Hesse instituted a harsh conscription system to keep its armies full. The system favoured a form of ultimo-geniture in which the elder sons were forced into the army from which they were unlikely to return, while the farm was kept intact as a dowry for the youngest daughter. Taylor and Rebel argue that the situation thus created was painful to the women involved. The tales serve not just as symbolic renderings of their situation but as an intellectual analysis which offered them a resolution: by marrying out of the area inheritance patterns would return to normal and the brothers could come home to their birth-right.[102]

Taylor and Rebel's article is closely argued and convincing, but it also highlights some of the difficulties which face historians when using folktales. AT451 is one of the most popular fairytales in the European tradition, and it is therefore hard to localise to Hesse. It is also, as we have already seen in *Dolopathos*, one of the earliest to be found in European literary sources. Its relationship with Hessian conscription in the eighteenth century, therefore, cannot be direct. In order to show how the tale was made to carry this partic-ular message in the particular circumstances of Hesse, one must show through comparisons that variations had been introduced to the tale-type. These points do not necessarily discredit Taylor and Rebel's thesis, but they do reveal the two characteristics of folktales which limit their value as sources; their lack of specificity in terms of time and space.

As we have seen, folklorists were often political nationalists or regionalists. One of their major purposes in pursuit of folklore was the assertion of a particular national or regional culture, which consequently warranted separate political institutions. Hence, when nineteenth-century

---

101 Peter Taylor and Hermann Rebel, 'Hessian peasant women, their families and the draft: a social-historical interpretation of four tales from the Grimm collection', *Journal of Family History* vi (1981), 353.
102 Ibid. 378.

collectors introduced their folktales, they often claimed that they reeked of the soil of the *pays* in which they were told. Unfortunately local references seldom appear in the tales themselves. When translated out of the local dialect, tales from one corner of Europe strongly resemble those told all over the continent (and beyond). Good performers localised events in order to give their narratives greater power, but this was certainly not necessary to the genre; indeed folktales could be divided from other treatments of similar themes precisely because of their refusal to provide a realistic setting.[103] In Cosquin's collection only three out of eighty-four tales make any mention of local places, rather a form of exoticism is in evidence, with Paris, Lyons, Calais and London all being more popular destinations than anywhere nearby. This lack of local specificity would not surprise a diffusionist like Cosquin, but they oblige historians to consider what relevance the communication contained within the folktale had to any particular community. A possible solution is offered by the concept of ecotypes.

This term was coined by the Swedish folklorist von Sydow to help understand why there are such marked differences in national canons of tales. He explained them in terms of tradition regions with definite boundaries; only one variant of a tale would be at home in any tradition region.[104] The concept was eagerly taken up by Dundes: 'In folklore, the term refers to local forms of a folktale, folksong or any other folkloristic genre . . . defined with reference to either geographic or cultural factors. Oicotypes could be on the village, state, regional, or national level.'[105] In other words, folklore adapts to its milieu, and assuming that there are distinct cultural communities we can expect that comparison of their oral traditions will highlight cultural differences. Any new oral narrative would either be rejected by a community satisfied with its existing ecotype, or, by altering its motifs, style or meaning, be changed to fit its new cultural context. The process of ecotypification, described by Roger Abrahams for the urban ghettos of North America, is a valuable way to connect the tradition with its specific social base, for similarities across tale-types (and even across genres) can be related to the particular

---

103 An example of the way a narrator localised the action of his tales is provided by one of Merkelbach-Pinck's informants who, before telling a tale about the fox and the wolf, took his juvenile audience to look at the supposed locus of the action, the cellar of their house: Merkelbach-Pinck, *Aus der lothringer Meistube*, ii. 180.

104 Carl Wilhelm von Sydow, 'Geography and folktale oicotypes', in *Selected papers on folklore*, Copenhagen 1948, 44–59. Sydow borrowed the idea from botany where the term is used to describe native variants. As well as *oicotype* one may also see *oikotype*, but *ecotype* is the commonly accepted spelling, and is already familiar as a concept to historians of the family.

105 Alan Dundes, *Life is like a chicken coop ladder: a portrait of German culture through folklore*, New York 1984, 2.

environment.[106] Ecotypes explain the distinct regional patterns in the almost universal distribution of folktale motifs.[107]

Folklorists have highlighted the existence of national ecotypes. In his introduction to the *Catalogue raisonné*, Delarue compared the style and content of French tales with those of Germany and Brittany. The German tales were strongly marked by their locus in the mysterious dark forest where a wealth of otherworld figures lurk. In France, however, 'the tale develops in lighter, more varied world, which corresponds to the more diversified and cheerful aspect of our landscape'.[108] He found that magic elements were much less common in French tales compared with their Germanic and Celtic counterparts, the emphasis being on humans finding solutions to their own difficulties. Robert Darnton's examination of the French tale of *Barbe Bleu*, in comparison with English, German and Italian variants, comes to a similar conclusion: 'Although each story adheres to the same structure, the versions in the different traditions produce entirely different effects – comic in the Italian versions, horrific in the German, dramatic in the French, and droll in the English.'[109] For Darnton these differences can be used to deduce something about national character: 'the French tale celebrates the trickster as a social type and suggests that tricksterism will work quite well as a way of life – or as well as anything in a cruel and capricious world'.[110]

An example of a regional ecotype may tell us something about the distinctive character of francophone Lorraine. A popular tale (forty-seven versions have been collected from France) concerns *The maiden without hands* (AT706). It can be found in Cosquin's collection, and is also one of Sadoul's

---

106 Roger Abrahams, *Deep down in the jungle: Negro narrative folklore from the streets of Philadelphia*, Chicago 1970, 173–4. James M. Taggart's comparisons between Nahuat (Mexico) Indian variants and the Spanish tradition from which they derive, demonstrates how stories vary according to the different conditions of family life and cultural antecedents of both societies: '*Hansel and Gretel* in Spain and Mexio', *Journal of American Folklore* ic (1986), 435–60.

107 Lauri Honko, 'Methods in folk narrative research', in Kvideland, Sehmsdorf and Simpson, *Nordic folklore*, 38.

108 'le conte se déroule dans un monde plus clair, plus varié, plus familier, qui correspond à l'aspect plus diversifié et plus riant de notre territoire': Delarue, *Le Conte populaire français*, i. 36.

109 Darnton, *The great cat massacre*, 53.

110 Ibid. 67. Darnton has been fiercely criticised among folklorists for falling into the trap laid by their nationalist predecessors by maintaining the connection between culture and territory. See, for example, Jack Zipes, 'The Grimms and the German obsession with fairy tales', in Bottigheimer, *Fairy tales and society*, 273. There is a potential flaw in Darnton's comparisons of tales, because his examples were drawn from collections edited with the intention of demonstrating 'national character', but his conclusions are in keeping with the work of some of the leading post-war scholars in folklore including Paul Delarue, Elisabeth Koechlin, Marianne Rumpf and Lutz Röhrich, not to mention Karl-Heinz Langstroff's study of the Merkelbach-Pinck collection and (earlier) Alice Sperber's of Cosquin's.

tales.[111] In the typical French version the daughter of a king is mutilated and expelled from her father's house by the machinations of her step-mother, is restored to health by miraculous intervention, marries a prince to whom she bears children, is again expelled from the marital home by the machinations of her mother-in-law, and is finally reunited with her husband. The versions collected by both Cosquin and Sadoul follow this basic outline but with the addition of one significant motif: their heroines escape from misery by dressing as soldiers and serving in their husbands' armies. This is a motif borrowed from another tale-type *The innocent slandered maiden* (AT883). This mixing of tale-types occurs in Lorraine and nowhere else. Songs about military maids were also extremely frequent in Lorraine and it would seem that the motif of the transvestite she-soldier had particular resonance there.[112]

Tying a particular tale to particular place is not easy, but relating it to a particular historical period is even more difficult. This is despite the fact that historical references abound. A standard opening phrase for Lorrainer folktales is 'Au temps jadis' or, in germanophone areas, 'Es ist schon lange', in other words a long time ago.[113] Occasionally the narrator would start with a more specific time-frame, usually setting the events before some great historic change.[114] Stories about discharged soldiers frequently cite real wars whose conclusion results in their redundancy.[115] For the tale to capture the interest of its audience, narrators often implied that the events really took place, but the precise period was not important. By interposing some seismic event about which their audience would have at least a hazy knowledge, such as wars of the empire, the narrator placed his story far enough away and thus the fantasy elements seemed to be within the realm of possibility. In one tale from Cosquin the hero lived in the same village as the narrator, but 3,000 years ago![116]

[111] Emmanuel Cosquin, *Contes populaires de Lorraine comparés avec les contes des autres provinces de France et des pays étrangers*, Paris 1886, ii. 323–4, no. 78: *La Fille du marchand de Lyon*; Charles Sadoul, 'Contes de Lorraine', *Revue des traditions populaires* xix (1904), 557–62, no. 4: *La Fille aux mains coupés ou l'hôtesse du dragon vert*.

[112] Explaining the significance of this ecotype in Lorraine would require a whole further chapter. Although Lorraine has produced more than its fair share of militarily active women, from Joan of Arc through Madame de Saint-Baslemont to Louise Michel, the motif of the transvestite she-soldier in folklore may have more to do with the distribution of authority within the domestic sphere than with public displays of power. It might, for example, be significant that it was in Lorraine that the anthropologist Susan Carol Rogers conducted the fieldwork for her seminal article 'Female forms of power and the myth of male dominance: a model of female/male interaction in peasant society', *American Ethnologist* ii (1975), 727–56.

[113] Lallement, *Contes rustiques*, 110; Merkelbach-Pinck, *Lothringer Märchen*, 205.

[114] For example, Pomeranian storytellers set their tales in times 'when people were still so dumb they were Catholic': Röhrich, *Folktales and reality*, 178.

[115] A tale from Nièvre starts 'C'étaient trois vieux soldats revenant d'Egypte', and similar opening sequences are not unusual: Marie-Louise Tenèze and Georg Hüllen, *Rencontre des peuples dans le conte*, I: *France/Allemagne*, Munster 1961, 71.

[116] Cosquin, *Contes populaires de Lorraine*, i. 82.

Not just the openings but the whole content appears old. Dégh found the 'most striking characteristic of the traditional tale lies in the fact that the social institutions and concepts which we discover in it reflect the age of feudalism'.[117] This is certainly true of Merkelbach-Pinck's tales, which abound in counts and castles. Cosquin's tales seem slightly more modern, but many of the social institutions, and even individual persons, can be dated to before 1789: in one tale the three heroes include an *appointé*, an army rank which was abandoned in 1792; in another tale, *Pou et pouce*, the nonsense round ends at the seigneurial oven run by père Quentin, its last operator before the institution was suppressed during the revolution.[118] The time-specific references in folktales are all to an earlier era: the king sits in the Louvre, not Versailles, where he doles out rewards in *livres* not *francs*.

The trouble with time-specific elements in a tale is that they do not always agree. One of Cosquin's tales is handily entitled *Les Deux Soldats de 1689*, but it also makes reference to a tree of liberty.[119] Kings and knights may look like indicators of a particular heritage, but the 'social oppositions in fairy tale plots are less an image of actual feudal attitudes than they are an artistic and narrative prerequisite'.[120] The position of king magnifies the opposition between the poor hero and the bride's father, while at the same time allowing the narrator to talk about his own position without giving offence to any social superiors present. Good narrators liked to introduce realistic details, to make their story more historical, and therefore believable, but the folktale king of France can no more be relied on as a historical character than the king of Australia who appears in a Lorrainer tale.[121]

Historical references are part of the language available to the narrator when telling a tale, but we cannot assume that by using them he intended to recall any historical reality. They may be a dissimulated way of referring to the current issues that affect him, and concerning which he wishes to communicate. That apparently historical narratives may disguise contemporary commentaries posed no problems for Taylor and Redel because at the time the Grimms were active the iniquities of the Hessian conscription system were within living memory. But France had to wait half a century or more for its collectors to get to work. Given folklore's inherent adaptability to new circumstances, are we entitled to consider that these tales are revealing of any period other than the one in which they were collected? The historian who wishes to use tales as sources of popular culture is caught in a cleft stick: he wants the tale to be closely related to the historical environment, but not

---

117 Dégh, *Folktales and society*, 65.
118 Cosquin, *Contes populaires de Lorraine*, i. 121, 203.
119 Cosquin treats this as evidence that the date should read 1789, but if this was the case the hero was extraordinarily ill-advised to marry the princess rather than take the monetary reward offered by the king: ibid. i. 84–6, no. 7 (AT613).
120 Lutz Röhrich, 'Introduction', in Bottigheimer, *Fairy tales and society*, 8.
121 Merkelbach-Pinck, *Lothringer Volksmärchen*, 160: *Die Königstöchter*.

the immediate historical environment. There are some reasons for believing that this is still a valid approach.

Narrators themselves often insisted on the historical accuracy of their tales, maintaining that they told them exactly as they heard them from their parents or grandparents. Jean Hilpert lay awake at night trying to recapture exactly how his father had told his tales in order to relay them to Merkelbach-Pinck. Like Cosquin, she found that tales might contain the names of known village characters dead for more than a century.[122] It was as important to narrators that they form part of a handed-down oral tradition as it is to the historian: 'You cannot change anything in a *Märchen*; we have to tell it exactly the way we have learnt it. How could you change it? It would no longer have its proper meaning.'[123]

Unfortunately the Hungarian narrator who made this statement had his repertoire recorded twice in twenty years, after which period many of his tales bore little relation to their former shape.[124] Whatever folktale narrators meant by 'unchanging' it certainly was not word-for-word memorisation. This variability is precisely what we should expect having seen how narrators recreate their tales for each new audience. The degree of flexibility may have varied from person to person, and from community to community.[125] But variability is a hallmark of the genre: whichever elements of a tale are no longer understood or lack credibility can simply be left out by the storyteller. Modern items replace out-of-date ones. In a Lorrainer tale the hero is provided not with a magic wand or cape, but a ticket which will take him wherever he wishes![126]

However, this example also highlights the other characteristic of folktales, their uniformity not only through space but also over time, for despite this change it is recognisably a variant of the same tale-type. While taking into account the variability of the oral tradition we should not ignore how durable are many of its features. Tale-types, and the ecotypes of particular regions, have preserved their identity over long periods. A tale may only exist within the context of a performance but this does not mean it has no history. Partly this can be accounted for by the method of transmission: in order to learn a tale the teller needs to keep in mind stock-phrases, scenes and plot-lines, so the degree of variability is kept in check by the tradition. Not only does the apprentice learn these from listening to existing narrators, but at the same time acquires his sense of what is good, 'a received and traditional aesthetic

---

[122] Idem, 'Wanderungen den Märchen', 226.
[123] Dégh, *Folktales and society*, 167.
[124] Ibid. 178.
[125] Merkelbach-Pinck found that most of her narrators were very faithful to their own versions, once they had acquired a shape and place in their repertoire: 'Wanderungen der Märchen', 224.
[126] Cosquin, *Contes populaires de Lorraine*, i. 123, no. 11, second variant (AT566).

which . . . barely tolerated variation'.[127] Nor should we forget Anderson's law of self-correction: folklorists working in tradition communities report that each narration can give rise to sharp discussion among the audience about the 'correct' version of a tale.[128] Taggart found, after witnessing many debates over deviations, that 'Narrators who introduce their private views into the stories known by others will not achieve renown if their views differ substantially from the expectations of their audience.'[129] The 'matrix', as it has been termed, of personality, tradition and milieu ensures stability as well as encouraging variation.[130]

This is one of the unresolved problems raised by Holbek's model: if a tale is tailored by its narrator for use before a particular audience, how do we account for the uniformity of tale-types? We may yet have to resurrect the concept of 'survivals in culture'. It is impossible to discover the original form of a tale, and thus make any plausible assertion as to its original meaning, for both change with each performance. Yet the stability of the tradition suggests that, because both narrators and audience were anxious that tales retain a recognisable form, they also felt that there was some essential content or meaning inherent to that form which was worth handing on. One way in which folklorists have accounted for this desire for stability is by picturing their narrators as part of a very long 'longue durée'. The tales told by the peasantry were (by-and-large) unchanging because, before 1900, the issues facing this section of society were (by-and-large) unchanging. The validity of this assertion in relation to the military is at the heart of this book.

Folktales do adapt to their environments, and if they are to have a value as historical sources these adaptations must be pinpointed. But they are also very conservative, and thus are good markers of the slow pace of cultural change. This at least was true up until the end of the nineteenth century when they rapidly disappeared as adult oral entertainment, an indication perhaps of the huge disruptions to long-established economic and social patterns which marked that era. Both characteristics – uniformity and variability – may be helpful to the historian in understanding the meaning of a tale in a particular historical community. However, first we must establish the context for its performance.

---

127 'C'était donc une esthétique reçue et traditionnelle qui. . . . ne souffrait guère de variation': Thomas, *Les Deux Traditions*, 61.
128 'several people would begin to interrupt, correcting the narrator and then telling the story in competition with the storyteller to see who could tell the best stories or the least known ones, or the best version (each person was convinced that his or hers was the only true version, of which the other versions were only variations, incorrect or badly told, citing authorities and names of very old, competent, and well-known storytellers to support their versions': Falassi, *Folklore by the fireside*, 53.
129 Taggart, 'Hansel and Gretel', 438.
130 William Bernard McCarthy, *The ballad matrix: personality, milieu, and the oral tradition*, Bloomington, Ind. 1990.

The soldier as storyteller

Unfortunately, nineteenth-century folklorists were largely unconcerned with the context of the tale. They considered tales as the common heritage of a whole region or nation; individual narrators were irrelevant. This was the case with the collection made by Emmanuel Cosquin. All we know of most of the texts is that they were found for him by a servant woman he employed during the 1860s to attend the *veillées* in the Barrois village of Montiers-sur-Saulx (Meuse). For only three of his eighty-four tales do we know anything more; in these cases the tales were told to him by a young man who had learnt them in the army.[131] One of the conscript's tales featured a soldier hero and in another soldier characters had an important role. The limited information supplied by Cosquin only hints at the ways in which the image of the soldier in folklore was formed, but already we can detect a pattern which would be reinforced by other folklorists, not only in relation to the occasions on which tales were told, but also about who was responsible for the telling.

Allowing for local variations it was the custom throughout Lorraine between All Saints and Easter for family and neighbours to gather together in one room after the evening meal, sharing fuel and lighting material while working and having fun. This occasion was known in various French and German dialects as the 'crègne', 'loure', 'pôle', 'Meistube', 'Spinnstube' or by a dozen different names which reflected the various practices in particular villages. For the sake of simplicity I have adopted the term *veillée* to cover them all. Lorrainer folklorists considered the *veillée* to be the prime place to hear folktales, and indeed other folk genres.[132] Eighty-five per cent of the tales collected by Merkelbach-Pinck were passed on in that context.[133] The local collectors who set fairytale telling in a context do so at the *veillée*.[134] Historians have followed folklorists in stressing the importance of the *veillée* among the social institutions of the village, as the place where the relationships between neighbours coalesced into a community. Social and cultural significance was linked because 'the more telling of Old Tales, the stronger

---

[131] Cosquin, *Contes populaires de Lorraine*, i, p. xxxv. The three tales are nos 3, 15 and 42.

[132] 'C'est pendant ces *veillées* que se racontent les histoires merveilleuses': L. Beaulieu, *Archéologie de la Lorraine ou recueil de notices et documens pour servir à l'histoire des antiquités de cette province*, i, Paris 1840, 268; 'Die Meistube war der Boden, auf dem die dörfliche Poesie wuchs und sich entfaltete in früherer Zeit': Angelika Merkelbach-Pinck, 'Vom Meien in Lothringen', *Zeitschrift für lothringische Volkskunde: organe du folklore lorrain de langue allemande* i (1937), 46.

[133] Langstroff, *Lothringer Volksart*, 57.

[134] The three writers who set tale-telling in a fictionalised context are Sauvé, *Le Folklore des Hautes-Vosges*, 320–40; Meyrac, *Traditions, coutumes, légendes*, 319–25; André Theuriet, *Madame Heurteloup (la bête noire)*, Paris 1882, 128–33.

the reminder of past generations to whose model the present is obliged to adhere'.[135]

At the same time those collectors who give details about their informants often name at least one former soldier among their main sources. Yet this presents something of a discrepancy, for the *veillée* was by and large a women's gathering and, to judge from reports on seventeenth-century pastoral visits, this had always been the case.[136] At Commercy, at the end of the eighteenth century, it was the women 'from the working classes' who got together during winter evenings to pass the 'quarail'.[137] In germanophone Lorraine the very names 'Spinnstube' – spinning-room – and 'Kunkelstube' – distaff-room – suggest that female-orientated work was central to the event.[138] Only in the Vosges do regular *veillées* appear to have been mixed sex events, but even here men and women divided into two groups, the women gathered round the light to work while the men retired to the cellar, to smoke and play cards.[139]

The anthropologist Colette Mechin characterises the *veillées* of Lorraine as 'feminine, nocturnal assemblies'.[140] This description may apply to other provinces of France, as Edward Shorter found that 'the *veillée* highlights a sexual division of sociability that runs through not just peasant life but all traditional French society'.[141] Where were the men of the village at the time? Many were away working, for winter was the season when Chamagnons and others set off on their travels. Those men left in the village got up too early in the morning to frequent late-night festivities.[142] Men had alternative meeting places: in particular the smithy was the 'Meistube der Männer' – the men's *veillée* – or 'le lavoir des hommes' –the men's washhouse (the washhouse being associated with gossiping women).[143] In Sierck while the women

---

135 Edward Shorter, 'The *veillée* and the great transformation', in Jacques Beauroy, Marc Bertrand and Edward T. Gargan (eds), *The wolf and the lamb: popular culture in France from the old regime to the twentieth century*, Saratoga, Ca. 1976, 135.

136 Guy Cabourdin, *La Vie quotidienne en Lorraine aux XVIIe et XVIIIe siècles*, Paris 1984, 299–301.

137 'de la classe ouvrière': [?] Lerouge, 'Notice sur quelque usages et croyances de la ci-devant Lorraine, particulièrement de la ville de Commercy', *Mémoire de l'Académie celtique* iii (1809), 448.

138 Lerond, *Lothringische Sammelmappe*, i. 29. Jaclot de Saulny and Raphaël de Wesphalen agree that in francophone Moselle the 'crégnes' were female affairs, as does Lallement for the Argonne.

139 Lepage and Charton, *Le Département des Vosges*, ii. 714; Lemasson, 'Anciennes Coutumes', 512.

140 Colette Mechin, 'Les Veillées', *Le Pays lorrain* lviii (1977), 199.

141 Shorter, 'The *veillée*', 131.

142 Westphalen noted that, around Metz, the *veilleuses* would wake their husbands on their return so the latter could get up to thresh the corn: *Petit Dictionnaire*, col. 154. In the Ardennes as well 'Les maris, fatigués par le labeur journalier, préféraient souvent se mettre au lit aussitôt après le souper': Georges Raillet, 'Miscellanées de folklore ardennais, II: Cycles saisonniers', *Etudes ardennaises* xxxix (1964), 31.

143 Merkelbach-Pinck, *Brauche und Sitte*, 43; Lucien Febvre, 'Une Enquête: la forge de village', *Annales d'histoire économique et sociale* vii (1935), 607. Raillet notes that in the

went to the 'Spinnstuf', the men retired to their 'Rauchstuf' – smoking-room, the room of an artisan such as a cobbler whose work demanded that he kept it warm and lit late into the night.[144] It should be understood that men were not just absent from the 'official' veillée; they were often purposefully excluded. They were considered 'in the way' because the matters under discussion might not be for their ears.[145] The occasion was used by women to plan marriage strategies and, as we will see later when considering conscription rituals, this was enough both to expel men on some occasions, but also to let them back in again on others.

As this last point suggests the all-female veillée was not a rigid rule; there were particular occasions when it was relaxed. Yet certainly women were in charge: it was the woman of the house who acted as host for the evening, it was she who controlled the materials which made it up, the fire, the lamp and the little supper or 'récine'.[146] That the woman was responsible for the dom-estic activities comes as no surprise for this division of labour was the basis of peasant households well beyond Lorraine.[147] In terms of the veillée, however, it meant that women were given a chance to exercise an authority not normally granted to them in a semi-public setting. To take one example, on the feast of Saint Agatha, which marked the end of the veillée season in the Argonne and the pays messin, the veilleuses (women at the wake) organised a party to which they invited the men and boys of the village: 'It goes without saying that, on this day, the women had priority and the choice of partners for the dance.'[148]

If women had control then we would expect the occasion to be dominated by female voices and indeed the picture presented by folklorists is of 'tongues and spinning-wheels busy together'.[149] The course of an evening in their

Ardennes 'Les hommes qui n'étaient pas au lit se réunissaient volontiers dans la boutique du maréchal où, à la lueur de la forge, il devisaient des questions du jour sans s'inquiéter du bruit du marteau sur l'enclume.'

144 Merkelbach-Pinck, 'Vom Meien', 42.

145 It has been conjectured that among these was illicit sexual knowledge such as means of birth control, though this element of female 'networking' is hard to trace: Warner, From the beast to the blonde, 36–43.

146 Thiriat, La Vallée de Cleurie, 330.

147 Martine Segalen, Love and power in the peasant family, Oxford 1983, 78–111, 137–54. For an informed discussion about how peasant conceptions of gender influenced the organisation of the veillée see Falassi's discussion of its Tuscan counterpart: Folklore by the fireside, 3–27.

148 'Il va sans dire que les femmes, ce jour-là, ont la priorité et le commandement de la danse': Jaclot de Saulny, Les Passe-Temps lorrains ou récréations villageoises: recueil de poésies, contes, nouvelles, fables, chansons, idylles, etc. en patois, Metz 1854, 56. The customs of 'la Sainte-Agathe' are also described in Lallement, Contes rustiques, 103–6. The similar customs of 'Fastnacht' in germanophone Lorraine are detailed in Lerond, Lothringische Sammelmappe, i. 33.

149 'Les langues et les tourets allaient bon train': Lallement, Contes rustiques, 103. Similar phrases are used by other folklorists, including Martin ('Pendant les loures, les bonnes vieilles, toutes occupées au tricot ou au rouet, avaient chacune leur conte à dire'), and

company is described in almost identical terms in the Argonne, in the Meuse, in the Vosges, in the *pays messin*, and in germanophone Lorraine. On arrival 'each woman recounted to the group what news she had learnt' which developed into 'the chronicle of scandal'.[150] Then came the stories, the 'fiauves' or fables as they were known in francophone areas, 'Geschichten' or stories in germanophone ones. Unfortunately folklorists of the nineteenth century did not distinguish between the genres of stories. The schoolteacher of Saint Remy in the Vosges listed among the 'fiauves' of his local *veillées* 'stories of ghosts or werewolves, the exploits of goblins or fairies, scoundrels, of brigands or sorcerers, clever tricks or jokes'.[151] The dominant tone, however, was one of fear, 'devilish tales to make one die of fear' which obliged children to hide under their mothers' aprons and young women to seek the reassurance of their fiancé's hand (if he had been allowed in).[152] Less often folklorists refer to other genres such as religious legends, etiological legends, local tragedies and, in one case, to 'fairytales, a hundred times retold', but stories of supernatural terror certainly left the greatest impression, with the Wild Hunt particularly popular.[153]

The threat of the supernatural was still in the air when the *dailleurs* arrived. The *dâyage*, a custom confined to Lorraine and bordering areas of Champagne and Franche-Comté, consisted of a ritualised conversation between the *veilleuses* and mystery (normally male) voices from outside. Their arrival, signalled by rattling shutters and spectral cries, might initially have added to the atmosphere of fear but their trade in love talk and mocking insults soon dispelled it.[154] If the *dailleurs* were permitted to enter the *veillée* this was the occasion for happier genres of folk literature, including riddles and humorous

Westphalen ('Pendant que les unes filaient, que les autres dévidaient, brodaient ou tricotaient, les langues allaient leur train'), while Jouve, Lerouge, Lemasson, Saulny and Gazin all strike the same note.

150 'chaque femme raconte à la société les nouvelles qu'elle a apprises': Lerouge, 'Notice', 449. The phrase 'la chronique scandaleuse' appears in Labourasse and Gazin. Lallement talks of 'cancans du village' while Westphalen refers to 'commérages'. Only Merkelbach-Pinck, perhaps because she was one of the few women folklorists in the region, avoids such derogatory terms, referring instead to 'Tagesereignisse, die Gegebenheiten in Dorf und Familie'.

151 'histoires de revenants ou de loup-garous, exploits de lutins ou de fées, scélérats, des brigands ou des sorciers, bon tours ou facéties': Eugène Martin, 'Folklore de Saint Remy (Vosges)', *Le Pays lorrain* iv (1907), 436.

152 'diableries à faire mourir de peur'. This phase of the evening is described by, among others, Lallement, Labourasse, Jouve, Westphalen, Saulny, Lerond and Merkelbach-Pinck.

153 'contes de fées cent fois répétés': Labourasse, *Anciens Us*, 78, and 'A. Joanne', 'L'Hiver dans les Vosges', 104. Angelika Merkelbach-Pinck published a whole book of stories of the Wild Hunt: *Wildjägersagen aus Lothringen*, Cassel 1942. Lerond noted that 'Die *Haute Chasse* oder die Lustgeister spielten eine grosse Rolle in der Spinnstubengesprächen.'

154 We will return to the *dailleurs* when considering conscript rituals. For the 'dayemans' themselves see Francesca Sautman, 'Rituels de dérision et langage symbolique dans les dayemans lorrains', *Cahiers de littérature orale* xxviii (1990), 97–125.

tales, some of which were distinctly blue, and which were accompanied by 'tâquinage' – physical and verbal teasing of the young women.[155] Even if the *dailleurs* remained excluded the lighter mood continued after their interruption with ballads and songs. Everyone was supposed to join in, 'it was the contribution imposed on all visitors and members', and we will see later that they could become a dialogue among those present.[156] Usually the boys would be obliged to leave after their rendition, and the evening would resume its quieter mood, perhaps ending with a prayer.[157] If, as was sometimes the case during the Carnival period, they were permitted to stay after the oil-lamp had died down then the evening closed in games and dancing, which sometimes carried on outside as the *veillée* broke up.[158]

As Falassi has shown, with the equivalent Tuscan *veglia*, there is a logic to the order in which *veillée* activities followed each other.[159] The earlier part of the evening, before the children went to bed, was more family-orientated while the latter part was for courting. Reports of recent happenings in the village and elsewhere would naturally give rise to comparisons with previous examples preserved in the oral tradition, and so local legends were introduced. These horror-stories provided an excellent introduction to the *dailleurs*, but whether they were admitted to the *veillée* or not, their conversation turned the *veilleuses* minds towards more amusing and erotic matters.

We are left with the discrepancy noted above: if the *veillée* was a female gathering – or at least dominated by female voices – how do we account for the role of Cosquin's soldier? And it is not just at Montiers-sur-Saulx that we find military storytellers: whenever individual storytellers were cited some turn out to have been in the army. The tales collected by Louis Lallement in the Argonne can mostly be traced back to the Soudant family of Neuville-le-Pont. The member of that family who contributed most was Eloi Soudant, a former *voltigeur de la garde*. His grandfather, Pierre-Joseph Soudant, had likewise been a soldier and was remembered as 'a no less talented storyteller'.[160] In Franche-Comté many of the tales told at the *veillée* in the 1930s were first introduced by ancestors who had been in the army: Adolphe Morgeotte of Burgille inherited his talent and his repertoire from his grandfather, an old soldier of the Crimean war who had learnt all his tales during his fourteen years in the army; at nearby Lantenne most tales came

---

155 An example of banter between the sexes can be found in Sauvé, *Le Folklore des Hautes-Vosges*, 212–14.
156 'c'est la contribution imposée a tous visiteurs et assistants': Saulny, *Les Passe-Temps lorrains*, 55. Exactly the same observation is made by Lallement, *Contes rustiques*, 226.
157 Saulny, *Les Passe-Temps lorrains*, 55; Lallement, *Contes rustiques*, 226; Labourasse, *Anciens Us*, 79.
158 Lerouge, 'Notice', 449; Edgard Gazin, 'Moeurs, traditions, légendes', in Léon Louis (ed.), *Le Département des Vosges*, Epinal 1889, iv. 564; Sauvé, *Le Folklore des Hautes-Vosges*, 344; Merkelbach-Pinck, 'Vom Meien', 43.
159 Falassi, *Folklore by the fireside*. . . . Each chapter represents a stage in the evening.
160 'un conteur non moins émérité': Lallement, *Contes rustiques*, 115, 134.

from two sources, one of whom, Jean-Jacques Malavaux, had sold himself as a replacement soldier sometime during the 1830s. His 'military life influenced his narratives', an influence still detectable when the tales were recorded from his descendants a century later.[161] Merkelbach-Pinck's 'best storyteller', Nicolas Jung, had served in the Bavarian army and at least some of his tales had been learnt there. Three of her other most important contributors, Louis Pfeifer, Nicolas Baro and Viktor Manque, all received part of their repertoire, either directly or indirectly, from former soldiers.[162]

If the tellers were not soldiers then they tended to be drawn from other male occupations, particularly those that required travel away from the village. Lallement's main sources apart from the Soudants were the Philiberts, a family of masons and sculptors.[163] Garneret's other sources included a 'confirmed bachelor' blacksmith who had made his *tour de France* as a journeyman.[164] Merkelbach-Pinck's collection was made up of tales told by men and women in equal proportion, but the majority of those whom she considered real storytellers (rather than persons who simply knew a story) were men. Usually they had learnt their repertoire from other men, including such travellers as a pedlar (in the case of Pfeiffer) and a shepherd (in the case of Manque). Even when they cited their father as their main source, as in the case of Baro and Jung, the tales had arrived in the village with vagrants, including discharged soldiers, who over-wintered on their farms.[165] It is therefore quite appropriate that the three local folklorists who present tale-telling in the context of the *veillée* none the less put their tales into a man's mouth. The name of one of these narrators, 'le père Ramette', suggests that he may have been a soldier.[166]

There are a number of related explanations for this apparent paradox. Nineteenth-century folklorists concentrated on collecting fairytales, that is folktales covered by numbers 300 to 750 of the Aarne-Thompson index. Yet as we have seen, the tales told at the archetypal *veillée* were of werewolves, ghosts and the sabbat, not fairytales at all but local, supernatural legends. Although fairytale narration did take place at the *veillée*, it was far from being the dominant genre that its disproportionate place in the collections makes it appear. Because of the neglect of these other genres it is difficult to establish

161 'sa vie militaire influençait ses récits': Jean Garneret, Contes recueillis en Franche-Comté, Besançon 1988, 13–19, 301–2. At Etrabonne Garneret found a teller who kept a list of the tales he had learnt in the army in the same notebook as his cavalry drill.
162 Angelika Merkelbach-Pinck, Volkserzählungen aus Lothringen, Münster 1967, 238–45. The German folklorist Matthias Zender, who collected in the nearby Eifel region, found that many of his narrators who had emigrated from Lorraine had learnt their tales during service in the French army: 'Quellen und Träger der deutschen Volkserzählung', in Leander Petzoldt (ed.), Vergleichende Sagenforschung, Darmstadt 1969, 117.
163 Lallement, Contes rustiques, 160.
164 Garneret, Contes recueillis en Franche-Comté, 13–19, 302.
165 Merkelbach-Pinck, Volkserzählungen aus Lothringen, 243–5.
166 Meyrac, Traditions, coutumes, légendes, 319.

whether women played a more important role in the narration of legends, though this is suggested by the descriptions offered of the *veillée* where it is usually 'une vieille' who knew the most frightening stories.[167]

Fairytales were rare because their narrators were few and far between. Merkelbach-Pinck, in nine years of research, assembled a collection of over 2,400 texts from more than 300 narrators, but only a hundred of these, supplied by thirty-two narrators, could be classed as 'Märchen'.[168] She found no tradition of fairytale-telling in many villages. Although she felt that it might have been more widespread in the past, evidence from other areas shows that narrators with both the talent and the repertoire to be considered as genuine tellers have always been rare.[169] Precisely because fairytales were considered to be at the apex of achievement in oral literature it could not be a talent shared by everyone. As we have already seen, in the case of the soldier ancestors of tale-tellers in Champagne and Franche-Comté, skilled narrators were remembered for generations. Considering their rarity one can understand why in the Vosges 'one hurried two or three leagues, despite the cold, the wind and the snow, to listen to a renowned storyteller'.[170] However, folklorists have found that in the absence of such a teller other genres were preferred; only a talented narrator could do a fairytale justice and command the attention that it required.[171]

The willingness of people to travel long distances to attend the *veillée* if a famous teller was present was recorded by other French folklorists. In Brittany Luzel found that if 'a renown singer or narrator arrived, a carpenter, thatcher, mason, or some wandering beggar', then 'all the neighbours were notified and, after their supper, they came in from the surrounding villages'.[172] In Lorraine the evidence is scanty for such open-house *veillées* where performance rather than work took centre stage, but in the *pays messin* 'the most important *veillées*' only took place on Saturday when the men could attend, and it was then that 'one mostly told stories, because during the week the women preferred to recount village gossip or relate the latest misdeeds of the "brownie" '.[173] In the Meuse, Labourasse noted that on certain holidays

---

167 Labourasse, *Anciens Us*, 78.
168 Langstroff, *Lothringer Volksart*, 73.
169 Holbek, *Interpretation of fairy tales*, 140.
170 'on accourait de deux et trois lieues, malgré le froid, le vent, la neige, pour entendre un conteur en renom': Sauvé, *Le Folklore des Hautes-Vosges*, 340.
171 Dégh, *Folktales and society*, 76.
172 'il arrivait quelque chanteur ou conteur renommé, un charpentier, un couvreur, un maçon, ou quelque mendiant ambulant. Alors tous les voisins étaient avertis et, après leur souper, ils arrivaient des villages environnants': François-Marie Luzel, 'Premier Rapport sur une mission en Basse-Bretagne, ayant pour objet de rechercher les traditions orales des Bretons-Amoricains, contes et récits populaires', *Archive des missions scientifiques et littéraires* 2nd ser. vii (1872), 104.
173 'c'est le samedi que l'on "fiauvait" le plus, car les femmes, en semaine, préféraient se raconter les petites histoires du village ou encore relater les derniers méfaits du "Sotre" ':

around Christmas and Carnival the women put their work away because 'the mice would eat the thread', and the men were invited in.[174] These larger, more entertainment-orientated events were of the type to which a renowned teller could be invited. But if they had to be invited, and their presence made it an important event, where were they the rest of the time?

One possible location, considering the role of men as narrators, were the male alternatives to the *veillée*. We have already seen how the excluded men were obliged – or preferred – to keep their own company at the smithy or some other artisan's shop. A teacher from Verdun described the smithy as the place to hear 'tales as old as the world'.[175] Another location frequented almost entirely by men was the bar or inn should the village possess one, and this was certainly an important venue for tale-tellers. One of Merkelbach-Pinck's informants, a twelve-year old girl, learnt her stock of tales from an innkeeper, who herself had learnt them from listening to the men who rested in the inn during bad weather.[176] In the tales themselves the *dénouement* is often sparked by the revelation of the hero's or villain's identity through telling their own story at an inn.[177] The role of male travellers as narrators, and the inn as a venue, should make us reconsider whether *veillées* were, in fact, the best places to hear tales.

Migrants told tales. Pedlars, vagrants and itinerant craftsmen (amongst whom we should include cobblers and tailors, for they preferred to work in the home of their customers rather than in their own shop) all had a reputation as tale-tellers. Those narrators who were settled in the village had often made long journeys in their youth, perhaps as journeymen or soldiers. Where we have information it also appears that it was during these absences that they acquired their repertoire of tales.

Nineteenth-century folklorists were local patriots: they wanted to find a treasury of tales that celebrated the wisdom and creativity of the people of their *pays*. Therefore the particular importance of migrants among tale-tellers was largely ignored. Happily, their successors of this century have been far more interested in the individual narrator, and in Russia, Germany, Hungary

Gérard Bolsinger, 'L'Image du peuple du pays messin à travers ses traditions', unpubl. *mémoire de maîtrise*, Nancy II 1972, 30.

[174] 'les souris mangeraient le fil': Labourasse, *Anciens Us*, 79. Exactly the same justification – 'das Garn sei zu fett, es würde von den Mäusen zernagt werden' – was used for the party held by the spinning-women on Shrove Tuesday in germanophone areas: Lerond, *Lothringische Sammelmappe*, i. 33.

[175] 'contes vieux comme le monde': Febvre, 'Une Enquête', 607. The only tale he mentions by name, *Christ and the blacksmith* (AT753), is a religious legend but one which often served as the introduction to wonder-tales.

[176] Merkelbach-Pinck, *Volkserzählungen aus Lothringen*, 237–8.

[177] In a Vosgian variant of *The hunter* (AT304), for example, the princess sets up a 'hôtellerie' for which the only payment is one's life-story, and thus she finds the man who had saved her life: Sauvé, *Le Folklore des Hautes-Vosges*, 335. The same motif is found in Cosquin, *Contes populaires de Lorraine*, ii. 69–71, no. 40: *La Pantoufle de la princesse* (AT304).

and Canada in-depth studies have been made of his (and it normally was a male) role. The conclusion reached by Linda Dégh, who has surveyed the bulk of this work, was that the real home of fairytale-telling was not the village *veillée*, but the male work-communities, such as journeymen's hostels, on board ships, in lumberjack cabins and, above all, barrack-rooms.[178]

This hypothesis does not accord with the statements made by folklorists concerning the importance of the *veillée*. One is, therefore, entitled to wonder whether twentieth-century research is applicable to earlier periods. The answer came as a shock to the German folklorist J. W. Wolf, a follower of the Grimms. After trudging from village to village in the forests of Hesse (where he believed the effects of the Enlightenment on the oral tradition would be minimised), he was amazed to find that his brother-in-law, an officer in the grand-duke's army, was able to provide for him an inexhaustible supply of tale-tellers from the soldiers under his command.[179] However, Wolf should not have been so astonished for one of the main contributors to the Grimms' collection, and one of the few who could not be described as middle-class, was an old sergeant of dragoons, Friedrich Krause.[180] One of the Grimms' earliest followers, the Hungarian György Gaal, made his initial collection from the members of a Hussar regiment stationed in Vienna in 1821.[181]

Sadly, despite these models, no French folklorist set out to collect fairytales in the barrack-rooms (although the bulk of Paul Sébillot's collection from francophone Brittany was made amongst sailors and fishermen who would equally fit Dégh's thesis). However the dormitory appeared in the earliest attempt to set French storytelling in its proper context. A book written by an officer, and designed to show the army 'as it is', took the reader to the Saint-Raphaël barracks in Bordeaux after lights-out sometime during the 1820s where, in order to fill the long hours of evening, the soldiers were expected to take the floor and narrate 'one of those new and marvellous stories in which the hero is always an old soldier who ends up by marrying a princess'.[182] There followed one of the longest and most detailed variants of the popular French tale *Jean-de-l'ours*, told by an Auvergnat soldier. He was

178 Dégh, *Folktales and society*, 79–80.
179 Johann Wilhelm Wolf, *Deutsche Hausmärchen*, Göttingen–Leipzig 1851, pp. v–vii.
180 Gonthier-Louis Fink, 'The fairy tales of the Grimms' sergeant of dragoons J. F. Krause as reflecting the needs and wishes of the common people', in James M. McGlathery (ed.), *The brothers Grimm and folktale*, Urbana, Ill. 1991, 146–7.
181 Linda Dégh, *Folktales of Hungary*, London 1965, p. xxvi. In consequence his manuscripts open with phrases like 'Private Jànos Kovàc humbly reports to the colonel that "There was once behind the beyond . . .".' It was still the practice for Hungarian soldiers to tell each other stories after lights out when Dégh started her folktale collecting.
182 'Il fallut chercher un moyen d'occuper les longues heures de la soirée, les invitations furent renvoyées de part et d'autre pour prendre la parole, et raconter une de ces nouvelles et merveilleuses histoires, dont le héros est toujours un vieux troupier, qui finit par épouser une princesse': J. Delmart and 'Léon Vidal' [Léon de Céran], *La Caserne: moeurs militaires*, Brussels 1833, 141.

clearly appreciated, for his comrades paid him for his stories in *eau-de-vie*, and he himself had a high opinion of his talent, or 'ma marchandise' as he termed it. In addition he used formulae to open and close his tales, as well as during the narrating; he involved his audience through eliciting responses, but at other times demanded complete silence; his tale was long, going on for hours; and he tailored his tales to his audience, introducing characters that he knew they liked. All these are characteristics of a teller in the 'public tradition'.[183]

Why was Wolf surprised at the number of soldier-narrators; why did no French folklorist pursue the significant source uncovered by this French officer? The explanation is that folklorists had inherited a preconceived idea of what a narrator should look like: an old countrywoman telling stories to children. The Grimms had perpetuated this 'Mother-Goose' image, but it did not originate with them, nor with Perrault who had likewise made use of it; rather it dates to classical times.[184] But Mother Goose is a figure of myth who has little to do with the actual storytelling tradition, at least in northern Europe. In Schleswig-Holstein, for example, 110 of the narrators featured in Kurt Ranke's enormous collection were male, forty-four female. Along the coast towards Hamburg, the folklorist Wilhelm Wisser wrote of his informants that 'the number of male narrators (190) exceeds that of the female narrators (50) to a striking extent. Therefore we have simply thrown out the dogma, prevalent until now, that female storytellers are superior to male storytellers and will assume the contrary'.[185] Both these collectors were male, and it may be that they had difficulty in establishing trust with female narrators, but in France women folklorists have noted the same pattern. Geneviève Massignon and Ariane de Félice, doing fieldwork in Brittany just after the Second World War, were unable to unearth more than two women narrators. When de Félice asked one of her male informants about this bias between the sexes she was told 'Girls are never interested in telling tales'.[186]

Surveying the growing body of evidence for fairytale-telling as a male pastime Dégh wrote 'it is obvious that storytelling is mostly connected with male occupations and the places of work for men. . . . The storytelling of women is only a secondary matter in the estimation of folk society; it is limited to the family, to the entertainment of children, and to the communal work of the women'.[187]

Why were earlier generations of folklorists so insistent, therefore, on the role of women as narrators? The answer is hinted at in this explanation from Dégh: there existed two oral traditions; the male, public tradition and the

---

183 Thomas, *Les Deux Traditions*, 16.
184 Warner, *From the beast to the blonde*, 12–25.
185 Dégh, *Folktales and society*, 91.
186 'Les filles ne sont jamais intéressées à dire des contes': Félice, *Contes de Haute-Bretagne*, p. v.
187 Dégh, *Folktales and society*, 92–3.

female, domestic tradition. As folklorists, from Perrault and the Grimms onwards, were drawn from the educated, urban middle and upper classes, they had very little direct contact with the culture of the rural world, to which they none the less ascribed their tales. The only members of the rural popular classes that they knew well were the wet-nurses and housemaids who looked after them as children, and who told them stories. Even when, as collectors, they came into contact with narrators in the male, public tradition their nostalgia for the nursery tales of their childhood blinded them to the importance of this source. This reaction is apparent in the work of one of the earliest French folklorists, Jean-François Bladé. Bladé was introduced to fairytales as an infant by his grandmother's maidservants who told him stories at her command. Though he was later introduced to storytelling in very different environments he dismissed those narrators who did not invoke the stories of his youth: 'For them, the integrity of the narrative is not preserved by any sacramental form ... they are always long, diffuse, and quite incapable of restarting their narration in the same terms.'[188] Luzel, in Breton-speaking Brittany, made a similar report:

> Not all narrators resemble each other. . . . Some are prolix, diffuse, gestural, dramatic. . . . These are the most sought after narrators, but not necessarily the best. The others, more calm, more sober, more spiritual . . . go straight to the end of their narrative and do not introduce personal reflections or extra episodes. They say that they narrate exactly as they heard it, a lesson learnt by heart. It is always this type of narrator that I consult by preference.[189]

[188] 'Pour eux, l'intégrité du récit n'est sauvegardée par aucune forme sacramentelle ... ils sont toujours longs, diffus, et tout à fait incapables de recommencer leur narration dans les mêmes termes': Jean-François Bladé, *Contes populaires de la Gascogne*, Paris 1886, i, p. xxxi.
[189] 'Tous les conteurs ne se ressemblent pas: chacun a sa manière et appartient à un système, à une école. . . . Les uns sont prolixes, diffus, prodigues de gestes, de déclamations et de mise en scène. Ils introduisent dans leurs récits des noms de lieux du pays, des personnes connues, quelquefois présentes dans l'auditoire, leur y font jouer un rôle, honorable ou coupable et honteux, suivant leur intérêt, leur caprice ou leurs passions. Souvent aussi pour allonger, ils empruntent des épisodes entiers à d'autres récits et mélangent ainsi deux ou trois contes. C'est ce qu'ils appellent: *reï tro*, c'est-à-dire *donner du tour*, autrement se donner carrière. Du reste, ceux-là ont souvent deux manières de débiter le même conte, et plus d'une fois des conteurs m'ont demandé s'il fallait *reï tro*, se donner carrière, ou conter tout simplement, *evel ann holl, comme tout le monde*. Ce sont là les plus généralement recherchés, mais ce ne sont sûrement pas les meilleurs. D'autres, plus calmes, plus sobres, mystérieux et ayant l'air de croire à ce qu'ils disent, y croyant même parfois, vont droit au but et n'embarrassent pas leurs récits de réflexions ni d'épisodes étrangers. On dirait qu'ils récitent exactement une leçon apprise par coeur. C'est toujours ceux-là que j'ai consultés de préférence. Ils ont mieux conservé la fable originelle et y ont mêlé moins d'éléments hétérogènes': Luzel, 'Premier Rapport', 103–4. Luzel returned to this distinction many times, for example in *Légendes chrétiennes de la Basse-Bretagne*, Paris 1881, ii. 243n. Luzel, working in the paradigm of communal creation, eschewed the obvious individual expressionism of the 'conteurs renommés'. The Grimms dropped several of the tales told by Sergeant Krause after the first edition of *Kinder- und Hausmärchen* for the same reason.

Although neither Bladé or Luzel drew a distinction on grounds of gender between 'these two schools of tale-telling', all the narrators of the first kind that they named were men, all those of the second kind were women.[190]

An investigation by the folklorist Gerald Thomas into storytelling in francophone Newfoundland has elucidated the origin and nature of these two schools. Thomas found that many people could tell a tale if pushed, but these same informants did not consider themselves as 'conteurs', rather they named others who had reputations as narrators.[191] The former group consisted mostly of women who told tales in their own home to their own family, but in a more public sphere left this genre to well-known narrators, usually 'vieux Français', men from metropolitan France who had deserted the French fishing fleet. There were, in fact, two traditions of tale-telling, one private or familial, the other public, though the latter had become more or less extinct. From the information supplied about the 'vieux Français', and one surviving narrator of this tradition, Thomas was able to establish what made 'un vrai conteur' as defined by the community. Although in both cases the context of telling was the veillée, the atmosphere was very different: at the private veillée the teller had to be coaxed into a fairytale, which competed with constant interruptions and other genres as each attendee got the chance to say or sing their piece. At the public veillée, to which an audience had been invited, the teller assumed centre-stage: he needed no coaxing and he brooked no interruptions, he had come to tell and they to listen, and the session could continue through the night. His repertoire would consist mostly of fairytales (AT 300–750) while a teller in the familial tradition drew on a much wider range. Despite hesitations and interruptions, tales at the private veillée tended to be short, around thirty minutes, whereas a 'conteur', without any such hesitations (which would have marred his reputation), would spin his out over hours, sometimes days. The ability to lengthen a tale to fit the occasion was considered the height of the teller's talent, and depended on a variety of stylistic techniques which are characteristic of the public tradition. These included recourse to formulaic expressions, not only at the beginning and end of narrating (though these in themselves tend to differentiate it from the domestic tradition), but throughout the tale; the use of triple repetition; introduction of new plot twists, even whole new tale-types, into the narrative. Above all a 'conteur' would turn each telling into a performance, using his face and his whole body to act out each character in the story, altering his

---

[190] Cosquin's initial contact with fairytales conforms to the pattern. In a letter to the brothers Grimm in 1862 he sent a copy of the tale Pou et Pouce (no. 18 of his collection), narrated to him by an 'old faithful maidservant' in his great-uncle's house. Servants were to remain his means of access to the storytelling environment, but he understood that although his experience fitted the model, this was not the complete picture: Nicole Odette Stein-Moreau, 'Les Frères Grimm, conteurs, et la France au dix-neuvième siècle', in Bruder Grimm Gedenken, Marburg 1963, 553–4.
[191] This same distinction was made in germanophone Lorraine: Merkelbach-Pinck, 'Wanderungen der Märchen', 224.

voice and even putting on costumes. His gestural range was denied to domestic tellers who were usually occupied with work during their narrating, but also because the kind of excited movements associated with a 'vieux Français' were frowned on in women. Thomas concluded that domestic telling was a way of passing time, of amusing the children, whereas public telling was an aesthetic experience: one went to hear (and see) a 'conteur' not so much for the story, which one already knew, but to appreciate his performance. Only by learning the stylistic and acting techniques to create such a performance did the 'conteur' earn the right to tell.[192]

One would expect to find this same distinction in the home country of the 'vieux Français', Brittany, and indeed Thomas's findings simply expand on the distinctions made by Luzel about the 'two schools' of narrators. In Brittany, as in Newfoundland, people drew a clear a distinction between respected 'conteurs' and those who, in the words of his informants, could tell a tale 'comme tout le monde'. Merkelbach-Pinck makes as similar point about the differences between men's and women's narration: women's tales were plainer and shorter; they told the tale as they heard it without ornament, whereas men used gesture, expression, tone, detail, colour to turn each narration into a performance.[193]

Soldier narrators belonged to the public tradition. Although we usually lack any information concerning the performance, stylistic differences associated with this 'school' of narration do show up in the texts. For example, the first of the three tales told to Cosquin by a soldier, *Le Roi d'Angleterre et son filleul*, uses repetition, formulae and additional motifs to make it the longest in the entire collection. Though it lacks the ritual introduction used during tale-telling in the barracks it ends with a closing formula common among soldier-tellers: 'Me, I was sentry at the princess' door; I got bored and I left.'[194] Such formulae helped Paul Delarue to distinguish 'a barracks' style' in the texts he catalogued. Indications included stock phrases such as the opening 'Il est bon de vous dire que' and the formula 'March today, march tomorrow, by dint of marching one goes a long way', every time the hero travels in the story.[195] References to garrison towns and the details of military life were further give-aways. Merkelbach-Pinck and Matthias Zender found that tales learnt in either the French or German armies retained the imprint of regimental life in the customs mentioned and the formulae used.[196] For example, Louis Pfeifer's version of *The ogre's heart in the egg* (AT302), learnt from the Napoleonic veteran Jean Lam, included a whole military parade: 'All at once he heard wonderful music. Bears arrived in regimental-style rank and file.

---

192 This is a summary of Thomas's findings: *Les Deux Traditions*, ch. ii.
193 Merkelbach-Pinck, 'Wanderungen den Märchen', 225–6.
194 Cosquin, *Contes populaires lorrains*, i. 43, no. 3 (AT513).
195 'Marche aujourd'hui, marche demain, à force de marcher on fait beaucoup de chemin': Delarue, *Le Conte populaire français*, i. 111, 246.
196 Merkelbach-Pinck, 'Wanderungen der Märchen', 225.

Thus they marched, and when our Karl came out of the ship, they presented arms before him.'[197]

How can we account for this difference in the way men and women told tales? In the case of the *veillée* one cannot say that, as in other public events, men's social power meant their voices predominated.[198] We can explain the role of men (and in particular men who have travelled) in the public tradition if we return to Dégh's contention that male work communities were the real home of tale-telling because these were the locations where a trainee-teller could serve his apprenticeship. 'The flowers of rhetoric' of the Auvergnat soldier 'are born nowhere except in the heart of the barrack'.[199] One needed to observe the performances of established narrators, and space to practice oneself. The only venues where one could acquire such mastery were those that brought individuals with talent together with those who had the leisure to learn. The *veillée*, with its local news and courting couples, not to mention the work which was at the heart of the gathering, were too distracting to allow such an apprenticeship. Better-suited environments were on board ship or in the mountain cabins of shepherds where long periods of inactivity, together with the mixing of persons from different localities, provided ideal opportunities. The boredom associated with such places also allowed the narrator to rehearse the tale in his mind, and when he felt sufficiently prepared his audience would be ready and waiting.[200] As it was men who served in the army, the navy, as shepherds and woodcutters, it was men who learnt the tales and brought them back to the village.

The soldier's reputation as a storyteller occurs in tales themselves; when a fairy reveals her identity to an old soldier he 'wasn't surprised at it, because at that time soldiers knew that fairies were true because they told stories around the camp-fire when on campaign, or in the dormitory in winter, when the candle was out but it was too early to sleep'.[201] Only someone who had served

---

[197] 'Auf einmal hörte er eine wunderschöne Musik. Da kamen Bären an, regimenterweise in Rieh und Glied. So marschierten sie, und als unser Karl aus dem Schiff herauskam, präsentierten sie vor ihm': Merkelbach-Pinck, *Lothringer Volksmärchen*, 230.

[198] Male narrators had their own explanations for the predominance of their sex in this genre, such as 'C'est bien rare qu'on entende parler qu'une femme dise des contes. Pour raconter ces trucs-là, il faut beacoup de patience': Félice, *Contes de Haute-Bretagne*, p. v.

[199] 'Les fleurs de rhétorique' . . . ne naissent qu'au sein des casernes': Delmart and Vidal, *La Caserne*, 141.

[200] Félice's informants, like Sauvé's, believed that to tell tales 'il faut avoir le temps de les rêver': *Contes de Haute-Bretagne*, p. vii.

[201] 'Il n'en fut pas étonné, car en ce temps-là les soldats savaient qu'il existait des fées dont ils se contaient les histoires autour des feux de camp lorsqu'ils étaient en campagne, ou dans la chambrée en hiver, quand, la chandelle éteinte, il était trop tôt pour dormir': Achille Millien and Paul Delarue, *Contes du Nivernais et du Morvan*, Paris 1953, 4, no. 1: *Les Princesses dansantes de la nuit* (AT306). This comment on the role of soldiers is particularly pertinent to this (rare) tale-type because the very first collected variant was noted for the Grimms by August von Haxthausen from a soldier on active service during the Napoleonic wars. He was killed the following day.

this apprenticeship could tell a tale, hence the father's disclaimer in the tale *Eine schöne Geschichte*, when called upon by a captain (in fact his daughter in disguise) to tell the company a tale: 'Oh I know nothing, I never was a soldier.'[202]

It follows therefore that women who had had the same opportunity would acquire similar skills (as is the case of the daughter in the above tale, who proves to be a master of suspense). In Lorraine we have already come across a female narrator whose job as an innkeeper gave just such a chance to learn her art. Yet the expectation was that a teller should be someone who 'had seen a hundred villages'.[203] One of Léon Zeliqzon's sources from the *pays messin* established the credentials of his tale by citing its source – his uncle the rag-gatherer – who 'knew lots of things which he had learnt on his travels, and during the winter, when we were gathered together at the *veillée*, he would tell them to us'.[204] Women, Merkelbach-Pinck found, had lived too little to become narrators, seldom having crossed the parish boundary. It was men who had the opportunity to travel and thus gain the necessary experience to give them authority as tellers. Luzel's main female informant was one of the few exceptions to the gender-division. As a professional pilgrim she had the opportunity to travel far and mix with new people.[205] But in a militarised province like Lorraine, the soldier was the man of experience par excellence.

The role of the itinerant as narrator was in part due to his position as an outsider in the community. In the folklore of Lorraine vagrants, blacksmiths and soldiers share many dubious qualities some of which we will explore in chapter 5. For the moment we simply need to note that their access to secret knowledge, which made them valued (but feared) as healers and witch-finders, also made them respected as narrators.

Recognising a person's experience does not necessarily entail giving them credence; the old soldier's stories were not always believed. Edgard Coulon's collection of legends from the Montbéliard region contained several contributions from a former soldier, but he added that his stories were not considered 'entirely truthful'.[206] In one of Cosquin's tales, told by a soldier, the hero is called Plumepatte, the legendary barber of the Zouaves to whom all improbable stories should be passed (as British sailors were told to 'tell it to the marines'). Cosquin's soldier-narrator is giving the audience a broad hint

202 'O ich weiss ja nichts, ich war ja nicht Soldat': Merkelbach-Pinck, *Lothringer Volksmärchen*, 159 (AT883).
203 Dégh, *Folktales and society*, 79.
204 'savait bien des choses qu'il avait appris dans ses voyages, et dans l'hiver, quand nous étions tous réunis à la *veillée* (crègne), il nous les racontait': Léon Zéliqzon and G. Thiriot, *Textes patois recueillis en Lorraine*, Metz 1912, 132.
205 Mary-Ann Constantine, *Breton ballads*, Aberystwyth 1996, 39.
206 Edgard Coulon, 'Légendes, croyances et contes populaires du pays de Montbéliard', *Revue du folklore français* i (1930), 230.

that what he is telling them is not entirely true.[207] The soldier's ability to lie was proverbial, hence the scepticism with which one greeted his stories. The soldier in the tales themselves is an expert liar, able to get the better of Saint Peter, Death and even the devil, yet none can cheat him. But because of the nature of fairytales as fantasy, the soldier's reputation for dishonesty only added to his skill as a narrator.[208]

The importance of itinerant narrators in the diffusion of tales may account for the popularity of certain plots, characters and even formulae throughout France, especially in those that concern soldiers. They had been learnt in barracks where Lorrainers and Normans rubbed shoulders with Gascons and Corsicans. The content of tales told by these men differed considerably from those popular in the domestic tradition. Most of the plots of the latter, like those of Perrault, concern children or young women, but those told by public narrators featured heroes similar to themselves: – journeymen or old soldiers. In some cases the heroes were exactly the same as themselves: the tale told by the 'conteur recherché' cited by Luzel, Gwilherm Garandel, has for its hero another Gwilherm; Garneret's tale *Adolphe du diable* was collected from Adolphe Mougeotte. The identification between narrator and his hero can go beyond names to pronouns. A stylistic trick used by public tellers to intensify the drama was to switch from third person to first person at moments of crisis for the hero, but it is plausible that as the excitement mounted the narrator unconsciously crossed the divide between himself and his lead character.[209]

The correspondence between the public narrator and his hero has been noted by a number of folklorists. Angelika Merkelbach-Pinck found that with men the 'folktale accurately reflects the narrator's hidden emotions. . . . He can present himself as he is in the folktale, without being shy and without pretence'.[210] Each narrator had made a selection of tales that meant most to him, and just as these usually reflected his gender, so they also reflected their social status and occupation.[211] This was because narrators were using tales to talk about themselves and their community. To quote the findings of Merkelbach-Pinck, a male narrator 'shaped the tale, formed it according to his fantasy, into which even his experiences and his ideals are brought, whereby, for example, his military service plays a significant role. He likes to

[207] Cosquin, *Contes populaires de Lorraine*, ii. 79, no. 42: *Les Trois Frères* (AT569). Plumepatte was army slang, so perhaps the meaning was lost on Cosquin: Léon Merlin, *La Langue verte du troupier: dictionnaire d'argot militaire*, Paris–Limoges 1886, 30, 55.

[208] One of the three types of narrator defined by the Hungarian folklorist Bano was the 'lying soldier or Munchausen type': Dégh, *Folktales and society*, 173.

[209] Henssen, *Überlieferung und Persönlichkeit*, 25.

[210] Röhrich, *Folktales and reality*, 202–3. This is also Röhrich's own conclusion: 'the folktale often becomes a concealed or even open statement about the narrator and reflects his or her personality throughout'.

[211] Holbek, *Interpretation of fairy tales*, 168–9.

portray himself through the tales' heroes'.[212] The soldier at the *veillées* of Lorraine put himself into the tale as the soldier hero, consciously shaping his character after his own image, or at least to suit his own tastes. Thereafter his tales were picked up and adapted in the domestic tradition so that they conformed to the local ecotype, but the portrait of the individual soldier thus preserved in folklore was one that returning soldiers had originally created. The soldier was himself the agent of cultural formation.

---

[212] 'gestaltet das Märchen um, formt es nach seiner Phantasie, indem er eben seine Erlebnisse, seine Wunschbilder hineinträgt, wobei z. B. seine Militärzeit eine grosse Rolle spielt. Er zeichnet sich in dem Helden des Märchens gern selbst': Merkelbach-Pinck, 'Wanderungen den Märchen', 225.

3

Conscripts and Volunteers

These surveys of French popular imagery and oral literature have demonstrated that the soldier was well represented in both. But in order to make sense of the image of the soldier as he appears in the folktales and cheap prints of Lorraine, we must first look at the social relationships to which these cultural products gave expression. The period under consideration saw important changes in the way armies were formed, supplied, housed and discharged – changes that were particularly marked in a border territory. How did these changes alter the relationships between peasant and soldier, and to what extent are these altered relationships reflected in the portrayal of the soldier? In other words, what were the connections between the changing world of experienced reality and the imagined world of rural popular culture?

Conscription was the point of greatest contact, and of greatest change in the nature of that contact, between civilian and military spheres between the eighteenth and nineteenth centuries. One might, therefore, expect to see in the response of the rural communities a cultural expression of this changing relationship. But these responses were themselves influenced by ideas and behaviour already current in society. An examination of conscription rites will show not only how new attitudes were formed, but also how they were informed by the pre-existing culture.

Conscription has a further interest in that it was cultural formation by law. The particular form of conscription under examination, the *tirage au sort* or military lottery, was originally introduced at the end of the seventeenth century to raise a militia force, but during the revolution it was extended to recruitment in general. Its initial purpose was to create a more effective fighting machine and the responses of the young men were, by and large, ignored by the administrators, except insofar as these affected their ability to fill their quota. However, the possibility that the army could be a tool for educating the population in ideas of nationhood was already current among some philosophers and officers during the 1770s and 80s.[1] The revolution gave great impetus in this direction, particularly under the Jacobin government for whom the ideological purpose of the army almost outstripped its role as a fighting force (or rather the two were intimately bound together in its

---

[1] Matthew S. Anderson, *War and society in Europe of the old regime, 1618–1789*, London 1988, 199.

rhetoric).[2] If military needs came to carry more weight with their successors, whether republican, imperial or royalist, the potential cultural role of the army was never ignored.[3]

The *tirage au sort* over time

Historians tend to date to 1798 the history of conscription and the first permanent system of military service in regular units.[4] Certainly the sheer numbers needed by the revolutionary armies make *ancien régime* attempts at imposing compulsory military service seem very limited, but it would be wrong to imagine that individual military obligation was simply another part of the new order between state and citizen. The form of conscription that the revolutionaries imposed was modelled on that introduced in 1688. It was in response to that first imposition, perceived as a feudal 'blood tax' by the peasants who had to bear its full force, that many of the rituals that would be elaborated during conscription were first developed.[5]

The *tirage au sort* was originally conceived by Louis XIV's minister Louvois as a temporary measure intended to free line troops for combat. The duties of the provincial militias in peacetime were light, but in wartime they included guarding coasts, garrison duty, chasing bandits and deserters, protecting baggage trains and prisoners of war. In practice the institution, with brief intervals, became a permanent feature of the *ancien régime*, and the kinds of service expected of the militia grew as the eighteenth century wore on, until it was little less than a reserve army.[6] Ducal Lorraine escaped the *tirage* until the beginning of the War of Austrian Succession. A French administration had been imposed on the duchy a few years previously, and while Lorraine

---

2 Alan Forrest, *Soldiers of the French revolution*, Durham, NC 1990, 89–124.

3 This is not the place to detail the debates among politicians, journalists and generals about the virtues or otherwise of a representative national army, issues which are already well covered in French military historiography; our interest is the role played by communities in the process. For further details (in English) see, among others, Isser Woloch, 'Napoleonic conscription: state power and civil society', *Past and Present* cxi (1986), 101–29; Richard Holroyd, 'The Bourbon army, 1815–1830', *Historical Journal* xiv (1971), 529–52; Douglas Porch, 'The French army law of 1832', ibid. 751–69. The best examination of the various strains of thought about the army after 1815 in political and intellectual circles remains Girardet, *La Société militaire*. It is important to be aware that these manipulations of the conscription system were not simply by-products of changing military needs: both the army and government had also considered what effects they wished to produce on society as a whole.

4 Jean-Paul Bertaud, 'Du Volontariat à la conscription', *Revue historique des armées* xxxviii (1982), 27.

5 The term 'corvée de sang' was frequently used in the *cahiers de doléances* of 1789: Alan Forrest, *Conscripts and deserters: the army and French society during the revolution and empire*, Oxford 1989, 11.

6 André Corvisier, *Armées et sociétés en Europe de 1492 à 1789*, Paris 1976, 65.

remained nominally independent under Louis XV's father-in-law, the former King Stanislas of Poland, the real power lay with the intendant, La Galaizière, who was anxious to force Lorraine into 'the French system' as quickly as possible.[7] The militia was part of this programme; the first *tirage* took place on 14 November 1742 in Nancy and it was to remain an all but annual ritual until suppressed by the revolution.[8]

The *tirage* usually fitted into an annual cycle starting in late autumn when the intendant sent out to his sub-delegates the order to raise the militia. The sub-delegate sent it on to the syndics of each *communauté*, and at the same time told them the number of militiamen to find, based on a rough division by population.[9] The syndics drew up a list of 'miliciables', persons to be entered for the *tirage*. These were only members of the third estate, no nobles or clerics were expected to serve, and there was a vast assortment of other group and individual exemptions ranging from whole towns (Lunéville, Bar and Nancy were excluded in 1742) through government officials, master craftsmen and monastery shepherds to the members of the Val-d'Ajol family of bonesetters, the Fleurots, who (according to legend) received this privilege as a reward for curing Louis XV in 1759.[10] Any individual with influence could pressurise the intendant to be excused, or, if all else failed, to accept a paid replacement. The result was that the greatest burden fell on the poorest elements of rural society.[11] A *miliciable* had to be between sixteen and forty, at least five feet tall, and in a fit state of health to serve. In normal circumstances only unmarried men or widowers without children were included, but if there were not enough then married men without children (and once, in 1752, even fathers) were added.[12]

The *tirage* took place in February or March of the following year. On the day the syndics of each *communauté* would march their *miliciables* to the main town of the sub-delegation. Anyone on the sub-delegate's list who did not appear for the *tirage* was declared a 'runaway', and would be automatically incorporated in the militia if caught. After a preliminary lottery to see in what order the *communautés* would pull their tickets, the *tirage* itself took place either at the home of the sub-delegate or at the *hôtel-de-ville*. Each man would step up to a hat held at head height. The ticket they pulled was either blank, a 'white ticket', or had the word 'Milicien' written on it, a 'black ticket'. The consequence of pulling the latter was six years' service.[13] A few

---

7 Guy Cabourdin, *Quand Stanislas régnait en Lorraine*, Paris 1980, 47.
8 Pierre Boye, *La Milice en Lorraine au XVIIIe siècle*, Nancy–Paris 1904, 17.
9 In 1742 the *communautés* were expected to find one militiaman for every thirty to thirty-five 'feux' or households: Ghislaine Grosdemange, 'Population et milice dans la subdélégation de Lunéville de 1737 à 1789', *Annales de l'est* 5th ser. iii (1952), 127.
10 Dom Pierre Tailly, *Lettres vôgiennes*, Liege 1789, 106.
11 Boye, *La Milice en Lorraine*, 48–9.
12 Although no married man over twenty was included after 1766, and no married men at all after 1773: Grosdemange, 'Population et milice', 126.
13 Even when service was reduced to five years in France in 1748 it remained at six years

weeks later the syndics would escort their militiamen to the spring muster to be incorporated.

It is difficult to gauge the impact of the militia. In the sub-delegation of Lunéville 102 militiamen were required in the first year, but only fifteen in the last year, 1788. With a population of 100,000 this does not seem a very heavy burden, but when one takes into account the evasion measures taken by *miliciables*, including emigration and even enlistment in line regiments, the drain on the population becomes much more marked. The curé of Neuville-aux-Bois reported: 'many farmers of my parish have been ruined for lack of sons or servants, particularly since the lottery for the militia or as a result of voluntary engagements or trickery [of the recruiting officers], having in a parish composed of ninety hearths more than twenty lads in the king's service'.[14] To judge from the reports of the sub-delegates to the intendant on the 'famine of subjects' this situation was not unusual.[15] It is perhaps surprising that young men would take such desperate measures to escape a service which in peacetime was not particularly onerous, but then they knew that, despite La Galaizière's ordinances, employers were unwilling to take a risk on a man who might at any moment be whisked off to the other end of the kingdom.[16] Worse, militiamen had to get an authorisation from the intendant before they could marry, which was not always forthcoming.[17] They may also have suspected that the militia was used as a recruiting ground for the regular army (as was indeed the case). By volunteering for the army they at least got to choose which regiment to serve in.

However, it was not primarily these features, which prompted the complaints of the miliciables who refused to submit to the *tirage* at Nancy in 1766, nor those made in the *cahiers de doléances* of 1789, but rather the obvious inequity in the way it was applied. The rioters demanded that all young men, included those exempted should be forced to submit to the lottery, while the *communauté* of Ananvillers demanded of the *Etats généraux* that 'the lottery for the militia, repugnant in itself and especially for the commonplace injustices [it gives rise to] should be suppressed'.[18]

---

in Lorraine, just one of several ways in which the institution weighed more heavily in the duchy: Boye, *La Milice en Lorraine*, 35.

[14] 'Plusieurs laboureurs de ma paroisse ont étés ruinés par le défaut de domestiques ou de garçons de famille, surtout depuis le tirage de la milice ou par suite d'engagements volontaires ou par surprise, ayant dans une paroisse composée de nonante feux, plus de vingt garçons au service de Roi': Désiré Mathieu, *L'Ancien Régime en Lorraine et Barrois d'après des documents inédits (1698–1789)*, Paris 1907, 226.

[15] Boye, *La Milice en Lorraine*, 94.

[16] Grosdemange, 'Population et milice', 132. Nor was a militiaman allowed to leave his parish without the written permission of his syndic.

[17] Pierre Bourgin, 'Milices et salpêtriers comtois sous l'ancien régime', *Barbizier: bulletin de liaison du folklore comtois* n.s. xv (1988), 67.

[18] Journal de Nicolas Durival aîné, lieutenant de police de Nancy, 1759–66, Bibliothèque municipale de Nancy, MS 1315 (863), vi, fo. 130v; 'Le tirage de la milice, très odieuse par elle-même et surtout par les injustices ordinaires': André Jeanmaire, *La Tradition en*

The militia was duly abolished by the revolution. Now patriotism was expected to be sufficient spur to arms. However, soon after the declaration of war in 1791 it became clear that patriotism would not be enough. It was not merely that the number of volunteers was insufficient, for on occasions the popular response, not least in Lorraine, could be huge, but the army required reliability as well as quantity. It needed time to train recruits and integrate them into their units, and it needed to know that they would not return home at the end of the campaigning season convinced that their patriotic duty was done. Already in 1792 the government, though still talking the language of patriotism, resorted to compulsion in those areas under direct threat of invasion. Several times in 1792 the young men in the Vosges were obliged to submit to the *tirage*.[19] In 1793 the revolutionary government broke even with the rhetoric of voluntary enlistment and organised two huge conscriptions of the population, the *levée de 300,000* in the spring and the *levée en masse* in the autumn. In Lorraine, this meant a return to the tried and tested system of the *tirage au sort*. As with the militia, the burden fell on unmarried men or widowers without children. These *levées* appear to have been far more equitable in practice than the militia, not least because the slightest suggestion of privilege for one young man resulted in a refusal to participate by the others.[20] However, only for the *levée en masse* was there no opportunity for the richer citizen to buy himself a replacement.[21]

The conscriptions of 1793 served their immediate purpose, and for a brief time there were only occasional and local *levées*. These could not, if the war was to continue, satisfy the demands of the army, and so the minister of war, Jourdan, drew up a system of conscription which, though incorporating elements of the earlier revolutionary *levées*, would provide a regular flow of recruits. The law of 1798 that bears Jourdan's name stipulated that all men between twenty and twenty-five belonged to one of five *classes*.[22] The numbers chosen by lottery from each *classe* would depend on the military situation, but those of the first *classe* (the twenty-year-olds) would always be

---

Lorraine: le cycle de vie; les proverbes, Colmar 1981, 33. The complaint of inequality in the organisation of the militia was very widespread; even the (exempt) nobility of the baili-wick of Bar demanded in their *cahier* that 'une répartition juste et égale pour le tirage des milices, le régime suivi jusqu'à ce jour étant d'une injustice sans exemple'.

[19] The irony was not lost on the unlucky few who found the word 'volontaire' written on their ticket: Lt Pasdeloup, 'Documents relatives aux levées de troupes de 1791, 1792 et 1793 dans les communes dépendant aujourd'hui de l'arrondissement de Saint-Dié', *Bulletin de la Société philomatique vosgienne* xxxix (1913–14), 21.

[20] Charles Pierfitte, 'Les Volontaires vosgiens en 1792', *Bulletin de la Société philomatique vosgienne* xxi (1895–6), 115.

[21] For a general discussion of the various means by which the revolutionary governments recruited see Jean-Paul Bertaud, *The army of the French revolution*, Princeton, NJ–Guildford 1988. For their impact on one area of Lorraine see Jean-Aimé Morizot, 'Les Volontaires du district de Remiremont', *Le Pays de Remiremont* xi (1992), 77–108.

[22] Those who had turned twenty by the first day of Vendémiaire (22 Sept.) formed the *première classe*, those who had turned twenty-one formed the *deuxième classe* and so on.

expected to march away first. If a young man made it to twenty-five without being chosen by the lottery, then he was free from the shadow of conscription. The law also granted certain exemptions, not least for those employed in the administration of the conscription process. Jourdan himself considered replacements an offence to revolutionary principle, but one year later the government bowed to pressure and permitted them.[23]

The *loi Jourdan* was to remain intact, with alterations, until the restoration. Bernard Kappaun has examined how it worked in practice in the department of the Moselle. Vaublanc, the prefect for most of the period, would receive the order for a certain number of men, and from which *classe* they should be drawn. He would divide the contingent between the arrondissements, and the sub-prefect then sub-divided it among the cantons. On the day of the *tirage*, the sub-prefect summoned the mayors to bring their young men to the *chef-lieu* of the canton. The mayors drew first among themselves to arrange in which order the communes would pull their tickets. Then each man stepped up to the urn and drew out a number. Those with a low number had a 'bad number', which meant that, unless they failed to meet the height and health requirements, or found some persuasive reason to convince the *conseil de recrutement* to excuse them (for instance, as only sons of widows), they would be drafted into the army. Those with a high or 'good number' could relax, until the next time. Anyone who received a 'bad number' and did not fall into an exempt category could, if rich, find a replacement, if poor they might run away.[24] In practice neither of these escape-routes were much used in Lorraine. Partly this is clearly due to the soldiering tradition which appears to have made military life more acceptable, but also there were few real choices: efficient administration made desertion unsafe, and what was the point of buying a rare and expensive replacement if one was only going to be called up in the next *tirage* in a few months' time?[25]

Vaublanc estimated that 47,000 inhabitants of the Moselle had served in the army between 1792 and 1813 (out of a total population of 399,201 in 1812). One third of these had been volunteers. How many of them returned is difficult to ascertain, but a guess sometimes proffered by historians is about one third.[26] The *tirage* was, therefore, taking most of the twenty to twenty-five age group and killing the majority of them, so that by 1813 even the loyal Vaublanc was forced to complain that his department was 'exhausted'.[27] Clearly no comparison can be made with the militia, or indeed the entire *ancien régime* military machine, in terms of destructiveness. It is

---

[23] Forrest, *Conscripts and deserters*, 34–5.

[24] Bernard Kappaun, 'La Conscription en Moselle sous le premier empire', unpubl. *thèse doctorale*, Nancy II 1967, 12–15; Forrest, *Conscripts and deserters*, 2.

[25] Kappaun, 'La Conscription en Moselle', 108–26.

[26] J. Houdaille, 'Le Problème des pertes de guerre', *Revue d'histoire moderne et contemporaine* xvii (1970), 418.

[27] Kappaun, 'La Conscription en Moselle', 74, 210–12.

perhaps surprising, therefore, that there was so little in the way of rejection of the process by the young men concerned. Unlike much of the rest of the country, which was in a state of semi-permanent civil disobedience over the issue of conscription, the Moselle consistently filled its contingent and sometimes exceeded it. Of course there is a great deal of difference between acceptance of one's fate and the patriotic fervour sometimes described by officials of the *tirage*, but even in 1813 men under the age of conscription were volunteering in large numbers in this border department – suggesting some degree of willingness.[28] If the *tirage* was accepted, one of the reasons seems to have been that many of the manifest inequalities of the militia had been done away with, even if the equality now on offer was the equality of 'bad numbers'.

Louis XVIII's 1814 *Charte* did away with conscription as one of the more loathed features of the usurper's regime, but almost immediately his government was faced with the same problem which dogged its predecessors: the army wanted a steady supply of recruits to turn into professional soldiers, but the country was not supplying sufficient volunteers. At the same time opposition to the Bourbons continued to demand an army representative of the nation. Louis's minister of war, Gouvion Saint-Cyr, drew up the legislative compromise, a form of conscription modelled on that of Jourdan, but adapted to the less bellicose needs of the restored regime. His law of 10 March 1818 was tweaked by his successors in 1824, in 1832 and in 1855, but apart from a fluctuation in the period of service required (from six to eight before finally settling on seven years), and a steady increase in the contingent demanded, their changes had little effect on the process of conscription as it was experienced in the countryside. There was now only one *classe*, made up of all the young men who turned twenty in the same calendar year. In the early spring of the following year the sub-prefect summoned the mayors of the communes together with their respective *classes* to the *chef-lieu* of the canton. Again the mayors held a preliminary ballot to fix the order in which the communes would approach the urn. Again low numbers were bad (the first ten being particularly unlucky as they meant service in the colonial marines), high numbers were good, but there was a grey area in between until the operation of the *conseil de révision* which would visit the *chef-lieu* a month or two after the *tirage*. At the *conseil* each number was called in turn, his height and health examined, any reasons for exemption heard and replacements accepted. The *conseil* proceeded until they had reached the number needed for the contingent. Those with 'bad numbers' would receive their marching orders towards the end of the year, the lucky ones could now get on with their lives, they had their *congé absolu* and could never again be threatened with conscription.[29]

---

[28] Ibid. 195–6.

[29] This timetable is based on the one given in Camille Maire, 'Conscrits en Amerique: le cas de l'arrondissement de Sarrebourg (Meurthe), 1829–1870', in Centre de recherches

131

The *tirage* of the constitutional monarchy and the second empire did not attempt to achieve the equality of chance demanded by the republican oppo-sition, but neither was there the mass of exemptions that characterised the *ancien régime*. Instead the steady growth in insurance against 'bad numbers' and the 'traders in human flesh' who dealt in replacements ensured that anyone whose opinion mattered (in the sense that they passed the property qualification and could vote) was in a position to buy their way out of the lottery. The resultant inequalities are less apparent in Lorraine than else-where; indeed, young Lorrainers were exported throughout the rest of France to replace less military-minded Frenchmen.[30] Perhaps this accounts for Lorraine's relative acceptance of post-revolutionary conscription, for throughout the period its four departments remained very efficient at reaching their quota. And Lorraine also continued to supply large numbers of volunteers.[31] When conscripts and volunteers from the city of Metz and surrounding areas are added together, one finds that no less than one third of twenty-year-old males served in the army (and this total does not include replacements sent to other departments).[32] The relatively high level of mili-tary experience among the male population of Lorraine, whether voluntary or obligatory, is one of the continuities over the period. In 1748 the man appointed by Galaizière to handle the raising of the militia, Nicolas Durival (whose brother was to contribute the article on the militia to the *Encyclopédie*), was able to record proudly in his *Journal*, 'No province of [Louis XV's] kingdom had supplied so many.'[33] This same claim could be made with justification about Lorraine's contribution to the defence of France at any time from then until she was cut in two by the defeat of 1870–1.

The *tirage* supplied the military needs of very different political regimes but changes in government had little effect on the response of the population. While Lorraine consistently supplied or even exceeded her quota, other areas of France, particularly in the south and west, consistently failed to meet the demands made of them. Lorrainers were not significantly influenced in their military duty by ideological considerations; they were equally ready to serve kings and republics.[34] The *tirage* was, therefore, a fixed element in an era of

d'histoire nord-américaine, *L'Emigration française*, Paris 1985, 229. A percentage of those designated, perhaps as much as half, would be left at home to act as a reserve.

[30] J.-C. Labate, 'Le Recrutement de l'armée à Metz, 1818–1870', unpubl. *mémoire de maîtrise*, Metz 1974, 26–38.

[31] Between 1819 and 1826 the departments of the Moselle and the Meurthe were the second and third highest *per capita* suppliers of volunteers: Aron, Dumont and Le Roy Ladurie, *Anthropologie du conscrit français*, map 7.

[32] Labate, *Le Recrutement de l'armée*, 19. The percentage was lower in rural areas of Lorraine, but the totals remained well above the national average.

[33] 'Aucune province de son royaume n'en avait tant fourni': Boye, *La Milice en Lorraine*, 84. The point Durival is making is, of course, that Lorraine was not part of the kingdom at that time.

[34] It is argued by political theoreticians that a readiness to be conscripted is a sign of the

political flux. The timetable remained stable from *ancien régime* to third republic: in the autumn the representative of central authority, whether intendant or prefect, ordered the lists to be drawn up by the representatives of local authority, whether syndic or mayor; the tirage proceeded early in the new year (usually in March); and any revision process would follow within a few weeks. The responsibilities of the syndics or mayors also remained constant: they had to draw up the lists, they had to attend the tirage and they had to account for any runaways.

The conjunction of the *tirage* with the month of Mars, god of war, did not pass unremarked by imagists. Their representations of the twelve months often used the conscripts on their way to the *tirage* to illustrate March.[35] The song accompanying one of Pellerin's versions of the *Douze mois* describes March in the act of summoning 'our young warriors'.[36] Originally this time-table was to fit in with the army's need for men to open the campaigning season. In later years the conscripts would be left at home for several months after their fate was decided, but the late autumn and early spring retained their connections with the conscription process. Therefore, the timing of the formation of the *classe* and the *tirage* itself slotted into the winter calendar of rural life, which was to prove significant for its reception.

We have seen how, throughout the period, the greatest expectations fell on young unmarried men, in particular the poorer elements of rural society. They were obliged by the authorities to act as a group, for example travelling to the *chef-lieu* as a commune. Every member of the *classe* was obliged to go through the process, even if he knew he would be exempted. Even those absent from the commune were represented in proxy by members of their family or the mayor. The behaviour demanded of them, originally to assist the officers in charge of the conscription by putting a body against every name on their lists, would also have important and sometimes unexpected results.

The continuities between the *ancien régime* and the nineteenth century explain why post-revolutionary conscripts in germanophone Lorraine were still called 'Milicebuben' – militia boys and the *tirage* 'Milicespielen' – militia lottery.[37] In francophone Moselle in the 1860s the *tirage* was known as 'the militia lottery.[38] In Franche-Comté conscripts were still singing on their way to the *Conseil de révision* in the first half of the twentieth century: 'I pulled in the militia lottery/ And I pulled the black ticket,/ I'm for seven year's service/

acceptance of the legitimacy of the regime. However, in France attitudes to conscription did not vary much with succeeding regimes: Lorraine was always among the best respondents, Corsica among the worst. The nature of the regime had nothing to do with it, local cultural attitudes were more significant.

35 MNATP 53.86.4733 D, *Les 12 Mois de l'année*, Gangel & Didion, Metz.
36 Coirault, *Formation*, 301.
37 Merkelbach-Pinck, *Brauch und Sitte*, 146.
38 'L'è tirieu lè Mèlice': Zéliqzon, *Dictionnaire*, 436.

[Before] I see you again poor darling.'[39] The resemblance between the militia and conscription was not lost on the rural community from whom these sayings were drawn, and we will see that the continuities in their response were not just at the level of language, but also of behaviour. But we also see that these responses borrow from traditional village groupings of young unmarried men dating back to before the introduction of the militia. In practice conscription fulfilled other functions in the peasant community than simply the requirements of the state. Even Jourdan, when he suggested that the *tirage* would form a part of normal civic life, a routine procedure for young men on the threshold of their adult lives, could not have foreseen just how important a rite it was to become.[40]

Conscription rites

There are few complete descriptions from before 1870 of the rituals surrounding conscription. Sub-delegates and sub-prefects focused only on the end result – recruits, while folklorists, anxious to find survivals of a more spiritual (whether Christian or pagan) past, largely ignored customs concerning a practice they connected with contemporary society. The record becomes fuller during the third republic as the army took on greater significance in national life, its representative function emphasised over and above demands for professionalism.[41] Commentators were keen to display the positive response of the *classe* to these changes, which is reflected in the wealth of surviving material on conscription from the last quarter of the nineteenth century.

The historian is faced with a quandary about whether to use the information gathered during the third republic to make sense of the brief descriptions of conscript rites before 1870.[42] I have tried to avoid material collected after 1870 unless the informants state that their evidence relates to that earlier period, or there is internal evidence to make this link. However, the resulting picture is something of a composite, drawing on information not only from various locations within Lorraine but also from those neighbouring provinces with whom cultural connections were closest. It is unlikely that the full range of conscript activities were undertaken in any one village,

---

[39] 'J'ai tiré à la milice au sort/ Et j'ai tiré le billet noir,/ J'ai pour sept ans de service/ Mon pauvre coeur pour te revoir': Jean Garneret, *Chansons populaires comtoises*, i, Besançon 1971, 138: *Je viens, l'objet de mes amours*.

[40] Forrest, *The soldiers of the French revolution*, 84.

[41] After 1873 almost all Frenchmen were called up, but the duration of service was reduced, diminishing the fears and antipathies that conscription had generated in the era of the *tirage*.

[42] The term conscript is here used to designate all members of the *classe*, as was the practice at the time, not just those actually selected for service by the *tirage*.

especially when many were not sufficiently populous to possess a *classe* at all.[43] 'Each village has its customs' goes the Champenois saying, and these included its own festive calendar with which conscript rituals were entwined.[44] The details below present a uniform picture that hides the responsiveness to local needs and inventiveness of local customs. On the other hand the underlying pattern in their rituals should become clear.

If this approach is revealing about the attitude of rural communities in Lorraine to conscription, it does not tell us how individual conscripts felt about this momentous event in their lives. Prefects reporting to their government on morale tended to see their conscripts through the rose-tinted spectacles of patriotic fervour, but there are few autobiographies by peasant-conscripts to tell us how they felt. I have, therefore, made use of the collections of conscript songs made by nineteenth-century folklorists to cover this silence, and occasionally I have borrowed concepts from the social sciences where I felt they may be revealing. Sociologists, looking at adolescents in modern societies, have characterised youth as a period of exploration and rebellion, because it is the age at which the individual personality emerges from the 'group or role identity' of the child.[45] Although such explanations may account for some of the behaviour of conscripts, they are not wholly satisfactory: conscription cannot be seen simply as an adventure in which youth indulged; it was an obligation enforced by law. On the other hand the activities of conscripts within their communities, though often boisterous, should not necessarily be seen as rebellion against parental authority, for the village as a whole expected, even encouraged them to behave in certain ways. Conscript rituals do not appear to have aided individualisation; on the contrary they reinforced traditional group and role identities. Conscripts were in many ways a conservative force within the community. This is not to suggest that sociological insights into the problems of youth are worthless in a historical context, but to understand, as Michael Mitterauer has shown, that youth itself has a history.

None the less there must be, in any social order, distinctions between adolescents and adults: one cannot be both at the same time and so there must be a transition. The boy, not responsible for his actions, not called upon to defend his community, and, above all, not able to marry, must be turned into a man. In modern European societies these transitions tend to be drawn out over a long period characterised by small but cumulative changes in the adolescent's social position, but in many other societies this change is effected 'once-and-for-all' through initiation ceremonies. Can comparisons

---

[43] Out of the twenty-six communes in the canton of Lorquin in 1860, ten were able to supply only one or two conscripts to take part in the lottery: Maire, 'Le contigent de 1860', 30.

[44] 'Chaque village a son usage': Louis Lallement, *Folklore et vieux souvenirs d'Argonne, arrondisement de Sainte-Ménéhould*, Châlons-sur-Marne 1921, 118.

[45] Michael Mitterauer, *A history of youth*, Oxford 1992, 24.

with such societies help us to understand the behaviour of conscripts? Anthropologists who have undertaken such comparative studies have found that initiation rituals follow a uniform structure, first enunciated by the folk-lorist Arnold Van Gennep: for persons to pass from one defined social position to another, they had to undergo a *rite de passage* involving three stages – separation, marginality (or liminality) and aggregation.[46] Conscript rituals, as Van Gennep himself noted, followed this pattern.[47] Similarities can be found between many of the specific elements of the rituals of the *classe* and male initiation ceremonies in tribal societies, but do these similar symbols carry similar meanings? Historians are naturally circumspect about drawing too many inferences from comparisons between societies which otherwise exhibit manifold differences. Initiation rites in tribal societies are assumed to have been designed to serve their overt purpose, to effect the change required. Historically there have been no widespread initiation rites in western Europe, only partial rites on the long road from boyhood to manhood, such as first communion, first job, first dance. If conscription became a full-blown *rite de passage*, we must explain how it emerged in a society with no history of such practices, and why it should form around an institution whose initial concern was not with social transitions but with the extraction of labour by governments from their subjects.

The *classe* and the annual cycle

The particular form taken by conscription rites arose partly from the dove-tailing of the government's timetable with the calendar of rural life, and partly because it affected precisely that group of persons who had traditionally taken a lead role in the communal life of the village, the young unmarried men. Between first communion and marriage it was common practice in north-eastern France (and far beyond) for men to form a recognisable unit within the village, responsible for organising its major public events: Carnival, the Lenten dances and the patronal fête. These events were also the occasions for courting, and the group's role in their organisation probably derives from its primary task as the regulator of couple formation and the protector of endogamous marriage patterns. It controlled access to the unmarried women of the community and ensured that its privileges were not infringed by similar groups in neighbouring villages. Its role in policing sexual mores extended to the whole village; it organised the charivari of remarried

---

[46] Arnold Van Gennep, *Les Rites de passage*, Paris 1909. Gennep's work achieved its great-est influence after the publication of the English translation in 1960. His translator, Monika Vizedom, subsequently carried out a large-scale comparison of initiation rites in many cultures which corroborated Gennep's model: *Rites and relationships: rites of passage and contemporary anthropology*, Beverly Hills 1976.

[47] Arnold Van Gennep, *Manuel de folklore français contemporain*, i, Paris 1943, 219.

widowers and others who offended village propriety. It also took a leading part in defending the community from outsiders, a duty that in times of peace might only involve stone-throwing at their neighbours, but in some areas developed into an armed defence force. In Lorraine the group might have a specific name related to one of its activities, such as the 'Kirmesbuben' – the fête-lads or the 'confrèrie des chetifs' – the confraternity of wretches, who were responsible for organising the annual fête, or to its primary function as 'garçons à marier'. But the most usual name was simply 'la jeunesse' – the youth (although not all were necessarily young). The history of these groups has received considerable attention in France.[48] I want only to look at the way conscription affected the behaviour of these groups, and how the conscript *classe* took over the functions previously exercised by 'la jeunesse' as a whole, as was the case in several parts of Lorraine.[49] I also wish to show how the *classe* reformulated these activities to create a genuine 'rite of passage'.

The timetable started in November/December, when the order went out to the communes to draw up the *recensement* which would decide who had to submit to the *tirage*.[50] As the conscription system became more regular, so the actions of the mayor could be predicted: every French boy born in nine-teenth-century France would know from an early age that he would be a member of the *classe* of the year in which he turned twenty.[51] None the less the formation of the *classe* as an active organisation within the village did not much precede their visit in December to the mayor's house to have their names inscribed on the table for that year.[52] The precise day on which the *classe* first met varied from area to area depending on the festive calendar of the village. In Alsace the feast of Saint Sylvester was the 'Conscrits-Tag', in Franche-Comté and Burgundy the first outing of the *classe* was New Year's Day.[53] The formation of the *classe* as a distinct group was the first stage on

---

[48] For an ethnological example see Daniel Fabre, ' "Doing youth" in the village', in Giovanni Levi and Jean-Claude Schmitt (eds), A *history of young people in the west*, ii, Cambridge, Mass. 1997, 37–65.

[49] 'Les conscrits menaient la fête, conduisaient la fête, c'est à dire organisaient toutes les réjouissances de la fête patronale et principalement le bal': Louis Lavigne, 'Petit Dictionnaire de folklore: notes alphabétiques de folklore recueillies à Cumières et Avillers Ste Croix (Meuse)', MNATP, MS 75.43.1.

[50] Thiriat, *La Vallée de Cleurie*, 333.

[51] This foreknowledge is expressed in a conscript song from Wirmingen, which starts 'Jetzt zwanzig Jahre sein ich alt/ Jetzt komme ich in der Kriegerzahl/ Milize müssen wir spielen': Pinck, *Verklingende Weisen*, iii. 381.

[52] The whole conscription process might be anticipated by a year, with the formation of a *classe* of nineteen-year-olds called the 'sous-conscrits', 'les au-devant' or the 'classe de balai'. As a formal organisation these groups only appear in descriptions from the end of the nineteenth century onwards, but it is suggested that younger adolescents had always played a part in conscript activities, even if in an informal manner: Georges L'Hôte, *La Tankiote: usages traditionnels en Lorraine*, Nancy 1984, 87.

[53] Roger Henninger, *Conscrits d'Alsace*, Strasbourg 1961, 14; Jean Garneret, *Un Village comtois: Lantenne: ses coutumes, ses patois*, Paris 1959, 293; J. Deshenry, 'Les Conscrits', *Folklore de France* ii (1961), 5.

their *rite de passage* as defined by Van Gennep – the act of separation. From this moment onwards their identity as a conscript group came before their normal kinship ties and other relationships. Their activities within the village, during the year that remained to them before the *classe* was disbanded, revealed them as 'liminaries'.[54]

At the first meeting a number of formalities had to be overcome. A president would be chosen who would liaise on behalf of the *classe* with the authorities, especially the mayor.[55] A treasurer was vital because the conscripts would be collecting and spending as a group until their final dissolution. They also had to decide on ceremonial roles: who would, on their marches, carry the cane, the flag, who would wear the aprons, beards and axes of the sappers? The role of drum major had of necessity to be given to the tallest, the role of standard-bearer normally went to the youngest or smallest.[56] If the *classe* had not inherited a flag from its predecessor then one would have to be ordered and appropriately decorated, and other ceremonial items would be bought, borrowed or constructed.[57] A venue had to be chosen which they would make their meeting-place: it might be a barn or specially constructed hut in the woods, but usually it was the village bar. However chosen, the meeting place would be the stage for some of the more private elements of their rites, house their equipment and witness their departure from – and hopefully their return to – the village.[58] The isolation of liminaries from their normal social relations, especially from their families, through removal to a secluded camp, or *telemenos*, is characteristic of the act of separation during initiation rites in tribal societies. The creation by conscripts of their own *telemenos* divided them from their previous relationships, but allowed them to indulge in activities not normally permitted them such as copious drinking, smoking and playing cards, all of which tended to reinforce their new-found group identity.[59] It is noteworthy that all these activities were associated with men, and in particular men removed from the restraints of family life, whose embodiment was the soldier.

Although within the *classe* each conscript might have a specific role, as far

[54] 'Liminaries' is a term borrowed from anthropology for those in the second or liminal stage of a rite of passage: Victor Turner, 'Variations on a theme of liminality', in Sally Moore and Barbara Myerhoff (eds), *Secular ritual*, Amsterdam 1977, 37.

[55] Michel Bozon, *Les Conscrits*, Paris 1981, 48.

[56] Comité du folklore champenois, *Travaux du comité du folklore champenois*, III: *Du berceau à la tombe*, Châlons-sur-Marne 1964, 45; Henninger, *Conscrits d'Alsace*, 16.

[57] In the late nineteenth century Pellerin and competitors made a good living out of orders from conscript *classes*: George, 'Conscription', 7–11.

[58] Paul Bailly, 'La Conscription aux alentours de Meaux au XIXème siècle', *Bulletin folklorique d'Ile-de-France* ix (1947), no. 3, 9. Carnival confraternities organised competitions between innkeepers for their custom, for instance during the nomination of the 'capitaine de la jeunesse' at Champey near Montbéliard: Edgard Coulon, 'Coutumes et croyances populaires au pays de Montbéliard', *Revue du folklore français* iv (1933), 238.

[59] Mme Simon de Riespach, 'D'Konscritzitt ou le temps des conscrits', *Folklore de France* xl (1991–2), 11.

as the community was concerned they appeared as a group. 'From the day on which their names are inscribed on the list, the conscripts of the same commune no longer step out without one another' wrote Xavier Thiriat of the young Vosgians.[60] Whatever they did they did in each other's company: they dressed in the same costume; they dined in rotation in each others' homes; often they would sleep together in a barn or shed; and when they danced, it was arm-in-arm.[61] Social divisions would be laid aside as members of the *classe* would 'tutoyer' each other, and references to political or religious differences were suppressed.[62] For the rest of their lives the relationship created in the *classe* would create a bond similar to that between godparents, so that one could, with the same strength of expression, say, 'c'est mon conscrit' as 'c'est mon compère'.[63] Anthropologists have given the term *communitas* to this new identity formed from the erosion of normal social roles and distinctions in favour of a communion among equals; it is characteristic of rites of passage.[64]

The conscription process itself fostered the sense of unity. Everyone had to be inscribed on the table, even the blind; everyone had to attend the *tirage*; and everyone had to return to the *chef-lieu* for the *conseil de révision*, even though many knew that their 'good numbers' made them safe. Even a conscript who wanted to be replaced had to introduce his replacement to the *conseil* in person. Yet the effort to create a group spirit could hardly hide the fact that the appearance of equality of chance before the *tirage* was false. Many stepped up to the urn safe in the knowledge that they would be replaced or exempted, and at every stage of the process the inequalities became more marked. The divisions created amongst them were recognised by the *classe*. They differentiated between the winner of the highest number – the 'râve' – and the most unlucky – the no. 1 or 'bidèt'.[65] The former would be fêted, the latter would be ragged. None the less they continued to act in concert, implying that their group existence rested on a deeper equality between them, one which the *tirage* could not breach.

In Lorraine and neighbouring Argonne some conscript groups were

---

[60] 'Depuis le jour de l'inscription sur le tableau, les conscrits d'une même commune ne marchent plus l'un sans l'autre': Thiriat, *La Vallée de Cleurie*, 333.

[61] Henninger, *Conscrits d'Alsace*, 14.

[62] Michel Bozon has found these requirements written into the constitutions of the 'amicales de conscrits' who continue to organise the 'fête des conscrits' at Villefranche: 'Conscrits et fêtes de conscrits à Villefranche-sur-Saône (Rhône)', *Ethnologie française* ix (1979), 29–46.

[63] Weber, *Peasants into Frenchmen*, 474. Nicolas Baro, one of Merkelbach-Pinck's most important informants, used the term 'conscrit' in this sense in his correspondence: Langstroff, *Lothringer Volksart*, 173.

[64] Turner, 'Variations on a theme', 46–8.

[65] Colonel Villemin, 'Bouquet des champs (Souvenirs et coutumes d'autrefois)', 1938, Bibliothèque municipale de Nancy, MS 293 (1545), fo. 158. The term in use in the rest of France for the highest number was 'le laurier', and laurels were carried in many regions instead of flags.

expected to take a role in the cult of the dead at All Saints (1 November) by, for instance, ringing the church bells the preceding evening (Halloween). But in general the first festive occasion at which the *classe* appeared was the feast of Saint Nicholas, the patron saint of Lorraine. He was also the protector of young children, but among adolescents his protective function became sex-specific: girls from first communion until marriage became the remit of Saint Catherine.[66] After first communion the adolescents sat together in two single-sex groups within the church, and acted as a juvenile confraternity with special duties towards their patron saint. As with other confraternities they also had a secular role, organising reciprocal dances.[67] It is clear, therefore, that in the part they played on the feast of Saint Nicholas, conscripts usurped the functions of – and the protection extended to – 'la jeunesse' as a whole, a pattern we will see repeated throughout the calendar. On the feast day itself, the *classe* would attend and sing a mass in honour of Saint Nicholas, and afterwards they would participate in the parade and organise the games, for it was a holiday in Lorraine and was celebrated in much the same way as the village fête.[68] In the evening, in the Argonne, the conscripts organised a dance to which they invited the young women who had previously invited them to the feast of Saint Catherine.[69]

Conscripts also invoked the protection of their patron during the lottery process itself. At Chicourt near Château-Salins, the day before the *tirage*, the *classe* offered a bouquet of flowers bound with ribbons (both items associated with conscripts) to the painting of Saint Nicholas in their church, and marched away firing pistols.[70] At Triaucourt in Argonne there was a relay of bouquets, the first was offered to the Saint Nicholas in the nave, the one which had been left there by the preceding *classe* was deposited at a stone statue of the saint at the door of the church, the one there was removed to a further statue in town, and the one there taken in procession to the priest's house and left with his personal Saint Nicholas. The last bouquet of all was divided up and the roses carried to every house in the village, starting with the mayor's.[71]

There are a number of elements in the fêting of Saint Nicholas that will reappear throughout the public performances of the conscripts at other village festivities. Although the fête of the village patron saint might be some way off the activities of the conscripts on both occasions were very similar. At Bourdons-sur-Rognon in Bassigny, for example, on the eve of the *fête*, the conscripts carried a bouquet of artificial flowers to the altar of the Virgin, and

---

66 Lerouge, 'Notice', 278.
67 Lallement, *Folklore et vieux souvenirs*, 170.
68 Labourasse, *Anciens Us*, 68.
69 Lallement, *Folklore et vieux souvenirs*, 170.
70 L'Hôte, *La Tankiote*, 87.
71 Conscripts preferred artificial flowers for their bouquets, hence their longevity: Comité du folklore champenois, *Travaux*, iii. 46.

would then sing serenades under the windows of the whole village, starting with the mayor, priest and schoolteacher, and making a special effort under the windows of the marriageable young women. In the morning they would attend mass, bedecked in ribbons, before going off to play festive games, especially the 'tir' (which involved shooting a bird with a cross-bow) and the 'jeu de l'oie' (in which a blindfolded participant tried to decapitate a goose hanging by its legs from a washing-line).[72] In the past both games appear to have been the prerogative of the local militia companies or confraternities of archers, and the conscripts had succeeded to their rights.[73] The role conscripts played in processions on religious feast days and pilgrimages also seems to be an appropriation of the role of local militias in previous centuries, before these formations were suppressed by governments jealous of their monopoly on violence.[74]

In other areas these processions, decorations and traditional pastimes were not the preserve of the conscripts. In the *pays messin*, it was the 'garçons de fête' who carried 'honours of the feast' (which appear to have been rosettes) to each house; dressed in ribbons ('aiguillettes'), they made the collection to pay for the games.[75] In Cons-la-Grandville in the Ardennes, the 'sergent de la jeunesse', carrying his 'royal cane', organised the fête, and in particular it was 'la jeunesse' who, with music at their head and with ribbons trailing, accompanied the girls to the dance.[76] At Breux in the Meuse it was 'la jeunesse' who went to 'round-up the girls' for the dances which followed the fête. The close connection between 'la jeunesse' and the *classe* was apparent at Breux, for if the first dance was reserved for 'la jeunesse', the second was for the conscripts.[77]

Conscripts played an organising role in the festivities of the community, but their activities had a characteristic look: the musical procession, the flowers and the ribbons, the gunfire. This uniformity was the result of their inheritance from earlier manifestations of the community of unmarried males that in some areas survived well into the nineteenth century. The conscript group took over the functions previously performed by other young men's associations, together with many of their accessories such as the cane of the 'sergent de la jeunesse', which reappears in the hands of the conscript drum-major.

The period of greatest intensity in conscript activities in Lorraine fell between the creation of the *classe* in December and the *tirage* and the *révision*

---

[72] Ibid.
[73] Labourasse, *Anciens Us*, 91–3.
[74] Etienne Fourier de Bacourt, *Les Sociétés de tir et les milices bourgeois dans l'ancien duché de Lorraine*, Bar-le-Duc n.d. In neighbouring areas of Champagne, Luxembourg and Belgium vestigial militia units still organised or participated in such events.
[75] Zéliqzon and Thiriot, *Textes patois*, 189.
[76] Meyrac, *Traditions, coutumes, légendes*, 93.
[77] François Houzelle, 'Breux: son histoire et sa seigneurie', *Mémoires de la Société des lettres, sciences et arts de Bar-le-Duc* 3rd ser. vii (1898), 299.

in February or March. Thus it overlapped with the *veillée* season which normally opened on All Saints, the 1 November.[78] Depending on the start of the agricultural season the *veillées* ended between 5 February and 12 March.[79] The regular 'working' *veillée*, when the wool was carded and the flax spun, was, as we have seen, largely a female occasion, partly in order that mothers and daughters could plan their marriage strategies.[80] It is precisely for this reason that the *veillée* women and the conscripts interacted, for the unmarried men wanted their voices heard in their counsels. The relationship has been admirably elucidated by Colette Mechin, who has examined the custom known as the *dâyage*. Around 8 p.m., when the *veillée* was under way, a tap would be heard at the shutter, and a voice disguised with a swazzle like Mr Punch would ask: 'Do you want to *dailler*?' To which one of the *veilleuses* replied: 'About what?' 'About love?' 'Seeing as you want to speak about love, tell me what it is to love?'[81] There followed a contest in which the person outside would pose quasi-riddles to which a *veilleuse* would have to reply, both using rhyming quatrains. Those in French were stereotyped and could be learnt, and several would be recognisable to medievalists as the game of courtly love called 'ventes d'amour'.[82] But the skilled *dailleur* was able to create his *dayemans* for the occasion, in which case his questions, posed in patois, were more personal.[83] The *dailleur* was out to embarrass the *veilleuse*, who in reply would try to guess the identity of her interlocutor. Unfortunately

[78] The following authors cite All Saints as the start of the *veillée* season: Beaulieu, *Archéologie de la Lorraine*, i. 267; Saulny, *Les Passe-Temps lorrains*, 51; Lallement, *Folklore et vieux souvenirs*, 229. Other authors mention other dates, both earlier and later.

[79] 5 February (Saint Agatha) is cited as the close of the *veillée* season by the following authors: Lallement, *Contes rustiques*, 222, Labourasse, *Anciens Us*, 77; Lavigne, 'Petit Dictionnaire de folklore'. The symbolic end of the season in the Vosges came either at the end of Carnival or during Easter week when the lamps or candles used to light the *veillée* were set in little boats on the river, a ceremony known as *Les Changolos*: A. Fournier, 'Vieilles Coutumes, usages et traditions populaires des Vosges provenant des cultes antiques et particulièrement de celui du soleil', *Bulletin de la Société philomatique vosgienne* xvi (1889–90), 159.

[80] All but one commentator agree that 'C'est aussi pendant ces réunions que se préparent les mariages': Beaulieu, *Archéologie de la Lorraine*, 268. However the one exception was a professional anthropologist of some note, and a native of Lorraine, who had made a special study of *veillées* and whose opinion, therefore, should carry some weight. Louis Marin rejected the received wisdom that 'le prinicpal attrait des *veillées* était de susciter ou de favoriser des relations courtoises entre jeunes gens et jeunes filles', indeed 'ils n'avaient absolument aucun rapport avec l'organisation de la jeunesse "par groupes" ': *Les Contes traditionnels en Lorraine*, 104. Marin also stated that there was little or no singing, drinking, eating, dancing or card-playing at the *veillées* of Lorraine, statements contradicted by every other report. I have suggested elsewhere some reasons why Marin's observations are so divergent from those of other folklorists: Hopkin, 'Identity in a divided province', 680.

[81] ' "V'leuz-ve dayeu!" "De què?" "D'émor?" "Pisque d'èmor ve v'leuz pâlé, d'heuz-me, tiat-ce ç'at d'ainmer?" ': Westphalen, *Petit Dictionnaire*, col. 176.

[82] Sautman, 'Rituels de dérision', 99–103.

[83] Théodore de Puymaigre, '*Veillées* de villages: les dayemans', *Archivio per lo studio delle tradizioni popolari* i (1882), 94.

these patois quatrains were largely left unrecorded by folklorists as too salty, but their ultimate purpose is clear from similar customs noted in Champagne. There the unknown voice would call from outside the shutter, but in this case his question was 'Women, women! Have you got any marriageable girls at your *veillée?*' The women inside would then propose one of their number, and the voice outside, spokesman for a group of village lads, would try to match it with a boy's name. The question and answer session would finish when the women announced 'she smiles' in response to a particular name.[84] This custom went by the apt if prosaic name of the 'arrangement of marriages' but sometimes it could take a more creative line, when a coupling was suggested between the local beauty and a hunchback. The connection with the *dayemans* of Lorraine is clear when compared with a text taken from an 1840 novelette (set in the 1770s), which opens with a gang of lads running arm-in-arm through the streets of Ligny knocking on windows and crying 'marriageable girls, hey, do you want to *dailler?*'[85]

Occasionally women might also *dailler*, but it was more usual for the person on the outside to be one of the young unmarried men who had been purpose-fully excluded from the *veillée*, and in practice it was an activity increasingly reserved to the conscripts. The *dâyage* can be seen as a negotiation between the group of unmarried men who oversaw courtship within the village, and the other villagers concerned with couple formation. Through the anony-mous *dayemans* 'one moved towards a semi-public declaration of affections kept secret until that day'.[86]

At a certain point, when it became clear that the suggested 'arrangement of marriages' were serious, and if they were acceptable to the *veilleuses* (mother as well as daughter), then the *dailleurs* would be allowed in.[87] Now no-one minded the teasing and horse-play which excluded them earlier, for as the Meusian proverb states '[He] who throws moths, throws cupid-arrows', releasing captured moths in the hair or under the skirts of the young women being a common practical joke.[88] Games would be played among the young people, such as 'la savate' in which a hidden object was passed from knee to knee under a row of handkerchiefs which encouraged physical contact

---

[84] 'Femmes, femmes! Avez-vous des filles à marier à votre *veillée?*': Alexis Guillemot, *Contes, légendes, vieilles coutumes de la Marne*, Châlons-sur-Marne 1908, 309. Similar exchanges appear in other works by folklorists: Lallement, *Contes rustiques*, 225; Meyrac, *Traditions, coutumes, légendes*, 14.

[85] 'Filles à marier, Hé! voulez-vous dailler?': F. d'Olincourt, 'Le Contrebandier de Ligny', *Les Veillées de la Lorraine, ou lectures du soir*, iii, Verdun 1842, 72.

[86] 'grâce à l'anonymat de la voix inconnue . . . du badinage amoureux on passe à une déclaration semi-publique des amours tenues secrètes jusqu'à ce jour': Mechin, 'Les Veillées', 201.

[87] Guillemot, *Contes, légendes, vieilles coutumes*, 311; Lemasson, 'Anciennes Coutumes', 512; Saulny, *Les Passe-Temps lorrains*, 55; Lallement, *Contes rustiques*, 226.

[88] 'Qu' jitte pîrottes, jitte amourottes': Labourasse, *Anciens Us*, 78.

between the boys and girls.[89] The more young people in attendance, the more the *veillée* took on a party atmosphere, particularly as the year moved into the carnival season.

However, if the *veillée* was not to get a bad reputation, the young men would have to leave after an hour or so. The *veillée* might continue for two more hours before breaking up. The *veilleuses* then had to find their way home in the darkness, now alive with the creatures from the tales they had just heard. And when the girls emerged the boys were waiting, dressed in sheets or carrying death-head's lanterns to send them scurrying home, if they did not stumble on the trip-wires they had erected.[90] But it was not just the girls they were after; men from other villages who had attended the *veillée* in a courting capacity would be scared off, and if they refused to be scared they would be beaten up under the cover of the disguise.[91]

The underlying purpose of the *dâyage* in couple formation, and the lead role taken by the conscripts, becomes clearer when one considers its logical culmination, the *dônage*, which was, in Mechin's words, 'a validation of the same order, but much more spectacular', and 'the revenge of natural inclination on the parent's more reasoned choice [of marital partner]'.[92] At Corcieux in the Vosges, after Vespers on the last Sunday before Lent, all the townsfolk gathered outside the church while the members of the *classe* ran from group to group, 'questioning the young women with a look and pretending to receive mysterious confidences from them'. The conscripts then divided into two bands, and invaded two houses opposite each other. The windows of an upper storey would be opened (though the shutters were kept closed) and a hidden representative of one of the bands cried: 'Give, who gives!' The first representative would then announce 'I give Pierre A to Louise B', the second responded 'I give Léonard X to Célestine Z' and so on, until everyone of an age and a condition to marry was paired off.[93] Similar customs have been reported throughout Lorraine and surrounding regions, normally on the first or second Sunday of Lent, that is to say at the close of the *veillée* season. In the Meuse and Champagne the young women themselves were usually not present when the *dônage* was called, but the presumption was that they had had a hand in the preparation of the list.[94] The caller would often include

---

89 Beaulieu, *Archéologie de la Lorraine*, i. 268; L'Hôte, *La Tankiôte*, 80.

90 Westphalen, *Petit Dictionnaire*, col. 153.

91 Ibid. col. 38.

92 'une officialisation du même ordre, bien plus éclatante . . . la revanche de l'inclination naturelle sur le choix plus raisonné des parents': Mechin, 'Les Veillées', 201.

93 'les conscrits de l'année vont d'un groupe à l'autre, graves affairés, interrogeant du regard les jeunes filles et feignant de recevoir d'elles de mystérieuses confidences. . . . jusqu'à ce que toutes les personnes en âge et en situation de contracter mariage y aient passé': Sauvé, *Le Folklore des Hautes-Vosges*, 42. In other areas of Lorraine the *dônâge* took place around a bonfire, in which case the criers were usually masked.

94 Charles Abel, 'Coutumes du pays messin: les valentins', *L'Austrasie* n.s. i (1853), 78–87; Labourasse, *Anciens Us*, 104; Comité du folklore champenois, *Travaux*, iii. 46; Westphalen, *Petit Dictionnaire*, cols 263–5.

joke couplings, of notorious bachelors and old spinsters, or he might make allusions to known liaisons among married people (which accorded with the conscripts' role in policing the sexual behaviour of the village); the crowd would be expected to express a view on the couple, either outrageously enthusiastic or violently hostile.[95]

The *dônage* might have consequences. If, as was often the case, it took place immediately before a Lenten dance, the parties named were expected to be partners for the evening, or even throughout the year.[96] In other areas the young men named would, the following Sunday, pay a visit to the house of their named partner, where they would hang about, perhaps making a racket or firing a pistol into the air, until the father appeared. If the father offered him his hand and invited him into the house for a drink, then it meant that the matchmaking might proceed.[97] As the Comité du folklore champenois concluded: 'this custom encouraged marriages'.[98]

Both the *dâyage* and the *dônage* long predate conscription; if the *classe* came to play a leading role in these village festivities it was because it replaced earlier groupings of young men. Carnival confraternities led the *dônage* in some areas of Lorraine throughout the nineteenth century, and there is evidence to suggest these were far more widespread before the revolution.[99] Here, as at other festive occasions, the *classe* had superseded existing groups while absorbing their function. They were structurally similar; like the earlier groups the conscripts were excluded from hearth and home, and wandered in the night during the dead season of winter until work began in the fields. Because of their exclusion from the domestic life of the village, Mechin draws a connection between the conscripts and the dead they mimicked when terrorising the *veilleuses*. The disguised voice of the *dailleur* represented the voice of the village's collective ancestors, because in Lorraine, where respect for the cult of the dead was marked, 'the community of the dead had the right to intervene in the affairs of the community of the living by means of the group of young men'.[100] Hence the need for their voices to remain anonymous. This conclusion can only be tentative, but

---

95   It was these scurrilous or even seditious aspects of the *dônage* which led the authorities to attempt to suppress the custom at Metz, Nancy, Toul and other places during the eighteenth and early nineteenth centuries: Meyrac, *Traditions, coutumes, légendes*, 15; Jean-Julien Barbé, *Coutumes populaires et ceremonies anciennes du pays messin*, Nancy 1910, 8; Abel, 'Coutumes du pays messin: les valentins', 86; Lepage and Charton, *Le Département des Vosges*, i. 713.
96   Labourasse, *Anciens Us*, 104; Comité du folklore champenois, *Travaux*, iii. 46.
97   Mechin, 'Les Veillées', 201; Eugen H. Huhn, *Deutsch-Lothringen. Landes-, Volks- und Ortskunde*, Stuttgart 1875, 92.
98   'cet usage favorisait les mariages': Comité du folklore champenois, *Travaux*, iii. 46.
99   In the village of Failly the 'Keulo' of the 'confrère des chaty' (the confraternity of wastrels) called the 'vausi'nates' or 'valentines': Anon., 'Promenade archéologique au village de Failly', *L'Austrasie* iv (1839), 201–2.
100 'la société des morts avait droit "d'intervention" dans les affaires de la communauté par groupe des jeunes gens interposé': Mechin, 'Les Veillées', 205.

certainly the conscripts were 'en marge', the second stage in Van Gennep's model of *rites de passage*, and their licence to intervene in the process of couple formation in part depended on the licence accorded them as liminaries. Perhaps it is worth noting that adolescent men undergoing initiation in tribal societies are often considered 'dead' until reintegrated with their everyday world.[101]

'The military lottery was young men's most beautiful day' a Comtois peasant told Jean Garneret.[102] The ability of the conscript to enjoy himself on these occasions has passed into proverbial speech. In a tale told in 1959 the 'Dummling' hero *Bruder Luschtich* 'danced and jumped and hopped the whole way, as if he was a conscript'.[103] There was, however, an air of desperation about many of the pleasures the conscript enjoyed at the *tirage*. After all, his attendance at this festival was not optional, it was an ordeal that he was obliged to endure and which gave rise to a high level of anxiety. It has been suggested that, in initiation rites in general, this state of fear is necessary for the rite to be effective, for it makes the liminary more receptive to the changes they are undergoing. By sharing the experience of the ordeal the bonds of the *classe* were reinforced.[104]

The evening before the *tirage* the *classe* united for a special mass to ensure their collective good luck.[105] The day of the *tirage* started early. From 4.00 a.m. the drummer and other musicians (as many as could be afforded or cajoled) were out on the streets waking up the conscripts and their families.[106] The early hours of the day of the *tirage* were anxious ones as families performed private rituals to ensure a propitious outcome. We first find the *classe* as a group assembled outside the *mairie* to give the mayor, their leader for the day, a 'dawn-chorus' of conscript songs.[107]

The cortège formed outside the *mairie*: at its head was the mayor himself in his regalia seated in a wagon. Behind him came the standard-bearer, and although he was often the smallest of the conscripts the flag was the biggest they could afford. The bigger and grander the flag, the more prestige reflected on the village. It would be decorated with the name of the commune and possibly with other symbols of local identity for, according to Michel Bozon,

---

101 Turner suggests that liminaries, stripped of their existing identities and removed from normal classifications, and thus reduced to a 'homogeneous social matter', become walking paradoxes, both human and animal, both living and dead, and, as we will see, both male and female: 'Variations on a theme', 37.

102 'Le tirage au sort c'était le plus beau jour des jeunes hommes': Garneret, *Un Village comtois*, 328.

103 'er . . . hedd gedonzt un ish g'shprunge un hedd g'hupst, de gonze Waih, ass wie e Gonskri': Merkelbach-Pinck, *Volkserzählungen aus Lothringen*, 21: *Dr Bruder Luschtich* (AT592).

104 Jean S. La Fontaine, *Initiation*, Manchester 1986, 77–81.

105 Richard, *Traditions populaires*, 88; Labourasse, *Anciens Us*, 21.

106 Bailly, 'La Conscription', 9.

107 Thiriat, *La Vallée de Cleurie*, 333.

'rather than a military emblem, the flag was the symbol of the connection created between the young conscripts of a commune'. In fact the flag served both purposes, as a 'traditional accessory of the fête, and no doubt also a symbol of virility', but also a means of demonstrating the new role the conscripts were assuming, not boys but men, and therefore in a new relationship with the state – represented by the flag – as its defenders.[108] Behind the standard-bearer came the drum-major with his cane, one of the attributes of the *classe* which may have been adopted from the military sphere (as the drum-major had become one of the most visible members of the military community).[109] As with the flag, and more rarely with the sappers' axes, there is a sense here that the conscripts, in a state between adolescence and manhood, were becoming men by doing what men do, and in particular by aping the army as an exclusively male activity. However the cane was also an important piece of regalia for the 'sergent de la jeunesse', the 'Keulo', and leaders of other carnival confraternities, as it was during the *rite de passage* for young French artisans, the 'compagnonnage', so it predated the *classe* as a virile symbol of male solidarity. The drum-major led the musicians and behind them came the rest of the *classe*, arm-in-arm and dressed in their full ceremonial costume.

The basic dress of the conscript was the peasant's Sunday best. However, it was always the accessories which were the subject of greatest care and attention, the bouquets of flowers and the multi-coloured ribbons which, when tied round the conscript's hat, might trail almost to the ground. Ribbons had always been a part of the costume of the soldier at the beginning of his career: we know that the *miliciables* wore ribbons on the way to the *chef-lieu* because a sub-delegate wrote to the intendant to ask if their cockades were chargeable to the *communauté* or not.[110] 'Aiguillettes' were a part of the festive dress of unmarried males throughout the calendar; the 'garçons de fête' wore them, so did the 'garçons de droit' at weddings.[111] However, it was more commonplace for young women in rural France to wear ribbons and flowers, and indeed the conscripts would distribute their own accessories among them after the ceremony. In the song *La Fiancée du conscrit*, the unfortunate winner of a 'bad number' announces the result to his lover: 'There! All these bouquets/ Will be for you, my darling,/ To prove to you/ How much I loved you.'[112] It is a

---

108 'Plus qu'un emblème militaire, le drapeau est le signe du lien qui se crée entre les jeunes conscrits d'une commune . . . objet concret, profane, accessoire traditionnel de la fête, et sans doute aussi symbole viril': Bozon, *Les Conscrits*, 52.
109 Drum-major Santini, Napoleon's companion on Sainte Helena and later ticket collector at Les Invalides, was known throughout eastern France from a myriad of cheap prints.
110 Grosdemange, 'Population et milice', 141. Ribbons, cockades and false pig-tails regularly turn up in the communal accounts for the day of the *tirage*: Bourgin, 'Milices et salpêtriers comtois', 167.
111 Westphalen, *Petit Dictionnaire*, col. 10.
112 'Va! tous ces bouquets/ Seront pour toi, ma belle,/ Pour te prouver/ Combien je t'ai

common feature of male initiation ceremonies for the initiates to mimic female activities; the wearing of traditional female items by conscripts is indicative of their liminal status.[113] This is not to suggest that conscripts were losing their male identity – on the contrary they were reinforcing it at every opportunity – but rather that while *en marge* one is permitted to play with the social boundaries of gender which in normal periods are fixed. This is particularly the case in male initiation rites where precisely these boundaries are at issue; the liminary conscripts were leaving behind the feminine domestic world of home and childhood to join the public world of men, citizens and soldiers. After they had undergone the ceremony they gave up these symbols, for now the boundaries of gender had become fixed.[114]

The journey to the *chef-lieu* itself physically separated the conscripts from their usual domestic setting and reinforced their liminal status. The procession might be joined by the conscripts' male relations, their fathers and godfathers, together with the boys of school age, for the day of the *tirage* was a holiday, the schoolteacher being one of those escorting his former pupils.[115] Before this crowd moved off, the mayor would give them a talking too: 'Lets go, lads, be brave today. If you are orderly, then there will be no curfew. If, however, you misbehave, I'll make 12 o'clock the curfew!'[116] Occasionally the *classe* would visit a local shrine to perform last minute prayers for a successful outcome.[117] However this was normally left to the mothers, sisters and girlfriends who, left at home, celebrated a mass or visited a local shrine while the *tirage* took place.[118] Though they had an important role in dressing and otherwise preparing the conscript, they could not accompany him, indeed even to see a woman on the street on that morning was considered bad luck.[119] Therefore, though all members of the community were involved

z-aimée.' She replies 'De tous ces beaux bouquets,/ Je t'en r'mercie, mon cher,/ J'aimerais mieux/ T'voir mourir sous mes yeux/ Que de te voir partir./ Adieu mon cher amant!': Charles Beauquier, *Chansons populaires recueillies en Franche-Comté*, Paris 1894, 34.

[113] Vizedom, *Rites and relationships*, 42. According to Terence Turner's remodelling of Van Gennep's structure, in order to move horizontally between two mutually incompatible classes (such as boy and man) one must, by means of a rite of separation, be temporarily removed to a higher level of the social system, where these two classes are not incompatible, but from which all social distinctions, including those between men and women, draw their origin: 'Transformation, hierarchy and transcendence: a reformulation of Van Gennep's model of the structure of rites of passage', in Moore and Myerhoff, *Secular ritual*, 53–70. As is well known, men wearing items of women's clothing were a feature of other liminal occasions, such as Carnival and riots, in early modern Europe.

[114] La Fontaine, *Initiation*, 120.

[115] Henninger, *Conscrits d'Alsace*, 15; Garneret, *Un Village comtois*, 328.

[116] 'Allez, ihr Bürslte, seid brav heute! Wenn ihr ordentlich seid, so habt ihr keinen Feierabend. Wenn ihr aber Sauereien macht, so mach ich um 12 Uhr Feierabend!': Auguste Kassel, *Conscrits, Musik und Tanz im alten Elsass*, Guebwiller 1929, 65.

[117] Comité du folklore champenois, *Travaux*, iii. 42.

[118] Martial Bayon, 'Sobriquets et superstitions militaires: le tirage au sort en France: le moyen d'avoir un bon numéro', *Revue des traditions populaires* iii (1888), 53.

[119] Paul Sébillot, *Coutumes populaires de la Haute-Bretagne*, Paris 1886, 80.

in the preparation for the *tirage*, there was a clear sexual division of labour: women were limited to the private concerns of the family – the wider community was the preoccupation of men.

The journey to the *chef-lieu* was a noisy affair, especially in the Vosges, where the ability to shout loudly from one hillside to another was highly developed: 'The conscripts came singing, and crying "Tiochichi!" (their war-cry and shout of joy), to pull their numbers when their *classe* was called.'[120] The greatest noise of songs and yodels was saved for the *chef-lieu* which they entered with a display of flag or mace throwing.[121] The effect they made was recalled by a visitor to Plombières during the last *tirage* for the royal militia in the val d'Ajol: 'a troop of 130 or 140, rigged out in the most grotesque manner, which made everybody laugh, they sang at the tops of their voices, and played on some rough instruments; they were so determined that the *gendarmerie* who were present scarcely worried them'.[122] For later periods it appears that the intended recipients of this display were not so much the officers of the conscription but the other villages. Many *classes* prepared special songs for the occasion, and there was considerable competition for new pieces that they hoped would impress the inhabitants of the *chef-lieu*, who commented on their presentation as they passed.[123]

After touring the town the mayors led their troupe to the main square outside the town hall; the *tirage* itself would take place inside. There sat the officers of the conscription all in their ceremonial regalia: the sub-prefect with his officials, an army officer, a member of the departmental council, as well as gendarmes to keep order. The mayors were the first to step up to the urn; they drew to see in what order the communes would draw their numbers. This was a moment of great importance for the conscripts, for it was widely believed that whoever drew first got the best numbers, and so rancour was injected into the already lively competition between the different communes.[124]

Then it was the conscript's turn to step up, pick a number, hand it to the sub-prefect who read it to the crowd of assembled dignitaries, and handed it back to the conscript. For that intensely personal if public moment, the

---

120 'C'est en chantant, c'est en proférant leur cri de guerre ou de joie 'Tiochichi!' que les conscrits viennent tirer leurs numéros au moment de l'appel de leur classe': Lepage and Charton, *Le Département des Vosges*, i. 706.

121 Comité du folklore champenois, *Travaux*, iii. 45.

122 'je les ai vu plusieurs fois de suite arriver en une troupe de plus de cent trente ou quarante qui étoient affublés d'une manière si grotesque, qu'ils faisoient rire tout le monde, ils chantoient à pleine tête, et jouoient de quelques mauvais instrumens; ils étoient tellement déterminés, que la Maréchaussée qui étoit présente ne les épouventoit guère': Tailly, *Lettres vôgiennes*, 104.

123 Paul Carru, *Les Chansons des conscrits du Haut-Revermont*, Bourg 1911, 10. Pinck's main informant, Papa Gerné, was employed by conscript *classes* of local villages to teach his least known, and therefore most impressive songs. Pinck found himself fulfilling this role after the publication of the first volume of *Verklingende Weisen*.

124 Pinck, *Verklingende Weisen*, iii. 382.

young man was alone, face-to-face with the embodiment of the power of the state that held his future in its hands. In the early years of conscription the authorities had drawn the tickets themselves and simply announced the results, but this gave rise to charges of bias.[125] Because the conscript was obliged to pull his own ticket it could be seen that he accepted the validity of the *tirage*. By his action of handing it to the sub-prefect he indicated he accepted the state's right to order his fate. As in oaths and tests in other initiations, he demonstrated his obedience to the initiator and the authority he represented. It was done before a congregation of representatives of authority, including those from his own community, who were witnesses to his acceptance and who were thus buttressed in their own authority.[126] Michel Bozon was quite right to identify 'an air of a lay sacrament to the ceremony' with the sub-prefect in the role of officiant.[127]

Now the conscript knew the worst, he had the number in his hand, and with the exception of some median numbers he could make an accurate guess as to whether it was good or bad. The first thing to do was to visit the crowd of pedlars in the square below. He may have already been, before the tirage, to buy a quick prayer or magic amulet: now he needed a decorative number to replace the one he had received from the urn. This he stuck on the front of his hat for all to see.[128] The original he would preserve, possibly decorated and framed, as a record of this fundamental turning point in his life.[129] He might also buy another ribbon, black for a 'mauvais numéro', red for a good one, which was added to the collection around his hat. The significance of the black ribbon does not need much elaboration: in the novel the *Histoire d'un conscrit de 1813*, the unfortunate winner of the number eight runs out of the town-hall demanding a black ribbon and crying 'This is what we need now. . . . We are all dead. . . . We should wear our mourning!'[130]

Whether lucky or unlucky, when the moment was over the *classe* needed to release tension in a bar. A favourite conscript song from germanophone Lorraine reports how they went to the Crown in Metz, and 'There we want to

---

[125] Michelle Mignot, 'La Conscription dans le département de la Meuse sous le directoire', unpubl. *mémoire de maîtrise*, Nancy II 1955, 22.

[126] La Fontaine, *Initiation*, 104.

[127] 'Le sous-préfet, par sa présence, conférait un caractère de sacrement laïque à la cérémonie': Bozon, *Les Conscrits*, 97.

[128] This custom apparently dates from the early years of the revolution when volunteers tied their 'billet d'enrôlement' to their hats with ribbons: Henninger, *Conscrits d'Alsace*, 3.

[129] The custom of decorating the *billet* and making a picture out of it was most developed in Alsace, but was practised in other areas, such as Champagne: Adolphe Riff, *L'Art populaire et l'artisanat rural en Alsace*, Strasbourg 1945, 12–13; Lallement, *Contes rustiques*, 229. Bozon suggests that during the period when the number contained a whole destiny (1800–72) the custom was far more widespread: *Les Conscrits*, 99.

[130] 'Voilà ce qu'il nous faut maintenant. . . . Nous sommes tous morts . . . nous devons porter notre deuil!': Emile Erckmann and Alexandre Chatrian, *Histoire d'un conscrit de 1813*, in the collected edn *Gens d'Alsace et de Lorraine*, ed. Jean-Pierre Rioux, Nancy 1993 (1st French edn, 1867), 919.

drink a round/ And we want to be merry.'[131] The significance of this occasion is suggested in the Comtois tale of *Adolphe du diable*: Adolphe the conscript had never previously left his home, 'he didn't know what fun was, nothing at all'. At the *chef-lieu* 'he had to go [to the bar] and dine as all the conscripts did'. Never having been in a bar before (many villages did not have one until the end of the nineteenth century) Adolphe gets drunk and loses all his money at cards, and as a result sells himself to the devil.[132] Gendarmes patrolled the streets to ensure that the increasingly drunken conscripts from rival villages did not have the chance to meet each other.[133] However, for many young men 'one can't have a good feast without a fight' and even though the gendarmes often escorted them a considerable way out of the town, they found an opportunity to come to blows.[134] The mace, the axes, the flag, were now objects of contention but also handy weapons in battles which frequently ended in bloodshed.[135] The drinking and other bad behaviour were generally tolerated; the licence they enjoyed was, according to Van Gennep, characteristic of all liminaries undergoing rites of passage.[136]

If the *classe* returned home in one piece then the party would continue into the night, sometimes starting with a male-only banquet (though more often this was held on the following evening, allowing the conscripts to make their *tournée*).[137] This banquet, attended by their male relatives and the notables of the village, is seen by Bozon as 'a way of publicly admitting the conscripts into adult society'.[138] They were now, as initiates, permitted to sit and drink in the public world of men, the process of aggregation had begun. One can imagine that for those with a bad number this was an ambiguous pleasure, but they still sang 'Today we'll play the fool,/ With our friends, with our brothers./ We'll be jolly, carefree lads,/ We'll forget our sweethearts.'[139] The guests wisely withdrew late in the evening to allow the conscripts to carry on drinking by themselves, until they slid under the table.

The day of the *révision* a few weeks later, followed a similar, if less exuberant pattern. The *classe* would again travel under escort to the *chef-lieu* where the officers of the conscription would process them one-by-one. Clear

---

131 'Da wollen wir eins trinken/ Und wollen wir Lustige sein': Pinck, *Verklingende Weisen*, iv. 47, no. 34: *Rekruten sind lustige Leute*.

132 'I n savait pas c que c'était que l'amusement, rien du tout. . . . I fallait aller dîner comme font tous les conscrits.': Garneret, *Contes recueillis en Franche-Comté*, 32, no. 3: *Adolphe du diable* (AT313).

133 Bozon, *Les Conscrits*, 94.

134 'Il n'y a pas de belle fête sans bataille': Ponchon, ' "A l'Veille!" ', 32.

135 Gennep, *Manuel de folklore français*, i. 215.

136 Ibid.

137 Thiriat, *La Vallée de Cleurie*, 333.

138 'ce qui était une manière d'admettre publiquement les conscrits parmi la société adulte': Bozon, *Les Conscrits*, 101.

139 'Aujourd'hui nous ferons les fous,/ Avec nos amis, avec nos frères./Soyons de francs lurons,/Oublions nos tendrons': Beauquier, *Chansons populaires*, 215: *Les Joyeux Conscrits*.

distinctions now appeared between the members of the *classe*: 'it was the bad numbers who wore the ceremonial trappings'.[140] Those passed as fit would visit the pedlars for further ribbons (especially black), and a new badge to replace the number on their hat, proclaiming them 'Bon pour le service'. 'If the lottery assigns us bouquets,/ We will choose fine panaches,/ Suspended from our hats/ As a sign of the flags [we will march under]' explained the Comtois conscript song.[141] Those passed as unfit not only had to remove their own regalia, but also had to pay for their comrades' accoutrements. Accounts of this moment surviving from the nineteenth century have described it as deeply shaming; the 'rejects' felt ostracised from the *classe*. In communities where success was based on hard physical labour, being rejected was tantamount to being unfit for work, and therefore undesirable as a marriage partner. The message was reinforced by another badge that could be purchased from the pedlars: 'Bon pour les filles'. As Michel Bozon has explained: 'in the eyes of the conscripts, military and sexual aptitude went hand in hand'.[142] However, throughout its usual run of activities the *classe* made use of dualisms, and the existence of just these two messages suggests that originally they had not been interchangeable but rather contrasted. A conscript who was 'Bon pour le service' was *ipso facto* not 'Bon pour les filles', for if he was engaged for the army for seven years or more, he could not become engaged to a woman. This distinction was maintained in Brittany, where on their return from the *chef-lieu* the conscripts were 'decorated with a cockade containing the words "fit for service" (for those who had been passed) or "fit for the girls" (for those who had been rejected)'. I will explain later why I believe this was the original meaning all over France.[143]

After the *conseil de révision* the *classe* might be expected to gain some sexual experience, often on the day itself since while in town they could visit the brothel.[144] Again there is a sense that the desired transition from boys to men could be achieved by doing what men do. Perhaps this explains why, when setting off on the day of the *tirage* or the *révision*, it was good luck to meet a woman of uncertain virtue and buy her a drink, when other encoun-

---

140 'C'étaient les mauvais numéros qui avaient des plumages': Garneret, *Un Village comtois*, 328.
141 'Si le sort nous donn' des bouquets,/Nous choisirons de belles panaches,/Flottant sur nos chapeaux/En signe de drapeaux': Beauquier, *Chansons populaires*, 215. The same theme is dealt with in other conscript songs: Westphalen, *Chansons populaires*, ii, no. 311: *Conscrits, soyons heureux*.
142 'aux yeux des conscrits, aptitude militaire et aptitude sexuelle allaient de pair': Bozon, *Les Conscrits*, 104.
143 'garni d'une cocarde avec la mention "Bon pour le service" (pour ceux qui avait été acceptés) ou "Bon pour les filles" (pour ceux qui avaient été refusés)': Susan Moroz, 'Analyse des chansons de conscrits de la commune de Saint-Vincent-sur-Oust (Haute-Bretagne)', *Cahiers de la littérature orale* xvi (1984), 84.
144 This visit was called 'la virée': Bozon, *Les Conscrits*, 104; Weber, *Peasants into Frenchmen*, 475.

ters with women were considered bad luck.[145] The sexual experience might be gained with the conscript's village 'maîtresse'. In the song of night-courtship entitled *Il fait froid, la nuit est sombre* a conscript asks his girlfriend to let him into her bedroom, to which she replies 'Yes, come into my little room,/ Don't wake my mother.' He replies 'Don't worry, my darling,/ She knows that I'm leaving this evening', implying that such behaviour was tolerated by the rest of the community.[146]

The conscripts' *tournée* was a close relative of other customary collections-cum-demonstrations that formed part of the Christmas and Easter cycles. Throughout the winter the conscripts had been organising festivities both for themselves and for the village, and the food, drink, music and other entertainments had to be paid for. So the *classe* went on the scrounge to supply their wants. The timing of their outings varied from district to district. On the eastern and southern slopes of the Vosges conscript *tournées* were associated with the period before the *tirage* when young men were allowed to 'play the conscript', and the results of the collection were put towards their own private parties.[147] In the wetter climes of Lorraine and Champagne the *tournée* usually waited until after the *tirage*, and helped to supply the wants of the season of dances between Carnival and Easter.

The *tournée* was a procession; the participants may not have decked themselves out in all the trappings of their trip to the *chef-lieu*, but they would wear their Sunday best and carry the flag and makeshift mace. They also needed to take with them something to carry all the produce they collected, usually a pole (called a *perche*) from which their booty hung like the quarry of hunters (the resemblance was probably not coincidental, for hunting like soldiering was an entirely male occupation). Birds would be tied to the pole, eggs and flour would be placed in baskets that hung from it.[148] The conscripts might also have with them a huge snuff-box, and passers-by would be offered a pinch in return for money. (As with other 'quêteurs' on festive occasions the conscripts had the right to 'tax' strangers.) Young unmarried women might get a pinch for free. These items were symbolic: throughout eastern France the offer of a snuff-box from a boy to a girl was a token of engagement.[149] The pole was more than just a means of transporting the booty – to the south of Lorraine a *perche* made from a laurel or a fir-tree was the symbol of the *classe* and would be given pride of place in front of the *mairie*, from where neigh-

145 Sébillot, *Coutumes populaires de la Haute-Bretagne*, 80.
146 ' "Oui, entrez dans ma chambrette,/ Ne réveillez pas ma mère."/ "Ne crains rien, oh ma chère,/ Elle sait que je pars ce soir" ': Schamber, *Chansons du folklore lorrain*, no. 21. 'Bundling' – night-visiting the girl of one's choice – was a common practice in Lorraine (and a popular theme in folksong), but in this case the conscript was after more than a kiss and cuddle, as less polite versions of this same song make clear.
147 'faire le conscrit': Garneret, *Un Village comtois*, 329.
148 Bozon, *Les Conscrits*, 59; Bailly, 'La Conscription', 14.
149 Deshenry, 'Les Conscrits', 8.

bouring village gangs would try to steal it.[150] A *perche* was also carried before a wedding couple in the Vosges by one of the 'garçons de droits'. A white hen, supposedly a symbol of the bride's virginity, was tied to the pole and was eaten by the 'garçons' after it had fulfilled its ceremonial function. As a wedding custom this practice died out in the first half of the nineteenth century, but it continued much later as part of the conscript *tournée*.[151] The 'garçons de droits' were often the unmarried members of the same *classe* as the bridegroom. They were allowed all kinds of privileges at weddings, including 'hunting the chicken', a kind of charivari in which if they did not receive food and drink from the wedding guests they would disrupt the reception.[152] In Lorraine, Champagne and Franche-Comté the conscripts' *tournée*, was also called 'hunting the chicken', and as the conscripts considered themselves 'cocks' so the hens in question were not just domestic fowl.[153]

Their march around the village followed the same order of priority as on the day of the *tirage*, first the mayor, followed by the priest and school-teacher, whom they treated to a serenade of conscript songs in order to oblige them to reach into their pockets. A patois poem composed by a Champagne postman in 1867 listed the things they were looking for: 'When I make our *tournée*,/ I will get for our good pot-full/ sausages, chitterlings and cutlets/ I will be able to make a complete feast/ With a peck of potatoes/ And of course plenty of cider until I'm fit to burst.' To this list one could add wine, beer, eggs, herrings and, of course, chickens.[154] The most important part of the *tournée* was, however, the visit to homes of the young women of the village. Again they treated them to a serenade, which often contained a far from subtle sexual threat. A song collected near Meaux demonstrates very clearly who the 'hen' was they had come to 'hunt': 'It's not eggs that we want,/ It's the daughter of the house,/ A day will come, we'll have her./ Alleluia!'[155] In areas where the *tournée* preceded the *tirage*, this was the occasion when the conscripts received their ribbons and cockades from the young women, but in Lorraine and Champagne it was the young women who were given the ribbons, taken from the conscripts' outfit 'by way of souvenir'. (In return she

---

150 Bozon, *Les Conscrits*, 48. Stealing this symbol of both the *classe* and the village was a provocation to violence: François Ploux, 'Rixes intervillageoises en Quercy (1815–1850)', *Ethnologie française* xxi (1991), 277.

151 Nicolas-Louis-Antoine Richard, 'Lettre à M. Eloi Johanneau sur un usage antique des Vosges relatif au mariage', *Mémoires de l'Académie celtique* iii (1809), 174–7. Van Gennep recorded similar customs among conscripts at the beginning of the twentieth century in the southern Vosges and around Montbéliard, as well as in Savoy and the Rhone valley: *Manuel de folklore français*, i. 215.

152 'courir la poule': Labourasse, *Anciens Us*, 48; Garneret, *Un Village comtois*, 341.

153 Comité du folklore champenois, *Travaux*, iii. 43.

154 'Quan j'aran fait nout' tournée/ J'aran pour nou n'boun potée/ D'sauciss, d'andouill' et de coût'lette/ J'pourran fair' enn' noce complette/ Av'in bichet d'poum'du terre/ Et don cid' plein n'seille à traire!': Lallement, *Folklore et vieux souvenirs*, 163.

155 'C'est pas des oeufs que nous voulons,/ C'est la fille de la maison,/ Un jour viendra, on la prendra./ Alleluia!': Bailly, 'La Conscription', 14.

usually gave a sausage for the *perche*.)[156] The value of the gift of ribbons appears in a song from the Montbéliard region: a conscript who had departed for the front without saying goodbye to his sweetheart returns love-sick, only to find she wants nothing more to do with him, so he tells her ' "my love I bring you here/ A ribbon for a smart young lady"/ "Stay here [with me]", his sweetheart said'.[157] If the soldier was called up then she would tie the ribbons to her distaff and carry them to the *veillée*, to kindle memories.[158] The *tournée* around the homes of the young women could turn into an impromptu party, with dancing and drinking, because being a conscript allowed one the licence typical of the Carnival period. Another conscript song, from Gérardmer in the Vosges, tells how they repeatedly went to 'to see the girls', and each verse records something they did on each occasion: 'we danced', 'we fought', 'I laid them out', and finally 'I kissed her'.[159] The potential for couple formation in the *tournée* is clear, particularly in those areas north of the Vosges where it came after the *tirage*, because by that stage many members of the *classe* were now eligible men, they had pulled a lucky number and so were in a position to consider marriage.

Whether during the *dâyage*, the *dônage* or the *tournée*, the conscript had plenty of opportunities to make the acquaintance of marriageable young women, and to discover whether any had taken a fancy to him. So when the night of the 30 April came (Walpurgisnacht, another occasion when conscripts mixed with the spirits of the dead), he knew to which house he should carry his *mais*. *Mais* were branches of trees, which would be planted in the manure pile outside the house of one's 'mistress'.[160] Again this was not specifically a conscript custom, at least in origin, but it gradually became the prerogative of the *classe*.[161] However, different *mais* carried different connotations: a laurel was the most sought after, a laurel branch being carried by the bride at weddings in Lorraine; a hawthorn meant that a boy felt he was being messed about; while a branch from a cherry-tree was the most insulting – it meant 'elle est à tous' – she goes with anyone.[162]

---

156 L'Hôte, *La Tankiote*, 87. In an image produced by Gangel & Didion of Metz in the 1860s, *Travaux et divertissements champêtres*, the second to last scene shows a conscript handing a ribbon to his *maîtresse*.

157 ' "Mai mie y vos aipoutche ci/ In bé riban de demoiselle"/ "Demeure ci li" dit lai belle': Beauquier, *Chansons*, 140: *Les Galants de Chèvremont*.

158 Kassel, *Conscrits, Musik und Tanz*, 17.

159 'vaûr le fêye . . . o z'on dansi . . . o s'on bèti . . . j lèzâ spandi . . . j'l'â èbrèssi': Menéstrels de Gérardmer, *Arts et traditions*, 191: *J'i â jö sti*.

160 Manure in eastern France and the Rhineland had meaning: if a pile was neat and tidy, this meant that marriageable women were within, and suitors could call. The larger the pile the more desirable the woman, or at least her dowry: Dundes, *Life is like a chicken coop ladder*, 13–16; Nicolas-Louis-Antoine Richard, 'Notice sur les cérémonies des mariages dans l'arrondisement de Remiremont, département des Vosges', *Mémoires de l'Académie celtique* v (1810), 252; Lepage and Charton, *Le Département des Vosges*, i. 715.

161 Comité du folklore champenois, *Travaux*, iii. 45.

162 Garneret, *Un Village comtois*, 297; Barbé, *Coutumes populaires*, 59. Other regions

These less sentimental messages remind us that the conscripts, as the successors to 'la jeunesse', were the persons responsible for turning communal opinion into communal judgement. But like the Carnival confraternities they resembled, conscripts were not above organising pranks simply for the fun of it.[163] Throughout the winter, and especially on 30 April, conscripts would smother a house in manure, take the wheels off carts, remove items of furniture and put them in the street, block doors from the outside and generally make a nuisance of themselves.[164] None the less, 'Mayor, schoolmaster, priest, field-guard, gendarmes, in fact the entire community, feigned blindness to the conscripts' rowdy behaviour and pleasure-seeking'; their liminal status was respected.[165]

After the *mais* there was a lull in conscript activities which in general were linked to the winter cycles of festivities – All Saints, Christmas, New Year, Carnival, Lent, Easter. However, in some regions the *classe* was called back into action for one major summer event – the feast of Saint John. Yet again, the role that became theirs was originally performed by other groupings of young men, such as the local militia, and in some areas of Lorraine these persisted in vestigial form into the nineteenth century.[166] Sometime before 24 June the conscripts collected wood to form a bonfire on top of a local hill. On the evening of the feast itself the village gathered behind the local notables to form a torch-lit parade up to the bonfire. Once lit, the conscripts, decked in flowers, their faces and hair covered against the flames, would leap over the pyre in turn.[167] Folklorists have suggested a number of origins for Saint John's bonfires, either as relics of pre-Christian sun-worship or (because in some regions of France newly married or engaged couples jumped through the fire) as a fertility rite. However, the explanation of the participants was that the fire was a preventative against magical harm, and the couples took part in the same way that animals were herded between fires and the ashes of the fire scattered in the fields, to protect against disease. Conscripts, particularly those with 'bad numbers', were probably in greater need of reassurance than most, but as with their other activities it may be that conscripts took on

ascribed different meanings to different branches: Raillet, 'Miscellanées de folklore ardennais', xxxix. 28.

[163] In Provence the conscripts' practical jokes were one of the most developed parts of their rituals, indicative of the important role played by 'abbayes de jeunesse' in this region before conscription: Claude Seignolle, *Le Folklore de Provence*, Paris 1967, 142.

[164] Garneret, *Un Village comtois*, 297; Gennep, *Manuel de folklore français*, iv. 2039.

[165] 'Maire, instituteur, curé, garde-champêtre, gendarmes, à l'image de toute la communauté d'ailleurs, fermaient les yeux sur les désordres et les amusements des conscrits': Bozon, *Les Conscrits*, 110.

[166] Lerouge, 'Notice', 448. The role of local militias in the feast of Saint John may have been the result of the desire of the authorities, local and ecclesiastical, to control the event, and prevent the sometimes dangerous carrying and throwing of fiery materials by 'la jeunesse'. Militias, or militia-like paramilitary groups, regularly assisted in other religious processions.

[167] Hélène Hemmerle, 'La Conscription', *Folklore de France* xl (1991/2), 8.

the role of agents for the whole community. Additionally, liminaries in other societies would often be expected to perform a feat of bravery and strength (such as stealing a horse) and it is feasible that the bonfire of Saint John fulfilled this role for conscripts, if in a slightly muted form. Not only was there the genuine element of danger, but it was also a performance witnessed by the whole village, including their 'mistresses', who had probably prepared their costume for the occasion. The 'Melissa' who jumped three times over the bonfire in the Munster valley of Alsace 'experienced a growing sense of bravery and were thus considered real men'.[168]

Between October and December those who had been designated by the lottery would receive their instructions on how to depart for the regimental depot. Before they left the *classe* would attempt to divine their future. In Burgundy each leave-taking was the occasion for one last party in the bar they had made their own for the year. An unopened bottle inscribed with the name of the conscript was hung from the ceiling, to await his return.[169] Bottles were particularly useful symbolic representations of the conscript, who had spent much of the past year learning to drink, because their contents could be enjoyed by the returning soldier (who often had a reputation for alcoholism in the village). As is often the case in magical symbolism, the role of the bottle could be reversed, not kept but destroyed. At Gespunsart in the Ardennes, when the time came to leave, the conscripts retired to a field outside the village with 'a respectable number of bottles' which they proceeded to empty. Each conscript would take an empty bottle and throw it with all his force against the ground, in an attempt to smash it. He who succeeded became indestructible himself, but he who failed would infallibly die in the army.[170]

Up to the last moments of the year the *classe* retained its unity. In some areas one last *quête* was made to collect money for the departing conscript (although the government wanted a professional army it was never willing to pay a professional wage, and the first few weeks in the regiment were very expensive).[171] Finally it was time to leave: each departing conscript was followed by a crowd of relatives and neighbours, above all the other members of the *classe*, who might travel as far as the next overnight stage on his

---

[168] 'les garçons connaissent une escalade de la bravoure et sont ainsi considérés commes des hommes accomplis': ibid. 8.

[169] Gennep, *Manuel de folklore français*, i. 216–19. In the Vendée the family of the conscript buried a bottle in a coffin in the garden when he left, to be disinterred when he returned: Geneviève Massignon, 'Coutumes et chants de conscrits', extract from the *Revue de Bas-Poitou* [1960], Fontenay-le-Comte 1961, 188.

[170] Meyrac, *Traditions, coutumes, légendes*, 25. A similar custom has been noted in Champagne, where on Easter Day the young men of the village would drink a whole bottle of wine at one go, and then try to smash it, but there seems not to have been any connection with divination: Guillemot, *Contes, légendes, vieilles coutumes*, 292.

[171] Labourasse, *Ancien Us*, 21.

journey.[172] They stopped at every bar on the way and stood him drinks, but when he came to the *mairie* of his first halt, conscripts from other communes would be waiting to be escorted to the same unit.[173] Now the *classe* had to be broken, the time spent *en marge* was at an end, and its members had to assume the adult roles dictated to them by the result of the *tirage*.

The *classe* and the life-cycle

As we have seen the *classe* played the central role in many village festivities, often inherited from earlier youth groups, whether Carnival confraternities or local militias. Despite attempts to suppress these earlier organisations, some survived as competitors to the *classe*. The latter's success was partly because it did not suffer from the disapproval of secular and religious authorities which affected the former, but this should not mask the essential similarity of its function within the village when compared with the pre-existing groups. We can see this more clearly by looking at three related activities undertaken by the conscripts, which, although often associated with the annual cycle of festivities, could take place at any time of the year: village rivalry, moral guardianship and wedding parties.

Throughout the medieval and early modern period Lorraine was divided by political borders which were constantly in dispute. Because the territories of both parties were so interwoven, the wars between the dukes of Lorraine and the city-state Metz (and its successor, the kingdom of France) set neighbouring villages against each other in violent conflict. The viciousness of these combats helped develop an antipathy between neighbouring communes, which did not necessarily end when the political boundaries became obsolete.[174]

The situation in Lorraine was not dissimilar to that examined by Robert Muchembled in Artois. He found that frequent conflict between neighbouring villages developed 'an intense xenophobia' between 'the French' and 'the Burgundians', which in turn gave rise to more violence.[175] As in Artois, so in Lorraine; a sense of communal solidarity was achieved in fighting. Local antipathies might be linked through the use of names and symbols to a larger unity. The most famous example is Joan of Arc, whose knowledge of herself as 'French' was enhanced when the young men of Domremy battled with the

---

[172] Thiriat, *La Vallée de Cleurie*, 333.
[173] Bailly, 'La Conscription', 10.
[174] The eagerness with which the *garde nationale* of Metz responded to Marshal Bouillé's call to suppress the Nancy mutiny in 1790 was seen, certainly by the inhabitants of Nancy, as typical of the rivalry between the two cities, which continues to this day: René Tournès, *La Garde nationale dans le département de la Meurthe pendant la révolution, 1789–1802*, Angers 1920, 94, 101.
[175] Muchembled, *La Violence au village*, 86–7.

'Burgundians' from the neighbouring Barrois.[176] Centuries later, when France and Lorraine were practically one country, the future abbé Grégoire discovered the residual strength of local identities in his home village on the border of the Three Bishoprics: 'Every year, in autumn when the fields had been laid bare, the young people of the French [meaning Messin] and Lorrainer villages sent challenges to one another which were always accepted; black eyes and a few broken arms ended the quarrel.'[177] In the constantly disputed commons of Lorraine village rivalries over access to economic resources became intertwined with larger disputes between Metz and Lorraine, France and the empire.[178] As a result all inhabitants had a clear sense of their communal identity and honour, whether insulting the next village or vaunting their own village's success. However, not all were called upon to defend it; this was a task devolved on to the young unmarried men of the commune.[179]

Conscripts would have grown up in a relationship of violence to their contemporaries in neighbouring villages. Numerous autobiographical accounts of childhood from Lorraine stress the importance of pasturing the village's flocks in developing their own group identity through rivalry with their neighbours.[180] If, by their own volition or through encouragement, cattle or sheep crossed the boundary into the common lands of the next village, this would be the excuse for a confrontation between their young herders. It started with a trade in insults 'worthy of the heroes of the Iliad'; insults either developed over generations and handed down in traditional form or created for the occasion by native wit.[181] (There was a whole genre of collective insults or 'blasons populaires' for neighbouring villages, which were turned into 'gospels' to be recited at length on communal occasions such as the fête and weddings.)[182] Stone-throwing might be followed by hand-to-

[176] Walter Sidney Scott, *The trial of Joan of Arc*, London 1986, 74.

[177] 'Tous les ans, lorsqu'en automne les campagnes étaient dépouillées, les jeunes gens de villages français et lorrains s'envoyaient des cartels toujours acceptés; des yeux pochés et quelque bras cassés terminaient la querelle': Henri Grégoire, *Mémoires ecclésiastiques, politiques et littéraires de M. Grégoire, ancien évêque de Blois, rédigés en 1808*, Paris 1840, 325. Grégoire's home village, was almost entirely surrounded by the hostile territory of ducal Lorraine. Perhaps his personal experience of the resulting hatreds helped shape the political enthusiasms of this leading critic of 'provincialism' during the revolution.

[178] For a comparable situation in the Pyrenees see Sahlins, *Boundaries*, 133–67.

[179] As such the situation was similar to, if not quite as bloody as, Quercy during the first half of the nineteenth century: Ploux, 'Rixes intervillageoises', 276–81.

[180] E. Froment, 'Les Rivalités entre Mandres et Norroy-sur-Vair', *Le Pays lorrain* xxii (1930), 37–9, and the response from Albert Troux in the same volume.

[181] 'L'approche des deux groupes antagonistes était digne des héros de l'Illiade se provoquant avant les combats': L'Hôte, *La Tankiote*, 64. Anyone who is familiar with Louis Pergaud's classic children's book *La Guerre au boutons* (or seen either of the two film versions) will be familiar with this kind of heroic banter.

[182] There are several collections of the *blasons populaires* used in Lorraine, the largest being Paul Rohr's *Blasons populaires et autres survivances du passé*, Nice 1970. Some of the

hand combat with traditional weapons – sabres made out of sticks with a rope hand-guard.

The greater the cohesion between members of the group, the greater the antagonism towards outsiders, and everything about the *classe* tended to increase the former and exacerbate the latter. They carried with them, in the shape of their flag, the symbol of their group loyalty and the honour of their home village. The group identity was reinforced in the songs they sang. Suzan Moroz found, in her analysis of conscript songs from Brittany, that the use of 'nous' – 'we' was stressed: 'through his adherence to the group, to the WE, each individual discovered his identity as conscript'. And the verb of which 'we' was the subject was usually an action verb, marching, fighting, drinking, acting together in a way to reinforce the sense of 'adherence to the group'.[183] The same concentration on group action can be found in the conscript songs of Lorraine: 'So it's to Gorze that we're going,/ Put the hand in the urn', or 'We must march to Saarguemines,/ To the *conseil* we really must go.'[184] Emphasising the 'we' in these songs, like the 'Tiou hi hie!' cry of Vosgian conscripts, was a way to outshine other villages.[185]

The rivalry already existent between groups of contemporaries was therefore greatly increased by the process of conscription. The state also added to the animus the *classe* felt towards its neighbours, for if one village was lucky in the *tirage*, it could only be at the expense of the others. The state even found them locations to vent their antagonisms by bringing them together on particular days. It is not surprising therefore to learn that battles between the various *classes* were a feature of conscription throughout the period. Although conscript punch-ups were not limited to the day of the *tirage*, the *classe* tended to stay aloof from the ritual confrontations of their juniors on the pastures. Instead they fought at public events such as the fête, or at night as groups tried to enter the *veillées* of neighbouring villages. In both these cases there was a particular issue at stake, access to the marriageable women of the commune.

A standard means of starting a fight at a village fête was for an outsider to try to get a dance with one of the local girls. The fête at Grandville in Ardennes started when the 'sergent de la jeunesse' invited all to 'Dance. . . . Outsiders come closer: you're permitted to dance, except for those from

'gospels' recited on communal occasions such as weddings have also survived: Louis Schely, 'Les Evangiles d'Imling, Moselle', *Le Pays lorrain* xxvi (1934), 139–41; Vital Collet, 'Evangile des sobriquets caractérisant les habitants de villages lorrains', ibid. v (1908), 442–3.

183 'Par son appartenance au group, au NOUS, chaque individu trouve son identité en tant que conscrit': Moroz, 'Analyse des chansons de conscrits', 91–3.

184 'C'est donc à Gorze que nous irons,/ Mett' la main dans le bocal': Westphalen, *Chansons populaires*, ii, no. 312; 'Wir müssen marschieren nach Saargemund,/ Zum Visitieren wohl müssen wir': Pinck, *Verglingende Weisen*, i. 139: *Wie ist doch die Falscheit so gross*.

185 Bozon, *Les Conscrits*, 67–8.

Aiglemont', Grandville's neighbouring village.[186] One can imagine that given that kind of invitation it was not long before a youth from Aiglemont attempted to butt in, and that the whole affair ended in a *mêlée* as was so often the case at these events. It is clear that 'la jeunesse' felt they were entitled to police the sexual habits of the village, particularly where these might threaten their monopoly over potential marriage partners. Westphalen described how 'if a young man from a neighbouring locality had the audacity to pay court to one or other of these girls [of the village], he had to expect to receive a punishment. Thus the gallants almost always took the precaution of being accompanied by their comrades from their own village'.[187]

This was not the only occasion on which 'la jeunesse' enforced its justice on those 'who trampled on what they considered to be their prerogative, their privileges'. They led the charivari ('bessnége' in local patois) if a widower or widow remarried, and it was they who went to visit the bridegroom 'to claim the recompense to which they had the right' (i.e. be paid to stop the noise).[188] All weddings could expect the 'garçons de droits' to come 'hunting the chicken', another phrase for a charivari, and if they were not paid off to suffer the consequences. As successors to 'la jeunesse', conscripts increasingly took on this role of policing marriages. In the Comtois village of Lantenne, for example, it was the conscripts who came to the wedding banquet to 'hunt the chicken', and they 'were quite happy if no one gave them anything, in order that they might have the pleasure of a charivari'.[189]

The 'garçons de droits' were particularly active at a wedding if the husband was from outside the village. Taxation was levied on 'foreign' husbands in the Vosges as the wedding cortège left the village for his home. The road would be barred with a ribbon, behind which 'a troop of young men', charged with bottles of spirits, invited the wedding guests to toast the bride, before approaching the husband and saying: 'The beautiful girl that we sell you,/ We'll give her for little money:/ We wish her many happy days,/ handsome children and to always be loved.' Again the new husband had to cough up if he wanted the procession to cross the ribbon.[190] As this little poem made clear, the young men believed that the young women of the village were

186 'Dansez. . . . Approchez les étrangers: c'est permis de danser, mais non pour . . . [sic] d'Aiglemont': Meyrac, *Traditions, coutumes, légendes*, 93.
187 'si un jeune homme d'une localité voisine se permettait de courtiser l'une ou l'autre de ces filles, il devait s'attendre à recevoir un châtiment. Aussi, les galants prenaient-ils presque toujours le précaution de se faire accompagner par des camarades de leur village': Westphalen, *Petit Dictionnnaire*, col. 38.
188 '. . . qui foulaient aux pieds ce qu'ils estimaient être leurs prérogatives, leurs privilèges . . . pour réclamer le salaire auxquels ils ont droit': Sauvé, *Le Folklore des Hautes-Vosges*, 99.
189 'Ils étaient tout contents qu'on ne leur donne rien pour avoir le plaisir d'un charivari': Garneret, *Un Village comtois*, 341. The same custom was reported throughout the Meuse.
190 'La belle fille que nous vous vendons,/ Pour peu d'argent nous vous la donnons;/ Nous lui souhaitons de bienheureux jours,/ De beaux enfants et d'être aimée toujours': Sauvé, *Le Folklore des Hautes-Vosges*, 93.

theirs, and could only be allowed into the hands of a stranger if he reimbursed them.

The 'garçons de droits' had more parts to play in the wedding preparations than taxing foreign bridegrooms. For example, they accompanied the bridegroom (if he was from the village) to the bride's father's house. The bride's unmarried female friends gave the men the ribbons, and 'from then on were considered "valentines", and chose their female "valentines" '.[191] At last the cortège could move off, led by the white hen on its *perche*, and followed by the musicians: 'their instruments were decorated with hanging white and red ribbons and they let joyous tunes ring out, some of which might be sung along to with more or less satirical words, which the young invited couples were fond of repeating'.[192] Then came the wedding couple themselves, followed by the 'lads' with their 'mistresses', the former 'not forgetting to "yoder", that's to say shouting and firing pistol shots from time to time, which they let off as close as possible to the bride'.[193] The 'garçons de droits' greeted the couple on their exit from the church with the same barrage of gunfire, and throughout the rest of the party played tricks on them, culminating in trying to prevent them ever getting to sleep, bursting in through the door, throwing things through the window and other 'persecutions'.[194]

The many resemblances between the behaviour of the 'garçons de droits' at a wedding and of the *classe* during the *tirage* did not pass unnoticed by contemporaries.[195] Not only their dress, but the musicians, the *perche*, the exchange of ribbons, the shouting and the shooting, the visit to the church (and the mayor for the civil ceremony), the dancing and singing, the gunpowder and the pranks, were common to the festive language of youth groups, whether for weddings or conscription rites. Of course one item was conspicuously absent from the *tirage* – a bride – or rather an alternative bride was on offer.

Much of conscript behaviour seems, therefore, to have less to do with the army and, like their predecessors, more to do with preservation of the endogamous balance of the community and the negotiation of couple formation. But why was the *classe* so successful in taking over the functions of

[191] 'Dès lors ils sont reconnus "valentins", et choisissent leurs "valentines"': Beaulieu, *Archéologie de la Lorraine*, 271.
[192] 'leurs instruments étaient ornées de rubans flottants blancs et rouges et laissent entendre de joyeux refrains dont certains pouvaient se chanter sur des paroles plus ou moins satiriques et que redonnaient volontiers les jeunes couples d'invités': Westphalen, *Petit Dictionnaire*, col. 523.
[193] '...n'oubliant pas de "yoder", c'est-à-dire de crier et de tirer de tems en tems des coups de pistolets qu'ils font partir le plus près possible de la mariée, parce que cette manière de temoigner leur joie lui est agréable, et qu'elle ne se croirait pas mariée convenablement si on ne brûlait pas de poudre à sa noce': Richard, 'Notice sur les cérémonies des mariages', 244.
[194] Sauvé, *Le Folklore des Hautes-Vosges*, 96.
[195] Henninger, *Conscrits d'Alsace*, 15.

traditional groups, and why were its activities tolerated, even encouraged by the same authorities who actively suppressed these earlier formations? Local militias were, in theory if not always in practice, finally disbanded when the French took over ducal Lorraine, while Carnival confraternities in many areas were fatally injured by the opposition of the revolutionary government; the looser organisation of 'la jeunesse' protected it for a time, but gradually its activities were supervised out of existence. This antagonism is in line with the Europe-wide trend of the political elite to withdraw from popular culture, and their subsequent displeasure at its manifestations.[196] Yet the *classe* not only survived but thrived and, as it did so under the protection of precisely those persons who were least tolerant of other marginal activities, we cannot simply see the *classe* as an alternative outlet for customary youthful exuberance. The use of similar symbols in the wedding cortege and during the *tirage* suggests one possible explanation.

Van Gennep compared societies to a house, each room being a stage in the life cycle and the threshold to each new room being a rite of passage. He also used this metaphor to differentiate between different societies: 'The more the society resembles ours in its form of civilisation, the thinner are its internal partitions and the wider and more open are its doors of communication. In a semi-civilised society, on the other hand, sections are carefully isolated, and passage from one to another must be made through formalities and ceremonies.'[197] If we accept the simile, we can see how, as France developed into the modern society known to Van Gennep, the existing organisations and rituals whose purpose was to forward the transition from one stage to the next, would become redundant. Their role in regulating courtship was no longer necessary now that the doors of society were increasingly wide open.

Men, as opposed to boys, could marry: this was the most important consequence of the transition to adulthood in societies where marriage strategies and economic strategies were intimately bound together. Both the *classe* and its predecessors were interested in courtship, but there was this difference between them: 'la jeunesse' included all young men who happened not to be married, even though some clearly were of an age to be so, but the *classe* consisted of young men who could not by law get married, until they had gone through the conscription process. A more concentrated experience of 'formalities and ceremonies' had to be undergone by conscripts before they could proceed to manhood and marriage. The *tirage* had to be endured; avoidance techniques such as running away would leave the conscript in a limbo as far as marriage prospects were concerned.[198] The government of France had,

---

[196] The growing disenchantment of European elites with popular culture has been traced by Burke, *Popular culture*, 207–43.

[197] Gennep, *The rites of passage*, 26.

[198] Before 1818 a militaman or a conscript could, in theory, marry before the *tirage* but only with the agreement of the authorities, which was seldom granted.

therefore, created a 'narrow door' from adolescence to manhood: conscription became a necessary rite of passage.

Of course it was in the nature of the *tirage* that individuals experienced the transition from boy to man in differing ways, depending on the luck of the draw. The conscript with a lucky number emerged from the *classe* into a new role within the village as a marriageable young man, but the one who drew the 'bad number' would not. Marriage was not, in normal circumstances, available for soldiers. The *tirage* selected between two types of manhood: the conscript could either marry or serve the nation, but not both. Some would be obliged to leave behind their homes and hopes, their reactions were captured in conscript songs which overwhelmingly tell of the sorrow of parting. Although some take the form of a catalogue of goodbyes, the particular focus of regret was usually the 'mistress' as in this common song, *Eugenie*: 'My darling mistress,/ I come, tears in my eyes,/ My heart full of misery,/ To say my goodbyes to you.'[199] Ten of the thirteen conscript songs collected by de Westphalen envisaged the moment when the conscript had to announce his departure (in songs, and as we will see in imagery, there was no gap between the *tirage* and receiving route instructions).[200]

However, although the folksong conscript Didiche was right to tell his fiancée Naniche, 'We can speak no further about our marriage neither', (or as the Ardennes conscript more bluntly told his Louise 'You can try and make yourself pleasing/ To other lads'), his bad luck in the *tirage* did not mean that no marriage was on offer.[201] Whether one received a good or bad ticket a wedding resulted; the 'bad ticket' was itself a certificate of marriage, but to an alternative woman – the regiment. When the conscripts of Vahl-lès-Faulquemont went to Gorze for the *tirage* they sang 'Put the hand in the urn,/ In the urn for seven years./ We'll choose as a wife/ A handsome regiment.' In the neighbouring village of Buchy the conscript told his sweetheart Julie 'Prepare my haversack, it's for departure./ Because I've chosen as a wife/ A handsome regiment.'[202]

We can understand now why the march to the *chef-lieu* and the cortège at a wedding appeared so similar – structurally they were similar. The two options appear in the songs as equal but opposite choices. This is why I stated earlier that the badges 'Fit for the girls' and 'Fit for service' were not originally

---

[199] 'Ma charmante maîtresse,/ Je viens, les larmes aux yeux,/ Le coeur plein de tristesse,/ Pour te faire mes adieux': Fourier de Bacourt, 'Anciens Chants populaires', no. 32. This particular song dates from the period of voluntary enlistment during the *ancien régime*, but the theme was adapted to the circumstances of conscription and proved immensely popular among conscripts: Garneret, *Un village comtois*, 307.

[200] Westphalen, *Chansons populaires*, ii, nos 310, 312–13, 316–22.

[201] 'Èco dè not mèriége,/ K'è n'an fauré pu pâlè': Jouve, *Chansons en patois*, 74; 'Tu peux bien chercher à plaire/ A d'autres garçons': Meyrac, *Traditions, coutumes, légendes*, 252.

[202] 'Mett' la main dans le bocal,/ Dans l'bocal pour sept ans./ Nous choisirons pour femme/ Un joli régiment', 'Prépare mon sac, c'est pour partir./ Car j'ai choisi pour femme/ Un joli régiment': Westphalen, *Chansons populaires*, ii, nos 312, 319.

synonymous, but contrasted. Although conscription deprived one of family and friends (and the opportunity of marriage with the social and economic connections that implied), the army supplied an entire new network of relations. Jean Poinsignon noticed in his study of popular song in Lorraine, that the phrases 'homme de père' (applied to the potential father-in-law) and 'homme de guerre' (applied to the commanding officer) occupied the same place in pairings of verses. From this he deduced that the father of the family and the father of the regiment had analogous roles in the mind of the singer: 'the conscript who had left his family discovered another family of which the father was the captain. This latter possessed, moreover, the traditional qualities of the family patriarch: he had authority – he was even sometimes severe – but he was understanding'.[203] If, as folksong seems to imply, the army was considered an alternative woman (and the officer an alternative father-in-law), it sheds new light on the comment of the Vosgian volunteer of Year II: 'I enjoyed myself as much in leaving as if I was going to a wedding as one of the guests.'[204]

However, if this new narrow door explains why the *classe* was able to take on the functions of earlier youth groups, we still have to account for the protection extended to it by the authorities. For an understanding of this phenomenon we must consider another traditional attribute of adult manhood, its military function. Male initiation is a feature of societies in which the burden of defence falls on clearly defined age-groups, whether in the Swiss cantons or the warrior age-sets of Africa. So far we have concentrated on the new identity that conscription gave to young men within their community. However, the transition from hearth and home to the public world of men also involved the conscript in a new relationship with the state. It was proclaimed in the symbols they used – the tricolour flag, the sappers' axes and the drum-major's mace – all borrowed from the one national institution the Lorrainer conscript knew well: the army. The songs which displayed their unity as a group also linked them to the wider community of the nation, for their 'we' contrasted with the 'they' who were the enemy. When germanophone conscripts sang on their way to the *tirage* 'We must leave behind mother and father/ And go on to the bloody field' it was not simply a statement of regret, but the assumption of a new role, not only male but French.[205]

---

[203] 'Le conscrit qui a quitté sa famille retrouve une autre famille dont le père est le capitaine. Celui-ci a d'ailleurs toutes les qualités traditionnelles de père de famille: il possède l'autorité – il est même parfois sévère – mais il est compréhensif': Jean Poinsignon, 'La Chanson populaire en Lorraine', unpubl. *mémoire de maîtrise*, Nancy II 1971, 25. Poinsignon's insight was inspired by an examination of the song *Trois Garçons de chez nous*: Westphalen, *Chansons populaires*, i, no. 3.

[204] 'je me réjouissais autant de partir que d'aller à la noce si j'y avais été invité': Jean-Claude Vaxelaire, *Mémoires d'un vétéran de l'ancienne armée (1791–1800)*, ed. H. Gauthier-Villars, Paris 1892, 16.

[205] 'Wir müssen Vater und Mutter verlassen/ Und müssen in das blutige Feld': Pinck,

Of course this was not a process without its dangers, as is apparent in another conscript song from germanophone Lorraine: three brothers pull their tickets together under the tricolour flag: the first gets the 'white' and so he wins, the second 'plays' and gets the 'blue', his fate is unclear, while the 'red' spells 'French blood' for the third.[206] The lottery, in other words, could condemn a man to die for his country. But if the song has tragic undertones, it does not hint that the conscript could escape his ordained fate. The central significance of this relationship between the youth and his country created through the *tirage* explains the attitude of the authorities towards the antics of the *classe*. When the conscript pulled his ticket he was accepting that the state had the power to order his future. As with the mass, at the heart of the *tirage* was an act of submission. No wonder that the sub-prefect was so often compared with an officiating priest, nor that the conscripts repeated Christ's words 'this is my body' as they pulled their ticket from the urn.[207] For the representatives of the state, whose authority rested on this submission, it was the most important part of the process, and they could afford to be tolerant of other conscript behaviour if they received it.

Considering how central the state and its expectations were to the conscription process, it is perhaps surprising that so few conscript songs contain any overt patriotic references. Conscript songs were much more expressive of longing and regret. This absence is particularly remarkable in warlike Lorraine. Although the germanophone population of Lorraine had a reputation for thirsting after martial glory, this is not conveyed in its conscript songs where one finds 'not one instance of euphoria, no over-flowing enthusiasm for the deeds of war to which it was [supposedly] dedi-cated'.[208] Indeed several conscript songs expressed a certain antagonism to those who obliged them to participate, not to mention anxiety about the fate that awaited them. At Varennes in the Argonne, the conscripts woke the mayor in the morning of the *tirage* with a rendition of 'To pull the ticket . . . to lead us to death.'[209] Reticence and fear are most marked in songs from

Verklingende Weisen, iv. 48, no. 35: *Rekrutenlied*. This was also the conclusion of Suzan Moroz's study of conscript songs in Brittany: 'Analyse des chansons de conscrits', 96.

[206] Pinck, *Verklingende Weisen*, i. 141.

[207] Lallement, *Folklore et vieux souvenirs*, 67.

[208] 'Réputée attachée à la vie, aux traditions et aux honneurs militaires, la population de l'Est mosellan ne manifeste, à travers ses chansons de conscrits, pas la moindre euphorie, ni le moindre débordement d'enthousiasme pour les hauts faits de guerre auxquels elle est promise': Laurent Mayer, 'Les Chansons de soldats et les chants à sujet historique, en Lorraine d'expression allemande avant 1870, d'après l'oeuvre de Louis Pinck', *Les Cahiers naboriens* iv (1990), 102. Although this statement is by-and-large correct, conscripts did occasionally sing soldiers' songs, which were more likely to contain patriotic and milita-ristic references.

[209] 'Tirer au sort . . . pour nous conduire à la mort': Comité du folklore champenois, *Travaux*, iii. 43. This refrain was borrowed from the most popular of all nineteenth-century conscript songs, distributed on thousands of 'images d'Epinal', entitled *Le Conscrit de l'an*

germanophone areas which complained 'Why is there so much deceit in the world/ That all we young lads/ Must march to the [battle-] field.'[210]

But if there was often apprehension, seldom was there outright rejection. Neither in song nor in deed did Lorrainer conscripts avoid the *tirage* and its potential consequences. In a number of songs their acceptance of their fate amounted to anticipation, change might after all be exciting. When the enthusiastic call went out 'Friends, friends, gather together,/ It's for departure, it's for departure', one feels that the conscript's later regrets expressed to his sweetheart are half-hearted.[211] This ambivalence is underlined in other conscript songs when the message of sorrow at parting is followed in the last verse by the question: 'Who composed this song?/ Three young soldiers of the squadron./ While drinking and singing/ With their pretty mistresses beside them.'[212] It reappears in one version of a germanophone song where the conscripts announced to their girlfriends (and reversing the usual emphasis of the song) 'Now we're going together into a regiment/ . . . And that's good luck for me and bad luck for you'.[213]

The *tirage* obviously gave rise to ambiguous feelings: on the one hand it was the process which gave status to the young man, recognised by both his community and the state, and put him in a position to pursue a relationship; on the other it might remove him from all he knew, perhaps for ever. Despite these worries, it appears that, in Lorraine at least, Jourdan's wishes were fulfilled and conscription became a regular stage in the lives of young men, an integrated part both of the annual cycle of the village and of the life cycle of the *classe*. With every passing year the ritual became a more institutionalised part of village life and, as with other public ceremonies it bound both participants and observers, because 'a common ritual tradition is an important element in a community's sense of its own identity'.[214]

In the examination of conscript rituals as a rite of passage I have concen-

---

dix, one verse of which went 'Le Maire, et aussi le Préfet,/ N'en sont aussi jolis cadets!/ Ils nous font tiré z'au sort,/ Pour nous conduit' z'à la mort.'

[210] 'Wie ist doch die Falschheit so gross in der Welt,/ Dass wir aller jungen Bürschlein/ Müssen marshieren ins Feld': Pinck, *Verklingende Weisen*, i. 139: *Wie ist doch die Falschheit so gross*. Conscript songs from germanophone Lorraine frequently ended in death on the bloody field of battle, an image that almost never appeared in francophone songs.

[211] 'Amis, amis rassemblons-nous, C'est pour partir, c'est pour partir': Westphalen, *Chansons populaires*, ii, nos 312, 319: *Amis, rassemblons-nous*.

[212] 'Qui a composé la chanson?/ Trois jeunes soldats de l'escadron./ Etant à boire et à chanter,/ Et leurs jolies maîtresses à leur côté': ibid. ii, nos 312, 319. This verse appears in later imagery versions of *Le Conscrit de l'an dix* from Pellerin, but not in the earlier versions from Pinot. This suggests that Pellerin picked it up from the local oral tradition. The virtue of this verse is that it could be tacked onto almost any conscript song: it appears in six of Westphalen's thirteen.

[213] 'Jetzt gehn wir mit einander unter ein Regiment/ . . . Und das ist Glück für mich und Unglück für dich,/ Ei zum Traleralera': Pinck, *Verklingende Weisen*, iii. 107, no. 33: *Conscritlied*.

[214] La Fontaine, *Initiation*, 11.

trated on the first and second stages of Van Gennep's model–separation and liminality. The period of aggregation was more muted because by that third stage the *classe* had been divided. For some their time as liminaries was at an end, they could return as full members of the community, but their unlucky 'conscrits' (in the nineteenth-century usage of the term as 'mates') could not. As soldiers, they were about to join a new group, and endure a further period *en marge* before being accepted by new comrades. In the eyes of his village peers the conscript's whole life was to be spent *en marge*.

The *degrés des âges* and the *âge viril*

Confirmation of the significance of conscription can be found in the images of *Les Degrés des âges – The steps of life* in the nineteenth century. The theme of the various ages of man was popular in medieval and Renaissance times, its best-known treatment, at least for English readers, being Jaque's speech in *As you like it*. While Shakespeare divided man's span of life into seven 'acts', others have given him three, four, nine and twelve ages to pass through. The various divisions drew on analogies with other number patterns, so that, for example, the seven ages of man were considered to be under the influence of the seven planets. In this case thirty, the period of young manhood, was the preserve of Mars and was visualised as particularly martial.[215] The design adopted by popular imagists over four centuries featured not seven ages but ten. Usually a couple were shown advancing over a stone bridge, mounting in stages of ten years from birth at the foot of the bridge to the crest at fifty years, then descending towards the death-bed at a hundred. If we consider the figures in their different ages as plotted on a graph, then the X-axis marked the passage of time, while the Y-axis could be read as social achievement.[216] The man-made bridge, therefore, represents the social world of human re-lations, while birth and death take place off the bridge in the realm of nature, shown on the left by a blossoming tree and on the right by a leafless tree. The bridge forms a tympanum in which is depicted the last judgement. Sometimes along the route five sacraments appear, acting as intermediaries between the couples and the cosmic order displayed under their feet: baptism, confirma-tion, marriage, communion and extreme unction (or burial).

The earliest known image to use the bridge of steps is a wood-engraved *Lebenstreppe* by Jörg Breu the younger, dated 1540.[217] The basic form was

---

215 The *Degrés des âges* has proved a popular theme over several centuries: Samuel Chew, *The pilgrimage of life*, New Haven, Conn. 1962; Elisabeth Sears, *The ages of man in medieval interpretations of the life cycle*, Princeton, NJ 1986.
216 Alain Charraud, 'Analyse de la représentation des âges de la vie humaine dans les estampes populaires du XIXe siècle', *Ethnologie française* i (1971), 61. Others have seen the pinnacle at fifty years as representing a physiological or intellectual peak.
217 Sears, *The ages of man*, fig. 98.

Plate 9. *Degrés des âges*: Pellerin (Epinal), *c*. 1800–14
This, the earliest of Pellerin's numerous versions, was based on a Parisian
copperplate print by Jean. Reproduced by permission of the Musée
départemental d'art ancien et contemporain, Epinal.

borrowed later in the century by the Italian copper-engraver Bertelli, whose
images inspired rue Saint-Jacques engravers in the seventeenth century.
Their major alteration was to combine the separate treatments of the ages of
man and woman into one image.[218] It probably entered the repertoire of
French provincial wood-engravers in the eighteenth century. Garnier of
Chartres remembered his uncle cutting a copy of this image in 1812 based on
a version by another Garnier brother in 1772, which itself was based on an
earlier copy of a copperplate original from the Parisian house of Basset. Basset
was, as far as I can ascertain, the first to give the name *Les Degrés des âges* to
the theme, a title that was retained by almost all later imagists.[219]

Angelika Merkelbach-Pinck recalled that images on the theme of *Les
Degrés des âges* could, at one time, be found on the wall of every inn in eastern
Moselle.[220] It was one of the most popular secular images in the nineteenth

218 Musée national des arts et traditions populaires, *Cinq Siècles d'imagerie française*, Paris
1973 (exhibition catalogue), 30–4.
219 Jusselin, *Imagiers et cartiers à Chartres*, 234, plate 17. The original Basset print was
made around 1700.
220 Merkelbach-Pinck, *Brauch und Sitte*, 17.

century and appears in the catalogue of almost every imagist. It has therefore received considerable attention from historians, who have seen in its alterations over time a reflection of changes in society.[221] During its progression from Italian copperplate to provincial French woodcut the natural and supernatural elements were gradually eroded, the social order became all important; Death, who had dominated the earliest representations of the theme, was dropped altogether, or perhaps recalled only in a tiny scene of burial. Only the figure of the Trinity presiding over the last judgement was preserved to remind viewers that all were finally subject to a higher power, and even this scene was dropped from some late nineteenth-century images. Despite these trends the personifications of the ages showed a remarkable degree of stability over time. As a typical example of the treatment from Bertelli onwards, let us take a copperplate image from the Parisian printers Jean, dating from the 1790s or the early empire, which was to be the model for most nineteenth-century imagists.[222] If we look at the ascending side we will see that the ages follow a set order: after birth and childhood the first step onto the bridge is ten (the age of 'adolescence' according to the inscription), and gender differences are already apparent as the girl carries a doll, the boy a drum. At twenty comes 'youth', pictured by a young man handing a rose, the standard symbol of courting in imagery, to a young woman. At thirty, termed the 'virile age' (a clear indication of the greater weight given to the consideration of the male's life-cycle), he is dressed in military uniform and accompanies his wife nursing their child. At forty, the 'age of discretion', the soldier has advanced up the hierarchy and wears a more gorgeous uniform of plumes and braid, but at fifty, the 'age of maturity' and the summit of his climb, he becomes a civilian again. This sequence had remained virtually unchanged over the centuries, and it accords with the first half of Shakespeare's description: the infant, the schoolboy, the lover, then, in his thirties, a soldier.[223]

This image should be compared with a contemporaneous print by one of Jean's main Parisian competitors, Basset.[224] Basset's new image had much in common both with earlier treatments from his own print-house and with that of Jean. The most significant difference occurs at age twenty. It was still the age of lovers, the man has his arms around the woman who has a rose, the symbol

---

[221] Barbara Ann Day, 'Representing ageing and death in French culture', *French Historical Studies* xvii (1992), 688–724.

[222] Jean's image (MDAACE 48.18.143) was copied by, among others, Rabier-Boulard of Orléans (MDAACE 57.3.1282), Martin-Delahaye of Lille (MDAACE 57.3.893), Clerc of Belfort (MDAACE 57.3.2609), Deckherr of Montbéliard (BN [estampes], Deckherr SNR) and Pellerin of Epinal twice, once during the empire (MDAACE 49.5.21), and again in 1826 (MDAACE 39.28.76).

[223] The suggestion that Shakespeare borrowed the idea from a cheap print or cloth-painting is certainly feasible.

[224] MDAACE 57.3.2774. Jean's contemporary, Genty of Paris, also produced an image of the *Degrés des âges* in which the man at twenty was represented by a revolutionary volunteer.

Plate 10. *Le Dégré* [*sic*] *des âges*: Desfeuilles (Nancy), 1825
This image also derives from a Parisian copperplate, but from Jean's rival,
Basset. Reproduced by permission of the Bibliothèque
nationale de France, Paris.

of love, in her hair; however, he is dressed in an infantryman's uniform, with a
musket in his hand, and the pack on his back indicates that this is a farewell
embrace. Picard-Guérin of Caen made a faithful copy of this image, while a
similar print was the inspiration for other popular imagists, such as Roiné of
Nantes, Dupont-Diot of Beauvais and Desfeuilles of Nancy.[225] Although
their treatments show some variation from Basset's, they have this in
common, that the young man of twenty years is both a lover and a foot-
soldier about to take his leave as he marches forward onto the next step. After
centuries in which these two activities – love and war – had been held as
characteristic of two different ages, in the aftermath of the *loi Jourdan* the
iconographic representative of twenty absorbed the military aspects of thirty.

During the first fifteen years of the nineteenth century, when almost every
fit twenty-year-old Frenchman would be called up as a soldier, it would make

---

[225] Hélot, *Notes sur l'imagerie*, 63; Musée départemental breton, *Imagerie populaire
bretonne*, 106; Garnier, *L'Imagerie populaire française*, i, no. 849; BN (estampes), Rd 61 pet.
fol. Desfeuilles, images de saints.

sense to depict this 'step of life' as a conscript. On the other hand, the notion that men experienced a 'martial age' around thirty had endured for three centuries even though during that time armies represented only a small percentage of the male population, many if not most of whom would have been younger than their allotted *degré*. While one cannot expect too much verisimilitude from an image that allowed mankind a life-cycle of a hundred years, none the less if the tradition-bound imagists altered the order of the ages it was to show some significant disturbance to the pattern. They now considered that his fate at twenty would have profound effects on the future life of the image's protagonist.

The iconographical connection between youth as a stage of life and conscription is made very clear in the work of a Messin imagist, Charles Thomas.[226] Instead of the ten ages of man he chose to depict four, linked to the seasons (a popular theme in French renaissance imagery, but which had been in abeyance in later periods). Winter, shown as the time for gathering wood, is linked to old age, depicted as an aged couple indoors with their grandchildren. Summer corresponds to 'youth', here shown as a crowd of conscripts on their way back from the *tirage*, their numbers secured to their hats with ribbons and with the tricolour at their head, marching into the village arm-in-arm behind three musicians.

As a way of looking at life these images are analogous to Van Gennep's metaphor of the house through whose doors one passes to the next stage of development. The link to *rites de passage* is even clearer in those images of *Les Degrés des âges* that include the sacraments at regular intervals.[227] Thus the social progression of the couple is brought into alignment with the supernatural powers which occupy the lower half of the image. A vestigial representation of the sacraments appears in a version from Dembour & Gangel of Metz.[228] On the left of the tympanum (once occupied by the Trinity and hosts of angels and devils) is shown a woman carrying a child and a couple making their way to church; they are labelled 'spring' and 'summer'. The right hand side, labelled 'autumn' and 'winter', depicts a burial. Man's arrival into, and

---

[226] MDAACE 57.3.963, *Les Saisons et les âges*. The image dates from the 1860s.

[227] These vignettes of the sacraments became increasingly rare in nineteenth-century images, and appear in none of those described above. In a contemporaneous image by Lefas of Rennes, however, a baptismal scene is shown at the foot of the children and a marriage hangs in the air above the lovers: Musée départemental breton, *Imagerie populaire bretonne*, 61.

[228] 'Au second entre dans le monde/ Le jeune Homme pour être heureux./ De tant de vices dont il abonde,/ Qu'il sorte sage et vertueux': MDAACE 57.3.2522. The image in the Musée départemental d'Epinal is in fact signed simply 'Gangel', and was passed by the *dépôt légal* on 21 Dec. 1854; at that time Gangel was having all Dembour's images, including this early woodcut, reissued in his own name. It was based on an 1835 copperplate engraving from the Nuremberg firm of Renner & Schuster: Landschaftsverbandung Rheinland, *Die Lebenstreppe: Bilder der menschlichen Lebensalter*, Cologne 1984 (exhibition catalogue), 132.

Plate 11. *Degrés des âges*: Gangel (Metz), 1854
Reproduced by permission of the Musée départemental
d'art ancien et contemporain, Epinal.

departure from, this world are mediated by rites of passage. Are the other transitions from stage to stage similarly achieved? The image from Metz is interesting for, unlike most other nineteenth-century versions, it follows the career of the man alone: his family appear at various stages but it is his story, and each stage is accompanied by a short poem. 'At twenty years, a young man', shows the youth not as a lover, but in the act of leaving home; his father pats him on the shoulder wishing him luck, he holds his downcast mother's hand in his left, while with his right he grasps his staff and raises his cap in farewell. Although not specifically dressed as a conscript, the association of the age twenty with departure for the army would have been natural in Metz, where more than a third of all young men entered the ranks at about this age. The accompanying rhyme stresses the importance of this departure, describing it as his 'entry' into the world. If conscription could be popularly described in terms of a second birth, then we are certainly entitled to consider it a rite of passage.

A process of transformation occurred in the conservative aesthetic of imagists during the nineteenth century. In their treatments of *Les Degrés des âges* the conscript gradually replaced the lover at the age of twenty, and the suitor replaced the warrior at the age of thirty. The most obvious explanation is that this ordering more accurately reflected the experience of their consumers since the introduction of conscription. Final confirmation of this switch can be found in a lithograph produced by the Paris firm Bés & Dubrueil around 1855. Their depiction of the couple at the age of twenty had been borrowed from contemporary images of the *Départ du conscrit*. The tearful conscript, wearing his beribboned hat with the unlucky number eighteen, is comforting his fiancée, before leaving to join his regiment (his pack is already on his back). We next see him at age thirty returned from the wars and leading his fiancée, now his bride, to the altar.[229]

Individual responses to conscription

When Xavier Thiriat asked a Vosgian farmer how old he was, he was told 'class of 1818 and an excellent year!'[230] Every young Frenchman in the nineteenth century grew up knowing that he would belong to a *classe* in his twentieth year, and he knew that this would be a defining experience in his life. It is probable, however, that the full importance of the *tirage* only impressed itself on the conscript as the day itself approached. Hence, perhaps, the reason why more men emigrated illegally from Lorraine at the age of twenty, using the passport obtained for a younger brother, than emigrated legally at the age of nineteen.[231] The growing awareness of what it will mean to him individually is vividly described in Erckmann-Chatrian's *Histoire d'un conscrit de 1813*: at first the apprentice gives no mind to the disasters of the retreat from Russia so wrapped up is he with the idea of marrying his Catherine, but this vision fades before the announcement of his forthcoming conscription. To his own fears are added the warnings of his boss, aunt, girlfriend, neighbours, and the threats of his rival, the pedlar Pinacle (who, as a seller of ribbons, had an economic as well as a personal interest in the conscription).[232] This fictional exception aside, the conversations which influenced the way the conscript approached the urn are lost to history, but echoes of them can be found in folktales and songs, and these suggest that he did not lack for advice.

In Lorraine and the surrounding provinces of eastern France there was little of the collective resistance to conscription that was so commonplace in the south and west of France (although there were occasional exceptions). This did not mean that every conscript stepped up willingly: there was a range of individual responses that tended to be less enthusiastic than those of the *classe* as a group. The French language does not draw a clear distinction between luck, destiny and magical intervention (all are *le sort*), so it is not surprising that conscripts believed their chances in the lottery could be influenced. Denied expression in the public sphere dominated by the activities of the *classe*, the 'hidden transcripts' of opposition (as defined by James Scott)

---

229 Duchartre and Saulnier, *L'Imagerie parisienne*, 106.
230 'classe de 1818 et un an de bon!': Thiriat, *La Vallée de Cleurie*, 333.
231 Maire, 'Conscrits en Amerique', 223.
232 Erckmann and Chatrian, *Histoire d'un conscrit*, 918.

were developed in 'sequestered places', particularly in the conscript's home.[233]

The day before the *tirage* the hero of a Picard folktale resolves to sell himself to the devil. Immediately the devil appears to remind him of all the reasons why he does not want to go:

> Right. You're going to pull a ticket tomorrow morning and I know that you must bring back a bad number. You'll be a soldier for seven years, seven years! . . . Have you really thought about it? I've no need to tell you how unhappy you'll be, obliged to obey the first corporal who comes along, sent to the guard house for the tiniest fault, poorly fed, exposed to the heat and the cold and I don't know what. And then war will come and you'll get yourself killed I don't know where and I don't know why. Furthermore you'll have to leave Catherine, your sweetheart, who will surely console herself rapidly, and at your return you'll find her married to someone other than you![234]

The devil, master of the lawyer's trick of making two irreconcilable facts appear as consequential, uses his persuasive skills to frighten the conscrpt into accepting his bargain – his soul for a high number. His words might easily have been borrowed from one of the numerous semi-legal 'traders in human flesh' or illegal 'swindlers' who made a living from the fears engendered by conscription. 'To better deceive the young men these wretches start by frightening them with tales of the country where they'll have to go, of the war to which they'll have to march' wrote Vaublanc, the prefect of the Moselle in 1806, who was conducting a personal crusade against swindlers.[235]

One group of 'professionals' who cashed in on conscription were the village dentists, blacksmiths and 'guérisseurs de secret' who, for a fee, would arrange or dissemble some injury or affliction that would earn a discharge at the *conseil*. Especially popular was the loss of the trigger finger or the two teeth necessary to tear open a cartridge. However, if the *conseil* suspected that these were self-mutilations the conscript would end up serving his seven years in the pioneers.[236] The range of temporary maladies that could be induced or

---

[233] James C. Scott, *Domination and the arts of resistance: hidden transcripts*, London 1990, 120–4.

[234] 'Voilà. Tu vas tirer au sort demain matin et je sais que tu dois ramener un mauvais numéro. Tu seras soldat pendant sept ans, sept ans! . . . y penses-tu bien? Je n'ai pas besoin de te dire combien tu seras malheureux, obligé d'obéir au premier caporal venu, mis à la salle de police ou à la prison pour la moindre faute, mal nourri, exposé à la chaleur, au froid, que sais-je? Et puis la guerre viendra, tu iras te faire tuer je ne sais où et pour je ne sais quoi. Et puis encore il te faudra laisser Catherine, ta bonne amie, qui se consolera bientôt sans doute et qu'à ton retour tu trouveras mariée à un autre que toi!': E. Henry Carnoy, *Littérature orale de la Picardie*, Paris 1883, 90: *Le Diable et le jeune homme qui ne voulait point être soldat*.

[235] 'Pour mieux tromper les jeunes ces misérables commencent par les effrayer sur le pays où ils doivent aller, sur la guerre à laquelle ils doivent marcher. Ils inspirent la peur à la plus brave jeunesse de l'univers': Kappaun, *La Conscription en Moselle*, 132.

[236] Bailly, 'La Conscription', 9.

simulated was far greater (oral knowledge as to how to induce some of these was still in circulation among conscripts at the end of the twentieth century). As with mutilation, particular methods were specific to particular areas, suggesting the influence of professional advice.[237] For example, the 'sorcerers' of Upper Brittany used bees to sting conscripts' testicles, but this practice does not seem to have caught on outside the region.[238] The numbers who tried trickery despite the potential penalties were significant; no less than one in ten of those declared 'fit for service' at the Meaux *conseil de révision* had presented themselves with some made-up malady, and of course there is no way of knowing the number who were successful.[239] However, the latter group was probably not very large, for the *conseil* quickly became wise to the more common frauds, and in addition could expect to receive denunciations from disgruntled fellow-members of the *classe*.[240]

At least the 'guérisseurs de secret' provided a service for their fee, the real con-men were those who, like the devil in the tale above, extorted money in return for a 'sure-fire' method of obtaining a high number. A local legend from the Ardennes records how a fugitive from justice, hiding in the woods near Montmédy, made a living from this source:

> People said that he had made a pact with the devil to stop the conscripts get-ting a bad number: and it's certain that the hands of his five sons had been lucky enough, when they took them out of the urn they discovered that they were legally exempt from all military service. Thus, for this reason it was easy for him to exploit public credulity and, so they say, under the cover of religion, or rather sorcery, he duped them shamelessly, making them pay with good money for his famous 'secret' which, however, was not always successful. For him, make no mistake, it was a matter of chance. So much the better if [Fate] smiled on the conscript.[241]

The fearsome reputation of this sorcerer meant he had little to fear from those conscripts for whom his formula was unsuccessful. In general those believed to have the power to conjure a high number out of the hat also had the power to condemn a conscript to a low one, so they were treated with respect. One young man from near Montbéliard blamed his unlucky number three in the

---

237 Aron, Dumont and Le Roy Ladurie, *Anthropologie du conscrit francais*, 32.
238 Sébillot, *Coutumes populaires de la Haute-Bretagne*, 83.
239 Bailly, 'La Conscription', 9.
240 Mignot, *La Conscription*, 25.
241 'On raconta qu'il avait fait un pacte avec le diable pour empêcher les conscrits de tirer un mauvais numéro: et il est certain que ses cinq fils, tant ils avaient eu la main heureuse, en la retirant de l'urne, s'étaient trouvés, de droit, exemptés de tout service militaire. Aussi, est-ce pour cela qu'il lui fut très facile d'exploiter la crédulité publique et, dit-on, sous le couvert de la religion, ou mieux de la sorcellerie, il l'exploita sans pudeur, faisant payer en bonne monnaie son fameux secret qui, cependant, ne fut pas toujours des plus efficaces. C'était pour lui, on le comprend, une affaire de chance. Tant mieux lorsqu'elle souriait au conscrit': Meyrac, *Traditions, coutumes, légendes*, 215.

tirage of 1863 (and subsequent seven years in the colonial marines) on his impoliteness to a fortune-teller.[242] But conscripts sometimes had the power to exact retribution: Thérèse Forget of Crèvechamps in the Meurthe was sent to prison for six months on the complaint of three young men for whom she had failed magically to supply high numbers, despite being paid 100 *francs* by each of them.[243]

The pedlars who sold ribbons and cockades on the day of the *tirage* were in an ideal position to trade in these formulae. They already specialised in selling similar magico-religious prayers, celestial letters and trinkets to ward off all kinds of dangers, and they were present at the very occasions when the conscript was most vulnerable to the conversation of 'swindlers', outside the town hall on the day of the *tirage*. Vosgian pedlars were famous for the efficacy of their 'formulae'.[244] A number of these have been preserved, including some from pre-revolutionary days. The folklorist Louis Lallement collected the following eighteenth-century injunction, which was still in use among conscripts at the end of the second empire:

> Learn the following by heart: in the name of God the father almighty, come out militia ticket, I conjure you that you have no more powers over me than the devil has over the priest during the sacrament of holy mass. . . . This is my body. Pull with your left-hand and make the sign of the cross with your tongue before you put your hand into the lottery. One must have confidence to succeed.[245]

Although the *classe* as a group made pilgrimages in order to obtain good luck, most attempts to alter the conscript's course were private, within the domestic setting.[246] The duty of protecting the conscript, or at least divining his

242 Coulon, 'Légendes, croyances et contes populaires', 231.
243 Camille Maire, 'Sept Ans de service . . . et comment y échapper', *La Revue lorraine populaire* xix (1993), 314.
244 Crampon, 'Le Culte de l'arbre', 292. The use of the word 'recette' (recipe or formula), rather than prayer, is a good indication of how people considered these items.
245 'Yvous aprendrés par couer ceci: au nom de Dieu le pere tout puissent sort billet de Milise, je te conjure que tus nca aucuns pouvoirs sur moy non plus que le Diable sur les praittre au Saint Sacréfices de la Sain Messe et que est a me quittée lorsque je [profèrerai]. Ce si hoc est meine Corpus me homme. Vous tirés de la main gauche et vus fairés le signe de la croix avec votre langue avant que de maitre la main au tirage. Hil faut avoir la confiance pour réucy': Lallement, *Contes rustiques*, 230. The same formula was found among conscripts in Moselle. Papa Gerné, Pinck's main informant, had a reputation as a sorcerer (or, as his son put it, 'er konn ebbes!'). He also sold conscripts formulae, but similarly he warned them 'Awer mr muss dron glawe!' – one must believe!: Merkelbach-Pinck, *Aus der lothringer Meistube*, i. 174.
246 According to Geneviève Massignon, those conscripts whose prayers on the feast of Saint Nicolas had been answered subsequently gave a blessed bread to the church: 'Coutumes et chants de conscrits', 173. On the way to the *tirage* conscripts did visit shrines such as the Virgin's oak in the forest of the Argonne. However, as in this case, most such *classe* activities (as opposed to individual behaviour) was concerned with divination rather than just protection: after making their requests the conscripts each lit a candle which, if it

future, largely fell to the women of his household, whose precautions were often supposed to be hidden from their object if they were to be efficacious. It was only after the *Conscrit de 1813* emerged from the town hall with his number seventeen that his aunt, confounded by her failure, revealed that she had placed 'a piece of rope' in his pocket which was supposed to protect him.[247] Michel Bozon has suggested that this was because 'the person concerned must meet his destiny as a "virgin" '.[248]

There was considerable variety among these domestic preventative measures. In part this was the result of the market in them – those who made a living from conscripts encouraged new and more powerful remedies – but there is also a sense in which, faced with a new danger, those charged with confronting it had not yet reached a consensus on the best line of defence. Not that there was much new in the responses they devised, the incantations, the talismans, the rituals were all borrowed from existing magic formulae. None the less, by the internal logic of magic, some mechanisms were more readily adaptable than others: for example the bones of toads and other reptiles hidden in the conscript's clothes on the day of the *tirage* probably derive from similar customs designed to protect soldiers in battle.[249] Thus it is possible to establish patterns in the variety.

The obvious source of supernatural help was God and the saints. Francophone conscripts from the Meurthe on pilgrimage to Xouaxange to implore the Virgin of Rinting passed germanophone Mosellans on their way to visit Notre-Dame des Hermites in Switzerland.[250] In the Vosges the conscript attended mass the evening before the *tirage*.[251] He also dipped the hand used to pull the ticket (the left because it was closest to the heart) into holy water.[252] Yet these religious practices were not separate from, nor considered different from, other magical practices. The Vosgian conscript not only went to his mass but also had to remember which foot to start out on in the morning (as for all successful journeys it had to be the right); the Messin conscript not only had to say five *Aves* and *Paters*, he had to give charity to the first beggar he met on the way to the *tirage*, and when in town buy a pack of cards and place the king of spades under his left shoe, all the time remembering a complex prayer to offer over the urn. In these incantations the names of saints were mixed with phrases drawn from magic, some with diabolical overtones: '*Resiété et rafité* in honour of Saint Escorbis. God give,

---

rose to the right, announced a high number. The candle revealed the conscript's fate but did not prevent it: Comité du folklore champenois, *Travaux*, iii. 42.

247 Erckmann and Chatrian, *Histoire d'un conscrit*, 918. The rope was probably from a hangman's noose, a widely respected magic talisman.

248 'l'intéressé devait arriver vierge face au destin': Bozon, *Les Conscrits*, 92.

249 Snakeskin, for example, which had long been used by soldiers as a talisman to ward off bullets, was subsequently used during the *tirage*: Seignolle, *Le Folklore de Provence*, 139.

250 L'Hôte, *La Tankiote*, 87; Merkelbach-Pinck, *Brauche und Sitte*, 146.

251 Richard, *Traditions populaires*, 88.

252 Lallement, *Folklore et vieux souvenirs*, 67.

preserve me from the black ticket. In honour of the blessed Virgin Mary: *satoné, potené, aperota arma et armatoria.*' Westphalen suggested that the last words were based on the magic square SATOR-AREPO-TENET-OPERA-ROTAS, often used in black magic.[253] As we have seen in the case of the Picard conscript, the devil could just as easily take a hand in destiny. There-fore, one should not look at the use of Catholic ceremonial and liturgy as simply the practices of the faithful: they were not done only in the hope of a Christian's reward, but with the specific intention of controlling the *tirage*. The prayers, the signs of the cross made with the tongue and the phrases derived from the mass were equal in importance to which hand one used to pick the number or which foot one started out on that morning.[254] If they failed 'the conscripts did not fail to accuse the sub-prefect of partiality', and in cases where money had changed hands the source of the magic 'recipe' might be pursued in the courts.[255] Yet the widespread use of the words 'Hoc est corpus meum' at the very moment that he was handed his ticket certainly reinforced the image of the *tirage* as a secular mass, with the sub-prefect as officiating priest, and acceptance of the ticket as incorporation into a group of initiates.

In addition to the prayers of the conscript himself were those of his female relatives, in particular his mother. We have seen that while the *classe* and almost the entire male population of the village readied themselves for their visit to the *chef-lieu* on the day of the *tirage*, women were often obliged to keep off the streets in case of bad luck. Once the cortège had set off, however, they had their own role to play, visiting local chapels (military saints were most favoured).[256] In Brittany and Normandy, mothers made pilgrimages to holy springs or rocks to make their prayers, often accompanied by complex perfor-mances.[257] Merkelbach-Pinck tells the cautionary tale of a woman who prom-ised to make a pilgrimage to the shrine at Lenzweiler if her son pulled a high number. Although her prayer was fulfilled, she neglected to keep her promise and her son died soon after.[258] But there were other ways for women to protect their men-folk. During the preparation of the conscript's attire, small items would be introduced into his clothing without his knowledge. In Brittany salt or the leaves of gladioli cut into tiny pieces were placed in his pocket; the number he pulled would be as high as number of grains.[259] More commonly a silver coin was hidden in his left shoe, as a talisman against the

[253] 'Resiété et rafité en l'honneur de St.-Escorbis. Dieu me donne, me préserve du billet noir. En l'honneur de la benoîte Vierge Marie: satoné, potené, aperota arma et armatoria': Westphalen, *Petit Dictionnaire*, col. 115.
[254] Lallement, *Contes rustiques*, 230.
[255] 'les conscrits ne manquaient pas d'accuser le sous-préfet de partialité': Bailly, 'La Conscription', 15.
[256] Bozon, *Les Conscrits*, 92.
[257] Bayon, 'Sobriquets et superstitions militaires', 53.
[258] Merkelbach-Pinck, *Aus der lothringer Maistube*, i. 195.
[259] Sébillot, *Coutumes populaires de la Haute-Bretagne*, 81.

evil eye.[260] Over the border at Charleroi in Belgium altar-boys were bribed to hide silver coins under the altar cloth during mass, so that they would be blessed with the host thus vastly increasing their protective power.[261] In the Ardennes a piece of wax from an Easter votive candle performed the same function.[262] The most telling of all these hidden additions to the conscript's costume was his own umbilical cord, carefully preserved after birth by his mother under the fire-place, the very physical symbol of his ties to hearth and home.[263]

The intention to preserve the links between the conscript and his community seems to be the inspiration behind many of the methods used. On the eastern slopes of the Vosges a wedding ring 'not having yet seen water' was hidden on the conscript.[264] Was the urn supposed to recognise the power of that alternative rite of manhood, marriage, and the bonds that it created to the community? In Champagne the conscript read the first part of the Gospel according to Saint John, while marking the place with the key of the house and thus making sacred his own ties to the household.[265]

The ties that the conscript tried to preserve were not just with his family, but with his physical home. In Belfort, each conscript took with him to the *tirage* a stone from the 'michotte', the ruined tower that overlooked the town. If, despite this precaution, he was called up he took his stone with him, in the hope that this talisman would keep him safe until he could see the tower again.[266] The conscript also looked to the wider network of community relationships to protect him, not least its dead. In the Ardennes the conscript visited the grave of the last person to die in the village and placed five nails in the form of a cross on it.[267] In Hohwarth in Alsace he visited the grave of the most recently deceased villager at midnight, and implored to be allowed to stay near him.[268] In germanophone Lorraine this prayer was repeated nine times, and the more daring would then descend into the crypt, to hear if the bones jangled (a sign that the prayer had been answered).[269] Often the

---

[260] Hemmerle, 'La Conscription', 4. Similar uses for silver coins are recorded by Lallement, Meyrac, Richard and de Westphalen.

[261] Alfred Harou, 'Sobriquets et superstitions militaires: le tirage au sort en Belgique', *Revue des traditions populaires* ii (1887), 457.

[262] Meyrac, *Traditions, coutumes, légendes*, 189.

[263] Jeanmaire, *La Tradition en Lorraine*, 35.

[264] 'un anneau de mariage n'ayant pas encore vu de l'eau était aussi cousu dans le vêtement du candidat': Hemmerle, 'La Conscription', 4; Bayon, 'Sobriquets et superstitions militaires', 54. Other, similar items used in Brittany included the wedding ring of a woman married that year, or the baptismal bonnet of the first male child born to a household: Sébillot, *Coutumes populaires de la Haute-Bretagne*, 81.

[265] Comité du folklore champenois, *Travaux*, iii. 42.

[266] Bozon, *Les Conscrits*, 93.

[267] Meyrac, *Traditions, coutumes, légendes*, 189.

[268] Alfred Pfleger, 'Conscritsaberglauben und alte Conscritslieder', *Neuer Elsässer Kalender* (1930), 99.

[269] Merkelbach-Pinck, *Brauche und Sitte*, 146.

conscript would carry away something from the grave, if not a bone as in Poitou then at least leaves of a plant growing on it which would be carried as a talisman on the day of the *tirage*.[270] Such talismans, which invoked the power of their ancestors as protectors of the community, had previously been carried by villagers when absent from the village, and continued to be used as such by conscripts in the army. However, the fairly widespread practice of placing iron nails on graves before the *tirage* may have been a way of preventing the dead claiming the conscript for themselves, death being his presumed fate if he was unlucky in the *tirage*.

The use of metals in such magic was commonplace. The silver coin and the gold wedding ring were inherently powerful. Iron, particularly in the form of meteorite stone, had been used as protection against the evil eye long before it was used as a talisman during the *tirage*.[271] In a series of prints issued by Wentzel of Wissembourg, an Alsatian conscript prepares for the *tirage* by taking an old trowel (which had dug the earth of home) at dawn to the blacksmith to turn into three nails which he knocks each day a bit further into a poplar (a custom normally associated in Alsace with death, but more generally in France with divination: if the head fell off before the conscript returned to the village, he would die in the army), and making his own amulet from the legs of three toads and a piece of his grandfather's felt hat.[272] Although there is no evidence that this complex formula was ever practised (Wentzel's prints were intended to satirise rustic customs), his choice of material is itself informative. That a nail should commonly become symbolic of the conscript's fate (rather than, for example, the votive candle) is, perhaps, the result of the relationship between soldiers, blacksmiths and iron, a relationship that we will examine later.

It is impossible to ascertain how commonly any of these customs were practised, but the numerous reported examples suggest that many conscripts took at least some precautions on the day of the *tirage*. Conscripts from all over Lorraine and surrounding regions, according to the widespread evidence of folklorists, left home on their right foot (avoiding women, priests and animals), with a silver coin in their left shoe, pulled their ticket with their left hand after making the sign of the cross with their tongue and repeating 'Hoc est corpus meum'. However, for those of a more practical bent of mind, there were alternative means of avoiding a high number.

Although Vaublanc detested all who preyed on the fears of the conscripts, his personal crusade to stamp out 'swindlers' concentrated on the people best placed to make a packet from the *tirage*, those involved in its administration. Mayors, army officers and doctors all appear on Vaublanc's list of suspects, but less frequently in subsequent criminal prosecutions, because the only person who could prove the accusation was the one with the least interest in doing

270 Bayon, 'Sobriquets et superstitions militaires', 53.
271 Ibid; Sébillot, *Coutumes populaires de la Haute-Bretagne*, 80.
272 Henninger, *Conscrits d'Alsace*, 17.

so, the conscript himself. Therefore reported cases probably represent only the tip of the iceberg. It did not take long for Captain Godet, charged with recruitment in the Vosges during the first empire, to be visited by a doctor hoping to come to an understanding (and the rather opaque language he used to describe this occasion in his memoirs might suggest that he was not altogether adverse).[273] It was partly to undermine the source of this corruption that replacements had been reintroduced by Jourdan's successor, Lacuée, in Year VIII, but during the war these were nearly impossible to find, and until their trade became free in 1832, bribery remained an option.[274] However, its very efficacy made it expensive: a military doctor serving with the conseil de révision in 1811 received, it was alleged, 3,150 and 4,500 francs to obtain discharges for two conscripts.[275] At these prices his services were well beyond the means of the average draft-dodger.

Bribery was not commonly dealt with in the folk literature of conscription, but the prospect of being replaced was a very popular theme. The soldier's sweetheart in a song from germanophone Lorraine goes to the captain and demands 'Give me a soldier, I'll pay what he costs,/ He is my heart's only comfort!'[276] Although almost entirely in the female voice, this song was sung by a man, as was another conscript song from Bresse: 'My father has some écus,/ They are for you, my dear./ . . . That will prevent you/ From going to the army.'[277] (A Vendéan variant of this song, which was sung by a woman, presents a rather different message: the man is not bought out but instead signs over his farm to his fiancée, who in return occasionally cries for him when at parties and dances.)[278] It should not be thought that putative wives or fathers-in-law rescuing conscripts by buying replacements were common. In practice it was his father to whom the conscript looked if he needed a replacement, as in this germanophone conscript song: 'Marching on manoeuvres/ And a note back home/ For my father to send me money/ That I buy myself out.'[279] However, the fact that, in song, it was usually his girlfriend who offered to buy the soldier out leads us again to see the army in opposition to potential relationships with women. The Vosgian conscript Nicolas Etienne sang 'I've still got some sous to buy myself [out]./ I don't give a toss for [the

273 Capitaine Godet, 'Mémoires du capitaine Godet', Carnets de la sabretache, fasc. 323, Paris 1928, 445.
274 Two doctors, Benoist of Lunéville and Toussaint of Saint-Nicolas-de-Port, were sentenced in 1826 for 'délit d'escroquerie en matière de recrutement': Maire, 'Conscrits en Amerique', 230.
275 Kappaun, La Conscription en Moselle, 142.
276 'Gebt mir ein Soldat, ich zahl, was es kost,/ Es ist meim Herz sein einzigster Trost!': Pinck, Verklingende Weisen, i. 135: Ich hab ein Schatz.
277 'Mon père a des écus,/Ils sont pour toi, mon cher./ . . . Ce sera pour t'empêcher/ D'y aller à l'armée': Carru, Les Chansons des conscrits, 17: La Veille du tirag.
278 Massignon, 'Coutumes et chants de conscrits', 174–6.
279 'Ins Manöver marschieret,/ Und ein Brieflein nach Haus,/ Dass mir mein Vater Geld schickt,/ Dass ich mich loskauf': Pinck, Verklingende Weisen, iii. 109, no. 34: Soldatenlied.

conscription],/ I want to marry.'[280] The song ends with the conscript being welcomed at the *veillée* of his potential father-in-law, so his hopes were probably well-placed.

Although in song replacement appears as an alternative to military service, it was an option little exercised by Lorrainer conscripts. In France as whole, from 1818 to the end of the second empire, between one fifth and a quarter of the *classe* on average found themselves replacements, but in Moselle the average was under 9 per cent. On the contrary many Lorrainers sold themselves as replacements in other departments. The germanophone arrondissement of Sarreguemines was the best source of replacements in Moselle, which was in turn one of the best in France. They were, in fact, an export industry of the region.[281] It is perhaps surprising, therefore, that the hope of replacement had a far more important place in germanophone songs (including the most popular local conscript song *Zum Strassburg*), than in francophone ones. The explanation lies in the fact that, although these songs seem to present the words of fathers, fathers-in-law and girlfriends, they were primarily sung by the conscripts themselves, who put the words they wanted to hear into the mouths of the other characters. This was not a real possibility, nor even just wishful-thinking, but rather the theme of replacement served in songs as a metaphor for the conscripts' desire to stay with their families and loved-ones. Hence in most of these songs the army keeps the soldier despite the offer of money. In practice, no one was going to pay to keep the conscript at home.

Price is one explanation for the low level of take-up. As a replacement cost between 500 and 2,500 francs only the well-off could avail themselves of one (which was precisely the government's intention, for only the sons of fathers who met the property voting qualification mattered). But in Lorraine many who could afford one none the less chose to serve, and over France as a whole there is no direct correlation between wealth and the demand for replacements. Indeed relatively wealthy Lorraine was covered in agents from insurance houses which specialised in protection against the *tirage*, looking for conscripts with lucky numbers willing to stand in for their less fortunate, and less militarily-minded compatriots in other regions.[282] The father of Papa Gerné, the main contributor to Pinck's *Verklingende Weisen*, was a 'dealer in human flesh', and Gerné learnt several of his songs from the young men who stayed with them before they were sent to replace conscripts in Normandy,

---

[280] 'Ja co dé sou pour mi rèchetè./ Jè m' fou bé d'clè,/ Jè m'vie mèriè': Louis Géhin, 'Gérardmer à travers les âges: 2eme partie', *Bulletin de la Société philomatique vosgienne* xx (1894–5), 10.

[281] Labate, *Le Recrutement de l'armée*, 26–31.

[282] The trade in replacements is admirably documented in Bernard Schnapper, *Le Remplacement militaire en France: quelques aspects politiques, économiques et sociaux du recrutement au XIXe siècle*, Paris 1968, with additional information supplied by Nuria Sales de Bohigas, 'Marchands d'hommes et sociétés d'assurance contre le service militaire au XIXe siècle', *Revue d'histoire économique et sociale* xlvi (1968), 339–80.

Burgundy and Paris.[283] Another innkeeper turned 'soul-merchant', Michel Matter of Alteckendorf, has left us his memoirs of the business during the second empire, when he persuaded many young Alsatians lucky in the *tirage* to replace rich but unlucky Norman youths 'who did not have much martial spirit'.[284] The army was not enthusiastic about replacements, who tended to have poor discipline records.[285] Matter likewise described his clients as not dissimilar to the 'Rowdies und Loafers' of the London docks. Selling one's services as a replacement was clearly an option which, as we will see with volunteering, appealed to more restless spirits.

Draft-dodging, either before or after the *tirage* was the poor man's alternative to bribery or replacement (though the economic repercussions on the conscript's family could be draconian). On average, about 1 per cent of the *classe* in Lorraine took this option, much less than in some other areas of France, such as Corsica, where up to a quarter of the *classe* regularly failed to turn up.[286] In the south and west of France draft-dodgers could rely on support from their community.[287] In Lorraine there was no such anti-conscription consensus; if Lorrainer conscripts stayed locally they would inevitably be denounced and caught. This does not mean that the thought did not cross the mind of young conscripts. In the memoirs of many veterans one can find allusions similar to Vaxelaire's confession that on the way to join his new battalion near Saint-Dié 'I looked towards the right, which was the Gérardmer side [his home region], I was on the verge of running away'.[288] Most, either for honourable or practical reasons, did not act on this momentary impulse, but Jean Carchon of Chermisey in the Vosges did, and luckily kept a record of his six years of evasion (before he finally received a pardon in 1799). If his original decision was the result of disgust with army life, his subsequent career as a draft-dodger was due to meeting his future wife while on the run.[289] In life as in popular culture, marriage and the military were counterpoised.

The only real alternative to conscription was emigration, an alternative form of even more long-term separation. Yet in folklore the army was placed in opposition to relations with the opposite sex. Conscripts in folksong chose draft-dodging out of love for their girlfriends, rather than to find their way to

---

283 Pinck, *Verklingende Weisen*, i. 277–8.

284 'welche nicht viel militärischen Geist haben': Kassel, *Conscrits, Musik und Tanz*, 43.

285 Schnapper, *Le Remplacement militaire*, 150.

286 Aron, Dumont and Le Roy Ladurie, *Anthropologie du conscrit francais*, map 6.

287 The patterns of resistance to conscription in the south-west of France which emerged during the revolution and first empire, were maintained during subsequent regimes: Forrest, *Conscripts and deserters*, 43–73.

288 'je regardai sur la droite, que c'était du côté de Gérardmer, je fus sur le point de m'évader': Vaxelaire, *Mémoires d'un vétéran*, 18. The moment when conscripts left their 'petit pays' was the critical point as far as those charged with their safe arrival at their depots were concerned.

289 Pierfitte, 'Les Volontaires vosgiens', 106–28.

Le Havre and a ship to the new world.[290] In a Messin conscript song the new soldier, on being told to swear loyalty to the fatherland, replies 'Yes, I swear my commandant,/ That in eight days I'm buggering off,/ There will be no gendarmerie nor national guards/ Who can stop me from seeing my darling under the elms.'[291] If he was to remain faithful to his Jeannette he could not make an alternative vow. However, the song should not be read as a sign of his actual plans, but again as a metaphor for his desire. It acted as a message between the conscript and his girlfriend, reassuring the latter that he intended to remain faithful, even if he could not prevent their separation.

Volunteers

With occasional exceptions, such as Georges Brodberger of Guéblange (who killed his father so that, as the eldest son of a widow, he would be discharged by the 1854 *conseil*), the conscripts of Lorraine did not take any of the more drastic courses of action to avoid the separation of military service.[292] Indeed the largest group of Lorrainers who failed to turn up for the *tirage* were the volunteers who had engaged before their twentieth year. Even in the dying years of the first empire between a quarter and a third of Mosellans had volunteered before their conscription.[293] This eagerness for military service was a feature of all subsequent regimes up to 1870. Between 1818 and the Franco-Prussian war, 13,318 Mosellans volunteered, 35 per cent of what was required from the department by conscription.[294] The other departments of Lorraine were not far behind: between 1818 and 1826, when Moselle was ranked second after Paris in the proportion of volunteers per *classe* (20.31 per cent), Meurthe came third with 16.33 per cent, and Meuse came seventh with 10.94 per cent.[295] The Vosges was some way down the list, but their martial reputation had already been secured when the Convention Nationale renamed the Place des Vosges in gratitude for the department's readiness to supply volunteers for the armies of the revolution. Captain Godet, who conducted five *tirages* in the Vosges between 1806 and 1809, amazed his colleagues in other departments by being able to report only one deserter

290 Maire, 'Conscrits en Amerique', 211–29.
291 'Oui, Je vous jur' mon commandant,/ Que dans huit jours je fous le camp,/Il n'y aura gendarmerie ni gardes nationaux/ Qui m'empêcher d'aller voir ma mie sous les ormeaux': Westphalen, *Chansons populaires*, ii, no. 326: *En arrivant au régiment*.
292 Brodberger was guillotined for his crime: Maire, 'Sept Ans de service', 315.
293 Kappaun, *La Conscription en Moselle*, 195–201. Kappaun calculates that 19,000 Mosellans donned the uniform of the empire, more than 6,000 of whom were volunteers. As the total number of voluntary enlistments in the French army in the period was only 52,000 (or 2.17% of its strength) one can appreciate the value of the Moselle's contribution: Girardet, *La Société militaire*, 16.
294 F.-Y. Lemoigne, 'Militaria', *Les Cahiers lorrains* n.s. xxvi (1974), 109.
295 Aron, Dumont and Le Roy Ladurie, *Anthropologie du conscrit français*, map 1.

during the whole period: 'Shouldn't one say it one more time, what a depart-ment!'[296]

This enthusiasm for army life, a complete contrast with the situation in many other areas of France, cannot be considered as a by-product of the revo-lution and the changes that it wrought in the relationship between citizen and state, for the regional tradition of military service long pre-dated it. In 1789 the chevalier des Pommelles noted that Lorraine supplied one soldier for every seventy-two members of the population (the second best result, after Alsace).[297] In 1764 1.327 per cent of the population of ducal Lorraine was serving in the armed forces of France, a higher proportion than any other region, and although it is hard to establish figures for the first half of the eighteenth century, before Lorraine came under French control, there is little doubt that the tradition of serving in the armies of France was already well established.[298]

Two questions are raised by these figures: firstly, why were young Lorrainers so keen to volunteer compared with other regions? Le chevalier des Pommelles ascribed this difference to the effects of climate, but other expla-nations may be more satisfactory. For example, the army's height require-ments favoured the men of the north over those of the south, who tended to be smaller. Far from the coasts, the men of Lorraine did not have a maritime alternative to compete with the army. More convincing is Samuel Scott's suggestion that the pattern resulted from the position of regiments on garrison duty. Under the *ancien régime* each regiment was responsible for raising its own volunteers, and they maintained a number of recruiters for this purpose. As the bulk of the army was in garrison on the north-eastern fron-tier, it was easier to employ one's recruiters locally. Hence, in 1789 when half of the infantry were garrisoned in the north-east, one third of the men were from that region.[299] However, exposure to soldiery does not necessarily make them endearing, so we have to face the even more fundamental question of why did young Lorrainers volunteer at all? Habituated to the army they may have been, but for that reason they would also have been aware of the low pay, the poor housing and the tiresome discipline, and that all this suffering frequently led to an early death. In these circumstances, what did they find attractive about the army?

When elite commentators wondered what drove men into the army, they frequently invoked the figure of 'recruiting-officer Misery'. Poverty seemed to be the only possible explanation for joining such a poorly paid, lowly regarded

---

[296] 'N'est-ce pas le cas de le dire encore une fois, quel département!': Godet, 'Mémoires du capitaine Godet', 484.

[297] Forrest, *Conscripts and deserters*, 14. The pattern observed by Pommelle, if not his figures, is confirmed by Corvisier, who calculated that more than 1.234% of the popula-tion of Lorraine were in the army in 1789, second only to Franche-Comté.

[298] Corvisier, *L'Armée française*, i. 430–1.

[299] The percentages were even higher in the other arms: Scott, *The response of the royal army*, 10.

organisation. Corvisier's examination of the value of bounties paid on engagement during the eighteenth century found that broadly they did follow fluctuations in the economy. The higher the price index, the easier it was to find volunteers, and there is clear evidence that local famines and sudden downturns in a local industry significantly eased the recruiters' problems.[300] More popular commentators sometimes invoked the same reasoning in folk-tales. In a tale from germanophone Lorraine a wife, disguised as an officer in the army, recruits her own husband now down on his luck: 'He had no clothes left, and nothing left to eat.'[301] However, considering how often poverty was the initial starting point of the hero, very few folktales in the French canon depict want as the reason for the volunteer's behaviour. This might be surprising if other sources did not considerably play down the role of 'recruiting-officer Misery'.

Although the economic depressions may have released men onto the labour market, recruiters were not keen to enlist the most desperate among them. Despite Enlightenment writers' frequent references to the army as the 'sweepings of prisons', the army tried hard to exclude vagabonds and crimi-nals.[302] Indeed, although Corvisier has shown that there was a gradual shift in recruitment towards the more popular end of the social scale over the century, the sons of day-labourers and servants never made up much more than 15 per cent, roughly equal to the contribution of upper and middle classes. The bulk came from the urban and rural artisanat, with a fair number of farmers and substantial peasants.[303] Changing economic circumstances may have made individuals consider the army, but absolute want was seldom the spur.

Labate's study of volunteers from Moselle after the end of the Napoleonic wars gives even less credit to poverty: 'What is remarkable is that there is absolutely no direct correlation between the economic difficulties of the population and [the number of voluntary] engagements.'[304] The numbers of volunteers rose to meet the political and international crises of 1830, 1840 and 1848, and continued at a high level throughout the bellicose reign of Napoleon III, but there was no marked rush to arms in the difficult years of

---

300 Corvisier, L'Armée française, i. 317–23.
301 'Er hatte keine Kleider mehr und nichts mehr zu essen': Merkelbach-Pinck, Lothringer Volksmärchen, 155: Eine schöne Geschichte (AT 883).
302 Le comte de Saint Germain, Mémoires, Amsterdam 1779, 183. Saint Germain was an experienced officer, and it is therefore surprising that he should characterise his own troops in this way, but such prejudices about soldiers were so much a part of 'enlightened' received wisdom that even those who knew better none the less repeated them. In fact, of 17,000 known beggars at the time of the revolution, only 88 joined the army, and had their history been discovered they would have been discharged: Scott, Response of the royal army, 19.
303 Corvisier, L'Armée française, i. 500–5.
304 'Ce qui est remarquable c'est qu'il n'y a aucune relation directe entre les difficultés économiques de la population et les engagements': Labate, Le Recrutement de l'armée, 43.

1846–7, 1857 or 1866, which suggests that volunteers had other motivations. Between 1818 and 1870 more than 2,000 volunteers came from the better-off sections of the population of the city of Metz.[305] In the rest of the country it was not from the most poverty-stricken regions that the volunteers came but, on the contrary, from the more prosperous cities of the north and east.[306]

This is not to say that there were not economic reasons behind a decision to join the army, but that absolute poverty was not commonly among them. It is noticeable that, although there were fluctuations between the proportions from the city and the country, town-dwellers were over-represented among volunteers throughout the whole period.[307] There are several reasons why a townsman might be more ready to enlist than his country compatriot: many were already migrants who, having made one gamble with their future were more willing to risk another. Joining the army was not such a great displacement for them as for the peasant who had never left his 'petit pays'. Centres of population drew recruiters and most towns, at least in the north-east, were also garrisons whose citizens were familiar with reviews and parades. Artisans and shopkeepers, who made up the bulk of the urban volunteers, were much more susceptible to the vagaries of the local economy than the peasant. The latter's wealth was in his land, in times of hardship he could probably get by, but if he gave it up he also gave up his economic independence. The wealth of an artisan was in his hands and his knowledge. In times of hardship he could temporarily make a living in the army, but with a bit of capital he could, on his discharge, get back to work again. And the army might supply the necessary capital. If the volunteer was careful and saved the bounty he received on engagement (or, in the case of replacements, the money paid by the family of the conscript he had replaced) he had the seed money for his own business.[308]

Unlike conscripts, volunteers could chose in which regiment they would serve. During the Napoleonic wars four regiments were most popular with Mosellans: the germanophone volunteers went into the first regiment of cuirassiers and second regiment of carabiniers; the francophones, mostly from the city of Metz, chose the second battalion of sappers and, above all, the first battalion of miners.[309] After the end of the wars Mosellans continued to opt for the technical arms, the artillery and especially the engineers (though

---

[305] Ibid. 53.
[306] Aron, Dumont and Le Roy Ladurie, *Anthropologie du conscrit français*, map 7.
[307] Corvisier calculates that 37.58% of soldiers were of urban origin in 1716, and 32.9% in 1763 (though it should be pointed out that the figures were much lower in Lorraine): *L'Armée française*, i. 408. The percentage had risen again by 1789, when 35% of the infantry were townsmen according to Scott: *The response of the royal army*, 15. Vaublanc noted the same pattern in the Moselle during the first empire.
[308] Between 1849 and 1855 58% of all new accounts at the Caisse d'épargne de Paris were opened by replacements: Schnapper, *Le Remplacement militaire*, 120.
[309] Kappaun, *La Conscription en Moselle*, 204–5.

germanophones still preferred the cavalry).[310] These regiments were all based in the region and had built up connections with the neighbouring population over years. Metz was the home to the some of the army's technical schools, and the presence of the teachers and cadets in the city probably gave these specialisms extra prestige. Knowing that there was a good chance that they would be called-up in any case, many young men decided to pre-empt the *tirage* in order to get into the regiment of their choice (and in which many of the friends and family were either serving or had served). This is how Georges Bangofsky reasoned in 1797: 'Having reached at this time the age of twenty I found I was of an age for conscription, and had to go [to the *tirage*] soon; as I preferred to serve in the cavalry, I volunteered for the seventh regiment of hussars and left Sarreguemines on 10 October, 1797, with several comrades who had taken the same decision.'[311] The preference of germanophone Lorrainers like Bangofsky for the hussars dated back to the *ancien régime* (when the language of command in many of these regiments was German). They even sang about it in their conscript songs: 'Now we're going together into a regiment/. . . . To the seventh regiment of hussars/ That is the best regiment.'[312]

Because of the high reputation these regiments enjoyed locally, because many young men had friends or family serving in them, they absorbed most of the department's volunteers, but there are also clear indications of economic calculation in their preferences. Conscripts chose to serve in regiments where their civilian skills would be most appreciated, so that, for example, large numbers of rural blacksmiths went into the cavalry while 90 per cent of the volunteers who entered the first battalion of miners already had a skill in wood or iron.[313] Not only did the army supply the capital to start a business, but it also equipped the volunteer with a very useful training in his chosen profession.

For a small number of volunteers the army itself would be their chosen profession. Most volunteers only did one tour of duty of seven years, but a sizeable proportion re-enlisted time after time. Even if the pay was not particularly good at least the soldier could count on being clothed, fed and housed, and there was always a chance that with long service there would come promotion, a pension or a place in Les Invalides. The large number of volunteers who were the sons of old soldiers may have been influenced by the posi-

---

310 Labate, *Le Recrutement de l'armée*, 61.
311 'Ayant, dans ce temps, atteint l'âge de vingt ans, je me trouvais de la conscription, obligé de partir bientôt; comme je préférais server dans la cavalerie, je m'engageai volontairement dans le 7e régiment de hussards et partais de Sarreguemines le 10 octobre 1797 avec plusieurs de mes camarades qui avaient pris la même décision': Roche du Teilloy, *Les Etapes de Georges Bangofsky*, 8.
312 'Jetzt gehen wir miteinander unter ein Regiment/. . . . Zum siebenten Regiment Husaren./ Das ist das schönste Regiment': Pinck, *Verklingende Weisen*, iii. 107, no. 33: *Conscritlied*.
313 Kappaun, *La Conscription en Moselle*, 205.

tive experiences of their fathers, but among those who stayed longest in the army were orphans, including the abandoned children adopted by the army. With no network of connections to start them in work or to anchor them in a community, they would have understood the sentiments of the germanophone soldier's song 'My regiment, my homeland/ My mother I never knew/ My father died in the field when I was young/ I'm all alone in this world.'[314] For most volunteers the army was an interlude of adventure before they returned to their normal civilian life, but for this group of soldiers the army was the only world they knew.[315]

However, although the army could be considered alongside other occupations, and a choice made on the basis of its relative advantages, this was not how it was usually treated in popular mentalities. If we turn to folktales and folksongs, we find other, more compelling reasons for the volunteers' behaviour.

In popular culture soldiering was depicted not as one occupation among many but as an alternative mode of life. A German ballad, well-known in Lorraine, starts, 'There was once two farmer's sons,/ That wanted to go to the war/ Right in the soldier's life'.[316] Why farm lads might wish to 'taste the life of the soldier' is explained by the heroes of a Picard tale: 'being quite adventurous and being bored to death in their village' each in turn decides to enlist. It is a blow to their father, who hoped that they would take over his farm, but as his second son tells him 'father, it's decided: I've really thought about it, but I can't resist the desire I have for the profession of soldier'.[317] Boredom, rather than poverty, is the most frequently cited folktale cause for volunteering, as in the tale of *Marchand*, 'who, being very bored in the village, asked his father one day for permission to go to town and volunteer for a regiment of dragoons'.[318] To François, the hero of another folktale, the excitement of the army appeared much more attractive than his father's job of rag-and-bone man, so he enrolled in the twenty-fourth colonial regiment at Perpignan.[319]

---

[314] 'Mein Regiment mein Heimatland/ Meine Mutter hab ich nicht gekant/ Mein Vater starb schon früh im Feld/ Ich bin allein auf diesser Welt': Archives départementales de la Moselle, 42/J/25, fonds Pinck, A 86, 917.

[315] Robert Laulan, 'Un Philanthrope militaire: le brigadier-général Merlet et la création des écoles d'enfants de troupe', *Actes du 83e congrès national des sociétés savantes, Aix–Marseilles, 1958*, Paris 1959, 170–80.

[316] 'Es war'n einmal zwei Bauernsöhn,/ Die hatten Lust, in den Krieg zu gehn,/ Wohl ins Soldatenleben': Pinck, *Verklingende Weisen*, i. 109: *Die Mordwirtin*.

[317] 'Les trois jeunes gens etaient assez aventureux et s'ennuyaient au diable dans leur village . . . . "Mon père, c'est tout résolu: j'y ai bien réfléchi, je ne puis résister au goût décidé que j'ai pour le métier de soldat" ': Carnoy, *Littérature orale de Picardie*, 292–3: *Le Château du diable* (AT566).

[318] 'L'aîné, qui s'ennuyait fort au village, demanda un jour à son père la permission d'aller à la ville s'engager dans un régiment de dragons': E. Henry Carnoy, *Contes français*, Paris 1885, 63: *Les Aventures de marchand* (AT935, from Berry).

[319] Geneviève Massignon, *Folktales of France*, Chicago 1968, 217: *The three deserters* (AT566).

The adventurous type evoked as the volunteer hero of many folktales could shade into the libertine. Corvisier found that, when called upon to explain the phenomenon of voluntary enlistment, men of the eighteenth century 'most frequently invoked libertinage and . . . some *philosophes* invoked only that'.[320] Drink clearly played a part in many decisions to enlist, and recruiting sergeants made fairs and fêtes their special haunt. One Messin singer was already a hardened drinker before volunteering: 'My mistress orders me to give up wine;/ To give up her charms but not wine/ . . . I'm going to war to serve king Louis.'[321] Corvisier cites the examples of a number of sons of good family, including several monks and priests, who ran away to join the army only to be dragged out by their families. Just such a young man features in a local legend, recorded by the Jesuit Father Abram in his history of the university of Pont-à Mousson. He had enlisted in the army to serve in the 'goujeats' (the valets of cavalrymen and considered the lowest of the low), only to be sent to school by his parents, 'but not liking the subjection which study requires, he quitted the school and returned to his former kind of life'.[322] Although this student repented he was not the last to long for the excitement of soldiering, as a popular patois song from Lorraine indicates: 'I have sworn by Saint Nicolas,/ patron of Lorraine,/ that I would rather become a soldier,/ a drummer or captain,/ than go to live in Toul/ with those old goat-beards/ To the devil with the seminarians/ and all the missionaries.'[323]

Soldier's autobiographies, such as that of Jean-Claude Vaxelaire, stress the excitement of volunteering which took the new soldier away from the tedium of everyday life. However, reading between the lines of his memoirs, one

---

[320] 'invoquaient le plus souvent le libertinage et . . . certains philosophes n'invoquaient que cela': Corvisier, *L'Armée française*, i. 331. It is interesting to note that, although it was replacements who usually got the bad press as 'mauvais sujets', volunteers actually had a worse record for military discipline, suggesting that there were many hot-heads among them: Schnapper, *Le Remplacement*, 150. Delmart, a lieutenant who had joined the army as a conscript, was particularly caustic in his judgement of volunteers: 'Pour un qui avait réellement le goût de l'art militaire et une vocation insurmontable pour la vie des camps, mille autres ont été poussés à s'enrôler par l'impossibilité de faire mieux dans le monde. Mauvais sujets dans la société, ils ont conservé leur caractère indisciplinable dans le régiment. . . . Ils ont apporté avec eux le goût et l'habitude de tous les désordres': *La Caserne*, 5.

[321] 'Ma maîtresse m'ordonne d'abandonner le vin;/ D'abandonner ses charmes mais pas le vin/ . . . Je m'en vais dans la guerre servir le roi Louis': Westphalen, *Chansons populaires*, i, no. 167: *J'ai fait une maîtresse*.

[322] It was at this moment that the devil appeared to him, tempting him to all sorts of crimes, but he saved himself by making the sign of the cross: Calmet, *The phantom world*, 214–15.

[323] 'J'aveuie jeuré pâ Saint Colàs,/ Patron de let Lôréyene,/ Que j'aie m'reuie meuie me mott' souldat,/ Tambour ou capitéyene,/ Que d'mon allie logic à Taoue,/ Avot ços vies barbeus de baoues;/ Au diabe los suminèyeres/ Ecot los misssiounèyeres': Archives départementales de Meurthe-et-Moselle, fonds de la Société d'archéologie lorraine MS 244, fonds Marchal, fo. 26v: *Le Seminaire de Toul*. At least two other versions of this song have been recorded.

senses that a difficult relationship with his father made his escape into uniform all the more pleasurable. If in their memoirs soldiers were guarded in their comments there was no such restraint in their songs. Germanophone schoolchildren sang 'And if my mother hits me one more time/ Then I'll pick up my bundle and go for a soldier.'[324] More commonly it was his relationship with his father that decided the young man to volunteer: 'To which ever side I turn,/ I feel my heart is disappointed:/ My father, who annoys me;/ My mistress, who has left me/ And me to the citadel/ I went to volunteer.'[325] For the adventurous, not to say wayward sons who are the heroes of many folk-tales, home-life (and in particular parental discipline) could be very trying. The superhuman strength of the adopted *Fils de diable* in Cosquin's tale of that name, was constantly getting him into trouble, but things came to a head when, following a fight at a village dance, he killed all but one of twenty-four gendarmes sent to arrest him:

> The following day it was announced, by the beating of a drum through the whole village, that those who wanted to volunteer would receive a generous bounty. So the young man said to his parents, 'I'd like to volunteer.' 'My son', replied his father, 'we are rich enough to support you, there's no need for that.' 'Father', said the young man, 'I clearly see that I will cause you nothing but unpleasantness: it's better that I leave the house.' So he left and reported to the regiment.[326]

If we are to trust the evidence of folksong and tales, one emotive reason made young men volunteer more than any other – being unlucky in love. This follows from the opposition in popular culture between the army on the one hand and lasting relationships with women on the other. The song of the Messin volunteer quoted above, although it mentions his father who made his life a misery, was actually addressed to his mistress who had left him. It was to revenge himself on his girlfriend that he enlisted, and in the last verse he tells her 'Of marrying you, charming beauty/ Never think again./ You played hard to get/ Now it's my turn/ I'm leaving you, charming beauty,/ Adieux, it's for ever!'[327] In neighbouring Franche-Comté, where the military tradition

---

324 'Hopsa, heisen Riewesalat,/ Un wann mi Mutter mich noch emol schlaht,/ Dann hol ich min Bindel un wäre Soldat': Josef Graf, 'Deutsche-lothringische Volkslieder, Reime und Sprüche aus Forbach und Umgegend', *Jahrbuch der Gesellschaft für lothringische Geschichte und Alterstumkunde* vi (1894), 106.
325 'De quel côté que je m'y tourne,/ J'y sens mon coeur embarrassé:/ Mon papa, qui me chagrine;/ Ma maîtresse, qui m'a quitté,/ Et moi à la citadelle/ Je me suis allé engager': 'Quépat', *Chants populaires messins*, no. 28: *Adieu, c'est pour toujours*.
326 'Le lendemain, on publia à son caisse par tout le village que ceux qui voudraient s'enroler auriant bonne récompense. La jeune homme dit alors à ses parents: "J'ai envie de m'enrôler." "Mon fils," répondit le père, "nous sommes assez riches pour te nourrir; tu n'as pas besoin de cela." "Mon père," dit le jeune homme, "je vois bien que je ne vous causerai que du désagrément: il faut mieux que je quitte la maison." Il parti donc et se rendit au régiment': Cosquin, *Contes populaires de Lorraine*, i. 161, no. 14: *Le Fils de diable* (AT650).
327 'De t'épouser, charmante belle/ Il n'y faut jamais plus penser./ Tu y as fait la difficile/ A

was almost as strong, the disappointed lover sang 'I will leave the fields for the town,/ And there make other girlfriends,/ And if these others don't want me,/ I'll go and be a soldier.'[328]

It is unlikely that the young men of Moselle were any more at risk of being jilted than those of other regions of France, so this factor in itself cannot account for the larger percentage of volunteers. However, the cultural models which described his situation, available to him through folktale and song, all suggest one course of action. As we will see in chapter 5, the opposition between the army and relations with women recurs in most songs from Lorraine that deal with soldiers. It is feasible that such models influenced the behaviour of those who knew them, and thus partially account for the regional patterns of enthusiasm for military service. Each generation of would-be soldiers who listened to the advice of singers and narrators went on to reinforce the pattern. Their own actions validated it and in turn became the material for future singers and narrators to use in their creations.

An example of the expression of the opposition between soldiering and marriage in popular culture can be found in the wedding customs of Lorraine. In many areas of Moselle, Meurthe and the Vosges it was the tradition for groups to serenade the couple during the wedding breakfast, in return for gifts of cake or money. Uninvited villagers (including the conscript *classe*) took up a position outside to give a rendition of *Reveillez-vous belle endormie*, the oblig-atory song on these occasions.[329] This song features a lover calling to the window of his mistress, only to be told by her that her father refuses to coun-tenance their relationship and is about to give him his 'congé'. In the context *congé* means his dismissal, but the word also means a discharge from the army, and was often used colloquially to describe a soldier's term of service (asked how long a man had served, he might reply one *congé*, meaning seven years). In a version of the song recorded in the city of Metz the lover leaves telling his mistress 'As I must take a *congé*/ I'll leave the country/ I'll go to those woods and hills,/ To finish my days, my dear loves' and it subsequently devel-oped as the popular conscript song *Le Portrait de la maîtresse*.[330] This combina-tion, in which the first verses of *Reveillez-vous belle endormie* became joined to

présent, c'est à mon tour./ Je te quitte, charmante belle,/ Or, adieu, c'est pour toujours!': 'Quépat', *Chants populaires messins*, no. 28: *Adieu, c'est pour toujours*. Many other folksongs from the same region, where volunteers were so numerous, cite the same causes, including this one, 'C'est le vingt-trois octobre/ Que ma maîtresse m'a quitté./ Tout droit en Angleterre/ Je m'en fus allé/ Trouver mon capitaine/ Pour m'engager': Westphalen, *Chan-sons populaires*, ii, no. 315: *C'est le vingt-trois octobre*.

[328] 'Je m'en irai de champs en ville,/ Pour y faire d'autres amies,/ Et si d'autres ne me veul'nt pas,/ Je m'en irai être soldat': Max Buchon, *Chants populaires de la Franche-Comté*, 2nd edn, Paris 1878, 63: *Propositions refusées*.

[329] Charles Bruneau, 'La Chanson populaire lorraine', *Le Pays lorrain* xxiii (1931), 239–40.

[330] 'Puisqu'un congé il me faut prendre/ Hors du pays je m'en irai,/ Je m'en irai dans ces bocages,/ Finir mes jours, mes chers amours': Barbé, *Coutumes populaires*, 59.

the latter verses of songs about soldiers, was, Van Gennep has suggested, the confusing result of the term *congé* being used in folksong in both senses. Yet I do not believe that there was any confusion in this mixing of themes; that the disappointed lover should go and join the army made perfect sense in the terms of the local popular culture.[331]

One motivating factor is noticeable by its absence from these sources: neither love of one's country nor loyalty to the presiding regime make many appearances in the oral literature of volunteering. It is not my intention to cast doubt on the patriotic reputation of 'our valiant populations of the east': statistically it was entirely justified. Napoleon called the Lorrainer town of Phalsbourg his 'nursery of warriors', but the same phrase could be applied to the whole of Lorraine. What I have hoped to establish from looking at folktales and songs are some of the reasons for their actions. The volunteer may well have loved his country but this was not a sufficient explanation for his behaviour.

There is, on the other hand, plenty of evidence of the attachment of the soldier to his 'pays', the little area he had grown up in and the people he knew, in the numbers who succumbed to the sometimes fatal disease of *nostalgie*.[332] Homesickness, the usual English translation of *nostalgie* or 'mal du pays', does not do justice to the seriousness of this common complaint which could rapidly lay waste an eighteenth-century army. But if *nostalgie* was more or less natural, love of one's country in the form of the nation-state was something that had to be learned, and often the army itself was the teacher. Folksong collections do contain patriotic references, but only in soldiers' songs which recount the battles they fought, the camaraderie of the regiment, and the victorious return home at the end of the campaign. Old soldiers carried these songs to their villages, bringing with them the idea of the wider nation that they felt they had served.

Sons and lovers

Conscription into the regular army established itself relatively quickly as a suitable topic for popular imagery. Among the images seized during the police raid on Pellerin's premises in 1816 was one entitled *Le Retour du conscrit*.[333] This was a reissue under a different title of an earlier image of Pellerin's, *Le Retour du soldat*, dating from the first years of the empire and which formed a pair with *Le Départ du soldat*.[334] Both were based on copperplate engravings by

---

331 Arnold Van Gennep, 'Deux Problèmes de folklore lorrain', *Le Pays lorrain* xxiii (1931), 425–37.

332 Marcel Reinhard, 'Nostalgie et service militaire pendant la révolution', *Annales historique de la révolution française* xxx (1958), 1–15.

333 Philippe, 'Jean-Charles Pellerin', 96. The image used in the subsequent prosecution is preserved: MDAACE 39.3244.

334 Perrout, *Trésors*, 56–7.

Plate 12. *Le Départ du soldat*: Pellerin (Epinal), *c*. 1800–10
Reproduced by permission of the Musée départemental
d'art ancien et contemporain, Epinal.

the Paris print-firm Noël.[335] *Le Départ du soldat* depicts a family at their meal
outside a country cottage. The family's attention is directed to the son of the
house, who, although he continues to embrace his wife and child, is turning
away from them to join his companion, a volunteer to judge by the cockade
in his hat. Although his family appear anxious, the soldier himself is joyful as
he raises a glass to his comrade. *Le Retour du soldat* shows the same family
group: the grandparents hurry from their cottage door to greet their 'worthy
son of victory' – now dressed in the uniform of a revolutionary dragoon. He
already has his wife and children (one of whom is noticeably younger than
when he left!) in his arms. In the background two neighbours rush from the
vineyard to welcome him home.

Pellerin used the same woodblock to illustrate the image which got him
into trouble, *Le Retour du conscrit*. The change in title implied a change in the
system of recruitment, but the only alteration to the image was the addition
of a song on the theme of *L'Arrivée d'un militaire chez sa mère*. The problem
with the image, as far as the authorities were concerned, was not the mention

335 Noël's work regularly formed the model for Pellerin's images; several suspect Noël
prints were among the items removed from Pellerin's office during the police raid:
Dumont, *La Vie et l'oeuvre*, 166.

Plate 13. *Le Retour du conscrit*: Pellerin (Epinal), *c.* 1810–14
Reproduced by permission of the Musée départemental
d'art ancien et contemporain, Epinal.

of conscription (although by 1816 conscription had been temporarily abandoned by Louis XVIII in a populist move), but the line in the accompanying
song where the mother addresses her son: 'How big you've grown,/ Defending
our empire', thus recalling the regime of the 'usurper'.[336]

This condemned image was the first appearance in popular imagery of a
title that was to be one of the mainstays of the industry throughout the nineteenth century. An inquiry into the contents of the packs of pedlars operating
in the department of the Bas-Rhin in 1869 found that versions of *Le Départ*
and *Le Retour du conscrit* were the most popular secular images they sold.[337]
The iconography of the theme became so well known that imagists could use
it on scraps, in children's games and, naturally, on tickets for the *tirage* itself,
and presume that it would be immediately recognised. It also served as a
model for many other images concerning the departure and return of a son,
whether moralising fictions such as the *Histoire du chasseur d'Afrique*, or the

336 'Que tu es devenu grand;/ Défendant notre empire': Perrout, *Trésors*, 57. Unfortunately the image, *Le Départ du conscrit*, was not among those seized, nor do any other
copies survive. It is mentioned in Pellerin's catalogue of 1814 and we can assume that it
was based on *Le Départ du soldat*, but we do not know what text he chose to complement
the picture.
337 Lerch, *Imagerie et société*, 197.

life stories of genuine military heroes such as *Trinquart*, the French-born commander-in-chief of the forces of the sultan of Lahore. Yet the standard representation of the theme, the version which would become familiar from literally hundreds of thousands of prints from Pellerin, Pinot, Gangel and Wentzel, took several decades to develop and then only among the print houses of eastern France.[338] The alterations in its iconography over this period may tell us something about changing attitudes to soldiering during the course of the nineteenth century.

Pellerin, his fingers burnt, did not replace *Le Départ du conscrit* in his catalogue until well after the 1830 revolution, even though conscription itself was reintroduced in 1818. However, a similar image by Desfeuilles, *Départ de conscrits* (112), was approved in September 1824, and had probably been engraved several years previously.[339] It also had a pendant, in this case the *Arrivée des conscrits au camp* (113). Both are made up of four lines of figures, rather in the manner of a sheet of cut-out soldiers in whose production Desfeuilles specialised. The top and bottom lines of both images were based, as usual, on Parisian copperplate engravings by Basset. In the top line of sheet 112 we see the departure of the conscripts for the *tirage*: with music at their head and cockades in their hats, they march or dance arm-in-arm, drinking as they go. In the last line we see the four conscripts designated by the *tirage* with their packs on their backs and their staves in their hands. We find them next, at the top of sheet 113, being welcomed into the new world of the regiment through a mixture of tiresome fatigue-duties and 'fraternisation' with the older soldiers, a euphemism for being obliged to buy them drinks. Similar scenes of initiation crop up regularly in the numerous images of the conscript's life-cycle issued up to the First World War.

The middle two lines of no. 112 are closer to Pellerin's image, though bizarrely the order has been reversed: the soldier returns before he has left. Again the image was copied from a Parisian copperplate engraving from the Napoleonic era, probably by Basset.[340] In the scene of departure two children, the conscript's younger brother and sister, grab his legs in an attempt to hold him back, his mother weeps into her hands, and the dog lifts its paw in farewell. The soldier is in that same uncomfortable pose seen in Pellerin's image, his head turned towards his family while his body marches in the direction he

---

[338] To my knowledge only one provincial imagist, outside Alsace and Lorraine, ever treated the subject of conscription, and that was Martin-Delahaye of Lille: Adolphe Aynaud, 'L'Imagerie lilloise ou Henri Porret père, 1768–1844', extract from *Le Vieux Papier*, Paris 1950, 7. I have not been able to trace a surviving copy of his version.

[339] MDAACE 57.3.1182, 57.3.1160. Nearly half Desfeuilles's total production was sent to the *dépôt légal* in the last four months of 1824, not because it was a particularly prolific year but because the law of censorship had finally caught up with him: Archives départementales de Meurthe-et-Moselle, 1/T/1233. The *Départ de conscrits* bears the address 'Rue de la Boucherie, à Nancy', where Desfeuilles lived before 1818, so the image probably predates the move.

[340] The Parisian copperplate original of this image is reproduced in Bozon, *Les Conscrits*, 114.

Plate 14. *Départ de conscrit[s] no. 112*: Desfeuilles (Nancy), c. 1818
Reproduced by permission of the Musée départemental
d'art ancien et contemporain, Epinal.

must travel following three soldiers, thus graphically depicting the
conflicting ties that bind him, to his family and to the nation. With one hand
he points after his comrades, but it is open in a gesture of helplessness as if
declaring that he has no choice but to go. However, his father, to whom he
looks, does not appear to be very understanding, for he wags his finger in what
looks like a gesture of admonition. At the soldier's return we see the same, if
slightly older family group rushing to welcome him home, even the dog is
there (a dog has always been there in stories of returning soldiers from the
Odyssey onwards). Although he left an infantryman he returns a hussar, just
as Pellerin's came back a dragoon, indicative of imagists' penchant for the
more dashing light cavalry.[341] The hussar leaps from his horse to embrace,
first and foremost, his grey-haired father, whom we last saw reproaching him.

341 In folksongs of the early nineteenth century, as well as in imagery, soldiers were almost

198

The central position of the father/son relationship in these early images of the returning conscript highlights the theme's connections to another profitable line for imagists, the story of the prodigal son. *L'Histoire de l'enfant prodigue* was among the first images which, despite its biblical origins, could not be classed as devotional, to enter the repertoires of provincial imagists: blocks, or copies of blocks, dating back to the sixteenth century were still in use among Pellerin's competitors at the beginning of the nineteenth.[342] But despite the theme's venerability, until the July Monarchy most imagists treated the parable as relevant to contemporary society. Their characters wore modern dress, as if the story of youthful rebellion and return to parental authority was immediately applicable to the image's potential customers.[343] However, when the Pellerin firm released their later versions in 1836, 1840, 1843 and 1860, all were resolutely set in New Testament times, which suggests a certain distancing between the viewer and the subject. The prodigal, having been visualised as a contemporary social problem in his earlier incarnations, now became once more a biblical parable of God's redeeming love. Is it fanciful to suggest that the conscript had replaced the prodigal in their experience, and therefore on their walls? Some of the elements in the iconography of the *enfant prodigue* suggest not.

In 1818 the Revd Thomas Frognall Dibdin was travelling through Normandy when he called in at the workshop of Jean-François Picard and his wife Marie-Françoise Guérin and bought two images, one of which was a comic-strip version of *L'Enfant prodigue*. He enclosed it in a letter home where he drew his correspondent's attention to the second scene of the story, because in it 'you will clearly perceive the military turn which seems to prevail throughout France in things the most minute. The prodigal is about to mount his horse and leave his father's house, in the cloke and cock'd hat of a French officer'.[344] Dibdin was wrong, I think, when he ascribed the prodigal's military apparel simply to the martial tastes of the French. He is also depicted in uniform in other contemporary images, from Leloup of Le Mans and Lecrêne-Labbey of Rouen, for example.[345] There is nothing in the Gospel to justify this. What led the imagists to dress their prodigals in this fashion?

The prodigal as soldier, or at least in the company of soldiers, was an iconographic commonplace in both the high and popular art of the sixteenth

---

always depicted as dragoons or hussars. The light cavalry seems to have grabbed the popular imagination in a way no other arm of the military could.

[342] The version of *L'Enfant prodigue* by Ledien-Canda of Amiens, though it probably dates from the first empire, was copied from a sixteenth-century original (which also inspired Letourmy's eighteenth-century version).

[343] For example, the Deckherrs' 1824 version of *L'Enfant prodigue* has the father and two sons dressed in the bourgeois fashion of the day: BN (estampes), Rc 36 L. fo., *L'Histoire du sauveur*.

[344] Revd Thomas Frognall Dibdin, A *bibliographical, antiquarian and picturesque tour in France and Germany*, London 1821, i. 318.

[345] Garnier, *L'Imagerie populaire française*, i, nos 293, 451.

Plate 15. *L'Enfant prodigue*: Picard-Guérin (Caen), *c.* 1820
'The prodigal is about to mount his horse and leave his father's house, in
the cloke and cock'd hat of a French officer' (Dibdin, 1821). Reproduced
by permission of Glasgow University Library (Special Collections).

and seventeenth centuries, and the reasons are not difficult to discover.
Flashily dressed troops were popular genre subjects for artists, particularly
when indulging the same picturesque bad habits – drinking, gambling and
whoring – which lost the prodigal his fortune.[346] If both Reformation and
Counter-Reformation authorities obliged later elite artists to stick more
closely to the text of Luke xv, at a popular level the identification between
soldiers and prodigals was not lost.

[346] Any number of sixteenth-century artworks demonstrate this connection: Konrad
Renger, *Zur Ikonographie des verlorenen Sohnes und von Wirtshausszenen in der
niederlandischen Malerei*, Berlin 1970.

For example, in the Basque country at the end of the nineteenth century, the prodigal's progress was a popular folk play in which the boy's valet, an old soldier, played a prominent part in leading him from the straight and narrow (such amateur productions were much more widespread at one time).[347] In general the prodigal's servant plays a much more important role in popular art and literature than that accorded him by Saint Luke, and was portrayed as a soldier. Through these plays and images the parable was widely available as a model of behaviour in rural popular culture, and its influence can be detected in forms of oral literature such as this introduction to a Basque folktale:

A king once had a son who was called Dragon. He was as debauched as it is possible to be. All the money that he had he had spent, and still more; not having enough, he demanded his portion from his father. His father gives it him immediately, and he goes off, taking with him a companion who had been a soldier, and who was very like himself. Very quickly they spent all their money.[348]

In popular culture prodigality and soldiering went hand in hand, and one may conjecture that the image of the *enfant prodigue* on the wall of the peasant home was a warning from parents to children who might be tempted to follow the drum. We have already seen this connection made in the explanations given by young men for voluntarily joining the army in folksong and tale. They complained of boredom and with being kept on too tight a lead at home, a situation that might easily be compared to the prodigal. In the Vosges they even had a proverbial phrase to describe just such situations – 'he wants to eat the mad cow', which according to the folklorist who collected it applied to 'a boy of good family, well provided for, but envying a condition which he believes is better than that allotted to him, loses patience and dons military uniform before his time. . . . Nineteen times out of twenty these "hot-heads" return sooner or later to the family home, disillusioned and sheepish, having seen hard times'.[349] The army provided the mechanism for

347 Julien Vinson, *Le Folklore du pays basque*, Paris 1881, 325.
348 Revd Wentworth Webster, *Basque legends, collected chiefly in the Labourd*, London 1887, 106: *Dragon* (AT401). The connection between prodigals and soldiers will be retained in popular culture as long as children read Johanna Spyri's *Heidi*. Heidi unwittingly uses the story to reconcile her grandfather to God and man; he had turned his back on both after he broken the hearts of his parents by wasting his inheritance, and so was forced to enlist in (and subsequently desert from, after a brawl in which he killed a man) the Swiss regiments in the Neapolitan service. Heidi tells the story, unaware of its personal significance, but it persuades him to pray to God for forgiveness and to move back to the village after many years on the mountains.
349 'È vue mingé d'lè vêche errêgie', a dialect phrase which applied to 'un garçon de bonne famille qui est bien chez lui; mais qui enviant une condition qu'il croit bien meilleure que celle qui lui est échue, "fait sa tête", et prend, avant l'heure, la tenue militaire. . . . Dix-neuf fois sur vingt, ces "èvaltonés" (écervelés) reviennent tôt ou tard, désillusionnés et penauds au foyer familial, après en avoir "vu de dures" ': C.-D. Petitjean, C.-J. Petitjean, H.-B.-D. Petitjean and Georges Petitjean, *Le Pays vosgien et ses habitants:*

prodigals to escape the parental home, and the parable provided their fathers with the biblical authority to warn them against such folly.

We can see how artists used Christ's interpretation of God's love and applied it to the secular character of the soldier in Greuze's *Le Fils ingrat*. When the original sketch of this well-known painting was shown at the salon of 1765, Diderot was deeply moved by its depiction of what he considered the unnatural act of the elder son who leaves his family to go off with the recruiting sergeant. Like other *philosophes*, the only explanation Diderot could offer for volunteering was profligacy. He described the son as 'violent, insolent, impetuous and heartless': 'despite the help he might, as the eldest son, be to his father, his mother and his brothers, has enrolled himself . . . this unnatural child, who no longer knows neither father, nor mother, nor duties, and returns insults for their reproaches'.[350] The prodigal soldier gets his just deserts in its pendant, *Le Fils puni*, when he returns from the wars to find his father on his deathbed and his family both poverty- and grief-stricken.

Interestingly Diderot's attitude had completely reversed by the time the finished pictures were exhibited in 1779: he declared himself revolted by Greuze when 'he shows a father cursing his son because he's gone for a soldier'.[351] Diderot's change of heart was a sign of a new concept of military service among certain members of the intelligentsia: the son should not be blamed for being a soldier for far from deserting his family he was serving the wider family – the nation. This was the message of much revolutionary propaganda, and the theoretical basis of the very institution of conscription, from where it found its way into the early images on the theme of the *Départ et retour du conscrit*. Pellerin's original returning soldier is described in the accompanying text, uttered by his parents, as a 'son of Mars' and a 'son of victory' – in other words his filial duties extended beyond the domestic sphere.

The scene of farewell in Desfeuilles's *Départ de conscrits* resembles Greuze's in many ways, with the son throwing out his hand in a gesture of helplessness, the angry father haranguing him. But the second part of the story is quite different to *Le Fils puni*, for in Desfeuilles's version the father rushes to embrace his son. Of course, the parental embrace is also the final scene of Desfeuilles's *Tableau de l'enfant prodigue*, the theme which may have inspired conscript imagery, but although the iconography is the same the logic is

origines – évolutions – descriptions, prises aux sources des lieux jusqu'ici inetudiés, no. 1: Granges, Epinal 1930, 68.

350 'Malgré le secours dont le fils ainé de la maison peut être a son vieux père, à sa mère et à ses frères, il s'est enrôlé. . . . Son père en est indigné; il n'épargne pas les mots durs à cet enfant dénaturé, qui ne connait plus ni père, ni mère, ni devoirs, et qui lui rend injures pour reproches. On le voit au centre du tableau; il a l'air violent, insolent et fougueux': Musée Bargoin, *Greuze et Diderot: vie familiale et éducation dans le deuxième moitié du XVIIIe siècle*, Clermont-Ferrand 1984 (exhibition catalogue), 99–100.

351 'quand il montre un père maudissant son fils parce qu'il s'est fait soldat': Denis Diderot, *Salons: text établi et presenté par Jean Seznec*, iv, Oxford 1967, 333.

Plate 16. *Départ et retour du conscrit*: Pellerin (Epinal), 1843
Reproduced by permission of the Musée départemental
d'art ancien et contemporain, Epinal

different. The prodigal chooses to leave his home and his father in order to enjoy himself, he does not deserve his father's forgiveness but none the less he receives it; the conscript, on the other hand, is obliged to go in order to do his duty to his other family, the nation, and so it becomes his father's duty to welcome him home.

This is the message of the next image issued on the theme of the conscript, edited by Nicolas Pellerin, Jean-Charles's son and successor, in 1843.[352] His

---

[352] 'Le départ d'un conscrit est une chose vraiment touchante dans le sein d'un hameau. Un père triste et rêveur, une mère désolée, une amante au désespoir et des amis qui pleurent; voilà l'intéressant cortège qui l'accompagne jusqu'à la colline. Voyez ce jeune soldat, il peut à peine s'arracher des bras de ceux qui l'aiment; on ne conserve aucune espérance de le revoir; chacun croit lui faire d'éternels adieux.' The accompanying song contains the following verses on departure: 'Il est cruel de quitter une mère/ Qui me berça dès mes plus jeunes ans;/ Avec douleur je m'éloigne d'un père/ Qui me retient dans ses bras caressans./ Mais quand la France (elle est aussi ma mère)/ Me dit: Marchons, marchons aux ennemis!/ Adieu! je pars, pour revenir, j'espère,/ Digne de vous, digne de mon pays.' On his return the conscript sings: 'Mère adorée, et vous père que j'aime,/ Dont si souvent j'ai rêvé le trépas,/ Plus, loin de vous, ma crainte fut extrême,/ Plus je ressens de bonheur dans vos bras./ Reposez-vous sur mon coeur qui palpite,/ Que mon amour baise vos cheveux blancs;/ Cette faveur votre fils la mérite,/ Car il revient fidèle à ses sermens. Viens à ton tour, viens ma fidèle amie,/ M'offrir ta flamme et recevoir mes feux;/ Viens partager la splendeur de ma vie,/ Ma croix d'honneur appartient à nous deux./ A te chérir mon âme s'abandonne,/ Je veux, d'hymen quand luiront les momens,/ Que mes lauriers te servent de couronne:/

Départ et retour du conscrit shows on the left a group of downcast conscripts, their sacks on their back, at the exit to a village. Their girlfriends sob nearby. The hero stands at the door of his father's cottage, his grieving mother covers her eyes, but the father, though mournful, looks his son straight in the eye while he clasps his hand. The text underneath explains:

> The departure of a conscript from the bosom of a village is a really touching scene. A sad and thoughtful father, a distressed mother, a lover in despair and friends who weep; this is the concerned cortège which accompanies him to the foot of the hill. See this young soldier, he can hardly drag himself away from the arms of those who love him; they have no hope of seeing him alive again; everyone believes that they are making their final farewells.

But they are happily mistaken for on the right we see the boy returning as a man. Dressed in a sumptuous uniform, he has grown a head taller than his now grey-haired father, a moustache has appeared where nothing came before, and on his chest shines a medal, the *croix d'honneur*. The imagist suggests both the time and distance which have separated the soldier from his family by having him exit 'stage right' and return 'stage left', so that his parents seem rooted to the spot, while he has made a full tour – a standard technique in imagery on this theme. As he strides across the floor his mother claps her hands, his fiancée puts hers together in a prayer of thanksgiving, but it is to the arms of his father that he rushes. His successful return, Pellerin says, is no more than his just desert, for he responded when the nation called. 'France is also my mother', the conscript tells his parents in the accompanying song, an idea whose powerful influence in the schoolrooms of the late nineteenth century we have already noted. And because the conscript has done his duty to his larger family, the nation, he has earned his father's embrace: 'Your son deserves this favour,/ Because he returns faithful to his vows.'

What has happened to the conscript in the intervening period is kept hidden from us here, but, to judge by the many images showing scenes from the career of the conscript, he spent his time in much the same way the prodigal son did. In Pellerin's 1841 image of *La Vie du conscrit*, for example, the hero spends his father's money drinking and getting into brawls. But whereas the prodigal's time away from home was depicted as a mistake which he regretted, here these youthful indiscretions are shown as necessary, because they turned the boy, the 'Jean-Jean' as raw country recruits were known, into a real man. As we will see in the next chapter, according to the imagists' idea of the conscript's life, his depravities harden his body, violence proves his bravery and crime demonstrates his intelligence. Thus, by the process of prodigality, the conscript not only becomes fit to fight for his country, he also

Reçois pour dot ma gloire et mes sermens': Garnier-Pelle, *L'Imagerie populaire française*, ii, no. 1176.

matures into a marriageable prospect. The last scene in this image shows the former conscript as a 'father of a family', emperor in his own home like Napoleon, whose image looks down on him from the wall, the secular saint of warriors. Thus the prodigal's vices became the soldier's ladder to social and sexual success. His development, therefore, from beardless youth to fully-grown moustachioed male was of less interest to his father than to another person he had left behind, his 'faithful girlfriend'.[353]

She is already present in Pellerin's second image: although relegated to the background her importance is established in the song the soldier sings on his return, for if the first verse is addressed to his parents the second is directed to his fiancée. He tells her 'Come share the splendour of my life,/ My *croix d'honneur* belongs to us both/. . . . Let my laurels serve you as a [wedding] crown:/ For a dowry receive my glory and my vows.' Pellerin implies that their separation and sufferings were all necessary for a successful marriage later. This image contains in fledgling form much of the iconography that would become standard over the next few decades, but whereas here the girlfriend plays second fiddle to the parents, in later versions it was the relationship between the two lovers that took centre stage.

Under the second empire four local imagists issued a number of closely related 'semi-fine' images of the conscript's departure and return. Their preference for higher quality imagery when dealing with this subject may reflect the value placed upon it by their customers, who surely included the family and friends of the conscripts themselves. Pellerin's lithographs appear to have been the first onto the market, but they were soon followed by those of Gangel & Didion of Metz, Wentzel of Wissembourg and Charles Pinot.[354] The most successful, to judge by the numbers which have survived, were Pinot's, both in their original semi-fine form and in a cheaper copy he produced two years later. These images were reprinted dozens of times in several languages under the second empire and (after Pinot's successors had sold his blocks to Pellerin) the third republic. In the first scene we find the conscript dressed in his Sunday best as if he had just returned from the *tirage* where he had drawn the unfortunate number three, stuck in his beribboned hat. Yet already he has his pack on his back as if he is about to leave this domestic scene for the army. Though crying himself he tries to comfort his lover who has a rose, symbolic of virginal love, in her breast (other imagists use a

---

353 Ibid. no. 1432. In the firm's later image, *Le Histoire de Grivet*, we see the conscript committing the additional faults of stealing, fighting duels and chasing women. But in his case he is not punished for his sins, but rewarded, for on return to his village he is elected mayor: see chapter 5.

354 Pellerin's images appear to have been first on the market (20 Oct. 1860), but they were quickly followed by Gangel & Didion, Pinot & Sagaire and Wentzel. Pellerin updated his own version on two further occasions. Both Pellerin's and Wentzel's images are reproduced in Lerch, *L'Imagerie populaire en Alsace*, 62, 65. The cheaper, and better known, of Pinot's versions, approved on 20 Jan. 1866, is illustrated in Perrout, *Trésors*, 57.

Plate 17. *La Vie du conscrit*: Pellerin (Epinal), 1841

Note the image of Napoleon behind the veteran in the last vignette.

Reproduced by permission of Bibliothèque nationale de France, Paris.

crucifix to convey the same meaning); she wipes her downcast eyes with her apron even as she gives him one final embrace.

All the second empire images combine the moment of the *tirage*, when the conscript's fate was decided, with the moment of departure, collapsing the intervening six months into one tearful moment. This dramatic sleight of hand also appears in Pellerin's illustration of the most popular of all conscript songs, *Le Conscrit de l'an dix*, which we have already heard the *classe* of Varennes singing to their mayor on the day of the *tirage*. Pellerin's shows the eponymous Languedocian stocking-weaver (whose authorship is asserted in the final verse) gazing in horror at the number two he has just pulled, but he already has a Dick Whittington-style stick and handkerchief over his shoulder, ready to follow the army guide waiting on his right. Even in 1810 conscripts were not expected to march away on the same day as the *tirage*, but in order to illustrate the song Pellerin had him ready to 'leave the Languedoc/ with sack on back'.[355]

Conscript songs similarly leapt movingly from the tirage straight to the departure: 'At the lottery for the militia/ I fell unfortunately/ Five years service/Goodbye for ever, my sweetheart.'[356] In both song and imagery the conscript's imminent departure is symbolised by the same piece of equipment – 'The soldier's haversack/ That speaks so much contempt/ To all the young girls/ Who are from our region.'[357] When the conscripts of Pournoy-la-Grasse (near Metz) returned from the *tirage* they announced to 'Julie, my sweet girl-friend' that 'my haversack is ready, in order to leave', even though they would not actually be saying their adieux for many months to come.[358] In popular culture the soldier's haversack, even more than his arms or his uniform, was his most vital accessory. It became a metaphor for the soldier's situation in life. The volunteer of 1792, Gabriel Noël, who was very alive to the conventions of soldiering (perhaps because he did not really feel himself to be one) wrote to his godmother that if he came across any curiosities, such as the ears of emigrés or the moustaches of uhlans, he would pop them in his haversack 'because a soldier must not travel without his haversack'.[359] When

---

355 'Je suis t'un pauvre conscrit,/ De l'an mille huit cent dit;/ Faut quitter le Languedo,/ avec le sac sur le dos': Bozon, *Les Conscrits*, 9. Pinot & Sagaire's better known version, *Le Départ du conscrit* (passed by the prefect on 17 Feb. 1866), does not make such a clear link between the *tirage* and the departure, for although the conscripts are decked in ribbons, they are not wearing their numbers.

356 'Au sort de la milice/ j'ai tombé par malheur/ cinq ans pour le service/ Adieu mon petit coeur': Garneret, *Chansons populaires comtoises*, i. 130: *Ma Charmante Maîtresse*.

357 'Le sac de militaire/ Qui cause tant de mépris/ A toutes les jeune filles/ Qui sont dans nos pays': L'Hôte, *La Tankiote*, 89.

358 'Mon sac est prèt, c'est pour partir./ J'ai vingt et un ans accomplis./ Mon numéro est pour partir': Westphalen, *Chansons populaires*, ii. no. 313: *Julie, ma douce amie*. The symbolism was as strong in germanophone songs as in francophone ones: 'Ach Vater, liebster Vater mein/ Soldaten müssen wir jetzt sein/ Tut ihr es den Hafersack richten': Pinck, *Verklingende Weisen*, iii. 381: *Conscritlied*.

359 'car un soldat ne doit point voyager sans son sac': Nöel, *Au Temps des volontaires*, 67.

Plate 18. *Le Départ du conscrit*: Pellerin (Epinal), 1875
Unusually, this woodcut version post-dates the original
lithograph by a decade. Reproduced by permission of the
Bibliothèque nationale de France, Paris.

his son was conscripted pastor Oberlin noted in his diary: 'My son
Henri-Gottfried, conscript, leaves Strasbourg haversack on back, but under
the auspices of divine providence.'[360] When the conscript put the pack on his
back he was separating himself from his family and home to join the vagabond community of the army.[361]

The conscript is still wearing his pack in Pinot's scene of return, but almost
everything else about him has changed. No longer a tearful boy, he sports a
Napoleon III goatee beard, and the emperor himself appears on three medals

[360] 'Mon fils Henri-Gottfried, conscrit, quitte Strasbourg le havre-sac sur le dos, mais sous
les auspices de la divine Providence': Mme Ernest Roehrich, 'Quelques Notes sur
Jean-Frédéric Oberlin', *Revue alsacienne illustrée* xii (1910), 59.
[361] In military slang the infantry were called 'Bifin' meaning rag-collector, because of the
pack they carried on their backs: Bayon, 'Sobriquets et superstitions militaires', 320.

Plate 19. *Le Départ du conscrit; Le Retour*: Pinot & Sagaire (Epinal), 1866
Reproduced by permission of the Musée départemental
d'art ancien et contemporain, Epinal.

on his chest. He seems very self-assured as he sweeps his sweetheart into his arms, and she surrenders to him with a look of ecstasy. And what is that baton which hangs down the conscript's trouser-leg? The answer is not obvious in Pinot's image but if we turn to Pellerin's lithographs we can see that it is the symbolic opposite of his haversack, it is the thing which will reunite him with his community, for this little metal cylinder contains his discharge papers. In slang it was known as 'the skittle'. 'Given the skittle' is still used in colloquial French to mean being sacked or released from prison, but it was originally a military term for one's discharge. To this day French conscripts begin to carve their own skittle, called the 'Père de Cent Jours', when there only remain a hundred days to their discharge. It is carried home proudly as proof that the conscript has accomplished his period of military service and has earned his freedom.[362] Pellerin makes clear its significance to the soldier's relationships, for if his fiancée's right hand points to the 'star of honour' on the zouave's chest (in the second empire colonials had replaced the light cavalry as the imagist's preferred representative of the armed forces) the other playfully taps the 'skittle' which he presents to her. Although Dominique Lerch has pointed out the resemblance between this image and contemporary lithographs of the *Madonna and Child*, I believe there is something more sexual than religious in the knowing look of joy that the conscript's fiancée's directs

---

[362] Bozon, *Les Conscrits*, 126. Bozon is, however, incorrect, I believe, about the derivation of this custom.

Plate 20. *Le Retour du conscrit*: Pellerin (Epinal), 1860
Reproduced by permission of the Mediathèque de Pontiffroy, Metz.

to the viewer. His 'skittle' represents not only the conscript's discharge, but also the manhood he acquired in the army. 'Skittle' is also a slang term for penis.

The shift of focus from the relationship between father and son to that between boyfriend and girlfriend may be indicative of a fundamental change in family relationships during the nineteenth century. In the opinion of historians of the family, it saw a dramatic decline in the power of the father. The control of patriarchs over their children's choice of spouses waned as increased mobility and new job opportunities in urban industries limited the importance of land inheritance in marriage strategies.[363] Conscription was

363 Mitterauer, *History of youth*, 111.

Plate 21. *Le Départ du conscrit; Le Retour du zouave*: Pellerin (Epinal), 1866
Reproduced by permission of the Musée départemental
d'art ancien et contemporain, Epinal.

itself a symptom of this change as sons left the control of their fathers to live
in towns, and many decided never to return to the land but to find work (and
wives) in their new environments.[364] The iconography of the theme lost its
overtones of the prodigal son as the primary concern of both conscript and
imagist was no longer to please the father, but the lover.

Pellerin seems to have thought that proof of the soldier's valour (a reflection, perhaps, on his manhood) was what young women really wanted. We
can see this very clearly in Pellerin's response to Pinot's cheaper, single sheet
version of *Le Départ du conscrit/Le Retour du zouave*, issued in 1866.[365]
Pellerin's version, like Pinot's, was based on his firm's own semi-fine lithographs, although the artist introduced some variations. In the scene of departure, the sad conscript has just returned from the *tirage* with his number
eleven, but again he has his bundle prepared ready to say goodbye. In the
scene of the return, the zouave enters from the right (in order to create the
feel of movement), his 'skittle' hanging down beside his pantaloons. His
fiancée, whom we last saw weeping into a hanky, rushes straight into his arms.
While she embraces him with one arm, the other points to the huge *croix
d'honneur* on his chest, and she turns to face the viewers, inviting them to
share her pleasure – one might even say to identify with her situation if, as I

364 Weber, *Peasants into Frenchmen*, 302.
365 MDAACE, no number.

presume, conscripts' fiancées were the target audience for this image. The conscript's mother has been erased from these images altogether; 'Mother-France' has entirely supplanted her. The father has been reduced to a tiny figure in the background of the second image, shown rushing from his cottage to greet his son, but he does not even warrant a glance from the zouave, his relationship with the girl he left behind him has become all-important. If there is a father-figure watching over their pairing it is not the peasant behind him but emperor who gave him his medal; the soldier as son of the nation has eclipsed the ties of blood. Barely recognisable as the boy who went away in the first image, the zouave sports a waxed moustache and a bushy beard, emphasising the maturity he has acquired during his absence. He is now a man and ready to marry. Looking at this image we can understand the confusion which led the originally contrasting badges worn by conscripts – 'Fit for the girls' and 'Fit for service' – to become interchangeable.

The process by which military service was a period of becoming a man, was also the conclusion of many conscript songs. Even when they give a dispiriting picture of military life, at the beck and call of any 'bugger of a sergeant', the days spent in pointless exercises and cold sentry-duty and often confined to the guardhouse, yet their conclusions are ambiguous.[366] The soldier who complains 'I feel too bad to stand up straight' looks forward to coming home a general, or at the very least a corporal.[367] The sufferings undergone by 'Jean-Jean' were necessary in order to turn him into a handsome soldier fit to marry his 'Naniche'.[368] The underlying message was the same as the reflection of the father of an 'thoughtless son' in a germanophone folktale: 'if he goes to the army as a soldier, then he will certainly grow up'.[369] This tale has the characteristic opening motif of *The return of the prodigal son* (AT935): the conscript pretends that he has been promoted to 'first soldier', then corporal and so on, and each time he writes to his father to ask for money to help equip him for his new post, which in reality he spends on loose living. The tale-type usually develops with the father, proud of his son's progress, coming to visit him, only to find he has either been imprisoned or deserted. Despite being abandoned by his angry parent, the son goes on to win the hand of the queen of England, but when he returns home to tell his father of his good fortune he is not believed, and sent to look after the pigs. Only when the queen herself arrives looking for her husband is he redeemed.[370]

Here we are face-to-face with some of the contradictions in the image of

---

[366] These examples of the miseries of the conscript's life (very similar, it should be noted, to those depicted in popular imagery) are taken from Zéliqzon and Thiriot, *Textes patois*, no. 19: *Lettre d'une recrue à ses parents*; Jouve, *Chansons en patois vosgien*, no. 77: *JeanJean*.

[367] 'J'a trop d'mau de m'tenin dreut': J. Thiriot, *Chansons lorraines*, Metz 1913, no. 11.

[368] Jouve, *Chansons en patois vosgien*, no. 77: *JeanJean*.

[369] 'Wenn er zum Militär kommt als Soldat, dann wird er schon erzogen werden': Merkelbach-Pinck, *Lothringer Volksmärchen*, 65: *Der eiserne Mann* (AT562).

[370] Although not common there are a few French variants of this tale type: Félice, *Contes de Haute-Bretagne*, 59–61: *Jean le fort* (AT935).

Plate 22. *Loterie alphabétique des 100 images*:
J = Jean Jean: Pellerin (Epinal), 1863
Reproduced by permission of the Archives
départementales des Vosges (photo: J. Laurençon).

the soldier: the conscript becomes a man by doing male things in the quintessentially male environment of the army – drinking, fighting, whoring and all the other vices which got Saint Luke's prodigal into so much hot water. But whereas in Christ's telling it was the prodigal's repentance which earned him forgiveness and reintegration into his original community, in the images and folktales the conscript is all but obliged to behave badly in order to mature and acquire the wherewithal to marry, and thus reintegrate himself. But there is yet another paradox, for the soldier's wild living is also character-istic of the periods of licence extended to liminals, such as the *classe*, during their rites of passage. Then the conscript's follies were tolerated because they were the preparation for his triumphs in life, and in both folktales and imagery his crowning achievement was marriage. But had the conscripts, who pulled lucky numbers in the lottery and remained in the village, continued to behave in this fashion after the *classe* had broken up they would have drawn the opprobrium of their fellow villagers. Conscripts aped the behaviour of soldiers in order to become men, but the same behaviour which made the *classe* marginal within the village community, made the army marginal to society as a whole.

4

The Serving Soldier: Friend and Foe

The images on the theme of *Le Départ et le retour du conscrit* make manifest the gulf of experience between the 'Blanc-bec' and the soldier, and hint at the processes by which the one was reshaped into the other. When 'Jean-Jean' joined his unit it was the start of a further series of rituals designed to separate him from his old world and initiate him into a different society. First his appearance would be completely transformed, his hair shorn, his peasant's smock discarded in favour of military uniform. The importance of this rite of separation was attested by numerous military writers: 'It is the transformation of the interior by the exterior. So do not deny the usefulness of uniform; it's the uniform that makes the soldier.'[1] The Vosgian conscript Louis Maugenre confirmed this officer's views when he wrote to his parents 'I do not know how to explain to you all my feelings while removing my civilian clothes one-by-one; it felt like I was taking leave of old friends.'[2] This was, of course, precisely the intention, to shed old relationships and form new ones within the regiment. However, although the recruit may, in his new uniform, have looked more like a soldier, he had a long way to go before he was accepted by his new comrades as an equal.

The first step was to visit the bar and buy a round of drinks: 'the gospel is less true than the article of military law that states: Conscript, you will pay for older comrade'.[3] This was a frequent scene in imagery; Dembour & Gangel's *Scènes de garnison* has a sergeant addressing a conscript: 'Conscript, I grant you the right to pay', to which the well-advised recruit replies 'Thank you Mister sergeant'.[4] Had he not he would no doubt have received the lesson illustrated by Pellerin in which a sergeant carefully explains to the archetypal conscript Nicolas Chauvin that money sent by his parents does not belong to

---

[1] 'c'est la transformation de l'intérieur par l'extérieur. Niez pas donc l'utilité de l'uniforme: c'est par l'uniforme qu'on est soldat': Delmart and Vidal, *La Caserne*, 26.

[2] 'Je ne saurais vous dire, toutes mes impressions en déposant un à un mes habits civils; il me semblait que je quittais de vieux amis': Louis-Marie-Auguste Maugenre, *Le Sergent Maugenre 1801–1887: trente-et-un ans au 36ème de ligne: récits et documents militaires inédits*, Saint-Dié 1891, 40.

[3] 'l'évangile est moins vrai que l'article de la loi militaire qui dit: Conscrit, tu paieras à ton ancien': Delmart and Vidal, *La Caserne*, 19.

[4] ' "Conscrit, je te donne le droit de payer." "Merci, monsieur le sergent" ': MDAACE, no number. See also Garnier-Pelle, *L'Imagerie populaire française*, ii, no. 1968: *Scènes de garnison*.

Plate 23. *Scènes militaires*: la prise d'uniforme:
Gangel (Metz), 1854
Reproduced by permission of the Musée
départemental d'art ancien et contemporain, Epinal

him personally.[5] The expectation that newcomers should supply their predecessors is also witnessed in folklore. In a Breton tale an old hand, Père-le-
Chique (a character we will meet again), offers to show the ropes to a Parisian
recruit in return for drinking money.[6] There was, therefore, a theoretical reci-
procity to these monetary exactions, but in many cases the tradition masked
the organised fleecing of new recruits, making their first weeks in the regiment a misery. Military memoirists tend to refer euphemistically to the more
unpleasant trials of their early career, in order to press on with the account of
their glory days once accepted into their new community.[7] Bangofsky was
unusually forthcoming about his arrival at the regimental depot in 1799:

---

[5] *Scènes militaires* (*dépôt légal* 1874), Archives départementales des Vosges, Epinal,
8/T/unnumbered.
[6] Paul Sébillot, 'Contes de marins recueillis en Haute-Bretagne', *Archivio per lo studio
delle tradizioni popolari* x (1891), 105: *Le Matelot qui épousa la fille du roi d'Angleterre*
(AT307, AT935).
[7] Maubec, a recruit for the Gardes françaises in 1760, is typical of the ironic mode
adopted by soldiers when dealing with this period of initiation: 'des âmes charitables
s'empressaient d'instruire le nouveau venu de ce qu'il ignorait et entreprenaient de le
former': Jean Chagniot, *Paris et l'armée au XVIIIe siècle: étude politique et sociale*, Paris 1985,
571.

Plate 24. *Scènes de garnison*: 'Conscrit je te
donne le droit de payer': Dembour & Gangel
(Metz), *c*. 1840–51
Reproduced by permission of the Musée
départemental d'art ancien et
contemporain, Epinal.

Until then we had only seen the good side of the military profession. But what a deception, on arriving at Gray, to see ourselves treated like slaves! I understood then the miseries of a poor soldier . . . under the cane of a heap of louts [*goujats* – which in cavalry parlance sometimes has the specific meaning of officers' servants] who, as long as you had the wherewithal to treat them, were friendly enough, but, as soon as money was lacking, became unbending.[8]

---

[8] 'Jusqu'alors on n'avait vu que le beau côté du métier militaire. En arrivant à Gray, quelle déception de se voir traités commes des esclaves! Je compris alors les privations d'un pauvre soldat . . . sous la férule d'un tas de goujats qui, tant que vous aviez de quoi les régaler, faisaient bonne mine, mais, dès que l'argent manquait, devenaient intraitables': Roche du Teilloy, *Les Etapes de Georges Bangofsky*, 8.

Maugenre's religious faith, but even more his physical strength, helped him get through the worst of it: 'On a peur de ma force et on me respecte: les chicaneurs et les solliciteurs de petits verres n'osent pas se frotter près de moi.' But neither stopped him being robbed by his sergeant-major: Maugenre, *Le Sergent Maugenre*, 40–1.

Plate 25. *Alphabet militaire comique: B = Blanc-bec*: Pinot & Sagaire (Epinal), 1864
The Blanc-bec is undergoing a rite of passage, the duel. Reproduced by permission of
the Archives départementales des Vosges (photo: J. Laurençon).

The ribbing and bullying carried on through the recruit's basic training, although his path might be eased by 'un pays', a compatriot from his home village or region already serving in the regiment who would arrange for him to have a decent bed-partner (vitally important!) and stick up for him in fights.[9] The value of 'un pays' was regularly recorded in folktales.[10] At some point he might well be expected to be blooded in a duel: 'the fight with cold steel was, in effect, a sort of initiation rite for the recruit from which he could not escape without losing face'.[11] Again, this initiation ceremony was frequently depicted by imagists.[12]

An obvious symbol of his initiation into his new life in the regiment was the replacement of the soldier's patronymic, his most personal link to his civilian life, with a *nom-de-guerre*. The birth certificate of Jean-Charles Pellerin, uncle of the future imagist, named the father as 'Charles le Ranconnier, carabinier', neglecting to mention his family name altogether.[13]

The custom was already well established in the seventeenth century when the use of *noms-de-guerre* was considered typical of the vaunting boastfulness of the military, and one of the army's particularisms that separated it from civilian society. The name was not chosen by the soldier himself, but given by either his comrades or his officer, so that joining the army was akin to being baptised anew, a clear indication that the soldier was moving into a new social world.[14] However, *noms-de-guerre* highlighted a very different set of values to Christian names, stressing the soldier's physical attributes, his womanising, his talent for violence, his drunkenness and his carelessness with his own life and property.[15]

This distinctive feature of military life declined in the second half of the eighteenth century, partly because officers of the period, influenced by the *philosophes*, started to give names drawn from classical literature which their troops considered silly.[16] But although officially abandoned during the revolution (when the authorities disapproved of such marks of distinction

---

9 Delmart and Vidal, *La Caserne*, 18.

10 The value of a 'pays' was emphasised in Breton tales, perhaps because Bretons as an ethnic minority felt greater need. This introduction is typical: 'Il y avait une fois deux soldats, à l'armée, qui étaient amis. Ils étaient de la même commune, de Pouvénez-Moïdec; ils étaient camarades de lit et on les voyait presque toujours ensemble': Francois-Marie Luzel, *Contes populaires de Basse-Bretagne*, Paris 1887, iii. 77: *L'Homme de fer* (AT562, AT560).

11 'Le combat à l'arme blanche était en effet, pour la recrue une sorte de rite initiatique, auquel il ne fallait pas se dérober, sous peine d'être discrédité': Chagniot, *Paris et l'armée*, 589.

12 Garnier-Pelle, *L'Imagerie populaire française*, ii, nos 1432, 1250.

13 Dumont, *La Vie et l'oeuvre*, 76 n. 24.

14 André Corvisier, *Les Contrôles des troupes de l'ancien régime*, Paris 1968.

15 Idem, *L'Armée française*, i. 848–61.

16 Jean-Paul Bois has also suggested that the decline in the use of *noms-de-guerre* may have been the result of a growing attachment and pride in patronymics: *Les Anciens Soldats dans la société française au XVIIIe siècle*, Paris 1990, 131–3.

Plate 26. *Les Quatre Vérités du siècle d'aujourd'hui*:
Pellerin (Epinal), *c.* 1816
This was the second of four versions of this image issued by Pellerin
during the nineteenth century. Reproduced by permission of the Musée
départemental d'art ancien et contemporain, Epinal.

between soldier and citizen), in practice *noms-de-guerre* survived as nick-
names well into the nineteenth century. And veterans kept them after their
discharge. Gabriel Richard's study of sobriquets in the four departments of
Lorraine between 1800 and 1850 reveals numerous *noms-de-guerre* still in
everyday use among veterans and their neighbours.[17] More important, for this
study, *noms-de-guerre* lived on in popular culture, as we will see in chapter 5.

Military initiation was often brutal and designed to be definitive. Painful
though these rites must have been to the homesick conscript, they were none
the less important in breaking his ties with home and creating the *esprit de*

[17] Gabriel Richard, 'Les Sobriquets en Lorraine dans la première moitié du XIXe siècle',
Annales de l'est, 5th ser. xv (1963), 357.

corps necessary for an effective fighting unit. They created the sense that the soldier was a member of a separate order of society. The distinctive place of soldiers within the social hierarchy was a frequent subject for imagists.

Soldiers and the second estate

When Dominique Lerch argued that imagery transmitted a norm he cited the example of a farmer from Alsace who declared with pride 'I feed you all', just like the peasant in Wentzel's lithograph of *Die verschiedenen Stände im menschlichen Leben* which hung on his wall.[18] The theme of *Die verschiedenen Stände* in German popular art – a graphic depiction of the various classes or estates who made up the social order – was related to the British print theme the *Four* or *Five* or *Six alls*. On eighteenth-century English pub-signs a king, bishop, lawyer and soldier each declared what they did for all, but the motto of the final figure, a 'poor countryman' (or, in some cases, John Bull) was 'I pay for all'.[19] In French imagery the theme is represented by *Les Quatre Vérités du siècle d'aujourd'hui*. *Les Quatre Vérités* were representatives of the different functional groups in society who, in turn, explained their contribution to the whole. The first figure was the priest, who declared 'I pray for you all'. Second came the soldier on sentry duty who declared 'I defend you all'. Third came the peasant, despised and neglected by the rest, but still able to claim that through his labours 'I feed you all'. Finally the lawyer was pictured at his desk. Initially he compared himself to the soldier, as the defender of his clients' interests, but finally admitted 'I eat you all'. The lawyer contributed nothing to society, he only took.

The Pellerin company produced four different versions of the *Quatre Vérités* between 1814 and 1892. They hardly altered in form over the course of the century, although the soldier's uniform was updated.[20] Similar images appeared in the catalogue of just about every other provincial imagist.[21] The

---

18 'Je vous nourris tous': Lerch, *Imagerie et société*, 203.
19 Watt, *Cheap print and popular piety*, 163; Francis Grose, A *classical dictionary of the vulgar tongue*, London 1796, *s.v.* 'Alls'. There still is a 'Five Alls' pub in Benwick, Cambridgeshire. Readers interested in folk music may also recognise the distant origins of the American folksinger Fiddlin' John Carson's 1929 song *The taxes on the farmer feeds them all*.
20 Garnier-Pelle, *L'Imagerie populaire française*, ii, nos 1396–8. Although the first image is considered to date from before 1814, the reference to the 'lys de français' in the text indicates that the print, if not the block, post-dates the Restoration. The second, by Georgin, certainly belongs to the Restoration as the grenadier has the fleur-de-lis on his cap. The third image was approved by the *dépôt légal* in 1875, but the soldier is in the uniform of the second empire, and as the engraver, Vanson, died in 1870 it must be a reissue of an earlier image. The final version, a lithograph, does not appear in the Garnier-Pelle catalogue but was still available from pedlars in the last decade of the century: Henri Gaidoz, 'Un Ancêtre du "quatrième état" dans l'imagerie populaire', *Mélusine* vi (1892), plate 3.
21 Imagists who issued versions of the *Quatre Vérités* include Deckherr (Montbéliard);

Plate 27. *Les Quatres Veritez du siecle d'apresent*:
Letourmy (Orléans), c. 1780
Reproduced by permission of the Musée départemental
d'art ancien et contemporain, Epinal.

satire was likely to prove popular among their peasant customers, for it reflected their widespread distrust and resentment of the law and its officers. It was the prayer of the French peasant to be delivered from 'all ill and from Justice'.[22] Their hostility was recorded in the *cahiers des doléances* prepared for the estates general in 1788–9 by rural assemblies; one village in Lorraine complained of the financial ruin wreaked by 'Jews, guards and lawyers'.[23]

Lecrêne-Labbey (Rouen, 1819, 1820); Picard-Guérin (Caen); Gangel (Metz, 1854, but almost certainly a reissue of an earlier image by J.-P. Clerc of Belfort [see frontispiece]); Mercier (Nantes, c. 1825); Rabier-Boulard (Orléans, 1820); Garson (Paris, 1840).

[22] Weber, *Peasants into Frenchmen*, 50–1.
[23] John Markoff, *The abolition of feudalism: peasants, lords and legislators in the French revolution*, University Park, Penn. 1996, 61.

Plate 28. *Les Quatre Veritez du siecle dapresent:*
Marteret? (Châtillon-sur-Seine), *c.* 1721
This is a reprint taken from an old woodcut found in a print-works at
Châtillon-sur-Seine. As no image made from this block is known it is
impossible to be entirely certain of its provenance, but it was copied from a
1721 copperplate print by Basset of Paris. Reproduced by permission of the
Musée départemental d'art ancien et contemporain, Epinal.

Partly this antagonism was due to the role played by lawyers as agents of land-
lords and seigneurs enforcing feudal dues, a major factor in exacerbating
tension in 1788 and 1789. But a more obvious reference in the images is to
lawyers' important role as rural moneylenders, made explicit in Pellerin's first
version, because behind the lawyer's desk is a notice of a bankruptcy sale.
Credit was becoming increasingly necessary for the functioning of the rural
economy, but it put peasants in the power of their creditors and, as the image
warns, lawyers eat country clowns who entrust their affairs to them.

Pellerin's first version was itself a faithful copy of Garnier-Allabre's, dating
from about 1812. Jacques-Marin Garnier credited one of his father's firm's
occasional engravers, the travelling puppeteer Boniot, with the original
concept for the image.[24] Unbeknownst to Garnier, however, the theme
already had a long history. Boniot probably got his inspiration from a late
eighteenth-century version by Letourmy of Orléans.[25] Earlier woodblocks

[24] Garnier, *Histoire de l'imagerie populaire*, 107–8.
[25] Boniot was co-owner of a puppet theatre which travelled all over western France,
giving him the opportunity to pick up themes from other centres: MDAACE 69.15.12, *Les
Quatres Veritez du siècle d'apresent.*

dating from the first quarter of the century have survived at Chalon-sur-Saône and Châtillon-sur-Seine, and they feature exactly the same cast of characters.[26] These were copied from a copperplate print by Basset of Paris, and dated 1721.[27] The *Quatre Vérités* had, therefore, been proclaiming their contemporary veracity from the walls of country cottages not only for the nineteenth century, but the eighteenth century, and perhaps even earlier.

Les Quatre Vérités developed out of the medieval *Danse macabre*, or rather combined this theme with representations of the various orders of men. Medieval representations of the three estates depicted Christ appearing in the sky above the assembled representatives of first two estates, the clergy and the nobility, to give them their respective functions – the spiritual and physical protection of mankind. A peasant appears in the background, hard at work, representing the third estate – those who 'labour' used in its original sense of turning the earth.[28] The ancestor of the *Quatre Vérités* was formed by simply replacing Christ with Death.[29] The transition had certainly taken place by the end of the sixteenth century, to judge from the reference in an English pamphlet, William Basse's 1619 *A helpe to discourse*. Basse's interlocutor poses the question 'Who are those that pray for all, Defend all, Feed all, Deuoure all?' to which the answer is given 'In an old picture, I found it thus written, The Pope with his Clergy, saies, I pray for you all; *Cæsar* with his Electors, I defend you all; The Clown [meaning a peasant] with his sack of Corne, I nourish you all: at last comes Death and sayes, I deuoure you all.'[30] The image referred to by Basse has not survived, but an analogous sixteenth-century French woodcut contains most of the same characters. A knight, the pope and the emperor – who respectively 'defend you all', 'absolve you all' and 'maintain you all' – sit at a table held up by two peasants who 'feed you all'. Above them hovers the skeletal figure of Death, who 'takes you all'.[31] At some point during the seventeenth century Death lost its position of dominance in the image, part of a wider trend that saw Death marginalised within popular culture.[32] Into his place, and borrowing his motto, stepped the lawyer. Within the framework of the image this substitution seems to suggest that the lawyer represented a kind of fourth estate.[33]

---

[26] Ferrand, *Les Bois gravés chalonnais*, no. 46; René Saulnier, 'Les Vieux Bois d'images populaires du Musée de Châtillon-sur-Seine', *L'Art populaire en France* iii (1931), no. 52.

[27] Jean Adhémar, *Imagerie populaire française*, Milan 1968, no. 54. A German copy of the Basset orginal is reproduced in Wolfgang Bruckner, *Populäre Druckgraphik Europas: Deutschland*, Munich 1969, no. 104.

[28] Ottavia Niccoli, *I sacerdoti, i guerrieri, i contadini: storia di un 'immagine della società'*, Turin 1979, figs 4–6, 8, 9.

[29] A Dutch painting, which dates from the 1620s and is now in the Bowes Museum, Barnard Castle, Co. Durham, demonstrates the connection.

[30] William Basse, *A helpe to discourse*, London 1619, 123. I am grateful to Dr Malcolm Jones for pointing out this reference.

[31] Gaidoz, 'Un Ancêtre du "quatrieme état" ', *Mélusine* vii (1895), plate 1.

[32] Day, 'Representing ageing and death', 694–6.

[33] The precise *ancien régime* meanings for the terms estate, corps and order, and the rela-

In common parlance there were but three estates: the clergy, the nobility and then the rest who formed the third estate. Among other things, the three estates provided the forum for political representation in France, at both local and national level. The political third estate was predominantly made up of townsfolk, with lawyers and officials of the administration particularly well represented. However, pictorially the third estate was always represented by a peasant – an iconographic tradition reactivated in 1789. Readers may be familiar with the numerous images depicting the conflict between the three estates at the time of the revolution, and in particular the series of copper-plate images issued by the Parisian Villeneuve in which a peasant (the third estate) turns the tables on his oppressors, the first and second estates, repre-sented by a priest and a noble army officer.[34] Interestingly, these copperplate images were not enthusiastically taken up by the provincial woodcut imagists, with the important exception of Letourmy of Orléans.[35] While urban revolu-tionaries were happy to see themselves symbolised by a peasant in the prints available in Paris, peasants may not have recognised themselves in the image.[36] Whatever their reactions to the revolution, it would have been diffi-cult for them to see themselves as forming part of the same estate as the urban deputies or the sans-culottes.

The urban–rural divide is one that runs through French history, and it may explain why, despite the legal status of the three estates, both bourgeois and peasant often preferred representations of four estates, achieved by splitting the political element of the third estate – the bourgeois – from the rest. This was an old idea.[37] In a fifteenth-century French panel painting, the emperor, a monk, a peasant and a lawyer take turns to explain their role in terms similar to those in Pellerin's image of the Quatre Vérités (the lawyer, in this instance, was depicted as an equally valuable member of society, declaring 'ie procure por tous quatre') only to be followed by Death and the announce-ment 'Je vous emporterai tous quatre'.[38] A woodcut of Les Quatre Estats

tionship between them, are not absolutely clear. Many historians seem to use the terms estate and order interchangeably, with corps as a sub-division of both. William Sewell has attempted to give more definition to these terms: 'Etat, corps and ordre: some notes on the social vocabulary of the French old regime', in Hans-Ulrich Wehler (ed.), Sozialgeschichte Heute: Festschrift für Hans Rosenberg zum 70. Geburtstag, Göttingen 1974, 49–68.

[34] They are very frequently used to illustrate the covers of books on the French revolu-tion, for example Markoff's The abolition of feudalism.

[35] Garnier, L'Imagerie populaire française, i, nos 91–4.

[36] Michel Vovelle, 'The countryside and the peasantry in revolutionary iconography', in Alan Forrest and Peter Jones (eds), Reshaping France: town, country and region during the French revolution, Manchester 1991, 26–36.

[37] In 1483, during Margaret of Austria's triumphal entry into Paris, four tableaux of figures marked her passage, representing the peasant, the clergy, merchants and nobility: Gaidoz, 'Un Ancêtre du "quatrieme état" ', vii, cols 147–8.

[38] Eustache-Hyacinthe Langlois, Essai historique, philosophique et pittoresque sur les danses des morts, Rouen 1852, ii. 146–9. A similar group of figures comprising a judge, merchant, bishop, knight and shepherd, was used to adorn Parisian death notices, implying that

Plate 29. *Die verschiedenen Stände im menschlichen Leben:*
Maÿ und Wirsing (Frankfurt-am-Main), 1851
This rearrangement of the orders of society proved popular in Germany and
Alsace during the nineteenth century. Reproduced by permission of
the Musée départemental d'art ancien et contemporain, Epinal.

figured in the 1598 inventory of the workshop of Denis de Mathonière, a
rue Montorgueil imagist.[39] This iconographic tradition suggests that the
lawyer in the *Quatre Vérités* was not merely a representative of a particular
obnoxious profession (as far as peasants were concerned) but the whole urban
world.

While the implication of the *Quatre Vérités* is that at least three of the four
estates or orders were equally necessary to the happiness of society, some
versions suggest that some were more equal than others.[40] In an eighteenth-century Dutch woodcut (adapted from a French original) the pastor,
lawyer and soldier all do their parts, but the peasant declares 'You may pray,

death comes to us all, regardless of rank. They have also been found on gravestones in
Brittany and Haarlem.
[39] Georges Wildenstein and Jean Adhémar, 'Les Images de Denis de Mathonière d'après
son inventaire (1598)', *Arts et traditions populaires* viii (1960), 156.
[40] In an uncharacteristically po-faced image engraved by Boulay for Clerc of Belfort (and
subsequently reissued by Gangel), the priest, the farmer, the dragoon and the lawyer each
claim for themselves the most important role, only to be informed by the legend underneath 'qu'ils ne sont supportable et nécessaires que réunis ensemble et se soutenant les uns
et les autres': MNATP 51.30.4 D (see frontispiece). Such even-handed treatments were
more popular in German imagery.

you may fight, you may plead, but it is I, the peasant, who has the eggs.'[41] German and Alsatian nineteenth-century imagists, including Wentzel, combined this message with an antisemitic satire in their images of *Die verschiedenen Stände*. By adapting the stone-bridge layout of *Les Degrés des âges*, they increased the number of orders to seven, and created a tympanum in which was pictured the foundation of society, a farmer pushing his plough. The other 'Stände' represented – the emperor, noble, priest, soldier and beggar – all contributed something to society, even if, as in the last figure, it was only to offer the others the opportunity for charity. A Jewish pedlar replaced the lawyer of French variants as the butt of the satire because he took 'profit from you all'.[42] But while all the other orders had a function, they only existed because of the more vital work of the farmer who, with his sack of corn, was the support of all.

Angelika Merkelbach-Pinck believed images similar to this, visible on the walls of every rural inn in germanophone Lorraine, embodied 'the proud self-consciousness of the peasant'.[43] They asserted the value of his contribution to society, but also served as a complaint that this went largely unrecognised and unrewarded. This message was made more forcibly in the song that sometimes accompanied images of the *Quatre Vérités – Le Pauvre Laboureur*. This song was first recorded in 1548, it appeared on Basset's 1721 copperplate image of the *Les Veritez du temps* (the inspiration for at least two eighteenth-century popular images), and continued to be hawked by market-singers well into the nineteenth century.[44] It was regularly recorded by folklorists, who noted that it was sung to accompany the rhythm of the plough. In versions from the upper Loire the ploughman proclaimed 'The poor *laboureur*,/ Considered a vile creature,/ Feeds the nobility:/ Nothing is more certain./ There is no king, nor prince,/ Nor bishop, nor lord/ Who lives without the effort/ Of the poor *laboureur*.'[45] The theme appealed to peasants of all language groups: variants were translated into Breton and German, transmitted by broad-sheets and eventually made their way into folksong collections.[46] The

---

41 Maurits de Meyer, *De Volks-en Kinderprent in de Nederlanden van de 15e tot de 20 eeuw*, Antwerp–Amsterdam 1962, 398.

42 MDAACE, no number. This may be the image referred to by Gaidoz: 'Un ancêtre du "quatrième état" ', vii, cols 153–4.

43 'Auf der obersten Stufe stand in stolzem Selbstbewusstein der Bauer. Unter dem Bild waren die Worte zu lesen: "Eine Hand muss lehren, die andere muss wehren,/ doch ich, ich muss euch alle ernähren" ': Merkelbach-Pinck, *Brauche und Sitte*, 17.

44 Julien Tiersot, *Chansons populaires recueillies dans les alpes françaises*, Grenoble 1903, 463. For a list of versions of this song consult Laforte and Champagne, *Le Catalogue de la chanson folklorique française*, ii. 609.

45 'Le pauvre laboureur,/ Passant pour un vilain,/ Nourrit la noblesse;/ N'y a rien de plus certain./ N'y a pas roi ni prince,/ Ni évêque, ni seigneur/ Qui ne vive de la peine/ Du pauvre laboureur': Victor Smith, 'Chansons populaires du Velay et du Forez', *Mélusine* i (1888), col. 458.

46 Joseph Ollivier, *Catalogue bibliographique de la chanson populaire bretonne sur feuilles*

affirmation of the peasants' social role expressed both in the song and the image may account for their long popularity in rural popular culture. To 'tell someone the four truths' survives in the colloquial French phrase meaning to tell someone how it really is: in this case that meant that peasants were the foundation of the social order.

However, if we accept that the *Quatre Vérités* corresponded to a peasant's eye view of the social hierarchy, does this mean that peasants possessed some sort of 'estate or order-consciousness'? If the analysis of the image is correct (and my assumption about its symbolic value as a statement of peasant self-awareness is true), it does seem that peasants considered function in society as the definition of social organisation, and that the shared role of the peasantry as the 'feeder of all' obviated other distinctions. Peasants, therefore, fulfil some of the conditions of the 'society of orders' which, according to Roland Mousnier, typified the *ancien régime* (even though peasants cannot be fitted into the legalistic framework of *états*, *corps* and *ordres* within which he worked).[47] It is feasible that it was this 'order consciousness' rather than their isolation that prevented peasants from becoming 'class conscious', as Marx and others wished they would. If so this would have important ramifications for the longstanding debate on peasant politicisation, but sadly this is far too big a subject to tackle within the parameters of this book. And there are many difficulties with this suggestion, not least the precise meaning of the word *laboureur*.[48] The concept of a peasant's imagined 'society of orders' is even more problematic when extended into the nineteenth century. The revolu-

volantes, Quimper 1942, 564; Pinck, *Verklingende Weisen*, ii. 142–6, 366–8, no. 45: *Bauernstand*.

[47] Roland Mousnier's formulation of a 'society of orders', although explored at length in numerous other works, is summarised in 'Les Concepts d'*ordres*, d'*états*, d'*fidélité*, et de *monarchie absolue* en France de la fin du XVe siècle à la fin du XVIIIe', *Revue historique* ccxlvii (1972), 289–312. Mousnier's work has been strongly criticised by numerous experts in the field, but I am inclined to agree with Peter Burke's view that in order to take an emic view of social solidarities and social conflicts in the past we must make use of 'contemporaries' social vocabulary, to recover "the insiders" models of society': 'The language of orders in early modern Europe', in Michael L. Bush (ed.), *Social orders and social classes in Europe since 1500: studies in social stratification*, London 1992, 11.

[48] Historians have found the term *laboureur* a useful designation for the small percentage of rural proprietors and small tenant farmers rich enough to own their own plough. Rather than an order, therefore, *laboureurs* appear to have been a kind of peasant-entrepreneur class. Peter Jones was largely responsible for introducing the term into English in this sense. However, as he points out, in the language of *ancien régime* France *laboureur* has a variety of meanings: *The peasantry in the French revolution*, Cambridge 1988, 10. In the Ile-de-France and in Lorraine it was certainly used by elite commentators to refer to richer peasants (as in La Fontaine's fable), but in many other areas it was used simply to refer to a ploughman, or to a peasant. In the regions where the song *Le Pauvre Laboureur* was mostly collected – Burgundy, Dauphiné, Brittany – it was clearly 'implied both in the text and the context in which it was sung' that the term applied to he who laboured in the sense of turning the earth.

tion swept away even the forms of a society of orders in one of its very first acts, the Tennis Court Oath of 20 June 1789. Jacques-Louis David's painting of this critical moment, when the representatives of the third estate in the estates-general declared themselves to be the National Assembly, has at its centre a symbolic union of orders.[49] Thereafter, in theory, orders were obsolescent, the entire citizenry was united in the body of the nation. Yet why, then, were images of the *Quatre Vérités* still on sale a century later? Perhaps we can understand why peasants, in their taste for imagery, seemed to argue for continuities with the *ancien régime* peasant when we recall that fully three-fifths of the delegates of the third estate who took the Tennis Court Oath were lawyers of one kind or another.

This digression into peasant attitudes to the social order is important to this study because the *Quatre Vérités* is one of the few images that puts peasants and soldiers side-by-side. However, the very presence of the soldier poses a further difficulty for this interpretation of the *Quatre Vérités* as a vision of a society of orders. In the versions closest to the *Danse des morts* the aristocratic order was represented by the emperor himself, or at the very least by a knight, clearly a representative of the second estate. However, by the time Basset issued his print of *Les Veritez du temps* in 1721 the knight had been replaced by the musketeer, and from that point on the soldier replaced the aristocrat in images of the *Quatre Vérités*. Basset's musketeer does seem very close to his noble predecessors: he occupies the same position in their visual order, and his motto, 'I guard you all', is the same. With the professionalisation of European armies in the seventeenth century the common soldier had taken over the warrior function of the nobility: the imagists were in this sense entirely justified in putting him in the place of the second estate. However, whatever their function in society, legally soldiers were not a separate estate, indeed the majority originated in the third estate, the same order of society as the peasants. Nor do soldiers meet the other requirement for membership of a distinct order – blood inheritance. Increasingly, from the end of the sixteenth century onwards, French nobles relied on 'race' as the defining quality which separated them from the *roture*, but even within the third estate there was a presumption that functions within society were inherited: the son of a potter became a potter, the son of a blacksmith became a blacksmith. Soldiering, however, was one occupation that was comparatively rarely inherited even under the *ancien régime*, and with the introduction of conscription even this weak sense of the army as membership of a distinct *corps* transmissible from generation to generation was lost. In what sense, then, did soldiers belong to a separate order? Yet if we do not accept the implication of the *Quatre Vérités* that this was indeed how soldiers were seen by peasants it is very difficult to make sense of the image of the military in rural popular culture. The message of these images was that soldiers and peasants were distinct orders of men,

---

[49] Emmet Kennedy, *A cultural history of the French revolution*, New Haven 1989, 247–54.

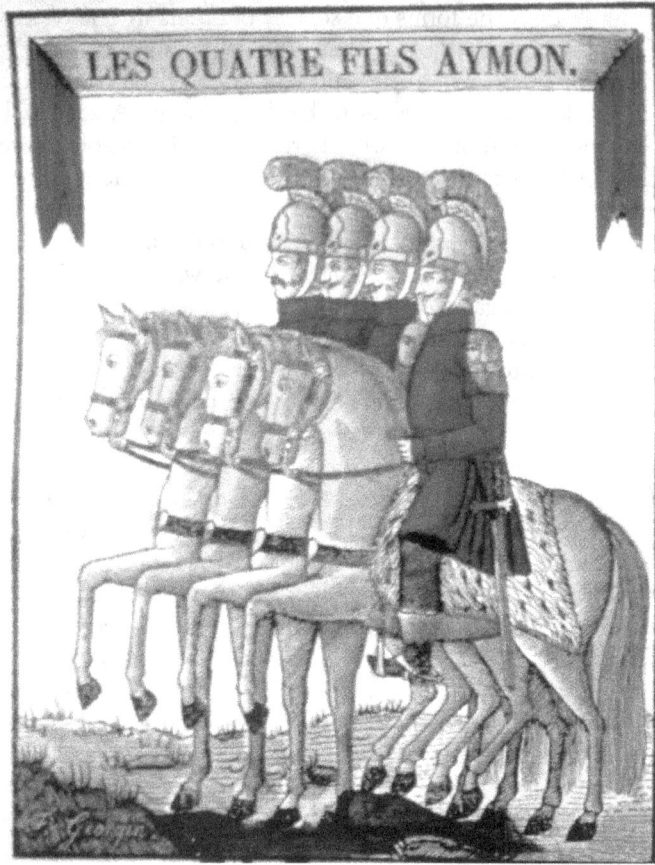

Plate 30. *Les Quatre Fils Aymon*: Pellerin (Epinal), 1830
Reproduced by permission of the Musée départemental
d'art ancien et contemporain, Epinal.

and that soldiers were closer to the second estate than the third. Popular attitudes towards soldiers were predicated on this relationship.

The connection between noble and soldier is readily apparent in popular
imagery. The hero of *Adélaïde et Ferdinand*, one of the most popular of the
secular 'carols', was supposed to be a Frankish nobleman of Neustria who,
driven by unjustified jealousy, kills first his son and then his wife. However,
the figure urging forward his horse in Diot of Beauvais's treatment is not a
Dark Ages warrior but very obviously a nineteenth-century army officer.[50]

[50] Henri Fromage, 'Un Maître de l'imagerie populaire au début du XIXe à Beauvais:
Côme-Lucien Diot', *Groupe d'étude des monuments et oeuvres d'art du Beauvaisis* xii (1981),
27. Diot's image was probably the model for Pellerin's first version which also depicts an
army officer (although in later versions, under the influence of nineteenth-century roman-

The practice of dressing the aristocratic heroes of the past in the uniforms of contemporary soldiers – in particular dragoons – was common among imagists. In Georgin's image of *Les Quatre Fils d'Aymon* the implacable enemies of Charlemagne are depicted in the plumes and epaulettes of the dragoons. They even have vestigial *fleurs-de-lis* on their helmets.[51]

Dragoons were the favoured arm of the military in French popular culture, and in particular in oral literature. In folksongs about soldiers the hero was commonly a 'beau dragon' and, as in imagery, they often stepped into the place vacated by earlier aristocrats.[52] *Germaine* is one of the very few medieval French ballads which survived in oral culture long enough to be collected by folklorists. The eponymous heroine no sooner marries her nobleman (a count or a baron according to two Lorrainer versions) than he is summoned away to the wars for seven years. On his return he is not recognised by either Germaine or her mother-in-law, and only reveals himself after testing his wife's fidelity. However, in one version collected in the Barrois, the returning husband is not a count or baron, but a captain of dragoons.[53] In the case of *Germaine*, soldiers and nobles were allomotifs.

Not only were soldiers able to replace aristocrats in particular songs and tales, but whole themes were transferred from the latter to the former. A standard theme in oral literature, made famous by Odysseus, was the return of the husband from the wars just in time to prevent his wife's remarriage. A variation on the theme, popular in germanophone Lorraine, was the ballad of *Graf Backewill*. Captured during the Hungarian wars, he was freed after seven years in a Turkish prison by the power of prayer and transported to his own castle just as the guests arrived for his wife's wedding banquet.[54] A similar story was told in francophone Lorraine about the lord of Réchicourt.[55] Although no ballad has survived about him, the theme had been as popular in medieval

---

ticism's chivalric revival, he was replaced by a medieval knight: Garnier-Pelle, *L'Imagerie populaire française*, ii, nos 918–20.

[51] Perrout, *Trésors*, 253.

[52] Dragoons were the preferred representatives of the military in oral literature. The most popular folktale regiments were the *Dragons verts* and the *Dragons dorés*.

[53] Etienne Fourier de Bacourt, 'Anciens Chants populaires du Barrois', *Bulletins de la Société d'archéologie lorraine* xliv (1894), no. 20. The more traditional aristocratic version can be found in Puymaigre, *Chants populaires*, i, no. 2, and Westphalen, *Chansons populaires*, i, no. 20. It is perhaps worth noting that Fourier de Bacourt's version may have been the earliest of the three to be recorded.

[54] Pinck, *Verklingende Weisen*, i. 81. Pinck was delighted to collect this song from the lips of his main informant, Papa Gerné; it provided proof that the oral tradition of Lorraine had preserved the Germanic culture of the Middle Ages, because the ballad was already recorded in the fourteenth century. Lorrainer versions had obviously adapted to local circumstances over time, for this story was also told as a local legend in which Backewill's salvation was attributed to the patron saint of the province, Saint Nicolas: Merkelbach-Pinck, *Lothringer Volksmärchen*, 102–10: *Der Türkengraf*.

[55] Louis Pitz, *Contes et légendes de Lorraine*, Paris 1956, 13–16.

and renaissance France as in Germany.[56] By the time the folksong collectors got active in France, however, the husband who arrived home and prevented the bigamous marriage was no longer a crusading knight, but a drunken soldier.[57] In the versions collected by Puymaigre, Westphalen and Lallement, the soldier has no supernatural aid but simply comes home at the end of a long campaign. Nor does he prove his identity with a gold ring like Graf Backewill (and Germaine's husband, for that matter), but instead offers to play the bridegroom at cards for the right to sleep with his wife!

These songs of returning soldiers cannot be seen just as up-dated versions of *Graf Backewill* or its French equivalents, rather they demonstrate that themes in oral literature which had been appropriate for nobles were adapted to suit soldier heroes. At one level the reasoning is obvious: soldiers, like crusading knights, left home for long periods of time in order to fight. Absences of seven years were particularly significant, perhaps related to canon law requirements for remarriage, but coincidentally the period of conscription. In many fairytales, such as *The maiden without hands* (AT706), the absence of the husband at the wars is a crucial plot device. It enables his mother to do away with the children of her unwanted daughter-in-law. In the vast majority of French variants of this tale-type the hero is a king, or at the very least a baron, but in one Breton version he is a soldier.[58] It is the soldier's periodic recall to the colours that enables the wicked mother-in-law to take revenge on his wife.[59] Crusaders and soldiers were the symbolic travellers of their eras, and they could be used as metaphors in oral culture for any departure.

This Breton soldier, it should be noted, behaves just like an aristocrat. He hunts, maintains servants and keeps a castle. He gets six months leave every two years, precisely the dispensation allowed to noble officers of the *ancien régime* army. Another explanation of the ease with which soldiers displaced noblemen in oral literature and imagery was that, in pre-revolutionary France, most officers were noblemen. The army was the main employer of the sons of the nobility of the sword, so the distinction between the nobility as an order in – and the military as a function of – society became blurred. In 1781 the Ségur decree limited all commissions to those who could prove four quarters, that is four generations of nobility.[60] The characterisation of the second

---

56 Puymaigre lists numerous examples in the notes to *Le Retour du mari: Chants populaires*, i, no. 3.
57 Westphalen, *Chansons populaires*, i, no. 8; Lallement, *Echoes rustiques*, 60: *Le Retour du mari soldat*.
58 Sébillot, *Contes populaires de la Haute-Bretagne*, i, no. 15: *La Fille aux bras coupés* (AT706).
59 This replacement of the noble allomotif by a soldier also occurs in other tales: MNATP, MS Millien-Delarue (Nivernais), AT451 version D: *La Femme du capitaine*.
60 This was a recognition of the long tradition of service by the old provincial nobility (who were anxious to prevent the one paid profession they could follow falling into the hands of the more recently ennobled), a tradition which was not entirely destroyed by the

estate as an army officer in the popular imagery of the revolution was entirely accurate.

However, when germanophone Lorrainers sang that 'Soldiers must be born/ Of a noble line', it is unlikely that they were referring to the Ségur decree.[61] The first verse of this song refers to the military's role in society in almost exactly the same terms as the soldier in Pellerin's *Les Quatre Vérités*: while the nation sleeps, he must keep watch. The explanation for the repeated assertion of the aristocratic heritage of soldiers in the song is at least partly related to their shared military function. However, the rest of the song dispenses with the duty to celebrate the liberties and pleasures of the soldier's life, pleasures all too often gained at someone else's expense. The ability to live without working (or, rather, to live off other people's hard work) was all but a definition of nobility in the eyes of the peasants, and it was likewise a quality of soldiers. As the Vosgian proverb explained, 'the laziest of the family, they'll make him a chief-soldier'.[62] However, the soldier's unwillingness to work was often expressed, in folk culture, as a blood inheritance, linking soldiers to aristocratic ideas of race (which were, of course, promoted above all by army officers). In a song from the Ardennes, a peasant comes home to find soldiers finishing off his geese, butter and wine: 'They will sleep in your bed/ With your pretty wife/ The children that you'll have/ Will be three cavalrymen.'[63] This is quite a common theme in folklore, and it does not simply reflect the belief that bastards and orphans would find a home in the army, although this was often the case.[64] Rather, the implication is that the offspring of the soldiers' aristocratic carelessness with the property and morality of others will live at the expense of the peasant, just as their fathers did.

The idea that soldiering was an inherited occupation, and in particular that it denoted some blood connection to the nobility, should obviously not be taken literally. Rather it was a metaphorical way of understanding why some young men were predisposed to a military career. Their habitual (if not actually genetically inherited) fecklessness and idleness made them suitable candidates.

It was not just peasants who made the connection between the military and the second estate. Soldiers were equally keen to assert the social difference between them. During the *ancien régime* the largely noble officer corps

revolution: David Bien, 'The army in the French Enlightenment: reform, reaction and revolution', *Past and Present* lxxxv (1979), 68–98.

61 'Soldaten müssen geboren sein/ Aus einem adeligen Stamm': Pinck, *Verklingende Weisen*, iii. 385: *Soldatenlied*.

62 'Le plus feignant de la famille, on en fera un chef-soldat': Jean Vartier, *Le Grand Livre des proverbes et dictons de Lorraine et du Bassigny*, Nancy 1985, 135.

63 'Ils coucheront dans ton lit/ Avec ta jolie femme/ Les enfants que tu auras,/ Ce sera trois gendarmes': Meyrac, *Traditions, coutumes, légendes*, 243: *C'etait un paysan*. A version is also recorded in Lallement, *Echoes rustiques*, 100.

64 Corvisier, *L'Armée française*, i. 343–7.

played a large part in defining the military ethic to which common soldiers ascribed. This can be seen in their obsession with honour that found expression in duelling. Duelling was originally an exclusively noble activity but, as we have seen, it became almost an initiation rite for recruits joining the army. Duels could only be fought between equals; it was unheard of for soldiers to take on civilians because the civilian was beneath them.[65]

The aristocratic ancestry of the military ethos also found expression in the soldier's uniform. The sumptuous dress and coiffeur of the musketeer in Basset's *Les Veritez du temps* was clearly borrowed from the fashions of the nobility, and in general soldier's uniforms owe at least as much to the desire to impress as to military functionality. The splendid uniform was one of the attractions of the soldier's life, emphasised in recruiting posters and exemplified in the ribbons, plumes and general swagger of the recruiting sergeant.[66] As we have seen, putting on uniform was not just a change of habits in the sense of dress, but also in the sense of a way of life. But the point is that the new way of life, symbolised in the uniform, was closer in spirit to that of the nobility. Common soldiers emulated aristocratic conspicuous consumption in dress. Flash clothes were the symbol of prodigality, a military virtue embodied in many *noms-de-guerre*.[67] However, the furnisher of both noble and soldier was often the peasant, who on the one hand paid dues to his *seigneur*, while soldiers rifled his wardrobe for fresh linen.[68] For this was another element of the noble's ethic that was adopted by soldiers – disdain for the peasant's labour and appropriation of its fruits.

The clash of military and peasant attitudes to property found expression in folktales. In the tale of *King Thrushbeard* (a folkloric version of *The taming of the shrew*), the princess of England, who had refused an offer of marriage from the dauphin, is seduced by him in the disguise of a hairdresser. They elope to Paris, where he forces her to keep an alehouse. Then, in his function as prince, he sends his soldiers to smash up the place, pull the bungs out of the barrels and insult her. He next obliges her to run a pottery stall in the market, and then sends his dragoons to ride over it. On both occasions she asks her husband to pursue the matter, but he simply shrugs his shoulders: this is how soldiers behave, what could possibly be done about it?[69] In practice it was very difficult for civilians to have their complaints against soldiers taken seriously, for the military authorities tended to look after their own. The contempt

---

[65] Pierre Chalmin, 'La Pratique du duel dans l'armée française au XIXe siècle', in *Actes du 80e congrès des sociétés savantes*, Lille 1955, 327–50.

[66] Daniel Roche, *The culture of clothing: dress and fashion in the ancien régime*, Cambridge 1994, 232–43.

[67] Corvisier, *L'Armée française*, i. 848–61.

[68] Roche, *The culture of clothing*, 251–2.

[69] Cosquin, *Contes populaires de Lorraine*, ii, no. 44: *La Princesse d'Angleterre* (AT900). See also Sébillot, *Contes populaires de la Haute-Bretagne*, i. 156: *La Dédaigneuse punie* (AT900); MNATP, Millien-Delarue (Nivernais), MS AT900 versions A, B, C.

shown by soldiers for 'pékins' (civilians) caused as much anger as their actual damage to property. Again the soldier was borrowing the ethic of his predecessor, the aristocrat, which was in complete opposition to the patient husbandry of the peasant.

Peasant resentment against the nobility was, therefore, readily transferred to soldiers as successors and emulators of the second estate.[70] The song *Le Pauvre Laboureur* suggested that, from the peasant point-of-view, the first and second estates were work-shy parasites living off the labour of the third, but in some versions soldiers were added to the list of burdens. The underlying hostility to soldiers as the offspring of the second estate is implied in *Les Quatre Vérités*, but it was spelt out in some German variants of *Die verschiedenen Stände* in which all the orders, from emperor to beggar, declare not what they do but on what they live: the moral of the image is that they all, in one way or another, live off the peasant.[71] The soldier, as one of the non-contributing orders, says 'I pay nothing'. However, as the image implies, and as the peasantry knew only too well, just because the soldier paid for nothing did not mean he cost nothing.

The population of Lorraine could hardly be unaware of the costs of the military establishment. In addition to their taxes, Lorrainers had to supply billets to the troops and forage for their horses, repair military roads, pay for the fortification of their towns, and loan their wagons to military convoys. The burdens were particularly heavy during the periods when ducal Lorraine was occupied by the French but not yet integrated into France.[72] The trend towards purpose-built barracks and more efficient systems of supply during the eighteenth century alleviated but did not remove the direct burden on this frontier population, particularly during times of war.[73] On the whole Lorraine bore these sacrifices with remarkably little dissent. And the army did bring benefits in the shape of the large market for local produce which it created. However, the soldiers' high-handed manner towards the locals sometimes led to tension. In 1809, three officers and NCOs of the second dragoons were billeted at the *Palais français* inn in Metz, they forced their way into the kitchen where, they said, they intended to sleep, made lewd suggestions to the landlady, pretended the roasting spits were swords and smashed the glass and crockery with them, and finally chased the maids with the pies which

---

[70] Yves-Marie Bercé, *History of peasant revolts: the social origins of rebellion in early modern France*, Ithaca, NY 1990, 195–6.

[71] The earliest variant of this type I have seen is by May & Wirsing of Frankfurt-am-Main, and dated 1851 (MDAACE 57.3.281). It became very popular in the second half of the century. Wentzel of Wissembourg's 1869 version is reproduced in Lerch, *L'Imagerie populaire en Alsace*, at p. 182. Interestingly, the prefect only approved Wentzel's image because it was intended for export.

[72] Gaston Zeller, 'Les Charges de la Lorraine pendant la guerre de Hollande', *Mémoires de la Société d'archéologie lorraine* lxi (1911), 13–65.

[73] Lee Kennet, *The French armies in the Seven Years' War*, Durham, NC 1967, 99–129.

had been prepared for the evening meal. The town guard sent to arrest them actually joined in their drunken spree.[74] The behaviour predicted of soldiers in popular culture was firmly based in experience.

Soldiers and bandits

It would be easier to accept the burden of the army if one appreciated the value of its contribution to society, if the peasant felt the benefit of the soldier's 'I defend you all'. An example of a soldier who could make this claim was Louis Gillet, sergeant in the Artois cavalry. Returning to his home in the Argonne through the forest (after forty-five years of service), he was attracted by piercing cries. An eighteen-year-old girl was about to be raped by two villains. Without hesitation the old soldier drew his sabre and launched himself at the brigands who fled. Releasing the young woman Gillet conducted her back to her parents who, in their joy, offered him their daughter's hand in marriage. He refused, saying that at seventy it was easier to fight two bandits than to keep an young wife happy, and he also refused the purse they offered; the only reward he required was in his heart.

I have taken the details of Gillet's escapade from a woodcut by the Orleans imagist Letourmy.[75] He copied it from a Parisian copperplate print by Deny, who in turn was inspired by a painting by Wille *fils* which was exhibited in the Salon of 1785.[76] Gillet was, at the time of the *Salon*, a resident at Les Invalides and his narration of his own adventures made him a well-known figure in Paris. He was even the subject of a play by Audinot, *Le Maréchal des logis*, to a performance of which he and forty fellow veterans were invited as guests of honour in 1785.[77] Yet, despite his fame, his story soon detached itself from his person to reappear in a variety of popular media without reference to the original hero. The scene illustrated by Letourmy also featured in the 1795 edition of the almanac *Le Messager boiteux de Berne et Vevey* under the title 'L'honnête homme et le scélérat'.[78] Later the soldier was reclothed in the

74 Paul Wiltzer, 'Petite Police et grande armée à Metz sous l'empire (1806–1815)', *Mémoires de l'Académie nationale de Metz* 5th ser. vi (1959–61), 154–5.

75 MDAACE 57.3.1249, *Le Maréchal-des-logis*; MDAACE 7.3.1674–5, *Le Maréchal des logis* and *La Jeune Villageoise*.

76 Wille's work is an example of the trend at the end of *ancien régime* for heroic paintings of individual soldiers, some real, others fictitious. It was the comparison of Wille's heroic treatment of a soldier in *La Double Récompense de mérite* with Greuze's *Le Fils puni* which prompted Diderot's caustic comments on the latter.

77 Friedrich Melchior von Grimm, Denis Diderot, Guillaume-Thomas Raynal and Jakob Heinrich Meister, *Correspondance littéraire, philosophique et critique par Grimm, Diderot, Raynal, Meistre, 1753–1790*, ed. Maurice Tourneux, xiv, Paris 1880, 293–4.

78 E. Gétaz, 'Monographie du *Messager boiteux de Berne et Vevey*, paraissant à Vevey depuis 1708', *Messager boiteux de Berne et Vevey* (1957), 5.

Plate 31. *Le Maréchal-des-logis*: Letourmy (Orléans), *c.* 1785
Reproduced by permission of the Musée départemental
d'art ancien et contemporain, Epinal.

uniform of a restoration hussar and painted onto the plates produced at Les Islettes, just a few miles from Gillet's home town of Sainte-Ménéhould.[79]

However, Gillet is a relatively lonely figure in popular culture. The heroism of individual soldiers was a commonplace in nineteenth-century painting, and in the Parisian print market, but comparatively rare in popular woodcut imagery. The concept clearly appealed to the urban and elite markets for these other genres, but made little impression on the rural market. Although there were plenty of *images d'Epinal* depicting French soldiers engaged in battles, there are very few Gillets who brought the general injunction to defend all down to the particular act of saving a damsel in distress.[80] One of the few other images that does depict an individually heroic

[79] *Le Journal du collectioneur* iv/31 (1994), 19.
[80] Pellerin was inspired by popular fiction (or rather Parisian engravings based on contemporary novels), such as *Marie ou la croix d'or* or the *Aventures d'un jeune officier*

soldier is Gangel & Didion's *L'Hospitalité bien payée*. It concerns a farmer who, having borrowed money from the notary, takes it home and then is lured away by bandits, who proceed to rob the house, unaware that a tired and hungry soldier has taken refuge there. With the help of the farmer's wife he captures the bandits, for which bravery he is promoted. Like Gillet he refuses the farmer's monetary reward, but unlike Gillet he does marry the daughter.[81]

This image was based on a *canard* popular in the 1820s under the title *Trait héroïque de courage d'un officier français*.[82] The *Trait héroïque* was one of a series of provincial *canards* that dealt with the theme of the returning soldier. They were among the Chamagnons' most requested items. However, most revolved around the false accusation and subsequent vindication of the soldier. Sergeant-major Jean Berthelier, for example, in the canard *Un Bienfait n'est jamais perdu*, was helped when drunk by a priest. When he calls on the priest to thank him, he arrives just in time to fight off a gang of murderers. However, the crowd that responds to the priest's cries mistakes the soldier for the attacker and arrests him. Only when the priest recovers his senses is the truth discovered, and the priest makes the soldier his adoptive son.[83] What is interesting about this *canard*, and dozens of others on similar themes, is the crowd's assumption that the soldier is the guilty party.[84] In popular mentalities the soldier was as likely to join in with the bandits as to oppose them. Peasants may well have found the soldier's declaration that he 'defends all' deeply ironic.

This is illustrated by a folktale from the Auvergne of a type which is closely related in subject matter to Gangel's image of the *Trait héroïque* (and may indeed have been its original inspiration). According to the Auvergnat narrative Marie's parents leave their house (not specified as a mill but a mill was the usual locus of the action in this tale-type, playing on the stereotype of mills as isolated and dangerous dwellings, and millers as rich) to go to a wedding. A band of robbers take advantage of their absence, but quick-witted Marie manages to trap their leader into putting his hand through the window, and promptly cuts off two fingers. (In folk culture heroines were not nearly so dependent on masculine help as they were portrayed in imagery which, like

---

français en Afrique, in which gallant soldiers save maidens and, in return, are loved and married by them. But in both cases his images were only produced in sets of four semi-fine quality lithographs: they were not among the subjects which were considered suitable for the cheaper end of the firm's market: Archives départementales des Vosges, fonds maison Pellerin, images militaires.

81 Musée historique lorrain, no code.

82 These *canards* were published in 1825, 1827 and 1828 at Lyon and Rocroi: Jean-Pierre Seguin, 'Les "Canards" de fait divers de petit format en France, au XIXe siècle', *Arts et traditions populaires* iv (1956), 34.

83 This *canard* was published in 1832 at Marseilles, Toulon, Bordeaux and Dijon, and, under the title *Le Curé et le militaire* in 1833 (Montpellier), 1834 (Le Mans), 1841 (Melun), 1849 (Lille) and 1850 (Montreuil-sur-Mer): ibid. 34.

84 Jean-Pierre Seguin, *Nouvelles à sensation: canards du XIXe siècle*, Paris 1959, 182–90.

the *Trait héroique*, tended to propose a more bourgeois notion of the proper behaviour for young women.) The robber captain flees into the night swearing that Marie will live to regret the day she tangled with Laramée. As we will see in chapter 5, this name is clear indication of the brigand's military background.[85]

The logic by which soldiers and bandits became associated in popular culture is not hard to follow, particularly given the prejudices of the period. Soldiers were, almost by definition, 'mauvais sujets' even before they joined up. Their immorality explained their presence in the ranks, and the army was not considered an environment conducive to curing their bad habits. During wartime they behaved as little more than licensed bandits, and at the end of war they were either unable, through disability, or unwilling, through habitual dissoluteness, to take up peacetime occupations. The *ancien régime* authorities' fear that discharged soldiers would form criminal bands was echoed at the popular level.[86] Les Invalides had been set up precisely to prevent soldiers behaving according to their worst instincts, but it was only available to a few. Deserters, in particular, could not rely on the discharged soldier's remedies – state or personal charity. Unable to regularise their situation they were forced into a life of wandering, which in the eyes of both the authorities and peasants was synonymous with crime. In addition, successful criminals had to possess some of the characteristics attributed to soldiers: discipline (many bandit gangs were organised along military lines); guile, in order to spot traps and fool the gendarmes; and they could not shrink from violence. The gangs run by Cartouche and Mandrin, the most famous French villains of the *ancien régime*, included several former (and sometimes serving) soldiers.[87] Recent research has highlighted the presence of veterans, serving soldiers, and above all deserters in the underworld of the Low Countries, England and France in the eighteenth century.[88] These soldier-brigands particularly thrived in times of war. Unfortunately, therefore, the turbulent history of Lorraine gave the local population plenty of opportunity to judge for themselves what value to attach to the soldier's 'I defend you all'.[89]

[85] Marie-Aimée Méraville, *Vie et oeuvres: contes populaires d'Auvergne, suivi d'un mémoire sur la langue et le patois*, Paris 1982, no. 16: *Laramée* (AT956b).
[86] Corvisier, *Armées et sociétés*, 96. The institution of Les Invalides was prompted by just such concerns. Bois notes that, until the second half of the eighteenth century, old soldiers in literature and official documents were almost always described as 'pauvre', but by the time of the revolution this had been replaced with 'brave': *Les Anciens Soldats*, 13.
[87] Ibid. 310. Cartouche had himself spent some time under arms. More than 150 *Gardes françaises* deserted on the night of his arrest for fear of being named as his accomplices: Corvisier, *L'Armée française*, ii. 891.
[88] Florike Egmond, *Underworlds: organised crime in the Netherlands, 1650–1800*, Cambridge 1993, 47–84; Douglas Hay, 'War, dearth and theft in the eighteenth century: the record of the English courts', *Past and Present* xcv (1982), 117–60; Cobb, *Paris and its provinces*, 141–210.
[89] Although it is not hard to find evidence of criminals with a military background, according to Bois the number of former soldiers brought before the courts of pre-1789

'Lets go to the war: all the others are going there!'[90]

'Great wind, great war' they warned in the Vosges.[91] Like all communities whose fortunes depended on the weather, the peasants of Lorraine had a large number of climatic prognostications. In January, as their thoughts turned to the coming year, they looked to the skies for omens of future trouble. The weather on the feast of the conversion of Saint Paul (25 January) was a useful guide: 'On Saint Paul's a clear day/ Promises us a good year/ If it snows or rains, famine on earth;/ If it's windy, we will have war;/ And if one sees thick fog/ Death in every quarter.'[92] This was a pessimist's charter; only one out of the four options could be considered a hopeful sign, but in this case pessimism was strengthened by experience: the wind on 25 January in each of the years 1870, 1914 and 1939 was so strong that it blew down church steeples.[93] Of course, in the stretch of hills running north from the Jura to the Ardennes, one did not need to be Nostradamus to predict bad weather on 25 January. And for long periods during Lorraine's history war seemed almost as certain.

The Thirty Years' War came late to Lorraine; it was not until the arrival of Richelieu's allies, the Swedes, in 1635 that Lorrainers felt its full destructive effects, but nowhere were its consequences more devastating. In the next ten years the province was fought over by seven different armies, not to mention local irregulars, who reduced her main towns to ruins and emptied her countryside. Famine followed as huge tracts of cultivated land were deserted because the villagers had fled before the soldiers and the attendant plague. It took decades of immigration from neighbouring territories for the population

France for crimes against property was not disproportionate when compared with other sections of society. Garrison cities like Metz had problems with rowdiness, but most soldiers picked up by the police were deserters, not bandits, their criminality limited to begging: *Les Anciens Soldats*, 312–16.

[90] 'Allons à la guerre: tous les autr' y vont!' This is the conclusion to a popular nursery rhyme in Champagne and Lorraine. This version was recorded at Chémery-sur-Bar, in the Ardennes: Bernard Poplineau, *Histoires et chansons populaires ardennaises*, Buzancy 1979, 102.

[91] 'Grand vent, grande guerre': Bibliothèque municipale de Nancy, MS 343 (721), les patois lorrains (Vosges): enquête de l'Académie Stanislas, 1877, fo. 122r. Similar statements have been recorded all over eastern France.

[92] 'De Saint-Paul la claire journée/ Nous dénote une bonne année;/ S'il neige ou pleut, cherté sur terre;/ S'il fait du vent, nous aurons guerre;/ Et si l'on voit d'épais brouillards,/ Mortalité de toutes partes': Sauvé, *Le Folklore des Hautes-Vosges*, 29. This is a commonly found maxim in Lorraine (a charter belonging the monastery of Clairlieu contains a medieval Latin version), though in some areas it applied to the eleventh day of Christmas and/or Saint Vincent on 22 January. It was carried in books such as the 1542 *Pronostication des anciens laboureurs* (and later almanacs based upon it), to every corner of France and beyond: J.-B. Kayser, 'A Propos de quelques règles et dictons météreologiques et agricoles', *Nos Traditions* i (1938), 45–50.

[93] Vartier, *Le Grand Livre des proverbes*, 177.

to return to its pre-war levels. For almost the whole of the rest of the century Lorraine remained in the hands of enemy soldiers.[94]

The profound impact of the prolonged Thirty Years' War coloured the attitudes to war of successive generations of Lorrainers. The surviving inhabitants preserved their opinions about warring soldiers in stories told at the *veillée* for centuries to come. Thus those Lorrainers who had not themselves witnessed its horrors, none the less knew what to expect when new enemies passed through Lorraine in 1743, 1792, 1814 and 1870. Each new invasion added to the store of legends that provided the population with models of survival in times of conflict. The vision of war invoked at the *veillée* played upon the horror rather than the humanity of foreign soldiers. Frightful stories about the Cossacks circulated in Lorraine in advance of the allied armies in the winter of 1813–14. Considering what they believed of the Cossacks, it is no surprise that the population fled to the woods rather than have to face the monsters they had been warned about.[95]

As it turned out the Cossacks were not quite as awful as the reputation that went before them. Although certainly guilty of some acts of theft, and occasionally of violence, they were relatively restrained. Although Merkelbach-Pinck's collections contains plenty of fearful legends from ' "the memorable epoch", when the Russians came through the land', in her more sober oral history accounts they appear more as objects of pity. Villagers had been terrified at their approach, but they ended up giving food and shelter to Cossack deserters.[96] The Cossacks were the victims of a shift in the object of local legends from historical to contemporary villains, whereby atrocities committed in former times were conflated with new threats. The way that 'memory overlays memory' is a well-known phenomenon to scholars of oral history.[97] The Cossacks, with their wild manners and strange dress, simply stepped into the stories already told about a succession of warriors from the fringes of Christendom, who had ravaged Lorraine in previous centuries. Just a few years before, during the 1792 invasion, the atrocities had been attributed to the imperial Croats who roamed the north-eastern corner of Lorraine. Before the Croats it had been Maria-Theresa's Pandours who had, under the orders of the brother of the former duke of Lorraine, pillaged this same area. In the 1960s the name of the Pandour was still used as a bogeyman to frighten

[94] There is, as yet, no full history of the impact of the Thirty Years War in Lorraine, although Gaber provides a useful introduction in *La Lorraine meutrie*.
[95] Merkelbach-Pinck, *Aus der lothringer Meistube*, i. 439.
[96] ' "der grossen Zeit", als die Russen im Lande durchkamen': ibid. i. 180, 293.
[97] James Fentress and Chris Wickham, *Social memory*, Oxford 1992, 58. Eugen Weber provides an example from the invasions in 1814–15 of the Mâconnais where 'the fairly benevolent presence of the Austrian troops seems to have left traumatic memories, so that in folktales the Austrians replace even Saracens as the prototypes of past conquerors, and vestiges of ancient monuments were often attributed to the Austrians': *Peasants into Frenchmen*, 425.

naughty children.[98] Before the Pandours, the Croats had had their first turn at devastating Lorraine as the allies of Duke Charles IV during the Thirty Years' War. The description given by Jean Bauchez, a Messin chronicler, would have been recognised by all subsequent generations of Lorrainers: 'pillaging, killing, raping and burning wherever they were met, this is a nation of people fearing neither God nor man, one would think that [they] were Turks, I think they were even worse, considering the evil they did'.[99] However, the soldiers with the worst reputation in Lorrainer oral history remained the Swedes of 1635: 'even today Lorrainer peasants speak of the Swedes as monstrous beings to which one attributes every vice' wrote Thiriat in 1869.[100] According to his informants the very standard of the Swedish armies showed the female representation of Lorraine cleft in two and carrying a torch and sword.[101]

One story told about the Swedes was the tale of the Wild Woman of Kerbach. Having just given birth, she was too weak to flee into the woods at their approach. The 'wild soldiers' grabbed her child and threw it into a house they had set on fire. When the villagers returned they found the mother crawling about on all fours and crying like an animal. She never recovered from the shock, and spent the rest of her life hiding in a pit in the forest. Henri Lerond heard this tale in the 1880s and Angelika Merkelbach-Pinck also collected it in the 1930s, the woman's trauma had left such a deep impression.[102] From such legends the audience learnt that if they did not flee or hide from the marauders, they were courting death.

Murder was not the only thing to fear, rape was also a threat. In their singing games, girls in the Argonne warned 'Young girls of Champagne/ Guard your houses well/ Because here come the soldiers/ Who will take you away.'[103] The result of failure to do so was, as we have seen, recalled in other

98 Charles François, 'Un Houzard en Lorraine', *Mémoires de l'Académie Stanislas* 6th ser. ii (1969–70), 87.
99 'pillant, tuant, viollant et brullant où ils se rencontroient, cest nation de gens ne craignant Dieu ny homme, on croioit que cestoient Turc, ie croy que pire estoient encour, veu le mal quils faisoient': Jean Bauchez, *Journal de Jean Bauchez, greffier de Plappeville au dix-septième siècle*, ed. Charles Abel and Edouard de Bouteiller, Metz 1868, 232. Bauchez had first-hand experience of their methods, his home was burned and his family murdered by Croats; he only survived because his pursuer's pistol misfired.
100 'aujourd'hui encore les paysans lorrains parlent des Suédois comme d'êtres monstreux auxquels on attribue tous les maux': Thiriat, *La Vallée de Cleurie*, 210.
101 I had imagined that this was a metaphor for Lorraine's sufferings, typical of the way oral culture concretises ideas and feelings, but in fact it is a fairly accurate description of the personal standard of Bernard of Saxe-Weimar, the commander of the Swedish forces. While folk history may not be as vigorous in its desire for accuracy as professional historians, it can sometimes be surprisingly reliable.
102 Lerond, *Lothringische Sammelmappe*, vi. 75; Merkelbach-Pinck, *Aus der lothringer Meistube*, ii. 111.
103 'Fillettes de Champagne/ Gardez bien vos maisons,/ Car voici les gens d'armes/ Qui vous emmèneront': Lallement, *Echoes rustiques*, 93.

songs.[104] In particular mothers warned their daughters against the hussars: 'If you see them coming,/ Flee/ Hide yourself in a corner,/ Far away.'[105] In French literature 'l'amour à la hussard', is still a euphemism for rape, though in the nineteenth century it might be replaced by the equally telling phrase – 'être cosaquer'.

The most common crime associated with soldiers was pillage. 'Unlucky the peasants who find themselves in the theatre of war!' declared the volunteer Vaxelaire, admitting to his own thefts from the fields and farmyards around Koblenz.[106] A children's rhyme from the Argonne announced that 'The soldiers are in the village/ Who make a terrible din', while on the other side of the province children warned ants to 'hide your eggs/ Here are the soldiers who are going to take them from you'.[107] Yet again the hussars stood accused as the worst thieves.[108] In another folksong the peasant who came home to find soldiers raiding his house exclaims 'These are all pillagers!', only to be told 'You lied in that, peasant/ These are all hussars!'[109] Georges Bangofsky, whom we last saw arriving at the regimental depot of the seventh hussars, revelled in his new role as sanctioned marauder. He wrote of his delight in seeing 'the hussars out pillaging, fighting each other for the booty', and boasted, like a medieval Landsknecht, that 'money is never lacking for hussars, particularly at the end of a campaign'.[110]

The insatiable hunger of soldiers became a standard motif in folk narratives, sometimes for comic effect. Folktale heroines, trying to impress the king, assured him that they could bake a loaf that would satisfy a regiment. The hero of another tale is able to complete a magical task with the help of an army of ants, 'with haversack on back and doing their drill', whom he had fed after seven years of hunger.[111] In a Provençal version of this tale it is actually an army of soldiers that the hero feeds, and who later come to his aid.[112] In

104 Meyrac, Traditions, coutumes, légendes, 243: C'était un paysan.

105 'Si tu les vois venir,/ Fuis/ Cache-toi dans un coin,/ Loin': Puymaigre, Chants populaires, ii, no. 79: La Cantinière. Chepfer and Quépat also collected versions of this popular song in eastern France.

106 'Malheureux les paysans qui se trouvent sur le théâtre de la guerre!': Vaxelaire, Mémoires d'un vétéran, 40.

107 'Les souldats [sic] sont dans les village/Qui faisont bien du tapage': Lallement, Folklore et vieux souvenirs, 139; 'cache tes oeufs/ Voici les soldats qui vont te les prendre': René Schamber, 'Formulettes enfantines du pays mosellan', Nos Traditions ii (1939), 21.

108 The first persons to be guillotined in Nancy were four Hungarians serving in the army who had freelanced as armed robbers: Charles François, 'Les Débuts de la guillotine dans le département de la Meurthe', Mémoires de l'Académie Stanislas 6th ser. i (1968–9), 177.

109 'Ce sont tous des pillards! Tu en as menti, paysan/ Ce sont tous des hussars!': Lallement, Echoes rustiques, 100: C'était un paysan.

110 'C'etait plaisir de voir les hussards au pillages, se battant pour le butin. . . . L'argent ne fait jamais défaut aux hussards, surtout au sortir de campagne': Roche du Teilloy, Les Etapes de Georges Bangofsky, 18, 29.

111 Cosquin, Contes populaires de Lorraine, ii. 284: Le Roi and ses fils (AT569).

112 James Bruyn Andrews, Contes ligures: traditions de la Rivière recueillies entre Menton et Gênes, Paris 1892, 9: Le roi d'Angleterre (AT531).

Plate 32. *Hobs gfost Bruder?*: Deckherr (Montbéliard), 1823
Reproduced by permission of the Musée départemental
d'art ancien et contemporain, Epinal.

oral history gluttony was the sin associated with soldiers. According to the peasants of the Argonne, the failure of the 1792 Prussian invasion was caused by diarrhoea brought on by guzzling unripe grapes.[113] The dragoon Marquant, who took part in the pursuit of the retreating enemy, concurred with the diagnosis.[114]

It was the allied armies of 1814 who gained the greatest notoriety for sheer greed. One of Boulay's woodcuts for the Deckherrs shows two soldiers of the Württemberg militia, part of the occupying forces in Montbéliard: a little fat soldier on the left, grasping a chicken in his mitten, asks his comrade 'Have you found (anything to eat), brother?' The thin soldier on the right, from whose webbing hangs a sausage and whose hat plume is made out of a knife, fork and spoon, replies 'Have you not seen the bread wagon?' No doubt the locals found this image funny when it was issued in 1823, several years after the Württembergers had left, but during the hard winters of 1814–15 and 1815–16 they probably would not have considered it a joking matter.[115] The

---

113 Lallement, *Folklore et vieux souvenirs*, 172.
114 One Prussian he found dead at the side of the road had seven pounds of uncooked bacon in his stomach: François-Etienne Marquant, *Carnet d'étapes du dragon Marquant*, ed. G. Vallée and G. Pariset, Paris–Nancy 1898, 172.
115 'Hobs gfost Bruder?' 'Hobts de Brod Wagen nit gsegn?': Lerch, *Almanachs, bibliothèque*

voracity of the Cossacks even found its way into proverbial speech: when something good was put on the table in Lorraine the diners might exclaim 'here's one that the Cossacks won't have!'[116]

Despite the miseries caused by marauding soldiers the crime which seems to have made the deepest impression on the devout Catholics of Lorraine was sacrilege. The memory of the Swedes was worse than that of other armies because they were Protestants. They were known to burn churches, pillage monasteries, disfigure statues and mutilate priests. The event that established their terrible reputation was the sack of Saint-Nicolas-de-Port in 1635, which included its famous church. However, their acts of sacrilege were countered by new miracles. As the Swedes hacked their way into the church where the population of the town had taken sanctuary, a Benedictine monk, Dom Moye, began to intone the mass. He took shelter behind a pillar in order to complete the service, but was spotted and pursued by a Swede. As the soldier rushed upon him the pillar opened to shelter the monk, and closed over him. The pillar still stands, though much of the rest of the church and town was destroyed, and according to legend it weeps at the approach of new invaders.[117] One hopes it gave warning of the arrival of the equally Protestant Prussians in 1792, who left a batch of new miracles in their wake. One Prussian soldier threw a bone (from a plundered ham) at the Madonna that adorned the Convent of the Annunciation outside Varennes. The statue opened its arms to receive the bone, where it remained for more than fifty years. Soon after the blasphemous soldier was drowned.[118]

The story of the Prussian at Varennes recalls the much better known miracle of Notre-Dame-de-la-Carole in Paris. According to legend, in 1418 an enraged soldier, who had gambled away his possessions, attacked the statue of the Virgin at the corner of the rue aux Ours with a knife. Her wounds ran with blood, and to celebrate the miracle, the local population burned a wicker soldier on the anniversary.[119] The celebrations surrounding the miracle demonstrate how a legend associated with one period might be transferred to another: in 1783 the wicker soldier was dressed up as Marlborough.[120] I also

---

bleue, imagerie, 84. Lerch incorrectly describes the image as a hunting scene. There is a long tradition in popular prints of portraying marauding soldiers equipped with eating utensils and armed with food: Dorothy M. George, English political caricature to 1792, Oxford 1959, plate 10: The English Irish souldier, 1642.

116 'en voilà un que les cosaques n'auront pas!': Hubert Vion, 'Patois messin, locutions, comparisons, proverbes', Jahrbuch der Gesellschaft für lothringische Geschichte und Altertumskunde ii (1890), 359; Zéliqzon, Dictionnaire, 160.

117 Emile Badel, 'Le Pilier qui pleure à Saint-Nicolas', Le Pays lorain xxii (1930), 167–9.

118 Labourasse, Anciens Us, 167. This story combines both the gluttonous and blasphemous behaviour of the Prussians.

119 Gaston, 'Les Images des confréries parisiennes', 86–8.

120 Grimm, Correspondance littéraire, xiii. 322. According to the correspondent the usual wicker figure was a Swiss soldier, though there is nothing in earlier versions of the legend to suggest that the soldier was foreign.

suspect that this transformation was the result of another trend – crimes originally associated with all soldiers, regardless of nationality, were increasingly ascribed only to foreign enemies. During the eighteenth century attitudes in Paris, if not in rural areas, had noticeably softened towards soldiers.[121] It was hard, in the period when Gillet and his ilk were being celebrated in the *Salon* and fêted in the theatre, to simultaneously burn in effigy one of his comrades.

However, this process was slow in the countryside and considerably hampered in Lorraine by the arrival of the 'bleus', the urban revolutionaries rushed to the frontiers in 1791, who were perceived as as much of a threat as the invaders they were supposed to forestall. Gabriel Noël, on patrol on the border near Sierck, wrote of the French regulars with whom he was serving: 'They comported themselves like Pandours would have done to us. I fear very much that our battalions will not make themselves loved by them [the peasants of the Low Countries]. At home even, we are not loved.'[122] Even Marquant, a Lorrainer dragoon and a convinced republican, wrote in his journal that 'I've seen several peasants say, tears of despair in their eyes, that they preferred the *ancien régime* a thousand times to our Constitution, at least one did not take all their property.'[123] Again, it was the revolutionaries' sacrilegious vandalism that left the strongest impression on the locals. In many stories the soldiers' destruction of chapels was associated with the miraculous rescue of the statues within: thus the Catholic faith was reaffirmed at the moment when it appeared to be under greatest attack.[124]

The legends and rumours about what to expect from invaders invoke one aspect of the relationship between peasants and soldiers – antagonism. Peasants viewed them as a threat to their lives, their livelihood, all that they held dear. This message was clearly expressed in the great anthem of the germanophone peasants of Lorraine, the *Bauernstand*, thematically akin to *Les Laboureurs*. When there is peace in the land then the peasant can nourish all the other orders of society. But when war breaks out, with its attendant 'robbing, plundering, burning, murdering', the peasant is forced to flee his house. His livestock is stolen, his fields left unploughed, he has nothing with which to feed himself let alone the populations of the towns. All must die if God does not listen to their prayers.[125] Neither in this song, nor in similar

121 Chagniot, *Paris et l'armée*, 534–50.
122 'Ils se sont conduits comme auraient fait chez nous des Pandours. Je crains bien que nos bataillons ne se fassent pas aimer si nous allons chez-euz. Chez nous même, nous ne sommes pas aimés': Noël, *Au Temps des volontaires*, 249.
123 'J'ai vu plusieurs paysans me dire, les larmes du désespoir aux yeux, qu'ils préféraient mille fois l'ancien régime à notre Constitution, qu'au moins on ne leur enlevait pas toutes leurs propriétés': Marquant, *Carnet d'étapes*, 80.
124 Meyrac, *Traditions, coutumes, légendes*, 55. Similar tales can be found in Merkelbach-Pinck, *Aus der lothringer Meistube*. For a useful discussion of this kind of legend see Philippe Raxhon, 'Folklore wallon et mémoire de la révolution française: le territoire de la légende', in Maurice Agulhon (ed.), *Cultures et folklores républicaines*, Paris 1995, 461–76.
125 'Rauben, plündern, brennen, morden': Pinck, *Verklingende Weisen*, ii. 144; Archives

statements from elsewhere in Lorraine, is there any indication that the nationality of the soldiers mattered. Francophone peasants on pilgrimage to the shrine of Saint Blaise outside Metz likewise prayed 'Blaise, chase war far away, break the weapons in the fist of the soldier who beats and kills him who drives the plough'.[126] In their Christmas carols they celebrated the time when Jesus would come 'with his great thing/ To brush away all the destroyers;/ He will repulse the soldiers,/ Kings will never again make/ War, war!'[127]

However, while waiting for this happier time to arrive, what should peasants do when they saw soldiers approaching? Another carol gave a detailed answer. When the alarm is given that soldiers are approaching, the shepherds fear that they have come to kill them and steal their flocks, so they send their womenfolk with the sheep into a ravine, while they themselves hide behind a hedge. Even when one *goujat* reassures them that the Three Kings he serves mean no harm but come to worship the infant Jesus, they refuse to come out: 'One cannot be too wary/ Of soldiers who would take even from the altar.'[128] The last phrase recalls a local proverbial expression, that soldiers would even steal off the altar, thus combining two of their characteristic faults – rapine and sacrilege.[129] Although this carol was first printed in Lorraine in the eighteenth century, the language dates it to at least a century before, when such alarms were only too common.[130] However, folklorists recorded it from oral recitation up to the First World War, and the model of behaviour it suggested was at least as long-lasting.

The danger run by peasants in taking to the woods was that the soldiers would pillage and burn their homes. The dragoon Marquant justified his own participation in the pillage of empty houses on the Luxembourg side of the border 'because by fleeing, we believed that they looked on us as rogues'. When the peasants reproached the French for the damage they had inflicted they were told 'You must be good people and not leave your houses.'[131] Local

---

départementales de la Moselle, 21/J/12, fonds de la Société d'histoire et d'archéologie de la Lorraine. Ironically, this second version was collected by P. Jacquemoth in July 1914.

126 'Blaise, chasse la guerre bien loin!/ Romps les armes dans le poing/ Du soldat, qui frappe et tue/ Celui que tient la charrue': Jean Lorraine, 'Nos Traditions: de le Saint-Blaise à Saint-Eucaire', *L'Austrasie* n.s. xiv (1910), 104.

127 'I vint avo s'gran iaque/ Pour r'gûgner tuertous los brisacs:/ I beurdré los soûdats,/ Los roïes nes' front pû jéma/ Lai guerre, lai guerre!': Fourier de Bacourt, 'Anciens Chants populaires, 343: *Noël d'Ormançon*. The exact meaning of 'un iacque' is unknown, though its purpose here is clear.

128 'Il ne se faut trop fier/ A des soldats qui en prendraient sur l'autel': G. Thiriot, 'Noël lorrain', *Le Pays lorrain* vi (1909), 770–5. Thiriot's carol is a translation from the 1777 patois version published by Barbie at Nancy under the title *Noëls et cantiques nouveaux sur la naissance de N. S. Jésus Christ*.

129 Jouve, *Noëls patois*, 76.

130 Laissy, *Noëls populaires lorrains*, 12.

131 'parce qu'en fuyant, nous crûmes qu'ils nous regardaient comme des scélérats. . . . "Il vous fallait être honnêtes gens et ne point quitter vos maisons" ': Marquant, *Carnet d'étapes*, 183. Marquant, who frequently found that the revolutionary army failed to live up

legends celebrated the cunning of those who, although unable to flee before the arrival of the soldiers, none the less escaped the consequences, such as the women of Godoncourt who cheated death when one of their number climbed out of the church in which they had been locked, killed the Swede on guard and let out the others.[132] Another legend from the Vosges recorded how one woman, unable to run away from the Cossacks, put green logs on the fire so that they were unable to see her through the smoke.[133]

A more practical way of avoiding destruction was to placate the advancing soldiers. When Niederfillen was in a panic at the approach of the Cossacks in 1814, one woman asked a Bavarian soldier what they should do. He advised them to meet the Cossacks with schnapps: 'they are thawed with schnapps'. The locals did as he suggested and indeed got on relatively well with the Russians who stayed in the village for many months.[134] Louise Tschenn remembered her mother greeting the invading Prussians in the same way in 1870.[135] Similar behaviour was reported from the departments on the German invasion route during the Franco-Prussian war, much to the horror of the provisional republican government in Paris, which had expected a 1792 style *levée en masse*.[136]

Both invaders and the authorities tended to misconstrue such gestures of friendliness. Marquant, who had taken the Luxembourgeois' presents of bread and wine as a mark of their support for the revolutionary cause, was furious when he later found out that the same peasants were deliberately misleading the French about Austrian positions.[137] He was even more disconsolate when he learned that some French towns, in particular Verdun, had greeted the allies in the same way in 1792. When the French retook the city later in the year, they took a dim view of the townsfolk's lack of patriotic resistance. The young women who, dressed in white gowns and decked in flowers, had led the procession to present the Prussians with the keys to the city, were guillotined.[138] For the revolutionary government it was a case of simple treachery, just as Marquant interpreted the gifts he received as support for his cause.

to his own high ideals, should have understood how this logic placed the Luxembourgeois in a quandary: if they feared the French were going to behave like brigands, then they would!

[132] Charles Charton, *Les Vosges pittoresques et historiques*, Paris 1862, 300. It was, apparently, the practice of the Swedes to lock the population into churches and then set them on fire.

[133] Thiriat, *La Vallée de Cleurie*, 243.

[134] 'sie sind mit Schnappes getaut': Merkelbach-Pinck, *Aus der lothringer Meistube*, ii. 292.

[135] Ibid. ii. 122.

[136] Sanford Kanter, 'Exposing the myth of the Franco-Prussian War', *War and Society* iv (1986), 13–30.

[137] Marquant, *Carnet d'étapes*, 14.

[138] The legend of the 'Vierges de Verdun' has exercised many commentators. They have been depicted as both counter-revolutionary martyrs and collaborators, depending on the political axes being ground. The fullest explanation of the affair is in Edmond Pionnier, *Essai sur l'histoire de la révolution à Verdun*, Nancy 1906, 241–53, 422–7.

However in both cases it is more likely that the inhabitants intended to show their submission. They were not supporting one cause over the other, simply trying to survive with their lives and property intact.

The peasants' last desperate option was to fight back against their enemies, as is shown in the second to last of Callot's series of prints *Les Misères de la guerre*.[139] The peasants, pushed beyond the limits of endurance by the soldiers' depredations, ambush and massacre them as, according to legend, the inhabitants of Fraize had done to the Swedes.[140] Usually it was not possible for the ill-armed peasant militias to face down whole units of soldiers.[141] Peasants were more successful at picking off small, detached groups of foragers or marauders. Marquant came across a troop of peasants on such duty south of Verdun in 1792. They were only armed with forks and flails, and their courage, he thought, was largely the product of drink. Fortunately the Prussians, thinking they were French soldiers, had fled before these irregulars could get to grips with them.[142] Enemy soldiers were most at risk when straggling behind a retreating army. Freed from the fear of retaliation the peasants took revenge on their now weakened oppressors.

The violence that existed between peasants and soldiers is, perhaps, easy to understand, but we must also account for a certain fascination which creeps into the retelling of the more horrific of military crimes. The willingness to believe the worst of the Cossacks, and later the Prussians, was the result not just of fear, but of excitement. Folk artists and imagists shared this fascination, in particular for those units that enjoyed the most fearsome reputations. It was the light cavalry regiments responsible for marauding who were the imagists preferred representatives of the military profession. The Cossacks made especially exotic subjects. Well before the 1814 invasion Hurez of Cambrai issued a series of images depicting the Cossacks, Kalmuks, Bashkirs and other irregular formations of the Russian army, some of which were copied by Pellerin.[143]

The notoriety of these – mostly irregular – units was part of their purpose. They existed in order to keep enemy (and sometimes domestic) populations in a state of terror, thus making them, in theory, more pliant. The success enjoyed by Maria-Theresa's Hungarian light infantry and cavalry in this role prompted the French military to form their own regiments of hussars and

139 Diane Wolfthal, 'Jacques Callot's *Miseries of war*', *The Art Bulletin* lix (1977), 232.
140 Gaber, *La Lorraine meutrie*, 75.
141 The Vadet brothers and the other *franc-tireurs* who resisted the 1814 invasion had some success, but it should be noted that the Vadets' recruits were mainly among town-dwelling veterans like themselves. In the countryside as a whole there was no sign of the hoped for 'levée en masse', and the brigandage of some *franc-tireurs* left a legacy of bitterness. In 1870, rather than supporting the *franc-tireurs*, some peasants, fearful of reprisals, arrested them and handed them over to the Germans.
142 Marquant, *Carnet d'étapes*, 99–101.
143 Duchartre and Saulnier, *Imagerie populaire française*, 250; Garnier-Pelle, *L'Imagerie populaire française*, ii, no. 1984. Hurez's images were copied from Engelbrecht of Augsburg.

chasseurs, modelled on their imperial equivalents. The *chasseurs* were the invention of one Fischer, a native of Lorraine. He came to the notice of French commanders while serving in the *goujats* at the siege of Prague in 1742, where he gave an impromptu display of his skills at irregular warfare, driving off the Croats and Pandours who preyed on the French camp. Given permission to raise his own command – 'les Chasseurs de Fischer' – he initially recruited from his Lorrainer compatriots, but during the Seven Years' War he added a battalion of gypsies, purely for their terror value.[144] Though feared by the Germans, Fischer was a hero in Lorraine where they sang songs in his praise.[145] However, the admiration he received could not mask the fact that Fischer was responsible for depredations around Hanover very similar to those of foreign invaders in Lorraine. The letters and memoirs of French soldiers on active service, such as those of Noël, Marquant and Bangofsky, did not hide from their readers that their own soldiers behaved in exactly the same way abroad as enemy troops did at home. As we have seen, there was little to distinguish, in rural popular culture, the revolutionary 'bleus' from the Prussians and Austrians. The opposition expressed to the military in the *Quatre Vérités* was not based on the nationality of the soldier, but on their way of life which was necessarily in conflict with that of the peasant. A certain ambiguity in the representation of French soldiers in popular sources can, therefore, be expected.

Marauders

In the images of *Les Quatre Vérités* one facial feature distinguishes the soldier from the cleric, the peasant and the lawyer, his moustache. The moustache was one of the army's particularisms which, like *noms-de-guerre*, set soldiers apart from civilians and identified the veteran even when he had resumed his peacetime occupation. Soldiers had to have a moustache: in Forbach school-children joked 'You think you could be a soldier/ and you have no moustache yet.'[146] Corvisier, looking at the distinguishing features of the Saintonge-infanterie in 1722, noted that recent recruits seldom had moustaches, but after enrolment they soon grew one.[147] It seems likely that the first group of French soldiers to distinguish themselves with moustaches were the grenadiers, considered the elite of the regiment. The grenadier's dress, in particular his brimless hat (useful for throwing grenades) was reminiscent of that of Turkish janissaries, the epitome of martial ardour. Borrowing the

---

[144] Capitaine Delphin-Charles Oré, *Fischer et l'origine des chasseurs*, Nancy–Paris 1911, 27.
[145] Puymaigre, *Chants populaires*, i. 238: *Le Gouverneur de Fischer*.
[146] 'Du mänscht, du werscht ä Soldätche,/ Un hascht noch kän Schnussbärtche': Graf, 'Deutsche-lothringische Volkslieder', 107.
[147] Corvisier, *L'Armée française*, ii. 861.

DE PAR LE ROI

CORPS DE   CHASSEURS

D E   FISCHER

A PIED ET   A CHEVAL

AVIS A LA BELLE JEUNESSE.

'ON fait à favoir à toutes Perfonnes, de quelle Qualité & Condition qu'elles puiffent être, qui voudront fervir SA MAJESTE dans le Corps de Chaffeurs de FISCHER, à Pied & à Cheval, n'auront qu'à s'adreffer à Monfieur   Officier dans ledit Corps, qui leur donnera toute forte de fatisfactions & d'agrémens : Congé de trois ans. Il eft logé   où pareilles Affiches font fur la Porte.

Plate 33. *Corps de chasseurs de Fischer: c.* 1757–63
The model for the chasseurs' uniform was the imperial Pandour.
Reproduced by permission of the Musée départemental
d'art ancien et contemporain, Epinal.

janissary's moustache was necessary to complete the awesome effect. Imperial Pandours and hussars cultivated moustaches for the same reason. It was part of their consciously created warlike image (elements of which were also learnt from the Turks), designed to inspire terror in their opponents.[148] Their French opposite numbers, such as Fischer's *chasseurs*, copied their dress and

[148] This suggestion was made by R. Frost in a paper given to the Forum on Early Modern Central Europe at the Warburg Institute, 12 Feb. 1997 entitled: ' "And these have such dreadful countenances": physiognomy of terror and the image of the Pole in the Thirty Years War'.

mannerisms.[149] These light troops were likewise considered the elite of the army, and were emulated by soldiers in other regiments. In eighteenth-century recruiting posters the moustache first appeared in appeals to 'la belle jeunesse' to enlist in Fischer's *chasseurs*, but from there it spread to all branches of the army.

Aspects of the French soldier's uniform were likewise borrowed from the exotic warriors encountered on the frontiers of European empires. French troops in the nineteenth century wore stylised versions of Hungarian (hussars), Polish (lancers) and Berber (zouave) ethnic dress. The process by which European armies adopted the costumes of their enemies is an interesting one, but the linking thread is that all the 'natives' they emulated were considered to be naturally warlike. Cossack and Arab societies were characterised by a high 'military participation ratio'; most adult males were expected to take part in their communities' armed conflicts. They were usually nomadic pastoralists, raised to the horse and the hunt. Violence was an integral part of their social relations, the result of a highly developed honour ethic, nurtured in constant raiding and resultant blood feuds. Personal acts of bravery were, therefore, highly prized.

European regular armies usually managed to defeat or control these 'hinterland warriors' as they have been called, but none the less admired their warlike behaviour. Their mobility, their commitment to individual action, were qualities that regular troops often lacked, and so efforts were made either to recruit former enemies directly, or at least to capture some of their qualities by adopting their dress. As we have seen, uniforms were expected to instil a military ethos into recruits. By dressing like a hussar, a Frenchman would become like a hussar. One consequence of this trend, which was common to all European armies, is that when they met in conflict soldiers of enemy nations actually resembled each other quite a lot. Bangofsky escaped twice from vengeful German peasants (after his wounds had prevented him from keeping up with the main body of the French army) because he was able to pass himself off as a German officer, thanks to his 'international' hussar uniform.[150] On other occasions the similarities of dress could have the opposite effect: in the heat of battle lancers, hussars and chasseurs from one side might easily be mistaken for the other. These difficulties in distinguishing domestic and enemy troops highlight the shared military ethic embodied in the uniform and based on opposition to the peasant. Cossacks and Pandours prided themselves on their 'free' status, which distinguished them from the enserfed population of their respective empires. Hussars and Polish lancers claimed noble descent. Contempt for the peasant was part of their

---

[149] When the seventeen-year-old future Baron de Marbot enlisted in the (germanophone) First Hussars in 1799, too young to have grown his own moustache, his comrades painted one on his face: Baron de Marbot, *The memoirs of Baron de Marbot*, London 1929, 28.

[150] Roche du Teilloy, *Les Étapes de Georges Bangofsky*, 43, 77.

way-of-life. All lived by raiding their more settled (and less warlike) neighbours. In theory they might be specifically employed to 'defend all', like the Croats and Pandours of the imperial military frontier in the Balkans, but in practice they were often guilty of depredations among the very people they were supposed to defend. In other words they were marauders by nature. It was for this purpose that they were often employed in European armies.[151]

As a consequence the ability to maraude effectively became a test of the martial qualities of European armies. Not only soldiers recruited in these hinterlands but those from the centre were expected to become efficient marauders in emulation of the quintessential warriors whose dress they had adopted. This injunction was well conveyed in numerous popular images on the subject.

Shortly after the Restoration Desfeuilles issued a series of woodcuts on the depredations of the allied soldiers. His *Distribution de la viande au camp* shows a farmer's family, armed with flails and pitchforks, on the heels of a group of Cossacks fleeing with the booty they have just filched (a lamb, two fowl and two sacks). In another *Tableau de la guerre* (no. 64) Cossacks are shown carrying off a young woman, and threatening an old lady and a child who offer purses in return for their lives. Although Desfeuilles copied these scenes from Paris copperplate prints depicting the Russo-Turkish war, there can be little doubt that he meant them to be seen as a record of events closer to home. However, almost exactly the same scenes reappear in Desfeuilles's *Tableaux des scènes militaires*. In the second of these two soldiers, one carrying a bedpan and duck, the other with a chicken and a cooking pot, are making their escape from a farm chased by the farmer and his wife, armed with brooms. The difference between this group of marauders and his earlier Cossacks is that these soldiers are in French uniforms of the restoration era.[152] An urge to steal, Desfeuilles implies, was common to all soldiers regardless of nationality.[153]

Nancy was a military town and Desfeuilles may well have had direct experience of pilfering soldiers. In nearby Metz minor thefts by soldiers (and subsequent confrontations with civilians) were common. Between 1806 and 1815, admittedly the period when the *grande armée's* comings and goings created rather unusual circumstances, two-thirds of all crimes involved soldiers. During the period in garrison of the second Westphalian infantry regiment (who, as Germans in the service of Napoleon, were both foreign and domestic at once), more than twenty complaints were made against them by local shopkeepers and householders. They stole fruit, cheese, bacon,

---

151 Thomas S. Abler, *Hinterland warriors and military dress: European empires and exotic uniforms*, Oxford 1999, 149–51.
152 BN (estampes), Li 10 pet. fo., images diverses chez Desfeuilles.
153 His image resembles medieval illustrations of another famous poultry-stealer, Renard the Fox, running away from the farmyard with Chanticlere in his jaws (a not inappropriate analogy given that Renard and the soldiers shared a reputation for cunning).

Plate 34. *Distribution de la viande au camp*: Desfeuilles (Nancy), 1824
Although derived from a Parisian copperplate print of the Turks, Desfeuilles
probably intended these marauders to be understood as Cossacks.
Reproduced by permission of the Bibliothèque nationale de France, Paris.

candles and scissors, upset stalls and accused the French of robbing poor
soldiers. When the locals attempted to detain them, they fled back to the
safety of the barracks where the guard denied all knowledge of their existence.[154] Such was the regular experience of civilians exposed to the military.

Images of genre-scenes illustrating the life of the soldier were one of the
mainstays of the imagery industry in the nineteenth century, and marauding
was almost always included alongside the fatigue-duties and duels. One of
their constant consolations for hot route marches and cold sentry duties, at
least according to imagists, was pilfering from peasants. French soldiers are
depicted in the act of stealing in no less than four images by Dembour and his
successor Gangel of Metz. In Dembour's initial selection of *Scènes militaires*,
issued on two sheets in 1842, we see a soldier enticing chickens out of their
coop with corn, while his comrade prepares to cut them down as they

154 Wiltzer, 'Petite Police et grande armée', 153–6.

Plate 35. *II.ème Tableau des scènes militaires*: Desfeuilles (Nancy), 1825
A similar scene, but now with French infantrymen engaged in marauding.
Reproduced by permission of the Bibliothèque nationale de France, Paris.

emerge.[155] Further down the same sheet two other soldiers stuff chickens and
rabbits into sacks. The scenario is repeated in Dembour & Gangel's 1849
Galerie militaire: les délassements du troupier, but on this occasion the soldiers
are spotted by the old lady whose hencoop they are robbing, and she goads
her dog into attacking them.[156] A further collection of *Croquis militaires* by
Gangel shows marauders at work among the grapevines (a genuine irritant to
the vintners of the wine-producing villages surrounding this garrison city).[157]
Finally, in one of Gangel & Didio's images celebrating the giant military
camp established in 1857 at Châlons-sur-Marne, we find a tiny scene of
soldiers 'fishing' for geese: a group of zouaves lead the flock with baited rods,
while others wait out of sight to grab their extended necks.[158] In none of
these images is it suggested that the population at risk from soldiers was
foreign, rather these were the people that, according to the *Quatre Vérités*, the
soldier was committed to defending. But it is difficult to detect any implied
criticism in these images. In Dembour's and Gangel's image, *Les Délassements
du troupier*, the soldiers' pilfering is set between duelling, getting drunk and

155 Archives départementales de la Moselle 1/T/92 (5 Oct. 1842). This image was based
on one of Horace Vernet's several lithographs on the theme of marauding 'grognards':
L.-M. Bruzard, *Catalogue de l'oeuvre lithographique de Horace Vernet*, Paris 1826, no. 88:
Petits, petits, petits.
156 Archives départementales de la Moselle 1/T/96 (*dépôt légal* 20 Dec. 1849). A
revamped version of this image is reproduced by Rafael de Francisco, *El recortable militar
espanol*, Madrid 1982, 203
157 Musée historique lorrain, no code. The image dates from between 1852 and 1858.
158 Ibid. no code: *Scènes de camp no.27*. The image dates from between 1858 and 1868.

Plate 36. *Scènes militaires*: 'Petits. . . petits. . . petits':
Dembour (Nancy), 1842
This scene is derived from a lithograph by Horace Vernet, c. 1826.
Scenes of marauding were a commonplace in the military imagery
of Dembour and his successors. Reproduced by permission of the
Archives départementales de la Moselle.

romancing nursemaids. It was simply an incident in military life like learning drill or cleaning stables, it was part of the learning experience which turned a conscript into a soldier. Marauding proved that the soldier was clever (if he escaped detection) or toughened him up (if he was caught and punished). As with the other activities depicted, marauding was the way by which the would-be warrior, the *Jean-Jean*, broke with his past life (and its humdrum moralities) and became more dangerous, more soldierly, and in the process more French.

There is a very clear demonstration of this process, and the part that marauding played in it, in a series of semi-fine images issued by the Pellerin firm between 1862 and 1864. The first showed the arrival of the clean-shaven rustic recruits – the *Jean-Jeans*, *Piou-Pious* and *Blanc-becs* at the regimental

Plate 37. *Les Provisions pour les amis*: Pellerin (Epinal), 1862
Reproduced by permission of the Archives départementales des Vosges
(photo: J. Laurençon).

depot, being mocked by the bemedalled soldiers. The next scene shows them
in military uniform, and their initiation has started with their first
fatigue-duty, collecting the soup. The third shows them in camp playing
cards, now with their full military quota of facial hair, and their military
education has proceeded apace for in addition to gambling they are drinking,
smoking and making love to the *cantinière*, all behaviour which their peasant
upbringing would have taught them was wasteful or immoral. A fourth image,
entitled *Les Provisions pour les amis*, shows a group of moustachioed zouaves
(to judge by their jackets) returning to camp with a pig, fowls, wine and other
pilfered provisions; an angry peasant gives chase. The final scene, entitled *Le
Passage difficile*, indicates the contempt in which the soldiers have learnt to
hold the peasant. A peasant and his pretty wife on their way to market are
forced to go through a camp of hussars. Although the peasant keeps his eyes
on the ground, one hussar accosts, him, another ties a frying pan to his dog's
tail, while a third sidles up to his wife and makes eyes at her. As a peasant is a
man without honour (in the military sense) one can insult him, abuse his
property and seduce his wife with impunity.[159] Indeed, the images imply, if

[159] Archives départementales des Vosges 8/T no code: *L'Arrivée des recrues au régiment/ Le
rata ou la soupe* (dépôt légal 1864); 8/T/443–6: *Le Passage difficile, Quinte et quatorze, Le
Camp des zouaves, Les Provisions pour les amis* (dépôt légal Jan. 1862).

Plate 38. *Le Passage difficile*: Pellerin (Epinal), 1862
Reproduced by permission of the Archives départementales des Vosges
(photo: J. Laurençon).

one wants to make a good French soldier one must learn to do so, for mocking and stealing from the peasant are shown as the very epitome of Gallic flair.

However, if all soldiers are marauders by nature, how can they become more French by marauding? A comparison of images of French and foreign troops engaged in the same actions indicates that it was not just the act that mattered, it was how it was done. Boulay's images of hungry Württembergers described above were clearly designed to be satirical: these amateur soldiers were unmilitary and the openness of their greed and theft was evidence of this. His fat militiaman was one of the earliest depictions of what would become a stock character in imagery, the heavy German soldier, always hunting for his sausage, too slow to outwit the clever Frenchman. On the other hand, a sense of superiority attaches to Boulay's illustrations of French marauders, such as his 1829 sapper of the guard. In a tall plumed bearskin and a long leather apron, with carefully groomed moustache and axe held nonchalantly over his shoulder, this sapper is a much more resplendent figure. Even the head of a recently stolen chicken peeping out from behind his back cannot detract from his manly figure.[160] Boulay thus admits that all soldiers were thieves by nature, but that the French were better at it, and this made them better soldiers.

[160] MDAACE 57.3.2597. Professor Michael Pavkovic has pointed out to me that the chicken's head is in fact the pommel of the sapper's sabre/saw combination, but unfortunately I learnt this too late to alter the text.

Plate 39. *Sapeur de la garde*:
Deckherr (Montbéliard), 1829
Reproduced by permission of the Musée
départemental d'art ancien et contemporain, Epinal.

A clear example of the failure of foreign soldiers as marauders is Pinot's 1871 image of a German uhlan rushing at a terrified Lorrainer peasant-woman with an open knife. The picture seems to threaten rape and murder, but, according to the text, all the soldier wanted was a piece of the woman's soap. In the imagists' imagination a French marauder would have got what he wanted with wit, and probably seduced the woman into the bargain, but the uhlan is German and therefore rough and clumsy – to get what he wants he can only bully.[161]

161 Reshef, ' "Le Hulan et la paysanne" ', 75–9.

Plate 40. *Le Hulan et la paysanne*: Pinot & Sagaire (Epinal), 1871
Reproduced by permission of the Musée départemental
d'art ancien et contemporain, Epinal.

Marauding was not, therefore, a blameworthy action in itself. Indeed if done well it added to a soldier's martial qualities. The soldier was supposed to be something of a rogue, a thief and a liar; this was part of his attraction. He was the model of an artful dodger, whose cunning helped him overcome his enemies. In one of Pellerin's *Scènes de garnison*, the trooper, caught by his officer with a stolen pig, replies 'Captain, it's my prisoner.'[162] If viewers were supposed to fear Desfeuilles's Cossacks, and laugh at Boulay's Württembergers, I think we can assume they were supposed to applaud this quick-witted cavalryman.

Two questions are raised by these images. First, as we have seen, the authorities kept a close eye on the production of imagery and were quick to condemn any image which smacked of immorality: why, therefore, did they allow past the censor prints which showed their own soldiers engaged in criminal acts against their own population? The answer must be that as far as governments was concerned military imagery served a useful propaganda purpose. Despite conscription, governments were anxious to encourage a military spirit among their subjects, and this included marauding. It therefore tolerated or even encouraged marauding as a suitable theme for illustration as one of the more exciting (but not dangerous) aspects of military life. Marauding was better than boring sentry-duty, or being shot at, features of

162 'Capitaine, c'est mon prisonnier': Garnier-Pelle, *L'Imagerie populaire française*, ii, no. 1968.

military life that tended not to be emphasised in the imagists' versions of the soldier's daily life. Governments were also keen to promote a sense of nation-hood, embodied in the figure of the soldier. But if the soldier embodied the nation, how could he commit crimes against it? Underlying these images was a sense that peasants were not truly French. They could become French by being soldiers, but until they did so their feelings were not a primary concern.

This leads us to the second question: who bought these images? In chapter 1 it was suggested that the audience for popular imagery was largely rural. But why would peasants wish to own prints which depicted their own humiliation? It is clear from the legends, songs and tales presented above that peasants resented marauders, but there is also the possibility that this aspect of military life simultaneously attracted them. The peasant's life was one of hard labour for meagre returns: the soldier's life was comparatively free and easy. Marauding for what one wanted must occasionally have seemed prefer-able to ploughing in wind and rain. Just as the myth of Robin Hood and his merry men provided for urban dwellers a useful model of a counter-commu-nity of liberty and ease inside the forest and outside the law, so the myth of the soldier, with his aristocratic airs, his exotic uniform, his loose morals and vagabond existence, existed as an alternative society in the imagination of peasants.[163] Let us now explore some of the other pleasures of the soldier's life, as envisioned in rural popular culture.

Wine, women and song

Soldiers pursued their pleasures at the expense of others. This is one of the messages of the best known theme in popular imagery – *Crédit est mort*. The image's apparent purpose was to enable shopkeepers to refuse credit without giving offence. It was commonly found in bars: a copy of *Crédit est mort* is visible on the wall of 'Dame Alison's Inn' in a mid seventeenth-century Pari-sian copperplate print, and again, a century later, in the print *Le Cabaret de Jean Ramponnaux*.[164] The point was not just that Credit was dead, and so

163 Without completely denying the usefulness of Eric Hobsbawm's notion of the 'social bandit', my understanding of the popular culture of Lorraine is more in line with the find-ings of social scientists and historians in Spain, Sicily, Corsica and the Low Countries which suggest that peasants seldom thought of bandits as heroes but rather detested them as threats to their lives and property: Anton Blok, 'The peasant and the brigand: social banditry reconsidered', *Comparative Studies in Society and History* xiv (1972), 494–506; Pat O'Malley, 'Social bandits, modern capitalism and the traditional peasantry: a critique of Hobsbawm', *Journal of Peasant Studies* ii (1978–9), 489–52. Indeed, in the folklore of Lorraine they appear closer to cannibals than to the 'noble bandit' archetype. This 'noble bandit', of whom Robin Hood is only the most famous example, seems to be largely the creation of urban popular culture for reasons which have been explored by Florike Egmond: 'The noble and ignoble bandit: changing literary representations of west-Euro-pean robbers', *Ethnologia Europaea* xvii (1987), 139–56.
164 Duchartre and Saulnier, *L'Imagerie parisienne*, 111.

Plate 41. *Crédit est mort*: Pellerin (Epinal), 1822
The second of five versions issued by Pellerin between 1811 and 1843, but the
cast of characters remained unchanged, as it had for a century before. The
fencing-master Mauvais Foy leads the assailants against Credit, whose murder
is witnessed by Gagne-Petit. Reproduced by permission of the Musée
départemental d'art ancien et contemporain, Epinal.

there was no point asking for him, but that he had been murdered by
defaulters. The image's subtitle was *Les Mauvais Payeurs l'ont tué*. The identity
of these villains was soon known. Credit's dying words were preserved in a
collection of sayings published in 1623, in which he accused 'Capitaine
Male-Paye', among others, of having struck the fatal blow.[165]

Prints on this topic are known from the mid-sixteenth century, but these
concentrate on Credit's funeral. In the versions from the Paris copperplate
print-houses, which began to appear in the first quarter of the eighteenth
century, the murder itself took centre-stage. In Crépy's version, which
appears to have been the model for all others, Credit lies battered and
bleeding in the road, surrounded by his three attackers: the painter
'Trompeur', the fiddler 'Renieur de dettes' and the fencing master 'Mauvaise
Foy' who dispatches the prostrate Credit with his rapier.[166] Fencing masters
were usually either serving or retired soldiers, so Saulnier was quite right to
see 'Mauvaise Foy' as the direct descendant of 'Capitaine Male-Paye'. An
Orléanist wood-engraver copied Crépy's print well before 1750, starting it on
its long and enormously successful career as a popular image. Pellerin issued
no fewer than five versions between 1811 and 1843.[167]

---

[165] Saulnier and Van der Zée, 'La Mort de crédit', 2, 8.
[166] Duchartre and Saulnier, *L'Imagerie populaire*, 99.
[167] Garnier-Pelle, *L'Imagerie populaire française*, ii, nos 1163–7.

Plate 42. *Crédit est mort*: Dembour (Metz), 1837
Reproduced by permission of the Musée départemental
d'art ancien et contemporain, Epinal.

In none of these images is it explained why fencing masters in particular should be such an enemy to Credit, although the extravagant dress and exaggerated gestures of 'Mauvaise Foy' cast him as a typical 'miles gloriosus'. Like the boasting, swaggering 'capitano' of the commedia dell'arte, 'Mauvaise Foy' would need credit to supply the elegant wardrobe with which he hoped to impress the ladies. This becomes clear in Dembour's 1837 addition to the *Crédit est mort* canon, in which 'Mauvaise Foy' is replaced by the army officer 'Gérôme Faux-Brillant' who declares that 'I wanted to dazzle the eyes;/ I wanted, through [their] desire and fury,/ to crush the envious/ By the brilliance of my attire!!'[168] Once more we can detect the soldier's descent from the aristocratic dandy.

In the background of *Crédit est mort* is the knife-grinder 'Gagne-petit'. He takes no part in the murder of Credit, preferring to work hard, earn little and spend less, 'Il n'est pas seul'. He was included to appeal to the peasant market, for his caution echoes their careful husbandry. Although the image was primarily designed for display in shops and bars it also found its way onto cottage walls.[169] Again the ethic of the peasant is contrasted with the soldier's showiness; his flamboyant appearance can only be achieved at the expense of others. Unfortunately, the image tends to undermine the moral of the text.

---

[168] 'Je voulais éblouir les yeux;/ Je voulais d'envie et de rage/ Faire crever les envieux/ Par l'éclat de mon equipage!!', MDAACE 57.3.2550 (*dépôt légal* 2 Mar. 1837).
[169] At least according to Balzac: *Le Peau de chagrin*, 279–80.

Plate 43. *Donnera-t-on quelque chose à crédit*: Pellerin (Epinal), 1822
The second of six versions issued by Pellerin during the nineteenth
century. Reproduced by permission of the Musée départemental
d'art ancien et contemporain, Epinal.

Frugality may be better than profligacy, but it is the attractive figure of
'Mauvaise Foy' who dominates the image.[170]

Soldiers were even more prominent in a later image designed to fill the
same space on the bar-room wall. In *L'Horloge de crédit* four figures gather
round a clock tower, on the spire of which stands a cockerel. The image
promises that when the clock strikes 12.00 and the cockerel crows the
publican will give his customers credit. The joke was, of course, that as both
were made out of paper, the clock would never advance beyond 11:25, the

---

[170] One of Pellerin's versions, and Dembour's version, overcame this problem by showing
both the murder and its consequences, as Mauvaise Foy and Gérôme Faux-Brillant have
their assets seized and are led off to the debtor's prison: Garnier-Pelle, *L'Imagerie populaire
française*, ii, no. 1165.

cock would never crow. The image is listed in Pellerin's 1814 catalogue, which is perhaps the oldest version.[171] In his first version the four expectant customers were a beadle, a pilgrim, a woodcutter and a hussar, the last puffing away at a pipe nearly half his height. This image was replaced in the catalogue soon afterwards with an almost identical image, the only significant alteration being the replacement of the hussar with an infantryman wearing the *fleur-de-lis* cap-badge of the restoration. Just one year later, in 1826, Georgin added a third version to the catalogue in which the infantryman was replaced by a grenadier sergeant. A fourth version, engraved by Vanson after a drawing by Pinot, was issued in 1850. In this the beadle was replaced by a beggar and the grenadier by another hussar. Finally Charles Maurin produced a lithograph version for the firm in 1875, in which the hussar was replaced by a zouave (part of the general preference for exotic colonial dress in the imagery of the second half of the century).[172] The personnel of the image varied little over three-quarters of a century, the texts that accompany each character even less. The soldier, always distinguished by his moustache, utters the same warning in the last version as he did in the first: 'While waiting for opening time/ I smoke my pipe;/ If the cock doesn't want to crow,/ I'll cut out his giblets.'[173] The other characters take different attitudes: the pilgrim approaches the cockerel in supplication, the beadle in forlorn hopelessness, only the woodcutter mirrors the soldier's aggression, threatening it with his axe.

As with other successful themes, imagists were quick to issue their own versions, so that by 1837 Blanc could report that *L'Horloge de crédit* was to be seen alongside *Crédit est mort* 'even in the least bar in the most obscure village'.[174] Bars were exactly the right location for this image, because it was

---

171 Duchartre and Saulnier, *Imagerie populaire française*, 180. As Jean-Charles Pellerin was also a clockmaker (and a manufacturer of paper clock faces) the humour of *L'Horloge de crédit* may have particularly appealed to him. Two versions from Brest and Nantes in Brittany, clearly copied from each other, appear more archaic than Pellerin's. They are more complex (six figures, including an additional fiddler and shepherdess, wait for the clock to strike), and combine the image of the clock with the earlier theme of *Crédit est mort*, because the fiddler is kneeling beside the grave of Credit. However, the grenadier who appears in both is clearly in the uniform of the Restoration era, and so the images must post-date Pellerin's 1814 catalogue. They suggest, however, that both Pellerin and the Bretons modelled their images on older prints of *L'Horloge de crédit*, now lost: Garnier, *L'Imagerie populaire française*, i, nos 339, 422.

172 Ibid. ii, nos 1183–6. The lithograph version can be found in BN (estampes), Tc mat.4 boite. Garnier-Pelle dates the second (infantryman) version to 1829, but it fits better the 1825 date given by Dumont, not least because it is a copy of an even earlier image issued by the Deckherrs (BN [estampes], Li 73 folio, images de Deckherr de Montbéliard): *Les Maîtres graveurs*, 60

173 'En attendant l'heure d'entrer/ Je fume ma pipe;/ Si le Coq ne veut pas chanter,/ Je lui coupe les tripes.'

174 '*Crédit est mort* et *L'horloge de crédit* se voient depuis longtemps en France, jusque dans le moindre cabaret du plus obscur village': Blanc, 'Rapport', 360. In addition to the version mentioned elsewhere in this chapter Boulay engraved a larger version featuring a hussar

Plate 44. *Horloge de crédit*: Dembour (Metz), *c.* 1836
Reproduced by permission of the Archives départementales de la Moselle.

apparent that all four characters wanted credit only in order to drink. The soldiers are waiting for 'opening-time' to the pub.[175] In Dembour's version the soldiers are actually shown in the garden of a country inn. An artilleryman, a lancer, a cuirassier and another cavalryman raise their glasses with a student and four other civilians to 'the union of the French' and 'the union of the peoples', while the innkeeper points to the *Horloge de crédit* hanging from the pergola to remind them that each toast must be paid for with ready cash.[176] Blanc was very struck with this idiosyncratic variant on the theme, and cited it in his report to the Académie royale de Metz as proof of the Dembour's attempts to improve the moral tone of the imagery industry:

for the Deckherrs (BN [estampes], Li 11 folio, imagerie populaire de Nancy: Desfeuilles; imagerie populaire de Montbéliard (Doubs): Deckherr), and Godard engraved a version for Hurez of Cambrai (reissued by Glémarec of Paris in 1858) in which, rather oddly, the sergeant was replaced by a bandit: René Faille, 'L'Imagerie populaire cambrésienne', *Le Vieux Papier*, fasc. 210, Paris 1964, 165.

[175] In Desfeuilles's version the hussar admits that 'Du Coq j'attends le chant,/ Pour boire un petit verre/ A crédit en passant': BN [estampes], Rd 61 pet. fo., Desfeuilles, images de saints.

[176] MDAACE 57.3.2551. This image, though unsigned, was almost certainly engraved by Wendling.

This idea, in its very simplicity, is it not of a nature to strike, in the bar itself, those souls soured by the heat of quarrel or over-excited by wine? It calls for peace, union; is that not a thousand times better than the financial censure which, since time immemorial, the old image of *Crédit est mort!* attached to musicians, painters and fencing-masters?[177]

Dembour's *Horloge de crédit* looks less like a reminder to pay than an invitation to buy, similar to some of the other images decorating the interior of the typical bar. Two such images, designed to advertise the publican's wares, were *Bonne Double Bière* and *Bonne Bière de mars*. In Deckherr's *Bonne Double Bière* two of the six companions around the table laden with bottles are soldiers.[178] Pierret *fils* of Rennes dispensed entirely with the civilians in his version to make way for a hussar, a *chasseur à pied*, an artilleryman and a drum-major, served by an Alsatian barmaid.[179] Later advertisements for all kinds of products from cocoa-powder to hair-tonic used soldiers as a kind of endorsement, linking particular products to martial virtues and French glory. However, images of *Bonne Double Bière* and *Bonne Bière de mars* were not related to any particular brand, and should be viewed more as a means of attracting a particular clientele. One can imagine that innkeepers in the garrison towns of Metz, Nancy, Epinal and Wissembourg (which were also home to the imagists) competed for the soldiers' pay. A prominently displayed image of *Bonne Double Bière* was more than just an assurance of the quality of the drink: it offered a promise of a good time in male company. Both the civilians and the soldiers in Deckherr's image seem in high spirits, singing, smoking and discussing, and in general partaking of the pleasures of the male-only environment of the bar-room.

Only occasionally do women join the scene, and then primarily for the benefit of soldiers. In another Deckherr image advertising *Bonne Bière de mars* two soldiers raise a glass of beer with one hand but have the other round the waist or touching the breast of a young woman.[180] Except on festive occasions, women who wanted to keep their good name steered clear of the inn.[181] Those women who did join the male company were generally judged loose-moralled seducers of men. Folksongs recalled the misery of a wife

---

[177] 'Cette idée, dans sa simplicité, n'est-elle pas de nature a frapper au cabaret même, des esprits aigris par l'ardeur de la dispute ou échauffés par le vin? Elle appelle la paix, l'union; ne vaut-elle pas mille fois mieux que celle de la réprobation financière dont l'image du vieux *Crédit est mort!* poursuivant de temps immémorial les musiciens, les peintres et les maîtres en fait d'armes?': Blanc, 'Rapport', 361.

[178] BN (estampes), Li 73 folio, images de Deckherr de Montbéliard (*dépôt légal* 1825, 1828).

[179] Garnier, *L'Imagerie populaire française*, i, no. 380 (*dépôt légal* 1869).

[180] Lerch, *Almanachs, bibliothèque bleue, imagerie*, 273.

[181] At least one regular customer preferred it that way. A peasant whom Marquant met on patrol could conceive of nothing more terrible than that his wife should come and hug him in the public bar: Marquant, *Carnet d'étapes*, 100.

Plate 45. *Bonne Bière de mars*: Deckherr (Montbéliard), c. 1825.
Reproduced by permission of the Musée départemental
d'art ancien et contemporain, Epinal.

finding her husband in the pub spending all his money on his 'darling', leaving their children to starve at home.[182] An image which showed a young woman sitting on the knee of a jolly (married) farmer would have represented every respectable woman's nightmare, and therefore was probably too *risqué* for the conservative imagists; soldiers were a different matter. Unmarried, away from home and with money in their pockets, they were expected to spend time with prostitutes (an expectation entirely confirmed by the army's centuries-old battle against venereal disease).[183] The promise of female company, and in particular of the kind that let breasts be felt, was no doubt part of the attraction of Deckherr's image, when used as an advert. A similar version of *Bonne Bière de mars*, in which 'a soldier offering a fountain of foam to a woman showing plenty of cleavage', made such an impression on Balzac that he put it in two of his novels, *La Rabouilleuse* of 1842 and *Les Souffrances de l'inventeur* of 1843.[184] In his mind, and probably those of other viewers, the image reinforced the soldier's reputation for licentiousness.

---

[182] Meyrac, *Traditions, coutumes, légendes*, 251: *La Femme du tambour*.
[183] Colin Jones, 'The welfare of the French foot-soldier from Richelieu to Napoleon', *History* lxv (1980), 203.
[184] 'un soldat offrant à une femme très décolletée un jet de mousse': Adhémar, 'L'Imagerie vue par l'écrivain', 410.

SCÈNES MILITAIRES.

Départ d'un conscrit.

La prise d'uniforme.

L'exercice du fusil.

Rencontre de la payse!

Le tambour-major et son épouse.

Le planton en fonction.

Les apprêts pour la revue.

La corvée des vivres.

En route pour la nouvelle garnison.

Le lieutenant vengé.

Décoré par son général!

Retour au pays.

Plate 46. *Scènes militaires*: Rencontre de la payse!: Gangel (Metz), 1854
Reproduced by permission of the Archives départementales de la Moselle.

269

The hope of the soldier's eventual return to his sweetheart was expressed in the image of *Le Retour du conscrit*. However, the images of *Bonne Bière de mars* imply that the hope that he would be faithful during the intervening period was wishful thinking. The same *Scènes de garnison* that depicts the conscript buying his sergeant a drink also shows soldiers making advances to a variety of maids and nurses. Because young women in domestic service were immigrants from the country, like soldiers, there was a good chance that some would be from the same area. Several images recall meeting with a 'payse' – a girl from one's region. In one of Gangel's life-cycles of the conscript he makes the acquaintance of his fellow countrywoman, a nursemaid, while she is taking her charge for a walk in the park. The pair are oblivious to the child who has fallen into a lake.[185] Unfortunately, such relationships tended to last only as long as the soldier's tour of duty. Once the soldier had changed garrison his promises were forgotten. Dembour & Gangel's *Scènes de garnison* shows a hussar telling his weeping sweetheart 'Don't cry little one, I'll look you up on my return', but contemporary songs were more realistic.[186] A mocking song from Metz advises 'Fanchon' not to cry when her 'guernadier' (a colloquial variation on grenadier) leaves: 'You can be sure that every lover/ Will remain faithful in the regiment', just as long, that is, as chickens have teeth![187] The false *Consolateur* of Metz was alluding to another song made famous through imagery, *Guernadier que tu m'affliges*. In Pellerin's 1851 version a Napoleonic grenadier comforts the weeping maid Fanchon, promising that although he cannot, as she wishes, be transferred to the permanent garrison, he 'does not have/ The heart capable,/ or so barbarous, or so treacherous,/ To forget all your attractions'.[188] Pinot copied the figure of Fanchon for his own firm's 1865 version, but his grenadier is a different character. Rather than trying to reassure Fanchon he twirls his moustache in a self-satisfied way. Pinot's version also included two further songs. In the first, *Le Retour du guernadier*, he does indeed come back to Fanchon, wounded in one eye but with his love intact. As she herself admits, this is a rare turn of events: 'Grenadier, I'm appreciative/ Of your rare honesty.' The oyster-girl in the other song is not as lucky. Having been seduced by a 'faithful trooper' she

---

[185] Archives du Musée historique lorrain, Nancy: Dembour & Gangel, *Scènes de garnison*, no. 228; Gangel, *Scènes militaires*, no. 125.

[186] 'Ne pleure pas, ma petite, je te donnerai de mes nouvelles à mon retour'. Pellerin's *Scènes de garnison* was, perhaps more accurate. It featured a corporal telling his 'payse' 'Ne pleure pas, Finfine, je donnerai ton adresse à un bon enfant': Garnier-Pelle, *L'Imagerie populaire française*, ii, no. 1968.

[187] 'Soyez en sûr, tout amant/ S'ra fidèle dans le régiment': Archives départementales de la Moselle 21/J/12, fonds de la Société d'histoire et d'archéologie de la Lorraine: 'Volkslieder – Westphalen'.

[188] 'Et crois bien qu'il n'aura pas/ Le coeur assez capable,/ Barbare, perfide,/ D'oublier tous tes attraits': Garnier-Pelle, *L'Imagerie populaire française*, ii, no. 1036.

Plate 47. *Guernadier que tu m'affliges*: Pinot & Sagaire (Epinal), 1865
Reproduced by permission of the Musée départemental d'art ancien et
contemporain, Epinal.

quickly learns that 'The lover changed his garrison,/It happens all the time!'[189]

The unfaithful soldier will leave you in the lurch, or so warned folksongs. 'Annemarie', in a germanophone song, goes to town to find herself a husband but meets a soldier. She comes home unmarried but pregnant.[190] The baker's daughter, when she notices that her skirt is riding high on her stomach, writes to her lover to rescue her from her predicament. But he unhelpfully replies 'Marry you, I can't do it,/ I'm in the service of the king.' As we have seen in the case of Jean-Charles Pellerin's grandfather, soldiers were forbidden to marry without their officer's consent, which was seldom given. But at least this soldier promises to return in two years and marry her (as the carabinier Pellerin did).[191] The young girl from the rue de la Monnaie who falls for a dragoon is not so lucky. When she confronts the soldier who got her pregnant he similarly replies 'Marry you, I can't do it,/ My captain doesn't want it' and he disappears, leaving her plaintively wailing after the baptismal linen he promised her.[192] The soldiers in garrison at Sanry were even more callous. They marched away to the sound of the local girls weeping, but when one of them wrote to her lover that she had become pregnant he advised her 'You will stay in Sanry/ You might find/ Some fool of a boy/ Who would be very pleased/ To have some unripe fruit.' The song refers to the children that the soldiers left behind them as 'little grenadiers'.[193] Similarly Annemarie's child, she says, will grow up to be a lieutenant, and there is no finer estate. We are back to the idea that occupation was devolved through blood or race, as was its place in the social hierarchy. More prosaically these songs comment on the assumption that illegitimate boys, without a family to give them a start in life, would have few opportunities except in the army. Abandoned children were brought up by foundling hospitals with this end in mind: the army would be their only family.

Songs contained warnings about the sexual threat posed by soldiers. In L'Epreuve, a son reproaches his mother for letting his sister guard the sheep in the fields: 'Mother, aren't you worried for her?/ The soldiers are there so often.'[194] In a dancing rhyme, popular in Lorraine, a girl is approached by a

---

189 'Guernadier, je suis sensible/ A ta rare honnêteté' . . . 'L'amant, de garnison,/ Changea, c'est bien possible': MDAACE D.37.584.

190 Archives départementales de la Moselle 42/J/25, fonds Pinck, A94,049.

191 'Pour t'épouser, je ne l'peux pas,/ Je suis au service du Roi': Westphalen, *Chansons populaires*, i, no. 138: *C'était la fille d'un boulanger*.

192 'Pour t'épouser, je ne le peux pas,/ Mon capitaine ne le veut pas': Quépat, *Chants populaires messins*, no. 12: *Florine*. The rue de la Monnaie was one of the main thorough-fares of Nancy old town, and where Desfeuilles had his workshop.

193 'A Sanry tu resterais,/ Tu trouverais peut-être/ Quelque garçon nigaud/ Qui s'rait encore bien aise/ D'avoir du fruit nouveau': Westphalen, *Chansons populaires*, ii. no. 324: *A Sanry, oh, quell' pitié*.

194 'Ma mère, n'avez-vous pas peur d'elle?/ Les soldats y sont si fréquents': Puymaigre,

nightingale, a frequent messenger between young women and soldier lovers in folksong. The nightingale offers her twice what she currently earns as a servant if she will come and share his camp-bed. Prudently she refuses, saying she will only sleep with a man after they have been married in church before God and her parents, and wearing her crown of virginity.[195] Not all folksong soldiers were willing to take no for answer. The possibility of rape is countenanced in an even more popular song, known in Lorraine as *Les Demoiselles du château de Bonfort*. One young gentlewoman is abducted by three officers who tell her 'With three captains/ You will pass the night.'[196] She only escapes by feigning death, but the song does not necessarily have a happy ending. In one variant her father refuses to release her from the grave saying 'Of any girl who gives herself up [to pleasure],/ One should speak no more.'[197]

Implicit in these songs is the sexual attraction of the soldier. The *demoiselle* of Bonfort claims that she is with the captains against her will, but the first two verses are couched as an invitation. The soldier is the model of the manliness that a woman expects in a lover, according to songs. Madelon, for instance, tells 'three handsome lads' that 'My forfeited heart is not for these boys./ It's for a man of war who has a beard on his chin./ And the pipe in mouth, smoking like a dragoon.'[198] A woman who has just spent the night with a *voltigeur* tells herself that she will plant her love in her garden, water it and tend it, and she will be able to give some 'to all these boobies/ Who don't have any'.[199] Country boobies are good enough to parent soldiers' bastard children, but one would not want to waste one's affections on them. Because a song is in the female voice does not necessarily mean that it was sung by women, and it is more than likely that several of these songs, such as the *Demoiselles de Bonfort*, originated in the army and so reflect the soldiers' own view of their irresistibility. But all three Lorrainer versions of the last song, *Ah, si l'amour prenait racine*, were collected from women.[200]

In the realm of love imagists drew a distinction between French soldiers and foreigners. When the French soldier marches out it is to the sound of

Chants populaires, i, no. 16. The inclusion of soldiers in this song-type is rather unusual, and points to a local ecotype in the area around Metz where soldiers were a frequent sight.
[195] Westphalen, *Chansons populaires*, ii, no. 271: *J'ai cueilli la rose rouge*; Meyrac, *Traditions, coutumes, légendes*, 289: *J'ai cueilli la rose rouge*.
[196] 'Avec trois capitaines/ Vous passerez la nuit': Puymaigre, *Chants populaires*, i, no. 28.
[197] 'Toute fille qui s'abandonne,/ Il n'en faut plus parler': Charles Bruneau, 'Pour nos patois lorrains', *Le Pays lorrain* xi (1914–19), 135; Westphalen, *Chansons populaires*, i, nos 223–4.
[198] 'Mon coeur en gage n'est point pour ces garçons./ C'est pour un homme de guerre qu'a d'la barbe au menton./ Et la pipe à la bouche, fumant comme un dragon': Westphalen, *Chansons populaires*, i, no. 168: *Madelon s'y baigne*.
[199] 'J'en donn'rais à tous ces nigauds/ Qui n'en ont point': Sadoul, 'Les Chansons lorraines', 225: *Ah, si l'amour prenait racine*.
[200] In addition to Sadoul's two versions Georges Chepfer collected a version: *Anciennes Chansons populaires recueillies en Lorraine*, in Jean-Marie Bonnet and Jean Lanher (eds), *Georges Chepfer: textes et chansons*, Nancy 1983, no. 3.

Plate 48. *L'Aimable Prussien*: Abadie (Toulouse), *c.* 1824–7
Reproduced by permission of the Musée départemental
d'art ancien et contemporain, Epinal.

broken hearts. In one of Pellerin's life-stories of the soldier when the
conscript Grivet leaves his garrison for Algiers, he leaves behind 'nothing but
tears and regrets', and the image shows three weeping women, one with a
baby.[201] Not only did Frenchwomen respond to the soldier's gallantry,
foreigners were equally likely to fall for his charms. The song which accompanies Pinot's *Le Retour du conscrit* describes the conquest of a town: 'when the
light of the moon appears,/ Each soldier chooses his [woman],/ In his condition as conqueror'. However, 'when we leave the town/ One should see the
effect of the partings . . ./ And all the women in line/ Compete in crying./

[201] 'Que de larmes et de regrets il laissa après lui, en partant pour l'Afrique':
Garnier-Pelle, *L'Imagerie populaire française*, ii, no. 1250: *L'Histoire de Grivet no. 2.*

274

Their tears make a river'.[202] Seduction, like marauding, was something
French troops did best, and relied on some of the same qualities – intelligence, dash and exotic uniforms. Foreign soldiers, at least according to
French imagists, did not have this effect (although in copperplate images
Highlanders are shown with some of the same qualities). Satires on the allied
occupation of 1815 show Prussian and British troops as very inept lovers.
How can they repeat the success of their French counterparts and seduce the
women of Tours by the light of the moon when with every word of love they
murder the language: 'Come on, one night only,/ Be gentle my soul, the moon
shines bright;/ A night shared is not long.'[203] The only means of seduction
they can command is abduction.

The road to hell

Soldiers, whether foreign or domestic, were addicted to the pleasures of life.
They were only too likely to be found on the broad way 'that leadeth to
destruction'. The popular imagery theme of *The broad and narrow way* owes its
origin to Jesus' instruction to his followers in Matthew vii.13, to enter at the
'strait gate' if they wish to enjoy everlasting life, and to avoid the 'wide gate'
which is the road to hell. It is one of the few themes illustrated by French
provincial imagists that might also be familiar to British readers.[204] It had first
been developed in Protestant Germany, under the influence of the international success of Bunyan's *Pilgrim's progress*. The German (and British)
versions were clearly designed for use in evangelical education. Each path was
littered with biblical references designed to help teachers instruct their
charges in the sins to avoid and the virtues to practice. With the help of a
Bible the message was laid bare: not only worldly pleasures, such as drinking,
dancing and gambling, but also worldly virtues, such as honour, respect and
fortune, could be pursued only at the risk of one's eternal soul. As the first
text which the traveller meets on his way explains, 'whosoever will be a
friend of the world is the enemy of God' (James iv.4).[205]

202 Quand vient le clair de lune,/ Chaqu' soldat choisit sa chacune,/ En qualité de
conquérant' . . . 'c'est quand nous quittons la ville/ Qu'il faut voir l'effet des adieux . . ./ Et
toutes les femmes à la file/ Se lamenter à qui mieux mieux./ C'est un' rivière que leurs
yeux': Perrout, *Trésors*, 57.
203 'Courache, éné nuit sélément,/ Gentil mon tam, la leun est claire;/ En nuit partié n'est
pas long-temps': MDAACE 57.3.2062, 57.3.1272: *L'Aimable Prussien* by Abadie of
Toulouse and Rabier-Boulard of Orléans respectively; D.52.85.5: *L'Ecossais galant* by
Abadie of Toulouse.
204 Lithograph versions from the early twentieth century can still occasionally be found
on the walls of old-fashioned Sunday-schools. Indeed it has been reprinted recently by the
Cotswold Printing Company.
205 Martin Scharfe, *Evangelische Andachtsbilder*, Stuttgart 1968, pp. lxxxvi–lxxxix, nos
149–52.

Plate 49. *La Nouvelle Jérusalem*: Pellerin (Epinal), 1824
Reproduced by permission of the Musée départemental d'art ancien
et contemporain, Epinal.

The layout of the variant of *The broad and narrow way* which proved popular
in France in the first half of the nineteenth century was rather different from
the usual German versions. It appeared in France first at Montbéliard, where
Boulay, then working for the Deckherr brothers, made a French-language
version of *Die beiden Wege und das neue Jerusalem*, shortly after his arrival in
the town in 1819. The likely model was an image by Christian Kräyenbühl, a
wood-engraver from the neighbouring canton Berne.[206] What is certain is
that Boulay was working from a German-language (and probably
Protestant) original, because one of the texts in his French version has been
mistranslated.[207] Along the top of Boulay's image floats the New Jerusalem of

---

[206] Ibid. p. lxxxiv, no. 146. Kräyenbühl probably copied it from an image by Enselin und
Laiblin of Reutlingen in Württemberg. The origins (and the identity of the engraver) of
the first French version of this image has been a topic of minor controversy, the details of
which can be discovered in David M. Hopkin, 'Reading difficulties', *Print Quarterly* xvii
(1998), 73–4.
[207] One of Boulay's sinners declares 'Plus je prend à droite, plus je me rapproche', but the
German original reads 'Recht verkehren, thut mich nähren'. The translator had obviously

276

Revelations. The Tree of Life grows in one of its squares, and Christ crowned waits to greet the few pious men and women who climb the thorny path to salvation. In the bottom right a small boy, refusing to be guided by his father towards things heavenly, points towards the multitude making their way through the wide gate and exclaims 'But everybody is going this way!' The crowd of sinners look like visitors to a local fête, couples take the air, pedlars sell their wares, a prostitute is eyed up by a priest, while musicians in berib-boned hats lead them on (as if for a wedding or the conscripts' march to the *tirage*). At the very head of the procession the Whore of Babylon, looking very like a market woman herself despite the seven-headed beast she rides, is the first to tumble into the pit of hell. The legend underneath explains that this is:

> the wide gate, ever open to all-comers: everyone can enter here without diffi-culty. Whoever wishes to win money and property should direct his steps there speedily. Thousands have already gone through, desirous of honour and for-tune; for pleasures, and ambition, there is no other route: song, dance and music provide the escort for the travellers.[208]

The main difference between this image and the more common British and German versions of *The broad and narrow way* is the addition of a third way. It runs parallel to the narrow way until, at the last moment, it falls away towards Death in person, who sweeps the unfortunate pilgrim into hell with his scythe. It might be called the 'path of false hope', illustrating Bunyan's claim that there is a way to hell 'even from the gates of Heaven'. In Boulay's woodcut this path is for those who do not have the faith necessary for salva-tion, symbolically represented in the empty lamps they carry. The pious voyagers on the upper path have burning torches, but those on the path of false hope, like the seven foolish virgins, have lost their oil. (In later variants on the theme, this way is followed by those sinners, lawyers, merchants and even kings, who appear outwardly virtuous but only in order to obtain worldly rewards: power, money, respectability. They are joined by pious non-believers, represented by a praying Turk.) A further important difference is that the French image no longer relies on biblical allusions, although the travellers are still accompanied by moralising statements.[209]

---

mistaken 'nähren' for 'nähern': Sigrid Metken, *Französische Bilderbogen des 19. Jahrhunderts*, Baden-Baden 1972 (exhibition catalogue), 35.

[208] 'Mais, tout le monde va de ce côté-ci! la porte large, sans cesse ouverte à tout venant: chacun y entre sans obstacle. Qui veut gagner argent et bien, doit y porter ses pas en hâte. Des milliers ont déjà passé, jaloux d'honneur et de fortune; pour la volupté, l'ambition, il n'est pas un autre chemin: les chants, la danse et la musique forment des passagers l'escorte.'

[209] MDAACE 57.3.2572: *La Nouvelle Jérusalem*. Boulay's image almost certainly provided the model for Georgin's 1824 version, but it was first passed by the *dépôt légal* in April 1830. It was common for images that had not previously been approved (due to the uncer-

Plate 50. *Le Chemin du ciel et le chemin de l'enfer*: Pellerin (Epinal), 1837
Reproduced by permission of the Musée départemental d'art ancien et
contemporain, Epinal.

In 1824 Boulay's image was copied by his former companion at the Pellerin
workshop, Georgin, for the firm's first version of *La Nouvelle Jérusalem*.[210] The
Pellerin version, including the errors that had crept in (for instance, now it
was the elect with their burning torches who turn to the reprobate to request
'Give us some of your oil') was almost immediately copied by Desfeuilles of
Nancy and Lefas of Rennes.[211] The theme quickly established itself in the
imagists' repertoire. Georgin cut another version for Pellerin just one year
later in 1825 (which was copied by Deckherr in 1830).[212] In 1837 Pellerin
issued a third and last version of the theme.[213] Other imagists followed the

tainties in application of the system, especially before 1822) to be resubmitted when
reprinted. Boulay had already left the Deckherrs to work for Clerc of Belfort in 1829.
[210] Garnier-Pelle, *L'Imagerie populaire française*, ii, no. 561 (*dépôt légal* 4 Sept. 1824). The
misplacing of the text 'Donnez-vous de votre huile' in this first Pellerin version is evidence
that it was copied from the Deckherr image, where it is positioned correctly.
[211] BN (estampes), Li 11 fo., imagerie populaire de Nancy: Desfeuilles; imagerie populaire
de Montbéliard (Doubs): Deckherr: *La Nouvelle Jérusalem*; MDAACE 50.4.1: *Le Chemin
du paradis*. The Lefas block was subsequently reused by Charles-Joseph Pierret: Musée
départemental breton, *L'Imagerie populaire bretonne*, 73.
[212] Garnier-Pelle, *L'Imagerie populaire française*, ii, no. 564. Deckherr's copy is BN
(estampes), Li 11 fo., imagerie populaire de Nancy: Desfeuilles; imagerie populaire de
Montbéliard (Doubs): Deckherr.
[213] Garnier-Pelle, *L'Imagerie populaire française*, ii, no. 553.

fashion. Louis Gondelfinger, the engraver who succeeded Boulay in Montbéliard, made a version for Jean-Pierre Clerc of Belfort in the 1830s.[214] It was subsequently sold to Dembour of Metz, replacing in his catalogue an earlier woodcut under the same title.[215] These rapid re-editions clearly demonstrate the theme's popularity. What is not clear is their intended market. It made sense for the Deckherrs to translate germanophone Protestant images into French because Montbéliard was still a largely Lutheran enclave in the 1820s. It is possible that Pellerin, Clerc and Dembour also expected their images to be bought by Protestants, as their images were bilingual and therefore suitable for export to Alsace and beyond. On the other hand, one of the few changes made to the theme in its migration to France was the substitution of Catholic clergy for pilgrims on the thorny path. This is particularly evident in the versions issued after 1825. The attempt to make the image acceptable in Catholic France failed to disguise its Protestant origins, for it left no room for good works, the sacraments, intercession, purgatory or many other essential Catholic dogmas. The newly appointed Commission du colportage banned the image when Gangel tried to reissue it in 1854, probably because it was doctrinally suspect.[216]

The reason I have spent so much time on the history of *The broad and narrow way* in French imagery is because of the prominent positions taken in it by soldiers (although not on the path to salvation). Kräyenbühl's woodcut already contained two soldiers sauntering along after the Whore of Babylon, but Boulay added a third and Georgin's 1824 version even squeezed in a fourth. The increase in the number of soldiers in French imagery is very noticeable when compared with Italian images, also based on Kräyenbühl's original, in which the number of soldiers was first reduced to one, before being eliminated altogether. Soldiers never seem to have acquired the significance in Italian popular culture that they have in French.[217] Soldiers appear in the traditional German and British versions of *The broad and narrow way*, but their presence is explained by reference to the biblical text John v.44: 'How can ye believe, which receive honour one of another, and seek not the honour that cometh from God only?' French imagists mentioned pursuit of honour, alongside ambition, wealth and sensual pleasure, in their general introduction to the 'wide gate', but in only one image does it appear that a soldier is being condemned for this sin. In Pellerin's 1837 version an officer dandy walks along the middle path, which though apparently leading to heaven, will in fact lead him to hell.[218] Officers were, perhaps, too far up the

214 MDAACE 57.3.2493 (a reprint by Dembour & Gangel).
215 BN (estampes), Td 24 t.2, allégories.
216 Bodé, *L'Imagerie messine*, 243.
217 Two Italian versions are preserved in the MDAACE: 63.22.2: *La via del paradiso*, by Barelli of Milan; the second, also named *La via del paradiso*, is unsigned and unnumbered.
218 Unfortunately the text beside him which warns that 'La mesure que vous emploierez envers les autres sera employée pour vous' is more apt for the man behind him, a draper,

Plate 51. *Les Trois Chemins de l'éternité*: Dembour & Gangel (Metz), *c.* 1840
Reproduced by permission of the Archives départementales de la Moselle.

social hierarchy to be shown mixing with the crowd on the 'broad way', where we see only common soldiers. And these soldiers are bound for hell because of their pursuit of worldly pleasures.

The crowds on the 'broad way' are always escorted by musicians, and soldiers are shown as their keenest followers. In both Clerc's and Pellerin's 1837 images, troopers are shown dancing to their music. Of course they are not dancing alone but with partners, and the other soldiers in the images are almost always in the company of young women. In Georgin's 1824 woodcut three soldiers walk arm-in-arm with women whose dress and gestures probably indicate that they are prostitutes. In his 1825 version a grenadier turns to a market-woman with a propositioning leer. Music, and particularly dancing, was widely associated with immodesty. Even the volunteer Vaxelaire, who earned his living as a violinist after he had been invalided out of the army, called dancing 'the torch of lasciviousness'.[219] Those soldiers without female

and so Pellerin's explanation for including the officer is lost. This is only one of several confusions in the positioning of the texts within French versions of *The broad and narrow way*, which suggests that Catholic imagists were not always entirely clear about its message, further evidence of the theme's Protestant origins.
[219] 'Je vous dirai que la danse est un amusement innocent en soi, mais que la suite en est bien funeste et, qu'en un mot, elle est le chef de la débauche et la perdition de beaucoup de jeunes gens. C'est le flambeau de l'impudicité': Vaxelaire, *Mémoires d'un vétéran*, 208.

companions could console themselves with the alcohol and tobacco. In Georgin's 1825 version a hussar standing in the middle of the 'broad way' puffs at a long German pipe. In Dembour's first image of *Les Trois Chemins de l'éternité* a soldier, waving a bottle in his hand, is literally carried to hell in a handcart because he is too drunk to walk. Even if not actually engaged in wrongdoing themselves, none the less soldiers are guilty by association, because of the bad company they keep on the 'broad way'. They mix not only with musicians but also with vagrants (a rag-picker is prominent in Dembour's image), thieves (Georgin's hussar is having his pocket picked), innkeepers, Gascons (who in the iconography of French imagery were synonymous with distillers), drunkards, smokers, lawyers and libertines of both sexes.

Unfortunately for the success of their message, these images exhibit the customary tendency for the fascination of evil to eclipse the good. With each succeeding version the sinners grew and the pious were dwarfed, the 'wide gate' became larger, and the 'narrow way' more hazardous and deserted. Looking at these images one feels some sympathy with the traveller in Clerc's version who, on arriving at the parting of the ways, exclaims 'What jollity! Follow the crowd.'[220]

220 'Quelle gaieté! Suivons la foule.'

5

The Veteran

Probably every inhabitant of Lorraine knew at least one veteran. In 1856 all but 5 per cent of communes of the department of the Meurthe were able to find someone to put forward for the Saint-Helena medal (awarded by Napoleon III to veterans of the revolutionary and Napoleonic wars).[1] As there had also been a continuous flow of Lorrainers into the army both before and after this period (and many veterans from outside the region also decided to settle near their former garrisons) the recipients of the medal were probably not the only inhabitants of their village with military experience.

It was often in their character as old soldiers that these veterans were considered by their neighbours. In the Comtois village of Lantenne 'Rank or military speciality marked their man for life in the period when not all "went as a soldier" (i.e. before 1873), so there was *lou dragon* (the dragoon) and his wife *lè dragoun*, *lou sapoer* (the sapper) . . . *lou karabi'nyé* (the carabinier).'[2] Lorraine soldiers, particularly those who had served in the armies of the *ancien régime* often retained their *noms-de-guerre* in the village (La Candeur, La Tulipe, la Renommée . . .). Others were identified by their rank (Lapointé, le Volontaire, Caporal . . .), their arm (le Cuirassier, le Zouave, le Tambour . . .), the battles in which they had fought or the places in which they had been imprisoned (la Vendée, l'Egyptien, l'Anglais . . .).[3] Military service may have only occupied a short period in the veteran's life, but it was considered fundamental to his identity.

There is no evidence that former soldiers objected to being labelled in this way. On the contrary it was a badge of pride in their achievements and proof of their experience. Their experience gave them status, and their status authorised them to speak of their experiences. As we have seen, veterans were among the most voluble participants at the *veillée*, but not always as narrators of fairytales. According to Gazin almost all the men who attended *veillées* in the Vosges had been soldiers: 'they love to recount their travels, the battles. They discuss the customs, the culture, and the industries of the countries they have visited, and this exchange of ideas makes up almost the entire

---

[1] Françoise Job, 'Les Anciens Militaires de la république et de l'empire dans le département de la Meurthe en 1857 et la médaille de Sainte-Hélène', *Le Pays lorrain* lxi (1981), 97.
[2] 'Le grade ou la spécialité militaire marquaient leur homme pour la vie quand tous "n'allaient pas soldats", ainsi *lou dragon* et sa femme *lè dragoun* le dragon, *lou sapoer* le sapeur . . . *lou karabi'nyé* le carabinier': Garneret, *Un Village comtois*, 262.
[3] Richard, 'Les Sobriquets en Lorraine', 347–96.

intellectual life of the village'.[4] Numerous other references from Lorrainer folklorists recall old soldiers 'still making war' around the stove.[5] In Sierck, Napoleonic veterans recalled their exploits under the emperor with the aid of images of Austerlitz, Russia and Waterloo that they hung on their walls.[6] Veterans did not renounce but rather traded on their experiences.

The old soldier reliving his 'great deeds', has become a stereotype of French art and fiction, familiar to us from the works of Diderot, Balzac, the Goncourt brothers, Zola and many others (including Lorrainer regionalist writers such as André Theuriet). The man who supplied Merkelbach-Pinck with information on Sierck, Michel Gregoire, included veterans of the War of Austrian Succession reminiscing at the *veillée* in his great-grandfather's fictional journal. Their presence gave it the air of veracity that it needed to be passed off as a true autobiography of the eighteenth century.[7] Such loquacious veterans were equally well known in oral literature. In a folksong from the Vosges a conscript resigns himself to his fate with the thought that when he was discharged he would no longer be embarrassed at the *veillée*; the marvels he had seen would give him something to tell.[8] However, the old soldier was not just a literary trope, he was certainly familiar to generations of Lorrainers as a significant figure within their own social world.

The soldier's experience of the world was not just valued as material for storytelling, it might also create a field of respect. Jean Parisot, a veteran of the first empire, was part of a group of old soldiers who gathered at the pub in Fresne-en-Woëvre during the restoration to reminisce about old times. Parisot went on to become mayor of his commune under Louis-Philippe.[9] Yet, despite Parisot's example of social triumph – which was not an isolated case – a more traditional image of the old soldier continued to circulate in which he was portrayed as an unredeemed prodigal at best, a menace to society at worst. For peasants, familiarity with veterans bred, if not exactly contempt, then at least circumspection. As we have already seen when looking at the figure of

---

4 'ils aiment à raconter leurs voyages, les batailles. On parle des moeurs, des procédés de culture, des industries des pays que l'on a visités, et cet échange d'idées a presque toute la vie intellectuelle du village': Gazin, 'Moeurs, traditions, légendes', 564.

5 'les anciens soldats faisaient encore la guerre': Lemasson, 'Anciennes Coutumes', 512. Similar comments appear in Louis Jouve, *Bussang*, (*Vosges*), Remiremont 1888, 15, and Géhin, 'Gérardmer à travers les âges', 156.

6 Merkelbach-Pinck, *Aus der lothringer Meistube*, ii. 441.

7 The *Journal d'un bourgeois de Sierck (1750–1843)* was supposedly written by Nicolas Gregoire, an eighteenth-century vintner, and was published as a true autobiography by Maurice Toussaint: *La Revue rhénane* iii (1922–3), 120–7. It was, in fact, almost certainly written by Michel Gregoire, and though it may contain elements of his family's history it is also riddled with factual errors. I am grateful to Line Skorka of the Archives départementales de la Moselle for supplying information on Michel and Nicolas Gregoire.

8 Jouve, *Chansons en patois*, 74: *Le Départ du conscrit Didiche*.

9 Jean Bohin, 'L'Invasion de 1815, et le parti royaliste à Fresne-en-Woëvre', *Le Pays lorrain* xiii (1921), 257–67.

the soldier-turned-pedlar, there remained ambiguities in the depiction of veterans.

Historians of government policy towards veterans have been somewhat puzzled by these ambiguities. Those who, like Corvisier, argue that the eighteenth century witnessed the integration of the army into the French nation (a process which the volunteers of Year II and Napoleon's conscripts merely completed), none the less recognise the dichotomy between the 'real' social situation of soldiers and the views expressed about them.[10] They have pointed to, in the words of Jean Chagniot, 'a rupture between facts and representations'.[11] Chagniot places the actual rehabilitation of the soldier firmly in the eighteenth century, when he was transformed from a 'bad lad into a patriot'.[12] Bois concurs in his assessment: just as better discipline on the battlefield and in garrison had raised the stock of the serving soldier, so the introduction of pensions for common soldiers after 1764, a process (theoretically) accelerated by the revolution, improved the social lot of veterans.[13] The state's reward gave the veteran a stake in society. By the end of the eighteenth century he had become an honoured defender of the nation, rather than the violent mercenary known to contemporaries of Louis XIV. Woloch, although less sanguine about the veteran's economic position, agrees that, as a consequence of the bellicose policies of the revolution and empire, he had become 'by far the state's most favored ward'.[14] In addition, post-revolutionary conscription had altered the make-up of veterans as a social group: not only were they more ubiquitous, they reflected French society as a whole rather than forming a distinct class apart.[15] Through the late eighteenth and into the nineteenth centuries, the social distance between veterans and civilians should have been ever-decreasing, yet people did not seem to be aware of it.

This failure is all the more surprising because the veteran, from at least the revolution onwards, was the beneficiary of a campaign of cultural rehabilitation. While succeeding regimes took a hand in directing the campaign, the soldier was not entirely reliant on state-sponsorship; he also benefited from the enthusiasm of generation after generation of intellectuals, journalists and writers. For example, Balzac in *Les Paysans* made a veteran into the standard-bearer of French civilisation in a recalcitrant countryside.[16] Artists such as Vernet and Charlet were particularly active promoters of the military, with a

---

10 Corvisier, *L'Armée française*, ii. 990.

11 'un décalage entre les faits et les représentations': Chagniot, *Paris et l'armée*, 653.

12 'Du mauvais garçon au patriote': ibid. 525.

13 Bois, *Les Anciens Soldats*, 318.

14 Woloch, *The French veteran*, 316.

15 Idem, *The new regime: transformation of the French civic order, 1789–1820s*, New York 1994, 380–426. However, Alan Forrest's study of resistance to conscription should make historians cautious about claims that the army had been 'nationalised', and the nation militarised: *Conscripts and deserters*, 219–37.

16 Lehning, *Peasant and French*, 18.

penchant for depictions of veterans as both idealised representatives of the nation and the epitome of contentment. From paintings and prints their vision made its way into the imagists' repertoire. However, as we will see, imagists were not able to entirely shake off the more dubious aspects of the soldier's reputation.

Yet popular attitudes took decades to conform to either the veteran's new social position as promoted by the state, or to his new cultural status as promoted by revolutionaries and nationalists. Was it simply a question, as Bois suggests, of generational lag, that 'mentalities transform themselves more slowly than realities or, to be more exact, with a gap which endures as long as memory, one or two generations'?[17] But the relationship between peasants and veterans is more complex than this explanation might suggest. Peasants did not merely respond to government propaganda and the cultural hegemony of national elites. They were able to form their own ideas about veterans according to rather different criteria. The veteran's economic well-being was only one of their concerns. Peasants remained ambivalent about the veterans in their midst because they were suspicious of what they had seen, what they done, the kind of persons they had become. A comparison between the image of the veteran promoted by imagists, and that articulated in folklore, highlights the rupture between how he was conceived of in urban, literate culture on the one hand, and rural, popular attitudes on the other. It also suggests some of the causes for this rupture.

The veteran in popular imagery: the *soldat-laboureur*

Imagists may have placed soldiers firmly on the road to hell, but it is clear that they did not consider their moral faults a bar to social success. The activities engaged in by the soldier following 'the Broad Way' – drinking, dancing and whoring – were, as we have seen, the same as those enjoyed by the prodigal-conscript. But in the case of the conscript these were depicted as formative experiences, turning him from a green recruit into a seasoned trooper. Only when that evolution was completed would he be man enough to return home and marry his faithful sweetheart. The domestic consequences of the conscript-cum-veteran's military achievements are shown in Pellerin's 1841 *La Vie du conscrit*. The final scene depicts him as the enthroned patriarch of his village home. His wife sits on his left, her role indicated by the symbols of household industry, the spinning wheel and distaff. A dog lies at his feet while with his right hand the veteran rocks his baby's cradle. He is the family's provider through his labours in the fields (in the previous scene he is shown with a scythe) but also their master; the image of the Emperor Napoleon on

---

17 'les mentalités se transforment plus lentement que les réalités, ou plus exactement, avec un décalage que dure le temps de la mémoire, une ou deux générations': Bois, *Les Anciens Soldats*, 17.

the wall behind his head echoes his own role within the household. And the presence of Napoleon, the patron of warriors, reminds us that the veteran remains a soldier: on his jacket is pinned the *croix d'honneur* and over the banister behind him hang his sabre. Having participated in the great history of the nation he has become a missionary to the countryside for the cult of the fatherland. A model citizen, he will bring up his children in an awareness of their duty to their country.[18]

This was the message underlying the image of *Le Retour du conscrit*: the 'Jean-Jean', transformed by his excesses and triumphs in the army, became ready to take on adult responsibilities, to work and provide a home as husband and father. Thus he would be reintegrated into his home community while none the less remaining, at some level, a soldier. The portrayal in *Les Quatre Vérités* of soldiers and peasants as opposed orders was being undermined by the single figure of the conscript-veteran in which the second and the third estates were confounded. The peasant becomes the soldier who becomes the veteran who marries and raises future generations of peasant-soldiers or, to use the contemporary term, *soldat-laboureurs*.

According to the historian Gerard de Puymège, the concept of the *soldat-laboureur* was a commonplace of the period.[19] The idea that peasants made the best soldiers, and *vice-versa*, was introduced into France by the *philosophes* from their readings of the ancients. Diderot, Holbach and Rousseau lifted whole chunks straight out of Cato, Pliny and Vegetius, for the benefit of their modern readers. They accepted the argument of the Roman authors that peasants were the best equipped for the rigours of military life, because they were inured by daily toil to hardship and violence. The attachment of the peasant to his little fatherland, the plot of earth that nourished him and his family, was supposed to make him more willing to defend the greater fatherland. City-dwellers, on the other hand, were effeminate and cosmopolitan, and on both grounds unsuited to military service. When the war was over the *soldat-laboureur* would turn his sword into a ploughshare and resume his other battle with the soil that he nourished with his sweat. And because conquest in war was analogous to conquest in love, and because the peasant had not been enervated by luxury, he was willing and able to procreate and thus produce a race of little *soldat-laboureurs*, whom he would school in the duties of the patriot. They, in turn, would reforge their swords from their ploughshares and march to the defence of the fatherland.

It is not hard to find evidence of the influence of the *soldat-laboureur* on the thinking of the French revolutionaries. Saint-Just's proposed education scheme, for example, was designed with the intention of producing a nation of identical *soldat-laboureurs*, each equally seized with the desire to give up his life for the fatherland. Although most of these projects came to nothing,

18 Garnier-Pelle, *L'Imagerie populaire française*, ii, no. 1432.
19 Puymège, *Chauvin*. The following paragraphs draw largely on Puymège's excellent work.

Napoleon did go some way towards creating agro-military colonies on the Roman model.[20] The colonies were evacuated with the approach of allied armies in 1813, but the idea of the *soldat-laboureur* survived the fall of the first empire. He became the darling of the liberal opposition under the restored monarchy, inspiring the songwriter Béranger, the artists Vernet and Charlet, and the historian Michelet. But one of the virtues of the *soldat-laboureur* was that he was equally appealing to the political right, and in time the same language and imagery found its way into the works of antisemitic nationalists such as Barrès, Deroulède and, finally, Pétain. Often those who celebrated him talk in quite specific terms about a reconciliation, or a melding of the third and second estates.[21]

Puymège argues that the *soldat-laboureur*, for all he represents a peasant, had no roots in peasant mentalities:

> although overtly plebeian, [he] was in truth neither of rural origin, nor proletarian extraction. . . . Rustic and warrior, he was not the product of provincial folklore. He was the fruit of an intellectual elite's nostalgia for Rome which, with its urbane and centralising tendencies, had absolutely no sympathy for local particularities which it hoped to destroy.[22]

However, considerable effort was made to plant the *soldat-laboureur* in the countryside. Revolutionary propaganda sheets, such as the 1790 *Feuille villageoise* (relaunched after the 1848 revolution) constantly invoked his model of republican virtue. The self-help manuals, produced in dozens of cheap editions in the first half of the nineteenth century, looked to him for inspiration. He was the hero of the collections of virtuous stories, distributed free to children by priests and schoolteachers, and to conscripts in the army. Above all he made his presence felt through conscription. Jourdan's draft proposal for the conscription system introduced in 1798 cited the Roman and Rousseauian model in its preamble.[23]

A wealth of pictorial representations of the *soldat-laboureur* has survived from the early nineteenth century. Balzac talked of a deluge of engravings,

---

[20] Woloch, *The French veteran*, 232–46. Woloch is less sure than Puymège that Napoleon was consciously copying a Roman model. The idea, whether Roman or not, resurfaced in the Napoleonic exiles' colony *Champ d'asile* in Texas and Bugeaud's plans for veterans' colonies in conquered Algiers.

[21] The point is made in one of the numerous vaudeville plays on the theme of the *soldat-laboureur* that appeared during the Restoration, *Le Laboureur ou tout pour le roi, tout pour la France* (1823): Puymège, *Chauvin*, 73.

[22] 'Tout au plus peut-on assurer que Chauvin, bien qu'ouvertement plébéien, n'est en vérité ni d'origine rurale, ni d'extraction prolétarienne. A destination populaire, le chauvinisme n'est pas issu d'une *tradition* populaire. Rustique et guerrier, il n'est pas le produit d'un folklore provincial. Il est le fruit des nostalgies romaines d'une élite intellectuelle urbaine et centralisatrice, qui n'a aucune sympathie pour les particularités locales qu'elle cherche a détruire': ibid. 280.

[23] Woloch, *The new regime*, 389.

clocks and statuettes, at least a million he estimated. The illustrator Charlet, one of the chief perpetrators of this flood, even joked about it in the foreword to one of his series of sketches illustrating the theme, 'I hear a passer-by call out to the public: "Don't buy this folder of sketches, it's yet another *soldat-laboureur*!" '[24] But can any of these innumerable images be classed as popular imagery, and did they find their way onto the walls of the homes of the peasants whose lives, in theory, they were celebrating?

The answer to the first part of the question is yes. In 1822 Fleuret engraved *Le Soldat laboureur* for the Chartres firm Garnier-Allabre.[25] The theme arrived in this popular medium by the usual path. Fleuret's image was a copy of an anonymous Parisian aquatint, which itself was modelled on a painting by Horace Vernet.[26] The painting was exhibited in Vernet's private show of 1822, set up in opposition to the Salon of that year from which he had been excluded on political grounds. Puymège's interpretation of the painting, and the image copied from it, is thought-provoking to say the least.[27] The setting is France after Waterloo, the ruins in the foreground are the consequence of the allied invasions of France in 1814 and 1815. They are home to a discharged veteran of the Napoleonic wars, identified by the military bicorne he wears. On returning to his village he has once more taken up the plough: having fought for his country he will now feed it. A second *soldat-laboureur*, identifiable by his forage cap, appears in the distance, thus indicating the ubiquity of the type. The veteran's plough has just turned up the body of one of his former comrades who sacrificed his life during the invasion. He is identified by the *croix d'honneur* which the *soldat-laboureur* has unearthed and which he holds pensively as he remembers his own past glories (symbolised by the laurel bush on the left). But, according to Vernet's guide to the exhibition, he is also dreaming of future revenge, when France, regenerated by his labours, will once more take her proper place in the world. All three figures, the two veterans and the skeleton, are quite literally sons of the soil, because France is their mother, 'a tender mother, invisible but ever present, who nourishes us always'. That is a quote from Michelet's *Le Peuple*, first published in 1846, but it is an idea we have already seen in the text accompanying Pellerin's 1843 image of *Le Départ et retour du conscrit*.[28] But the soil is also the spouse of the *soldat-laboureur*. He ploughs her female body, and fertilises her with his labour, so that she gives birth to the food that feeds him, and, by extension, to the children who will replace him. The 'Frenchman has married France' says Michelet, and from their coupling comes forth a new race of *soldat-laboureurs*. So the soil of France is both wife and mother, but a mother

[24] 'J'entends un railleur dire au public: n'achetez donc pas ce cahier de croquis, c'est *encore* un soldat-laboureur!': Puymège, *Chauvin*, 245–6.
[25] Garnier, *L'Imagerie populaire française*, i, no. 1102.
[26] Day, 'Political dissent', 424.
[27] Puymège, *Chauvin*, 251–71.
[28] Garnier-Pelle, *L'Imagerie populaire française*, ii, no. 1176.

Plate 52. *Le Soldat laboureur*: Bloquel-Castiaux (Lille), 1828
Derived from Horace Vernet's 1822 painting of the same title
(now in the Wallace Collection), this image was originally
engraved by the Parisian *canardier* Fleuret in 1822 for the
Chartrian firm of Garnier-Allabre. Reproduced by
permission of the Musée départemental
d'art ancien et contemporain, Epinal.

who eats her own children, for it is made up of the sweat, blood and bones of
sons who have sacrificed their lives in her defence. Their bodies are ploughed
back into the earth to become the humus that produces the bread to nourish
future generations. Thus the *soldat-laboureur* becomes 'his own communion
wafer'. Again, that is Michelet's metaphor.[29]

It is no exaggeration to say that Puymège, one of the few historians willing
to use psychoanalytic techniques in history, is deeply concerned about the

[29] 'Nous avons une mère commune . . . une mère tendre qui nous nourrit toujours, invisible et présente' . . . 'le Français a épousé la France' . . . 'sa propre hostie'. The quotes from
Michelet are provided by Puymège: *Chauvin*, 175, 219, 292.

mental health of Vernet and Michelet, and all the other politicians and writers who devoted themselves to the *soldat-laboureur*. However, the theme did not prove very popular with the people the *soldat-laboureur* was supposed to represent. Despite his manifold representations, from 1820 to 1840, in paintings, statues, bronzes, lithographs and shop-fronts, Fleuret's image is one of only two *soldat-laboureurs* ever to appear under that title in popular imagery. Jacques-Pierre Garnier, the manager of the Chartrian firm that produced the woodcut version, was born in Versailles and trained in Paris, and was open to currents from the nearby metropolis. The engraver Fleuret was a Parisian born and bred; he only worked in the provinces for a short time, and normally he sold his songs on the banks of the Seine.[30] Although the block was reused by Blocquel-Castiaux of Lille after 1828, and so one must assume it had a continuing market, it was not copied by any other provincial imagist.[31] This contrasts with another image engraved for Garnier-Allabre at about this period (and subsequently sold to Blocquel-Castiaux), Boniot's *Les Quatre Vérités*, which formed the model for Pellerin and many others. We can, perhaps, deduce that the peasants who bought *Les Quatre Vérités* considered it a fairer representation of their attitudes to soldiers than the *soldat-laboureur*.

However, if the *soldat-laboureur* in his most blatant form failed to find a market among the customers of imagists, this is not to say he left no trace on the genre. The authorities, as we know, kept a close rein on the imagists, and the military career was one they were keen to promote. Imagists were often themselves connected to the military. In the workshops of the Pellerin firm in particular, veterans had influence on what subjects were depicted.[32] So images informed by the mythology of the *soldat-laboureur* did become more common, particularly from the 1840s onwards. Yet at the same time imagists felt it necessary to reissue again and again a more traditional representation of the soldier which rejected the rapprochement between the second and third estates. These two contradictory currents of thought, one emanating from the Parisian intellectual and artistic circles to which imagists looked for their inspiration, the other reflecting the persistence of more ambivalent attitudes among their rural clientele, can be perceived in the imagists' treatments of the veteran. One might compare, for example, Pellerin's histories of two old soldiers, Grivet and La Ramée.

---

[30] Garnier, *Histoire de l'imagerie populaire*, 116.

[31] I have only been able to find one other representation of the *soldat-laboureur* in coloured woodcut form; it is one of twelve tiny *Scènes militaires* issued for the juvenile market by Dembour of Metz in 1842. However, in Dembour's version there is no skeleton, no ruins, no *croix d'honneur*, only a soldier with a spade: Archives départementales de la Moselle 1/T/92, no. 68 (dépôt légal 5 Sept. 1842). Around 1860 Dembour's successor, Didion, produced an image of the *Camp de Châlons* that included an even tinier *Soldat jardinier*.

[32] Day-Hickman, *Napoleonic art*, 36–47.

The *Histoire de Grivet* was issued in 1858. Grivet was a Breton conscript, brought up by his uncle, a former sapper, to appreciate the military life. His career in the army follows the well-trodden path – minor offences and tiresome fatigue duties, duels and love affairs with children's nannies – before he is sent to Algiers. While there he does not receive a baptism of fire, the most ferocious enemies he has to face are pariah dogs and medical orderlies. So, unlike most of Pellerin's other conscripts, when he returns home it is without the *croix d'honneur*, but this does not prevent his social triumph. In the last scene we see him 'happy husband, happy father, mayor of his commune, on Sundays he reviews his *garde nationale* and sometimes modestly tells them of his exploits'.[33]

The name Grivet derives from a series of lithographs issued in 1819 by Horace Vernet on the life-cycle of a *soldat-laboureur*, the conscript *Jacques Grivet*.[34] But the last scene, in which the conscript-cum-veteran becomes mayor of his home village, owes more to Charlet's 1838 series of drawings on the theme of the conscript, *La Vie civile, politique et militaire de caporal Valentin* (whom Charlet himself described as a *soldat-laboureur*).[35] The *soldat-laboureur* was supposed to instruct his neighbours, who had not had his good fortune to be educated in the army, to love their country and know their patriotic duty.[36] Grivet's threat to treat the *garde nationale* to his service reminiscences fulfils the *soldat-laboureur's* supposed pedagogic function, but it also conforms to the old soldier's reputation as a *raconteur*.

The belief that former soldiers made ideal material for positions of responsibility, including mayoral office, owes much to the revolution. In the *ancien régime* veterans were more likely to be considered by the authorities as utterly incapable of looking after their own affairs let alone anyone else's. If they were given a pension they immediately spent it on drink, if they were found a job (as a lay-brother in a monastery or on garrison duty) they ran away and rapidly fell back into destitution. Louis XIV's plans to house some veterans in Les Invalides were couched in exactly these terms. Veterans might prefer their liberty but they were a danger to themselves and a nuisance to others, and a very poor advertisement for a military career. It was better for them and for everyone else that they should be cared for by the state.[37]

The second half of the eighteenth century saw a slight shift in attitudes. In 1788 the *commissaire des guerres* de Zaiguelius suggested that the king should

[33] 'Aujourd'hui heureux époux, heureux père, Maire de sa commune, il passe en revue la dimanche, sa garde nationale et parfois lui raconte modestement ses exploits': Garnier-Pelle, *L'imagerie populaire française*, ii, no. 1250.

[34] Bruzard, *Catalogue*, nos 172–5.

[35] Colonel de La Combe, *Charlet, sa vie, ses lettres, suivi d'une description raisonnée de son oeuvre lithographique*, Paris 1856, 362, no. 964: *Valentin père et maire de sa commune*.

[36] An image which Puymège has identified as forming part of the myth of the *soldat-laboureur* was *Le Soldat instituteur*, a common theme in Charlet's art and in Parisian prints in general, though not in popular imagery: Puymège, *Chauvin*, fig. 18.

[37] Bois, *Les Anciens Soldats*, 41.

Plate 53. *Histoire de Grivet* 1–2 (opposite): Pellerin (Epinal), 1858
Reproduced by permission of the Réunion des musées nationaux
(photo: Danièle Adam).

Il eut ses jours d'émotion.

Ses succès dans les armes lui donnent l'envie d'autres triomphes.

Que de larmes et de regrets il laissa après lui, en partant pour l'Afrique.

En débarquant le cœur faillit lui manquer, les marins soutiennent son courage.

Il trouve sur cette terre nouvelle, des ennemis inconnus.

Les plus terribles, furent le choléra, l'hôpital et les infirmiers.

Il s'en tira heureusement, et revit avec joie le clocher de son village.

Aujourd'hui heureux époux, heureux père, Maire de sa commune, il passe en revue le dimanche, sa garde nationale et parfois lui raconte modestement ses exploits.

reserve for injured veterans such posts as gate-keepers in military towns and concierges in public buildings. De Zaiguelius was partly prompted by the fear that idleness among veterans led to crime and disorder, but he also believed that soldiers, trained in the need for discipline and order, might really be the best candidates for these kinds of official positions. After the revolution a further consideration was added – the recompense of a grateful nation.[38] This led to the policy of preferential employment that was followed not only by the National Convention but by all succeeding governments, whether republican, royalist or imperial. Veterans were given first consideration for public appointments, particularly to uniformed jobs that called for the exercise of authority, including the gendarmerie, *gardes champêtres* and *forestiers*, church beadles and postmen. Many of the individual soldiers we have met in the course of this book benefited from this policy. Pierre-Joseph Soudant, the Argonne storyteller, was appointed *garde forestier* under Charles X; his grandson Eloi Soudant, another former soldier, was a postman.[39] Even the Vosgian deserter Jean Carchon became a *garde forestier* in 1804 on the strength of the few months he served in 1792, 'and his desertion, which lasted six years (from 1793 to 1799), was counted as a peccadillo'.[40]

The same logic, that soldiers were by nature upholders of order, and that service in the name of the fatherland fitted one to represent the state, led to the selection of veterans to elected positions of responsibility. The choice of a former soldier for mayor was not just a fantasy of Charlet, it was a definite pattern during the empire and even more so under the restoration, at least in Lorraine. Whereas veterans provided only 2 per cent of mayors nationally in 1824, in the arrondissement of Commercy 16 per cent of mayors had served as soldiers.[41] The example of Jean Parisot has already been mentioned, but the careers of several of the soldiers whose paths we have crossed followed similar trajectories. Gabriel Noël, for example, volunteer of 1791, was mayor of Sommerviller from 1806 until his death in 1850.[42] His namesake, Colonel Noël, born in Saint-Dié in 1778, became mayor of Nancy under Louis-Philippe.[43]

The veteran's social triumph as mayor of his commune, both in imagery

---

[38] Woloch discusses this preferential employment policy: *The French veteran*, 154–63.

[39] Lallement, *Contes rustiques*, 110, 154.

[40] 'et sa désertion, qui dura six années (de 1793–1799), fut comptée comme peccadille': Pierfitte, 'Les Volontaires vosgiens', 128.

[41] Michel Salviac, 'Les Maires anciens soldats: l'arrondissement de Commercy', in Maurice Agulhon, L. Girard, J.-L. Robert and W. Serman (eds), *Les Maires en France du consulat à nos jours*, Paris 1986, 329–42.

[42] Isabelle Roger-Noël, 'La Révolution aux frontières vue par un volontaire de 1792–1796', *Revue historique des armées* xlii (1986), 15. Most veteran-mayors were officers, though in the case of Gabriel Noël he had risen through the ranks. Noël, both in his actions and aspirations, was the embodiment of the *soldat-laboureur*.

[43] Jean-Nicolas-Auguste Noël, *Souvenirs militaires d'un officier du premier empire (1795–1832)*, Paris–Nancy 1895, p. vii.

and in reality, might be seen as the final proof of the public's change of heart towards the soldier, the sea-change detected by Corvisier, Bois and Chagniot during the last third of the eighteenth century. The soldier was no longer a threat to civil society but rather its protector (and so was duly rewarded). However, his new-found respectability was not the only reason why the veteran was being elected to public office. He was also chosen for the same reason that people listened to soldier-storytellers. Although he may have started life as just a local lad, the soldier had become, through his travels and experiences, a man of the world. The regiment was a school, often quite literally. In the *ancien régime* some regiments advertised for recruits with the promise to teach them reading and writing.[44] *Ecoles régimentaires* were promised by the revolution, although the promise was not fully kept until after 1818. Under their auspices, according to Furet and Ozouf, well over a million illiterate soldiers learnt to read in the period up to 1869.[45] Pauline Schwartz-Bonneville of Wölflingen recalled that her father had only 'first learnt to read and write German and French like a notary while a soldier'.[46] To speak French, and even more to write in it, was to communicate in the language of authority, which made the old soldier very helpful to his neighbours. But there were other skills the soldier learnt in the army. As we saw in the case of the marauding soldier, he was supposed to be crafty, able to negotiate himself out of difficulties and get the better of his superiors. In the army he had learnt 'to function in terms which characterise any complex stratified society in which individuals can improve their status through the judicious manipulation of social ties'.[47] He could therefore serve as a 'broker' between centre and periphery, between the nation and the community, between the prefecture and the villagers.

The concept of culture-broker was proposed by the anthropologist Eric Wolf, commenting on the role of political operators in post-revolutionary Mexico, but his description equally applies to soldier-mayors:

> The position of these 'brokers' is an exposed one, since, Janus-like, they face in two directions at once. They must serve some of the interests of groups operating on both the community and the national level, and they must cope with the conflicts raised by the collision of these interests.[48]

The soldier's knowledge of the world and its ways enabled him to resolve the problems of his fellow villagers who had not had the benefit of his education

---

[44] MDAACE 57.3.2790: *Corps royal d'artillerie, en garnison à Brest* (c. 1760s).
[45] François Furet and Jacques Ozouf, *Reading and writing: literacy in France from Calvin to Jules Ferry*, Cambridge 1982, 254–7.
[46] 'Er erst beim Militär deutsch und französisch lesen und schreiben gelernt wie ein Notar': Merkelbach-Pinck, *Aus der lothringer Meistube*, ii. 391.
[47] Eric Wolf, 'Aspects of group relations in a complex society: Mexico', *American Anthropologist* lviii (1956), 1072.
[48] Ibid.

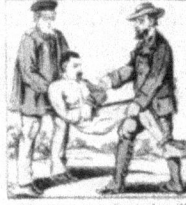

Plate 54. *Le Sergent Laramée*: Pellerin (Epinal), 1864
Reproduced by permission of the Musée départemental
d'art ancien et contemporain, Epinal.

in the 'university of life'. But it also separated him from the villagers who could never quite believe that his interests were the same as their own, making him an object both of wonder and suspicion.

This is the latent message of another Pellerin image, *Le Sergent Laramée*, first issued in 1864.[49] During the second empire Pellerin's production had became increasingly geared towards children, and favourite subjects with this new audience were fairytales delivered in comic-strip form. At first glance *Le Sergent Laramée* is just such a fairytale. It opens with the traditional formula 'Once upon a time' and goes on to tell how an old soldier, returning home after thirty years in the army, shares his ration-loaf with two old women and a young beggar boy. These characters turn out to be one-and-the-same fairy in disguise, testing Laramée's generosity. In return for his kindness she grants him the power to resolve all difficulties with the magic word 'Caritas'. Laramée uses his gift to triumph over numerous obstacles and help the people he meets on his travels, before receiving an ecstatic welcome home from his fellow villagers. They make him mayor, and the last vignette shows him in his sash of office, reconciling two bickering neighbours with the word 'Caritas'. Like so many of Pellerin's later images, which were often distributed by schoolmasters and priests, *Le Sergent Laramée* has a moralising message: be charitable.

Yet if *Le Sergent Laramée* was typical of Pellerin's production in its didactic intention, in another respect it was very unusual. Most of Pellerin's fairytale images derived from Charles Perrault's *Tales of Mother Goose* or other salon *conteurs* of the seventeenth and eighteenth centuries (which had long been a mainstay of the firm's *bibliothèque bleue* production), but there was no literary source for the old soldier.[50] The original inspiration for this print must have come from the contemporary oral tradition in a tale told, perhaps, by one of the numerous veterans employed in the Pellerin workshop. The influence of the imagist's oral source is most apparent in the first five frames where sergeant Laramée is tested and rewarded. This is closely related to the standard opening of a popular folktale, *The devil in the knapsack* (AT330B). In the typical French version Christ, Saint Peter or God himself is the disguised beggar who benefits from the traveller's generosity. Twenty-seven variants of this tale-type have been recorded in France, fifteen of which feature a soldier as hero (eight of whom are named La Ramée).[51] Only three had appeared in

---

[49] Garnier-Pelle, *L'Imagerie populaire française*, ii, no. 1418.

[50] The rarity of an imagist turning to the oral tradition is attested by a study of Dutch and Belgian popular imagery which found that, although dozens of images feature fairytales, only one was not obviously derived from a literary source: Maurits de Meyer, 'Le Conte populaire dans l'imagerie populaire hollandaise et belge', *Fabula* i (1958), 183–92. There are a handful of other Pellerin images for which the source may be the local oral tradition, such as the *Aventures de Fanfan Bêtinet* and the *Histoire de M. Rignolet* (both issued in 1860), but these are the exceptions that prove the rule: Garnier-Pelle, *L'Imagerie populaire française*, ii, nos 1114, 1263.

[51] Delarue, *Le Conte populaire français*, i. 346–64. There is also an Italian variant in which

print before 1864, and none of these can be considered the source of the Pellerin image.[52]

Although this image shares the introduction with the folktale, its subsequent development owes more to printed sources. The various incidents on the sergeant's journey, which include his attempted murder, his rescue of a child from a burning farm, and the saving of an old man expiring at the wayside, derive from a series of *canards*. As we have seen the theme of the returning soldier falling under the suspicion of a crime, only to have his innocence revealed at the *dénouement*, was particular popular among the *canardiers* of the second empire.[53] The Pellerin firm did not deal in the genre but it had extensive contacts with print houses and the local *chamagnon* pedlars who did.[54] The *canards* played on the community's fear of strangers, in particular the soldier as vagabond and criminal, but the *dénouement* reversed the expectation. The *canards* were one step in the direction of the rehabilitation of the soldier's reputation in popular culture, but the image of *Laramée* goes further, for in his case the soldier is never even suspected of firing the farmhouse or killing the traveller. The last vignette, in which Laramée becomes mayor, links this print back to the theme of the *soldat-laboureur*.

However, whereas the mayoral veterans so far discussed were brokers between the village and the nation, Laramée was also a broker between the natural and supernatural worlds, and it was for his supernatural abilities in particular that his neighbours turned to him. While presented here in a benign form the soldier's contacts with supernatural power were a recurrent theme in folklore, but one that also made him an object of fear. His very name would have invoked in the mind of its purchasers a very different concept of the veteran to that proposed by the *soldat-laboureur*, for Laramée was a character already familiar from folklore. This, for example, is how he makes his first appearance in Cosquin's collection, which was being made at almost exactly the same time as Pellerin's print saw the light of day, and not far away. The story so far is that the place of the godson of the king of England has been usurped, and the impostor has set the genuine godson, Adolphe, a number of impossible tasks. He has been told to find the ring of the daughter of the king of England, lost during a sea voyage. Adolphe has called on the

the hero is named La Ramée, but he is not a soldier: Andrews, *Contes ligures*, no. 48: *La Ramée, grand fumeur.*

[52] The three are Emile Souvestre, *Les Derniers Bretons*, Paris 1836, 143: *Histoire de Moustache* (although Delarue considers this a variant of AT330); Trollope, *Summer in Brittany*, ii: *Troadec* (this variant is not included in Delarue's *Catalogue raisonné*); Justin-Édouard-Mathieu Cénac-Moncaut, *Contes populaires de la Gascogne*, Paris 1861, 57: *Le Sac de la Ramée*. In the two Breton variants the hero is a soldier (but not called La Ramée), whereas in the Gascon tale the hero is named La Ramée but is a pedlar.

[53] For details on the *canards* of the soldier's return see Seguin, *Nouvelles à sensation*, 182–90.

[54] Picoche, *Le Monde des chamagnons*, 30–51.

kingdom of fish, which he previously saved from starvation, to seek their help:

> The call to arms was beaten among the fish: they arrived in a crowd, but not one of them knew where the ring was. Someone noticed that two old soldiers were missing on parade, La Chique and La Ramée: they were made to come. La Ramée, who was drunk, declared that he didn't know where the ring was, but neither did he care; so he was put in prison. La Chique arrived next, even more drunk; he said that he had the ring in his haversack, but first La Ramée had to be taken out of prison. When his comrade was free, La Chique gave the ring to the young man. Adolphe gave him a hundred francs to drink to his health.[55]

The soldier-fish in this extract (from a soldier's narration; the reference to the call to arms is a typical regimental detail of barracks tale-telling) exemplify many of the characteristics of the soldier in French folktales, as we will discover.

The veteran in folklore: La Ramée and his comrades

An indication of La Ramée's place in the oral tradition is suggested by Delmart's description of barrack-room narrating in the 1820s. By the time the Auvergnat soldier had finished telling the tales of *Jean de l'Ours* and *CriCri* (mentioned in chapter 2) all but one of his audience were sound asleep. The exception, a young conscript, still hoped to hear the classic tale of *La Ramée*, but that pleasure had to be put off until the morrow.[56] This passing mention is the first reference to La Ramée in folklore.

Thereafter La Ramée made an appearance in most French folktale collections. Cénac-Moncaut's 1861 collection of Pyrenean tales is, despite its literary overtones, considered the first to be based in the oral tradition. It includes one story about La Ramée (although in this case he is a pedlar rather than a soldier).[57] Cosquin's more vigorous collecting unearthed five tales that

---

[55] 'On battit la générale parmi les poissons: ils arrivèrent en foule, mais aucun d'eux ne savait où etait l'anneau. On s'aperçut alors qu'il manquait à l'appel deux vieux soldats, La Chique et La Ramée: on les fit venir. La Ramée, qui etait ivre, déclara qu'il ne savait où était l'anneau, mais que peu lui importait; on le mit en prison. La Chique arriva ensuite, encore plus ivre; il dit qu'il avait la bague dans son sac, mais qu'il fallait d'abord tirer La Ramée de prison. Quand son camarade fut en liberté, La Chique remit la bague au jeune homme. Adolphe lui donna cent francs pour boire à sa santé': Cosquin, *Contes populaires de Lorraine*, i. 42, no. 3: *Le Roi d'Angleterre et son filleul* (AT531).

[56] Delmart and Vidal, *La Caserne*, 141–68.

[57] Cénac-Moncaut, *Contes populaires*, 57: *Le Sac de la Ramée* (AT330B). As we have seen, both in elite and popular culture there was a perceived connection between soldiers and pedlars.

concerned La Ramée, out of the eighty-four he recorded at Montiers.[58] At least one of these was from a former soldier who had learnt it in the army. La Ramée also figures three times in Léon Pineau's tales collected around Lussac-les-Châteaux (Vienne).[59] He is the hero of no less than sixteen of Achille Millien's manuscript collection of tales made in the Nivernais in the 1880s.[60] Altogether folklorists have noted at least forty-five tales which feature La Ramée in some capacity. Most were recorded between 1861 and 1914, although a handful have been collected since the end of the Second World War, in the Pays de Retz, the Auvergne and Savoy, although in these post-1945 tales La Ramée's military connection appears to have been forgotten.[61]

As these examples indicate, La Ramée tales were collected from all over France: from Breton-speaking Tréguier in the west to germanophone Lorraine in the east, from French Flanders in the north to the Italian Riviera in the south, almost everywhere where folklorists have been active.[62] We can perhaps deduce that La Ramée was at home in the oral tradition of all these regions because he originated inside the one national institution that men from every part of France had experienced – the army. Not only does Delmart mention his presence, but La Ramée was also the hero of other nineteenth-century accounts of storytelling in the barracks.[63] La Ramée was an *enfant de troupe*, born and raised in the army, but his tale travelled back to the village with the veterans themselves. His is, therefore, something of a self-image, actively promoted by old soldiers. However, not every narrator who knew him was an old soldier. Tales of La Ramée were also collected from peasants, their wives and their children. The idea of the old soldier encapsulated in the figure of La Ramée was readily adopted into rural popular culture.

Unlike other folktale characters, such as Cinderella or Blue Beard, La Ramée was not limited to one particular story. He appeared, sometimes as the

---

58 La Ramée features in tales 3, 31, 33, 52 (notes) and 82.
59 Léon Pineau, *Les Contes populaires de Poitou*, Paris 1891, 59–68, 127–30, and 'Contes populaires de Poitou', *Revue des traditions populaires* xii (1897), 487–9: *Vive Sans-Souci La Ramée.*
60 This collection, MNATP, MS Millien-Delarue (Nivernais), contains approximately 920 tales and is housed in the Musée national des arts et traditions populaires at Neuilly. I only searched through those tale-types usually associated with soldier heroes, so it may contain more than sixteen La Ramée tales.
61 Delarue and Ténèze *Le Conte populaire français*, ii. 386–8; Méraville, *Vie et oeuvres*, nos 16, 23; Charles Joisten and Alice Joisten, 'Quelques Traditions orales de Savoie', *Revue de Savoie* iv (1959), 324–6.
62 The major lacunae in La Ramée's wanderings are Corsica and the Basque country. Tales of La Ramée are exceedingly rare in Provence and the Mediterranean Languedoc, but these have proved fairly barren areas for fairytales of any kind. On the other hand, considering the amount of time folklorists have spent traipsing over Brittany, one might have expected them to find rather more than two La Ramée tales, one from the gallophone Côtes-du-Nord, the other from the Breton-speaking portion of the same department.
63 Charles Leroy, *Faits et gestes du sergent Roupoil*, Paris n.d., 159.

hero, sometimes as a bit-player, once as the villain (and once as the name of God himself), in twenty-two different tale-types.[64] So La Ramée, the vaga-bond soldier, was a wanderer across the folktale catalogue just as he was through the regions of France. As hero he tended to be associated with tale-types which involve descents into an underworld, or a meeting with a supernatural personage (often the devil), and the receipt of a magic gift.[65] The presence of soldiers in tales that feature these motifs is not coincidental but a revealing pattern, indicative of popular attitudes to this occupational group. However, as a secondary character he can appear in almost any male tale-type – that is a tale whose primary hero is male. In one Lorrainer variant La Ramée even has a minor part to play in the favourite female tale *The maiden without hands* (AT706).[66] But throughout his travels La Ramée main-tained his distinctive character; he became the oral-cultural model by which both soldiers and civilians judged veterans. This is the value of folktales for historians: because texts collected from many locations and over a long period display many similarities, they indicate a widespread and enduring pattern of thought. They reflect how veterans (as storytellers) presented themselves, and how the rest of the population (as their audience and narra-tors in their turn) perceived them. Everybody knew La Ramée. As one Breton priest told a folklorist: 'You who hunt for fairytales and legends, and you don't know the story of Fanfan and the inseparable La Ramée? You astound me! The whole world knows that tale.'[67]

Who was La Ramée that he should enjoy such nationwide fame? There are at least two historical contenders; the first known La Ramée was a Breton soldier for the Catholic League and pretended son of Charles IX. He was hanged in Paris in 1596.[68] Another La Ramée, a cavalry sergeant, was gaoler of the duke of Beaufort while imprisoned at Vincennes, and was trussed up during the latter's escape in June 1648.[69] From history this La Ramée passed into literature as an important figure in Dumas's *Twenty years on*, the sequel to

---

64 The villainous *Laramée* is the eponymous subject of one tale: Méraville, *Vie et oeuvres*, no. 16 (AT956b). La Ramée as God appears in Sylvain Trébucq, 'Contes du Languedoc', *Revue des traditions populaires* xxxiv (1919), 298: *La Ramée* (AT785).

65 In the folktale catalogue these cluster in the region of types AT300–65 ('supernatural adversaries') and AT562–621 ('magic objects').

66 Sadoul, 'Contes de Lorraine', 67, no. 4: *La Fille aux mains coupés ou l'hôtesse du Dragon Vert*.

67 'Vous qui êtes à la recherche des contes et légendes, vous ne connaissez pas l'histoire de Fanfan et de l'inséparable La Ramée? Vous m'étonnez! Tout le monde sait cette historiette': Cerny, *Contes*, 139: *Fanfan et La Ramée* (AT401).

68 Yves-Marie Bercé, *Le Roi caché: sauveurs et imposteurs: mythes politiques populaires dans l'Europe moderne*, Paris 1990, 168–75, 418–20. The pretender had been brought up by a Breton noble named La Ramée. I am grateful to Professor Bonney for bringing this work to my attention. The folktale La Ramée also frequently ends up on the scaffold in front of a king, but then makes a daring escape.

69 La Ramée was an 'éxempt', meaning a cavalry NCO appointed to an officer's functions but without the rank. He is mentioned by name in several of the memoirs of the period

The three musketeers.[70] But Dumas's novel was not La Ramée's first outing in the arts: in 1695 the recruiting-sergeant La Ramée had a part in Dancourt's play *La Femme d'intrigues*, where he spent the regimental pay trying to acquire a rich wife. As he explained to a comrade, 'One must not be scrupulous, Jolicoeur, when one wants to make one's fortune.'[71]

However, it is unlikely that the folktale La Ramée owed much to these historical or literary prototypes. It is apparent from Dancourt's drama that the name La Ramée, like that of Jolicoeur, had already become a representative term for a soldier, particularly an old soldier or NCO. Both names originated in the army as *noms-de-guerre*. Unlike other professions that had similar rites of entry, the soldier's new name was recognised by the authorities. It was included in the regimental muster-lists after 1716.[72] Thus we know that almost every regiment in the eighteenth century could boast at least one genuine La Ramée in its ranks.[73] Some other genuine *noms-de-guerre* – such as Tranche-Montagne, La Tulipe and Sans-Souci – passed from the army into art and literature as representatives of military types. They had joined that elect group of names that are both genuine and generic. As such they were all occasionally used as the names of folktale soldier-heroes, but in this particular genre La Ramée dominated. His nearest rivals, La Chique (ten references) and Pipette (six references, including two from Italy), clearly derived their names from another military particularism, the use of tobacco, although both have other appropriate meanings in a folktale context. So, before 1789, the name La Ramée was used both by real soldiers and to designate an archetype. The continued use of an eighteenth-century *nom-de-guerre* in nineteenth-century folklore suggests that, whatever the changes in government policy, ordinary people perceived little difference between the *ancien régime* and the post-revolutionary soldier. But whereas the qualities of Tranche-Montagne and Sans-Souci are readily apparent, the meaning of La Ramée may not be quite so obvious. Slang definitions of the term may offer some clues as to his identity.

In modern dictionaries the word 'ramée' occurs most often in the phrase

including that of Madame de Motteville: *Mémoires sur Anne d'Autriche et sa cour*, ed. Francis-Marie Riaux, Paris 1886, ii. 57–8.

[70] Alexandre Dumas père, *Vingt Ans après*, Paris 1962 (1st edn, Paris 1845), 203, 219. Dumas's La Ramée shares some of the characteristics of the folktale hero, 'joyeux vivant, franc convive, buveur reconnu, grand joueur de paume, bon diable au fond'.

[71] 'Il ne faut point être scrupuleux, Jolicoeur, quand on veut faire sa fortune.' Jolicoeur, sincerely impressed by this lack of morality, replies 'Oh, tu es comme il faut être': 'Palapat' [Dancourt], *La Femme d'intrigues*, The Hague 1695, 24. Unfortunately for La Ramée, the object of his game is the very 'femme d'intrigues' of the title, an adventuress after a rich husband, but all is revealed at the *dénouement*.

[72] A page from the 'Contrôle du régiment de Vivarais (infanterie)', including one 'La Ramée', originally from Moulin, recruited in 1715 and discharged in 1724, is reproduced in Corvisier, *Les Contrôles des troupes*, i, illustration 4.

[73] Corvisier, *L'Armée française*, i. 852.

'ne pas foutre une ramée', to do absolutely nothing. Thus 'un ramier' is a lazy-bones.[74] La Chique had similar qualities, for a 'chiqueur' was likewise a synonym for an idler.[75] As we have seen, idleness was a widespread prejudice against soldiers under the *ancien régime*. Among the intellectual elite ideas were transformed through the influence of the Roman model of the *soldat-laboureur*, which posited that hard work in the fields was the ideal training for the army. However, the soldier's lazy reputation certainly survived in folk culture well into the nineteenth century. In one tale, when La Ramée is asked by a comrade how he is going to live now he has left the army after twenty-one years service, he replies, 'I've no idea! Things are going badly at the moment; I can't be bothered to work, but I don't know what to do to get a living.'[76] His solution is to go begging, but the peasant's attitude to such vagabonds is again expressed in folktales: 'you're as fit to work as I am!'[77] The old saw, 'young soldier, old beggar', continued to be repeated in rural society, long after the military pension alleviated the burden of absolute destitution from veterans.

The soldier's habitual laziness was the precursor to a life of crime, or so it was widely believed. It may be appropriate, then, that one folktale brigand-captain goes by the name Laramée.[78] Yet more usually in folklore the relationship between bandits and soldiers was antagonistic. In more than one tale La Ramée ends up beheading an entire robber-band, while his king cowers under the bed.[79] What peasants objected to in soldiers was not so much organised crime as the petty pilfering in the market and crop-fields, which soldiers could commit with impunity because of their force, and the tacit protection offered by the military authorities. La Ramée is, naturally, a marauder, using his magic sack to plunder bakeries and cook-shops, and laughing while others get the blame.[80] But in the folktale world this kind of

74 Alain Rey and Jacques Cellard, *Dictionnaire du français non conventionnel*, Paris 1980, 690; Gaston Esnault, *Dictionnaire historique des argots français*, Paris 1965, 533. The compilers are unsure of the origin of these terms, though Rey and Cellard suggest that 'ne pas en fiche une ramée' may have originated with a lazy woodcutter.
75 According to Esnault 'chiqueur' may also mean a 'fainéant': *Dictionnaire*, 158.
76 'je n'en sais rien! Les affaires vont mal de ce moment-là; ça m'embête de travailler, mais je ne sais pas que faire pour gagner ma vie': Pineau, *Les Contes populaires*, 59: *La Ramée* (AT613A).
77 'T'es aussi capable *comme* moi de travailler!': Félice, *Contes de Haute-Bretagne*, 88, no. 8: *La Belle Kévale* (AT613A, AT531).
78 Méraville, *Vie et oeuvres*, no. 16: *Laramée* (AT956b).
79 Cosquin, *Contes populaires de Lorraine*, ii, no. 33: *La Maison de la forêt* (AT952); Merkelbach-Pinck, *Lothringer Märchen*, no. 35: *Le Vieux La Ramée* (AT952); MNATP, MS Millien-Delarue (Nivernais), AT952, versions A, C, D.
80 Cénac-Moncaut, *Contes populaires*, 60: *Le Sac de la Ramée* (AT330B); Charles Deulin, *Contes du roi Cambrinus*, Lausanne 1935, 136–7: *Le Sac de La Ramée* (AT785). Deulin's books are extremely unreliable guides to the oral tradition, but he did have a knack for spotting folkloric themes.

behaviour does not count as crime but as cunning, and the old soldier has more than his fair share of that.

'On a ramé' is also a common expression meaning to work until exhausted, while 'avoir la rame' was military slang for 'knackered'.[81] La Ramée could only be an old soldier, decrepit even.[82] This is how the eponymous *Vieux Raramé* is introduced in a Comtois tale: 'He was an old soldier who'd served twenty-five years and then by God he was tired, he wanted to leave the regiment. He had already tried to leave, but kept coming back [in other words, a habitual deserter].'[83] The name, La Chique, likewise suggests something old and ill functioning: in the dialects of eastern France if a gun 'fait chic' then it has misfired.[84] Old age as a characteristic of a folktale hero has some rather unusual consequences for such a conservative genre. It is all but axiomatic that a fairytale should end with a wedding: the youngest son frees the princess and marries her; that is the basic plot. Hence in Propp's extremely influential *Morphology*, the final plot function is designated 'W: Wedding'.[85] But we usually meet soldiers when they are too old to fight and have been discharged from the army. It is because they are old that they are poor and homeless, which is the starting point for many tale-types. This puts the veteran in a difficult position when the princess he has just saved suggests marriage, because he feels obliged to tell her, in the words of one of La Ramée's rivals, *Pipet, der alter Franzos*, 'I'm much too old for you.'[86] In another germanophone tale the eponymous Hungarian hussar is offered the princess's hand in marriage only to tell her bluntly 'I'm too old! I'd much rather have a big load of gold.'[87] In another tale, collected in Brittany, the hero was a young man when he volunteered for the army. Three days later, after freeing the enchanted princess, he announces 'I will not marry, because I'm too old, but I

81 Centre national de la recherche scientifique, *Trésor de la langue française: dictionnaire de la langue du XIXe et du XXe siècles*, Paris 1990, xiv. 324–5, 328–9. The compilers were somewhat puzzled that the same word, 'ramée', could come to mean both 'exhausted by hard work', and 'absolute laziness'. However, when applied to the old soldier La Ramée, there is no real contradiction.

82 The diminutive of La Ramée, Ramollot, was applied to old soldiers who had lost the full use of their mental faculties. The term derives from a comic character invented by the humorist Charles Leroy: *Le Colonel Ramollot: recueil de récits militaires suivi de fantaisies civiles*, Paris 1881.

83 'C'était un vieux soldat qu'avait vingt-cinq ans d'service, et puis ma foi il était fatigué, i' voulait quitter le régiment. Il avait déjà cherché d'quitter, puis i' r'venait toujours': Garneret, *Contes recueillis en Franche-Comté*, 44, no. 5: *Le Vieux Raramé* (AT330, AT753). Garneret recorded the tale from Louis Morgeotte of Burgille in 1938. Louis had learnt his repertoire of tales from his father, an old soldier who had acquired the whole of his extensive repertoire during his fourteen years of military service.

84 Zéliqzon, *Dictionnaire*, 136, 653; Lavigne, *Le Patois de Cumières*, 226.

85 Vladimir Propp, *Morphology of the folktale*, Austin, Tx 1968, 63–4.

86 'Ich bin schon zu alt für dich': Merkelbach-Pinck, *Lothringer Märchen*, 236, no. 38: *Pipet, ein alter Franzos* (AT330, AT326).

87 'Ich bin zu alt! Ich hätte grösseren Spass an einer guten Ladung Gold', ibid. 145, no. 29: *Der ungarische Husar* (AT307).

will stay with you always.'[88] The idea that military experience brought maturity is here taken to extremes! This peculiarity of soldiers' tales is apparent even in the barrack-room narration of the Auvergnat Piquenot. In his story of *Cricri*, the eponymous old soldier ends up not married to the princess but serving as her aide-de-camp. His conscript-audience, clearly influenced by his previous experiences of the genre, disappointedly declares 'Well, I would have preferred it if he had married the princess' (to which the more elderly storyteller replies 'Imbecile! It's the same thing').[89]

However, age is not always the issue. In the Breton tale of *Fanfan et La Ramée*, La Ramée frees the princess Irène and she reluctantly agrees to marry him, despite being 'not at all pleased to marry a soldier'. However, when the time comes for the wedding service La Ramée is fast asleep, and so Irène escapes her fate. As he philosophically tells his comrade, 'I'm not made for marrying princesses!'[90] Although Holbek defined the fairytale as the story of a misalliance, La Ramée was not the only soldier-hero who felt himself unfit for this kind of social elevation. In a Nivernais tale three soldiers who have saved some princesses from the clutches of the devil likewise tell the king 'we are not for marrying your princesses and we can live without that'.[91] In this instance the soldiers prefer to retain their liberty as single men.

This is a serious breakdown of genre expectations, and it challenges some commonly held assumptions among folklorists. Scholars of oral narrative have argued that the character of the hero has no significance. According to Max Lüthi, 'The figure is nothing more than a vehicle for the plot . . . . The folktale's millers, bakers, soldiers, and officers of state . . . do not typify a profession but exhibit traits that for the most part could be found as easily in one trade as in another.'[92] Lutz Röhrich agreed:

> The folktale's depiction of occupations is also so varied that it does not allow us to draw a precise picture of some historical or social reality . . . discharged soldiers who apparently fought as mercenaries in the Thirty Years War meet craftsmen who could have lived in the late Middle Ages as well as the nineteenth century. All of these figures are largely interchangeable.[93]

---

88 ' "Je ne me marierai pas, car je suis trop vieux," dit-il, "mais je resterai toujours avec vous et avec ma mère" ': Joseph Frison, 'Contes et légendes de la Basse-Bretagne', *Revue des traditions populaires* xxviii (1913), 281, no. 180: *La Veillée de la princess morte* (AT307).
89 ' "Tiens", dit le conscrit, "j'aurais voulu qu'il épousât la princesse." "Imbécile! c'était la même chose" ': Delmart and Vidal, *La Caserne*, 168 (AT1641).
90 'peu flattée d'épouser un soldat . . . "je ne suis pas fait pour épouser des Princesses!" ': Cerny, *Contes*, 153: *Fanfan et La Ramée* (AT401).
91 'nous ne sommes pas pour épouser vos princesses et nous pouvons vivre sans cela': Tenèze and Hüllen, *Rencontre des peuples*, 74, no. 13: *Les Trois Soldats dans le château hanté* (AT566).
92 Lüthi, *The European folktale*, 72. Propp agreed that 'one character is easily replaced by another': *Morphology*, 87.
93 Röhrich, *Folktales and reality*, 93.

It is true that the heroes of particular tale-types are not always restricted to one profession.[94] For example, in most French variants of the story *The ogre's heart in the egg* (AT302) the hero is a soldier, but in others he is a cobbler, a fisherman, a valet, a nobleman or a prince. If we accept Lüthi's argument that the character of the hero is just 'a vehicle for the plot' then we would expect that his occupation would have no impact on the development of the story. By-and-large this is the case: the hero, whether prince or soldier, rescues the princess from the ogre and is rewarded with her hand in marriage. However, in one Breton variant, when the king wants to marry his daughter to the old soldier Emile, the latter replies 'I'm too old to marry, but I will stay with you'.[95] This same pattern, of soldiers excusing themselves when non-military heroes invariably marry can be found in several other tale-types.[96]

Although the soldier himself often rejects marriage, either on grounds of age or because he preferred his bachelor lifestyle, just as frequently it was the woman who refused the match. In one tale where La Ramée actually weds the daughter of a baron, the bride complains to her father that the soldier has failed in his conjugal duties: 'What am I going to do with this old man you've given me? He's an old lump of wood. My God! I don't want him anymore!'[97] However, it was not always his age that was at issue: the soldier had lived too long in all-male company, he spat, he swore, he got drunk, he showed his arse in public, he was generally unfit for the conventions of married life. This became readily apparent at La Chique's wedding to a princess: 'he, next to her, was always spitting and the servants had a hard job to clean up, he spat in the dishes, after dinner he gets up on the table, drunk, shits in the dishes and the wedding was finished'.[98] Hence the dissatisfaction of several fairytale princesses with their soldier bridegrooms, and their repeated attempts to end the misalliance. One princess, for example, found Pipette clumsy, lacking

---

94 However, some tale-types do seem to require particular kinds of heroes. If it were true that the *dramatis personae* were interchangeable allomotifs we might anticipate that they would crop up in equal proportion across the Aarne-Thompson index, but this is far from the case. Although some tale-types can have either a high-born or low-born hero, in other tale-types social groups do not mix. Only a prince can take the leading role in AT516, *Faithful John*, but many other tale-types are reserved to the poverty-stricken. Not only are some tale-types associated with particular social groups, in many cases they are limited to particular professions. All French variants of AT562, *The spirit in the blue light*, concern a soldier, while AT670, *The animal languages*, always features a shepherd.

95 'Je suis trop vieux pour me marier, mais je resterai avec vous': Frison, 'Contes et légendes', xxix (1914), 307, no. 203: *Le Corps sans âme* (AT302).

96 These include AT307, AT326, AT401 and AT566.

97 'Qu'est-ce que je vais faire de ce vieux que tu m'as donné? C'est une vieille bûche de bois. Ma foi! je n'en veux plus!': Pineau, *Les Contes populaires*, 65: *La Ramée* (AT613, AT559).

98 'Lui, à coté d'elle crachait toujours et valets avaient beau essuyer, [il] crachait dans le plats, [il] monte sur la table, saoul, après diner, [il] chie dans les plats et la noce fut fermé': MNATP, MS Millien-Delarue (Nivernais), AT952, version B: *Le Père la Chique et le petit chasseur*.

'either rank or distinction', and so as soon as possible wishes him to the middle of the Saharan forest [sic].[99] Often a prince, her lover, encourages the princess's actions: she was as suspicious of misalliances as the soldier was.[100]

The soldier's difficulties in forming a lasting relationship with a partner of the opposite sex often diverts the tale from its usual conclusion. It is not the creation of a misalliance that provides the motive force for many tales concerning soldiers, but the remorseless hunt for a duplicitous wife or lover. For example, in one tale La Ramée and his girlfriend are crossing a forest when a gang of brigand-giants sets upon them. La Ramée kills five of them and lets the sixth live as his servant, but in a short time 'the woman was comrade with the giant, [she] detested La Ramée'.[101] They plot to murder him and finally she blinds him with a dining-fork. This fairytale, like so many others, is resolved not by the traditional happy ending of a wedding but rather by revenge.

Revenge on a false wife is the finale to tale-type *The three snake leaves* (AT612), which in France was always associated with soldiers. It concerns a merchant, married to a beautiful woman who dies. While watching over her grave the merchant sees a snake resurrect one of its family with a leaf. He tries the method on his wife, who revives. Soon after, while he is away on business, the wife is seduced by a colonel and elopes. The merchant joins the regiment in disguise, but is spotted by his wife, and court-martialled on a trumped-up charge. While in prison he entrusts his leaf to a habitual offender, La Ramée (or sometimes La Chique). After the execution his comrade digs up the merchant's body and applies the leaf. The merchant then joins a Guards regiment, where he attracts the attention of a princess. She promotes him to Field-Marshal and they marry. He returns to inspect his old regiment. His saviour is, of course, in the guardhouse. The new prince insists that La Ramée be invited to dinner with the colonel and his wife, where he encourages the soldier to climb on the table, smash plates, and throw wine in the faces of the other guests. Finally the king reveals his true identity and has the guilty couple either shot, burnt in a white-hot oven or torn to pieces by wild horses (whipped on by La Chique in one Corsican version).[102] Obviously, for some soldier-narrators, this was what constituted a happy ending.

---

99 'La princesse ne paraissait pas bien satisfaite de lui: elle le trouvait lourd, et qu'il ne tenait ni rang ni distinction': Léopold Dardy, *Anthologie populaire de l'Albret (sud-ouest de l'Agenais ou Gascogne landaise)*, Agen 1891, ii. 193, no. 50: *Pipèto* (AT562). Similar marital breakdowns occur frequently in tales concerning soldiers, particularly in tale-types AT562 and AT566.

100 Luzel, *Contes populaires*, iii. 77: *L'Homme de fer* (AT562).

101 'la femme était camarade avec le géant, [elle] détestait La Ramée': MNATP, MS Millien-Delarue (Nivernais), AT590, version B: *La Ramée et les géants*.

102 Geneviève Massignon, *Contes corses*, Aix-en-Provence 1963, 226, no. 101: *Le Marchand et la fille du roi* (AT612, AT307). La Ramée appears in three out the six variants collected in France, La Chique in the other three.

Such bloodthirsty conclusions are relatively rare; soldier heroes are usually as happy as other lowborn heroes to accept their misalliance. Yet a handful of French tales featuring soldiers conclude not with a wedding but instead descend into an orgy of violence during which the prospective bride is annihilated. When three soldiers fail to impress the king of England and his daughters with their magic gifts they beat the princesses and declare war instead. With their magic army of deathless men they are inevitably successful, the king is forced to flee while 'the three brothers went and looted his palace, then they lit a great fire and threw onto it the queen and her three daughters'.[103]

This is one of three of Cosquin's tales that was learnt by a young man of the village during his time in the army. It was also part of the repertoire of another soldier, Sergeant Krause, a contributor to the Grimms' collection. Krause's version is even more destructive, the hero using his magic horn to bring down vengeance on everyone: 'in his fury he blew it with all his might. Instantly everything collapsed – walls and fortifications, towns and villages – and the king and his daughter were crushed to death. If he had blown the horn a little longer . . . everything would have been destroyed and not one stone would have been left standing on another'.[104] Gonthier-Louis Fink, who has studied Krause's repertoire, highlights this idiosyncratic conclusion as 'entirely unusual' but indicative of the old soldier's personality:

> What we have of Krause's repertoire appears rather uniform and reflects both the misery and wishes of the old soldier and his discontent with the world and with society (not least of all, his joy in depicting destruction bespeaks his misogyny). This contrasts with his consciousness of his worth, his ability, and his cunning, though his consciousness of his subservient position also remains evident.[105]

This statement applies with equal force to La Ramée in French folktales. As old soldiers were among the narrators of these tales we must assume that this

---

103 'Les trois frères allèrent piller son château, puis ils allumèrent un grand feu et y jetèrent la reine et ses trois filles': Cosquin, *Contes populaires de Lorraine*, ii. 84: *Les Trois Frères* (AT569).
104 Jacob Grimm and Wilhelm Grimm, *The Penguin complete Grimms' tales for young and old*, London 1984, 195, no. 54: *The knapsack, the hat and the horn* (AT569). This is one of two of the dragoon's tales in which the hero (in one case an old trooper like Krause himself), ends up a king ruling over an empty kingdom.
105 Fink, 'The fairy tales', 160. Krause's contribution to the Grimms' collection includes nos 48, *Old Sultan* (AT101); 54, *The napkin, the knapsack, the little canon hat and the horn* (AT569); probably 92, *The king of the golden mountain* (AT401); possibly 16, *The three snake leaves* (AT612); and possibly 111, *The skilled huntsman* (AT304). He also told one tale which did not make it into the final collection, *Herr Fix und Fertig* (Mr Ready and Waiting), about an old soldier who woos a princess on behalf of a prince, and ends up as aide-de-camp to the couple. Interestingly, at least three of these tales (AT401, AT569, AT612) might be considered 'soldiers' tales' in France.

is how veterans saw themselves and, through their narratives, how their audience saw them.

The moral of these stories appears to be that the old soldier was unfit for marital relations with women. He had been debauched by his time in the army, he could not be domesticated. This goes against the mythology developed by elite French authors who found it difficult to avoid the analogy between military and sexual conquests: the French army did not just beat its male opponents, it successfully wooed their women as well. Imagists played on this analogy, but this conflation had no place in folk culture where, as we have seen, military service and marriage were considered two, mutually exclusive, paths to maturity. Many French soldiers obviously did marry after their discharge (though often to women met during their service, and thus far from their home community), but the cultural models available in folklore suggested that they were better suited to remaining bachelors. The folktale soldier's frequent failure to marry (or marry happily) suggests that both veterans and peasants had difficulties conceiving how soldiers might be reintegrated into the village community, for whom the conjugal unit was an essential element.

However, it was not just with prospective brides that the old soldier had problems forming a viable relationship: all his contacts with female characters retained the possibility of violence. In most fairytales the role of the donor (the fairy-godmother of *Cinderella* fame) is an important one. Holbek has suggested, following the opinion of Freudian folklorists, that the character of the donor is achieved by splitting contradictory aspects of the parent figures (in the case of Cinderella, the fairy-godmother represents the good aspects of the mother figure, the wicked stepmother the bad). He added 'If hero and donor are of opposite sexes . . . the relation between them is as a rule friendly; it may have sexual overtones. If they are of the same sex . . . their relation is often hostile.'[106] This may be true for the fairytale tradition as a whole, but it is certainly not the case in French tales concerning soldiers. In one of Cosquin's tales La Ramée is asked by an old woman to fetch a candle from the well. Although he has no inkling of the candle's magic powers La Ramée decides to keep the candle to light his pipe, and when the old woman insists he hands it over he murders her. His act is made all the worse because he is a deserter and, as in all the other French versions, the old woman gave him food and shelter, as well as advice.[107] Usually rewards are given by donors in response to an act of generosity, which is why some people view folktales as moralising fictions. But often the folktale soldier does nothing to deserve his good luck; indeed the reverse is true. Witness the soldier's discourteous treatment in a Nivernais tale of the old woman who advises him how to avoid being eaten by a vampire princess. Instead of being grateful 'he swears at her,

---

106 Holbek, 'The language of fairy tales', 48.
107 Cosquin, *Contes populaires de Lorraine*, i. 121, no. 11: *La Bourse, le sifflet et le chapeau* (AT566).

old whore, etc. [*sic*]'.[108] The language of the soldier in an Auvergnat version of the same tale is even worse: 'Let me pass, you old witch, or I'll pass my sabre through your stomach.'[109] Not only old women but even soldiers' mothers or sisters were quite likely to be on the receiving end of his anger.[110]

La Ramée has other, related, meanings. To be 'ramè', in the dialects of eastern France (where the bulk of the *ancien régime* army was recruited or garrisoned), meant to be dissatisfied.[111] Of course a common term for a veteran was a *grognard* or grumbler, and the old soldier in folktales is a habitual grumbler. Many tales open with a discharged soldier returning to the barracks to get what is due to him. For example, in the Breton tale of *Fanfan et La Ramée*, after spending three days on the road La Ramée suddenly realises he has been cheated of two liards (two and half centimes). He immediately sets off back to camp, promising to stick his sabre into the cashier's stomach up to the hilt. Fanfan remonstrates with him, 'Are you mad, my poor La Ramée! You would go sixty leagues for the sake of two liards?' but La Ramée declares 'They're due to me, I want them, and I will have them!' Once La Ramée has extracted his due he tells his comrades 'one doesn't make a fool out of an old moustache like me'.[112] This introduction is not linked to any particular tale-type but rather to the place where the tale was learnt, the barracks.[113] It gave the soldier-storyteller the opportunity to round on his superior officers and the conditions in which he was forced to live. In a story of La Ramée set in the context of barrack-room narrating, this introduction is expanded to become the whole tale and gives the teller, Sergeant Mistouflard (itself a name suggestive of misery), the opportunity to complain about promotion, pay (and deductions from pay), pensions, uniform and food.[114]

The principle objects of the soldier's complaints were, however, his officers. The tale of *Le Vieux La Ramée* from germanophone Lorraine opens with a tirade of abuse directed by the hero towards his superiors who have just

---

108 'Il la jure, vieille putain etc. [*sic*]': MNATP, MS Millien-Delarue (Nivernais), AT307, version D: *Le Corps sans âme*.

109 'Laisse-moi passer, vieille sorcière, ou je te passe mon sabre à le ventre': François Pommerol, 'Contes d'Auvergne', *Revue des traditions populaires* xv (1900), 641, no. 5: *L'Enfant du diable* (AT307).

110 Sébillot, *Contes populaires de la Haute Bretagne*, iii. 201, no. 21: *Jean le soldat* (AT590).

111 Zéliqzon, *Dictionnaire*, 552. The term probably derives from a widespread dialect usage of the world 'ramener', meaning to grouse or moan: Olivier Leroy, *Dictionary of French slang*, London 1935, 195.

112 ' "Et-tu fou, mon pauvre La Ramée! tu ferais soixante lieues pour deux liards?" "Ils me sont dûs, je les veux et je les aurai!" . . . "C'est bien," dit La Ramée aux soldats, "ce n'est pas à une vieille moustache comme moi qu'on fait la nique" ': Cerny, *Contes*, 145: *Fanfan et La Ramée* (AT401).

113 It serves regularly to introduce La Ramée tales: *Contes populaires de Lorraine*, ii. 29, no. 33: *La Maison de la forêt* (AT952); Garneret, *Contes recueillis en Franche-Comté*, 44, no. 5: *Le Vieux Raramé* (AT330, AT753); MNATP, MS Millien-Delarue (Nivernais), AT330, version E: *La Ramée et son sac* (+ AT613).

114 Leroy, *Faits et gestes*, 159: *Histoire de la Ramée*.

discharged him without any reward for his years of service: 'The rogues, the wastrels, the wretches! Twenty-four years service without blemish and now they send me away without a pension or a place [in Les Invalides]. I'm not going to take it from them!' He sets off to Paris in order to bring this injustice to the attention of the king. His complaints build to a crescendo throughout the tale until, while dining with the king, he explodes into a frenzied rant.[115] And of course he cannot make his complaints without at the same time 'swearing like a trooper', a soldier's habit in tales which is always getting him into trouble with his more pious travelling-companions. Saint Peter leaves La Ramée in one tale because he 'was continuously blaspheming'.[116]

A common cause of complaint among genuine soldiers in the nineteenth century was lack of promotion. According to Douglas Porch this, rather than any ideological commitment, was at the core of the republican conspiracies among troops garrisoned at Lunéville in 1834 and Strasbourg in 1836.[117] Although I have been at pains to show how, for the peasant, soldiering was an alternative way of life, for the professional soldier it was his job: terms and conditions of employment were, therefore, at the top of his personal agenda. Promotion opportunities were certainly a preoccupation of folktale soldiers: another La Ramée, realising he was not going to be promoted to corporal after twenty-one years' service, shouts at his captain 'The devil with enlisting! I'm leaving. I'd prefer to serve the devil for seven years than to stay a year longer with you.'[118] The devil is only too happy to take up the soldier's offer. The folktale soldier's relations with the devil are quite complex: he may even appear, if not as the soldier's friend, at least as his patron, giving him the magic gift vital to the development of the story. In one, admittedly rare, variant of the tale that usually ends with the soldier tricking his way past Saint Peter into Heaven, La Ramée actually prefers to stay in hell![119] But at

---

115 'Der Lump, die Liederlichen, das miserabel Volk! Vierundzwanzich Johr Diescht un keen Schtrof un schicken mich jetz ob ohne Pension un ohne Pletz. Un lo, den schenk ich's awer net!': Merkelbach-Pinck, *Lothringer Märchen*, 194, no. 35: *Le Vieux La Ramée* (AT952).
116 'il ne cessait de blasphémer': Filleul de Pétigny, 'Contes de la Beauce et du Perche', *Revue des traditions populaires* xiii (1898), 182: *La Ramée* (AT330B).
117 Douglas Porch, *Army and revolution: France, 1815–1848*, London 1974, 138. Samuel Scott makes a similar point about the revolutionary militancy of the army in 1789, while stressing that demands for political change cannot be dissociated from a desire for redress of other grievances: *Response of the royal army*, 112.
118 Paul Delarue, *The Borzoi book of French folktales*, New York 1956, 252, no. 33: *La Ramée and the phantom* (AT307). A large number of La Ramée tales from the Nivernais (in particular those in the repertoire of the Briffault family of Montigny-aux-Amognes) have the same motif: Millien and Delarue, *Contes du Nivernais*, 3, no. 1: *Les Princesses dansantes de la nuit* (AT306); MNATP, MS Millien-Delarue (Nivernais), AT952, version D: *La Ramée et les voleurs*; AT590 version B: *La Ramée et les géants*; AT330 version C: *Le Diable boiteux*. However, it is also found in other regions such as Lorraine and Brittany.
119 MNATP, MS Millien-Delarue (Nivernais), AT613, no version number: *La Ramée et son sac* (+ AT330).

the same time there are overtones of the parade-ground in their relationship. For example, the devil may reward the soldier but only when he has performed his military duty properly.[120] In several tales the devil addresses La Ramée familiarly, as if they were already known to each other. When the devil finds La Ramée sleeping in a haunted castle he exclaims 'Well, its you, La Ramée! I wasn't expecting to find you here. How's your friend La Tulipe, and all the comrades of the regiment, and the king, and the great lords of France? Are you sleeping, come on, wake up, answer!'[121] The hierarchical nature of their relationship is even clearer in another variant of this tale-type, in which the devil addresses the soldier: 'Miserable rogue, is that how one speaks to one's superiors?'[122] The folktale devil provided a replacement figure for the soldier's superior officer, both in his capacity as a father-figure or donor, and as his tormentor. He can become, therefore, the victim of the soldier's simmering resentment at years of bad treatment. In a Breton tale a soldier and the devil play cards; the devil drops one on the floor hoping that the soldier will stoop to pick it up, giving him the opportunity to steal his money back. The soldier refuses, shouting 'No, no, no! I've been a servant long enough, its about time it was my turn to be the master.' When the devil bends down the soldier leaps upon him crying 'It's your turn to suffer; me, I've suffered for twenty-one years!'[123]

Folktales were usually only found among the poorer members of society; they are the record of the voices of subordinate social groups. They reveal the desires and the hatreds of the dominated, which could not be expressed openly for fear of the consequences, and so found outlets in fantasy. Hence historians of slavery have turned to the tales of Brer Rabbit and the tricks he played on his numerous enemies to 'overhear' what blacks in the ante-bellum South really thought about their masters.[124] The disciplined atmosphere of the army might be considered an analogous situation. Any direct resistance to the military hierarchy could result in massive retaliation on the individual, but soldiers could channel their aggression into stories and thus share their feelings with their comrades and perhaps, indirectly, communicate them to

---

[120] Cosquin, *Contes populaires de Lorraine*, ii. 79, no. 42: *Les Trois Frères* (AT569). In this tale, narrated by a veteran, a soldier is mounting guard over a tower when he hears chains dragging. He gives the 'Qui vive?' and when he gets no reply threatens 'Si tu ne réponds pas, je te brûle la cervelle', to which the devil replies 'Ah! tu as du bonheur de bien faire ton service!' and gives the soldier a magic purse.

[121] 'Tiens, c'est toi, La Ramée! je ne m'attendais pas à te trouver ici. Comment va ton ami La Tulipe, et tous les camarades du régiment, et le Roi, et les grands Seigneurs de France? Dors-tu, allons, réveille-toi, réponds!': Cerny, *Contes*, 147: *Fanfan et La Ramée* (AT401).

[122] 'Malheureux coquin, est-ce ainsi que l'on parle à ses supérieurs?': Paul Sébillot, *Contes des landes et des grèves*, Rennes 1900, 15, no. 1: *Le père Décampe* (AT326, AT401).

[123] 'Non, non, non! J'ai été assez longtemps domestique, c'est bien à mon tour d'être le maître. . . . C'est bien à ton tour de souffrir; j'ai souffert pendant 21 ans moi!': Pineau, *Les Contes populaires*, 156: *Le Vieux Soldat et le diable* (AT326).

[124] Scott, *Domination*, 162–6.

their officers.[125] This may help to explain why storytelling was such a prevalent form of leisure in the barracks. The soldier's frustration with the discipline and fatigues of army life finds its voice in folktales. They reveal the soldiers' utmost desire in the face of the restrictions placed on his life – complete liberty. In many tales the soldier volunteers for a particularly dangerous mission in return for a day's permission to do exactly as he pleases. The eponymous hero of the Breton tale *La Rose* (the protégé of père La Chique) 'made the most of his liberty: he went from bar to bar, and when he was tipsy he amused himself by breaking bottles, and by throwing wine on the gentlemen's trousers, and no one said anything to him'.[126] Even more important, folktale soldiers had the opportunity their real life counterparts yearned for but never had – revenge – the tale's real *dénouement*. In a tale from the Nivernais La Ramée, having saved the life of the prince, asks a favour, the right to inspect his former regiment. He makes his colonel and other officers stand as targets for live-firing practice, and when they are dead he makes his old comrade La Chique colonel in their place.[127]

In military parlance the phrase 'il ne vaut pas une ramée' meant not worth a damn, and La Ramée habitually could not care less.[128] The soldier's devil-may-care attitude is summed up in the Poitevin story of *Vive Sans-Souci la Ramée*: 'Vive Sans-Souci la Ramée went everywhere in the battles, [when] the musket-balls touched him, he went like that: "take that, fly!" He thought that it was flies, and the bullets too.'[129] His fearlessness is the quality that enables La Ramée to face his supernatural opponents. In another variant of this tale-type La Ramée volunteers to sleep in the haunted house with the words 'An old soldier like me cannot be frightened; I've seen plenty of others.'[130] Death itself held few terrors for the professional soldier for whom it

---

[125] It is difficult to recover the interaction between soldiers and their officers as communicated through tales, but an example cited by one of my students may illustrate the general point. Living on a hop farm in Kent she often attended storytelling sessions held by Gypsy hop-pickers whose tales invariably included a character 'King Hedgehog'. She noticed that when the farmer himself was present the narrator took pains to stress what a good and generous employer King Hedgehog was!

[126] 'La Rose profita largement de la permission: il alla de débit en débit, et quand il fut gris, il s'amusait à casser les bouteilles, à jeter du vin sur les pantalons des messieurs, et personne ne lui disait rien': Sébillot, *Contes populaires de la Haute-Bretagne*, iii. 39, no. 32: *La Rose* (AT612).

[127] MNATP, MS Millien-Delarue (Nivernais), AT952, version A: *Le Vieux Soldat et le fils du roi*.

[128] Centre national de la recherche scientifique, *Trésor de la langue française*, xiv. 323–5. Similarly, if something 'ne pas valoir pipette' then it was not worth a damn: Moses J. Leitner and J. R. Lamen, *Dictionary of French and English slang*, London 1965, 238.

[129] 'Vive Sans-Souci la Ramée passait partout dans les batailles, les balles qui le joigniant, il faisait comme ça: à mouche! Il croyait qu'ol [sic] était des mouches et les boulets aussi': Pineau, 'Contes de Poitou', 487: *Vive Sans-Souci la Ramée* (AT326).

[130] 'Un vieux soldat comme moi, dit-il, ne peut pas avoir peur; j'en ai vu bien d'autres': Joannès Plantadis, 'Contes populaires du Limousin', *Revue des traditions populaires* xvii (1902), 400, no. 6: *La Ramée* (AT326).

was but an occupational hazard. As another soldier-hero in the same situation puts it, 'Me, I'm an old soldier and I'm not scared; to die here or elsewhere, it matters little to me.'[131] There is no point avoiding challenges or duties, 'one only dies once'.[132]

In the constant presence of death, the folktale soldier naturally has no thoughts for tomorrow, he lives for today. Real soldiers were often presumed to live in the same way. In war he could make no plans which depended on his survival and even in peacetime his future was uncertain. He was unable to marry and raise a family, so he had little reason to save his money, and as his regiment never stayed in one place he had no opportunity to invest in land or a home. This being the case he could not take the misfortunes of this world too seriously, and this military pattern of thought remained with him even after he had left the army. As La Ramée says to himself on arrival in a town in mourning (for a princess about to be sacrificed to a monster): 'Here are people who don't know how to take life as it comes.'[133] This sounds like an echo of the opinion of the most famous veteran in French literature, Jacques the Fatalist, whose mantra was 'everything which happens to us on this earth, both good and bad, is written up above'.[134] The 'militaire-philosophe' was a commonplace of eighteenth-century literature. Many Enlightenment tracts were published under military pseudonyms, partly to invoke the tradition of Descartes and Montaigne, but also because the soldier was by nature a cosmopolitan, a witness to the plurality of beliefs and therefore expected to be both tolerant and sceptical.[135] One might say that his wider experience of the world was supposed to give him a deeper understanding of it. The idea lived on into the art and literature of the nineteenth century in the form of the 'philosophic rag-picker', whose missing limb reveals his previous calling as a soldier.[136] However, in folktales the old soldier was 'philosophical' in the more colloquial sense of being indifferent to the turns of fortune.

It is this attitude which brings him to the attention of his occasional travelling-companions, Jesus and Saint Peter, who appear dressed as beggars to test the soldier's charity. The Comtois soldier Raramée is quite happy to share his ration loaf with the disguised saint, but perhaps less out of charity than

---

131 'Moi, je suis un vieux soldat et je n'ai pas peur; mourir ici ou ailleurs, peu m'importe': Sébillot, *Contes des landes et des grèves*, 2, no. 1: *Le Père Décampe* (AT326, AT401).

132 'on ne meurt qu'une fois': François Cadic, *Nouveaux Contes et légendes de Bretagne*, ii, Paris 1922, 90: *Cadeaux des morts* (AT401).

133 'Voilà des gens qui ne savent pas prendre la vie comme elle vient': Méraville, *Vie et oeuvres*, 161, no. 23: *Le Retour de la Ramée* (AT302).

134 Denis Diderot, *Jacques the fatalist*, London 1986, 21. Jacques learned his philosophy from his captain. The novel was written during the 1760s and 1770s, and the military characters are based in part upon Diderot's acquaintances in Les Invalides. It is worth noting that Jacques, like other veterans, was a superb storyteller.

135 Chagniot, *Paris et l'armée*, 629–39.

136 Robert L. Herbert, *Peasants and 'primitivism': French prints from Millet to Gauguin*, South Hadley, Mass. 1995, 74–5.

simple unconcern about what the future may bring.[137] His generosity is the flip side of the soldier's habitual prodigality. When folktale soldiers do occasionally get their hands on cash they immediately spend it in riotous living. As La Ramée's colonel remarks in one tale, money for him was 'like a strawberry in the jaws of a wolf' – soon gone.[138] The eponymous hero of Cosquin's tale *Victor La Fleur*, while sharing a prison cell with La Ramée, gives the latter his money on condition that he digs up his corpse after his execution and rubs it with ointment. Instead 'He rummages in La Fleur's trunk and, as he finds gold and silver there, he goes on a spree for eight days, then he's put in the guard-house for nine days.' Only on the eighteenth day does he remember his former comrade, now in an advanced state of decomposition.[139] The need to protect soldiers from their own improvidence was one of the most persistent prejudices against veterans, and not just in folktales. The military committee of the National Assembly abandoned plans to abolish Les Invalides because, as Clermont-Tonnerre put it, its residents' 'past deeds have earned them a subsistence which their future imprudence must not be permitted to jeopardise'.[140] In the nineteenth century special banks were set up to dissuade soldiers from dissipating their engagement money. These were particularly aimed at the replacements who sold themselves to take the place of others who had been unlucky in the *tirage au sort*. As volunteers in a largely conscript army, replacements bore the brunt of many of the negative attitudes developed towards soldiers in general under the *ancien régime*. Why would anyone willingly join the army unless he was an incorrigible rogue?[141]

The soldier's imprudence did not just concern material matters, it even extended to his eternal salvation. In many tales Saint Peter offers the soldier a guaranteed place in heaven, but as far as La Ramée is concerned 'if he had nothing but that to give him, he could get lost'.[142] The soldier is too concerned with enjoying himself in the here-and-now to give any thought to what comes after.

The soldier's prodigality with both his money and his life is another continuing connection between military virtues and aristocratic culture. But however noble it might be, it was anathema to the culture of the village. As

---

137 Garneret, *Contes recueillis en Franche-Comté*, 44, no. 5: *Le Vieux Raramé* (AT330, AT753).
138 'C'est comme une fraise à la gueule d'un loup': MNATP, MS Millien-Delarue (Nivernais), AT952, version A: *Le Vieux Soldat et le fils du roi*.
139 'La Ramée, qui n'est pas ivre, vise bien au coeur. Il fouille dans la malle de La Fleur, et, comme il y trouve de l'or et de l'argent, il va se divertir pendant huit jours, puis il est mis pour neuf jours à la salle de police': Cosquin, *Contes populaires de Lorraine*, ii. 343, no. 82: *Victor La Fleur* (AT612).
140 Woloch, *The French veteran*, 52.
141 Schnapper, *Le Remplacement*, 120–4. Schnapper considers that these initiatives were quite successful, but among army officers replacements retained a disreputable reputation for prodigality.
142 'qu'il n'avait que cela à lui donner, il pouvait se le mettre au derrière': MNATP, MS Millien-Delarue (Nivernais), AT330 version C: *Le Diable boiteux*.

Alan Forrest has explained, 'Peasants understood with unerring clarity that for them security meant the investment of years of back-breaking labor. . . . Military service could condemn a young peasant to a lifetime of labor for the account of someone else, and with it to a position of marginality in the village community.'[143] Not for them the sprees that punctuated the soldier's life, but rather the close husbandry which made the peasant, in French culture, synonymous with greed.[144]

A clear instance of attitudinal opposition between villagers and soldiers is provided by the veterans' use of tobacco. The stereotypical image of the soldier puffing away on his pipe was familiar from hundreds of popular images, and it was one readily recognised by the soldiers themselves. In 1792 the volunteer Gabriel Noël wrote to his godmother 'Here are our smokers smoking their pipes. They do nothing but that. It's an infection. . . . There's hardly a young volunteer who doesn't smoke like the old soldiers.'[145] Smoking, or chewing tobacco, was another military particularism that became enshrined in folktales.[146] When Pierre Lelièvre, a veteran himself, talked about old soldiers in his tales he would describe them as 'a famous tobacco-chewer [chiqueur] like me'.[147] This addiction was particularly obvious in the case of La Ramée's two rivals in the genre, Pipette and La Chique. According to one storyteller Pipette got his name 'because he always had his pipe in his mouth', while Sébillot explained that old sailors (and old sailor characters in folktales) were known as Père la Chique 'because they were constantly chewing tobacco'.[148] La Ramée was also fond of the weed, as we learn from the title of a Genoese tale – La Ramée, grand fumeur.[149] In folk-lore smoking became a symbol for the soldier's fearlessness. When young conscripts marched off to join their regiments they sang 'Friends, fear not the storm,/ Neither the musket nor the cannons;/ I'm going to light my pipe/ At the head of our battalions.'[150] But it was also an indication (and perhaps a cause) of his philosophical nature. When imps play skittles around him with

---

[143] Forrest, Conscripts and deserters, 90–1.

[144] Lehning, Peasant and French, 14–20.

[145] 'Voilà nos fumeurs qui fument leurs pipes. Ils ne font que cela. C'est une infection. . . . Il n'y a presque pas de jeune volontaire qui ne fume comme les vieux soldats': Noël, Au Temps des volontaires, 15.

[146] Tobacco use had already become associated with the army by the end of the seventeenth century. A copperplate image of the period, Le Portrait universel, asks 'Charmant tabac sans toy que ferait une armée?/ Les troupes sont sans toy des troupes désolées': Duchartre and Saulnier, L'Imagerie parisienne, 151. Again there is a connection to the second estate, the other social group that took tobacco, though in their case usually in the form of snuff.

[147] 'un fameux chiqueur comme moi': Félice, Contes de Haute-Bretagne, p. xi.

[148] Dardy, Anthologie populaire, ii. 189, no. 50: Pipèto (AT562, AT566); Sébillot, 'Contes de marins' x (1891), 105.

[149] Andrews, Contes ligures, 226, no. 48: La Ramée, grand fumeur (AT330).

[150] 'Amis, ne craignons pas l'orage,/ Ni le mousquet ni les canons;/ Je m'en vais allumer ma pipe/ A la tête de nos bataillons': Fourier de Bacourt, 'Anciens Chants', no. 8: L'Enrôlé.

skulls and skeletons, 'La Ramée watched them tranquilly from his bed while smoking his pipe.'[151] Needless to say his *sang-froid* infuriates the devil. But however much the peasant-audience for these exploits might admire the folk-tale soldier and his pipe, they could not afford to emulate him. As Joseph Creusot noted in his portrait of his home village in the Haute-Marne 'Our people hardly ever smoked. How could one be mad enough to change pennies into smoke! Soldiers, however . . . returned to the village conquered by tobacco.'[152] It was the conscription system of the third republic, which required all Frenchmen to spend some time in the ranks, that made smoking a national addiction in France.

It is perhaps not surprising that La Ramée is so little fazed by his dealings with death, devils and saints, for he himself had connections to the supernatural. In the Vosges La Ramée was a name given to the Wild Hunt, the furious night ride across the sky of men, animals and spirits.[153] Although folk belief seems rather uncertain about who exactly the participants in the Wild Hunt were, some sources suggest that they were the souls of those who have died violent deaths. Hence soldiers featured prominently in several descriptions.[154] Although the use of this term for the Wild Hunt is very localised (and may have nothing to do with soldiers), it does fit a pattern. La Ramée's access to unknown powers was not just a folktale motif, it was a matter of belief. In a local legend (told as a true story) from the nearby Argonne, La Ramée owes his superhuman strength, which allows him to brush away bullets with his trademark exclamation 'Really, the flies in this country are vicious', to a pact made with the devil.[155] The soldier's relationship to the supernatural is one to which we will return.

Folktale soldiers, like their real life counterparts, were likely to have been educated in the army. For example, the eponymous hero of Sébillot's *Jean-le-soldat* learnt to read in the regiment and thus was able to decipher the message on the blade of the magic sabre.[156] But it was the skills learnt in the

---

151 'La Ramée les regardait tranquillement de son lit en fumant sa pipe': Pétigny, 'Contes de la Beauce', 182: *La Ramée* (AT330B). Smoking, in folk culture, is generally associated with sang-froid.
152 'Nos gens ne fumaient guère. Peut-on être assez fou pour changer des sous en fumée! Les soldats pourtant . . . revenaient au village conquis par le tabac': Joseph Cressot, *Le Pain au lièvre*, Paris 1943, 115.
153 Charles Sadoul, 'Dangers de la nuit: les apparitions de la nuit dans les Vosges', *Revue des traditions populaires* xix (1904), 87. It may be that, in this instance, the name derives merely from 'ramée' in the sense of linked (as in trains). Sadoul did not draw any inferences, although he had collected tales that featured La Ramée.
154 These include its first ever recorded appearance, at Bonneval in Normandy in 1091: Jean-Claude Schmitt, *Ghosts in the Middle Ages: the living and the dead in medieval society*, Chicago–London 1998, 93–9. However, Sadoul's informants only specifically mentioned unbaptised infants.
155 'Qu lè mouche son don méchante da ç'tu pailly-là': Lallement, *Contes rustiques*, 80–7: *La Ramée*. This story has aspects of AT650, but it was told as a local legend.
156 For example, the eponymous hero of Sébillot's *Jean-le-soldat* learnt to read in the regi-

university of life that were most valued in the folktale world, above all craftiness. Naturally an 'old moustache' like La Ramée was also a 'fin poil' – a
'smart hair', hairiness being a sign of wit.[157] The soldier was deviousness
personified, no one could hoodwink him. Cosquin's *Une Militaire avisée* (clev-
erness being this soldier's defining characteristic) tricks a fox, usually the last
word in folktale cunning, into a cherry-tree and leaves him skewered on a
sharp stick.[158] The devil should offer more of a challenge, yet the old soldier
who volunteers to free a princess from his clutches, even though 'it was
written that she would be delivered by whoever showed himself to be more
cunning than the devil', had little difficulty in proving the prophecy
correct.[159] Another old soldier who falls in with the devil manages to overcome the tasks he sets him. The devil, having been fooled again, is impressed
by the soldier's talents: 'Aha, Christian, you've worked well!' to which the
soldier replies, 'Do you think so, my master? It's because I got an education
during my travels.'[160] As we have seen, the belief that 'it is rare that one does
not learn through travel' was important to the veteran's credibility both as
mayor and as storyteller.[161]

Craftiness was not considered a fault among the inhabitants of the folktale
world. For Robert Darnton these clever characters 'constitute an ideal type,
the little guy who gets ahead by outwitting the big', and indicate the value of
folktales to their audience: they 'told peasants how the world was put
together, and they provided a strategy for coping with it'.[162] Certainly the
only way that the old soldier, with a reputation for drinking, fighting and
swearing, could hope to get to Heaven was by craftiness. *Pipet, ein alter
Franzos* tricks his way past Saint Peter by wishing himself inside his own
magic haversack which he had thrown through the gates, 'and [thus] Pipet
was cleverer than Peter!'[163] However, if cunning was not perceived as a fault,
it was certainly morally ambivalent. In one tale an old soldier and God share
a meal of mutton. While his companion's back is turned the soldier gobbles
down the liver, but when God asks where it is the soldier denies that this
sheep ever had one. God exclaims ' "A sheep that has no liver! That's never

---

ment and thus was able to decipher the message on the blade of the magic sabre: *Contes
populaires de la Haute Bretagne*, iii. 201: no. 21 (AT590).
157 Vartier, *Le Grand Livre des proverbes*, 127.
158 Cosquin, *Contes populaires de Lorraine*, i, no. 2: *Le Militaire avisé* (AT151).
159 'Il était écrit qu'elle serait délivrée par celui-là qui se montrerait plus rusé que le
Diable et qui triompherait de ses artifices': Cadic, *Contes et légendes de Bretagne*, iii. 159: *La
Reine des trois montagnes d'or* (AT401). While it is often the case that the devil is depicted
as a bit dim in folktales, in those concerning soldiers it is sometimes implied that he has
purposely let the soldier off the hook.
160 Delarue, *The Borzoi book*, 11: *La Belle Eulalie* (AT313).
161 'il est rare qu'on ne s'instruise pas en voyageant': Meyrac, *Traditions, coutumes,
légendes*, 491: *Jean-Sans-Peur* (AT326).
162 Darnton, *The great cat massacre*, 59–71.
163 'Und Pipet ist klüger gewesen als Petrus!': Merkelbach-Pinck, *Lothringer Märchen*,
239, no. 38: *Pipet, ein alter Franzos* (AT330, AT326).

been seen." "Me," said the soldier, "I've already seen it." '[164] This is the folk-tale soldier's answer to the world: he has travelled, he has seen it all before, nothing can surprise him and he knows better than anyone else. However, in this case the soldier's travels have also taught him, like his comrade Pipette, to 'piper', to lie; like his comrade La Chique he is too 'chicant' or tricksy for God.[165] 'Faire du chiqué' means to bluff, to boast, to fake, while 'une piperie' is an outrageous falsehood. Whenever La Chique and Pipette were named they immediately recalled the status of folktales as lies, and the soldier-narra-tor's reputation as the best liar of all.[166]

Laramée in Pellerin's print is wearing his haversack. The folktale soldier La Ramée is inseparable from his. When he temporarily forgets it in one of Cosquin tales he immediately requests 'Caporal, I left my haversack on the table in my room; that has never happened to me before. . . . Would you allow me to go and fetch it?'[167] Even when La Ramée ventured into the other world (as he frequently did) he took his haversack with him. As we have seen in the case of Pipet, the magic haversack, given to him by Jesus and into which he could wish anything he desired, became the means by which he slipped into heaven and if, one Italian tale informs us, you get to the pearly gates yourself, you will find La Ramée hanging behind the door in his haversack, smoking his pipe.[168] The pedlar La Ramée goes into rhapsodies over his haversack when Saint Peter offers to grant him a wish: 'If you separate me from my old haversack, my faithful companion through pleasure and pain, the greatest wish I can make is that you should give me another one, as soon as possible.'[169] Saint Peter becomes infuriated by another La Ramée's solicitude for his haversack (which the soldier used as a metaphor for his physical well-being) rather than his eternal salvation: 'Your haversack, your haver-sack! You think of nothing but that damned haversack.'[170] The haversack was an essential part of his character: as one folktale puts it, 'La Ramée had never

---

164 ' "Un mouton qui n'a pas de foie! cela ne s'est jamais vu." "Moi," dit le militaire, "je l'ai déjà vu." ': Cosquin, *Contes populaires de Lorraine*, i. 285, no. 30: *Le Foie de mouton* (AT 785).

165 Zéliqzon, *Dictionnaire*, 136. The same idea is implied in the English 'to have one's tongue in one's cheek', or simply 'cheeky'.

166 La Ramée can be caught telling lies in the tales themselves, boasting, for example, that 'Oh, your phantom, I was scarcely afraid of it. I took it by the shoulders and I said: "You run along back into your hole" ', when he had in fact hidden from it behind the altar: Delarue, *The Borzoi book*, 254, no. 33: *La Ramée and the phantom* (AT307).

167 'Caporal, j'ai oublié mon sac sur la table de ma chambre; cela ne m'arrive pourtant jamais. . . . Me permettez-vous de l'aller chercher?': Cosquin, *Contes populaires de Lorraine*, ii. 1, no. 31: *L'Homme de fer* (AT562).

168 Andrews, *Contes ligures*, 229, no. 48: *La Ramée, grand fumeur* (AT330B).

169 'Si vous me séparez de mon vieux sac, mon fidèle compagnon de plaisir et de peine, le meilleur souhait que je puisse former, c'est que vous m'en donniez un autre au plus tôt': Cénac-Moncaut, *Contes populaires*, 60: *Le Sac de la Ramée* (AT330B).

170 'Ton sac! ton sac! tu ne songes qu'à ce maudit sac': Deulin, *Contes du roi Cambrinus*, 130: *Le Sac de La Ramée* (AT785). Again Deulin, although an author rather than a collector, put his finger on the significance of a folkloric motif.

been scared in his life, and was even less so now that he had the famous haversack on his back.'[171]

As we have seen, in folk culture to have 'pack on back', was used as a metaphor for the soldier's condition. Therefore, the old soldier's desire to hold onto his haversack indicated his unwillingness, or his inability, to quit the military life to settle down in the village. Only when the old soldier hung up his haversack would it signal that he was rejoining his original community. However, this reunion could not be straightforward for either party, because neither could ignore what had happened in the meantime. The soldier had acquired a new name, new clothes, new facial hair, new habits (like smoking) and, above all, new knowledge. The haversack, which appears hanging on a peg in the background to so many images, could be resumed at any moment, and in folktales it often was.[172] The haversack remained a badge of his belonging to a separate estate.

The soldier kept his craft in his haversack, at least metaphorically. When the hero of a tale, narrated in a barracks-dormitory in 1912, is confronted with a giant he warns him 'you'll see that I've got more than one trick in my pack'.[173] But the soldier kept more than that in there. As we have seen, soldiers were famous as narrators, a reputation that is confirmed in the tales themselves. Where did veterans keep their tales? In their haversack of course! Hence when storytellers finished their tales they used the formula: 'Cric, Crac!/ That's the story from out of my pack!'[174]

La Ramée is the quintessence of the popular idea of the soldier: a wanderer, a prodigal, lazy, dissolute, addicted to wine and tobacco, unable to form settled relationships, a happy-go-lucky fellow, unless crossed in which case he readily resorted to violence. The only quality that he has in common with the *soldat-laboureur*, at least in his most Roman conception (for his representation in urban popular culture did borrow more widely from the folkloric archetype), is bravery. One noticeable absentee from La Ramée's list of martial qualities, compared with the *soldat-laboureur*, is patriotism. La Ramée, though he might (accidentally) save the life of his king, is basically a mercenary. His politics are neither monarchist nor republican, he serves best who rewards him most. If, as has been suggested, La Ramée was a projection of soldiers' own ideas of themselves, can we assume from this absence that soldiers were not motivated by patriotism? Not necessarily. It may be that folktales are

---

171 'La Ramée n'avait jamais eu peur de sa vie et encore moins maintenant qu'il avait le fameux sac sur le dos': Pétigny, 'Contes de la Beauce', 183: *La Ramée* (AT330B).

172 Garnier-Pelle, *L'Imagerie populaire française*, ii, no. 1432.

173 'tu verras que j'ai plus d'un tour dans mon sac': Millien and Delarue, *Contes du Nivernais*, 18, no. 2: *Le Géant à la barbe d'or ou le Petit Fûteux* (AT328). It was told to Paul Delarue while on national service.

174 'Cric, Crac!/ Voilà l'histoire sortie d'mon sac!': Francesca Sautman, 'Variabilité et formules d'ouverture et de clôture dans le conte populaire français', in Veronika Görög-Karady (ed.), *D'Un Conte . . . à l'autre: la variabilité dans la littérature orale*, Paris 1990, 140 n. 33.

simply the wrong genre for the expression of this kind of feeling. Perhaps ironically, given the uses to which they have been put by nationalists and regionalists of every ilk, folktales have little to say about national (or religious, or ethnic, or political) identities. In Delmart's re-creation of barrack-room narrating he mentions that some in the audience would have preferred to hear some personal account of France's military adventures in Spain from one of the older soldiers present.[175] Perhaps these might have been more likely to emphasise national differences and chauvinistic self-worth. But Delmart did not record them. Throughout the rest of the nineteenth century folklorists hint at an audience tired of fantasy and more enthusiastic about historical narrative in which issues of national identity were likely to have loomed larger. However, it is difficult to know whether this reflected a widespread change in popular taste, as the Romantic historical imagination with its nationalist concerns took hold in the nineteenth century, or if it was merely personal.

However, if soldiers chose not to emphasise national difference in their tales, they certainly did articulate a sense of social difference. La Ramée may fight for any or all of the kings of France, Spain and England, but he can never be a peasant. The issue at stake in being a soldier was not whose uniform you wore, but the social distance that any uniform placed between the soldier and the peasant. La Ramée's attitudes, his morality, his way-of-life were often implicitly, and sometimes explicitly, contrasted with those of the rural world. Soldiers, at least those who told folktales, and those who eagerly listened to them, revelled in this distinction.

What can one say, then, about La Ramée's role in rural popular culture, for unlike the *soldat-laboureur* it is clear that La Ramée did find a home in the village? Two possibilities suggest themselves. Firstly, although peasants may not have accepted the hierarchy associated with the society of orders, they also defined themselves through the contrast with their anti-type – the soldier – embodied in the figure of La Ramée. They were what he was not: hard-working, thrifty, pious, hardy, forced to accept the insults and injuries offered by social superiors (including soldiers), and unable to escape because bound to a particular place by a dense network of reciprocal relationships, above all the conjugal partnership of the peasant family household. All these peasant qualities are emphasised in the various versions of the song *Les Laboureurs*.[176] Bizarrely, given that the song is little more than a string of complaints, it sometimes ends with the suggestion that the peasant puts up with all these miseries without a murmur, yet another contrast with La Ramée the grumbler.[177]

This does not mean, however, that peasants utterly rejected La Ramée and

---

175 Delmart and Vidal, *La Caserne*, 154.
176 Donatien Laurent, *Aux Sources du Barzaz-Breiz: la mémoire d'un peuple*, Douarnenez 1989, 91–2.
177 Julien Tiersot, *Histoire de la chanson populaire en France*, Paris 1889, 155.

all he stood for. Instead, it may be that telling tales about him allowed villagers temporary and imaginative escape from the burdens of daily life. There is, perhaps, an element of envy in their portraits of La Ramée. They too might like to escape their constant round of back-breaking toil and the incessant bickerings of a close-knit community to, as one folktale soldier puts it, 'travel at one's leisure, to eat when hungry, to sleep as one liked'.[178]

The second role that La Ramée may have performed in rural communities was to act as a messenger. I have argued that folktales were not merely fictions but formed communications between narrators and audiences, often representing troubled relationships in a symbolic fashion. The fact that La Ramée was able to do what the peasant would like to do but in reality could not, meant that he carried meaning without the act itself being performed. In particular La Ramée's hostility and violence towards women meant that male narrators were able to give voice to the tensions in their relationships with their female kin. Given the relish with which narrators imaginatively entered into such assaults one can but hope that the description of them proved cathartic.

Without knowing much more about the personal lives of narrators and their families, it is difficult to go beyond this general supposition. We may be able to understand more clearly how the members of rural communities used the idea of the soldier in their metaphorical communications if we turn to folksongs.

Soldiers' homecomings in song:
absent lovers and unrecognisable prodigal sons

While misalliances are not as dominant as plot devices in songs as they are in folktales, they none the less feature in a sizeable proportion of the catalogue. One of the most popular of all folksongs in Lorraine, according to Charles Sadoul, was *Joli Capitaine*. It concerns an officer returning from war to find his beloved locked in a tower by her father because she refuses to renounce her lover. When the captain confronts the father, a marshal of France, the latter becomes so angry that he throws his daughter into the river, from where the captain rescues her. He promises her 'I will marry you/ Despite your parents', and takes her to the army where 'She passed for a queen/ In the regiment.'[179] Doncieux believed that *Joli Capitaine* originated as an eighteenth-century soldiers' song.[180] Soldiers' songs, like their tales, revealed

---

178 'de voyager à son aise, de manger à sa faim, de dormir à sa paresse': Meyrac, *Traditions, coutumes, légendes*, 501: *Belle-Humeur et Sans-Chagrin* (AT613).
179 ' "Je t'épouserai/ Malgré tes parents". . . . Elle passait pour reine/ Dans le régiment': Sadoul, 'Les Chansons lorraines', 226: *Joli Capitaine*. This song was also recorded by Puymaigre and Westphalen (twice).
180 *Joli Capitaine* is thematically related to an older song, known as *La Fille du roi Loys*, in

their singers' desires (for a good match) and their expectations (for their sweethearts' fidelity). But the continuing popularity of *Joli Capitaine* in the village, among female singers as well as male, may have rested on its ability to deliver messages without causing bad feeling. In the charged triangular relationship between father, daughter and potential son-in-law the song could be deployed by both the woman to promise faithfulness, and by the young man to promise to overcome the difficulties that separate them.

Folklorists have demonstrated that songs could serve as messages from the singer to a very specific audience, particularly where courting was concerned. Alessandro Falassi concluded from observation of the Tuscan *veglia* that 'As in many other genres of folklore, love songs acted as impersonal carriers of very personal communications.' Singers could make a declaration without either opening themselves up to emotional attack, or offending the guardians of moral etiquette, because 'they were able to pretend to sing without reference to the sentimental situation of those present, because the *stornello*, or folk song, "goes like this" '.[181] Is it possible to recover similar communications in Lorrainer folksongs? That songs in general were used at the *veillée* and other occasions to impart messages was witnessed by the Vosgian folklorist Géhin: 'if a young person was actively sought in marriage for her fortune or her beauty, the ousted suitors revenged themselves on the *ingrate*, by putting her and her chosen-one into song; song also served the petty personal jealousies of the mountain inhabitants, or their natural desire to make fun of their neighbour's misfortunes'.[182] Géhin does not mention courting songs directly but Lorrainer song collections are similar to their Tuscan counterparts in which 'it is easily recognisable that their contents cover without omissions all the possible situations of courting and love'.[183] It is also true that the majority of such songs appear in the form of conversations between the man and the woman; thus singers could, through this impersonal form, suggest the answers they hoped for to questions that they dared not ask directly.

In order to recover these messages we must know who sang what song on what occasion and to what audience. As a rule this is just the kind of infor-

---

which the girl fakes death in order to escape the tower and be reunited with her lover: her sham funeral turns into her wedding. Her lover, in the older song, is either a knight or a prince. In the later song, 'les choses sont arrangées à la mode militaire. . . . Le franc chevalier est devenu un brave capitaine' (a transfer of heroic roles from noble to military with which we should now be familiar): George Doncieux, *Le Romancéro populaire de la France*, Paris 1904, 427.

181 Falassi, *Folklore by the fireside*, 106. Falassi gives an example in which a woman dismissed her new love and reinstated her old one in a four-line stanza: both men immediately understood her intention.

182 'si une jeune personne était activement recherchée en mariage pour sa fortune ou sa beauté, les prétendants évincés se vengeaient de l'*ingrate* en la chansonnant ainsi que son *préféré*; la chanson servait aussi les petites rancunes personnelles des montagnards ou leur penchant naturel à ridiculiser les travers de leur prochain': Géhin, 'Gérardmer à travers les ages', 9.

183 Falassi, *Folklore by the fireside*, 114.

mation that folksong collections lack. Fortunately in the case of conscript songs we know both the persons who sang the song – the *classe* – and the occasion – the *tirage*. In their songs the conscripts gave voice to the fears and recriminations of their lovers: 'You promised to me as a pledge/ Your hand, your heart and you fidelity,/ And now you join up/ To go far away from me.'[184] This song shows how different persons might use a text: it could be sung by a woman to express her worries, and also her hope that those worries would be allayed by the departing soldier's promise to her. On the other hand it was popular among the conscripts themselves, in which case it implied their intention to return safe and sound to the village and their girlfriends – 'I'll return here, I hope,/ All covered in laurels/ In military dress/ Like a valiant warrior.'[185] We can surmise that these were the words that their girlfriends wanted to hear: a female dancing rhyme from Raon-l'Etape even put them into the mouth of a soldier: 'Before I leave/ I will be engaged to you./ At my happy return/ I will marry you.'[186] But as the soldier cannot marry during his period of service while his girlfriend can, in some ways he has more to worry about, so it is not surprising that many conscript songs end with the entreaty and promise 'Julie, Julie, my sweet girlfriend,/ Will you always think of me?/ I'm going from here to the frontier/ I will write to you from far away/ I will write you letters/ Letters of love.'[187]

However, the happy homecoming and marriage were dependent on proof of the woman's fidelity during his absence. Several songs – including, as we have seen, the ballad of *Germaine* – contain a test to which the woman is put before the soldier reveals his true identity. In a related theme common in germanophone songs, the pair, unlike Germaine and her count, are not yet married. The man returns unrecognised after seven years to find his true-love wandering in the woods and tells her that he saw her fiancé getting married the day before in the city. Only when she wishes the couple 'as much luck and happiness,/As there are grains of sand in the sea' does he reveal that he himself is her (still unmarried) 'heart's desire'. The song is called, appropriately, *Liebesprobe* – Love test.[188] Neither this heroine nor Germaine get a chance to put their men to a similar test. On the contrary, as we have seen the

184 'Tu m'avais promis pour gage/ Ta main, ton coeur et ta foi,/ Et à présent tu t'engages/ Pour t'éloigner loin de moi': Westphalen, *Chansons populaires*, ii, no. 318: *Eugénie, les larmes aux yeux*.

185 'J'y reviendrai, j'espère,/Tout couvert de lauriers/Sous l'habit militaire/Comme un vaillant guerrier': Garneret, *Un Village comtois*, 307.

186 'Avant que d'm'en aller/ Je vous fiancerai./ A mon joli retour/ Je vous épouserai': Charles Sadoul, 'Chansons populaires lorraines: *Au bout du village* (Ronde)', *Le Pays lorrain* xxi (1929), 521.

187 'Julie, Julie, ma douce amie,/ Penseras-tu toujours à moi?/ J'y pars pour la frontière./ De loin je t'écrirai,/ Je t'écrirai des lettres,/ Des lettres d'amitié': Westphalen, *Chansons populaires*, ii, nos 312, 319: *Amis, rassemblons-nous*.

188 'so viel Glück und Heil,/ Als Sandkörner an dem Meere sind': Pinck, *Verklingende Weisen*, ii. 245, no. 83.

expectation was that the soldier's life would be one of constant amorous adventures. He fulfilled his part of the promise by returning, not through his chastity.

If conscript songs did, as I have suggested, act as messages, then the conversation of which they formed part took place in the brief existence of the *classe*. Promises and plans made during this highly charged time might not survive the actual separation, as a Messin *trimazo* (Mayday songs sung by the young women of the village during their own *tournée*) makes clear: 'I've seen how many handsome boys/ Blown away by the cannons,/ I've seen their beauties distraught/ Three months later totally consoled.'[189] Such unromantic statements are very much less common in folksong collections than lovers who remain loyal even unto death. One may wonder whether they are more realistic but this is to miss the point. 'Song-messages' had their meaning at a particular moment, in a particular set of circumstances, and in their context the declarations of love and fidelity were true, or at least metaphorically so. In the case of the woman her future conduct would remain under the observation of the conscript's friends and family, as Richard's description of a Vosgian *veillée* recalls:

> Often as well a young girl . . . sings some extremely touching and sad laments like the farewells of the volunteers (conscripts) of Vagney. . . . Or again the old ballad that one always listens to with deep interest, of a young and handsome prisoner to whom the gaoler's daughter threatens that she will bury herself in a convent if he does not escape: 'Another lover [I]'ll not have,/ I swear and protest it,/ I'll go into a convent/ There to pray to God for my lover.'[190]

Given that Richard had stated just before that the memory of absent conscript-boyfriends was an important theme for the women present at the *veillée* her song may have been meant as a reassurance that her feelings towards her absent soldier-lover were unchanged. This message could be passed on to him by his family.

However, songs about soldiers (and songs sung by soldiers), as opposed to conscript songs, did not always enjoy the same idyllic ending. There would be no reintegration of the soldier into his community, his initial separation from his home and family would become permanent. There was, after all, the very real possibility that he might die in the service. *La Pauvre Fiancée* in a song from Foville has lost her lover in the wars, so while her contemporaries marry

---

189 'J'ai vu combien de beaux garçons/ Flambés d'un coup par les canons,/ J'ai vu leurs belles désolées/ Trois mois après toutes consolées': Charles Abel, 'Coutumes du pays messin: les trimazos', *L'Austrasie* n.s. i (1853), 260.

190 'Souvent aussi une jeune fille . . . chante quelques complaintes très-touchantes et très-tristes comme celle des adieux des volontaires (conscrits) de Vagney. . . . C'est encore la vieille romance que l'on entend toujours avec un vif intérêt, d'un jeune et beau prisonnier que le fille d'un geolier menacé d'aller s'ensevelir dans un couvent, s'il ne s'enfuit pas: "Un autre amant ne ferai pas,/ Je le proteste et jure,/ Je m'en irai dans un couvent/ Y prier Dieu pour mon amant" ': Richard, *Traditions populaires*, 169.

and have children she will 'remain alone, poor bereaved woman./ Their children will be their joy,/ Seeing them, I will be miserable/ But I will remain a spinster,/ And I will die a true virgin'.[191] Fidelity remained the promise, even after death. Perhaps surprisingly the possibility of the man's death away from home was seldom entertained in francophone folksongs. In songs from germanophone Lorraine, and in particular in soldiers' songs, death was a much more insistent presence. Those from the French side of the language divide were more concerned with the village and its inhabitants.[192]

Events in the village could, however, lead to the death of the soldier. In one song the departing soldier promises fidelity to his 'darling', only to hear that as soon as he had left 'There's her father who marries her off/ He gave her to an old man/ Who was not to her taste.' The news is enough to break his heart fatally.[193] The pressure that fathers put on daughters to marry against their will is as common a theme in folksong as parents' opposition to the object of their children's desires. The possibility that the soldier's girlfriend would willingly be unfaithful to him is, in fact, seldom considered in folksong, but when it does occur the soldier has a ready answer: 'It's me who's wandered the open road so much/ My shiny sword at my side/ My gun on my left shoulder;/ And I make love, to another.'[194]

An alternative marriage was not the only threat hanging over their relationship. In desperation over the soldier's long absence the woman might enter a convent. When, after seven years, the soldier returns to her father's house to ask her hand in marriage, he is told: 'Seeing how you'd been gone so long,/ She took herself into a convent,/Into a convent of Ursulines,/ Where one can see her languishing.' The soldier immediately goes to the convent to confront her 'in a very frosty mood', and to give her the traditional ring as 'proof of my fidelity' during his absence. No sooner has he told her that 'I will never love anyone anymore,/ Sweetheart, remember me' than he falls down dead, leaving his lover lamenting 'If I am held here/ It's me alone who wanted it/ I alone am the cause', absolving the absent soldier of any responsibility for the tragedy.[195] The soldier makes it clear that the choice to enter the convent

---

191 'Je veura mes compegnes meriayes,/ Mas j'pourtra tojos m'chegrin/ Et rest'ra seule, poure andeuyaye./ Zoute jwes s're dans zous-afants,/ An les weyant, j'era mau tamps,/ Mas j'rest'ra tojos bacele,/ Et je meurra an vra pucele': Zéliqzon and Thiriot, *Textes patois*, 260–4, no. 7: *Le poure fiancaye*.

192 Mayer, 'Les Chansons de soldats', 113. A representative song of this morbid kind, often found in *Liederheften*, is offered by Pinck: *Verklingende Weisen*, i. 147: *Soldatenlos*.

193 'Voilà son pèr' qui la marie/ A un vieillard il l'a donnée/ Et qui n'était pas à son gré': Puymaigre, *Chants populaires*, i, no. 5: *Le Dragon*; Westphalen, *Chansons populaires*, i, no. 9: *L'Autre Jour, en m'y promenant*. Puymaigre's variant is in the male voice, Westphalen's in the female.

194 'C'est moi qu'a tant roulé l'pavé,/ Mon épée claire à mon côté,/ Mon fusil sur l'épaule gauche;/ Et je fais l'amour, c'est pour un autre': Westphalen, *Chansons populaires*, i, no. 176: *Ce sont trois garçons de chez nous*.

195 'Vous voyant parti si longtemps,/ Elle s'est rendue dans le couvent,/ Dans un couvent des Urselines,/ Où l'on vit qu'en languissant . . . d'une humeur très froid . . . "preuve de ma

is just as much an act of infidelity by the woman as marriage to another man. The young girl in another messin song is made of sterner stuff. Her mother tells her 'a lover, my girl, you will not have./ Don't speak to me of those men of war!'; instead she intends to put her in a convent, but the girl replies 'To the convent, mother, I will not go;/ The chasseur that I love will prevent me.' The song ends with the soldier in the girl's bedroom and a promise of fidelity on both sides.[196] In folk culture, a woman's marriage to Christ is akin to the soldier's marriage to his regiment.

The drama inherent in the conflict between the lover's vows and the vows of the nun has made this motif popular in local legends about knights and ladies of Lorraine as elsewhere. The best known version of the story was that of the knight in *Damon et Henriette*, one of the most popular of the secular carols distributed by *Imagerie d'Epinal*.[197] This is a further example of how soldiers and nobles became interchangeable. It is also an example of how a song, though largely in the female voice, can express the man's expectations that she will wait for him. A German song that contains this motif puts a slightly different spin on the story: after the woman has entered the convent she dreams that her 'rider' has been killed in Bohemia. Her decision to enter a convent is not just the natural conclusion to 'a sad life' as in the francophone songs but is justified in terms of her ability to pray for his soul and sing him 'a grave-song'.[198] This different treatment of similar motifs on both sides of the language divide is characteristic of the different cultures, often as in this case, in the more overt religiosity of the germanophone songs.

This difference is again apparent in the motif of the soldier returning to find his lover dead. Francophone songs open with the soldier requesting leave of his captain to go and visit his girlfriend. The captain is a father-figure: in reality and in the song he took on the father's role of deciding whether the soldier could go courting and marry.[199] Francophone and germanophone songs initially develop in much the same way: the soldier returns to his lover's house only to be told by her parents that she is dead, he then goes to her grave to mourn her. But in germanophone songs the soldier joins her in death: 'Now give me my love in my arms,/ I wish to rot beside her.'[200] In francophone songs the soldier returns to the army to tell his captain 'Since

---

foi. . . . Je n'aimerai plus personne,/ La belle, souvenez-vous de moi?" . . . "Si je suis détenue/ C'est moi seule qui l'ai voulu,/ C'est moi seule qui en est l'auteur" ': Puymaigre, *Chants populaires*, i, no. 9: *L'Amant fidèle*; Westphalen, *Chansons populaires*, i, no. 10: *Je suis un fillette délaissée*. In Westphalen's version the nun bathes her lover with her tears, he awakes and abducts her from the convent.

[196] ' "un amant ma fille tu n'en auras pas./ De ces hommes de guerr' va, ne m'en parle pas!" . . . "Au couvent, ma mère, non, je n'irai pas;/ Le chasseur que j'aime m'en empêchera" ': Westphalen, *Chansons populaires*, i, no. 172: *Un Amant, ma fille*.

[197] Labourasse, *Anciens Us*, 78.

[198] 'ein Grabgesang': Pinck, *Verklingende Weisen*, i. 117: *Ich ging einstmals spazieren*.

[199] Poinsignon, 'La Chanson populaire en Lorraine', 25.

[200] 'Jetzt gebt ihr mir mein Liebchen in meine Arme,/ Bei ihr will ich verfaulen': Pinck, *Verklingende Weisen*, i. 71: *Nun adje, jetzt muss ich reiten fort*; iii. 209: *Feinslieb im Grab*.

my girl is dead/ I will serve you for ever.' In this song the soldier's original choice of an alternative woman – the regiment – proves irreversible.[201]

This theme is developed in the most popular of all French folksongs, *Le Retour du mari soldat*.[202] It was translated into Italian, Dutch and German and so (unusually) was sung on both sides of the language divide in Lorraine. It concerns a man who goes to war leaving a wife and child, and returns like the prodigal son 'one foot shoed the other naked' to find her running a bar. Initially he does not reveal his identity but sells his horse and pistols because he cannot pay for her wine. With wine the soldier becomes cheerful and starts to sing (soldiers' reputations as singers appear in their songs, just as their talent as narrators is lauded in folktales). His wife recognises the song and thus her husband, and starts to cry, because in the meantime she has remarried and has had at least two more children. Different versions have the soldier threatening to kill the replacement husband, his wife, her new children or their own children, or to divide them and take the eldest to enrol in the army, but the conclusion of the song is always the same: 'I'm going back to the regiment.'[203]

Le Retour du mari soldat started life, like *Joli Capitaine*, as an eighteenth-century soldiers' song which passed into general circulation during the nineteenth.[204] Unlike *Joli Capitaine*, but in common with the tales told about La Ramée, the song suggests that the soldier's reintegration into his home community would be difficult, if not impossible. Songs about soldiers and their loves were not exclusively sung by soldiers and their lovers, but rather singers were able to use the image of the returning warrior to symbolically represent their own relationships. Conscript songs, therefore, were not just used by the *classe* but to express feelings at any parting, because the soldier had become the archetypal traveller. Any jilted boyfriend could use soldiers' songs that renounced false love. The metaphor of the soldier was available to all, but it relied on a popular conception of the soldier as separate from the

---

201 'Puisque la belle est morte/ J' vous servirai toujours': Puymaigre, *Chants populaires*, i, no. 6: *Trop tard*; Westphalen, *Chansons populaires*, i, no. 2: *C'étaient trois jeunes dragons*.
202 *Le Retour du mari soldat* has been recorded fifty-seven times in France alone, according to the far from complete catalogue, not to mention in Belgium, Switzerland and innumerable times in Canada: Laforte and Champagne, *Le Catalogue de la chanson folklorique française*, ii. 415–22. The catalogue lists two versions from Lorraine. I have found another four (not to mention two in German), which gives some indication of the popularity of this song.
203 'Un pied chaussé et l'autre nu/ Je m'en retourne au régiment': Puymaigre, *Chants populaires*, i, no. 4; Menéstrels de Gérardmer, *Arts et traditions*, 213; Westphalen, *Chansons populaires*, i, nos 11, 12, 23; Tiersot, *Histoire de la chanson populaire*, 18. The German variant appeared in Pinck, *Verklingende Weisen*, i. 153. The presence of this song on both sides of the language divide led to insinuations during the Second World War that Puymaigre's collection was really a translation of germanophone folksongs. In fact Puymaigre himself had mentioned that the song was popular among both language groups: 'Chansons populaires du pays messin', *Revue de l'est* n.s. v (1868), 17.
204 Doncieux, *Le romancéro populaire*, 407.

village. His new identity has marked him for life. Initiation into the alternative world of the army, marriage to the alternative woman, the regiment, were not reversible processes. One could not be, in the language of the conscripts' badges, 'fit for the girls' as well as 'fit for service'. In popular mentalities the peasant husband and father and the soldier were not, as the propagandists for the *soldat-laboureur* believed, two facets of the same person. Rather they were two contrasted, even contradictory identities. The soldier had become a different man.

At one level the transformation undergone by the soldier was a physical one. It was not just the imagists, with their returning conscripts, who liked to dwell on this metamorphosis. *Le Retour du mari soldat* reminds us that the soldier, after seven or more years in the army, dressed and looked very differently from the young man who had gone away. He returned under a different identity, to the point that he was frequently unrecognisable, even among those who had known him best. The changes in his appearance meant that he could, if he wished, remain incognito, as in the song of the soldier returning after seven years to find his wife on the point of remarrying. Neither the soldier's mother, who lodges him, nor his in-laws, who invite him to the feast, nor his brother, at whose table he sits, recognise the soldier. Only the bride recognises him as her first husband.[205]

The soldier hides his former identity – as the husband – behind his new identity as a soldier. One might assume that this motif belongs to the realm of folklore, popular only because it makes the final revelation more dramatic. However, real soldiers behaved in ways not dissimilar to their folksong counterparts. When Vaxelaire returned to Vagney after ten years in the revolutionary army he did not go straight home but holed up in a local inn for three days: 'I thought that I could stay there, incognito, until the day of the fair [when he expected his father to come to town].'[206] He does not explain his reasons for behaving thus, but what is revealing is that he was able to remain hidden in the town and among people he had known almost since birth. To the people of Vagney he appeared as a soldier, and only as a soldier, and therefore, by definition, unfamiliar.

That returning soldiers faced problems of recognition (in the era before photography) is not unknown to historians, nor to the wider public since Natalie Zemon Davis's exploration of the case of Martin Guerre was turned, first, into a film and, more recently, a musical.[207] Lorraine has its own Martin Guerre in the shape of Claude-Nicolas Mique. Claude-Nicolas was the son of a well-connected Nancy builder. He was a hot-headed youth who did not get

---

[205] Puymaigre, *Chants populaires*, i. 60, no. 3: *Le Retour du mari*; Westphalen, *Chansons populaires*, i, no. 8: *Le Jour de mes noces*; Lallement, *Echoes rustiques*, 60: *Le Retour du mari*.
[206] 'je m'imaginais que je devais rester là, incognito, jusqu'au jour de la foire': Vaxelaire, *Mémoires d'un vétéran*, 216. His behaviour may have been provoked by the shame of going home on crutches, knowing the burden he was likely to prove to his family.
[207] Natalie Zemon Davis, *The return of Martin Guerre*, Cambridge, Mass. 1983.

along with his father's second wife. In 1745 he joined the *volontaires de Maurepas*, an elite unit which was supposed to form the bodyguard of the Young Pretender. On their way to Scotland their ship was involved in a gun-battle with a British coastguard cutter, in which the *volontaires* were all but annihilated. Claude-Nicolas Mique, along with most of his comrades, was reported to have been buried at sea. Yet in 1775 Claude-Nicolas Mique returned from the dead to claim his share of the inheritance from his brother Richard. Richard Mique was then an architect working for the king at Versailles, and was not at all pleased to be confronted with a long-lost brother and demands for a share of his fortune. Unfortunately his attempts to suppress the latter's claims only made the scandal more public, and the affairs of the Mique family became a sensation in both Paris and Nancy.

The new Mique had some difficulty in establishing his credentials. He was much younger than the real missing soldier, he was several inches shorter and his eyes were of a different colour. His story of his miraculous escape was full of holes, including a period spent on a desert island in the middle of the English Channel, and it was flatly contradicted by the surviving members of the *volontaires* who had witnessed the unequivocal death of Claude-Nicolas. The newcomer was not even sure of his own name, initially calling himself Charles-François. In fact it was rapidly established that his real name was Charles-François Mougenot, born in Epinal in 1733. He married in 1752, but shortly after ran away to join the army. He deserted from the *Gardes-Lorraines* in 1762, and from the *Lyonnais-Infanterie* in 1765. He ended up in Copenhagen six months later where he joined the Danish royal guard, and bigamously married Caroline Ahrenfeld. Although these facts were widely canvassed it did not prevent Mougenot from duping a great many people. When he was tried for imposture in Nancy in 1776 the *lieutenant de police* dryly noted that 'many people born after the date at which he fixes his departure from Lorraine, testify that they recognise him perfectly for ensign Mique'.[208]

Claude-Nicolas Mique had been absent for thirty years, so the people of Nancy might be forgiven for their uncertainties about his identity. But even much shorter lengths of time in the army were sufficient to transform the civilian into an unrecognisable soldier. Ulrich Bräker, a Swiss recruit for the army of Frederick the Great, had been in the Prussian army no more than a year when he deserted after the battle of Lowositz in 1756. Yet when he returned home 'not a single one of my own brothers and sisters recognised

---

[208] 'beaucoup de personnes nées depuis l'époque à laquelle il fixait son départ de Lorraine, assuraient qu'elles le reconnaissaient parfaitment pour le sous-lieutenant Mique': Alfred Hachette, *L'Affaire Mique (1745–1794)*, Paris 1928, 32. Although the imposture was ultimately unsuccessful, Mougenot kept up the mask until his death, and his cause was pursued by his daughter by his second marriage, Catherine Verguier. The Terror provided her with a chance for revenge on the family that had refused to acknowledge her father. She laid false information about the political behaviour of Richard Mique and his son, and they were both guillotined in 1794.

me, and that they were pretty scared at the unusual spectacle of a Prussian soldier addressing them there in full kit, with a large pack on back, hat pulled down low, and a luxuriant moustache'. Bräker kept up the deception with his mother, asking for lodgings for the night. When she demurred, 'I couldn't restrain myself any longer, seized her hand, saying: "Mother! Mother! Don't you know me any more?"' [209]

It is not just the rarity of French soldier's memoirs from the pre-revolutionary era which has led me to quote the example of Bräker, but that his behaviour on his homecoming conformed exactly to the expectations of soldiers expressed in the popular culture of the late eighteenth and early nineteenth centuries. The problems of identity surrounding soldier-sons appealed to the Romantics, whose works may have influenced Bräker's memory. Schlotterbeck's *Walter, der verlohrne Sohn* was probably the most successful of the sentimental ballads composed in huge numbers in Germany between 1770 and 1825. It rose to fame when it was included in the second edition of an anthology of *Lieder für Volksschulen,* published in 1800 and frequently reprinted in the first half of the nineteenth century. From there it made its way into the repertoire of the *Bänkelsanger,* and from their broadsides into the hand-written song books and performances of folksingers, dozens of which were recorded by the *Deutsches Volksliedarchiv* The ballad tells of how Walter, after many years service as an officer in a far-off land, returns to his parents' cottage. The door is opened by his mother, who immediately asks for news of her son whom she fears has died in the army. She does not recognise his voice when he asks for a night's lodging and, although pleading poverty, grants his request. Inside the cottage he finds his father, too old and exhausted to get up from his bed. But although he is moved to tears by their plight and their heartbreaking requests for news of their child, he remains incognito, claiming instead that he knows Walter, he serves in his regiment as a common soldier. He only reveals his identity after he has offered the parents money to relieve them from their misery and they refuse it; they want nothing but their son. [210]

It is possible, but unlikely, that *Walter* was the model for the numerous French folksongs on a similar theme, several of which date from the early

[209] Ulrich Bräker, *The life story and real adventures of the poor man of Toggenburg,* ed. Derek Bowman, Edinburgh 1970, 146. Bräker's account of his metamorphosis highlights only the changes in his appearance: his uniform, his kit, his moustache. However, the army had marked him in ways that would prove longer lasting. As his editor recalls, the months he stayed 'in the service of Frederick the Great were never far from his mind: on the slightest provocation he was likely to start recalling them; they had opened up a new world to him, a world that demanded expression. Once, he got so carried away by his memories that he fell to drilling Prussian-style with a kitchen-knife as a musket, and, presenting arms, gave his hand a bad gash'. Although he was a deserter he remained proud of his identity as a Prussian soldier.

[210] Tom Cheesman, *The shocking ballad picture show: German popular literature and cultural history,* Oxford 1994, 97–106.

years of the first empire, if not the republic. We have already seen one in the margin of Pellerin's print *Le Retour du conscrit*. François the soldier asks a night's lodging of his mother who fails to recognise him after ten years' absence. Initially she refuses – her home is too poor, her nourishment too meagre – but when he asks her if she too has a child who might that night be begging a roof, she relents. Only then does he take her into his arms and tell her that her son has come back to provide for her old age.[211] Lallement collected a version of this song in a manuscript songbook in the Argonne. The differences between Pellerin's version and Lallement's are telling: while Pellerin's mother congratulates her son on his accomplishments and the transformation he has undergone, Lallement's asks anxiously 'Do you return with your papers in order?'[212] However, in both printed and hand-written versions the soldier tests his mother's feelings before he makes her his offer: does she remember her son with sufficient affection to grant hospitality to stranger in his name?

A similar song from the first empire was collected by Puymaigre. Franc-Coeur similarly hides his identity from both his parents when, after fourteen years at the wars, he sits down at table with them in their humble cottage. In his case his mother, after some hesitation, recognises him. Mothers, the song implies, should know their own children, even if they come in the guise of soldiers.[213] The theme was taken up and refashioned for use during France's subsequent wars and military expeditions. Westphalen's collection contains a later song on the theme dating from the invasion of Algiers.[214] It is probable that all these songs, like *Walter*, had their origins in the chapbooks of pedlars and the performances of fair-ground singers. An even later edition, which places the return of the soldier (a zouave), after the Franco-Prussian war, was printed by Claude of Charmes in 1872 for distribution by the Chamagnons. In this version his mother is an innkeeper and the soldier, like Walter, claims to know her son before she guesses his identity for herself.[215]

---

[211] MDAACE 39.3244. This was one of the images used in the prosecution of Pellerin in 1816.

[212] 'Reviens-tu bien en règle?': Lallement, *Folklore et vieux souvenirs*, 171–2: *Le Retour du soldat*. The soldier reassures her that not only does he have his discharge papers in order but also a pension of 500 *francs*, enough to keep them both in comfort.

[213] Puymaigre, *Chants populaires*, i. 208, no. 52: *Joie inespérée*.

[214] Westphalen, *Chansons populaires*, i, no. 21: *En arrivant dans mon pays*. Beauquier collected three versions of this song in Franche-Comté.

[215] Picoche, *Le Monde des chamagnons*, 169–70. The song was clearly designed to inspire confidence in the recently defeated army. Its final verse reads: 'Vous autres garçons du village,/ Vous qui allez servir la patrie,/ Armez-vous toujours de courage/ En allant contre l'ennemi./ Montrez de la vaillance/ En arrivant au champ d'honneur,/ Vous aurez comme moi pour récompense/ La belle étoile de l'honneur.' The song was printed on the back of a *canard*, to the contents of which it was indirectly related. It tells the story of a zouave named Charles Martel, a virtuous and religious soldier, who is falsely accused of firing a commune on the Metz road while marching home from imprisonment in Germany. His

Tom Cheesman, who has studied the ballad of Walter, relates it to the period in European history when 'unprecedented numbers of young people (mainly males) of the lower and middle classes became able to escape paternal authority'. As soldiers (or, increasingly, as factory-workers) they lived in new, urban communities where they were exposed to radical ideas and earned more portable wealth than their parents ever had. No longer were such young men's identities 'constituted by patrilineal descent, tied to place and community, and defined by conferred status', rather they had become fluid and changeable: 'fathers entirely ceased to command symbolic authority as representatives of absolute power sanctioned by tradition. The family as it had always been conceived threatened to disintegrate'. A new model of the family was needed, and was supplied by Rousseau in *La Nouvelle Héloïse* and *Emile*. His ideal family was one bound by affection and virtue, with the mother at the centre as nurturer and teacher. The new model was propagated by a generation of bourgeois intellectuals, such as Schlotterbeck. Hence it is to his mother that Walter, and the French soldiers in the songs above, first appear on their return, rather than the patriarch of the parable of the prodigal son.[216]

In neither the German ballad nor the French folksongs does the soldier give his reasons for hiding his kinship with his parents. His behaviour can only be understood, Cheesman says, if the audience already knew another ballad, *Die Mordeltern*. Pinck recorded the ballad from Pierre Gangloff in 1918.[217] The story concerns two peasant lads who 'wanted to go to the war/ Right in the soldier's life'. They return home after many years, loaded down with their plunder. One lodges with his parents, now innkeepers, but he retains his incognito. Foolishly he shows his wealth to his parents before retiring to bed for the night. The sight of the gold is too much for the mother (in the songs, but not always in other versions of this story, the woman, being 'naturally' the more given to temptation, is the most forward in vice). It drives her to murder the soldier, an act performed by pouring burning fat down his throat while he sleeps, thus underlining the horror. In the Rousseauian world of domestic morality the pan of fat should be used by the mother to nurture her family, not destroy it. Early next morning his comrade comes to see how the family reunion went, only to be told by the innkeeper's wife that the soldier left even earlier. His comrade is worried, the soldier's horse is still in the stable and where should he go, her own son? Only now does she realise the horror of her crime. Overcome by remorse she hangs

innocence is proved on the executioner's scaffold by Sister Marthe, a saintly (and patriotic) nun attached to a military hospital. As we have seen, Charles Martel was only one in a long line of soldiers to suffer the false accusation of arson in the *canards* of nineteenth-century France. Only when he can prove his other identities, as a good Christian and as a dutiful son, is he saved from his unmerited fate.

[216] Cheesman, *The shocking ballad picture show*, 87, 95–6, 100.
[217] Pinck, *Verklingende Weisen*, i. 109, 297.

herself in the attic and the father drowns himself in the brook. The last verse is a curse on gold for bringing so much misery into the world.

Pinck recorded this song from eight singers, and collected many more versions in manuscript songbooks.[218] It was certainly one of the most popular ballads of germanophone Lorraine. According to one of his sister's sources, Katherina Bour, the song had been introduced to the province by a *Bänkelsanger* who had visited her village of Gebenhausen in the years immediately before the Franco-Prussian war. He had a canvas portraying the vital scenes of the story, and he sold for two sous a songsheet for subsequent use in the spinning-room.[219] This version of the song first appeared in print in *Des Knaben Wunderhorn*, but it was certainly older, probably dating from the first half of the eighteenth century. And it is only one of at least sixteen different songs on the theme of *The murdered son* which appeared in cheap print in Germany between 1633 and the late nineteenth century, many of which also passed into oral tradition.[220]

Pinck related the ballad to two reported events, the murder of an (incognito) son by the keeper of the 'Zum güldenen Sieb' in Leipzig in the spring of 1618, and a similar case from Thermels (now Cernolice) in Bohemia dating from 1649, in which a mother unwittingly murdered her soldier-son.[221] It is unlikely that either of these two tragedies ever took place, for these news stories were but two examples of the international tale-type *The murdered son* (AT939a). Since 1618 the story has turned up at different places and times in religious *exempla*, local legends and songs, and may occasionally appear even today as a *fait-divers* in provincial newspapers.[222] It should be classed, according to the definitions used by folklorists, as a 'memorabile' rather than a tale because, unlike most tales, it was always told as a 'true story'. Its ability

---

[218] In addition to the three versions mentioned in *Verklingende Weisen* others remain in Pinck's manuscript collection: Archives départementales de la Moselle 42/J/25, fonds Pinck, A 158,952, A 158,951, A 158,950, A 158,949, A 158,954.

[219] Merkelbach-Pinck, *Lothringer Volksmärchen*, 146: *Der Soldat* (AT939a). Katherine Bour, who narrated this story, knew another on the theme of the murdered son, likewise learnt from a broadside ballad, but in which the son was not a soldier but a returned emigrant who had made his fortune in America: Merkelbach-Pinck, *Aus der lothringer Meistube*, ii. 82: *Die Ruckkehr des Sohnes* (AT939a).

[220] Tom Cheesman, 'The return of the transformed son: a popular ballad complex', *Oxford German Studies* xviii–xix (1989), 88–91. It is probable that at least one of these other songs was already known in Lorraine: Gangloff's version contains borrowed phrases from another ballad on the same theme.

[221] The Leipzig murder was first reported in the *Historische Chronica* of 1634; the Thermels murder first appeared in the *Lübecker Chronica* of 1650. Both reports are reproduced in summary in Maria Kosko, *Le Fils assassiné (AT 939A): étude d'un thème légendaire* (Folklore Fellows Communications cxcviii), Helsinki 1966, 91–3.

[222] The first appearance of *The murdered son* was in a 1618 pamphlet, printed by Edward Allde of London, entitled *News from Perin* [Penryn] *in Cornwall*. It is also summarised in Kosko, *Le Fils assassiné*, 40–9. It was still doing the rounds after the Second World War: Albert Camus read a newspaper version set in Czechoslovakia, which subsequently appeared in his fiction.

to detach itself from historical circumstances only reinforced its credibility for new audiences. Most of the authors, narrators and singers who have repeated the story seem to have believed it; Pinck and Katherina Bour certainly did.[223] Its air of veracity was essential to its purpose: 'the plot could only be credible, and beyond that, popular (and prior to credible, imaginable), in a society where the normative role of sons was to inherit the position and possessions of their fathers, but where this norm was threatened by the emergence of markedly increased chances of upward mobility for young men, away from their home communities'.[224]

The story, although not as popular as in Germany, was certainly well-known in France and in particular in Lorraine.[225] Its first appearance in France was in the form of a *canard*, printed in Paris in 1618, supposedly relating true events from Nîmes.[226] That *canard* also concerned a soldier, returning from years of loyal and well-paid service in Sweden to be murdered by his innkeeper parents. His sister, whom he had met earlier in town, revealed the identity of their victim. Newspaper accounts, setting the murder in Corbeil and in Marseilles, appeared, respectively, in 1727 and in 1732.[227] General Hugo, father of Victor Hugo, told the story as a true narrative of events in Chateaubriant in 1795, witnessed by his fellow officers.[228] A *canard* printed at Lons-le-Saulnier in 1824 set the murder after the fall of Napoleon, the victim an officer returning from imprisonment in Siberia to his father's inn in Montpellier. Implicit in this *canard* is an attack on the breakdown of family relations, repeatedly blamed during the restoration for the 'parricide' of the execution of the king.[229] Three further *canards*, printed in Toulouse, Valence and Quimper (in 1848, 1870 and 1876 respectively), tell the story as happening to François Joseph Richard, zouave, veteran of the wars in Algiers, or Italy or Mexico, and proud wearer of the *étoile d'honneur*.[230]

Both Westphalen and Schamber in the *pays messin* noted a ballad on the

---

223 This, for Kosko, is the essence of the story: 'Son caractère essentiel, en effet, est de vouloir se faire passer pour authentique et d'y réussir à merveille': *Le Fils assassiné*, 348.
224 Cheesman, 'The return of the transformed son', 68.
225 Details of most of the following French versions can be found in Kosko, but an additional seven have been listed by Daniel Fabre and Jacques Lacroix: 'Sur la production du récit populaire: à propos du fils assassiné', *Arts et traditions populaires* xviii (1970), 131–40.
226 The *canard* is reproduced by Jean-Pierre Seguin: *L'Information en France avant le périodique: 517 canards imprimés entre 1529 et 1631*, Paris 1964, no. 69.
227 Kosko, *Le Fils assassiné*, 104–7.
228 Adèle Hugo, *Victor Hugo raconté par un témoin de sa vie, avec oeuvres inédités de Victor Hugo*, Brussels–Leipzig 1863, i. 11. Hugo gave his narrative a political twist; the victim was a republican soldier and the murderer was his *chouan* father.
229 Kosko, *Le Fils assassiné*, 193.
230 Seguin, *Nouvelles à sensation*, 189; 'Les "canards" de fait divers', 36. In a later *canard*, entitled *André le mécanicien*, the returning son is not, for once, a soldier but a successful emigrant back from America.

same theme, which almost certainly had its origins in pedlars' songbooks.[231] In this version the mother is a professional criminal who murders travellers for gain, while the witness of her son's return is his aunt. Again the mother begs the aunt not to denounce her, but she is executed. Although rare in French oral tradition (only one other version has been collected to my knowledge), Maria Kosko discovered several Italian versions which had clearly been translated from French originals dating from period of the revolution and first empire.[232]

The story of *The murdered son* is, according to Cheesman, a reworking of the parable of the prodigal son. We have already seen how the parable, so popular throughout post-Reformation Europe, could be adapted to refer to hot-headed youths seeking adventure in the army, before finding their way home to their families. However, whereas the parable offers

> a utopia of perfect domestic, social and cosmological harmony under a sublime patriarchal authority . . . [*The murdered son*], reversing all the attributes, gives a brutally realistic picture of insoluble conflict between individualists incapable of giving expression to the experience of kinship, in either the profane or spiritual sense, who are driven by egotistical whims.[233]

Cheesman dates the appearance of the story to precisely that period in European history when social and geographical mobility were undermining patriarchal authority. Both the victim and perpetrators had been corrupted by the different values of the emerging capitalist economy. The son rebels against patriarchal authority and runs off to the army to forge a new identity for himself. He grows rich on plunder and returns home in this new guise, the thieving soldier, only to be robbed and murdered by his own parents who are blinded by their own lust for gold. In the early German versions, and in particular those picked up by Jesuits as good material for *exempla*, it is clear that all three, the soldier as well as the parents, deserve their fates because of what they have become.[234] The story was told as a warning of the consequences of urban capitalism destroying the traditional patriarchal values of rural communities: 'The family is not reintegrated in a utopian harmony but annihilated. So the legend articulates a deep anxiety about the very possibility of sustaining any legitimate social order or cultural continuity in the face of the advance of economic and moral individualism.'[235]

The validity of Cheesman's claims is, in part, born out by the memoirs of

231 Westphalen, *Chansons populaires*, i. no. 22: *C'était un pauvre jeun' garçon*; Schamber, *Chansons du folklore lorrain*, 49, no. 19: *C'était un pauvre garçon*.
232 Kosko, *Le Fils assassiné*, 209.
233 Cheesman, 'The return of the transformed son', 68.
234 Kosko, *Le Fils assassiné*, 85–7. In nineteenth-century French versions the son is usually an idealised soldier (he is, after all, a member of the *Légion d'honneur*), and all the blame attaches to the mother, but in those from germanophone Lorraine the son was still depicted as meriting punishment.
235 Cheesman, *The shocking ballad picture show*, 89.

the Parisian glazier Jacques-Louis Ménétra. Something of a prodigal son himself, he spent most of the period between 1757 and 1764 as a journeyman enjoying the many pleasures offered by the towns of southern France. Ménétra includes the tale of *The murdered son* in his account of his travels, written up on his return to Paris, but as if he himself had visited the scene, in a village in the Cevennes, just days after the event. This is unlikely. Ménétra almost certainly read the story in a pamphlet or heard it declaimed by a pedlar at a fair, but he internalised it to the extent that he retold it as true, and even vouched for its veracity by claiming he was actually there. Slightly earlier he told a similar story, again probably acquired from a chapbook or *canard* but narrated as personal testimony, of another prodigal who runs away from home to join the army. Fourteen years later he comes back, but incognito. He refuses to reveal his real identity until he has tested his parents' affections, until his mother says she would know her own son in ten thousand. Only then does he show her the mark by which she might know him. The story does not have the ending that we might expect from our reading of similar narratives, for here the mother dies of shock and the son runs away again. The significance of this second story, according to Ménétra's editor Daniel Roche, was that he himself was on the way home, having become quite rich during his years of travel. As he had left Paris under a cloud he was not sure of the reception he would receive from his father, with whom he was always on difficult terms, nor from his maternal grandmother, his surrogate mother. Ménétra used the story to structure his own behaviour towards his family, promising himself that he would not frighten his grandmother in the same way. The personal meaning of *The murdered son* is not so clear in the text, but it is reasonable to surmise that it reflected some of Ménétra's anxieties about his relationships with his family.[236]

We can now see why the actions of Walter and his French counterparts need the story of *The murdered son* to be comprehensible. As Cheesman says, '*Walter* only makes sense because Walter himself arrives home suspecting the parents will be predisposed to kill him. . . . In demonstrating that such fears need not be justified, the song evidently performed a function that was highly valued in nineteenth-century Germany.'[237] The need was likely to be all the greater in France, where the revolution had (according to Lynn Hunt) ushered in something of a crisis in familial relationships.[238] In these dangerous circumstances songs on the *Walter* theme offered reassurance. The young man's new identity as a soldier (and by metaphorical extension any wanderer) need not completely sever him from his former relationships, nor definitively prevent the resumption of his former identities as son and peasant.

---

236 Jacques-Louis Ménétra, *Journal of my life*, ed. Daniel Roche and Robert Darnton, New York 1986, 78, 94–5, 248.
237 Cheesman, *The shocking ballad picture show*, 105.
238 Lynn Hunt, *The family romance of the French revolution*, London 1992.

In the first two decades of the nineteenth century, the period that saw the flourishing popularity of *canards* and folksongs on the theme of the unrecognisable soldier (whether murdered, falsely imprisoned or simply welcomed home), one song bucked the trend. Again spread by fairground-singers, *Le Soldat Simon* remained, according to Garnier, a popular number for many years.[239] Lallement found a version in an Argonne songbook, and Puymaigre recorded another near Metz.[240] Simon is a prisoner-of-war recently released from captivity in England.[241] On his return he makes no attempt to disguise himself, hammering on his parents' door and shouting 'I'm your man Simon,/ Who's returned from England'. Nor do his family entertain any doubts that he is telling the truth, his mother cries 'Here's Simon, our grown-up lad'. There is one aspect of his identity, however, which is in doubt: whether or not he is alive. Unfortunately, Simon's arrival has been preceded by his death-certificate, and his family are convinced that it is a ghost knocking at their door. They bar the way, sprinkle holy water over the threshold, promise to pay for a mass for the dead, anything to make him go away. Only when they see Simon eat and drink are they reassured that the certificate was a mistake and that it is really their son before them, because 'I know full well that down there/ The dead don't eat!'

Simon is reunited and reintegrated with his family and home through the symbol of community and togetherness, the shared meal, or as Simon puts it, 'Since I sup [with you],/ Let's all embrace!'[242] *Le Revenant*, as this song was also known, was written in a kind of pastiche rural dialect, used by street-singers to mock the habits of the peasantry. *Le Soldat Simon* is a humorous swipe at the superstitions of country bumpkins, and yet the family's initial reaction towards their son is revealing. He had been to places and seen things they would never see and could only know about from his stories. He had almost certainly witnessed the death of others, possibly at his own hands, and more than likely come close to death himself. He had, therefore, been intimate with the realm of the supernatural. Simon was not the first soldier to come back from the other side.

[239] Garnier, *Histoire de l'imagerie populaire*, 300.
[240] Lallement, *Echoes rustiques*, 55: *Le soldat Simon*; Puymaigre, *Chants populaires*, 205, no. 51: *Le Revenant*.
[241] The earliest version of this song to be discovered is in a manuscript song-book dated 1814, the year when large numbers of prisoners-of-war were making their way home: Coirault, *Notre Chanson folklorique*, 23.
[242] ' "J' suis vot' grand Simon,/ Qui r'viens d'Angleterre" . . . "V'là Simon, not' grand gas' . . . j'sais bien qu'là-bas/ Les morts ne mangent pas!" . . . "Puisque j'casse la croûte,/ Embrassez-moi tourtous!" '

The soldier and the supernatural

Not all soldier-sons got the chance to return home; that is the tragedy under-lying this comic tale told in the Vosges about a couple whose only son was killed in the army. One day another soldier passes their door, and in response to the mother's question, tells her he comes from Paris. The woman, however, mishears, and, thinking he said Paradise, enquires if he had seen her son: 'Oh yes, definitely I saw him, he's at the gate of Paradise, he can't go in . . . because he doesn't have the pennies to enter.' The woman is horrified but, as she happens to have some cash from the sale of a cow, asks the soldier to take the necessary money to her son, to which he readily agrees. When her husband returns home he is furious with her, and sets off after the soldier at a gallop. The soldier, guessing that he might be pursued, reverses his jacket, so it now looks grey rather than blue. The man accosts him unwittingly, asks whether he has seen a soldier in a blue jacket: 'Absolutely, we're travelling together; he's taking his trousers down behind that hedge.' The man asks the soldier to hold his horse while he goes to find him, but as soon as the man is out of sight the soldier mounts the horse and rides off. The man returns home in a very bad mood and announces 'you gave him the cow to go to Paradise, and I gave him the horse to go to the devil'.[243]

This tale is an old joke. It was told by the Alsatian monk Pauli in his 1522 collection entitled *Schimpf und Ernst*, and appeared in many other sixteenth-century jest books, such as Hans Sachs.[244] In these literary Renaissance versions the traveller is a student from Paris. One can imagine that, in the urban and scholarly circles in which Pauli and Sachs were read, the story provided a few laughs at the expense of simple country-folk. In those versions subsequently collected from the oral tradition, including Cosquin's, the cheating traveller becomes just a vagabond. As we have seen in relation to pedlars, vagabonds often claimed supernatural knowledge and used their supposed powers to beg food from unwilling farmwives, which is precisely what Cosquin's tramp does.[245] It is easy to see how a veteran came to replace the tramp in this Vosgian version, for to many people there was little differ-ence between them.[246] This tale exemplifies the popular verdict on the

---

[243] ' "Oh! si fait je l'ai vu, il a d'sus l'heuch do Pérédis et i n's'ra-mé rontret . . . paceque i n'et point d'sous pou rontret." . . . "Si fait," dit lo soudère, "i fait route évo mé; il a derr' lé hâye to-la qui pose si châse." . . . "t'li et d'net lé torech' pou n'allet o Pérédis, et mé j'li et d'net lo chwouà pou'n allet au diàle" ': Charles Sadoul, *Traditions et vieilles histoires du pays lorrain*, Nancy 1906: *Lo soudère qu'vet o Perédis* (AT1540). Another version of this tale-type that has a soldier as the protagonist can be found in Méraville, *Vie et oeuvres*, 51–3, no. 5: *La Veuve remariée et le soldat* (AT1540).

[244] Johannes Pauli, *Schimpf und Ernst*, ed. Johannes Bolte, Berlin 1924, i. 271–2, no. 463: *Der Man gab ein das Pferd* (AT 1540).

[245] Cosquin, *Contes populaires de Lorraine*, i, no. 22: *Jeanne et Brimboriau* (AT1540, AT1653).

[246] A thorough listing and comparison of variants from different regions can be found in

soldier as a thieving vagabond, but also confirmed his reputation for cunning and storytelling (story also meaning a fib). Like the returning soldiers we have just examined he was a master of disguise, changing his identity to suit his purpose. And at least some people took him seriously when he told them he could visit the other side.

Although *The student from paradise* (AT1540) remained a joke even after the soldier replaced the student, other folktales took the soldier's claims to supernatural travel more seriously. A Breton version of *The man as heater of hell's kettle* (AT451) illustrates the point. An old soldier returns home after seventeen years in the army, thinking about his old officer: 'Oh! the wicked captain, he was bad, yes, as bad as the devil!' Soon after he meets a well-dressed man who offers him employment keeping the fires under his cauldrons well fuelled. The stranger turns out to be a good master, 'even coffee and tobacco were not forgotten'. One day he hears a voice from inside the cauldron: 'Soldier, moderate the fire.' It turns out to be his old captain and at first the soldier intends to double the heat, but the captain explains he is in hell. He also tells him how he can get the better of the devil: when he comes to be paid he should refuse the gold but ask instead for the pair of old worn trousers hanging over the fireplace. The devil is surprised: 'You have spoken to someone smarter than yourself; but it's all the same to me, you served me well, I'll repay you for that if the occasion arises.' The trousers turn out to be magic, their pockets are always full of gold coins. An innkeeper discovers the secret and steals them, then claims the soldier stole all his money. The soldier is about to be hanged when the devil turns up and rescues him.[247]

As Marie-Louise Tenèze has demonstrated, *The man as heater of hell's kettle* is one of the tale-types that cross the boundary between fantasy and belief, with some variants being told as testimonies to the real existence of hell and damnation.[248] Although none of the French versions in which soldiers visit hell were recorded as factual accounts, some motifs shared with the tale certainly crop up in popular beliefs about soldiers. For example, a legend from Boulay recorded at the beginning of the nineteenth century tells of a soldier who, returning home to his parents' home at Saarlouis, stopped to pick up some grains of wheat under the walls of the 'the devil's castle'. When he got

Antti Aarne, *Der Mann aus dem Paradies* (Folklore Fellows Communications xxii), Helsinki 1915.

247 ' "Ah! le méchant capitaine, il était méchant, oui, méchant comme le diable!" ... même le café et le tabac n'étaient pas oubliés ... "Soldat, modère le feu!"..... "Tu as parlé à plus fin que toi; mais c'est égal, tu m'as rendu service, je te revaudrai cela si l'occasion s'en présente" ': Paul Sébillot, 'Contes et légendes de Haute-Bretagne', *Revue des traditions populaires* xvi (1901), 123–5: *Le Vieux Militaire* (AT475).

248 Marie-Louise Tenèze, 'The devil's heater: on the "contexts" of a tale', *Journal of Folklore Research* xx (1983), 197–219.

home he found that they had changed into so many gold coins.[249] This is a common motif relating to dealings with the devil: refuse the gold coins he offers you as they will turn into old leaves; instead take the pile of wood-shavings for these will become gold. Another young soldier learnt this to his cost when, having accepted a purse of gold from the devil, he opened it to find only pieces of copper.[250] This story was related in the chronicles of the university of Pont-à-Mousson, about a boy of good family who ran away from home to join the army. It concludes with the message that 'he returned home to his mother, did penance and changed his conduct'. The moral of the tale seems to be that military prodigal sons put themselves at risk from the devil.

Several of the motifs that we have seen in tales of La Ramée can also be found in stories told as true legends or even personal narratives. The *Devil in the knapsack* (AT330B, one of La Ramée's preferred vehicles) was a variation on the tale the more usual version of which concerns a boy who has never experienced fear and wants to know what it is, so he agrees to spend a night in a haunted castle. As fearlessness is one of the soldier's main characteristics it is not surprising that in eleven of the fifty-six French versions he takes the boy's place. The hauntings are usually resolved by the discovery of bodies buried in non-sanctified land, or a stolen treasure that the ghost insists must be returned to its rightful owner. The same motif plays an important part in legends that place soldiers in similar environments. According to a story told to Henry Bardy, the ghost of a father whose son refused to pay for a mass for his soul haunted a room in a house in the village of Meroux, near Belfort. During the Thirty Years War, when Swedes occupied the village, a cavalryman was billeted on the house. The inhabitants tried to persuade him not to sleep in the haunted room, but the soldier laughed at their fears: 'Is it nothing but that? Quick, let them give me this room! God be praised! We won't sleep out this evening, neither my beast or me.' During the night, however, the ghost appears to him and forces the Swede, despite being a Protestant, to have a mass said for the rest of his soul.[251] A similar story, although without such a conclusive ending, was told by the Count Despilliers (to anyone who would listen) about his experiences in his regiment's winter quarters in Flanders.[252] In a story told to Merkelbach-Pinck and supposed to have taken place in 1869, a ghost appeared to a soldier and asked him to have three masses said for his soul. Interestingly, his non-military companion was unable to see the ghost; he only appeared to the soldier.[253]

The connections between soldiers and the devil, revenants, and more

---

[249] Ernest Auricoste de Lazarque, 'Histoires surnaturelles de Boulay, Moselle', *Revue des traditions populaires* xx (1905), 168–9: *Le Château du diable*.

[250] Calmet, *The phantom world*, i. 215.

[251] 'N'est-ce que cela? allons vite qu'on me donne cette chambre! Dieu soit loué! nous ne coucherons dehors, ce soir, ni ma bête ni moi': Henri Bardy, 'Deux Légendes alsaciennes, et une bretonne', *Revue d'Alsace* viii (1857), 273–8.

[252] Calmet, *The phantom world*, i. 209.

[253] Merkelbach-Pinck, *Aus der lothringer Meistube*, i. 172: *Dr Soldad*.

generally with the darker side of the supernatural, were not just folktale fantasies, they were also matters of belief. At Mourot in the Vosges the story was
told of an old soldier of the empire who had picked up a 'grimoire' or
spell-book during his plunder of a German monastery. He had literally come
back with forbidden knowledge in his knapsack, and that he had obtained it
by sacrilege made it all the more terrible. Once when he was obliged to clear a
field of stones, he decided to get the devil to undertake it for him. Using his
spell-book he summoned the devil who put a legion of little demons to work.
While they busied themselves he desperately tried to find the spell to make
the devil disappear, but unfortunately that page was missing from the book.
Seeing his chance, the devil fell on the soldier thinking to kill him and take
his soul, 'but the devil was tangling with a tough customer. He who had
valiantly beaten the Russians and Austrians at Austerlitz had no more fear of
Lucifer or of Satan in person than of Cossacks and Kaiserlicks [a derogatory
term for Austrian soldiers].'[254] The soldier of legend was as much a match for
the devil as his folktale counterpart. He cried out to a passer-by to go and
fetch the priest, and just as the soldier was about to succumb, the priest drove
off the devil with holy water. The peasant who told this legend to Thiriat
pointed to the very field where the battle took place; it was still called the
'champ de diable', thus stressing the validity of his tale.[255]

One reason why soldiers were presumed to have access to supernatural
power was their proximity to death. We have seen in chapter 3 that it was the
custom in western France to hold a wake as if for the dead when a conscript
left his village. In the Vendée, even in recent years, a bottle would be buried
in the garden of the conscript's home, to be disinterred from its coffin only if
he safely returned.[256] Exile from his community was akin to death, particularly in the case of the soldier who might very well die during his absence. If
he survived it was in part because he adjusted to the ways of the army, which
were anathema to the code of the village. The soldier was thieving, licentious
and lazy, and spent his time in bad company, the company of those seduced by
the devil. He became a prodigal son, lost to God. He might have learnt to
read, itself a suspicious talent because it gave access to illicit knowledge. And
he had broken the taboo on killing men. Both in the army and after his
discharge he was a nomad, so he shared the bad reputation of other vagabonds, and also the fear they inspired because of the supernatural powers they

---

254 'mais le diable avait affaire à forte partie. Celui qui avait vailliamment battue les
Russes et les Autrichiens à Austerlitz n'avait pas plus peur de Lucifer ou de Satan en
personne que des Cosaques et des Kaiserlicks': Thiriat, *La Vallée de Cleurie*, 359.
255 This story, although from a different source, is substantially repeated by L. Godat
where a Christian name – Nicolas or 'Coliche' – is given to the soldier. His sister was a
well-known local witch in the eighteenth century: *Notice historique sur la commune de
Tholy, Vosges*, Remiremont 1899.
256 Massignon, 'Coutumes et chants de conscrits', 188. Apparently this ritual burial was
still commonplace in the 1970s (personal communication), and remnants of similar practices can be found in other parts of France.

claimed for themselves. A marginal in the life of the community he was between the worlds of the living and the dead. This position gave him supernatural power. In 1874 the former marine and postman in the southern Vosges, Emile N . . ., was warned by the *garde-champêtre* about three families of local witches, from whom he should never accept hospitality. Foolishly he visited one farm, and found himself under a spell that forced him to leap into a chasm. Miraculously he was unharmed. When he told a local wise-woman about his experiences she asked him ' "Have you been under arms honestly?" "Yes", said N. . ."I [took part in] five campaigns in the colonies." "For this reason," said she, "these people have no authority over you, without that they would have many cruelties against you." '[257]

The suggestion here is that the soldier's 'mastery of fire' saved him from evil. But it was also a skill he shared with the devil.[258] As we have seen, the matter of his trade – iron – was widely used in the performance of magic. In an earlier period soldiers' power to deliver death through fire and iron made them objects of superstitious horror. According to Robert Muchembled: 'Soldiers inspire in other men a strange terror, a little supernatural, even if they do not have the real means to impose their force.'[259]

Soldiers' skills with these materials made them akin to blacksmiths, and in reality there were strong connections between these two professions: service in the cavalry, artillery and specialist arms was used as an apprenticeship in the metal trades, particularly in Lorraine.[260] Blacksmiths shared several character traits with soldiers. They enjoyed reputations as freethinkers and as storytellers, or at least their forge was the place to hear tales told. When Jesus visited the smith (and future saint) Eloi in order to take his pride down a peg, he found 'a . . . gossip-shop of men in the lean-to'.[261] Smiths were also feared for their supernatural knowledge: they often combined their work with a vocation as a healer. Conscripts resorted to them for a means, magical or physical, to avoid the draft. Although this made the blacksmith a figure of respect, it also made him feared. Even at the beginning of this century 'One

---

[257] ' "Avez-vous porté les armes honnêtement?" "Oui", fit N. . . [*sic*] "J'ai cinq campagnes aux colonies." "Pour cette cause," dit-elle, "ces gens n'ont eu aucune autorité sur vous, sans cela ils auraient commis bien des cruautés à votre égard." ': Coulon, 'Légendes, croyances', 229–30.

[258] Mircea Eliade, *The forge and the crucible: the origins and structures of alchemy*, 3rd edn, Chicago 1978, 106.

[259] 'Les militaires inspirent bien aux autres hommes une terreur étrange, un peu sacrée, même s'ils n'ont pas les moyens réels de s'imposer de force': Muchembled, *La Violence au village*, 117.

[260] Kappaun, *La Conscription en Moselle*, 205; Labate, *Le Recrutement de l'armée*, 50.

[261] 'in quoiraïe d'hommes dans lè râwe': Adam, *Les Patois lorrains*, 441: *Lé Conversion dé St Eloué* (AT753). 'Couarail' is a common dialect term in Lorraine where it is usually applied to gatherings of women. See also Merkelbach-Pinck, *Brauche und Sitte*, 44–5.

ran back to him very often, because he was at once sorcerer, healer, doctor and vet. He inspired such fear that his counsels were always followed.'[262]

It is not surprising, therefore, that smiths and soldiers are interchangeable characters in a number of tale-types. In the Auvergnat soldier Piquenot's tale of *Jean de l'Ours*, quoted above, the hero is a smith endowed with superhuman strength, but in another variant of the same tale-type the hero is La Ramée.[263] A similar transition took place when the legend of Saint Eloi, patron of blacksmiths, crossed the genre boundary into folktale. According to legend Jesus proved to the smith Eloi that he was not, as he claimed 'master of all masters', by performing the miracle of recasting an old woman young again. When Eloi put his mother (or wife or mother-in-law) in the forge she, of course, burnt to death.[264] However, in France, the upshot of this miracle usually concerned, not a smith, but a soldier. In a Beauceron variant, La Ramée, having been deserted by his travelling companion Christ, tries his luck as a 'recaster of old women'. Unfortunately his customers stay dead and he is about to be executed when Christ returns to resuscitate the patients.[265] In a Comtois variant of the same tale Saint Peter scolds Raramée for attempting the miracle. Raramée responds, with the same unconcern which characterises all his utterances: 'You've got no reason to worry, I don't want to retry it, whether they die or don't die, it's all the same to me.'[266]

One folktale hero who follows the path of professional advancement leading from the army to the blacksmith's forge is the Breton soldier *Sans-Souci*, so-called 'because of his jolly temperament and happy character'. Travelling back from the army, perhaps with his papers in order, perhaps not – the storyteller claims such matters are unimportant – he is invited to spend the night in a castle haunted by the devil. Sans-Souci agrees: 'I never was a coward, and it would not displease me to see the Devil up close, I've heard him spoken of many times and I still don't know him. Perhaps he's not as bad as people say, after all.' As we might have suspected the devils know Sans-Souci well, addressing him familiarly in the 'tu' form as 'old friend': none the less Sans-Souci expels them from the castle with the help of some holy water he had picked up the night before. In recompense Sans-Souci is offered one of the seigneur's daughters in marriage. The old soldier replies (characteristically refusing a misalliance), 'My lord, I have not merited so much honour, and I don't aspire so high. I'm a blacksmith by trade, like my father, and if you

---

[262] 'On recourait très souvent à lui, car il était à la fois sorcier, guérisseur, médecin et vétérinaire. Il inspirait une telle crainte qu'on suivait toujours ses conseils': Febvre, 'Une Enquête', 606.

[263] Cosquin, *Contes populaires de Lorraine*, ii, no. 52: *La Ramée* (AT301B, only in note form).

[264] Tenèze, *Le Conte populaire française*, iv. 148–52.

[265] 'fondeur de vieilles': Pétigny, 'Contes de la Beauce', 182–3, no. 15: *La Ramée* (AT753, AT330).

[266] 'T'as pas besoin d'avoir peur, j'en veux jamais rentreprendre, qu'i' meurent ou qu'i' meurent pas, ça m'est égal': Garneret, *Contes recueillis en Franche-Comté*, 46, no. 5: *Le Vieux Raramé* (AT330, AT753).

want to make me happy build me a forge by the side of the main road. The lord agrees, and Sans-Souci sets up in business. One day his forge is visited by two travellers, who much admire his work. The younger offers him three wishes, the elder prompts 'Paradise' but instead the soldier wishes that his pear-tree should bear fruit all year round, that whoever sits down on his bench can not get up again unless he says so, and for a magic pack of cards. His wishes are granted, the travellers being none other than Jesus and Saint Peter. Sans-Souci works away until Death comes to fetch him. Sans-Souci asks him to wait while he finishes shoeing a horse, so Death takes a seat on the bench, and becomes stuck there. This situation continues for months and years, and every time Death suggests that it is time to go Sans-Souci 'amused himself by whistling and laughing in his face, and this went on for a long time'. In the meantime Death is absent from the world, people age but get no relief. In the end Sans-Souci shuts up his forge and, leaving Death there, goes out into the world. He meets a well-dressed man who offers to play him at cards for his soul. Sans-Souci quickly realises that this is 'old William', a local name for the devil, but says to himself 'No problem, you don't know who you're dealing with, you who they call cunning.' The devil may have hoped that he was sure to win when using 'the devil's picture-book', but cards are also the 'soldier' gospel', and Sans-Souci still has his magic pack. The devil keeps raising the stakes, until hell is emptied. Then, in a fury, he disappears in a puff of smoke. Sans-Souci continues to wander and is struck by the suffering of all the aged waiting to die, so he returns home and releases Death. Death starts catching up with his back-log by taking Sans-Souci himself. At heaven's gate the soldier-smith is turned away by Saint Peter for having refused Paradise when it was offered, but when he reaches hell the devil wants nothing more to do with him. So he goes back to Saint Peter, and while the latter is chatting, he throws his cap in. Saint Peter tells him to go and fetch it but instead he sits on it, and when the angels try to dislodge him he claims 'Here I am on my own property, and nobody has the right to chase me off.' God agrees, and thus Sans-Souci found his place in heaven.[267]

If the collector Luzel had quizzed the narrator of this tale, the cobbler Jean le Person, or the audience gathered in his workshop in Plouaret 1869, as to

---

[267] 'Il y avait une fois un soldat breton nommé Sans-Souci, à cause de son humeur joyeuse et de son heureux caractère, qui revenait de l'armée. . . . Les uns disent qu'il avait son congé en règle; d'autres prétendent qu'il avait déserté; mais peu nous importe. . . . "Je n'ai jamais été poltron, et je ne serais même pas fâché de voir un peu de près le diable, dont j'entends parler si souvent et que je ne connais pas encore. Peut-être n'est-il pas aussi méchant qu'on le dit, après tout." . . . "Monseigneur, je n'ai mérité tant d'honneur, et je n'aspire pas si haut. Je suis maréchal-ferrant de mon état, comme l'était mon père, et si vous voulez me rendre heureux, faites-moi bâtir une forge au borde de la grande route." . . . il se contentait de siffler et de lui rire au nez; et cela dura longtemps ainsi. . . . "N'importe! tu ne sais pas ce qui t'attend, toi que l'on nomme le malin." . . . "Je suis ici sur mon bien, et personne n'a le droit de m'en chasser" ': Luzel, *Légendes chrétiennes*, i. 311–28: *Sans-Souci où le maréchal-ferrant et la mort* (AT326, AT330).

whether they believed the story, the answer would probably have been no. This does not mean that we can dismiss it as a fantasy, because the fantasy drew on the audience's preconceptions about soldiers and their doings. The same story could not be told about a tailor and still be credible within the terms of the genre, which called for a suspension of disbelief. The motifs involving fearlessness, cunning, generosity, vagrancy, cheerfulness and informality even in the face of Death himself would have made sense to their audience when related to an old soldier because they fitted the image that they already had in their minds. This was not of the *soldat-laboureur*, the patriotic embodiment of national virtue, but the vagabond prodigal son turned 'vieux moustache' of folklore.

And at least the tale of Sans-Souci and Death explains one fact that everybody knows about old soldiers: they do not die, 'they simply fade away'.[268]

268 Frank Richards, *Old soldiers never die*, London 1933, 324.

Conclusion: 'Two Races of Men'?

With the apotheosis of the old soldier some readers may feel that history has been left far behind; we have opted for the world of fantasy. Although the longevity of soldier-memorialists such as Gabriel Noël and Jean-Claude Vaxelaire was impressive (they represented, after all, a select band of survivors), finally even they could not escape the inevitable conclusion of the life-cycle. Although I have tried throughout this book to show when and how popular attitudes towards the military were shaped by material factors such as wars and laws, not every aspect of soldiers' representation is readily connected to historical reality. Contrary to the folktale-image, not only did old soldiers die, but before they did so many of them had also settled down in their home village, re-adapted to agriculture, married and raised a family, and finally become pillars of the community. The disreputable tramp La Ramée was not necessarily an accurate characterisation of all veterans: he was a mythic figure. But if popular attitudes to soldiers were formed around myths, what is the significance of this study to understanding the history of modern France?

One subsidiary purpose has been to encourage an appreciation of the products of popular culture. Not everyone will respond to the aesthetic qualities of a coloured woodcut, nor enjoy reading a collection of folktales, but it may help if one can visualise the place that these objects held in the lives of the people who created or used them. When written down and edited, a folksong is in danger of being judged according to the values of the literary critic and found wanting. We are unsure what the song is supposed to tell us. But the explanation for this difficulty is precisely why the song is such a valuable historical source. Because a writer intends his work for posterity, to communicate with unknown people in unknown situations, it loses its historical specificity. Every new generation of readers is invited to engage with the text and take what it wants from it. A singer, on the other hand, does not expect anyone other than those immediately present to hear his song: and while the song may have a history as part of a tradition, it is created in that moment for that moment alone. Our participation is merely secondary. This is why folksongs, and other forms of oral literature, are such wonderful windows onto the past. Only if we can imagine hearing the song in its original context, as a communication between a particular singer and a particular audience at a particular time, will we be able to glimpse the outlines of its possible meanings. If we understand more clearly the meaning, it is easier to admire the form.

However, those readers still not convinced of the qualities of oral literature may none the less recognise how the soldier of popular imagination has influenced better known artists. The relative ease with which the popular conception of the soldier has entered into 'high art' (compared with the limited impact of the elite's preferred model – exemplified by Puymège's Chauvin – on the oral tradition), might lead us to reconsider our notions of elite cultural hegemony. Several examples of literature's borrowing's from popular culture have been mentioned in the course of this book, from Diderot's *Jacques the fatalist* to the grandfather of Spyri's *Heidi*. However, traces of the folkloric soldier can be found over a wider area and time-span: Charles Ramuz presents an obvious starting point, Thomas Hardy only slightly less so, but not everyone might immediately detect his influence on Alain Robbe-Grillet for instance. And yet, once one is familiar with *La Ramée*, it is difficult not to see *In the labyrinth* as a modernist reworking of the folktale. But perhaps literature's clearest debt to folklore is offered by Jaroslav Hašek in the figure of *The good soldier Svejk*. The hero of this masterpiece has not always been well-served by his critics: they have tried (as in Bertolt Brecht's *Schweyk in the Second World War*) to turn Svejk into an 'everyman' figure, whereas he more closely resembles the old soldier of popular culture: a marauder, a vagabond, a storyteller. The contradictions of Svejk's character, which so many commentators explore at length, simply dissolve when compared with the tales of *La Ramée* or his cognates in other languages such as the Grimms' *Bruder Lustig*.[1] The war was not an environment that Svejk merely survived, it was where he thrived. Hašek, a habitual wanderer, was well acquainted with the oral tradition of many communities, from gypsy camps to prison dormitories, not to mention the army.

But Svejk's *Anabasis* has once again led us away from the particular realities of eighteenth- and nineteenth-century France. For the historian it is not enough to suggest how collective myths inspire particular fictions: they must be shown to generate actions that can be recorded and (ideally) measured. The characterisations that peasants and soldiers held about themselves and each other should not only fill their dreamscapes, but also affect their actual social relations. To demonstrate how the popular concept of the soldier may have actually influenced peasant behaviour, let us consider two related debates about the history of France.

The first debate has largely been framed by military historians: when did the French army and the French nation become reconciled? It is assumed (and confirmed by the collective memories of Lorrainer peasant communities) that in the reign of Louis XIV relations between peasants and soldiers were similar to Grimmelshausen's vision of 'two races of men in the world . . . pursuing one another so cruelly'.[2] Although John Lynn has shown that Louis XIV took steps to reduce the sources of conflict between his army and his

---

[1] For two such explorations by leading critics of Hašek's work see Radko Pytlík, *Jaroslav Hašek and the good soldier Schweik*, Prague 1983, 44–58; Cecil Parrott, *Jaroslav Hašek: a study of Svejk and the short stories*, Cambridge 1982.

[2] Hans Jacob Christoph von Grimmelshausen, *The adventures of Simplicissimus*, 1st English edn, London 1912 (1st German edn, 1668), 33.

subjects (even though the *dragonnades* and the Cévennes campaign suggest some serious limitations to his sympathies) he found little evidence of popular enthusiasm for the military in the seventeenth century.[3] When, then, was 'the enmity which there is ever between soldiers and peasants' overcome? Was it in 1709 as Corvisier has tried to argue, or in the last decades of the *ancien régime* as Bois and Chagniot suggest, or was it the declaration of 'la patrie en danger' and the volunteer armies of Year II which finally fused citizen and soldier into one republican mass, as Bertaud urges? Should we look to the Napoleonic centralisation and bureaucratisation of the military described by Woloch, or to the development of national culture in the nineteenth century as explored by Puymège, or the heightened awareness of international tensions in the 1840s put forward by Girardet, or the arrival of mass society in the 1860s as implied by Michael Howard (for Europe in general rather than just France)? Or, following Weber, was the third republic really responsible for this union, the necessary precursor to the mass slaughter of 1914? In fact none of these historians takes quite such a linear view of the changing relationship between French peasant and French soldier as this; they are all quite aware of the potential fluctuations, continuities, survivals and revivals which add shades and tones to their general assertions. Yet each implicitly accepts that there was, or there should be, a time when a society and its army becomes as one. But in rural popular culture the distinctions between peasants and soldiers were still being articulated at the very end of the nineteenth century. When was the moment of fusion as far as our singers and narrators were concerned?

Perhaps, on the evidence presented here, one might argue that throughout the eighteenth and nineteenth centuries peasants continued to view soldiers with a mixture of hostility and admiration. This is not really a paradox, the two often go hand-in-hand as we have already noted in the French army's enthusiasm for the dress (and attitudes) of its enemies, whether Hungarian hussars or North African zouaves. Just as the French military defined itself as the civilised antithesis to these barbarian warriors while at the same time aping them, so peasants defined themselves as the opposite to soldiers by their acknowledging different qualities. But by this very process they were in danger of acquiescing in the social hierarchy that the military itself asserted: that as successors to the second estate soldiers were not just different from peasants, they were superior, and for this reason allowed, obliged even, to fasten on them. Thus is superiority articulated. Peasants resented the impositions the military laid on them, but could not help but respond to the glamorous uniform and aristocratic swagger of the soldier, who brought colour and excitement to the routine miseries of their daily lives. They both despised and envied the soldier. Again there is no real contradiction: the oral culture of rural France simmers with hostility to seigneurs, but the resolution of these

---

[3] John A. Lynn, *Giant of the 'grand siècle': the French army, 1610–1715*, Cambridge 1997, 417, 444–50.

stories is seldom expressed in a revolutionary concern for equality and social justice, rather the previously oppressed becomes the new oppressor. Presumably their narrators wanted the chance to become that which (in their current circumstances) they loathed.

Peasants envied soldiers precisely because the latter were able to do things that the former could not: they could avoid the prying eyes that upheld village morality, they could escape the minor tyrannies of neighbourly status conflicts. It is surprising that the army, one of the most disciplined environments imaginable, was none the less consistently associated with a level of personal liberty that the peasant could only dream of – to travel, to drink, to rob, to loaf, to hit, to rape even. While condemning such behaviour, those caught up in the rigidities of peasant society might sometimes yearn for the licence that the soldier considered his privilege. This is why peasants endowed the soldier of popular culture with mythic characteristics, so that he could be the vehicle for their own longings. In reality life in the army might have very little to do with such imaginings, but this did not prevent some soldiers from trying to live up to their wild reputations.

That both positive and negative elements continued to shape peasant attitudes to the military throughout the period does not mean that nothing changed with the revolution, but it may help to explain how things changed. Consciously or unconsciously, governments and administrators took advantage of peasant desires by promoting the army, not just as duty, but also as liberation. Conscription in particular offered young men the opportunity to live the life of the prodigal while still expecting the reward of a dutiful son. Not every participant in the *tirage* was necessarily enthusiastic, but because the process was credible in the peasant's own cultural terms, it became acceptable. There may have been many drawbacks to becoming a soldier, but recruits familiar with the songs, tales and images we have examined would have expected compensations.

The question of the relationship of the army to society, and the role of conscription within it, leads onto another debate: was the army one of the agents of modernisation, turning peasants into Frenchmen? In the original republican conception peasants (and everyone else) became French citizens by taking on public responsibilities, such as military service. But the nation in arms was not supposed to result in the militarisation of the citizenry, but rather the assertion of rustic values such as hard work and patriotism in that den of aristocratic and cosmopolitan vice, the army. However, it never quite worked like that. In the memoirs of the volunteers of 1792 one can already see citizen-soldiers accommodating themselves to the military style. With conscription that process became explicit, for to turn the recruit into a soldier it was necessary to break his connections with his civilian life. To perform his duty as a French citizen he had to repudiate his peasant upbringing and adopt the military ethos. Perhaps this helps explain why, during the nineteenth century, to be French increasingly meant to be martial. Moustaches became commonplace as French men were expected to have the daring of a marauder, the sexual prowess of a hussar, the insouciance of a *Sans-Souci*. Military vices became national virtues.

Thus it became harder for peasants to assert their own self-worth on the basis of their antagonism to soldiers, for as a consequence they would be turning their backs on the French state and all the benefits which it might bring. Not every peasant had to become a soldier, but they had to take part in the *tirage* either directly or as witnesses to this military celebration, they had to tolerate military propaganda particularly in schools, and finally they had to accept that their sons might leave them to serve their country. In return the state recognised them as French men, the gender element of this acquired identity being as least as important as the nationality. Although the 'Peasants into Frenchmen' debate has tended to focus on politics, schools and railways, the army may also have been a significant factor, and not just for the material differences it made to peasants' lives. It was not only because peasants learned to read in the army, or mixed with their fellows from other regions, or drank alongside Bonapartists and republicans in city bars, that military service became an engine for national integration, but also because of the role it played in peasants' understanding of what it meant to be French.

And yet, despite the army's role as the premier national institution, the absence of patriotic sentiments in the folklore surrounding soldiers is note-worthy. Tricolour flags may have abounded on the day of the *tirage*, but it is extremely difficult to find chauvinist statements in conscript songs sung prior to 1870. Even in Lorraine, supposedly the heartland of militaristic nation-alism, there are few references either to the nation or the regime that the soldier was supposed to be serving, and even fewer suggesting that such service possessed a virtue not available to the foreigner. Monarchs, empires and republics made fleeting appearances in the oral literature of conscription, but they seldom took centre-stage.

Despite providing France with so many of its leading patriots, it is difficult to establish any clear sense of the loyalties of Lorrainers through their exem-plary record of military service. More inhabitants of Lorraine chose to serve in the army than of almost any other region regardless of the regime in power: in no way can their response be analysed as a comment on the perceived legitimacy of the regime. Even more strikingly the military tradition of Lorraine, established when the province was an independent dukedom, con-tinued not only through the period of French control but even, for those parts which formed the imperial *Reichsland* after 1870, under the Germans. For although evasion from the draft in Alsace-Lorraine has often been cited as an example of resistance to Germanisation, it largely affected urban recruits: rural areas not only filled their quotas but exceeded them by providing numerous volunteers.[4]

The strength of the military tradition in Lorraine, despite the vicissitudes

[4] Dan Silverman, *Reluctant union: Alsace-Lorraine and imperial Germany, 1871–1918*, University Park, Penn. 1972, 71.

of its history, might lead one to conclude that the issues that matter so much to the historian – national identity and political allegiance – were not always at the forefront of the peasants' minds. Their attitudes to the army were formed around much more pressing matters: family relationships, communal loyalties, leaving home, marriage, making a living. . . . Propagandists could make use of these concerns to introduce national or political messages, for example when Napoleon III takes the place of the father in images of the returning conscript. But this was subsidiary to the main purpose of the print; it's appeal was more personal. The soldier certainly played a large part in peasant culture, particularly in Lorraine, but not because he was the standard bearer for the emperor, or the republic, or the nation, or the fatherland. It was because he was the representative of an alternative way of life.

Bibliography

Unpublished primary sources

Epinal, Archives départementales des Vosges
8/T   Images du dépôt légal
9bis/M/14   Presse et imprimerie
18/R/4   Deniers lettres des soldats
48/J   Fonds de l'imagerie d'Epinal S.A.

Epinal, Musée départemental d'art ancien et contemporain (MDAACE)
The museum at Epinal is home to an enormous collection of popular images. A part of the collection has, at various times in the past, been organised according to age, size, theme or place of origin, but much of it has not. Therefore, although most of my knowledge of the images derives from time spent in the museum (and almost all of my illustrations are taken from its collection), in the footnotes I prefer to cite published sources which include reproductions of the images, where these are available. If not I refer to the image in the museum's collection by accession number, followed by name of imagist, title and date (if known), for example MDAACE 57.3.2550: Dembour, *Crédit est Mort*, 2 Mar. 1837.

Metz, Archives départementales de la Moselle
1/T/91–110   Fonds du dépôt légal du département de la Moselle
12/J/102   Fonds Puymaigre; Varia literae
21/J/12   Fonds de la Société d'histoire et d'archéologie de la Lorraine; chants populaires, patois messin
42/J/22–35   Fonds Pinck; Chansons populaires, cahiers et textes originaux fournis par diverses personnes

Nancy, Archives départementales de Meurthe-et-Moselle
1/T/1207   Documents concernant l'imprimerie etc.
1/T/1209   Documents concernant l'imprimerie etc.
1/T/1210   Documents concernant l'imprimerie etc.
1/T/1233   Registre d'inscription des titres de gravures, cartes, plans, 1823–57
SAL 244   Société d'archéologie lorraine, fonds Marchal
SAL 408   Société d'archéologie lorraine, fonds Piernot

Nancy, Bibliothèque municipale de Nancy
MS 293 (1545)   Colonel Villemin   Bouquet des champs (souvenirs et coutumes d'autrefois), 1938
MS 326–9 (419)   Lerouge   Glossaire lorraine
MS 343–8 (721)   Académie Stanislas   Les patois lorrains: enquête de l'Académie Stanislas, 1877

MS 354 (1662)		Monographes des communes de Meurthe-et-Moselle rédigées en 1889 par les instituteurs pour l'exposition de 1900
MS 768 (619)	l'abbé Jeannin	Mélanges sur l'histoire de Lorraine: legendes, cérémonies, usages, superstitions, patois
MS 1256 (888)	P. le Gendre	Origines de dictons et mots populaires
MS 1709 (1088)	Anne Barbe Pierron	Recueil de noëls anciens composé par Anne Barbe Pierron à Luneville en 1757

Nancy, Musée historique lorrain

The museum at Nancy holds a small collection of imagery, which is unnumbered.

Paris, Bibliothèque nationale, département des estampes

Li 10 petit folio	Images diverses chez Desfeuilles
Li 11 folio	Imagerie populaire de Nancy: Desfeuilles
	Imagerie populaire de Montbéliard (Doubs): Deckherr
Li 58 folio, tomes 1–4	Imagerie populaire
Li 59 folio, tomes 1–11	Images d'Epinal
Li 63 folio	Dembour & Gangel, Metz, 1835–51
Li 73 folio	Images de Deckherr de Montbéilard
Rc 36 L. folio	L'histoire du Sauveur
Rd 61 petit folio	Desfeuilles; Images de saints
SNR	Boulay, Caroline Boulay, J. B. Clerc, Deckherr, Dembour, Dembour[g] & Gangel, Gondelfinger, Lacour, Maurin, Noël, Thiébault, Wendling
Tc 23 petit folio	Ages de la vie humaine
Td matière 1–1a	Ages de la vie humaine
Td matière 4, boite 1	Chansons
Td matière 24, tomes 1–9	Allegories

Paris, Musée national des arts et traditions populaires (MNATP)

MS 43.7	Demange	Baptême, fiancailles, mariage à Cirey (Meurthe et Moselle)
MS 43.102	Anon.	Coutumes, dictons, proverbes, usages locaux (Vosges, Remiremont)
MS 43.106	Anon.	Folklore de Meurthe-et-Moselle
MS 43.277	Raphaël de Westphalen	Dictons recueillis dans le pays messin
MS 75.43. 1–2	Louis Lavigne	Petit Dictionnaire de folklore: notes alphabetiques de folklore recueillies à Cumières et Avillers Ste Croix (Meuse)
MS Millien-Delarue (Nivernais)	Achille Millen and Paul Delarue	Folktales collected by Achille Millien in the Nivernais in the last quarter of the nineteenth century, subsequently organised by Paul Delarue. Delarue arranged the collection according to

Aarne-Thompson tale-type and gave each version a different letter. These are used for citations in the footnotes, for example: MS Millien-Delarue (Nivernais), AT302, version B.

The Iconothèque of the Musée national des arts et traditions populaires houses an extensive collection of popular imagery. Each image is catalogued separately and where cited in the footnotes its inventory number is given followed by the name of imagist, the title of the image and its date, for example, MNATP 53.86.2818 C: Pellerin, *Scènes de garnison*, 1842.

Printed primary sources

Abel, Charles, 'Coutumes du pays messin: les trimazos', *L'Austrasie* n.s. i (1853), 258–69

——— 'Coutumes du pays messin: les valentins', *L'Austrasie* n.s. i (1853), 78–88

——— 'Revue rétrospective des vieilles chansons populaires du pays mosellan à propos d'un concours ouvert en 1888', *Mémoires de l'Académie de Metz*, 3rd ser. xxvii (1887–8), 107–18

Adam, Lucien, *Les Patois lorrains*, Nancy–Paris 1881

Andrews, James Bruyn, *Contes ligures: traditions de la Rivière recueillies entre Menton et Gênes*, Paris 1892

Anon., 'Promenade archéologique au village de Failly', *L'Austrasie* iv (1839), 92–206

Auricoste de Lazarque, Ernest, 'Usages et superstitions populaires de la Lorraine: pays messin', *Revue des traditions populaires* xvi (1901), 12–24

——— 'Histoires surnaturelles de Boulay, Moselle', *Revue des traditions populaires* xix (1904), 257–68, 403–16, 494–7; xx (1905), 167–71; xxiii (1908), 236

Badel, Emile, 'Le Pilier qui pleure à Saint-Nicolas', *Le Pays lorrain* xxii (1930), 167–9

Balzac, Honoré de, *Le Peau de chagrin*, first edn, Paris 1831; Paris 1984

(Barbé), 'Jean-Julien', 'Lo Conscrit d'1812', *Le Pays lorrain* ix (1912), 531

——— 'Vieux Dictons et proverbes dans les chroniques de la ville de Metz', *Nos Traditions* n.s. i (1947), 9–11

Bardy, Henri, 'Deux Légendes alsaciennes, et une bretonne', *Revue d'Alsace* viii (1857), 269–80

——— *Les Traditions et la littératures populaires, le roman et la poésie dans l'arrondisement de Saint-Dié*, Saint-Dié 1882

——— *Le Folklore du Val de Rosemont*, Belfort 1890

——— *Le Folklore du Val de Vaudémont*, Belfort 1898

Basse, William, *A helpe to discourse*, London 1619

Bauchez, Jean, *Journal de Jean Bauchez, greffier de Plappeville au dix-septième siècle*, ed. Charles Abel and Edouard de Bouteiller, Metz 1868

Beaulieu, L., *Archéologie de la Lorraine ou recueil de notices et documens pour servir à l'histoire des antiquités de cette province*, Paris 1840–3

Beauquier, Charles, *Chansons populaires recueillies de Franche-Comté*, Paris 1894

——— *Flora et fauna populaire de Franche-Comté*, Paris 1910

Beyle Henri ('Stendhal'), *Histoire de la peinture en Italie*, first edn, Paris 1817; Geneva–Paris 1969

Bladé, Jean-Francois, *Contes populaires recueillis en Agenais*, Paris 1874
—— *Contes populaires de la Gascogne*, Paris 1886
Bloch, Oscar, *Lexique français: patois des Vosges méridionales*, Paris 1917
Bräker, Ulrich, *The life story and real adventures of the poor man of Toggenburg*, first edn 1789–92; ed. Derek Bowman, Edinburgh 1970
Brod, Robert, *Die Mundart der Kantone Château-Salins und Vic in Lothringen*, Halle 1912
Brondex, Albert and Didier Mory, *Chan Heurlin ou les fiançailles de Fanchon: poëme patois messin, en sept chants*, first edn, Metz 1787; ed. Maurice Cressot, Nancy 1948
Buchon, Max, *Chants populaires de la Franche-Comté*, first edn, Salins 1863; 2nd edn, Paris 1878
Cadic, François, *Contes et légendes de Bretagne*, Paris 1906
—— *Contes et légendes de Bretagne*, Paris 1914–22
—— *Nouveaux Contes et légendes de Bretagne*, Paris 1922–5
Calmet, Dom Augustin, *Histoire ecclesiastique et civile de Lorraine*, Nancy 1728
—— *The phantom world or the philosophy of spirits, apparitions, etc.*, ed. H. Christmas, London 1850
Carnoy, E. Henry, *Littérature orale de la Picardie*, Paris 1883
—— *Contes français*, Paris 1885
Carru, Paul, *Les Chansons des conscrits de Haut-Revermont*, Bourg 1911
Cénac-Moncaut, Justin-Édouard-Mathieu, *Contes populaires de la Gascogne*, Paris 1861
—— *Littérature populaire de la Gascogne*, Paris 1868
Cerny, Elvire de, *Contes et légendes de Bretagne*, Paris 1898
Charton, Charles, *Les Vosges pittoresques et historiques*, Paris 1862
—— and Henri Lepage, *Le Département des Vosges, statistique historique et administrative*, Epinal 1845
Chepfer, Georges, *Anciennes Chansons populaires recueillies en Lorraine*, in Jean-Marie Bonnet and Jean Lanher (eds), *Georges Chepfer: textes et chansons*, Nancy 1983
Coignet, Capitaine Jean-Roch, *Les Cahiers du Capitaine Coignet*, first edn, Paris 1883; 2nd edn, ed. Jean Mistler, Paris 1968
Collet, Vital, 'Evangile des sobriquets caractérisant les habitants de villages lorrains', *Le Pays lorrain* v (1908), 442–9
Comité du folklore champenois, *Travaux du comité du folklore champenois*, III: *Du berceau à la tombe*, Châlons-sur-Marne 1964
Cosquin, Emmanuel, 'Contes populaires de Lorraine recueillis dans un village du Barrois à Montiers-sur-Saulx', *Romania* v (1876), 82–107
—— *Contes populaires de Lorraine comparés avec les contes des autres provinces de France et des pays étrangers*, Paris 1886
Coulon, Edgard, 'Légendes, croyances et contes populaires du pays de Montbéliard', *Revue du folklore français* i (1930), 226–57
—— 'Coutumes et croyances populaires au pays de Montbéliard', *Revue du folklore français* iv (1933), 235–43
Dardy, Léopold, *Anthologie populaire de l'Albret (sud-ouest de l'Agenais ou Gascogne landaise)*, Agen 1891
Delarue, Paul, *The Borzoi book of French folktales*, New York 1956

Delmart, J. and 'Léon Vidal' [Léon de Céran], *La Caserne: moeurs militaires*, Brussels 1833

Delvau, Alfred, *Du Pont des arts au pont de Kehl*, Paris 1866

Deulin, Charles, *Contes du roi Cambrinus*, first edn, Paris 1874; Lausanne 1935

Dibdin, Revd Thomas Frognall, *A bibliographical, antiquarian and picturesque tour in France and Germany*, London 1821

Diderot, Denis, *Jacques the fatalist*, first edn, Paris 1796; London 1986

—— *Salons: texte établi et présenté par J. Seznec et J. Adhémar*, Oxford 1957–67

Dumas, Alexandre (père), *Vingt Ans après*, first edn, Paris 1845; Paris 1962

Duvernoy, Emile, *Les Légendes de l'histoire de Lorraine*, Nancy 1925

Erbrich, Emil, 'Uber Volks- und Dialektdichtung im Metzer Lande', *Jahrbuch der Gesellschaft für lothringische Geschichte und Alterstumkunde* xiv (1902), 301–18

Erckmann, Emile and Alexandre Chatrian, *Histoire d'un conscrit de 1813, L'Histoire d'un paysan, L'Ami Fritz* and *Le Blocus de Phalsbourg*, in the collected edn *Gens d'Alsace et de Lorraine*, ed. Jean-Pierre Rioux, Paris 1993

Félice, Ariane de, *Contes de Haute-Bretagne*, Paris 1954

Flaubert, Gustave, *Bouvard and Pécuchet*, first edn, Paris 1881; London 1976

Fleury, Jean, *Littérature orale de la Basse-Normandie*, Paris 1883

Fontaine, A.-L., 'Us et coutumes d'une village d'Aouze', *Le Pays lorrain* xxiii (1931), 482–99

Fourier de Bacourt, Etienne, 'Anciens Chants populaires du Barrois', *Bulletins de la Société d'archéologie lorraine* 3rd ser. xxii (1894), 339–83; xxiv (1896), 269–314; xxvi (1898), 207–56

—— 'Anciennes Chansons patoises du Barrois', *Le pays lorrain* ii (1905) 33–6

Fournier, A., 'Vieilles Coutumes, usages et traditions populaires des Vosges provenant des cultes antiques et particulièrement de celui du soleil', *Bulletin de la Société philomatique vosgienne* xvi (1890–1), 137–60

Frison, Joseph, 'Contes et légendes de Basse-Bretagne', *Revue des traditions populaires* xxi–xxxi (1906–16)

Garneret, Jean, *Un Village comtois: Lantenne: ses coutumes, ses patois*, Paris 1959

—— *Contes recueillis en Franche-Comté*, Besançon 1988

—— and Charles Culot, *Chansons populaires comtoises*, Besançon 1971–85

Gazin, Edgard, 'Moeurs, traditions, légendes', in Léon Louis (ed.), *Le Département des Vosges*, Epinal 1889

Géhin, Louis, 'Gérardmer à travers les âges: 2ème partie', *Bulletin de la Société philomatique vosgienne* xx (1894–5), 9–15, 144–60

—— 'Vieilles Chansons lorraines: les adieux du conscrit', *Le Pays lorrain* iv (1907), 595–6

Godat, L., *Notice historique sur la commune de Tholy, Vosges*, Remiremont 1899

Godet, Captaine, 'Mémoires du capitaine Godet', *Carnets de la sabretache*, fasc. 323, Paris 1928, 442–84

Graf, Josef, 'Deutsche-lothringische Volkslieder, Reime und Sprüche aus Forbach und Umgegend', *Jahrbuch der Gesellschaft für lothringische Geschichte und Alterstumkunde* vi (1894), 95–110

Grégoire, Henri, *Mémoires ecclésiastiques, politiques et littéraires de M. Grégoire, ancien évêque de Blois, rédigés en 1808*, Paris 1840

Grimm, Friedrich Melchior von, Denis Diderot, Guillaume-Thomas Raynal and Jakob Heinrich Meister, *Correspondance littéraire, philosophique et critique par*

Grimm, Diderot, Raynal, Meistre, 1753–1790, ed. Maurice Tourneux, Paris 1877–82

Grimm, Jacob and Wilhelm Grimm, The Penguin complete Grimms' tales for young and old, London 1984

Grimmelshausen, Hans Jacob Christoph von, The adventures of Simplicissimus, 1st German edn, 1668; 1st English edn, London 1912

Guillemot, Alexis, Contes, légendes, vieilles coutumes de la Marne, Châlons-sur-Marne 1908

Haillant, Nicolas, Essai sur un patois vosgien, Epinal 1882–1901

—— Les Sobriquets, prénoms et noms de famille patois d'un village vosgien, Urimenil n.d.

—— and Albert Virtel, Choix de proverbes et dictons patois de Damas près de Dompaire, Vosges, Epinal 1902

'Heurlin, Chan' [Frédéric Estre], Lo Couâraie pè Chan Heurlin et des autes boin zig, Strasbourg 1860

—— Lo pia ermonèk lourain, Strasbourg 1877–81

Hingre, le chanoine, Vocabulaire complet du patois de la Bresse, Saint-Dié 1907

Houpert, N., 'Das deutsche Volkslied in Lothringen', Jahrbuch der Gesellschaft für lothringische Geschichte und Altertumskunde ii (1890), 347–56

Houzelle, François, 'Breux: son histoire et sa seigneurie', Mémoires de la Société des lettres, sciences et arts de Bar-le-Duc 3rd ser. vii (1898), 299

Hugo, Adèle, Victor Hugo raconté par un témoin de sa vie, avec oeuvres inedités de Victor Hugo, Brussels–Leipzig 1863

Hugo, Victor, Oeuvres completes: édition chronologique, ed. Jean Masson, Paris 1967–70

Huhn, Eugen H., Deutsch-Lothringen: Landes-, Volks- und Ortskunde, Stuttgart 1875

Joanne, A. [Louis Jouve], 'L'Hiver dans les Vosges', L'Illustration, 16 Feb. 1850, 103–7

Joisten, Charles and Alice Joisten, 'Quelques Traditions orales de Savoie', Revue de Savoie iv (1959), 319–41

Jouve, Louis, Noëls patois: anciens et nouveaux chantés dans la Meurthe et dans les Vosges, Paris 1864

—— Chansons en patois vosgien, recueillies et annotées avec un glossaire et la musique des aires, Epinal–Remiremont 1876

—— Recueil nouveau de vieux noëls inédites en patois de la Meurthe et des Vosges, Paris n.d.

Kassel, Auguste, Conscrits, Musik und Tanz im alten Elsass, Guebwiller 1929

Kiesel, Frédéric, Légendes d'Ardennes et Lorraine, Gembloux 1974

Köhler, Carl and John Meier, Volkslieder von der Mosel und Saar mit ihren Melodien aus dem Volksmunde gesammelt, Halle 1896

L'Herubel, Michel, Contes populaires de toutes les Normandie, Rennes 1978

L'Hôte, Georges, La Tankiote: usages traditionnels en Lorraine, Nancy 1984

Labourasse, Henri, Glossaire abrégé du patois de la Meuse, Arcis-sur-Aube 1887

—— Anciens Us, coutumes, légendes, superstitions, préjugés, etc. du département de la Meuse, Bar-le-Duc 1903

Ladoucette, Jean-Charles-François de, 'Notes sur des camps, voie romains, châteaux, objexts et inscriptions antiques dans les Vosges et la Moselle', Mémoires de la Société des antiquaires de France x (1834), 15–169

Lallement, Louis, *Echoes rustiques de l'Argonne*, Châlons-sur-Marne 1910
────── *Contes rustiques et folklore de l'Argonne*, Châlons-sur-Marne 1913
────── *Folklore et vieux souvenirs d'Argonne, arrondisement de Sainte-Ménéhould*, Châlons-sur-Marne 1921
Lancy, Paul and Geneviève Lancy, *Récits-légendes d'Alsace-Lorraine et pays messin*, Nancy 1903
Laukhard, Frédéric-Christian, *Un Allemand en France sous le Terreur: souvenirs de Frédéric-Christian Laukhard, professeur d'université saxon et sans-culotte francais, 1792–1794*, ed. W. Bauer, Paris 1915
Laurency, Robert, *Sagen aus Lothringen*, Strasbourg 1918
Laurent, Donatien, *Aux Sources du Barzaz-Breiz: la mémoire d'un peuple*, Douarnenez 1989
Lavigne, Louis, *Le Patois de Cumières et du Verdunois*, Verdun 1940
Le Braz, Anatole, *La Légende de la mort chez les bretons armoricains*, Paris 1923
Lemasson, C., 'Anciennes Coutumes de la paroisse de Champ-le-Duc (Vosges)', *Le Pays lorrain* xxiv (1932), 505–18
Lerond, Henri, *Lothringische Sammelmappe*, Metz 1890–1911
────── *Sagenborn lothringischer Burgtrümmer*, Metz 1912–21
Lerouge, [?], 'Notice sur quelques usages et croyances de la ci-devant Lorraine, particulièrement de la ville de Commercy', *Mémoires de l'Academie celtique* iii–iv (1809), 441–53, 84–92; vi (1812), 102–20
Leroy, Charles, *Le Colonel Ramollot: recueil de récits militaires suivi de fantaisies civiles*, Paris 1881
────── *Faits et gestes du sergent Roupoil*, Paris n.d.
Lorraine, Jean, 'Nos Traditions: de Saint-Blaise à Saint-Eucaire', *L'Austrasie* n.s. xiv (1910), 101–5
────── 'Nos Traditions: décembre et janvier', *L'Austrasie* n.s. xiv (1910), 105–12
Luzel, François-Marie, 'Premier Rapport sur une mission en Basse Bretagne, ayant pour objet de rechercher les traditions orales des Bretons-Armoricains, contes et récits populaires', *Archive des missions scientifiques et littèraires* 2nd ser. vii (1872), 101–24
────── 'Quatrième Rapport sur une mission en Basse Bretagne, ayant pour objet de rechercher les traditions orales des Bretons-Armoricains, contes et récits populaires', *Archive des missions scientifiques et littèraires* 2nd ser. vii (1872), 173–206
────── *Veillées bretonnes: moeurs, chants, contes et récits populaires des Bretons armoricains*, Paris 1879
────── *Légendes chrétiennes de la Basse-Bretagne*, Paris 1881
────── *Contes populaires de Basse-Bretagne*, Paris 1887
Marbot, Baron de, *The memoirs of Baron de Marbot*, London 1929
Marchal, l'abbé Laurent, 'Poésies populaires de la Lorraine', *Bulletins de la Société d'archéologie lorraine* iv (1853–4), 383–539
────── 'Poésies populaires de la Lorraine', *Bulletins de la Société d'archéologie lorraine* 2nd ser. vii (1865), 43–87
Marquant, François-Etienne, *Carnet d'étapes du dragon Marquant*, ed. G. Vallée and G. Pariset, Paris–Nancy 1898
Martin, Eugène, 'Folklore de Saint-Remy (Vosges)', *Le Pays lorrain* iv (1907), 316–19, 366–70, 435–43

——— 'La Vie autrefois dans le canton de Provendères-sur Fave', *Le Pays lorrain* xxii (1930), 98–106

Massignon, Geneviève, *Contes de l'ouest*, Paris 1954

——— 'Coutumes et chants de conscrits' (extract from the *Revue de Bas-Poitou* [*1960*]), Fontenay-le-Comte 1961, 170–90

——— *Contes corses*, Aix-en-Provence 1963

——— *Folktales of France*, Chicago 1968

Maugenre, Louis-Marie-Auguste, *Le Sergent Maugenre, 1801–1887, trente-et-un ans au 36eme de ligne: récits et documents militaires inédites*, Saint-Dié 1891

Menéstrels de Gérardmer, *Arts et traditions de la vallée des lacs*, Colmar–Ingersheim 1978

Méraville, Marie-Aimée, *Vie et oeuvres: contes populaires de l'Auvergne, suivi d'un mémoire sur la langue et le patois*, Paris 1982

Merkelbach-Pinck, Angelika, *Lothringer erzählen*, Saarbrück 1936

——— *Lothringer Volksmärchen*, Cassel 1940

——— *Wildjagersagen aus Lothringen*, Cassel 1942

——— *Aus der lothringer Meistube: Sagen, Schwänke, Legenden, Bauerngeschichte, Redensarten, Sprichwörter*, Cassel 1943

——— *Volksmärchen aus Lothringen*, Munich 1943

——— *Lothringer Volksmärchen*, Dusseldorf–Cologne 1961

——— *Volkserzählungen aus Lothringen*, Münster 1967

Meyrac, Albert, *Traditions, coutumes, légendes et contes des Ardennes*, Charleville 1890

Michon, L., 'Quelque Dictons de l'ancienne Lorraine', *Mémoires de l'Académie Stanislas* 6th ser. x (1912–13), 51–73

Millien, Achille and Paul Delarue, *Contes du Nivernais et du Morvan*, Paris 1953

Minsmer, J., *Choix de chansons vosgiennes*, Paris 1918

Motteville, Françoise Bertault, madame Langlois de, *Mémoires sur Anne d'Autriche et sa cour*, ed. Francis-Marie Riaux, Paris 1886

Noël, François-Jean-Baptiste, *Mémoires pour servir à l'histoire de Lorraine*, Nancy 1837–41

Noël, Jean-Nicolas-Auguste, *Souvenirs militaires d'un officier du premier empire (1795–1832)*, Paris–Nancy 1895

Noël, Joseph-Louis-Gabriel, *Au Temps des volontaires: lettres d'un volontaire de 1792*, ed. J. Noël, Paris 1912

Oberlin, Jérémie-Jacques, *Essai sur le patois lorrain des environs du comté du Ban de la Roche, fief royal d'Alsace*, Strasbourg 1775

Olincourt, F. d', *Les Veillées de la Lorraine, ou lectures du soir*, Verdun–Paris 1840–2

'Palapat' [Dancourt], *La Femme d'intrigues*, The Hague 1695

Paris, Gaston, 'La Chanson du chevreau', *Romania* i (1872), 218–25

Peters, F., *Aus Lothringen: Sagen und Märchen*, Leipzig 1887

——— *Märchen aus Lothringen, dem Volke nacherzählt*, Strasbourg 1888

Pétigny, Filleul de, 'Contes de la Beauce et du Perche', *Revue des traditions populaires* xiii (1898), 180–4

Petitjean, C.-D., C.-J. Petitjean, H.-B.-D. Petitjean and Georges Petitjean, *Le Pays vosgien et ses habitants: origines–évolutions–descriptions, prises aux sources des lieux jusqu'ici inetudiés: no 1: Granges*, Epinal 1930

Pfleger, Alfred, 'Conscritsaberglauben und alter Conscritlieder', *Neuer Elsässer Kalender* (1930), 99–106

Pinck, Louis, *Verklingende Weisen; Lothringer Volkslieder*, Metz–Strasbourg–Cassel 1926–39 (a fifth volume was edited by Angelika Merkelbach-Pinck, Frankfurt-am-Main, 1965)

——— *Volkslieder von Goethe im Elsass gesammelt mit Melodien und varianten aus Lothringen und dem faksimiledruck der Strasburger Goethe-Handschrift*, Metz 1932

Pineau, Leon, *Les Contes populaires du Poitou*, Paris 1891

——— *Le Folklore de Poitou*, Paris 1892

——— 'Contes populaires de Poitou', *Revue des traditions populaires* xii (1897), 487–9

Pitz, Louis, *Contes et légendes de Lorraine*, Paris 1956

Plagnard, Ernest, *Vieux Contes de l'Aubrac*, Rodez 1959

Plantadis, Joannès, 'Contes populaires du Limousin', *Revue des traditions populaires* xvii (1902), 399–401

Poirier, M., 'Traditions et croyances lorraines: environs de Metz', *Revue des traditions populaires* xi (1896), 258–9

Pommerol, François, 'Contes d'Auvergne', *Revue des traditions populaires* xv (1900), 641–2

Ponchon, Alexandre, ' "A Veille!": la veillée vers 1850: contribution à l'étude des traditions populaires de l'Amienois', *Conferences des rosatis picards* xli (1909), 1–51

Poplineau, Bernard, *Histoires et chansons populaires ardennaises*, Buzancy 1979

Prost, Auguste, *Etudes sur l'histoire de Metz: les légendes*, first edn, Nancy 1865; 2nd edn, Brionne 1972

Puymaigre, Théodore de, *Poésie populaire: chants allemandes recueillis dans le departement de la Moselle*, Metz 1864

——— 'Chansons populaires du pays messin', *Revue de l'est* n.s. v (1868), 1–43

——— *Chants populaires recueillis dans le pays messin*, first edn, Metz 1865; 2nd edn, Paris–Nancy–Metz 1881

——— 'Veillées de villages: les dayemans', *Archivio per lo studio delle tradizioni popolari* i (1882), 93–8

——— *Folk-lore*, Paris 1885

——— 'Chansons populaires du pays messin', *Archivio per lo studio delle tradizioni popolari* v (1886), 227–37

——— 'Chansons populaires du pays messin', *Archivio per lo studio delle tradizioni popolari* vi (1887), 81–93

Quépat, Nérée [René Paquet], *Chants populaires messins, recueillis dans le Val de Metz en 1877*, Paris 1878

——— 'Contes du pays messin', *Mélusine* i (1878), cols 41–2, 424–5

Richard, Nicolas-Louis-Antoine, 'Lettre à M. Eloi Johanneau sur un usage antique des Vosges relatif au mariage', *Mémoires de l'Académie celtique* iii (1809), 174–7

——— 'Notice sur les cérémonies des mariages dans l'arrondisement de Remiremont, département des Vosges', *Mémoires de l'Académie celtique* v (1810), 236–48

——— *Traditions populaires, croyances superstitieuses, usages et coutumes de l'ancienne Lorraine*, Remiremont 1848

Roche du Teilloy, Alexandre de, *Les Etapes de Georges Bangofsky, officier lorrain: fragments de son journal de campagnes (1797–1815)*, Paris–Nancy 1905

Rohr, Paul, *Blasons populaires et autres survivances du passé*, Nice 1970

Romy [Didier Mory], *Le P'tiat ermonek messin*, Metz 1817–18

Sadoul, Charles, 'Chanson contre-révolutionnaire en patois lorrain', *Le Pays lorrain* i (1904), 274–6

——— 'Chansons populaires de la Lorraine', *Revue des traditions populaires* xix (1904), 203–9

——— 'Contes de Lorraine', *Revue des traditions populaires* xix (1904), 67–72, 367–70, 555–62

———'Dangers de la nuit: les apparitions de la nuit dans les Vosges', *Revue des traditions populaires* xix (1904), 87–90

——— 'Vieilles chansons lorraines: les garçons de Raon', *Le Pays lorrain* ii (1905), 333–4

——— *Traditions et vieilles histoires du pays lorrain*, Nancy 1906

——— 'Chansons populaires lorraines: *Au bout du village* (Ronde)', *Le Pays lorrain* xxi (1929), 521

——— 'Les Chansons lorraines', *Le Pays lorrain* xxv (1933), 213–30

Saint Germain, le comte de, *Mémoires*, Amsterdam 1779

Saulny, Jaclot de, *Le Lorrain peint par lui-même*, Metz 1853

——— *Les Passe-Temps lorrains ou récréations villageoises: recueil de poésies, contes, nouvelles, fables, chansons, idylles, etc. en patois*, Metz 1854

Sauvé, Léopold-François, *Le Folklore des Hautes-Vosges: sorcellerie, croyances et coutumes populaires*, Paris 1889

Schamber, René, 'Formulettes enfantines de pays mosellan', *Nos Traditions* ii (1939), 20–3

——— *Chansons du folklore lorrain*, Metz 1953

Schely, Louis, 'Les Evangiles d'Imling, Moselle', *Le Pays lorrain* xxvi (1934), 139–41

Sébillot, Paul, *Contes populaires de la Haute-Bretagne*, Paris 1880–2

——— *Littérature orale de la Haute-Bretagne*, Paris 1881

——— *Coutumes populaires de la Haute-Bretagne*, Paris 1886

——— 'Chansons de conscrits', *Revue des traditions populaires* iii (1888), 74–6

——— 'Contes de marins recuellis en Haute-Bretagne', *Archivio per lo studio delle tradizioni popolari* ix (1890), 226–39, 420–34, 509–17; x (1891), 103–16, 169–77

——— 'Contes résumés de la Haute-Bretagne', *Revue des traditions populaires* ix (1894), 167–83, 267–83, 336–53

——— *Contes des landes et des grèves*, Rennes 1900

——— 'Contes et légendes de Haute-Bretagne', *Revue des traditions populaires* xvi (1901), 119–31

Smith, Victor, 'Chansons populaires du Velay et du Forez', *Mélusine* i (1888), cols 27–8, 409–15, 458–60

Souvestre, Emile, *Les Derniers Bretons*, Paris 1836

Tailly, Dom Pierre, *Lettres vôgiennes*, Liège 1789

Tenèze, Marie-Louise and Georg Hüllen, *Rencontre des peuples dans le conte*, I: *France/Allemagne*, Munster 1961

Theuriet, André, *Madame Heurteloup (la bête noire)*, Paris 1882

Thiriat, Xavier, *La Vallée de Cleurie; statistique, topographie, histoire, moeurs et idiomes des communes du Syndicat de Saint-Ami, de Lalorge, de Cleurie et de quelques localités voisines, canton de Remiremont, Vosges,* Mirecourt–Remiremont–Paris 1869

—— *Les Kédales et les Voinraux, conte saussuron,* Remiremont 1872

Thiriot, G., 'Noël lorrain', *Le Pays lorrain* vi (1909), 770–5

—— 'Les Fêtes du keulo à Failly', *Le Pays lorrain* viii (1911), 547–58

—— 'La Chanson des sabots', *Jahrbuch der Gesellschaft für lothringische Geschichte und Alterstumkunde* xxv (1913), 55–66

—— *Chansons lorraines,* Metz 1913

Thuriet, Charles, *Traditions populaires du Doubs,* Paris 1891

—— *Traditions populaires de la Haute-Saône et du Jura,* Paris 1892

Tiersot, Julien, 'Chansons de conscrits', *Revue des traditions populaires* iii (1888), 13–17

—— 'Le Portrait de la maîtresse, chansons des conscrits de Rochegude, Drome', *Revue des traditions populaires* viii (1893), 72–4

—— *Chansons populaires recueillies dans les alpes françaises,* Grenoble 1903

Töppfer, Rodolphe, *La Vie et les oeuvres de Töppfer d'après des documents inédits, suivies de fragments de littérature et de critique inédits ou inconnus,* ed. l'abbé Relave, Paris 1886

Trébucq, Sylvain, 'Contes du Languedoc', *Revue des traditions populaires* xxxiv (1919), 298–9

Troux, Albert, 'A Propos des rivalités entre villages lorrains', *Le Pays lorrain* xxii (1930), 121

Vartier, Jean, *Le Grand Livre des proverbes et dictons de Lorraine et du Bassigny,* Nancy 1985

—— *Le Grand Livre des sobriquets et quolibets de Lorraine et du Bassigny,* Nancy 1989

Vaxelaire, Jean-Claude, *Mémoires d'un vétéran de l'ancienne armée (1791–1800),* ed. H. Gauthier–Villars, Paris 1892

Vion, Hubert, 'Patois messin, locutions, comparisons, proverbes', *Jahrbuch der Gesellschaft für lothringische Geschichte und Altertumskunde* ii (1890), 359–63

—— 'Patois lorrain–messin: daillements recueillis sur place par Fr. Bonnardot', *Jahrbuch der Gesellschaft für lothringische Geschichte und Altertumskunde* iv (1892), 251–5

Virtel, Albert, 'Proverbes lorrains recuellis à Dams-devant-Dompaire', *Le Pays lorrain* viii (1911), 176, 376, 440; x (1913), 288, 363, 683, 774

Webster, Revd Wentworth, *Basque legends, collected chiefly in the Labourd,* London 1877

Westphalen, Raphaël de, 'Les Trimazos', *Jahrbuch der Gesellschaft für lothringische Geschichte und Altertumskunde* xxv (1913), 335–75

—— *Petit Dictionnaire des traditions populaires messines,* Metz 1934

—— 'Notes folkloriques', *Nos Traditions* ii (1939)

—— *Chansons populaires lorraines,* Nancy 1977

Wolf, Johann Wilhelm, *Deustche Märchen und Sagen,* Leipzig 1845

—— *Deutsche Hausmärchen,* Göttingen–Leipzig 1851

Zéliqzon, Léon, *Lothringische Mundarten,* Metz 1889

—— 'Patois Lieder aus Lothringen', *Jahrbuch der Gesellschaft für lothringische Geschichte und Alterstumkunde* xiii (1901), 124–44

—— 'Zur Lothringischen Volkskunde', *Jahrbuch der Gesellschaft für lothringische Geschichte und Alterstumkunde* xxv (1913), 67–129

————— *Dictionnaire des patois romans de la Moselle*, Strasbourg 1924

————— 'Quatre Noëls en patois saulnois', *Annuaire de la Société historique et archéologique lorraine* xxxiii (1924), 63–97

————— 'Miscellanées patoises', *Annuaire de la Société historique et archéologique lorraine* xl (1931), 93–139

————— and G. Thiriot, *Textes patois recueillis en Lorraine*, Metz 1912

Secondary sources

Aarne, Antti, *The types of the folktale: a classification and bibliography* (Folklore Fellows Communications iii), Helsinki 1910; rev. Stith Thompson (Folklore Fellows Communications clxxxiv), Helsinki 1961

————— *Der Mann aus dem Paradies* (Folklore Fellows Communications xxii), Helsinki 1915

Abélès, Luce, *Champfleury: l'art pour le peuple*, Paris 1990

Abler, Thomas S., *Hinterland warriors and military dress: European empires and exotic uniforms*, Oxford 1999

Abrahams, Roger, *Deep down in the jungle: Negro narrative folklore from the streets of Philadelphia*, Chicago 1970

Adhémar, Jean, 'Pellerin était un dangereux franc-maçon', *Le Vieux Papier*, fasc. 167, Paris 1954, 171–2

————— 'La Rue Montorgueil et la formation d'un groupe d'imagiers parisiens au XVIe siècle', *Le Vieux Papier*, fasc. 166, Paris 1954, 25–34

————— 'Hypothèses sur la formation des imagiers provinciaux français du XVIIe et du XVIIIe siecle', *Arts et traditions populaires* iii (1955), 208–10

————— *Imagerie populaire française*, Milan 1968

————— 'L'Imagerie vue par l'écrivain au siècle dernier', *Le Vieux Papier*, fasc. 270, Paris 1978, 407–19

Agulhon, Maurice, *The republic in the village: the people of the Var from the French revolution to the second republic*, Cambridge 1982

————— (ed.), *Cultures et folklore républicains*, Paris 1995

Anderson, Matthew S., *War and society in Europe of the old regime, 1618–1789*, London 1988

Anderson, Walter, *Kaiser und Abt* (Folklore Fellows Communications xlii), Helsinki 1923

Arnoult, Jean-Marie, *Histoire et traditions de Champagne*, Châlons-sur-Marne 1979

Aron, Jean-Paul, Paul Dumont and Emmanuel Le Roy Ladurie, *Anthropologie du conscrit francais*, Paris 1972

Auvray, Michel, *Objecteurs, insoumis, déserteurs: histoire des réfractaires en France*, Paris 1983

Aynaud, Adolphe, 'L'Imagerie lilloise ou Henri Porret père, 1768–1844', extract from *Le Vieux Papier*, Paris 1950, 1–7

————— 'L'Imagerie de Beauvais', *Le Vieux Papier*, fasc. 156, Paris 1951, 145–56

————— 'L'Imagier inconnu de Metz', *Le Vieux Papier*, fasc. 166, Paris 1954, 1–11

————— 'Les Thiébault, graveurs nancéiens', *Le Vieux Papier*, fasc. 170, Paris 1955, 105–10

—— 'Notes sur l'imagerie d'Epinal', *Le Vieux Papier*, fasc. 178, Paris 1956, 337–40

—— 'Epinal: Georgé ou Georgin?', *Le Vieux Papier*, fasc. 179, Paris 1957, 357–9

—— 'Notes sur l'imagerie de Nancy', *Le Vieux Papier*, fasc. 181, Paris 1957, 3–6

—— 'Notice sur l'imagerie de Hinzelin', *Le Vieux Papier*, fasc. 205, Paris 1963, 483–4

—— 'Le Saint Napoléon', *Le Vieux Papier*, fasc. 209, Paris 1964, 93–7

—— 'Notes sur l'imagerie d'Epinal (suite et fin)', extract from *Le Vieux Papier*, Paris 1966

Bailly, Paul, 'La Conscription aux alentours de Meaux au XIXe siècle', *Bulletin folklorique d'Ile-de-France* ix (1947), no. 2, 14–15; no. 3, 9–11

Baker, Alan, 'Military service and migration in nineteenth-century France: some evidence from Loir-et-Cher', *Transactions of the Institute of British Geographers* n.s. xxiii (1998), 193–206

Barbé, Jean-Julien, *Coutumes populaires et cérémonies anciennes du pays messin*, Nancy 1910

—— *La Lithographie à Metz*, Metz 1910

—— *L'Imagier de Metz*, Metz 1950

Barbier, Frédéric, 'Le Colportage de libraire dans le Bas-Rhin sous le second empire', in *105e Congrès national des sociétés savantes*, Caen 1980, i. 283–99

—— 'Un Exemple d'émigration temporaire: les colporteurs de libraire pyrénéens (1840–1880)', *Annales du Midi* xcv (1983), 289–307

Barral, Pierre, *L'Esprit lorrain: cet accent singulier du patriotisme français*, Nancy 1989

Bauchez, Jean, Magdelaine Clermont-Joly and Marie-Emmanuelle Meyer, *Images de Metz*, Metz 1987

Baudin, François, *Histoire économique et sociale de la Lorraine*, Nancy 1992–7

Bayon, Martial, 'Sobriquets et superstitions militaires: armée française', *Revue des traditions populaires* ii (1887), 319–24

—— 'Sobriquets et superstitions militaires: le tirage au sort en France: le moyen d'avoir un bon numéro', *Revue des traditions populaires* iii (1888), 53–4

Beauroy, Jaques, Marc Bertrand and Edward T. Gargan (eds), *The wolf and the lamb: popular culture in France from the old regime to the twentieth century*, Saratoga, Ca. 1977

Becker, Jean-Jacques and Stéphane Audoin-Rouzeau, *La France, la nation, la guerre: 1850–1920*, Paris 1995

Bell, David, 'Recent works on early modern French national identity', *Journal of Modern History* lxviii (1996), 84–113

Belmont, Nicole, 'The symbolic function of the wedding procession in the popular rituals of marriage', in Robert Forster and Orest Ranum (eds), *Ritual, religion, and the sacred: selections from the Annales: economies, sociétés, civilisations*, Baltimore 1982, 1–7

Bercé, Yves-Marie, *Revolts and revolution in early modern Europe: an essay on the history of political violence*, Manchester 1987

—— *History of peasant revolts: the social origins of rebellion in early modern France*, Ithaca, NY 1990

—— *Le Roi caché: sauveurs et imposteurs: mythes politiques populaires dans l'Europe moderne*, Paris 1990

Bertarelli, Achille, *L'Imagerie italienne*, Paris 1929

Bertaud, Jean-Paul, *La Vie quotidienne des soldats de la révolution, 1789–1799*, Paris 1985

—— *The army of the French revolution*, Princeton, NJ–Guildford 1988

—— *Valmy: la démocracie en armes*, Paris 1970

—— 'Du Volontariat à la conscription', *La Revue historique des armées* xxxviii (1982), 25–33

Best, Geoffrey, *War and society in revolutionary Europe, 1770–1870*, London 1982

Bettelheim, Bruno, *The uses of enchantment: the meaning and importance of fairy tales*, London 1976

Bibliothèque historique de la Ville de Paris, *Imagerie parisienne, XVIe–XIXe siècle*, Paris 1977 (exhibition catalogue)

Bien, David, 'The army in the French Enlightenment: reform, reaction and revolution', *Past and Present* lxxxv (1979), 68–98

Binder, Heinke, 'Deutsche-Französische Liedverbindungen', in R. W. Brednich, Lutz Röhrich and W. Suppan (eds), *Handbuch des Volkslieder*, Munich 1975, ii. 285–337

Blanc, M., 'Rapport sur les images de M. Dembour', *Mémoires de l'Académie royale de Metz* xix (1837–8), 357–62

Blaudez, François, Jean Mistler and André Jacquemin, *Epinal et l'imagerie populaire*, Paris 1961

Blok, Anton, 'The peasant and the brigand: social banditry reconsidered', *Comparative Studies in Society and History* xiv (1972), 494–506

Bode, Gérard, *L'Imagerie messine, 1838–1871: exposition d'images conservées aux archives départementales*, Metz 1987

Bohin, Jean, 'L'Invasion de 1815, et le parti royaliste à Fresne-en-Woëvre', *Le Pays lorrain* xiii (1921), 257–67

Bois gravés du Musée de Châtillon, Châtillon-sur-Seine 1946

Bois, Jean-Paul, *Les Anciens Soldats dans la société française au XVIIIe siècle*, Paris 1990

Bolte, Johannes and Georg Polivka, *Anmerkungen zu den Kinder und Hausmärchen der Brüder Grimm*, Leipzig 1913–32

Bottigheimer, Ruth B. (ed.), *Fairy tales and society: illusion, allusion and paradigm*, Philadelphia 1986

—— 'Cupid and Psyche vs. Beauty and the beast: the Milesian and the modern', *Merveilles et contes* iii (1989), 4–44

Bouchot, Henri, *Le Bois Protat, un ancêtre de la gravure sur bois: étude sur un xylographe taillé en Bourgogne vers 1370*, Paris 1902

Bourgin, Pierre, 'Milices et saltpêtriers comtois sous l'ancien régime', *Barbizier: bulletin de liaison du folklore comtois* n.s. xv (1988), 66–74

Boye, Pierre, *La Milice en Lorraine au XVIIIe siècle*, Nancy–Paris 1904

Bozon, Michel, 'Conscrits et fêtes de conscrits à Villefranche-sur-Saône (Rhône)', *Ethnologie française* ix (1979), 29–46

—— *Les Conscrits*, Paris 1981

Braudrillart, Cardinal, *Vieux Bois gravés, achetés, ou échangés par les imagiers du Châlon-sur-Saône*, Châlon-sur-Saône 1939

Briggs, Katharine M., *The anatomy of Puck*, London 1959

—— *Pale Hecate's team*, London 1962

—— *A dictionary of British folktales in the English language*, London 1970–1

Briggs, Robin, *Witches and neighbours*, London 1996

Brochon, Pierre, *Le Livre de colportage en France depuis le XVIe siècle*, Paris 1954

Browning, Reed, *The War of Austrian Sucession*, Stroud 1994

Bruckner, Wolfgang, *Populäre Druckgraphik Europas: Deutschland*, Munich 1969; trans. as *Imagerie populaire allemande*, Milan 1969

Bruneau, Charles, 'Pour nos patois lorrains', *Le Pays lorrain* xi (1914–19), 129–37

—— 'Les Parlers lorrains anciens et modernes: bibliographie critique 1908 à 1924', *Revue de linguistique romane* i (1925), 348–413

—— 'Essai d'une bibliographie de la chanson populaire francaise et allemande', *Annales de l'est* xliv (1930), 439–41

—— 'La Chanson populaire lorraine', *Le Pays lorrain* xxiii (1931), 121–32, 192–204, 237–49

—— 'Le Folklore lorrain', *Le Pays lorrain* xxiii (1931), 22–6

Bruzard, M.-L., *Catalogue de l'oeuvre lithographique d'Horace Vernet*, Paris 1826

Burke, Peter, *Popular culture in early modern Europe*, London 1978

—— 'Strengths and weaknesses of the history of mentalities', *History of European Ideas* vii (1986), 439–52

—— 'The language of orders in early modern Europe', in Michael L. Bush (ed.), *Social orders and social classes in Europe since 1500: studies in social stratification*, London 1992, 1–12

Cabourdin, Guy, *Quand Stanislas régnait en Lorraine*, Paris 1980

—— *La Vie quotidienne en Lorraine aux XVIIe et XVIIIe siècles*, Paris 1984

Calame-Griaule, Geneviève, Veronika Görög-Karady and Michèle Chiche (eds), *Le Conte, pourquoi? Comment? Folktales, why and how? Actes des journées d'études en littérature orale (Paris, 23–26 March, 1982)*, Paris 1984

Canetti, Elias, *Crowds and power*, 1st edn, Munich 1960; 2nd English edn, London 1962

Centre national de la recherche scientifique, *Trésor de la langue française: dictionnaire de la langue du XIXe et du XXe siècles*, Paris 1990

Cerquand, Jean-François, 'L'Imagerie populaire à Avignon et dans le Comtat aux XVIIe et XVIII siècles', *Mémoires de l'Académie de Vaucluse* i (1882), 45–71

Chagniot, Jean, *Paris et l'armée au XVIIIe siècle: étude politique et sociale*, Paris 1985

Chalmin, Pierre, 'La Pratique du duel dans l'armée française au XIXe siècle', in *Actes du 80e congrès des sociétés savantes*, Lille 1955, 327–50

'Champfleury' [Jules-François-Félix Husson], *Histoire de l'imagerie populaire*, Paris 1869

Charnay, Jean-Paul, *Société militaire et suffrage politique en France depuis 1789*, Paris 1964

Charraud, Alain, 'Analyse de la représentation des âges de la vie humaine dans les estampes populaires du XIXe siècle', *Ethnologie française* i (1971), 59–78

Chartier, Roger, *The cultural uses of print in early modern France*, Princeton, NJ 1987

Chauvet, Jean-Yves, *Les Loups en Lorraine: histoire et témoignages*, Le Coteau 1986

Cheesman, Tom, 'The return of the transformed son: a popular ballad complex', *Oxford German Studies* xviii–xix (1989), 60–91

—— '*Bänkelsang*: seeing, hearing, telling and singing in the German ballad picture show', *Lore and Language* xii (1994), 41–57

—— *The shocking ballad picture show: German popular literature and cultural history*, Oxford 1994

Chesnutt, Michael (ed.), *Telling reality: folklore studies in memory of Bengt Holbek*, Copenhagen–Turku 1993

Chew, Samuel, *The pilgrimage of life*, New Haven, Conn. 1962

Childs, John, *Armies and warfare in Europe, 1648–1789*, Manchester 1982

Choux, Jacques and Adolphe Riff (eds), *Art populaire de Lorraine: recueil d'études*, Strasbourg–Paris 1966

Christiansen, Reidar T., *The tale of the two travellers or the blinded man: a comparative study* (Folklore Fellows Communications xxiv), Helsinski 1916

—— *The migratory legends* (Folklore Fellows Communications clxxv), Helsinski 1958

Cobb, Richard, *The police and the people: French popular protest, 1789–1820*, Oxford 1970

—— *Reactions to the French revolution*, London 1972

—— *Paris and its provinces, 1792–1802*, London 1975

Cochin, Jacques, 'Monde à l'envers, mondes à l'endroit', *Arts et traditions populaires* xvii (1969), 233–57

Coirault, Patrice, *Recherches sur notre ancienne chanson populaire traditionnelle*, Paris 1927–33

—— *Notre Chanson folklorique*, Paris 1941

—— *Formation de nos chansons folkloriques*, Paris 1953–63

Collado, Marian García, 'Le Conte entre l'oral, le représenté et l'écrit: l'histoire du conte *Jean de l'ours*', *Merveilles et contes* vii (1993), 341–81

Collet, Vital, *Les Communes du canton de Charmes*, Epinal 1905

Collins, Roger, 'Simon Blocquel, imagier et éditeur lillois', *Journal de la Société des océanistes* xli (1985), 235–40

Collot, Gérald, 'L'Imagerie populaire de Metz', in Choux and Riff, *Art populaire*, 203–10

Constantine, Mary-Ann, *Breton ballads*, Aberystwyth 1996

Corbin, Alain, 'L'Histoire de la violence dans les campagnes françaises au XIXe siècle: esquisse d'un bilan', *Ethnologie française* xxi (1991), 224–36

Cordonnier-Détrie, Paul, 'Imagerie et colportage', *Revue historique et archéologique du Maine* 2nd ser. xxxiii (1953), 3–36

Corvisier, André, *L'Armée française de la fin du XVIIe siècle au ministère de Choiseul: le soldat*, Paris 1964

—— *Les Contrôles des troupes de l'ancien régime*, Paris 1968

—— 'La Mort du soldat depuis la fin du moyen âge', *Revue historique* ccliv (1975), 3–30

—— *Armées et sociétés en Europe de 1492 à 1789*, Paris 1976

Crampon, Maurice, 'Le Culte de l'arbre et de la forêt: essai sur le folklore picard', *Mémoires de la Société des antiquaires de Picardie* xlvi (1936), 1–562

Cressot, Joseph, *Le Pain au lièvre*, Paris 1943

Crick, Lucien, 'Monsieur de Marlborough', *Bulletin des musées royaux d'art et d'histoire* 3rd ser. iii (1931), 117–22

—— 'Exposition d'images populaires', *Bulletin des musées royaux d'art et d'histoire* 3rd ser. xv (1943), 131–40

Darmon, Jean-Jaques, *Le Colportage de libraire en France sous le second empire: grand colporteurs et culture populaire*, Paris 1972

Darnton, Robert, *The great cat massacre and other episodes in French cultural history*, London 1984

Davis, Natalie Zemon, *The return of Martin Guerre*, Cambridge, Mass. 1983

Day [-Hickman], Barbara Ann, 'Representing ageing and death in French culture', *French Historical Studies* xvii (1992), 688–724

―――― 'Political dissent and Napoleonic representations during the restoration monarchy', *Historical Reflections – Réflexions historiques* xix (1993), 409–32

―――― *Napoleonic art: nationalism and the spirit of rebellion in France (1815–1848)*, Newark, Del. 1999

Dégh, Linda, *Folktales of Hungary*, London 1965

―――― *Folktales and society: story-telling in a Hungarian peasant community*, Bloomington, Ind. 1969

Dejob, Charles, 'Le Soldat dans la litterature française au XVIIIe siècle', *Revue bleue, revue politique et littéraire* lxiv (1899), 449–58

Delarbre, Léon, 'L'Imagerie populaire belfortaine', in Riff, *France*, 183–94

Delarue, Georges, 'La Longue Errance d'un chanteur ambulant du XIXe siècle', *Le Monde alpin et rhodanien* x (1982), 359–68

Delarue, Paul and Marie-Louise Tenèze, *Le Conte populaire français: catalogue raisonné des versions de France et de pays de langue francais d'outre-mer*, Paris 1957–2000

Demard, Jean Christophe, *Tradition et mystères d'un terroir comtois au XIXe siècle: les Vosges méridionales*, Langres 1981

Depreaux, Albert, *Les Affiches de recrutement de XVIIe siècle à nos jours*, Paris 1911

Descaves, Lucien, *L'Humble Georgin, imagier d'Epinal*, Paris 1932

Desfeuilles, André, 'Les Desfeuilles, graveurs-imagistes nancéiens (1800–1840)', *Le Vieux Papier*, fasc. 174, Paris 1956, 209–24

―――― 'L'Imagerie populaire en Lorraine: centenaire de François Desfeuilles (1779–1855)', *Arts et traditions populaires* iv (1956), 143–4

―――― 'Du Classement des images populaires: les images de la fabrique de Desfeuilles de Nancy conservées au Cabinet des Estampes à Paris', *Le Vieux Papier*, fasc. 184, Paris 1958, 1–16

―――― 'Images et almanachs dans l'est sous le 1er empire', *Revue de l'Institut Napoléon* (1958), 10–19

Deshenry, J., 'Les Conscrits', *Folklore de France* ii (1961), 4–12

Despiques, Paul, *Soldats de Lorraine*, Nancy–Paris 1899

Doncieux, George, *Le Romancéro populaire de la France*, Paris 1904

Dorson, Richard, *The British folklorists: a history*, Chicago 1968

Drouillet, Jean, *Folklore du Nivernais et du Morvan*, La Charité-sur-Loire 1959–68

Ducatel, Paul, *Histoire de la IIIe république vue à travers l'imagerie populaire et la presse satirique*, Paris 1973–8.

Duchartre, Pierre-Louis and René Saulnier, *L'Imagerie populaire*, Paris 1925

―――― *L'Imagerie parisienne: l'imagerie de la rue Saint-Jacques*, Paris 1944

Duffy, Christopher, *The military experience in the age of reason*, London 1987

Dumont, Jean-Marie, *La Vie et l'oeuvre de Jean-Charles Pellerin (1756–1836)*, Epinal 1956

―――― *Les Maîtres graveurs populaires, 1800–1850*, Epinal 1965

Dundes, Alan, *Life is like a chicken coop ladder: a portrait of German culture through folklore*, New York 1984

―――― 'The symbolic equivalence of allomotifs: towards a method of analysing folktales', in Calame-Griaule, Görög-Karady and Chiche, *Le Conte, pourquoi?*, 187–99

―――― 'Fairy tales from a folkloristic perspective', in Bottigheimer, *Fairy tales and society*, 261–72

Ecomusée Nord-Dauphiné, *Salut la classe!*, Villefontaine 1986

Egmond, Florike, 'The noble and ignoble bandit: changing literary representations of west-European robbers', *Ethnologia Europaea* xvii (1987), 139–56

—— *Underworlds: organised crime in the Netherlands, 1650–1800*, Cambridge 1993

Eich, Jean, 'Un Littérateur et érudit lorrain: Théodore de Puymaigre', *Annuaire de la Société d'histoire et d'archéologie de la Lorraine* liii (1953), 111–27

Eliade, Mircea, 'Les Savants et les contes de fées', *Nouvelle revue française* iv (1956), 884–91

—— *The forge and the crucible: the origins and structures of alchemy*, 1st edn, London 1962; 3rd edn, Chicago 1978

—— *Shamanism: archaic techniques of ecstasy*, 1st edn, London 1964; 2nd edn, London 1989

Ellis, John M., *One fairy story too many: the Brothers Grimm and their tales*, Chicago 1983

Esnault, Gaston, *Dictionnaire historique des argots français*, Paris 1965

Fabre, Daniel, ' "Doing youth" in the village', in Giovanni Levi and Jean-Claude Schmitt (eds), *A history of young people in the west*, ii, Cambridge, Mass. 1997, 37–65

—— and Jaques Lacroix, 'Sur la production du récit populaire: à propos du fils assassiné', *Arts et traditions populaires* xviii (1970), 91–141

Faille, René, 'L'Imagerie populaire cambrésienne', *Le Vieux Papier*, fasc. 210, Paris 1964, 141–76

Falassi, Alessandro, *Folklore by the fireside: text and context of the Tuscan veglia*, Austin, Tx 1980

Febvre, Lucien, 'Une Enquête: le forge de village', *Annales d'histoire economique et sociale* vii (1935), 603–14

Fentress, James and Chris Wickham, *Social memory*, Oxford 1992

Fernandez, James W, 'Folklorists as agents of nationalism: Asturian legends and the problem of identity', in Bottigheimer, *Fairy tales and society*, 133–45

Ferrand, Louis, *Les Bois gravés châlonnais préservés au Musée de Châlon-sur-Saône*, Châlon-sur-Saône 1973

Fink, Gonthier-Louis, 'The fairy tales of the Grimms' sergeant of dragoons J. F. Krause as reflecting the needs and wishes of the common people', in James M. McGlathery (ed.), *The brothers Grimm and folktale*, Urbana, Ill. 1991, 146–63

Fischer, John L., 'Sociopsychological analysis of folklore', *Current Anthropology* iv 1963, 235–95

Fishman, J. Susannah, *Boerenverdriet: violence between peasants and soldiers in early modern Netherlands art*, Ann Arbor, Mich. 1982

Fontaine, Laurence, *History of pedlars in Europe*, Cambridge 1996

Ford, Caroline, *Creating the nation in provincial France: religion and political identity in Brittany*, Princeton, NJ 1993

Forrest, Alan, *Conscripts and deserters: the army and French society during the revolution and empire*, Oxford 1989

—— *Soldiers of the French revolution*, Durham, NC 1990

Fourier de Bacourt, Etienne, *Les Sociétés de tir et les milices bourgeois dans l'ancien duché de Lorraine*, Bar-le-Duc n.d.

Francisco, Rafael de, *El recortable militar espanol*, Madrid 1982

François, Charles, 'Les Débuts de la guillotine dans le département de la Meurthe', *Mémoires de l'Académie Stanislas* 6th ser. i (1968–9), 173–80

———— 'Un Houzard en Lorraine', *Mémoires de l'Académie Stanislas*, 6th ser. ii (1969–70), 83–92

Fromage, Henri, 'Un Maitre de l'imagerie populaire au début du XIXe siècle à Beauvais: Côme-Lucien Diot', *Groupe d'étude des monuments et oeuvres d'art du Beauvaisis* xii (1981), 19–36

Froment, E., 'Les Rivalités entre Mandres et Norroy-sur–Vair', *Le Pays lorrain* xxii (1930), 36–9

Fromm, Erich, *The forgotten language: an introduction to the understanding of dreams, fairy tales and myths*, New York 1951

Furet, François and Jacques Ozouf, *Reading and writing: literacy in France from Calvin to Jules Ferry*, Cambridge 1982

Gaber, Stéphane, *La Lorraine meutrie: les malheurs de la guerre de trente ans*, Nancy 1979

Gaidoz, Henri, 'Un Ancêtre du "quatrième etat" dans l'imagerie populaire', *Mélusine* vi (1892–3), cols 49–50, 97–9; v (1894–5), 147–54, 190–1, 222–3

Garnier, Jacques-Marin, *Histoire de l'imagerie populaire et des cartes à jouer à Chartres*, 1st edn, Chartres 1869; 2nd edn, Toulouse 1991

Garnier [-Pelle], Nicole, 'Les Bois d'imagerie populaire de François Desfeuilles de Nancy (1800–1837)', *La Revue du Louvre et des musées de France* v–vi (1987), 389–96

———— 'Aux Origines de l'imagerie populaire: la gravure de la rue Montorgueil à Paris au XVIe siècle', *Revue du Louvre* iv (1989), 225–32

———— *L'Imagerie populaire française, I: Gravures en taille-douce et en taille-d'épargne: catalogue du fonds du Musée national des arts et traditions populaires*, Paris 1990

———— *L'Imagerie populaire française, II: Images d'Epinal gravées sur bois*, Paris 1996

Gaston, Jean, *Les Images des confréries parisiennes avant la révolution*, Paris 1909

Gastoué, Amédée, *La Cantique populaire en France: ses sources, son histoire; augmentée d'une bibliographie générale des anciens cantiques et noëls*, Lyon 1924

Gebelin, Jacques, *Histoire des milices provinciales (1688–1791): le tirage au sort sous l'ancien régime*, Paris 1882

Geographical section of Naval Intelligence Division, Naval Staff, Admiralty, *A manual of Alsace-Lorraine atlas*, London 1920

George, Dorothy M., *English political caricature to 1792*, Oxford 1959

George, Henri, 'Conscription, tirage au sort et imagerie populaire', *Le Vieux Papier*, fasc. 279, Paris 1981, 133–43

———— 'Un Catalogue de l'imagerie Pellerin d'Epinal de 1842', *Le Vieux Papier*, fasc. 340, Paris 1996, 257–62

Georgel, Chantal, *L'Enfant et l'image au XIXe siècle*, Paris 1988 (Musée d'Orsay exhibition catalogue)

Gérard, Pierre (ed.), *L'Armée à Nancy, 1633–1966: mélanges d'histoire militaire*, Nancy–Paris 1967

Gétaz, E., 'Monographie du *Messager boiteux de Berne et Vevey*, paraissant à Vevey depuis 1708', *Messager boiteux de Berne et Vevey* (1957), 1–8

Ginzburg, Carlo, 'Clues: roots of an evidential paradigm', in *Clues, myths and the historical method*, Baltimore 1989

Girard, Georges, *Racolage et milice: le service militaire en France à la fin du règne de Louis XIV, 1701–1715*, Paris 1912

Girardet, Raoul, *La Société militaire dans la France contemporaine, 1815–1939*, Paris 1953

Gooch, John, *Armies in Europe*, London 1980

Görög-Karady, Veronika (ed.), *D'un Conte . . . à l'autre: la variabilité dans la littérature orale*, Paris 1990

'Gregoire, Nicolas' [Michel Gregoire], *Journal d'un bourgeois de Sierck (1750–1843)*, ed. Maurice Toussaint, *La Revue rhénane* iii (1922–3), 120–7, 190–6, 337–45, 401–7, 483–5

Grosdemange, Ghislaine, 'Population et milice dans la subdélégation de Lunéville de 1737 à 1789', *Annales de l'est* 5th ser. iii (1952), 119–48

Grose, Francis, *A classical dictionary of the vulgar tongue*, London 1796

Hachette, Alfred, *L'Affaire Mique (1745–1794)*, Paris 1928

Hale, John R., 'The soldier in Germanic graphic art of the Renaissance', *Journal of Interdisciplinary History* xvii (1986), 85–114

—— *Artists and warfare in the Renaissance*, New Haven–London 1990

Hansen, William, 'Bengt Holbek: obituary', *Journal of American Folklore* cvi (1993), 184–89

Harou, Alfred, 'Sobriquets et superstitions militaires: l'armée belge', *Revue des traditions populaires* ii (1887), 49–52

—— 'Sobriquets et superstitions militaires: le tirage au sort en Belgique', *Revue des traditions populaires* ii (1887), 457–61

Harp, Stephen, *Learning to be loyal: primary schooling as nation building in Alsace and Lorraine, 1850–1940*, Dekalb, Ill. 1998

Hartland, E. Sidney, *The science of fairy tales*, London 1890

Hay, Douglas, 'War, dearth and theft in the eighteenth century: the record of the English courts', *Past and Present* xcv (1982), 117–60

Hayward Gallery, *French popular imagery: five centuries of prints*, London 1974 (exhibition catalogue)

Hélot, René, *Notes sur l'imagerie populaire en Normandie*, Lille 1908

Hemmerle, Hélène, 'La Conscription', *Folklore de France* xl (1991/2), 4–9

Henninger, Roger, *Conscrits d'Alsace*, Strasbourg 1961

Henssen, Gottfried, *Ueberlieferung und Persönlichkeit: die Erzählungen und Lieder des Egbert Gerritz*, Munster 1951

Herbert, Robert L., *Peasants and 'primitivism': French prints from Millet to Gauguin*, South Hadley, Mass. 1995

Herranen, Gun, 'A blind storyteller's repertoire', in Kvideland, Sehmsdorf and Simpson, *Nordic folklore*, 63–9

—— 'A blind storyteller's perception of reality', in Chesnutt, *Telling reality*, 113–20

Hiegel, Henri, 'Bibliographie du folklore mosellan', *Les Cahiers lorrains* n.s. xvi (1964), 11–24

—— 'Deux Folkloristes lorrains: Henri Lerond et Angelika Merkelbach', *Les Cahiers lorrains* n.s. xxvii (1975), 108–14

—— 'L'Oeuvre du folkloriste lorrain Louis Pinck (1873–1940)', *Les Cahiers lorrains* n.s. xxxiii (1981), 199–218, 249–63

Hobsbawm Eric J., *Bandits*, London 1969

Holbek, Bengt, *Interpretation of fairy tales: Danish folklore in a European perspective* (Folklore Fellows Communications ccxxxix), Helsinki 1987

—— 'The language of fairy tales', in Kvideland, Sehmsdorf and Simpson, *Nordic folklore*, 40–62

—— 'Variation and tale type', in Görög-Karady, *D'Un Conte . . . à l'autre*, 471–86

Holmes, Richard, *The road to Sedan: the French army, 1866–70*, London 1984

Holroyd, Richard, 'The Bourbon army, 1815–1830', *Historical Journal* xiv (1971), 529–52

Holzapfel, Otto, 'Nachlasse Pinck im Deutschen Volksliedarchiv: Ammerkungen zum deutschen Volkslied in Lothringen', *Jahrbuch für Volksliedforschung* xxii (1977), 119–30

Honko, Lauri, 'Methods in folk narrative research', in Kvideland, Sehmsdorf and Simpson, *Nordic folklore*, 24–38

Hopkin, David M., 'Reading difficulties', *Print Quarterly* xvii (1998), 73–4

———— 'Identity in a divided province: the folklorists of Lorraine, 1860–1960', *French Historical Studies* xxiii (2000), 639–82

Houdaille, J., 'Le Problème des pertes de guerre', *Revue d'histoire moderne et contemporaine* xvii (1970), 411–23

Hunt, Lynn, *The family romance of the French revolution*, London 1992

Hutton, Ronald, *The shamans of Siberia*, Glastonbury 1993

———— 'The English Reformation and the evidence of folklore', *Past and Present* cxlviii (1995), 89–116

Jameson, R. D., 'Cinderella in China', in Alan Dundes (ed.), *Cinderella: a casebook*, London 1988, 71–97

Jeanmaire, André, *La Tradition en Lorraine: le cycle de la vie; les proverbes*, Colmar 1981

Jehan de la Haute Selve, *Li Romans de Dolopathos*, ed. Charles Brunet and Anatole de Montaiglon, Paris 1856

———— [Latin text] Johannis de Alta Silva, *Dolopathos sive de rege et septem sapientibus*, ed. Hermann Oesterley, Strasbourg–London 1873

Joachim, J., 'Les Images de Sainte Agathe en Alsace', in Riff, *Alsace*, 133–55

Job, Françoise, 'Les Anciens Militaires de la république et de l'empire dans le département de la Meurthe en 1857 et la médaille de Sainte-Hélène', *Le Pays lorrain* lxi (1981), 97–108

Jones, Colin, 'The welfare of the French foot-soldier from Richelieu to Napoleon', *History* lxv (1980), 193–213

Jones, Peter, *Politics and rural society: the southern Massif Central, 1750–1880*, Cambridge 1985

———— *The peasantry in the French revolution*, Cambridge 1988

Jouve, Louis, *Bussang (Vosges)*, Remiremont 1888

Jusselin, Maurice, *Imagiers et cartiers à Chartres*, Paris 1957

Kanter, Sanford, 'Exposing the myth of the Franco-Prussian War', *War and Society* iv (1986), 13–30

Kappaun, Bernard, 'La Conscription en Moselle sous le premier empire', *Les Cahiers lorrains* n.s. xxxix (1987), 181–224

Karnoouh, Claude, 'L'Etranger ou le faux inconnu: essai sur la définition spatiale d'autrui dans un village lorrain', *Ethnologie française* i (1972), 107–22

Kayser, J.-B., 'A Propos de quelques règles et dictons météorologiques et agricoles', *Nos Traditions* i (1938), 45–50

Kennedy, Emmet, *A cultural history of the French revolution*, New Haven 1989

Kennet, Lee, *The French armies in the Seven Years War*, Durham, NC 1967

Koechlin, Elisabeth, *Wesenszüge des deutschen und des französischen Volksmärchens: eine vergleichende Studie zum Märchentypus von 'Amor und Psyche' und vom 'Tierbräutigam'*, Basel 1945

373

Kosko, Maria, *Le Fils assassiné (AT939a): étude d'un thème légendaire* (Folklore Fellows Communications cxcviii), Helsinki 1966

Krohn, Kaarle, *Folklore methodology*, Austin, Tx 1971

Kvideland, Reimund, Henning Sehmsdorf and Elizabeth Simpson (eds), *Nordic folklore: recent studies*, Bloomington, Ind. 1989

La Combe, Colonel de, *Charlet, sa vie, ses lettres, suivi d'une description raisonnée de son oeuvre lithographique*, Paris 1856

La Fontaine, Jean S., *Initiation*, Manchester 1986

Laforte, Conrad, 'La Coutume antique et médiévale des couronnes de fleurs retrouvées dans la chanson de tradition orale', *Folklore canadien – Canadian Folklore* xvi (1994), 89–102

——— and Edith Champagne, *Le Catalogue de la chanson folklorique française*, Quebec 1977–84

Laissy, Marie, *Les Noëls populaires lorrains*, Nancy 1977

Landschaftsverbandung Rheinland, *Die Lebenstreppe: Bilder der menschlichen Lebensalter*, Cologne 1984 (exhibition catalogue)

Lang, Andrew, *Custom and myth*, London 1904

Langlois, Eustache-Hyacinthe, *Essai historique, philosophique et pittoresque sur les danses des morts*, Rouen 1852

Langstroff, Karl Heinz, *Lothringer Volksart: Untersuchung zur deutsch-lothringischen Volkserzählung an Hand der Sammlung von Angelika Merkelbach-Pinck*, Marburg 1953

Lapadu-Hargues, Francoise and Georges Henri Riviere, 'Imagerie, cartes à jouer, toiles imprimées: problèmes d'évolution et d'interdépendance des centres de production et des styles', *Arts et traditions populaires* xiii (1965), 217–28

Laulan, Robert, 'Un Philanthrope militaire: le brigadier-général Merlet et la création des écoles d'enfants de troupe', *Actes du 83e congrès national des sociétés savantes, Aix–Marseilles, 1958*, Paris 1959, 170–80

Lavisse, Emile, *Tu seras soldat*, Paris 1888

Le Journal du collectionneur iv/31 (1994), 19

Le Roy Ladurie, Emmanuel, *Le Territoire de l'historien*, Paris 1975

——— *Love, death and money in the pays d'oc*, London 1984

——— and A. Zysberg, 'Anthropologie des conscrits français (1868 à 1887)', *Ethnologie française* ix (1979), 47–68

Lehning, James, *Peasant and French: cultural contact in rural France during the nineteenth century*, Cambridge 1995

Leitner, Moses J. and J. R. Lamen, *Dictionary of French and English slang*, London 1965

Lemoigne, F.-Y., 'Militaria', *Les Cahiers lorrains* n.s. xxvi (1974), 104–10

Léonard, Emile-G., 'La Question sociale dans l'armée française au XVIII siecle', *Annales d'histoire economique et sociale* iii (1948), 135–49

Lepage, Henri and Charles Charton, *Le Département des Vosges, statistique historique et administrative*, Epinal 1845

Lerch, Dominique, *Imagerie et société: l'imagerie Wentzel de Wissembourg au XIXe siècle*, Strasbourg 1982

——— 'L'Historien et l'imagerie: quelques réflexions suivies d'une relecture (et d'une reécoute!) de l'imagerie amiénoise', *Mémoires de la fédération des sociétés d'histoire et d'archéologie de l'Aisne* (1987), 172–88

——— 'Du Colportage à l'errance: réflexions sur le colportage en Alsace au XIXe siècle', *Revue d'Alsace* cxiii (1987), 163–89

—— Almanachs, bibliothèque bleue, imagerie: une famille d'éditeurs de la France de l'est, les frères Deckherr de Montbéliard, Montbéliard 1990

—— L'Imagerie populaire en Alsace et dans l'est de la France, Nancy 1992

—— 'La Représentation de la guerre par l'imagerie populaire (1854–1945)', Ethnologie française xxiv (1994), 263–75

Leroy, Olivier, Dictionary of French slang, London 1935

Les Colporteurs de Chamagne: étude d'après leurs passeports, 1824–1861, Chamagne 1990 (exhibition catalogue)

Lesueur, Jacqueline, 'Une Figure populaire en Lorraine au siècle dernier, le colporteur ou chamagnon', Bulletin de la Société lorraine des études locales dans l'enseignement public n.s. xxxvi (1969), 29–39

—— 'La Chanson populaire et les marchands de chansons dans les Vosges au siècle dernier', Bulletin de la Société philomatique vosgienne lxxiii (1970), 88–109

Lévi-Strauss, Claude, 'L'Analyse morphologique des contes russes', International Journal of Slavic Linguistics and Poetics iii (1960), 122–49

Lionnais, Georges, Fêtes lorraines, Nancy 1920

Lloyd, Geoffrey E. R., Demystifying mentalities, Cambridge 1990

Lord, Albert B., The singer of tales, Cambridge, Mass. 1960

Lüthi, Max, The European folktale: form and nature, Bloomington, Ind. 1986

Lynn, John A., The bayonets of the republic: motivation and tactics in the army of revolutionary France, 1791–94, Urbana, Ill. 1984

—— Giant of the 'grand siècle': the French army, 1610–1715, Cambridge 1997

McCarthy, William Bernard, The ballad matrix: personality, milieu, and the oral tradition, Bloomington, Ind. 1990

Mackenzie, John M. (ed.), Imperialism and popular culture, Manchester 1986

Mcphee, Peter, The politics of rural life: political mobilization in the French countryside, 1846–1852, Oxford 1992

—— Revolution and environment in southern France: peasants, lords, and murder in the Corbières, 1780–1830, Oxford 1999

Magnien, Gabriel, 'Les Ecrivains romantiques et l'imagerie populaire', Le Vieux Papier, fasc. 194, Paris 1961, 27–40

Maire, Camille, 'Le Contigent de 1860 dans le canton de Lorquin', Les Cahiers lorrains n.s. xlvi (1984), 29–35

—— 'La Mobilité des jeunes lorrains au XIXe siècle: l'example des conscrits des cantons d'Albestroff et de Dieuze (1830–70), Le Pays lorrain lxiv (1984), 246–250

—— 'Conscrits en Amerique: le cas de l'arrondisement de Sarrebourg (Meurthe), 1829–70', in Centre de recherches d'histoire nord-américaine, L'Emigration francaise, Paris 1985

—— 'Sept Ans de service . . . et comment y échapper', La Revue lorraine populaire xix (1993), 312–16

Mandrou, Robert, De la Culture populaire aux 17e et 18e siècles: la bibliothèque bleue de Troyes, Paris 1964

Maradan B., 'Chamagne et les chamagnons: colporteurs en livres', in Les intermédiaires culturels, actes du colloque du centre méridional d'histoire sociale, des mentalités et des cultures, 1978, Aix-en-Provence 1981, 277–87

Margadant, Ted, French peasants in revolt: the insurrection of 1851, Princeton, NJ 1979

—— 'Tradition and modernity in rural France', Journal of Modern History lvi (1984), 667–97

Marin, Louis, Les Contes traditionnels en Lorraine, Paris 1964

Markoff, John *The abolition of feudalism: peasants, lords and legislators in the French revolution*, University Park, Penn. 1996

Martin, Auguste, *L'Imagerie orléanaise*, Paris 1928

Martin, Paul, *Les Petits Soldats de Strasbourg*, Strasbourg 1950

—— 'L'Imagerie militaire de Wissembourg (1831–1920)', in Riff, *La France de l'est*, 151–66

Mathias, François, *Notice sur l'imagerie d'Epinal*, Epinal 1904

Mathieu, Désiré, *L'Ancien Régime en Lorraine et Barrois d'après des documents inédits (1698–1789)*, Paris 1907

Mauriange, Edith, 'Sources d'inspiration de François Georgin pour quelques estampes de l'épopée napoléonienne', in Riff, *La France de l'est*, 367–83

Mayer, Laurent, 'Les Chansons de métiers en Lorraine germanophone avant 1870 d'après l'oeuvre de Louis Pinck', *Les Cahiers naboriens* iii (1986), 35–74

—— 'Les Chansons de soldats et les chants à sujet historique, en Lorraine d'expression allemande avant 1870, d'après l'oeuvre de Louis Pinck', *Les Cahiers naboriens* iv (1990), 100–30

Mechin, Colette, 'Les *Veillées*', *Le Pays lorrain* lviii (1977), 199–205

Medick, Hans, 'Village spinning bees: sexual culture and free time among rural youth in early modern Germany', in Hans Medick and David Sabean (eds), *Interest and emotion: essays on the study of family and kinship*, Cambridge 1984

Ménétra, Jacques-Louis, *Journal of my life*, ed. Daniel Roche and Robert Darnton, New York 1986

Merkelbach-Pinck, Angelika, 'Von Meien in Lothringen', *Zeitschrift für Lothringische Volkskunde: organe du folklore lorrain de langue allemande* i (1937), 40–4

—— 'Wanderungen der Märchen im deutschsprachigen Lothringen', *Folk-Liv* ii–iii (1939), 224–31

—— *Brauche und Sitte in Ostlothringen*, Frankfurt-am-Main 1968

Merlin, Léon, *La Langue verte du troupier; dictionnaire d'argot militaire*, Paris–Limoges 1886

Metken, Sigrid, *Französische Bilderbogen des 19. Jahrhunderts*, Baden-Baden 1972 (exhibition catalogue)

Meyer, Maurits de, 'Le Conte populaire dans l'imagerie populaire hollandaise et belge', *Fabula* i (1958), 183–92

—— *De Volks-en Kinderprent in de Nederlanden van de 15e tot de 20 eeuw*, Antwerp–Amsterdam 1962

Mignot, Michelle, 'La Conscription dans le département de la Meuse sous le directoire', *Annales de l'est* 5th ser. vi (1955), 145–9

Mitterauer, Michael, *A history of youth*, Oxford 1992

Moore, Sally F. and Barbara G. Myerhoff (eds), *Secular ritual*, Amsterdam 1977

Morgan, David, *Visual piety: a history and theory of popular religious images*, Berkeley–Los Angeles 1998

Morizot, Jean-Aimé, 'Les Volontaires du district de Remiremont', *Le Pays de Remiremont* xi (1992) 77–108

Moroz, Susan, 'Analyse des chansons de conscrits de la commune de Saint-Vincent-sur-Oust (Haute-Bretagne)', *Cahiers de la littérature orale* xvi (1984), 83–103

Mousnier, Roland, 'Les Concepts d'*ordres*, d'*états*, d'*fidélité*, et de *monarchie absolue* en France de la fin du XVe siècle à la fin du XVIIIe', *Revue historique* ccxlvii (1972), 289–312

Moxey, Keith, *Peasants, warriors and wives: popular imagery in the Reformation*, Chicago 1989

Muchembled, Robert, *Culture populaire et culture des élites dans la France moderne (XVe–XVIIIe siècle)*, Paris 1978

—— *La Violence au village: sociabilité et comportements populaires en Artois du XVe au XVIIe siècle*, Turnhout 1989

Muller, M., *La Défense des Vosges en 1814–1815: Wolff, Brice, les frères Vadet, Vatot et Rouyer*, Epinal 1911

Musée Bargoin, *Greuze et Diderot: vie familiale et éducation dans le deuxième moitié du XVIIIe siècle*, Clermont-Ferrand 1984 (exhibition catalogue)

Musée Carnavalet, *Paris raconté par l'image d'Epinal*, Paris 1990 (exhibition catalogue)

Musée départemental breton à Quimper, *L'Imagerie populaire bretonne*, Quimper 1992 (exhibition catalogue)

Musée du Louvre, *Nouvelles Acquisitions du département des Peintures, 1983–6*, Paris 1987

Musée national des arts et traditions populaires, *Cinq siècles d'imagerie francaise*, Paris 1973 (exhibition catalogue)

Niccoli, Ottavia, *I sacerdoti, i guerrieri, i contadini: storia di un 'immagine della società'*, Turin 1979

Nisard, Charles, *Histoire des livres populaires et de la littérature de colportage*, Paris 1864

Noël, Maurice, 'L'Imagerie de Pont-à-Mousson', in Riff, *La France de l'est*, 381–93

Nordman, Daniel, 'Des Limites d'état aux frontières nationales', in Pierre Nora (ed.), *Les Lieux de memoire*, II: *La nation*, Paris 1986

O'Malley, Pat, 'Social bandits, modern capitalism and the traditional peasantry: a critique of Hobsbawm', *Journal of Peasant Studies* ii (1978–9), 489–52

Oinas, Felix J. and Stephen Soudakoff (eds), *The study of Russian folklore*, The Hague 1975

Ollivier, Joseph, *Catalogue bibliographique de la chanson populaire bretonne sur feuilles volantes*, Quimper 1942

Oré, Capitaine Delphin-Charles, *Fischer et l'origine des chasseurs*, Nancy–Paris 1911

Palais des Beaux-Arts, Lille/ Musée des arts et traditions populaires, Paris, *L'Image de Lille*, Paris 1957 (exhibition catalogue)

Parrott, Cecil, *Jaroslav Hašek: a study of Svejk and the short stories* , Cambridge 1982

Pasdeloup, Lt, 'Documents relatives aux levées de troupes de 1791, 1792 et 1793 dans les communes dépendant aujourd'hui de l'arrondissement de Saint-Dié', *Bulletin de la Société philomatique vosgienne* xxxix (1913–14), 15–42

Pauli, Johannes, *Schimpf und Ernst*, 1st edn, Strasbourg 1522; ed. Johannes Bolte, Berlin 1924

Percheval, Maurice, *La Tradition gothique dans l'imagerie populaire: les images éditées à Amiens*, Cayeux-sur-Mer 1908

Pergaud, Louis, *La Guerre des boutons*, Paris 1912

Perrout, Réné, *Les Images d'Epinal*, Nancy 1912, repr. as *Trésors des images d'Epinal*, Paris 1985

Philippe, André, 'Jean-Charles Pellerin poursuivi pour vente d'images seditieuses (1816)', *La Révolution dans les Vosges* xv (1926–7), 1–15, 97–107

—— 'Colportage de fausses nouvelles', *La Révolution dans les Vosges* xviii (1928–9), 1–7

———— 'Les Débuts de l'imagerie populaire à Epinal: images napoléoniennes de Jean-Charles Pellerin (1810–1815)', *L'Art populaire en France* i (1929), 161–78

———— 'Mésadventures d'un colporteur à Mirecourt (Janvier 1792)', *La Révolution dans les Vosges* xix (1930–1), 33–9

———— 'Quelques Images des Deckherr de Montbéliard, éditées de 1820 à 1832', *L'Art populaire en France* iv (1932), 109–17

Picoche, Philippe, *Le Monde des chamagnons et des colporteurs au XIXe siècle dans les Vosges*, Raon–l'Etape 1992

Pierfitte, Charles, 'Les Volontaires vosgiens en 1792', *Bulletin de la Société philomatique vosgienne* xxi (1895–6), 101–30

———— 'Chamagne: les chamagnons', *Bulletin mensuel de la Société d'archéologie lorraine* iii (1903), 280–3

Pinck, Louis, 'La Circulation des chants vue de la Lorraine', *Folk-Liv* iii (1939), 208–214

Pionnier, Edmond, *Essai sur l'histoire de la révolution à Verdun*, Nancy 1906

Pitsch, Marguerite, 'Credit est mort: image d'Orléans inspirée par *Les Cris de Paris* de Bouchardon', *Arts et traditions populaires* vi (1958), 264–8

Planhol, Xavier de, 'Aux Origines de l'habitat rural de type lorraine', in Franz Dussart (ed.), *L'Habitat et les paysages ruraux d'Europe*, Liège 1971

———— *An historical geography of France*, Cambridge 1984

Ploux, François, 'Rixes intervillageoises en Quercy (1815–1850)', *Ethnologie française* xxi (1991), 276–81

Porch, Douglas, 'The French army law of 1832', *Historical Journal* xiv (1971), 751–69

———— *Army and revolution, France, 1815–1848*, London 1974

Poulet, Henry, *Les Volontaires de la Meurthe aux armées de la révolution (levée de 1791)*, Nancy–Paris 1910

Price, R. D., 'The French army and the revolution of 1830', *European Studies Review* iii (1973), 243–67

Price, Roger, *The modernisation of rural France: communications, networks and agricultural market structures in nineteenth-century France*, London 1983

———— *A social history of nineteenth-century France*, New York 1987

Propp, Vladimir, *Morphology of the folktale*, Austin, Tx 1968

———— *Theory and history of folklore*, Manchester 1984

Puymège, Gérard de, *Chauvin, le soldat-laboureur: contribution à l'étude des nationalismes*, Paris 1993

Pytlík, Radko, *Jaroslav Hašek and the good soldier Schweik*, Prague 1983

Raillet, Georges, 'Les Mauvais Souvenirs de l'histoire dans le langage populaire', *La Grive* xxviii (1956), 21–5

———— 'Miscellanées de folklore ardennais, I: Du berceau à la tombe', *Etudes ardennaises* xxxiv (1963), 5–19

———— 'Miscellanées de folklore ardennais, II: Cycles saisonniers', *Etudes ardennaises* xxxix (1964), 19–34

———— 'Miscellanées de folklore ardennais, IV: Fêtes patronales', *Etudes ardennaises* xlv (1966), 17–32

Ranke, Kurt, *Folktales of Germany*, Chicago 1966

Raxhon, Philippe, 'Folklore wallon et mémoire de la révolution française: le territoire de la légende', in Agulhon, *Cultures*, 461–76

Reinhard, Marcel, 'Nostalgie et service militaire pendant la révolution', *Annales historique de la révolution française* xxx (1958), 1–15

Renan, Ernest, 'Qu'est-ce qu'une nation?', in John Hutchinson and Anthony D. Smith (eds), *Nationalism*, Oxford 1994

Renger, Konrad, *Zur Ikonographie des verlorenen Sohnes und von Wirtshausszenen in der niederlandischen Malerei*, Berlin 1970

Reshef, Ouriel, *Guerre, mythes et caricatures: au berceau d'une mentalité française*, Paris 1984

———— '*Le Hulan et la paysanne*: lectures d'une image éditée chez Pinot et Sagaire', *Gazette des beaux-arts* cix (1987), 75–9

Rey, Alain and Jacques Cellard, *Dictionnaire du français non conventionnel*, Paris 1980

Richard, Gabriel, 'Les Demi-Soldes en Lorraine dans la première moitié du XIXe siècle', *Annales de l'est* 5th ser. vii (1956), 187–216

———— 'Les Sobriquets en Lorraine dans la première moitié du XIXe siècle', *Annales de l'est* 5th ser. xv (1963), 347–96

Richards, Frank, *Old soldiers never die*, London 1933

Riespach, Mme Simon de, 'D'Konscritzitt ou le temps des conscrits', *Folklore de France* xl (1991–2), 11–13

Riff, Adolphe, *L'Art populaire et l'artisanat rural en Alsace*, Strasbourg 1945

———— (ed.), *Art populaire en France*, Strasbourg 1960

———— (ed.), *Art populaire d'Alsace*, Strasbourg–Paris 1963

———— (ed.), *Art populaire de la France de l'est*, Strasbourg–Paris 1969

Robert, Raymonde, 'Emmanuel Cosquin et les contes lorrains', in Roger Marchal and Bernard Guidot (eds), *Lorraine vivante: hommage à Jean Lanher*, Nancy 1993, 201–7

Roche, Daniel, *The culture of clothing: dress and fashion in the ancien régime*, Cambridge 1994

Roehrich, Mme Ernest, 'Quelques Notes sur Jean-Frédéric Oberlin', *Revue alsacienne illustrée* xii (1910), 48–61

Roger-Noël, Isabelle, 'La Révolution aux frontières vue par un volontaire de 1792–1796', *Revue historique des armées* xlii (1986), 12–27

Rogers, Susan Carol, 'Female forms of power and the myth of male dominance', *American Ethnologist* ii (1975), 727–56

Röhrich, Lutz, *Folktales and reality*, Bloomington, Ind. 1991

Ronsin, Albert, 'Almanachs populaires vosgiens au XIXe siècle', in Choux and Riff, *Lorraine*, 215–24

Rooth, Anna B., *The Cinderella cycle*, Lund 1951

Ross, Steven T., *French military history, 1661–1799: a guide to the literature*, New York–London 1984

Roth, François, *La Lorraine annexée: étude sur la presidence de Lorraine dans l'empire allemand (1870–1918)*, Nancy 1976

———— 'Nation, armée et politique à travers les images d'Epinal, 1860–1914', *Annales de l'est* 5th ser. xxxii (1980), 195–213

Rozanov, Ivan N., 'From book to folklore', in Oinas and Soudakoff, *Russian folklore*, 65–75

Rumpf, Marianne, *Rotkäppchen: eine vergleichende Märchenuntersuchung*, Frankfurt-am-Main 1989

Ryan, Edward, *Paper soldiers*, London 1994

Sabourin de Nanton, *Notice sur l'imagerie Pellerin à Epinal*, Epinal 1857

———— *Epinal et l'imagerie dans les Vosges*, Strasbourg 1868

Sadoul, Charles, 'Les Rebouteux de Val d'Ajol', *Revue des traditions populaires* xix (1904), 118

Sahlins, Peter, *Boundaries: the making of France and Spain in the Pyrenees*, Berkeley–Los Angeles 1989

—— *Forest rites: the war of the Demoiselles in nineteenth-century France*, Cambridge, Mass. 1994

Saintyves, Pierre, *Les Contes de Perrault et les récits parallèles*, Paris 1923

Sales de Bohigas, Nuria, 'Marchands d'hommes et sociétés d'assurance contre le service militaire au XIXe siècle', *Revue d'histoire économique et sociale* xlvi (1968), 339–80

Salies, Pierre, 'Imagerie populaire et confréries toulousaines', *Gazette des beaux-arts* lix (1962), 258–76

Salviac, Michel, 'Les Maires anciens soldats: l'arrondissement de Commercy', in Maurice Agulhon, L. Girard, J. L. Robert and W. Serman (eds), *Les Maires en France du consulat à nos jours*, Paris 1986

Sandt, Capitaine de, *Les Soldats de Vézelise en l'an II*, Nancy 1912

Saulnier, René, 'De l'Imagerie populaire à l'imagerie enfantine', *L'Art populaire en France* ii (1930), 161–78

—— 'Les Vieux Bois d'images populaires du Musée de Châtillon-sur-Seine', *L'Art populaire en France* iii (1931), 124–35

—— 'Crédit est mort: thème international d'imagerie populaire', *Le Folklore vivant* i (1945), 33–54

—— *L'Imagerie populaire du Val-de-Loire (Anjou, Maine, Orléanais et Touraine)*, Angers 1945

—— 'L'Imagerie populaire en Ile-de-France: Beauvais (Oise)', *Bulletin folklorique d'Ile-de-France* xii (1949), 59–62

—— and Adolphe Aynaud, 'Prototypes de l'imagerie populaire', *Arts et traditions populaires* i (1953), 59–69

—— and H. Van der Zée, 'La Mort de crédit: image populaire, ses sources politiques et économiques', *Dawna Sztuka* ii (1939), 1–25

Sautman, Francesca, 'Le Conte 425B: rites de mariage et parcours magique', *Merveilles et contes* iii (1989), 28–44

—— 'Rituels de dérision et langage symboliques dans les dayemans lorrains', *Cahiers de la littérature orale* xxviii (1990), 97–125

—— 'Variabilité et formules d'ouverture et de clôture dans le conte populaire français', in Görög-Karady, *D'un Conte . . . à l'autre*, 133–44

Sauvy, Anne, *Le Miroir du coeur: quatre siècles d'images savantes et populaires*, Paris 1989

Savigneur, P., 'Carbonarism and the French army', *History* liv (1969), 198–211

Schamber, René, 'Migration de la chanson populaire', *Nos Traditions* n.s. i (1947), 80–3

Schapiro, Meyer, 'Courbet and popular imagery', *Journal of the Warburg and Courtauld Institutes* iv (1940), 164–91

Scharfe, Martin, *Evangelische Andachtsbilder*, Stuttgart 1968

Schenda, Rudolf, 'Ein französischer Bilderbogenkatalog aus dem Jahre 1860', *Schweizerisches Archiv für Volkskunde* lxii (1966), 49–61

Schmitt, Jean-Claude, *Ghosts in the Middle Ages: the living and the dead in medieval society*, Chicago–London 1998

Schnapper, Bernard, *Le Remplacement militaire en France: quelques aspects politiques, économiques et sociaux du recrutement au XIXe siècle*, Paris 1968

Scott, James C., *Domination and the arts of resistance: hidden transcripts*, London 1990

Scott, Samuel F., *The response of the royal army to the French revolution: the role and development of the line army, 1787–93*, Oxford 1978

Scott, Walter Sidney, *The trial of Joan of Arc*, London 1986

Scribner, Bob, *For the sake of simple folk: popular propaganda for the German reformation*, Cambridge 1981

——— 'Is a history of popular culture possible?', *History of European Ideas* x (1989), 175–92

Sears, Elisabeth, *The ages of man in medieval interpretations of the life cycle*, Princeton, NJ 1986

Sébillot, Paul, 'Sobriquets et superstitions militaires', *Revue des traditions populaires* ii (1887), 128–30

——— 'L'Imagerie en Haute-Bretagne', *Revue des traditions populaires* iii (1888), 407–17

——— 'L'Imagerie populaire: l'imagerie en Basse-Bretagne', *Revue des traditions populaires* iii (1888), 305–17

Segalen, Martine, *Love and power in the peasant family*, Oxford 1983

Seguin, Elise, 'Images et imagiers à Lille avant 1800', *Arts et traditions populaires* ix (1961), 27–56

——— 'Imagerie et vie sociale à Lille: Louis Melino, 1790–1859', *Arts et traditions populaires* xvii (1969), 179–232

Seguin, Jean-Pierre, 'Les Debuts de graveur lillois Josue Henry Porret', *Arts et traditons populaires* iii (1955), 243–5

——— 'Les "Canards" de fait divers de petit format en France, au XIXe siècle', *Arts et traditions populaires* iv (1956), 30–44, 115–35

——— *Nouvelles à sensation: canards du XIXe siècle*, Paris 1959

——— *L'Information en France avant le périodique: 517 canards imprimés entre 1529 et 1631*, Paris 1964

Seignolle, Claude, *Le Folklore de Provence*, Paris 1967

Senn, Harry, 'Folklore beginnings in France: the Académie Celtique, 1804–1813', *Journal of the Folklore Institute* xviii (1981), 23–33

Sewell, William, 'Etat, corps and ordre: some notes on the social vocabulary of the French old regime', in Hans-Ulrich Wehler (ed.), *Sozialgeschichte Heute: Festschrift für Hans Rosenberg zum 70. Geburtstag*, Göttingen 1974, 49–68

Shorter, Edward, *The making of the modern family*, London 1976

——— 'The *veillée* and the great transformation', in Beauroy, Bertrand and Gargan, *The wolf and the lamb*, 127–40

Silverman, Dan, *Reluctant union: Alsace-Lorraine and imperial Germany, 1871–1918*, University Park, Penn. 1972

Sperber, Alice, *Charakteristik der Lothringer Märchensammlung von E. Cosquin*, Vienna 1908

Spyri, Johanna, *Heidi*, first edn 1880; London 1956

Stein-Moreau, Nicole Odette, 'Les Frères Grimm, conteurs, et la France au dix-neuvième siècle', in *Bruder Grimm Gedenken*, Marburg 1963

Sternhell, Zeev, *Maurice Barrès et le nationalisme français*, Brussels 1985

Sturgill, Claude, 'Le Logement des troupes chez l'habitant à Metz en 1750, premier examen des résultats', *Mémoires de l'Académie nationale de Metz* 6th ser. ii (1974), 115–22

Stuttgart Staatsgalerie, *Bänkelsang und Moritat*, Stuttgart 1975 (exhibition catalogue)

Sydow, Carl Wilhelm von, *Selected papers on folklore*, Copenhagen 1948

Taggart, James M., 'Hansel and Gretel in Spain and Mexico', *Journal of American Folklore* ic (1986), 435–60

——— *Enchanted maidens: gender relations in Spanish folktales of courtship and marriage*, Princeton, NJ 1990

Taylor, Peter and Hermann Rebel, 'Hessian peasant women, their families and the draft: a social-historical interpretation of four tales from the Grimm collection', *Journal of Family History* vi (1981), 347–78

Tenèze, Marie-Louise, 'De Quelques Coutumes et croyances se rattachant aux cierges en Moselle', *Annales de l'est* 5th ser. ii (1951), 317–26

——— 'The devil's heater: on the "contexts" of a tale', *Journal of Folklore Research* xx (1983), 197–219

Thomas, Gerald, *Les Deux Traditions: le conte populaire chez les franco-terreneuviens*, Montréal 1983

Thompson, Stith, *Motif-index of folk literature: a classification of narrative elements in folktales, ballads, myths, fables, medieval romances, exempla, fabliaux, jest-books, and local-legends* (Folklore Fellows Communications cvi–cxvii), Helsinki 1932–6

——— *The folktale*, New York 1946

Tiersot, Julien, *Histoire de la chanson populaire en France*, Paris 1889

Tombs, Robert, *France, 1814–1914*, London 1996

Toschi, Paoli, *L'Imagerie populaire italienne*, Paris 1964

Tournès, René, *La Garde nationale dans le département de la Meurthe pendant la révolution, 1789–1802*, Angers 1920

Tribout de Morembert, Henri, 'Raphaël de Westphalen (1873–1949)', *Nos Traditions* n.s. ii (1949), 25–30

Trollope, Thomas Adolphus, *A summer in Brittany*, London 1840

Turner, Terence, 'Transformation, hierachy and transcendence: a reformulation of Van Gennep's model of the structure of rites of passage', in Moore and Myerhoff, *Secular ritual*, 53–70

Turner, Victor, 'Variations on a theme of liminality', in Moore and Myerhoff, *Secular ritual*, 36–52

Urtel, Hermann, 'Lothringen kritischer Uberblick bis 1908', *Revue du dialectologie romane* ii (1910), 131–48, 437–55

Vallantin, Catharine, 'Lecture et tradition orale: le conte en France en milieu rural aux XVIIe–XVIIIe siècles', *Merveilles et contes* iii (1989), 212–25

Van Gennep, Arnold, 'Deux Problèmes de folklore lorrain', *Le Pays lorrain* xxiii (1931), 425–40

——— *Manuel du folklore français contemporain*, Paris 1937–46

——— *Les Rites de passage*, Paris 1909; trans. as *The rites of passage*, Chicago–London 1960

Van Heurck, Emile H. and Gerrit J. Boekenoogen, *Histoire de l'imagerie populaire flamande et de ses rapports avec les imageries etrangères*, Bruxelles 1910

——— *L'Imagerie populaire des Pays-Bas*, Paris 1930

Varlet, Charles Jules, *Dictionnaire du patois meusien*, Verdun 1896

Vartier, Jean, *La Vie quotidienne en Lorraine au XIXe siècle*, Paris 1973

Verdier, Yvonne, *Façons de dire, façons de faire: la laveuse, la couturière, la cuisinière*, Paris 1979

Vernus, Michel, 'Colporteurs et marchands merciers dans le Jura au XVIIIe siècle', *La Nouvelle Revue franc-comtoise* xviii–xix (1980), 209–18, 25–33

Vigneulles, Philippe de, *Les Cent Nouvelles Nouvelles de Philippe de Vigneulles*, ed. Charles Livingston, Geneva 1972

Villemin, Martial, 'Les Assurances contre le recrutement et le replacement en Moselle avant 1870', *Les Cahiers lorrains* n.s. xxxix (1987), 309–39

Vingtrinier, Joseph, *Chants et chansons des soldats de France, 1789–1905*, Paris 1902

Vinson, Julien, *Le Folklore du pays basque*, Paris 1881

Vizedom, Monika, *Rites and relationships: rites of passage and contemporary anthropology*, Beverly Hills, Ca. 1976

Vovelle, Michel, 'The countryside and the peasantry in revolutionary iconography', in Alan Forrest and Peter Jones (eds), *Reshaping France: town, country and region during the French revolution*, Manchester 1991, 26–36

Waquet, J., 'Une Source d'histoire politique, institutionelle et sociale: les états d'engagements volontaires pour l'armée de 1818 à 1832', in *Actes de 92e congrès des sociétés savantes*, Strasbourg 1967, iii. 41–53

Warner, Marina, *From the beast to the blonde: on fairytales and their tellers*, London 1994

Watt, Tessa, *Cheap print and popular piety, 1550–1640*, Cambridge 1991

Weber, Eugen, *Peasants into Frenchmen: the modernization of rural France, 1870–1914*, Stanford, Ca. 1976

────── 'Fairies and hard facts; the reality of folktales', *Journal of the History of Ideas* xlii (1981), 93–113

Wesselski, Albert, *Märchen des Mittelalters*, Berlin 1925

Westphalen, Raphaël de, 'Le Culte de l'arbre dans nos coutumes populaires', *Annuaire de la Société historique et archéologique lorraine* xxxii (1923), 143–260

────── 'Frédéric Estre', *Nos Traditions* i (1938), 9–25

Wildenstein, Georges and Jean Adhémar, 'Les Images de Denis de Mathonière d'apres son inventaire (1598)', *Arts et traditions populaires* viii (1960), 150–7

Wiltzer, Paul, 'Petite Police et grande armée à Metz sous l'empire (1806–1815)', *Mémoires de l'Académie nationale de Metz* 5th ser. vi (1959–61), 149–63

Wolf, Eric, 'Aspects of group relations in a complex society: Mexico', *American Anthropologist* lviii (1956), 1065–78

Wolfram, Georg and Werner Gley, *Elsass-lothringischer Atlas: Landeskunde, Geschichte, Kultur und Wirtschaft Elsass-Lothringens*, Frankfurt-am-Main 1931

Wolfthal, Diane, 'Jacques Callot's *Miseries of war*', *The Art Bulletin* lix (1977), 222–33

Woloch, Isser, *The French veteran from the revolution to the restoration*, Chapel Hill, NC 1979

────── 'Napoleonic conscription: state power and civil society', *Past and Present* cxi (1986), 101–29

────── *The new regime: transformation of the French civic order, 1789–1820s*, New York 1994

Zeller, Gaston, 'Les Charges de la Lorraine pendant la guerre de Hollande', *Memoires de la Société d'archéologie lorraine* lxi (1911), 13–65

Zender, Matthias, 'Quellen und Träger der deutschen Volkserzählung', in Leander Petzoldt (ed.), *Vergleichende Sagenforschung*, Darmstadt 1969

Zipes, Jack, 'The Grimms and the German obsession with fairy tales', in Bottigheimer, *Fairy tales and society*, 273–85

Zonabend, Françoise, *The enduring memory: time and history in a French village*, Manchester 1984

Unpublished theses etc.

Bauchez, Jean, 'Légende napoléonienne et propagande bonapartiste à Metz et en Moselle de 1832 à 1852', *mémoire de maîtrise*, Metz 1986

Bolsinger, Gérard, 'L'Image du peuple du pays messin à travers ses traditions', *mémoire de maîtrise*, Nancy II 1972

Chlemaire, Karine, 'La Répresentation de la femme dans l'imagerie populaire: exemple de l'imagerie Pellerin', *mémoire de maîtrise*, Paris IV 1993

Frost, R., ' "And these have such dreadful countenances": physiognomy of terror and the image of the Pole in the Thirty Years War', paper given to Forum on Early Modern Central Europe, Warburg Institute, 12 Feb. 1997

Kappaun, Bernard, 'La Conscription en Moselle sous le premier empire', *thèse doctorale*, Nancy II 1967

Labate, J.-C., 'Le Recrutement de l'armée à Metz, 1818–1870', *mémoire de maîtrise*, Metz 1974

Martin, Lucien, 'Contribution à l'étude des images d'Epinal sous la troisième republique, 1870–1914', *mémoire de maîtrise*, Tours 1971

Mayer, Laurent, 'La Chanson populaire en Lorraine germanophone d'après le recueil *Verklingende Weisen* de Louis Pinck', *thèse doctorale*, Metz 1984

Mignot, Michelle, 'La Conscription dans le département de la Meuse sous le directoire', *mémoire de maîtrise*, Nancy II 1955

Poinsignon, Jean, 'La Chanson populaire en Lorraine', *mémoire de maîtrise*, Nancy II 1971

General Index

Aarne, Antti, folklorist, *see* folktale: historical-geographic ('Finnish') school; folktale: indexes
Abrahams, Roger, folklorist, *see* ecotypes
Académie Stanislas (Nancy), 77
Allabre, Marin, imagist (Chartres), 22, 33, 48
allied invasions and occupations (1814–15), 241, 244, 275
almanacs, 71, 76
Aynaud, Adolphe, historian of imagery, 21

Balzac, Honoré de, 39, 45, 48, 268, 284, 287
Bangofsky, Georges, soldier-writer, 100, 189, 216, 243, 252
Bänkelsänger, 67, 334. *See also* pedlars
Barc, André-Sébastien, imagist (Chartres), 22, 55
Baro, Nicolas, storyteller, 85
Barrès, Maurice, 15–16
Basset, copperplate imagist (Paris), 29, 169–71
Beauvais: popular imagery, *see* Dupont-Diot, Frédéric
Belfort: popular imagery, *see* Clerc, Jean-Pierre
Bés & Dubrueil, lithographers (Paris), 173
Bettelheim, Bruno, *see* folktale: psychoanalytic interpretation
bibliothèque bleue, *see* chapbooks
blacksmiths, 109, 175, 189, 343–4
Bladé, Jean-François, folklorist, 118
'blasons populaires', 159
Blocquel & Castiaux, imagists (Lille), 51
Bois, Jean-Paul, 284–5
Boniot, engraver (Chartres), 223
Boulay, 340
Boulay, Caroline, engraver (Paris), 23
Boulay, Charles, engraver (Epinal–Montbéliard–Belfort), 23, 30, 226 n. 40, 244, 258, 276–8
Bräker, Ulrich, soldier-writer, 330–1
Bruneau, Charles, Lorrainer dialectologist, 77

Caen: popular imagery, *see* Picard-Guérin, François
cahiers de doléances, 128
Callot, Jacques, 17, 249
Calmet, Dom Augustin, 76
Cambrai: popular imagery, *see* Hurez, Armand-François
Camus, Albert, 334 n. 222
canards, 20 n. 16, 66, 69, 238, 298, 332, 335
Carchon, Jean, soldier-writer, 184, 294
Cardinet, Claude, imagist (Epinal), 22
cards: card-making, 19, 21; card-playing, 346
carnival, 145
carols, 76, 247
Cartouche, bandit, 239
Chagniot, Jean, 284
Chamagnons (Vosgian pedlars), 62–71, 238
Champfleury, historian of imagery, 20
Chan Heurlin, 75. *See also* Mory, Didier
chapbooks, 93–4
charivari, 161. *See also* wedding ceremonies
Charlet, Nicolas, 287–8, 291
Chartier, Roger, 36, 94 n. 74
Chartres: popular imagery, *see* Allabre, Marin; Barc, André-Sébastien; Boniot; Fleuret; Garnier, Jacques-Marin; Garnier, Jacques-Pierre
chasseurs, 250–2
Chateaubriand, François-René, 42, 66 n. 220
Chauvin, Nicolas, legendary soldier, 11, 13, 215. *See also soldat-laboureur*
Cheesman, Tom, 333, 336
Christiansen, Reidar, folklorist, *see* folktale: historical-geographic ('Finnish') school
Claude, *canardier* (Charmes), 332. *See also* Chamagnons
Clerc, Jean-Pierre, imagist (Belfort), 23, 28 n. 43, 32

Index of Imagery Titles

Index of Tale-Types (Aarne-Thompson)

Index of Song Titles

www.ingramcontent.com/pod-product-compliance
Lightning Source LLC
Chambersburg PA
CBHW050624280326
41932CB00015B/2512